Western Civilizations

Their History & Their Culture

Joshua Cole
Carol Symes

Western Civilizations

Their History & Their Culture

EIGHTEENTH EDITION

VOLUME C

W. W. NORTON & COMPANY ▪ NEW YORK ▪ LONDON

W. W. Norton & Company has been independent since its founding in 1923, when William Warder Norton and Mary D. Herter Norton first published lectures delivered at the People's Institute, the adult education division of New York City's Cooper Union. The firm soon expanded its program beyond the Institute, publishing books by celebrated academics from America and abroad. By midcentury, the two major pillars of Norton's publishing program—trade books and college texts—were firmly established. In the 1950s, the Norton family transferred control of the company to its employees, and today—with a staff of four hundred and a comparable number of trade, college, and professional titles published each year—W. W. Norton & Company stands as the largest and oldest publishing house owned wholly by its employees.

Printed in Canada

Editor: Jon Durbin
Associate editor: Justin Cahill
Editorial assistant: Penelope Lin
Project editor: Melissa Atkin
Managing editor, College: Marian Johnson
Copyeditor: Jude Grant
E-media editors: Steve Hoge, Tacy Quinn
Ancillary editor: Lorraine Klimowich
Assistant editor, E-media: Stefani Wallace
Photo editor: Evan Luberger
Photo research: Rona Tucillo
Marketing manager, History: Sarah England
Production manager, College: Sean Mintus
Design director: Rubina Yeh
Book designer: Judith Abbate / Abbate Design
Composition: Jouve
Cartographers: Mapping Specialists
Manufacturing: Transcontinental

Library of Congress has catalogued the one-volume edition as follows:

Cole, Joshua, 1961–
Western civilizations : their history & their culture / Joshua Cole and Carol Symes. —Eighteenth edition.
pages cm
Includes bibliographical references and index.

ISBN 978-0-393-92213-4 (hardcover)
1. Civilization, Western—Textbooks. 2. Europe—Civilization—Textbooks. I. Symes, Carol. II. Title.
CB245.C56 2013
909'.09821—dc23

2013029952

This edition:
ISBN: 978-0-393-92218-9 (pbk.)

W. W. Norton & Company, Inc., 500 Fifth Avenue, New York, N. Y. 10110
wwnorton.com

W. W. Norton & Company Ltd., Castle House, 75/76 Wells Street, London W1T 3QT

1 2 3 4 5 6 7 8 9 0

To our families:

Kate Tremel, Lucas and Ruby Cole
Tom, Erin, and Connor Wilson

with love and gratitude for their support.
And to all our students, who have also been our teachers.

About the Authors

JOSHUA COLE (Ph.D., University of California, Berkeley) is Associate Professor of History at the University of Michigan, Ann Arbor. His publications include work on gender and the history of the population sciences, colonial violence, and the politics of memory in nineteenth- and twentieth-century France, Germany, and Algeria. His first book was *The Power of Large Numbers: Population, Politics, and Gender in Nineteenth-Century France* (Ithaca, NY: Cornell University Press, 2000).

CAROL SYMES (Ph.D., Harvard University) is Associate Professor of History and Director of Undergraduate Studies in the history department at the University of Illinois, Urbana-Champaign, where she has won the top teaching award in the College of Liberal Arts and Sciences. Her main areas of study include medieval Europe, the history of information media and communication technologies, and the history of theater. Her first book was *A Common Stage: Theater and Public Life in Medieval Arras* (Ithaca: Cornell University Press, 2007).

Brief Contents

Contents

Chapter 26 ▪ THE SECOND WORLD WAR 873

Chapter 27 ▪ THE COLD WAR WORLD: GLOBAL POLITICS, ECONOMIC RECOVERY, AND CULTURAL CHANGE 911

Chapter 28 ▪ RED FLAGS AND VELVET REVOLUTIONS: THE END OF THE COLD WAR, 1960–1990 947

Maps

Primary Sources

Preface

This new edition of *Western Civilizations* sharpens and expands the set of tools we have developed to empower students—our own and yours—to engage effectively with the themes, sources, and challenges of history. It presents a clear and vigorous narrative, supplemented by a compelling selection of primary sources and striking images. At the same time, as the authors of this book's previous edition, we have worked to develop a unified program of pedagogical elements that guide students toward a more thorough understanding of the past, and of the ways that historians reconstruct that past. This framework helps students to analyze and interpret historical evidence on their own, encouraging them to become active participants in the learning process.

Moreover, the wide chronological scope of this book offers an unusual opportunity to trace central human developments (population movements, intellectual currents, economic trends, the formation of political institutions, the power of religious belief, the role of the arts and of technologies) in a region of the world whose cultural diversity has been constantly invigorated and renewed by its interactions with peoples living in other places. Students today have a wide selection of introductory history courses to choose from, thanks to the welcome availability of introductory surveys in Latin American, African, and Asian history, alongside both traditional and innovative offerings in the history of the United States and Europe. Global history has also come into its own in recent years. But our increasing awareness that no region's history can be isolated from global processes and connections has merely heightened the need for a richly contextualized and broad-based history such as that represented in *Western Civilizations*.

As in previous editions, we have attempted to balance the coverage of political, social, economic, and cultural phenomena with extensive treatment of material culture, daily life, gender, sexuality, art, science, and popular culture. And following the path laid out by the book's previous authors, Judith Coffin and Robert Stacey, we have insisted that the history of European peoples must be understood through their interactions with peoples in other parts of the world. Our treatment of this history is accordingly both deep and dynamic, attentive to the latest developments in historical scholarship.

Given the importance of placing human history in a global context, those of us who study the histories of ancient, medieval, and modern Europe are actively changing the ways that we teach this history. For good reasons reflected in the title of this book, few historians today would uphold a monolithic vision of a single and enduring "Western civilization" whose inevitable march to domination can be traced chapter by chapter through time. This older paradigm, strongly associated with the curriculum of early twentieth-century American colleges and universities, no longer conforms to what we know about the human past. Neither the "West" nor "Europe" can be seen as distinct, unified entities in space or time; the meanings attributed to these geographical expressions have changed in significant ways. Moreover, historians now agree that a linear notion of any civilization persisting unchanged over the centuries was made coherent only by leaving out the intense conflicts, extraordinary ruptures, and dynamic changes that took place at the heart of the societies we call "Western." Smoothing out the rough edges of the past does students no favors; even an introductory text such as this one should present the past as it appears to the historians who study it—that is, as complex panorama of human effort, filled with possibility and achievement but also fraught with discord, uncertainty, accident, and tragedy.

We know that current and future users of our text will be enthusiastic to see the efforts made in this new edition to update and reorganize the Late Medieval and Early Modern periods in order to place them in a larger Atlantic World context. The major highlight of this reorganization is a brand new chapter, entitled "Europe in the Atlantic World, 1550–1650." It places the newly integrated space of the Atlantic at the center of the story, exploring the ways, that religious warfare, economic developments, population movements, and cultural trends shaped—and were shaped by—historical actors on this dynamic frontier. Another significant result of the reorganization of these two periods is to provide a clearer chronological framework for the narrative, so that the students can better see how major topics and events emerge from their historical contexts. This, of course, was part of a larger effort begun across the entire text in the previous edition. These revisions demonstrate our dual commitment to keep the book current and up-to-date, while striving to integrate strong pedagogical features that help students build their study and history skills.

New and Revised Pedagogical Features

In our ongoing effort to shape students' engagement with history, this book is designed to reinforce your course objectives by helping students to master core content while challenging them to think critically about the past. In order to achieve these aims, our previous edition augmented the traditional strengths of *Western Civilizations* by introducing several exciting new features. These have since been refined and revised in accordance with feedback from student readers and teachers of the book. The most important and revolutionary feature is the pedagogical structure that supports each chapter. As we know from long experience, many students in introductory survey courses find the sheer quantity of information overwhelming, and so we have provided guidance to help them navigate through the material and to read in meaningful ways.

At the outset of each chapter, the ***Before You Read This Chapter*** feature offers three preliminary windows onto the material to be covered: *Story Lines*, *Chronology*, and *Core Objectives. Story Lines* allow the student to become familiar with the primary narrative threads that tie the chapter's elements together, and the *Chronology* grounds these *Story Lines* in the period under study. *Core Objectives* provide a checklist to ensure that the student is aware of the primary teaching points in the chapter. The student is then reminded of these teaching points upon completing the chapter, in the ***After You Read This Chapter*** section, which prompts the student to revisit the chapter in three ways. The first, *Reviewing the Core Objectives*, asks the reader to reconsider core objectives by answering a pointed question about each one. The second, *People, Ideas, and Events in Context*, summarizes some of the particulars that students should retain from their reading, through questions that allow them to relate individual terms to the major objectives and story lines. Finally, *Thinking about Connections*, new to this edition, allow for more open-ended reflection on the significance of the chapter's material, drawing students' attention to issues that connect it to previous chapters and giving them insight into what comes next. As a package, the pedagogical features at the beginning and end of each chapter work together to enhance the student's learning experience, by breaking down the process of reading and analysis into manageable tasks.

A second package of pedagogical features is designed to capture students' interest and to compel them to think about what is at stake in the construction and use of historical narratives. Each chapter opens with a vignette that showcases a particular person or event representative of the era as a whole. Within each chapter, an expanded program of illustrations and maps has been enhanced by the addition of ***Guiding Questions*** (following these illustrations' and maps' captions) that urge the reader to explore the historical contexts and significance of these features in a more analytical way. The historical value of images, artifacts, and material culture is further emphasized in another feature we introduced in our previous edition, ***Interpreting Visual Evidence***. This section provides discussion leaders with a provocative departure point for conversations about the key issues raised by visual sources, which students often find more approachable than texts. Once this conversation has begun, students can further develop their skills by ***Analyzing Primary Sources***, through close readings of primary texts accompanied by cogent interpretive questions. The dynamism and diversity of Western civilizations are also illuminated through a look at ***Competing Viewpoints*** in each chapter, in which specific debates are presented through paired primary-source texts. The bibliographical ***Further Readings***, located at the end of the book, has also been edited and brought up-to-date.

In addition to these features, which have proven successful, we are delighted to introduce an entirely new segment with this eighteenth edition. The new ***Past and Present*** features in the main text prompt students to connect events unfolding in the past with the breaking news of our own time, by taking one episode from each chapter and comparing it with a phenomenon that resonates more immediately with our students. To bring this new feature to life for students, we have also created a new series of **Author Videos**, in which we describe and analyze these connections across time and place. There are a number of illuminating discussions, including, "Spectator Sports," which compares the Roman gladatorial games with NFL Football; "The Reputation of Richard III," which shows how modern forensics like those we see used on numerous TV shows were recently used to identify the remains of Richard III;

"The Persistence of Monarchies in a Democratic Age," which explains the origins and evolution of our ongoing fascination with royals like Louis XIV and Princess Diana; and "The Internet and the Enlightenment Public Sphere," which compares the kinds of public networks that helped spread Enlightenment ideas to the way the Internet can be used today to spread political ideas in movements such as the Arab Spring and Occupy Wall Street. Through this new feature, not only do we want to encourage students to recognize the continuing relevance of seemingly distant historical moments, but also we want to encourage historically-minded habits that will be useful for a lifetime. If students learn to see the connections among their world and the past, they will be more apt to place unfolding developments and debates in a more informed and complex historical context.

A Tour of New Chapters and Revisions

Our previous edition of *Western Civilizations* featured significant changes to each of the book's first five chapters, and this process of revision has continued in the present edition. In Chapter 1, the challenge of locating and interpreting historical evidence drawn from nontextual sources (archaeological, environmental, anthropological, mythic) is a special focus. Chapter 2 further underscores the degree to which recent archeological discoveries and new historical techniques have revolutionized our understanding of ancient history, and have also corroborated ancient peoples' own understandings of their past. Chapter 3 offers expanded coverage of the diverse polities that emerged in ancient Greece, and of Athens' closely related political, documentary, artistic, and intellectual achievements. Chapter 4's exploration of the Hellenistic world includes an unusually wide-ranging discussion of the scientific revolution powered by this first cosmopolitan civilization. Chapter 5 emphasizes the ways that the unique values and institutions of the Roman Republic are transformed through imperial expansion under the Principate.

With Chapter 6, a more extensive series of revisions has resulted in some significant reshaping and reorganization, so that the book's narrative reflects recent scholarship. The story of Rome's transformative encounter with early Christianity has been rewritten to ensure clarity and also to emphasize the fundamental ways that Christianity itself changed through the Roman Empire and in contact with peoples from northwestern Europe. Chapter 7, which examines Rome's three distinctive successor civilizations, now offers more extensive coverage of the reign of Justinian and emergence of Islam. Balanced attention to the interlocking histories of Byzantium, the Muslim caliphates, and western Europe has carried forward in subsequent chapters. Chapters 8 contains an entirely new section, "A Tour of Europe around the Year 1000," with coverage of the Viking diaspora, the formation of Scandinavian kingdoms and the empire of Cnute, early medieval Rus' and eastern Europe, and the relationship among Mediterranean microcosms. It also features greatly expanded coverage of economy, trade, and the events leading up to the First Crusade. Chapter 9, which now covers the period 1000–1250, features a new segment on the Crusader States and crusading movements within Europe.

Chapter 10's treatment of the medieval world between 1250 and 1350 is almost wholly new, reflecting cutting-edge scholarship on this era. It includes a fresh look at the consolidation of the Mongol Khanates, new images and maps, some new sources, and a new ***Interpreting Visual Evidence*** segment on seals and their users. Chapters 11 and 12 have been thoroughly reorganized and rewritten to ensure that the narrative of medieval Europeans' colonial ventures (from the western Mediterranean to the eastern Atlantic and Africa, and beyond) is integrated with the story of the Black Death's effects on the medieval world and the impetus for the intellectual and artistic innovations of the Renaissance. In previous editions of the book, these concurrent phenomena were treated as separate, as though they took place in three separate periods (the later Middle Ages, the Renaissance, and the Age of Exploration). This made the connections among them almost impossible to explain or appreciate. In this eighteenth edition, therefore, the voyages of Columbus are firmly rooted in their historical contexts while the religious, social, and cultural upheavals of the Reformation (Chapter 13) are more clearly placed against a backdrop of political and economic competition in Europe and the Americas.

This program of revisions sets the stage for the most significant new chapter in the book: Chapter 14, "Europe in the Atlantic World, 1550–1650." This chapter, the hinge between the book's first and second halves, resulted from a close collaboration between us. It is designed to function either as the satisfying culmination of a course that surveys the history of Western civilizations up to the middle of the seventeenth century (like that taught by Carol Symes) or to provide a foundation for a course on the history of the modern West (like that taught by Joshua Cole). The chapter illuminates the changing nature of Europe as it becomes fully integrated into the larger Atlantic world that dramatically impacts all of its internal political, social, cultural, and economic development. In addition to greatly enhanced treatment of the transatlantic slave trade and the Columbian

Exchange, it also features new sections on the different models of colonial settlement in the Caribbean and the Americas, as well as expanded coverage of the Thirty Years' War.

The new emphasis on the emergence of the Atlantic world carries over to Chapter 15, which covers the emergence of powerful absolutist regimes on the continent and the evolution of wealthy European trading empires in the Americas, Africa, and Asia. This material has now been reorganized to clarify developments over time, as the early successes of the Spanish empire are gradually eclipsed by the successes of the Dutch, the French, and the British empires. A new document on the Streltsy rebellion, meanwhile, allows students to better understand the contested nature of power under the Russian tsars during the absolutist period. We have retained the emphasis on intellectual and cultural history in Chapter 16, on the Scientific Revolution, and in Chapter 17, on the Enlightenment. In Chapter 16 we have enhanced our treatment of the relationship between Christian faith and the new sciences of observation with a new primary-source document by Pierre Gassendi. In Chapter 17, meanwhile, we have sought to set the Enlightenment more clearly in its social and political context, connecting it more explicitly to the theme of European expansion into the Americas and the Pacific. This helps, for example, in connecting a document like the American Declaration of Independence with the ideas of European Enlightenment thinkers.

Chapters 18–19 cover the political and economic revolutions of the late eighteenth and early nineteenth centuries. Chapter 18 covers the French Revolution and the Napoleonic empires in depth, while also drawing attention to the way that these central episodes were rooted in a larger pattern of revolutionary political change that engulfed the Atlantic world. Chapter 19 emphasizes both the economic growth and the technological innovations that were a part of the Industrial Revolution, while also exploring the social and cultural consequences of industrialization for men and women in Europe's new industrial societies. The ***Interpreting Visual Evidence*** feature in Chapter 19 allows students to explore the ways that industrialization created new perceptions of the global economy in Europe, changing the way people thought of their place in the world.

Chapters 20–21 explore the successive struggles between conservative reaction and radicals in Europe, as the dynamic forces of nationalism unleashed by the French Revolution redrew the map of Europe and threatened the dynastic regimes that had ruled for centuries. Here, however, we have sought to clarify the periodization of the post-Napoleonic decades by focusing Chapter 20 more clearly on the conservative reaction in Europe after 1815, and the ideologies of conservatism, liberalism, republicanism, socialism, and nationalism. By setting the 1848 revolutions entirely in Chapter 21 (rather than split between the two chapters as in previous editions) instructors should be able to demonstrate more easily the connection between these political movements and the history of national unification in Germany and Italy in subsequent decades. While making these changes in the organization of the chapters, we have retained our treatment of the important cultural movements of the first half of the nineteenth century, especially Romanticism.

Chapter 22 takes on the history of nineteenth-century colonialism, exploring both its political and economic origins and its consequences for the peoples of Africa and Asia. The chapter gives new emphasis to the significance of colonial conquest for European culture, as colonial power became increasingly associated with national greatness, both in conservative monarchies and in more democratic regimes. Meanwhile, Chapter 23 brings the narrative back to the heart of Europe, covering the long-term consequences of industrialization and the consolidation of a conservative form of nationalism in many European nations even as the electorate was being expanded. The chapter emphasizes the varied nature of the new forms of political dissent, from the feminists who claimed the right to vote to the newly organized socialist movements that proved so enduring in many European countries.

Chapters 24 and 25 bring new vividness to the history of the First World War and the intense conflicts of the interwar period, while Chapter 26 uses the history of the Second World War as a hinge for understanding European and global developments in the second half of the twentieth century. The ***Interpreting Visual Evidence*** feature in Chapter 24 allows for a special focus on the role of propaganda among the belligerent nations in 1914–1918; and the chapter's section on the diplomatic crisis that preceded the First World War has been streamlined to allow students to more easily comprehend the essential issues at the heart of the conflict. In Chapter 25 the ***Interpreting Visual Evidence*** feature continues to explore the theme touched on in earlier chapters, political representations of "the people," this time in the context of fascist spectacles in Germany and Italy in the 1930s. These visual sources help students to understand the vulnerability of Europe's democratic regimes during these years as they faced the dual assault from fascists on the right and Bolsheviks on the left.

Chapters 27–29 bring the volumes to a close in a thorough exploration of the Cold War, decolonization, the collapse of the Soviet Union and the Eastern Bloc in 1989–1991, and the roots of the multifaceted global conflicts that beset the world in the first decade of the twenty-first century. Chapter 27 juxtaposes the Cold War with decolonization, showing how this combination sharply diminished the ability of European nations to control events in the international arena, even as they succeeded in rebuilding their economies at home. Chapter 28 explores the vibrancy of European culture in the crucial period of the 1960s to the early 1990s, bringing new attention to the significance of 1989 as a turning point in European history. Finally, extensive revisions to Chapter 29, add to the issues covered in our treatment of Europe's place in the contemporary globalized world. The chapter now includes a new section on efforts to deal with climate change, as well as expanded discussion of the impact of global terrorism, and recent developments in the Arab-Israeli conflict. The discussion on the financial crisis of 2008 and the presidency of Barack Obama has been brought up to date, and two new sections have been added to allow students to think about the Arab Spring of 2011 and the European debt crisis of recent years in connection with the broader history of European democracy, nation-building, and colonialism in the modern period.

Media Resources for Instructors and Students

LMS COURSEPACKS WITH STRONG ASSESSMENT AND LECTURE TOOLS

- **Dynamic Author Videos (55 total)** in which the authors discuss two of the main topics or themes in each chapter. New to this edition, illustrations, maps, and other types of media are integrated into the interviews to make them richer and more dynamic. These segments can serve as lecture launchers or as a preview tool for students before and after they read a chapter. (Available in PowerPoint and on Norton StudySpace.)
- **NEW *Past and Present* Author Videos (29 total)** that connect topics across time and place and show why history is relevant to understanding our world today (see further explanation above). Examples include "Spectator Sports," "Medieval Plots and Modern Movies," "Global Pandemics," and "The Atlantic Revolutions and Human Rights" (Available in PowerPoint and on Norton StudySpace.)
- **NEW Guided Reading Exercises** by Scott Corbett (Ventura College) are designed to help students learn how to effectively read a textbook. The reading exercises, which are keyed to each chapter's *People, Ideas, and Events in Context* questions, instill a three-step Note-Summarize-Assess pedagogy. Exercises are based on actual passages from the textbook (three exercises per chapter). Feedback will provide model responses with direct page references. (Available only in the Norton Coursepack.)
- **NEW 36 Map Exercises** can be assigned for assessment. These activities ask students a series of questions about historical events that must be answered by clicking on the map to record the answer. (Available only in the Norton Coursepack.)
- **NEW Chrono-Quiz** improving on the ever-popular Chrono-Sequencer, the Chrono-Quiz is now available as an assessment activity that will report to the school's native LMS. (Available only in the Norton Coursepack.)
- **NEW *StoryMaps*** break complex maps into a sequence of four to five annotated screens that focus on the *story* behind the *geography*. There are ten StoryMaps that include such topics as The Silk Road, The Spread of the Black Death, and Nineteenth-Century Imperialism. (Available only on wwnorton.com/web/westernciv18/instructors.)

INSTRUCTOR'S MANUAL

Bob Brennan (Cape Fear Community College)
Bruce Delfini (Rockland Community College)
Christopher Laney (Berkshire Community College)
Alice Roberti (Santa Rosa Community College)

The Instructor's Manual for *Western Civilizations*, Eighteenth edition, is designed to help instructors prepare lectures and exams. The Instructor's Manual contains detailed chapter outlines, general discussion questions, document discussion questions, lecture objectives, interdisciplinary discussion topics, and recommended reading and film lists. **This edition has been revised to include sample answers to all of the student-facing comprehension questions in the text.**

TEST BANK

Geoffrey Clark (SUNY Potsdam)
Donna Trembinski (St. Francis Xavier University)

The Test Bank contains over 2,000 multiple-choice, true/false, and essay questions. This edition of the Test Bank has been completely revised for content and accuracy. All test questions are now aligned to Bloom's Taxonomy for greater ease and effectiveness of assessment.

FOR STUDENTS

wwnorton.com/web/westerncivl8

Free and open to all students, Norton StudySpace includes

- **Author Videos (over 80 in all)** for every chapter, including the new *Past and Present* segments that connect topics. Examples include
  - "Medieval Plots and Modern Movies"
  - "Controlling Consumption" (the legalization of controlled substances, from sixteenth-century regulations to contemporary marijuana policy)
  - "The Internet and the Enlightenment Public Sphere"
- **Chapter Outlines and Quizzes.** Quiz feedback is aligned to student learning outcomes and core objectives, along with page references.
- **World History Tours,** powered by Google Earth™, now operate from within the browser, eliminating the need to download third-party applications or files.
- **iMaps** allow students to view layers of information on each map.
- **Map Worksheets** provide each map without labels for offline re-labeling and quizzing.
- **Flashcards** align key terms and events with brief descriptions and definitions.
- Over **400 primary-source documents and images**
- **Ebook links** tie the online text to all study and review materials.

A FEW WORDS OF THANKS

Our first edition as members of *Western Civilizations'* authorial team was a challenging and rewarding one. Our second edition has been equally rewarding in that we have been able to implement a number of useful and engaging changes in the content and structure of the book, which we hope will make it even more student- and classroom-friendly. We are very grateful for the expert assistance and support of the Norton team, especially that of our editor, Jon Durbin. Melissa Atkin, our fabulous project editor, has driven the book beautifully through the manuscript process. Justin Cahill has provided good critiques of the illustrations and the new *Past and Present* features in addition to all the other parts of the project he has handled so skillfully. Evan Luberger and Rona Tucillo did an excellent job finding many of the exact images we specified. Lorraine Klimowich did an expert job developing the print ancillaries. Sean Mintus has efficiently marched us through the production process. Steve Hoge has done a great job developing the book's fantastic emedia, particularly the new *Past and Present* Author Videos, the new Guided Reading Exercises, and the new StoryMaps. Jude Grant and John Gould were terrific in skillfully guiding the manuscript through the copyediting and proofreading stages. Finally, we want to thank Sarah England for spearheading the marketing campaign for the new edition. We are also indebted to the numerous expert readers who commented on various chapters and who thereby strengthened the book as a whole. We are thankful to our families, for their patience and advice, and to our students, whose questions and comments over the years have been essential to the framing of this book. And we extend a special thanks to, and hope to hear from, all the teachers and students we might never meet—their engagement with this book will frame new understandings of our shared past and its bearing on our future.

REVIEWERS

17th Edition Consultants

Paul Freedman, Yale University
Sheryl Kroen, University of Florida
Michael Kulikowski, Pennsylvania State University
Harry Liebersohn, University of Illinois, Urbana-Champaign
Helmut Smith, Vanderbilt University

17th Edition Reviewers

Donna Allen, Glendale Community College
Ken Bartlett, University of Toronto
Volker Benkert, Arizona State University
Dean Bennett, Schenectady City Community College
Patrick Brennan, Gulf Coast Community College
Neil Brooks, Community College of Baltimore County, Essex
James Brophy, University of Delaware
Kevin Caldwell, Blue Ridge Community College
Keith Chu, Bergen Community College
Alex D'Erizans, Borough of Manhattan Community College, CUNY
Hilary Earl, Nipissing University
Kirk Ford, Mississippi College
Michael Gattis, Gulf Coast Community College
David M. Gallo, College of Mount Saint Vincent
Jamie Gruring, Arizona State University
Tim Hack, Salem Community College
Bernard Hagerty, University of Pittsburg
Paul T. Hietter, Mesa Community College

Paul Hughes, Sussex County Community College
Kyle Irvin, Jefferson State Community College
Llana Krug, York College of Pennsylvania
Guy Lalande, St. Francis Xavier University
Chris Laney, Berkshire Community College
Charles Levine, Mesa Community College
Michael McKeown, Daytona State University
Dan Puckett, Troy State University
Dan Robinson, Troy State University
Craig Saucier, Southeastern Louisiana University
Aletia Seaborn, Southern Union State College
Victoria Thompson, Arizona State University
Donna Trembinski, St. Francis Xavier University
Pamela West, Jefferson State Community College
Julianna Wilson, Pima Community College

18th Edition Reviewers

Matthew Barlow, John Abbott College
Ken Bartlett, University of Toronto
Bob Brennan, Cape Fear Community College
Jim Brophy, University of Delaware
Keith Chu, Bergen Community College
Geoffrey Clark, SUNY Potsdam
Bill Donovan, Loyola University Maryland
Jeff Ewen, Sussex County Community College
Peter Goddard, University of Guelph
Paul Hughes, Sussex County Community College
Michael Kulikowski, Penn State University
Chris Laney, Berkshire Community College
James Martin, Campbell University
Derrick McKisick, Fairfield University
Dan Puckett, Troy University
Major Ben Richards, US Military Academy
Bo Riley, Columbus State Community College
Kimlisa Salazar, Pima Community College
Sara Scalenghe, Loyola University Maryland
Suzanne Smith, Cape Fear Community College
Bobbi Sutherland, Dordt College
David Tengwall, Anne Arundel Community College
Pam West, Jefferson State Community College
Julianna Wilson, Pima Community College
Margarita Youngo, Pima Community College

Western Civilizations

Their History & Their Culture

Before You Read This Chapter

STORY LINES

- The French Revolution of 1798–1799 overthrew Louis XVI and created a government committed in principle to the rule of law, the liberty of the individual, and an idea of the nation as a sovereign body of citizens. These political changes also opened the way for the expression of a wide variety of social grievances by peasants, laborers, women, and other social groups in Europe.
- The French Revolution encouraged the spread of democratic ideas, but it also led to an increase in the power of centralized nation-states in Europe. The pressures of the revolutionary wars led governments to develop larger national bureaucracies, modern professional armies, new legal codes, and new tax structures.
- The French Revolution was part of a broader set of changes that rocked the Atlantic world at the end of the eighteenth century. Along with the Haitian Revolution and the American Revolution, this wave of cataclysmic change reshaped the political order of Europe and the Americas.

CHRONOLOGY

May 1789	The Estates General meets
June 1789	The Tennis Court Oath
July 1789	The Fall of the Bastille
September 1792	First French Republic
January 1793	Execution of King Louis XIV
September 1793–July 1794	The Terror
1798–1799	Napoleon's invasion of Egypt
January 1804	Haitian independence
1804	Napoleon crowned emperor
1804	Civil code
1808	Invasion of Spain
1812	Invasion of Russia
1814–1815	Napoleon's abdication and defeat

18

The French Revolution

CORE OBJECTIVES

- **UNDERSTAND** the origins of the French Revolution in 1789.
- **EXPLAIN** the goals of French revolutionaries and the reactions of people elsewhere in Europe and the Atlantic world.
- **DESCRIBE** the events that made the Revolution more radical in 1792–1794.
- **IDENTIFY** the connections between the Revolution and Napoleon's regime after 1799, and the effects of Napoleon's conquests on Europe.
- **CONSIDER** the links between the French Revolution and the Atlantic world, which also saw revolutions in the Americas and in the Caribbean during these decades.

When a crowd of Parisians attacked the antiquated and nearly empty royal prison known as the Bastille on July 14, 1789, they were doing several things all at once. On the one hand, the revolt was a popular expression of support for the newly created National Assembly. This representative body had only weeks earlier declared an intention to put an end to absolutism in France by writing a constitution that made the nation, rather than the king, the sovereign authority in the land. But the Parisians in the street on July 14 did not express themselves like members of the National Assembly, who spoke the language of the Enlightenment. The actions of the revolutionary crowd were an expression of violent anger at the king's soldiers, who they feared might turn their guns on the city in a royal attempt to restore order by force. When the governor of the Bastille prison opened fire on the attackers, killing as many as a hundred, they responded with redoubled fury. By the end of the day, the prison had fallen, and the governor's battered body was dragged to the square before the city hall, where he was beheaded. Among the first to meet such an end as a consequence of revolution in France, he would not be the last.

This tension between noble political aspirations and cruel violence lies at the heart of the French Revolution. The significance of this contradiction was not lost on the millions of people throughout Europe who watched in astonishment as France was engulfed in turmoil in the 1790s. In 1789, one European out of every five lived in France, a kingdom that many considered to be the center of European culture. Other kingdoms were not immune to the same social and political tensions that divided the French. Aristocrats across Europe and the colonies resented monarchical inroads on their ancient freedoms. Members of the middle classes chafed under a system of official privilege that they increasingly saw as unjust and outmoded. Peasants fiercely resented the endless demands of central government on their limited resources. Nor were resentments focused exclusively on absolutist monarchs. Bitter resentments and tensions existed between country and city dwellers, between rich and poor, overprivileged and underprivileged, slave and free. The French Revolution was the most dramatic and tumultuous expression of all of these conflicts.

This age of revolution opened on the other side of the Atlantic Ocean. The American Revolution of 1776 was a crisis of the British Empire, linked to a long series of conflicts between England and France over colonial control of North America. It led to a major crisis of the old regime in France. Among "enlightened" Europeans, the success with which citizens of the United States had thrown off British rule and formed a republic based on Enlightenment principles was a source of tremendous optimism. Change would come, many believed. Reform was possible. The costs would be modest.

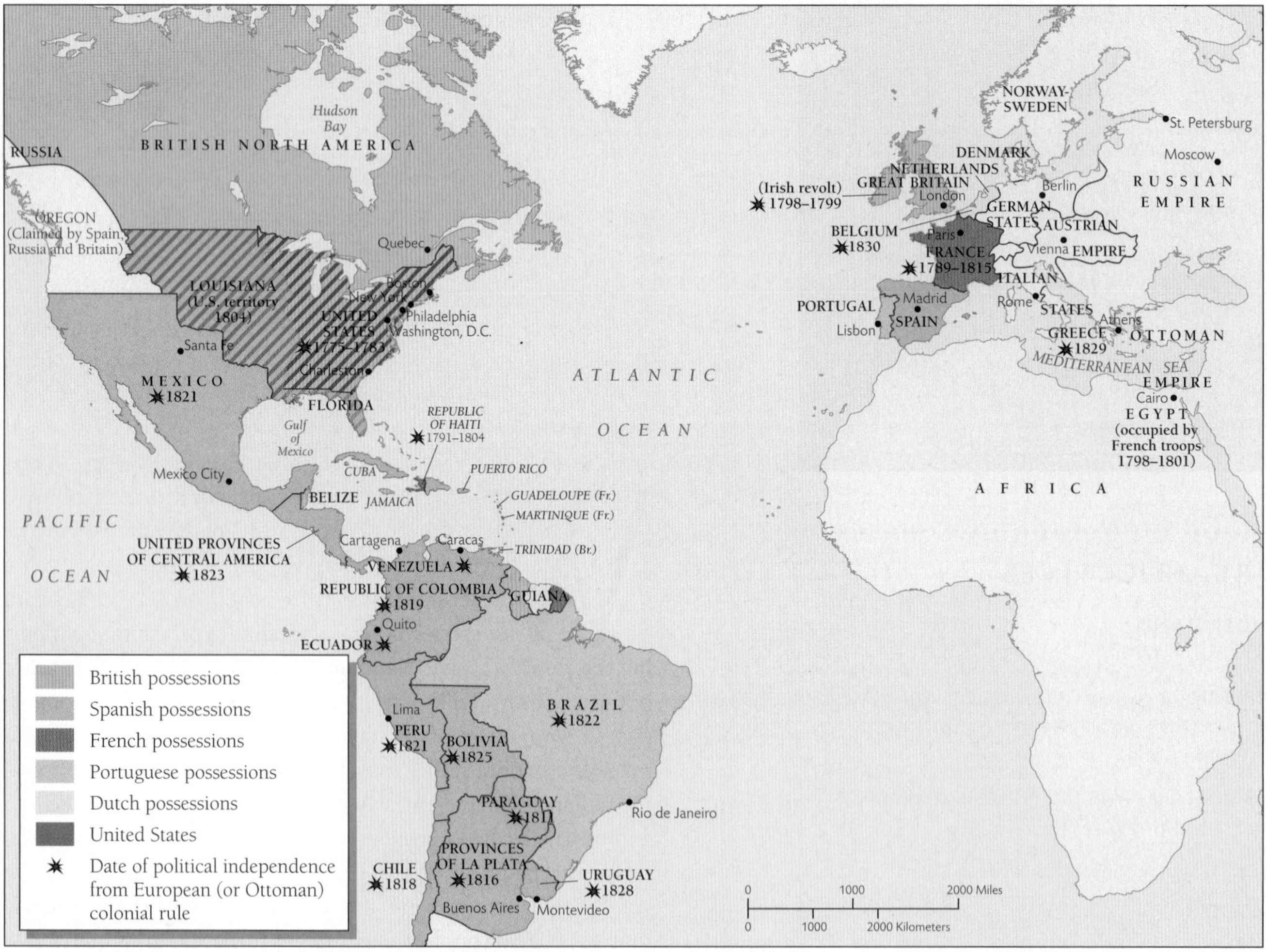

THE ATLANTIC REVOLUTIONS. The Atlantic revolutions shook nations and empires on both sides of the ocean, challenging the legitimacy of Europe's dynastic realms, lending further support to notions of popular sovereignty and forcing contemporaries to rethink the meanings of citizenship in a context of intense political and economic struggle. ▪ ***How many of these struggles took place within Europe?*** ▪ ***How many appear to have taken place on the periphery of the Atlantic world?*** ▪ ***What circumstances may have made it more difficult for such revolutionary movements to develop within Europe itself?***

The French Revolution did not live up to these expectations, though change certainly did come. By any measure, the accomplishments of the revolutionary decade were extraordinary: it successfully proved that the residents of an old monarchy in the heart of Europe could come together to constitute themselves as citizens of a new political idea, the nation. Freed from the shackles of tradition, revolutionaries in France posed new questions about the role of women in public life, about the separation of church and state, about the rights of Jews and other minorities. A slave revolt in the French colonies convinced the revolutionaries that the new liberties they defended so ardently also belonged to African slaves, though few had suggested such a thing at the outset. Meanwhile, the European wars precipitated by the revolution marked the first time that entire populations were mobilized as part of a new kind of devastating international conflict, the first "total wars." In other words, in spite of the optimism of those who began the revolution in 1789, it quickly became something much more costly, complex, and violent. Its effects were to resonate throughout Europe for the next half century.

THE FRENCH REVOLUTION: AN OVERVIEW

The term *French Revolution* is a shorthand for a complex series of events between 1789 and 1799. (Napoleon ruled from 1799 to 1814–1815.) To simplify, those events can be divided into four stages. In the first stage, running from 1788 to 1792, the struggle was constitutional and relatively peaceful. An increasingly bold elite articulated its grievances against the king. Like the American revolutionaries, French elites refused taxation without representation; attacked despotism, or arbitrary authority; and offered an Enlightenment-inspired program to rejuvenate the nation. Reforms, many of them breathtakingly wide ranging, were instituted—some accepted or even offered by the king, and others passed over his objections. The peaceful, constitutional phase did not last. Unlike the American Revolution, the French Revolution did not stabilize around one constitution or one set of political leaders, for many reasons.

Reforms met with resistance, dividing the country. The threat of dramatic change within one of the most powerful countries in Europe created international tensions. In 1792, these tensions exploded into war, and the crises of war, in turn, spelled the end of the Bourbon monarchy and the beginning of the republic. This second stage of the revolution, which lasted from 1792 to 1794, was one of acute crisis, consolidation, and repression. A ruthlessly centralized government mobilized all the country's resources to fight the foreign enemy as well as counterrevolutionaries at home, to destroy traitors and the vestiges of the Old Regime.

The Terror, as this policy was called, did save the republic, but it exhausted itself in factions and recriminations and collapsed in 1794. In the third phase, from 1794 to 1799, the government drifted. France remained a republic. It continued to fight with Europe. Undermined by corruption and division, the state fell prey to the ambitions of a military leader, Napoleon Bonaparte. Napoleon's rule, punctuated by astonishing victories and catastrophes, stretched from 1799 to 1815. It began as a republic, became an empire, and ended—after a last hurrah—in the muddy fields outside the Belgian village of Waterloo. After Napoleon's final defeat, the other European monarchs restored the Bourbons to the throne. That restoration, however, would be short lived, and the cycle of revolution and reaction continued into the nineteenth century.

THE COMING OF THE REVOLUTION

What were the long-term causes of the revolution in France? Historians long ago argued that the causes and outcomes should be understood in terms of class conflict. According to this interpretation, a rising bourgeoisie, or middle class, inspired by Enlightenment ideas and by its own self-interest, overthrew what was left of the aristocratic order. This interpretation drew on the writings of the nineteenth-century philosopher Karl Marx and on much twentieth-century sociology.

Historians have substantially modified this bold thesis. To be sure, the origins of the revolution lie in eighteenth-century French society. Yet that society was not simply divided between a bourgeois class and the aristocracy. Instead, it was increasingly dominated by a new elite or social group that brought together aristocrats, officeholders, professionals, and—to a lesser degree—merchants and businessmen. To understand the revolution, we need to understand this new social group and its conflicts with the government of Louis XVI.

French society was legally divided into Three Estates. (An individual's *estate* marked his standing, or status, and it determined legal rights, taxes, and so on.) The First Estate comprised all the clergy; the Second Estate, the nobility. The Third Estate, by far the largest, included everyone else, from wealthy lawyers and businessmen to urban laborers and poor peasants. Within the political and social elite of the country, a small but powerful group, these legal distinctions often seemed artificial. To begin with, in the upper reaches of society, the social boundaries between nobles and wealthy commoners were ill defined. Noble title was accessible to those who could afford to buy an ennobling office. For example, close to 50,000 new nobles were created between 1700 and 1789. The nobility depended on a constant infusion of talent and economic power from the wealthy social groups of the Third Estate.

To preserve their elite status, aristocrats spoke of a distinction between the nobility of the sword and of the robe, the former supposedly of a more ancient and distinguished lineage derived from military service, the latter aristocrats because they had purchased administrative or judicial office (hence the robe).

Nevertheless, wealth did not take predictable forms. Most noble wealth was proprietary—that is, tied to land, urban properties, purchased offices, and the like. Yet noble families did not disdain trade or commerce, as historians long thought. In fact, noblemen financed most industry, and they also invested heavily in banking and such enterprises as ship owning, the slave trade, mining, and metallurgy. Moreover, the very wealthy members of the Third Estate also preferred to invest in secure, proprietary holdings. Thus, throughout the century, much middle-class wealth was transformed into noble wealth, and a significant number of rich bourgeois became noblemen. Wealthy members of the bourgeoisie did not see themselves as a separate class. They thought of themselves as different from—and often opposed to—the common people, who worked with their hands, and they identified with the values of a nobility to which they frequently aspired.

There were, nonetheless, important social tensions. Less prosperous lawyers—and there were an increasing number of them—were jealous of the privileged position of a favored few in their profession. Over the course of the century, the price of offices rose, making it more difficult to buy one's way into the nobility, and creating tensions between middling members of the Third Estate and the very rich in trade and commerce who, by and large, were the only group able to afford to climb the social ladder. Less wealthy nobles resented the success of rich, upstart commoners whose income allowed them to live in luxury. In sum, several fault lines ran through the elite and the middle classes. All these social groups could nonetheless join in attacking a government and an economy that were not serving their interests.

The Enlightenment had changed public debate (see Chapter 17). Although ideas did not cause the revolution, they played a critical role in articulating grievances. The political theories of Locke, Voltaire, and Montesquieu could appeal to both discontented nobles and members of the

PREREVOLUTIONARY PROPAGANDA. Political cartoons in late-eighteenth-century France commonly portrayed the Third Estate as bearing the burden of taxation while performing the bulk of the nation's productive work. On the left, a peasant bears the burden of his tools and his harvest, as a cleric and a nobleman look on; on the right, the commoner is literally carrying his social superiors. ▪ ***What visual cues indicate the status of individuals in these images?*** ▪ ***Would one expect the nobility or the clergy to defend their status on the basis of their usefulness to society?*** ▪ ***Can one detect the power of certain Enlightenment ideas behind these forms of social critique?*** ▪ ***Which ones?*** ▪ ***How might an opponent of Enlightenment thought have confronted such arguments?***

middle class. Voltaire was popular because of his attacks on noble privileges; Locke and Montesquieu gained widespread followings because of their defense of private property and limited sovereignty. Montesquieu's ideas appealed to the noble lawyers and officeholders who dominated France's powerful law courts, the *parlements*. They read his doctrine of checks and balances as support for their argument that parlements could provide a check to the despotism of the king's government. When conflicts arose, noble leaders presented themselves as defenders of the nation threatened by the king and his ministers.

The campaign for change was also fueled by economic reformers. The "physiocrats" urged the government to simplify the tax system and free the economy from mercantilist regulations. They advocated an end to price controls in the grain trade, which had been imposed to keep the cost of bread low. Such interventions, they argued, interfered with the market's ability to find an equilibrium between supply and demand.

In the countryside, peasants did not think in terms of markets. They were caught in a web of obligations to landlords, church, and state: a tithe, or levy, on farm produce owed to the church; fees for the use of a landlord's mill or wine press; fees to the landlord; and fees when land changed hands. In addition, peasants paid a disproportionate share of both direct and indirect taxes—the most onerous of which was the salt tax—levied by the government. (For some time, the production of salt had been a state monopoly; every individual was required to buy at least seven pounds a year from the government works. The result was a commodity whose cost was often as much as fifty or sixty times its actual value.) Further grievances stemmed from the requirement to maintain public roads (the corvée) and from the hunting privileges that nobles for centuries had regarded as the distinctive badge of their order.

Social and economic conditions deteriorated on the eve of the revolution. A general price increase during much of the eighteenth century, which permitted the French economy to expand by providing capital for investment, created hardship for the peasantry and for urban tradesmen and laborers. Their plight deteriorated further at the end of the 1780s, when poor harvests sent bread prices sharply higher. In 1788, families found themselves spending more than 50 percent of their income on bread, which made up the bulk of their diet. The following year the figure rose to as much as 80 percent. Poor harvests reduced demand for manufactured goods, and contracting markets in turn created unemployment. Many peasants left the countryside for the cities, hoping to find work there—only to discover that urban unemployment was far worse than that in rural areas. Evidence indicates that between 1787 and 1789 the unemployment rate in many parts of urban France was as high as 50 percent.

Failure and Reform

An inefficient tax system further weakened the country's financial position. Taxation differed according to social standings and varied from region to region—some areas were subject to a much higher rate than others. Special exemptions made the task of collectors more difficult. The financial system, already burdened by debts incurred under Louis XIV, all but broke down completely under the increased expenses brought on by French participation in the American Revolution. The cost of servicing the national debt in the 1780s consumed 50 percent of the nation's budget.

Problems with the economy reflected weaknesses in France's administrative structure, ultimately the responsibility of the country's absolutist monarch, Louis XVI (1774–1792).

LOUIS XVI. The last prerevolutionary French king, who was to lose his life in the Terror, combined in his person a strong attachment to the monarchy's absolutist doctrine with an inability to find workable solutions to the financial crisis facing his government. His royal portrait mimicked the forms of spectacular display that proved so useful to Louis XIV in shoring up the power of the monarchy. ▪ ***What made this display so much less potent in the late eighteenth century?*** ▪ ***What caused the monarchy to lose its aura?***

Analyzing Primary Sources

What is the Third Estate? (1789)

The Abbé Emmanuel-Joseph Sieyès (1748–1836) was, by virtue of his office in the Church, a member of the First Estate of the Estates General. Nevertheless, his political savvy led him to be elected as a representative of the Third Estate from the district of Chartres. Sieyès was a formidable politician as well as a writer. His career during the revolution, which he ended by assisting Napoleon's seizure of power, began with one of the most important radical pamphlets of 1789. In What Is the Third Estate?, *Sieyès posed fundamental questions about the rights of the estate, which represented the great majority of the population and helped provoke its secession from the Estates General.*

The plan of this book is fairly simple. We must ask ourselves three questions.

1. What is the Third Estate? *Everything.*
2. What has it been until now in the political order? *Nothing.*
3. What does it want to be? *Something.*

It suffices to have made the point that the so-called usefulness of a privileged order to the public service is a fallacy; that without help from this order, all the arduous tasks in the service are performed by the Third Estate; that without this order the higher posts could be infinitely better filled; that they ought to be the natural prize and reward of recognized ability and service; and that if the privileged have succeeded in usurping all well-paid and honorific posts, this is both a hateful iniquity towards the generality of citizens and an act of treason to the commonwealth.

Who is bold enough to maintain that the Third Estate does not contain within itself everything needful to constitute a complete nation? It is like a strong and robust man with one arm still in chains. If the privileged order were removed, the nation would not be something less but something more. What then is the Third Estate? All; but an "all" that is fettered and oppressed. What would it be without the privileged order? It would be all; but free and flourishing. Nothing will go well without the Third Estate; everything would go considerably better without the two others.

Source: Emmanuel-Joseph Sieyès, *What Is the Third Estate?*, ed. S. E. Finer, trans. M. Blondel, (London: 1964), pp. 53–63.

Questions for Analysis

1. How might contemporaries have viewed Sieyès's argument that the Three Estates should be evaluated according to their usefulness to the "commonwealth"?
2. Was Sieyès's language—accusing the privileged orders of "treason" and arguing for their "removal"—an incitement to violence?
3. What did Sieyès mean by the term *nation*? Could one speak of France as a nation in these terms before 1789?

Louis wished to improve the lot of the poor, abolish torture, and shift the burden of taxation onto the richer classes, but he lacked the ability to accomplish these tasks. He appointed reformers like Anne-Robert-Jacques Turgot, a physiocrat, and Jacques Necker, a Swiss Protestant banker, as finance ministers, only to arouse the opposition of traditionalists at court. When he pressed for new taxes to be paid by the nobility, he was defeated by the provincial parlements, who defended the aristocracy's immunity from taxation. He allowed his wife, the young but strong-willed Marie Antoinette—daughter of Austria's Maria Theresa—a free hand to dispense patronage among her friends. The result was constant intrigue and frequently reshuffled alliances at Versailles. By 1788, a weak monarch, together with a chaotic financial situation and severe social tensions, brought absolutist France to the edge of political disaster.

THE DESTRUCTION OF THE OLD REGIME

The fiscal crisis precipitated the revolution. In 1787 and 1788, the king's principal ministers, Charles de Calonne and Loménie de Brienne, proposed new taxes to meet the growing deficit, notably a stamp duty and a direct tax on the annual produce of the land.

Hoping to persuade the nobility to agree to these reforms, the king summoned an Assembly of Notables from among the aristocracy. This group insisted that any new tax scheme must be approved by the Estates General, the representative body of the Three Estates of the realm, and that the king had no legal authority to arrest and imprison arbitrarily. These proposed constitutional changes echoed the English aristocrats of 1688 and the American revolutionaries of 1776.

Faced with economic crisis and financial chaos, Louis XVI summoned the Estates General (which had not met since 1614) to meet in 1789. His action appeared to many as the only solution to France's deepening problems. Long-term grievances and short-term hardships produced bread riots across the country in the spring of 1789. Fear that the forces of law and order were collapsing and that the common people might take matters into their own hands spurred the Estates General. Each of the three orders elected its own deputies—the Third Estate indirectly through local assemblies. These assemblies were charged as well with the responsibility of drawing up lists of grievances (*cahiers des doléances*), further heightening expectations for fundamental reform.

The delegates of the Third Estate, though elected by assemblies chosen in turn by artisans and peasants, represented the outlook of an elite. Only 13 percent were men of business. About 25 percent were lawyers; 43 percent were government officeholders of some sort.

By tradition, each estate met and voted as a body. In the past, this had generally meant that the First Estate (the clergy) had combined with the Second (the nobility) to defeat the Third. Now the Third Estate made it clear it would not tolerate such an arrangement. The Third's interests were articulated most memorably by the Abbé Emmanuel Sieyès, a radical member of the clergy. "What is the Third Estate?" asked Sieyès, in his famous pamphlet

THE TENNIS COURT OATH* BY JACQUES LOUIS DAVID (1748–1825).** In June 1789, the members of the Third Estate, now calling themselves the National Assembly, swear an oath not to disband until France has a constitution. In the center stands Jean Bailly, president of the new assembly. The Abbé Sieyès is seated at the table. In the foreground, a clergyman, an aristocrat, and a member of the Third Estate embrace in a symbol of national unity. The single deputy who refused to take the oath sits at far right, his hands clasped against his chest. ▪ ***What is the significance of this near unanimity expressed in defiance of the king? ▪ ***What options were available to those who did not support this move?***

of January 1789. Everything, he answered, and pointed to eighteenth-century social changes to bolster his point. In early 1789, Sieyès's views were still unusually radical. But the leaders of the Third Estate agreed that the three orders should sit together and vote as individuals. More important, they insisted that the Third Estate should have twice as many members as the First and Second.

The king first opposed "doubling the Third" and then changed his position. His unwillingness to take a strong stand on voting procedures cost him support he might otherwise have obtained from the Third Estate. Shortly after the Estates General opened at Versailles in May 1789, the Third Estate, angered by the king's attitude, took the revolutionary step of leaving the body and declaring itself the National Assembly. Locked out of the Estates General meeting hall on June 20, the Third Estate and a handful of sympathetic nobles and clergymen moved to a nearby indoor tennis court.

Here, under the leadership of the volatile, maverick aristocrat Mirabeau and the radical clergyman Sieyès, they bound themselves by a solemn oath not to separate until they had drafted a constitution for France. This Tennis Court Oath, sworn on June 20, 1789, can be seen as the beginning of the French Revolution. By claiming the authority to remake the government in the name of the people, the National Assembly was asserting its right to act as the highest sovereign power in the nation. On June 27, the king virtually conceded this right by ordering all the delegates to join the National Assembly.

First Stages of the French Revolution

The first stage of the French Revolution extended from June 1789 to August 1792. In the main, this stage was moderate, its actions dominated by the leadership of liberal nobles and men of the Third Estate. Yet three events in the summer and fall of 1789 furnished evidence that their leadership would be challenged.

POPULAR REVOLTS

From the beginning of the political crisis, public attention was high. It was roused not merely by interest in political reform but also by the economic crisis that, as we have seen, brought the price of bread to astronomical heights. Many believed that the aristocracy and the king were conspiring to punish the Third Estate by encouraging scarcity and high prices. Rumors circulated in Paris during the latter days of June 1789 that the king's troops were mobilizing to march on the city. The electors of Paris (those who had voted for the Third Estate—workshop masters, artisans, and shopkeepers) feared not only the king but also the Parisian poor, who had been parading through the streets and threatening violence. The common people would soon be referred to as *sans-culottes* (*sahn koo-LAWTS*). The term, which translates to "without breeches," was an antiaristocratic badge of pride: a man of the people wore full-length trousers rather than aristocratic breeches with stockings and gold-buckled shoes. Led by the electors, the people formed a provisional municipal government and organized a militia of volunteers to maintain order. Determined to obtain arms, they made their way on July 14 to the Bastille, an ancient fortress where guns and ammunition were stored. Built in the Middle Ages, the Bastille had served as a prison for many years but was no longer much used. Nevertheless, it symbolized hated royal authority. When crowds demanded arms from its governor, he procrastinated and then, fearing a frontal assault, opened fire, killing ninety-eight of the attackers. The crowd took revenge, capturing the fortress (which held only seven prisoners—five common criminals and two people confined for mental incapacity) and decapitating the governor. Similar groups took control in other cities across France. The fall of the Bastille was the first instance of the people's role in revolutionary change.

The second popular revolt occurred in the countryside. Peasants, too, expected and feared a monarchical and aristocratic counterrevolution. Rumors flew that the king's armies were on their way, that Austrians, Prussians, or "brigands" were invading. Frightened and uncertain, peasants and villagers organized militias; others attacked and burned manor houses, sometimes to look for grain but usually to find and destroy records of manorial dues. This "Great Fear," as historians have labeled it, compounded the confusion in rural areas. The news, when it reached Paris, convinced deputies at Versailles that the administration of rural France had simply collapsed.

The third instance of popular uprising, the "October Days of 1789," was brought on by economic crisis. This time, Parisian women from the market district, angered by the soaring price of bread and fired by rumors of the king's continuing unwillingness to cooperate with the assembly, marched to Versailles on October 5 and demanded to be heard. Not satisfied with its reception by the assembly, the crowd broke through the gates to the palace, calling for the king to return to Paris from Versailles. On the afternoon of the following day the king yielded and returned to Paris, accompanied by the crowd and the National Guard.

Each of these popular uprisings shaped the political events unfolding at Versailles. The storming of the Bastille persuaded the king and nobles to agree to the creation of the National Assembly. The Great Fear compelled the most

WOMEN OF PARIS LEAVING FOR VERSAILLES, OCTOBER 1789. A crowd of women, accompanied by Lafayette and the National Guard, marched to Versailles to confront the king about shortages and rising prices in Paris. ▪ ***Did the existence of the National Assembly change the meaning of such popular protests?***

sweeping changes of the entire revolutionary period. In an effort to quell rural disorder, on the night of August 4 the assembly took a giant step toward abolishing all forms of privilege. It eliminated the Church tithe (tax on the harvest), the labor requirement known as the corvée, the nobility's hunting privileges, and a wide variety of tax exemptions and monopolies. In effect, these reforms obliterated the remnants of feudalism. One week later, the assembly abolished the sale of offices, thereby sweeping away one of the fundamental institutions of the Old Regime. The king's return to Paris during the October Days of 1789 undercut his ability to resist further changes.

THE NATIONAL ASSEMBLY AND THE RIGHTS OF MAN

The assembly issued its charter of liberties, the Declaration of the Rights of Man and of the Citizen, in September 1789. It declared property to be a natural right, along with liberty, security, and "resistance to oppression." It declared freedom of speech, religious toleration, and liberty of the press inviolable. All citizens were to be treated equally before the law. No one was to be imprisoned or punished without due process of law. Sovereignty resided in the people, who could depose officers of the government if they abused their powers. These were not new ideas; they represented the outcome of Enlightenment discussions and revolutionary debates and deliberations. The Declaration became the preamble to the new constitution, which the assembly finished in 1791.

Whom did the Declaration mean by "man and the citizen"? The constitution distinguished between "passive" citizens, guaranteed rights under law, and "active" citizens, who paid a certain amount in taxes and could thus vote and hold office. About half the adult males in France qualified as active citizens. Even their power was curtailed, because they could vote only for "electors," men whose property ownership qualified them to hold office. Later in the revolution, the more radical republic abolished the distinction between active and passive, and the conservative regimes reinstated it. Which men could be trusted to participate in politics and on what terms was a hotly contested issue.

Also controversial were the rights of religious minorities. The revolution gave full civil rights to Protestants, though in areas long divided by religious conflict those rights were challenged by Catholics. The revolution did, hesitantly, give civil rights to Jews, a measure that sparked protest in areas of eastern France. Religious toleration, a central theme of the Enlightenment, meant ending persecution; it did not mean that the regime was prepared to accommodate religious difference. The assembly abolished serfdom and banned slavery in continental France. It remained silent on colonial slavery, and although delegations pressed the assembly on political rights for free people of color, the assembly exempted the colonies from the constitution's provisions. Events in the Caribbean, as we will see, later forced the issue.

The rights and roles of women became the focus of sharp debate, as revolutionaries confronted demands that working women participate in guilds or trade organizations, and laws on marriage, divorce, poor relief, and education were reconsidered. The Englishwoman Mary Wollstonecraft's milestone book *A Vindication of the Rights of Woman* (see Chapter 17) was penned during the revolutionary debate over national education. Should girls be educated? To what end? Wollstonecraft, as we have seen, argued strongly that reforming education required forging a new concept of independent and equal womanhood. Even Wollstonecraft, however, only hinted at political representation, aware that such an idea would "excite laughter."

Only a handful of thinkers broached the subject of women in politics: the aristocratic Enlightenment thinker the Marquis de Condorcet and, from another shore, Marie Gouze, the self-educated daughter of a butcher. Gouze became an intellectual and playwright and renamed herself Olympe de Gouges. Like many "ordinary" people, she found in the explosion of revolutionary activity the opportunity to address the public by writing speeches, pamphlets, or newspapers. She composed her own manifesto, the *Declaration of the Rights of Woman and the Citizen* (1791). Beginning with the proposition that "social distinctions can only be based on the common utility," she declared that women had the same rights as men, including resistance to authority, participation in government, and naming the fathers of illegitimate children. This last demand offers a glimpse of the shame, isolation, and hardship faced by an unmarried woman.

DECLARATION OF THE RIGHTS OF MAN (1789). Presented as principles of natural law inscribed on stone, this print gives a good indication of how the authors of the Declaration wished it to be perceived by the French people. Over the tablets is a beneficent and all-seeing deity accompanied by two female allegorical figures representing strength and virtue on one side and the French nation on the other. Two armed soldiers wear the uniform of the newly created National Guard. The image's symbols refer to Masonic lore (the triangle or pyramid with an eye at the center, the snake grasping its tail), and a set of historical references from the Roman Republic: a Phrygian cap, used by Romans as a symbol of liberty, is mounted on a spear emerging from a bundle of sticks. This bundle was known as a *faisceau* and was carried in ancient Rome by magistrates as symbols of their authority. ▪ ***Given the absence of any monarchical symbolism or references to the Catholic Church, why was it important for the authors to come up with an alternative set of historical references?***

De Gouges's demand for equal rights was unusual, but many women nevertheless participated in the everyday activities of the revolution, joining clubs, demonstrations, and debates and making their presence known, sometimes forcefully. Women artisans' organizations had a well-established role in municipal life, and they used the revolution as an opportunity to assert their rights to produce and sell goods. Market women were familiar public figures, often central to the circulation of news and spontaneous popular demonstrations (the October Days are a good example). Initially, the regime celebrated the support of women "citizens," and female figures were favorite symbols for liberty, prudence, and the bounty of nature in revolutionary iconography. When the revolution became more radical, however, some revolutionaries saw autonomous political activity by women's organizations as a threat to public order, and in 1793 the revolutionaries shut down the women's political clubs. Even so, many ordinary women were able to make use of the revolution's new legislation on marriage (divorce was legalized in 1792) and inheritance to support claims for relief from abusive husbands or absent

Analyzing Primary Sources

Declaration of the Rights of Man and of the Citizen

One of the first important pronouncements of the National Assembly after the Tennis Court Oath was the Declaration of the Rights of Man and of the Citizen. *The authors drew inspiration from the American Declaration of Independence, but the language is even more heavily influenced by the ideals of French Enlightenment philosophers, particularly Rousseau. Following are the* Declaration's *preamble and some of its most important principles.*

The representatives of the French people, constituted as the National Assembly, considering that ignorance, disregard, or contempt for the rights of man are the sole causes of public misfortunes and the corruption of governments, have resolved to set forth, in a solemn declaration, the natural, inalienable, and sacred rights of man, so that the constant presence of this declaration may ceaselessly remind all members of the social body of their rights and duties; so that the acts of legislative power and those of the executive power may be more respected... and so that the demands of the citizens, grounded henceforth on simple and incontestable principles, may always be directed to the maintenance of the constitution and to the welfare of all....

Article 1. Men are born and remain free and equal in rights. Social distinctions can be based only on public utility.

Article 2. The aim of every political association is the preservation of the natural and imprescriptible rights of man. These rights are liberty, property, security, and resistance to oppression.

Article 3. The source of all sovereignty resides essentially in the nation. No body, no individual can exercise authority that does not explicitly proceed from it.

Article 4. Liberty consists in being able to do anything that does not injure another; thus the only limits upon each man's exercise of his natural laws are those that guarantee enjoyment of these same rights to the other members of society.

Article 5. The law has the right to forbid only actions harmful to society. No action may be prevented that is not forbidden by law, and no one may be constrained to do what the law does not order.

Article 6. The law is the expression of the general will. All citizens have the right to participate personally, or through representatives, in its formation. It must be the same for all, whether it protects or punishes. All citizens, being equal in its eyes, are equally admissable to all public dignities, positions, and employments, according to their ability, and on the basis of no other distinction than that of their virtues and talents....

Article 16. A society in which the guarantee of rights is not secured, or the separation of powers is not clearly established, has no constitution.

Source: Declaration of the Rights of Man and of the Citizen, as cited in K. M. Baker, ed., *The Old Regime and the French Revolution* (Chicago: 1987), pp. 238–239.

Questions for Analysis

1. Who is the Declaration addressed to? Is it just about the rights of the French, or do these ideas apply to all people?

2. What gave a group of deputies elected to advise Louis XVI on constitutional reforms the right to proclaim themselves a National Assembly? What was revolutionary about this claim to represent the French nation?

3. Article 6, which states that "law is the expression of general will," is adapted from Rousseau's *Social Contract*. Does the Declaration give any indication of how the "general will" can be known?

fathers, claims that would have been impossible under the prerevolutionary legislation.

THE NATIONAL ASSEMBLY AND THE CHURCH

In November 1789 the National Assembly decided to confiscate all Church lands to use them as collateral for issuing interest-bearing notes known as *assignats*. The assembly hoped that this action would resolve the economy's inflationary crisis, and eventually these notes circulated widely as paper money. In July 1789, the assembly enacted the Civil Constitution of the Clergy, bringing the Church under state authority. The new law forced all bishops and priests to swear allegiance to the state, which henceforth paid their salaries. The aim was to make the Catholic Church of France a national institution, free from interference from Rome.

These reforms were bitterly divisive. Many people resented the privileged status of the Church, and its vast monastic land holdings. On the other hand, for centuries the parish church had been a central institution in small towns and villages, providing poor relief and other services, in addition to baptisms and marriages. The Civil Constitution of the Clergy sparked fierce resistance in some parts of rural France. When the pope threatened to excommunicate priests who signed the Civil Constitution, he raised the stakes: allegiance to the new French state meant damnation. Many people, especially peasants in the deeply Catholic areas of western France, were driven into open revolt.

The National Assembly made a series of economic and governmental changes with lasting effects. To raise money, it sold off Church lands, although few of the genuinely needy could afford to buy them. To encourage the growth of economic enterprise, it abolished guilds. To rid the country of local aristocratic power, it reorganized local governments, dividing France into eighty-three equal departments. These measures aimed to defend individual liberty and freedom from customary privilege. Their principal beneficiaries were, for the most part, members of the elite, people on their way up under the previous regime who were able to take advantage of the opportunities, such as buying land or being elected to office, that the new one offered. In this realm as elsewhere, the social changes of the revolution endorsed changes already under way in the eighteenth century.

A NEW STAGE: POPULAR REVOLUTION

In the summer of 1792, the revolution's moderate leaders were toppled and replaced by republicans, who repudiated the monarchy and claimed to rule on behalf of a sovereign people. Why this abrupt and drastic change? Was the revolution blown off course? These are among the most difficult questions about the French Revolution. Historians have focused on three factors to explain the revolution's radical turn: changes in popular politics, a crisis of leadership, and international polarization.

First, the revolution politicized the common people, especially in cities. Newspapers filled with political and social commentary multiplied, freed from censorship. From 1789 forward, a wide variety of political clubs became part of daily political life. Some were formal, almost like political parties, gathering members of the elite to debate issues facing the country and influence decisions in the assembly. Other clubs opened their doors to those excluded from formal politics, and they read aloud from newspapers and discussed the options facing the country, from the provisions of the constitution to the trustworthiness of the king and his ministers. This political awareness was heightened by nearly constant shortages and fluctuating prices. Prices particularly exasperated the working people of Paris who had eagerly awaited change since their street demonstrations of 1789. Urban demonstrations, often led by women, demanded cheaper bread; political leaders in clubs and newspapers called for the government to control rising inflation. Club leaders spoke for men and women who felt cheated by the constitution.

A second major reason for the change of course was a lack of effective national leadership. Louis XVI remained a weak monarch. He was forced to support measures personally distasteful to him, in particular the Civil Constitution of the Clergy. He was sympathetic to the plottings of the queen, who was in contact with her brother Leopold II of Austria. Urged on by Marie Antoinette, Louis agreed to attempt an escape from France in June 1791, hoping to rally foreign support for counterrevolution. The members of the royal family managed to slip past their palace guards in Paris, but they were apprehended near the border at Varennes and brought back to the capital. The constitution of 1791 declared France a monarchy, but after the escape to Varennes, Louis was little more than a prisoner of the assembly.

The Counterrevolution

The third major reason for the dramatic turn of affairs was war. From the outset of the revolution, men and women across Europe had been compelled, by the very intensity of events in France, to take sides in the conflict. In the years immediately after 1789, the revolution in France won the enthusiastic support of a wide range of thinkers. The British poet William Wordsworth, who later became disillusioned, recalled his initial mood: "Bliss was it in that dawn to be alive." His sentiments were echoed across the Continent by poets and philosophers, including the German Johann Gottfried von Herder, who declared the revolution the most important historical moment since the Reformation. In Britain, the Low Countries, western Germany, and Italy, "patriots" proclaimed their allegiance to the new revolution.

Others opposed the revolution from the start. Exiled nobles, who fled France for sympathetic royal courts in Germany and elsewhere, did all they could to stir up counterrevolutionary sentiment. In Britain, the conservative cause was strengthened by the publication in 1790 of Edmund Burke's *Reflections on the Revolution in France*. A Whig politician who had sympathized with the American revolutionaries, Burke deemed the revolution in France a monstrous crime against the social order (see ***Competing Viewpoints*** on pages 594–95).

Analyzing Primary Sources

Social Grievances on the Eve of the Revolution (1789)

During the elections to the Estates General, communities drew up "notebooks of grievances" to be presented to the government. The following comes from a rural community, Lignère la Doucelle.

For a long time now, the inhabitants have been crushed beneath the excessive burden of the multiplicity of taxes that they have been obliged to pay. Their parish is large and spread out, but it is a hard land with many uncultivated areas, almost all of it divided into small parcels. There is not one single farm of appreciable size, and these small properties are occupied either by the poor or by people who are doing so poorly that they go without bread every other day. They buy bread or grain nine months of the year. No industries operate in this parish, and from the time they began complaining, no one has ever listened. The cry of anguish echoed all to the way to the ministry after having fruitlessly worn out their intendants. They have always seen their legitimate claims being continuously denied, so may the fortunate moment of equality revive them.

* * *

That all lords, country gentlemen, and others of the privileged class who, either directly or through their proxies, desire to make a profit on their wealth, regardless of the nature of that wealth, pay the same taxes as the common people.

* * *

That the seigneur's mills not be obligatory, allowing everyone to choose where he would like to mill his grain.

* * *

That the children of common people living on a par with nobles be admitted for military service, as the nobility is.

That the king not bestow noble titles upon someone and their family line, but that titles be bestowed only upon those deserving it.

That nobility not be available for purchase or by any fashion other than by the bearing of arms or other service rendered to the State.

* * *

That church members be only able to take advantage of one position. That those who are enjoying more than one be made to choose within a fixed time period.

That future abbeys all be placed into the hands of the king, that His Majesty benefit from their revenue as the head abbots have been able to.

That in towns where there are several convents belonging to the same order, there be only one, and the goods and revenue of those that are to be abolished go to the profit of the crown.

That the convents where there are not normally twelve residents be abolished.

That no tenth of black wheat be paid to parish priests, priors or other beneficiaries, since this grain is only used to prepare the soil for the sowing of rye.

That they also not be paid any tenths of hemp, wool, or lamb. That in the countryside they be required to conduct burials and funerals free of charge. That the ten sous for audit books, insinuations, and the 100 [sous] collected for the parish be abolished.

* * *

That grain be taxed in the realm at a fixed price, or rather that its exportation abroad be forbidden except in the case where it would be sold at a low price.

Source: Armand Bellée, ed., *Cahiers de plaintes & doléances des paroisses de la province du Maine pour les Etats-généraux de 1789*, vol. 2 (Le Mans: 1881–1892), pp. 578–582.

Questions for Analysis

1. Do these grievances reflect the interests of only one social group, or can one hear demands being made from different groups within this rural community?
2. What do you think were the main problems faced by this community?
3. How did the revolutionaries receive these grievances?

Competing Viewpoints

Debating the French Revolution: Edmund Burke and Thomas Paine

The best-known debate on the French Revolution set the Irish-born conservative Edmund Burke against the British radical Thomas Paine. Burke opposed the French Revolution from the beginning. His Reflections on the Revolution in France *was published early, in 1790, when the French king was still securely on the throne. Burke disagreed with the premises of the revolution. Rights, he argued, were not abstract and "natural" but the results of specific historical traditions. Remodeling the French government without reference to the past and failing to pay proper respect to tradition and custom had, in his eyes, destroyed the fabric of French civilization.*

Thomas Paine was one of many to respond to Burke. The Rights of Man *(1791–1792) defended the revolution and, more generally, conceptions of human rights. In the polarized atmosphere of the revolutionary wars, simply possessing Paine's pamphlet was cause for imprisonment in Britain.*

Edmund Burke

You will observe, that from the Magna Carta to the Declaration of Rights, it has been the uniform policy of our constitution to claim and assert our liberties, as an entailed inheritance derived to us from our forefathers.... We have an inheritable crown; an inheritable peerage; and a house of commons and a people inheriting privileges, franchises, and liberties, from a long line of ancestors....

You had all these advantages in your ancient states, but you chose to act as if you had never been moulded into civil society, and had every thing to begin anew. You began ill, because you began by despising every thing that belonged to you.... If the last generations of your country appeared without much luster in your eyes, you might have passed them by, and derived your claims from a more early race of ancestors.... Respecting your forefathers, you would have been taught to respect yourselves. You would not have chosen to consider the French as a people of yesterday, as a nation of low-born servile wretches until the emancipating year of 1789.... [Y]ou would not have been content to be represented as a gang of Maroon slaves, suddenly broke loose from the house of bondage, and therefore to be pardoned for your abuse of liberty to which you were not accustomed and ill fitted....

... The fresh ruins of France, which shock our feelings wherever we can turn our eyes, are not the devastation of civil war; they are the sad but instructive monuments of rash and ignorant councel in time of profound peace. They are the display of inconsiderate and presumptuous, because unresisted and irresistible authority....

Nothing is more certain, than that of our manners, our civilization, and all the good things which are connected with manners, and with civilization, have, in this European world of ours, depended upon two principles; and were indeed the result of both combined; I mean the spirit of a gentleman, and the spirit of religion. The nobility and the clergy, the one by profession, the other by patronage, kept learning in existance, even

Burke's famous book aroused some sympathy for the counterrevolutionary cause, but active opposition came slowly. The first European states to express public concern about events in revolutionary France were Austria and Prussia, declaring in 1791 that order and the rights of the monarch of France were matters of "common interest to all sovereigns of Europe." The leaders of the French assembly pronounced the declaration an affront to national sovereignty. Nobles who had fled France played into their hands with plots and pronouncements against the government. Oddly, perhaps, both supporters and opponents of the revolution in France believed war would serve their cause. The National Assembly's leaders expected an aggressive policy to shore up the people's loyalty and bring freedom to the rest

in the midst of arms and confusions. . . . Learning paid back what it received to nobility and priesthood. . . . Happy if they had all continued to know their indissoluble union, and their proper place. Happy if learning, not debauched by ambition, had been satisified to continue the instructor, and not aspired to be the master! Along with its natural protectors and guardians, learning will be cast into the mire, and trodden down under the hoofs of a swinish multitude.

Source: Edmund Burke, *Reflections on the Revolution in France (1790)* (New York: 1973), pp. 45, 48, 49, 52, 92.

Thomas Paine

Mr. Burke, with his usual outrage, abuses the *Declaration of the Rights of Man*. . . . Does Mr. Burke mean to deny that man has any rights? If he does, then he must mean that there are no such things as rights any where, and that he has none himself; for who is there in the world but man? But if Mr. Burke means to admit that man has rights, the question will then be, what are those rights, and how came man by them originally?

The error of those who reason by precedents drawn from antiquity, respecting the rights of man, is that they do not go far enough into antiquity. They stop in some of the intermediate stages of an hundred or a thousand years, and produce what was then a rule for the present day. This is no authority at all. . . .

To possess ourselves of a clear idea of what government is, or ought to be, we must trace its origin. In doing this, we shall easily discover that governments must have arisen either *out* of the people, or *over* the people. Mr. Burke has made no distinction. . . .

What were formerly called revolutions, were little more than a change of persons, or an alteration of local circumstances. They rose and fell like things of course, and had nothing in their existance or their fate that could influence beyond the spot that produced them. But what we now see in the world, from the revolutions of America and France, is a renovation of the natural order of things, a system of principles as universal as truth and the existance of man, and combining moral with political happiness and national prosperity.

Source: Thomas Paine, *The Rights of Man (1791)* (New York: 1973), pp. 302, 308, 383.

Questions for Analysis

1. How does Burke define *liberty*? Why does he criticize the revolutionaries for representing themselves as slaves freed from bondage?
2. What does Paine criticize about Burke's emphasis on history? According to Paine, what makes the French Revolution different from previous changes of regime in Europe?
3. How do these two authors' attitudes about the origins of human freedoms shape their understandings of the revolution?

of Europe. Counterrevolutionaries hoped the intervention of Austria and Prussia would undo all that had happened since 1789. Radicals, suspicious of aristocratic leaders and the king, believed that war would expose traitors with misgivings about the revolution and flush out those who sympathized with the king and European tyrants. On April 20, 1792, the assembly declared war against Austria and Prussia. Thus began the war that would keep the Continent in arms for a generation.

As the radicals expected, the French forces met serious reverses. By August 1792, the allied armies of Austria and Prussia had crossed the frontier and were threatening to capture Paris. Many, including soldiers, believed that the military disasters were evidence of the king's treason.

On August 10, Parisian crowds, organized by their radical leaders, attacked the royal palace. The king was imprisoned and a second and far more radical revolution began.

The French Republic

From this point, the country's leadership passed into the hands of the more egalitarian leaders of the Third Estate. These new leaders were known as Jacobins, the name of a political club to which many of them belonged. Although their headquarters were in Paris, their membership extended throughout France. Their members included large numbers of professionals, government officeholders, and lawyers; but they proclaimed themselves spokesmen for the people and the nation. An increasing number of artisans joined Jacobin clubs as the movement grew, and other, more democratic clubs expanded as well.

The National Convention, elected by free white men, became the effective governing body of the country for the next three years. It was elected in September 1792, at a time when enemy troops were advancing, spreading panic. Rumors flew that prisoners in Paris were plotting to aid the enemy. They were hauled from their cells, dragged before hastily convened tribunals, and killed. The "September Massacres" killed more than a thousand "enemies of the Revolution" in less than a week. Similar riots engulfed Lyons, Orléans, and other French cities.

The newly elected convention was far more radical than its predecessor, and its leadership was determined to end the monarchy. On September 21, the convention declared France a republic. In December, it placed the king on trial, and in January 1793 he was condemned to death by a narrow margin. The heir to the grand tradition of French absolutism met his end bravely as "citizen Louis Capet," beheaded by the guillotine. Introduced as a swifter

THE EXECUTION OF LOUIS XVI. The execution of Louis XVI shocked Europe. Even committed revolutionaries in France debated the necessity of such a dramatic act. The entire National Convention (over 700 members) acted as jury, and although the assembly was nearly unanimous in finding the king guilty of treason, a majority of only one approved the final death sentence. Those who voted for Louis XVI's execution were known forever after as "regicides." ▪ ***What made this act necessary from the point of view of the most radical of revolutionaries?*** ▪ ***What made it repugnant from the point of view of the revolution's most heated enemies?***

and more humane form of execution, the frightful mechanical headsman came to symbolize revolutionary fervor.

The convention took other radical measures. It confiscated the property of enemies of the revolution, breaking up some large estates and selling them on easier terms to less-wealthy citizens. It abruptly canceled the policy of compensating nobles for their lost privileges. It repealed primogeniture, so that property would not be inherited exclusively by the oldest son but would be divided in substantially equal portions among all immediate heirs. It abolished slavery in French colonies (see below). It set maximum prices for grain and other necessities. In an astonishing effort to root out Christianity from everyday life, the convention adopted a new calendar. The calendar year began with the birth of the republic (September 22, 1792) and divided months in such a way as to eliminate the Catholic Sunday.

Most of this program was a hastily improvised response to crisis and political pressure from the common people in the cities and their leaders. In the three years after 1790, prices had risen staggeringly: wheat by 27 percent, beef by 136 percent, potatoes by 700 percent. While the government imposed its maximums in Paris, small vigilante militias, representing the sans-culottes, attacked those they considered hoarders and profiteers.

The convention also reorganized its armies, with astonishing success. By February 1793, Britain, Holland, Spain, and Austria were in the field against the French. Britain came into the war for strategic and economic reasons: it feared a French threat to Britain's growing global power. The allied coalition, though united only in its desire to contain France, was nevertheless a formidable force. To counter it, the revolutionary government mustered all men capable of bearing arms. The revolution flung fourteen hastily drafted armies into battle under the leadership of newly promoted, young, and inexperienced officers. What they lacked in training and discipline they made up for in organization, mobility, flexibility, courage, and morale. In 1793–1794, the French armies preserved their homeland. In 1794–1795, they occupied the Low Countries; the Rhineland; and parts of Spain, Switzerland, and Savoy. In 1796, they invaded and occupied key parts of Italy and broke the coalition that had arrayed itself against them.

The Reign of Terror

In 1793, however, those victories lay in a hard-to-imagine future. France was in crisis. In 1793, the convention drafted a new democratic constitution based on male suffrage. That constitution never took effect—suspended indefinitely by wartime emergency. Instead, the convention prolonged its own life year after year and increasingly delegated its responsibilities to a group of twelve leaders, the Committee of Public Safety. The committee's ruthlessness had two purposes: to seize control of the revolution and to prosecute all the revolution's enemies—"to make terror the order of the day." The Terror lasted less than two years but left a bloody and authoritarian legacy.

Perhaps the three best-known leaders of the radical revolution were Jean Paul Marat, Georges Jacques Danton, and Maximilien Robespierre, the latter two members of the Committee of Public Safety. Marat was educated as a physician and by 1789 had already earned enough distinction in that profession to be awarded an honorary degree by St. Andrews University in Scotland. Marat opposed nearly all of his moderate colleagues' assumptions, including their admiration for Great Britain, which Marat considered corrupt and despotic. Persecuted by powerful factions in the constituent assembly who feared his radicalism, he was forced to take refuge in unsanitary sewers and dungeons.

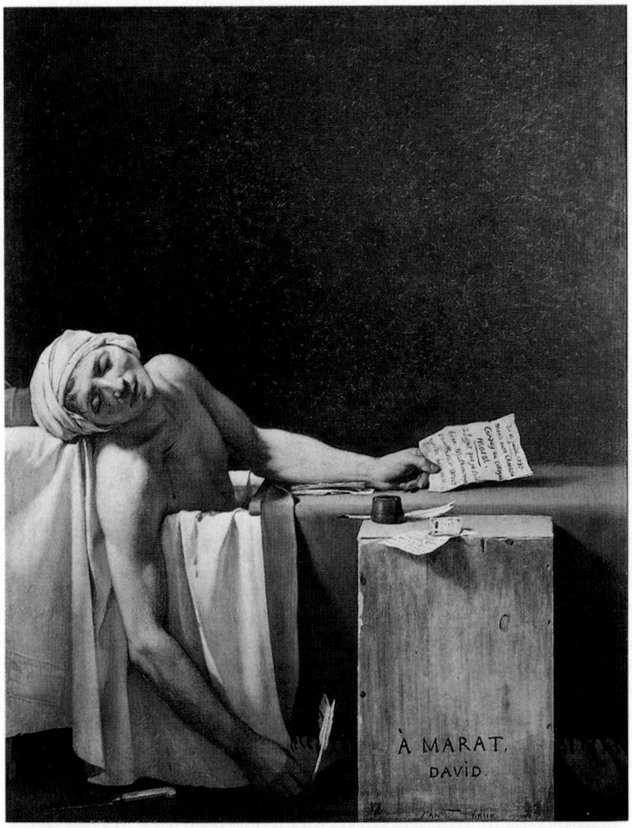

THE DEATH OF MARAT. This painting by the French artist Jacques-Louis David in 1793 immortalized Marat. The note in the slain leader's hand is from Charlotte Corday, his assassin. ▪ ***Why was it important to represent Marat as a martyr?***

He persevered as the editor of the popular news sheet *The Friend of the People*. Exposure to infection left him with a chronic and painful skin disease, from which baths provided the only relief. In the summer of 1793, at the height of the crisis of the revolution, he was stabbed in his bath by Charlotte Corday, a young royalist, and thus became a revolutionary martyr.

Danton, like Marat, was a popular political leader, well known in the more plebian clubs of Paris. Elected a member of the Committee of Public Safety in 1793, he had much to do with organizing the Terror. As time went on, however, he wearied of ruthlessness and displayed a tendency to compromise, which gave his opponents in the convention their opportunity. In April 1794, Danton was sent to the guillotine. On mounting the scaffold, he is reported to have said, "Show my head to the people; they do not see the like every day."

The most famous of the radical leaders was Maximilien Robespierre. Born of a family reputed to be of Irish descent, Robespierre trained in law and quickly became a modestly successful lawyer. His eloquence and his consistent, or ruthless, insistence that leaders respect the "will of the people" eventually won him a following in the Jacobin club. Later, he became president of the National Convention and a member of the Committee of Public Safety. Though he had little to do with starting the Terror, he was nevertheless responsible for enlarging its scope. Known as "the Incorruptible," he came to represent ruthlessness justified as virtue and necessary to revolutionary progress.

The two years of the radical republic (August 1792–July 1794) brought dictatorship, centralization, suspension of any liberties, and war. The committee faced foreign enemies and opposition from both the political right and left at home. In June 1793, responding to an escalating crisis, leaders of the "Mountain," a party of radicals allied with Parisian artisans, purged moderates from the convention. Rebellions broke out in the provincial cities of Lyons, Bordeaux, and Marseilles, mercilessly repressed by the committee and its local representatives. The government also faced counterrevolution in the western region known as the Vendée, where movements enlisted peasants and artisans, who believed their local areas were being invaded and who fought for their local priest or against the summons from the revolutionaries' conscription boards. By the summer, the forces in the Vendée posed a serious threat to the convention. Determined to stabilize France, whatever the cost, the committee redeployed its forces, defeated the counterrevolutionaries, and launched murderous campaigns of pacification—torching villages, farms, and fields and killing all who dared oppose them and many who did not.

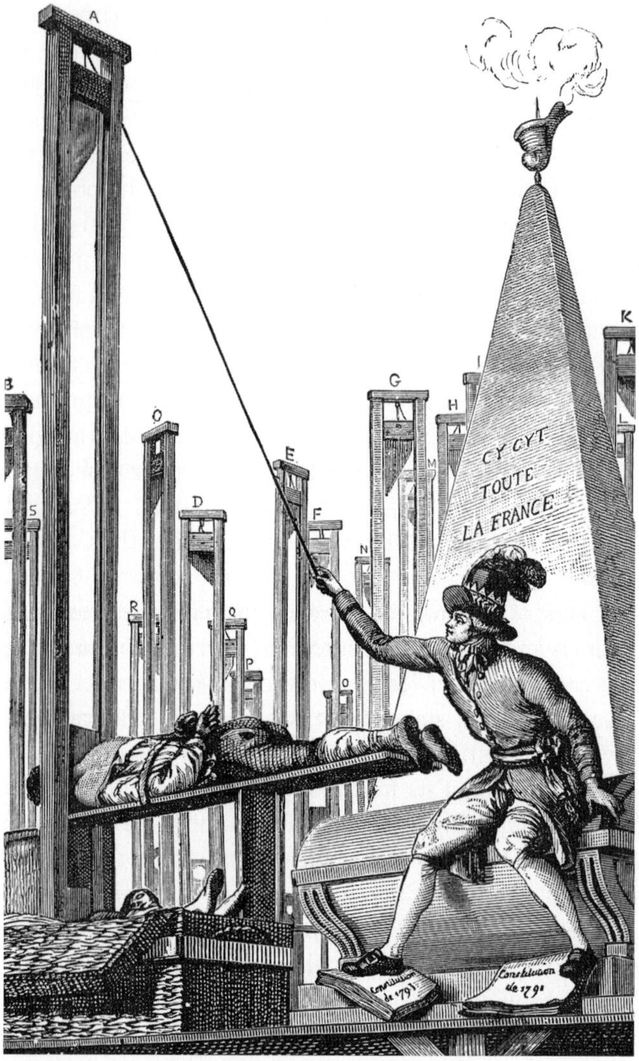

ROBESPIERRE GUILLOTINING THE EXECUTIONER. The original caption for this 1793 engraving read "Robespierre guillotines the executioner after having had all the French guillotined." In fact, Robespierre himself was guillotined after his fall from power in July 1794. ▪ ***What made the struggle for power and authority among revolutionaries so merciless and uncompromising?***

During the period of the Terror, from September 1793 to July 1794, the most reliable estimates place the number of deaths at close to 40,000 to about 16,500 from actual death sentences, with the rest resulting from extra-judicial killings and deaths in prison. Approximately 300,000 were incarcerated between March 1793 and August 1794. These numbers, however, do not include the pacification of the Vendée and rebellious cities in the Rhone Valley, which took more than 100,000 lives. Few victims of the Terror were aristocrats. Many more were peasants or laborers accused of hoarding, treason, or counterrevolutionary activity. Anyone who appeared to threaten the republic, no matter what his or her social or economic position, was at risk. When some time later the Abbé Sieyès was asked what he had done to distinguish himself during the Terror, he responded dryly, "I lived."

The Legacy of the Second French Revolution

The "second" French Revolution affected the everyday life of French men, women, and children in a remarkably direct way. Workers' trousers replaced the breeches that had been a sartorial badge of the middle classes and the nobility. A red cap, said to symbolize freedom from slavery, became popular headgear, and wigs vanished. Men and women addressed each other as "citizen" or "citizeness." Public life was marked by ceremonies designed to dramatize the break with the Old Regime and celebrate new forms of fraternity. In the early stages of the revolution, these festivals seem to have captured genuine popular enthusiasm for new ways of living and thinking. Under the Committee of Public Safety, they became didactic and hollow.

The radical revolution of 1792–1793 also dramatically reversed the trend toward decentralization and democracy. The assembly replaced local officials, some of them still royalist in sympathy, with "deputies on mission," whose task was to conscript troops and generate patriotic fervor. When these deputies appeared too eager to act independently, they were replaced by "national agents," with instructions to report directly to the committee. In another effort to stabilize authority, the assembly closed down all the women's political clubs, decreeing them a political and social danger. Ironically, those who claimed to govern in the name of the people found the popular movement threatening.

Finally, the revolution eroded the strength of those traditional institutions—church, guild, parish—that had for centuries given people a common bond. In their place now stood patriotic organizations and a culture that insisted on loyalty to one national cause. Those organizations had first emerged with the election campaigns, meetings, and pamphlet wars of 1788 and the interest they heightened. They included the political clubs and local assemblies, which at the height of the revolution (1792–1793) met every day of the week and offered an apprenticeship in politics. The army of the republic became the premier national institution.

On the one hand, the revolution divided France, mobilizing counterrevolutionaries as well as revolutionaries. At the same time, the revolution, war, and culture of sacrifice forged new bonds. The sense that the rest of Europe, carrying what the verses of the "Marseillaise," the most famous anthem of the revolution, called the "blood-stained flag of tyranny," sought to crush the new nation and its citizens unquestionably strengthened French national identity.

FROM THE TERROR TO BONAPARTE: THE DIRECTORY

The Committee of Public Safety might have saved France from enemy armies, but it could not save itself. Inflation became catastrophic. The long string of military victories convinced growing numbers that the committee's demands for continuing self-sacrifice and Terror were no longer justified. By July 1794, the committee was virtually without allies. On July 27 (9 Thermidor, according to the new calendar), Robespierre was shouted down while attempting to speak on the floor of the convention. The following day, along with twenty-one other conspirators, he met his death by guillotine.

Ending the Terror did not immediately bring moderation. Vigilante groups of royalists hunted down Jacobins. The repeal of price controls, combined with the worst winter in a century, caused widespread misery. Other measures that had constituted the Terror were gradually repealed. In 1795, the National Convention adopted a new and more conservative constitution. It granted suffrage to all adult male citizens who could read and write. Yet it set up indirect elections: citizens voted for electors, who in turn chose the legislative body. Wealthy citizens thus held authority. Eager

PATRIOTIC WOMEN'S CLUB. The members of this patriotic club wear constitutional bonnets to show their support for the revolution and the reforms of the convention. ▪ ***What can one conclude about the atmosphere in Paris during the revolution from the existence of such associations?***

to avoid personal dictatorship, it vested executive authority in a board of five men known as the Directory, chosen by the legislative body. The new constitution included not only a bill of rights but also a declaration of the duties of the citizen.

The Directory lasted longer than its revolutionary predecessors. It still faced discontent on both the radical left and the conservative right. On the left, the Directory repressed radical movements to abolish private property and parliamentary-style government, including one led by the radical "Gracchus Babeuf." Dispatching threats from the right proved more challenging. In 1797, the first free elections held in France as a republic returned a large number of monarchists to the councils of government, alarming politicians who had voted to execute Louis XVI. Backed by the army, the Directory annulled most of the election results. After two years of more uprisings and purges, and with the country still plagued by severe inflation, the Directors grew desperate. This time they called for help from a brilliant young general named Napoleon Bonaparte.

FRANCE AND ITS SISTER REPUBLICS. ▪ ***The French revolutionaries, fighting against the conservative monarchs of Europe, conquered and annexed large sections of what three countries?*** ▪ ***Who were potential supporters of the French Revolution in areas outside France during the Napoleonic era?*** ▪ ***Who was most likely to oppose it in these areas?***

Bonaparte's first military victory had come in 1793, with the recapture of Toulon from royalist and British forces, and had earned him promotion from captain to brigadier general at the age of twenty-four. After the Terror, he was briefly arrested for his Jacobin associations. But he proved his usefulness to the Directory in October 1795 when he put down an uprising with "a whiff of grapeshot," saving the new regime from its opponents. Promoted, he won a string of victories in Italy, forcing Austria to withdraw (temporarily) from the war. He attempted to defeat Britain by attacking British forces in Egypt and the Near East, a campaign that went well on land but ran into trouble at sea, where the French fleet was defeated by Admiral Horatio Nelson (Abukir Bay, 1798). Bonaparte found himself trapped in Egypt by the British and unable to win a decisive victory.

It was at this point that the call came from the Directory. Bonaparte slipped away from Egypt and appeared in Paris, already having agreed to participate in a coup d'état with the leading Director, that former revolutionary champion of the Third Estate, the Abbé Sieyès. On November 9, 1799 (18 Brumaire), Bonaparte was declared a "temporary consul." He was the answer to the Directory's prayers: a strong, popular leader who was not a king. Sieyès declared that Bonaparte would provide "[c]onfidence from below, authority from above." With those words Sieyès pronounced the end of the revolutionary period.

NAPOLEON AND IMPERIAL FRANCE

Few figures in Western history have compelled the attention of the world as Napoleon Bonaparte did during the fifteen years of his rule in France. Few men lived on with such persistence as myth, not just in their own countries, but across the West. Why? For the great majority of ordinary Europeans, memories of the French Revolution were dominated by those of the Napoleonic Wars, which devastated Europe, convulsed its politics, and traumatized its peoples for a generation.

Yet Bonaparte's relationship to the revolution was not simple. His regime consolidated some of the revolution's political and social changes but sharply repudiated others. He presented himself as the son of the revolution, but he also borrowed freely from very different regimes, fashioning himself as the heir to Charlemagne or to the Roman Empire. His regime remade revolutionary politics and the French state; offered stunning examples of the new kinds of warfare; and left a legacy of conflict and legends of French glory that lingered in the dreams, or nightmares, of Europe's statesmen and citizens for more than a century.

Consolidating Authority: 1799–1804

Bonaparte's early career reinforced the claim that the revolution rewarded the efforts of able men. The son of a provincial Corsican nobleman, he attended the École Militaire in Paris. In prerevolutionary France he would have been unable to rise beyond the rank of major, which required buying a regimental command. The revolution, however, abolished the purchase of military office, and Bonaparte quickly became a general. Here, then, was a man who had risen from obscurity because of his own gifts, which he lent happily to the service of France's revolution.

Once in power, however, Bonaparte showed less respect for revolutionary principles. After the coup of 1799, he assumed the title of "first consul." A new constitution established universal white male suffrage and set up two legislative bodies. Elections, however, were indirect, and the power of the legislative bodies sharply curbed. "The government?" said one observer. "There is Bonaparte." Bonaparte instituted what has since become a common authoritarian device, the plebiscite, which put a question directly to popular vote. This allows the head of state to bypass politicians or legislative bodies who might disagree with him—as well as permitting local officials to tamper with ballot boxes. In 1802, flush with victory abroad, he asked the legislature to proclaim him consul for life. When the Senate refused to do so, Bonaparte's Council of State stepped in, offered him the title, and had it ratified by plebiscite. Throughout, his regime retained the appearance of consulting with the people, but its most important feature was the centralization of authority.

That authority came from reorganizing the state, and on this score Bonaparte's accomplishments were extraordinary and lasting. Bonaparte's regime confirmed the abolition of privilege, thereby promising "careers open to talent." Centralizing administrative departments, he accomplished what no recent French regime had yet achieved: an orderly and generally fair system of taxation. More efficient tax collection and fiscal management also helped halt the inflationary spiral that had crippled the revolutionary governments, although Bonaparte's regime relied heavily on resources from areas he had conquered to fund his military ventures. As we have seen, earlier revolutionary regimes began to reorganize France's administration—abolishing the ancient fiefdoms with their separate governments, legal codes, privileges, and customs—setting up a uniform system of departments. Bonaparte continued that work, pressing it further and putting an accent on centralization. He replaced elected officials and local self-government with centrally appointed prefects and subprefects, who answered directly to the Council of State in Paris. The prefects wielded considerable power, much more than any elected representative: they were in charge of everything from collecting statistics and reporting on the economy and the population to education, roads, and public works. With more integrated administration, in which the different branches were coordinated (and supervised from above), a more professional bureaucracy, and more rational and efficient taxation (though the demands of war strained the system), Napoleon's state marked the transition from Bourbon absolutism to the modern state.

Law, Education, and a New Elite

Napoleon's most significant contribution to modern state building was the promulgation of a new legal code in 1804. Each revolutionary regime had taken up the daunting task of modernizing the laws; each had run out of time. Napoleon tolerated no delays, and threw himself into the project, pressing his own ideas and supervising half the meetings. The Napoleonic Code, as the civil code came to be called, pivoted on two principles that had remained significant through all the constitutional changes since 1789: uniformity and individualism. It cleared through the thicket of contradictory legal traditions that governed the ancient provinces of France, creating one uniform law. It confirmed the abolition of feudal privileges of all kinds: not only noble and clerical privileges but the special rights of craft guilds, municipalities, and so on. It set the conditions for exercising property rights: the drafting of contracts, leases, and stock companies. The code's provisions on the family, which Napoleon developed personally, insisted on the importance of paternal authority and the subordination of women and children. In 1793, during the most radical period of the revolution, men and women had been declared "equal in marriage"; now Napoleon's code affirmed the "natural supremacy" of the husband. Married women could not sell property, run a business, or have a profession without their husbands' permission. Fathers had the sole right to control their children's financial affairs, consent to their marriages, and (under the ancient right to correction) to imprison

Interpreting Visual Evidence

Representing the People during the French Revolution

From the moment the population of Paris came to the assistance of the beleaguered National Assembly in July 1789, representations of "the people" in the French Revolution took on an overwhelming significance. Building a new government that was committed to an idea of popular sovereignty meant that both the revolution's supporters and its opponents were deeply invested in shaping perceptions of the people. And of course, Article III of the Declaration of the Rights of Man ("The principle of sovereignty resides essentially in the nation") meant that any individual, group, or institution that could successfully claim to represent the will of the people could wield tremendous power, as long as others accepted that claim.

Of course, revolutionary crowds did not always conform to the images of them that circulated so widely in prints and paintings during the period 1789–1799. Some were spontaneous, and others were organized; some were made up of recognizable social and professional groups with clear political goals, and others were a hodgepodge of conflicting and even inarticulate aspirations. Many were nonviolent; some were exceedingly threatening and murderous. All politicians sought to use them to support their political programs, and many learned to fear their unpredictable behavior.

These four images give a sense of the competing visions of the people that appeared in the public realm during the French Revolution. The first (image A) shows the killing of Foulon, a royal official who was lynched and beheaded by an enthusiastic crowd barely a week after the fall of the Bastille because he was suspected of conspiring to starve the Parisian population as punishment for their rebellion against the king. The second (image B) shows a more care-

A. The punishment of Foulon (anonymous print, 1789).

B. *The Festival of Federation* by Charles Thévenin, 1790.

fully choreographed representation of the people during the Festival of Federation, organized in July 1790 by the revolutionary government to commemorate the first anniversary of the fall of the Bastille. Finally, the last two documents show contrasting images of the revolutionary sans-culottes, the working-class revolutionaries who supported the government during the Terror in 1792–1794. The first (image C), a sympathetic portrait of a sans-culottes as a virtuous and self-sacrificing working man, standing with an eye to the future, seems completely incongruous when paired with the British satirist James Gilray's portrait of a cannibalistic sans-culottes family (image D), drawn literally "without pants," feasting on the bodies of their victims after a hard day's work.

Questions for Analysis

1. Image A depicts an event from July 1789—that is, before the August publication of the Declaration of the Rights of Man. How does this image portray the crowd's vengeance on Foulon? What possible political messages are contained in this image?
2. Image B, on the other hand, chooses to display the people celebrating their own birth as a political body, by convening on the anniversary of the fall of the Bastille. What emotions is this painting designed to invoke, and how is it related to more disturbing images such as image A?
3. How are the positive and negative portrayals of sans-culottes as political actors (images C and D) constructed? Can one imagine a painting of a worker like image C being produced before 1789? What does image D tell us about how the revolution was viewed from Britain?

C. A typical sans-culotte, painting by Louis-Léopold Boilly, 1792.

D. A family of sans-culottes [*sic*] refreshing after the fatigues of the day. (British satirical cartoon by James Gilray, 1793).

them for up to six months without showing cause. Divorce remained legal, but under unequal conditions; a man could sue for divorce on the grounds of adultery, but a woman could do so only if her husband moved his "concubine" into the family's house. Most important to the common people, the code prohibited paternity suits for illegitimate children.

In all, Napoleon developed seven legal codes covering commercial law, civil law and procedures, crime, and punishment. Like the civil code, the new criminal code consolidated some of the gains of the revolution, treating citizens as equals before the law and outlawing arbitrary arrest and imprisonment. Yet it, too, reinstated brutal measures that the revolutionaries had abolished, such as branding and cutting off the hands of parricides. The Napoleonic legal regime was more egalitarian than law under the Old Regime but no less concerned with authority.

Napoleon also rationalized the educational system. He ordered the establishment of *lycées* (high schools) in every major town to train civil servants and army officers and a school in Paris to train teachers. To supplement these changes, Napoleon brought the military and technical schools under state control and founded a national university to supervise the entire system. It is not surprising that he built up a new military academy. He reorganized and established solid financing for the premier schools of higher education: the polytechnic (for engineers) and the normal (for teachers), to which students would be admitted based on examinations and from which would issue the technical, educational, and political elites of the country. Like almost all his reforms, this one reinforced reforms introduced during the revolution, and it intended to abolish privilege and create "careers open to talent." Napoleon also embraced the burgeoning social and physical sciences of the Enlightenment. He sponsored the Institute of France, divided into four sections, or academies: fine arts, sciences, humanities, and language (the famous Académie française). These academies dated back to the age of absolutism—now they were coordinated and put on a new footing. They acquired under Napoleon the character that they have preserved to this day: centralized, meritocratic, and geared to serving the state.

Who benefited from these changes? Like Bonaparte's other new institutions, the new schools helped confirm the power of a new elite. The new elite included businessmen, bankers, and merchants but was still composed primarily of powerful landowners. What was more, at least half of the fellowships to the high schools went to the sons of military officers and high civil servants. Finally, like most of Bonaparte's reforms, changes in education aimed to strengthen the empire: "My object in establishing a teaching corps is to have a means of directing political and moral opinion," Napoleon said bluntly.

Bonaparte's early measures were ambitious. To win support for them, he made allies without regard for their past political affiliations. He admitted back into the country exiles of all political stripes. His two fellow consuls were a regicide of the Terror and a bureaucrat of the Old Regime. His minister of police had been an extreme radical republican; his minister of foreign affairs was the aristocrat and opportunist Charles Talleyrand. The most remarkable act of political reconciliation came in 1801, with Bonaparte's concordat with the pope, an agreement that put an end to more than a decade of hostility between the French state and the Catholic Church. Although it shocked anticlerical revolutionaries, Napoleon, ever the pragmatist, believed that reconciliation would create domestic harmony and international solidarity. The agreement gave the pope the right to depose French bishops and to discipline the French clergy. In return, the Vatican agreed to forgo any claims to Church lands expropriated by the revolution. That property would remain in the hands of its new middle-class rural and urban proprietors. The concordat did not revoke the principle of religious freedom established by the revolution, but it did win Napoleon the support of conservatives who had feared for France's future as a godless state.

Such political balancing acts increased Bonaparte's general popularity. Combined with early military successes (peace with Austria in 1801 and with Britain in 1802), they muffled any opposition to his personal ambitions. He had married Josephine de Beauharnais, a Creole from Martinique and an influential mistress of the revolutionary period. Josephine had given the Corsican soldier-politician legitimacy and access among the revolutionary elite early in his career. Neither Bonaparte nor his ambitious wife were content to be first among equals, however; and in December of 1804, he finally cast aside any traces of republicanism. In a ceremony that evoked the splendor of medieval kingship and Bourbon absolutism, he crowned himself Emperor Napoleon I in the Cathedral of Notre Dame in Paris. Napoleon did much to create the modern state, but he did not hesitate to proclaim his links to the past.

In Europe as in France: Napoleon's Empire

The nations of Europe had looked on—some in admiration, others in horror, all in astonishment—at the phenomenon that was Napoleon. Austria, Prussia, and Britain led two coalitions against revolutionary France in 1792–1795 and in 1798, and both were defeated. After Napoleon came to power in 1799, the alliance split. Russia and Austria withdrew from the fray in 1801, and even the intransigent British were forced to make peace the following year.

By 1805, the Russians, Prussians, Austrians, and Swedes had joined the British in an attempt to contain France. Their efforts were to no avail. Napoleon's military superiority led to defeats, in turn, of all the continental allies. Napoleon was a master of well-timed, well-directed shock attacks on the battlefield: movement, regrouping, and pressing his advantage. He led an army that had transformed European warfare; first raised as a revolutionary militia, it was now a trained conscript army, loyal, well supplied by a nation whose economy was committed to serving the war effort, and led by generals promoted largely on the basis of talent. This new kind of army inflicted crushing defeats on his enemies. The battle of Austerlitz, in December 1805, was a triumph for the French against the combined forces of Austria and Russia and became a symbol of the emperor's apparent invincibility. His subsequent victory against the Russians at Friedland in 1807 only added to his reputation.

Out of these victories, Napoleon created his new empire and affiliated states. To the southeast, the empire included Rome and the pope's dominions, Tuscany, and the Dalmatian territories of Austria (now the coastline of Croatia). To the east, Napoleon's rule extended over a federation of German states known as the Confederation of the Rhine and a section of Poland. These new states were presented as France's gift of independence to patriots elsewhere in Europe, but in practice they served as a military buffer against renewed expansion by Austria. The empire itself was ringed by the allied kingdoms of Italy, Naples, Spain, and Holland, whose thrones were occupied by Napoleon's brothers, brothers-in-law, and trusted generals.

The empire brought the French Revolution's practical consequences—a powerful, centralizing state and an end to old systems of privilege—to Europe's doorstep, applying to the empire principles that had already transformed France. Administrative modernization, which meant overhauling the procedures, codes, and practices of the state, was the most powerful feature of changes introduced. The empire changed the terms of government service (careers open to talent), handing out new titles and recruiting new men for the civil service and the judiciary. It ended the nobility's monopoly on the officer corps. The new branches of government hired engineers, mapmakers, surveyors, and legal consultants. Public works and education were reorganized. Prefects in the outer reaches of the empire, as in France, built roads, bridges, dikes (in Holland), hospitals, and prisons; they reorganized universities and built observatories. In the empire and some of the satellite kingdoms, tariffs were eliminated, feudal dues abolished, new tax districts formed, and plentiful new taxes collected to support the new state.

In the realm of liberty and law, Napoleon's rule eliminated feudal and church courts and created a single legal system. The Napoleonic Code was often introduced, but not always or entirely. (In southern Italy measures against the Catholic Church were deemed too controversial.) Reforms eliminated many inequalities and legal privileges. The Duchy of Warsaw in Poland ended serfdom but offered no land reform, so former serfs became impoverished tenants. In most areas, the empire gave civil rights to Protestants and Jews. In Rome, the conquering French opened the gates of the Jewish ghetto—and made Jews subject to conscription. In some areas, Catholic monasteries, convents, and other landholdings were broken up and sold, almost always to wealthy buyers. In the empire as in France, and under Napoleon as during the revolution, many who benefited were the elite: people and groups already on their way up and with the resources to take advantage of opportunities.

In government, the regime sought a combination of legal equality (for men) and stronger state authority. The French and local authorities created new electoral districts, expanded the suffrage, and wrote constitutions, but newly elected representative bodies were dismissed if they failed to cooperate, few constitutions were ever fully applied, and political freedoms were often fleeting. Napoleon's regime referred to revolutionary principles to anchor its legitimacy, but authority remained its guiding light. All governmental direction emanated from Paris and therefore from Napoleon.

Finally, in the empire as in France, Napoleon displayed his signature passions. The first of these was an Enlightenment zeal for accumulating useful knowledge. The empire gathered statistics as never before, for it was important to know the resources—including population—that a state had at its disposal. That spirit had been evident already in Bonaparte's extraordinary 1798 excursion into Egypt. He took hundreds of scholars and artists along with the army, founded the Egyptian institute in Cairo, and sent researchers off to make a systematic inventory of the country (its geology, rivers, minerals, antiquities, animal life) and to conduct archaeological expeditions to Upper Egypt, where they sketched the pyramids and excavated what would turn out to be the Rosetta Stone (see Chapter 20). Napoleon's second passion was cultivating his relationship to imperial glories of the past. He poured time and energy into (literally) cementing his image for posterity. The Arc de Triomphe in Paris, designed to imitate the Arc of Constantine in Rome, is the best example; but Napoleon also ordered work to be undertaken to restore ruins in Rome, to make the Prado Palace in Madrid a museum, and to renovate and preserve the Alhambra in Granada.

Such were Napoleon's visions of his legacy and himself. How did others see him? Europe offered no single reaction. Some countries and social groups collaborated enthusiastically, some negotiated, some resisted. Napoleon's image as a military hero genuinely inspired young men from the elite, raised in a culture that prized military honor. By contrast, Catholic peasants in Spain fought him from the beginning. In many small principalities previously ruled by princes—the patchwork states of Germany, for example, and the repressive kingdom of Naples—reforms that provided for more efficient, less corrupt administration, a workable tax structure, and an end to customary privilege were welcomed by most of the local population. Yet the Napoleonic presence proved a mixed blessing. Vassal states contributed heavily to the maintenance of the emperor's military power. The French levied taxes, drafted men, and required states to support occupying armies. In Italy, the policy was called "liberty and requisitions"; and the Italians, Germans, and Dutch paid an especially high price for reforms—in terms of economic cost and numbers of men recruited. From the point of view of the common people, the local lord and priest had been replaced by the French tax collector and army recruiting board.

It is telling that even Napoleon's enemies came to believe that the upstart emperor represented the wave of the future,

NAPOLEON'S EUROPEAN EMPIRE AT ITS HEIGHT. At the height of his power in 1812, Napoleon controlled most of Europe, ruling either directly or through dependent states and allies. ▪ ***Compared to the map on page 600, by what means had Napoleon expanded French control on continental Europe?*** ▪ ***Which major countries remained outside of French control?*** ▪ ***Which areas felt the most long-lasting impact of Napoleon's reign?***

NAPOLEON ON HORSEBACK AT THE ST. BERNARD PASS* BY JAÇQUES-LOUIS DAVID, 1801, AND *LITTLE BONEY GONE TO POT* BY GEORGE CRUIKSHANK, 1814.** The depth of Napoleon's celebrity in Europe can be measured in the equal shares of adulation and hatred that he stirred up within Europe among his supporters and his enemies. David's portrait, painted before he became emperor of France, captures the ardent hopes that many attached to his person. The painting explicitly compared Napoleon to two previous European conquerors, Charlemagne and the ancient Roman emperor Hannibal, by evoking their names in the stones at the base of the painting. In George Cruikshanks's bitter caricature, published after Napoleon's exile to Elba, the devil offers him a pistol to commit suicide, and the former emperor, seated on a chamber pot, says he might, but only if the firing mechanism is disabled. Both images use assumptions about virility and masculine authority to make their point. ▪ ***Who are the intended audiences for these images, and how do they convey their respective arguments?

particularly in regard to the reorganization of the state. Though they fought Napoleon, Prussian and Austrian administrators set about instituting reforms that resembled his: changing rules of promotion and recruitment, remodeling bureaucracies, redrawing districts, eliminating some privileges, and so on. Many who came of age under Napoleon's empire believed that, for better or worse, his empire was modern.

THE RETURN TO WAR AND NAPOLEON'S DEFEAT: 1806–1815

Napoleon's boldest attempt at consolidation, a policy banning British goods from the Continent, was a dangerous failure. Britain had bitterly opposed each of France's revolutionary regimes since the death of Louis XVI; now it tried to rally Europe against Napoleon with promises of generous financial loans and trade. Napoleon's Continental System, established in 1806, sought to starve Britain's trade and force its surrender. The system failed for several reasons. Throughout the war, Britain retained control of the seas. The British naval blockade of the Continent, begun in 1807, effectively countered Napoleon's system. While the French Empire strained to transport goods and raw materials overland to avoid the British blockade, the British successfully developed a lively trade with South America. A second reason for the failure of the system was its internal tariffs. Europe divided into economic camps, at odds with each other as they tried to subsist on what the Continent alone could produce and manufacture. Finally, the system hurt the Continent more than Britain. Stagnant trade in Europe's ports and unemployment in its manufacturing centers eroded public faith in Napoleon's dream of a working European empire.

The Continental System was Napoleon's first serious mistake. His ambition to create a European empire, modeled on Rome and ruled from Paris, was to become a second cause of his decline. The symbols of his empire—reflected in painting, architecture, and the design of furniture and clothing—were deliberately Roman in origin. Where early revolutionaries referred to the Roman Republic for their imagery, Napoleon looked to the more ostentatious style of the Roman emperors. In 1809, he divorced the empress Josephine and ensured himself a successor of royal blood by marrying a Habsburg princess, Marie Louise—the great-niece of Marie Antoinette. Such actions lost Napoleon the support of revolutionaries, former Enlightenment thinkers, and liberals across the Continent.

NAPOLEON ON THE BATTLEFIELD OF EYLAU. Amid bitter cold and snow, Napoleon engaged with the Russian army in February 1807. Although technically a victory for the French, it was only barely that, with the French losing at least 10,000 men and the Russians twice as many. This painting, characteristic of Bonaparte propaganda, emphasizes not the losses but the emperor's saintlike clemency—even enemy soldiers reach up toward him.

Over time, the bitter tonic of defeat began to have an effect on Napoleon's enemies, who changed their own approach to waging war. After the Prussian army was humiliated at Jena in 1806 and forced out of the war, a whole generation of younger Prussian officers reformed their military and their state by demanding rigorous practical training for commanders and a genuinely national army made up of patriotic Prussian citizens rather than well-drilled mercenaries.

The myth of Napoleon's invincibility worked against him as well, as he took ever greater risks with France's military and national fortunes. Russian numbers and Austrian artillery inflicted horrendous losses on the French at Wagram in 1809, although these difficulties were forgotten in the glow of victory. Napoleon's allies and supporters shrugged off the British admiral Horatio Nelson's victory at Trafalgar in 1805 as no more than a temporary check to the emperor's ambitions. But Trafalgar broke French naval power in the Mediterranean and led to a rift with Spain, which had been France's equal partner in the battle and suffered equally in the defeat. In the Caribbean, too, Napoleon was forced to cut growing losses (see below).

A crucial moment in Napoleon's undoing came with his invasion of Spain in 1808. Napoleon overthrew the Spanish king, installed his own brother on the throne, and then imposed a series of reforms similar to those he had instituted elsewhere in Europe. Napoleon's blow against the Spanish monarchy weakened its hold on its colonies across the Atlantic, and the Spanish crown never fully regained its grip (see Chapter 20). But in Spain itself, Napoleon reckoned without two factors that led to the ultimate failure of his mission: the presence of British forces and the determined resistance of the Spanish people, who detested Napoleon's interference in the affairs of the church. The Peninsular Wars, as the Spanish conflicts were called, were long and bitter. The smaller British force learned how to concentrate a devastating volume of gunfire on the French pinpoint attacks on the open battlefield and laid siege to French garrison towns. The Spanish quickly began to wear down the French invaders through guerrilla warfare. Terrible atrocities were committed by both sides; the French military's torture and execution of Spanish guerrillas and civilians was immortalized by the Spanish artist Francisco Goya (1746–1828) with sickening accuracy in his prints and paintings. Though at one point Napoleon himself took charge of his army, he could not achieve anything more than temporary victory. The Spanish campaign was the first indication that Napoleon could be beaten, and it encouraged resistance elsewhere.

The second, and most dramatic, stage in Napoleon's downfall began with the disruption of his alliance with Russia. As an agricultural country, Russia had suffered a severe economic crisis when it was no longer able to trade its surplus grain for British manufactures. The consequence was that Tsar Alexander I began to wink at trade with Britain and to ignore or evade the protests from Paris. By 1811, Napoleon decided that he could no longer endure this flouting of their agreement. He collected an army of 600,000 and set out for Russia in the spring of 1812. Only a third of the soldiers in this "Grande Armée" were French; nearly as many were Polish or German, joined by soldiers and adventurers from the rest of France's client states. It was the grandest of Napoleon's imperial expeditions, an army raised from across Europe and sent to punish the autocratic tsar. The invasion ended in disaster. The Russians refused to make a stand, drawing the French farther and farther into the heart of their country. Just before Napoleon reached the ancient Russian capital of Moscow, the Russian army drew the French forces into a bloody, seemingly pointless battle in the narrow streets of a town called Borodino, where both sides suffered terrible losses of men and supplies, harder on the French who were now so far from home. After the battle, the Russians permitted Napoleon to occupy Moscow. But on the night of his entry, Russian partisans put the city to the torch, leaving little but the blackened walls of the Kremlin palaces to shelter the French troops.

THE DISASTERS OF WAR* BY FRANCISCO GOYA (1746–1828).** Goya was a Spanish painter and political liberal who had initially supported the French revolution. After Napoleon invaded Spain in 1807, Spaniards rose up in revolt, leading to the Peninsular War of 1808–1814. Between 1810 and 1820, Goya documented the war's violence in a series of black-and-white prints containing stark images of atrocity, rape, and the aftermath of famine. Note the absence of political imagery and the pointed and bitter irony of Goya's caption: "A great heroic feat! With dead people!" ▪ ***Who or what is the target of Goya's sarcasm here?

Hoping that the tsar would eventually surrender, Napoleon lingered amid the ruins for more than a month. On October 19, he finally ordered the homeward march. The delay was a fatal blunder. Long before he had reached the border, the terrible Russian winter was on his troops. Frozen streams, mountainous drifts of snow, and bottomless mud slowed the retreat almost to a halt. To add to the miseries of frostbite, disease, and starvation, mounted Cossacks rode out of the blizzard to harry the exhausted army. Each morning the miserable remnant that pushed on left behind circles of corpses around the campfires of the night before. Temperatures dropped to −27°F. On December 13, a few thousand broken soldiers crossed the frontier into Germany—a fragment of the once proud Grande Armée. Nearly 300,000 of its soldiers and untold thousands of Russians lost their lives in Napoleon's Russian adventure.

After the retreat from Russia, the anti-Napoleonic forces took renewed hope. United by a belief that they might finally succeed in defeating the emperor, Prussia, Russia, Austria, Sweden, and Britain renewed their attack. Citizens of many German states in particular saw this as a war of liberation, and indeed most of the fighting took place in Germany. The climax of the campaign occurred in October 1813 when, at what was thereafter known as the Battle of the Nations, fought near Leipzig, the allies dealt the French a resounding defeat. Meanwhile, allied armies won significant victories in the Low Countries and Spain. By the beginning of 1814, they had crossed the Rhine into France. Left with an army of inexperienced youths, Napoleon retreated to Paris, urging the French people to resist despite constant setbacks at the hands of the larger invading armies. On March 31, Tsar Alexander I of Russia and King Frederick William III of Prussia made their triumphant entry into Paris. Napoleon was forced to abdicate unconditionally and was sent into exile on the island of Elba, off the Italian coast.

Napoleon was back on French soil in less than a year. In the interim, the allies had restored the Bourbon dynasty to the throne, in the person of Louis XVIII, brother of Louis XVI. Despite his administrative abilities, Louis could not fill the void left by Napoleon's abdication. It was no surprise that when the former emperor staged his escape from Elba, his fellow countrymen once more rallied to his

Analyzing Primary Sources

Napoleon the "Liberator"?

Did Napoleon continue the work of the French Revolution? These two documents, from early and late moments in Napoleon's career, allow one to judge the extent to which Napoleon's regime shared the goals of revolutionaries who preceded him.

The first document concerns Napoleon's decision to reestablish slavery in French colonies. The slaves of Saint-Domingue had freed themselves by insurrection in 1791, and the French revolutionary government made this freedom official by abolishing slavery on French territory in 1794. In 1802, Napoleon launched an expeditionary force to reimpose French control over the colony, and in the course of this conflict it became clear that his goal was reenslavement. The former slaves of Saint-Domingue defeated Napoleon's troops and established Haiti as an independent nation, but in the nearby French colonies of Tobago, Martinique, and Guadeloupe, as well as in French holdings in the Indian Ocean, Napoleon reinstituted slavery. The first excerpt below is from a preliminary draft for the law on reenslavement that Napoleon drew up himself.

The second selection is excerpted from a proclamation that Napoleon addressed to the sovereigns of Europe on his return to France in March 1815, after escaping from his exile on the island of Elba. It is an excellent illustration of Napoleon's self-image at the end of his career, his rhetoric, and his belief that he represented the force of history itself.

Letter to Consul Cambacères, April 27, 1802

The consuls of the Republic and informed council of State decree:

Article One: According to the reports made to the captain-general of the colony of ________ by those individuals who will commit to this result, a list will be composed comprising first the names of black people who enjoyed freedom before 26 Pluviôse, Year II, and second, the names of blacks who have united to defend the territory of the Republic from its enemies, or who, in any other matter, have served the state.

Article Two: All the individuals named on this list will be declared free.

Article Three: Those among them who do not own property, and who have not trade or skill which can assure their subsistence, will be subjected to the regulations of the police who will assign them to property owners who will support them in agricultural work, determine their pay, and will stipulate above all arrangements for preventing vagabondage and insubordination.

Article Four: Insubordinates and outspoken vagabonds will be, in cases determined by the regulations, struck from the list and deprived of the advantages which result from it. One can substitute for this arrangement deportation to colonies where the emancipation laws have not been enacted.

Article Five: All blacks not included on the aforementioned list in article one will be subjected to the laws which in 1789 comprised the Black Code in the colonies [the Black Code was the law regulating the practice of slavery].

Article Six: It will be permitted to import blacks in the colony of ________ in accordance with the laws and regulations of the trade which were in place in 1789. The minister of the marine is charged with the execution of the present order.

Source: Laura Mason and Tracey Rizzo, *The French Revolution: A Document Collection* (Boston: 1999), pp. 349–50.

side. By the time Napoleon reached Paris, he had generated enough support to cause Louis to flee the country. The allies, meeting in Vienna to conclude peace treaties with the French, were stunned by the news of Napoleon's return. They dispatched a hastily organized army to meet the emperor's typically bold offensive push into the Low Countries. At the battle of Waterloo, fought over three bloody days from June 15 to 18, 1815, Napoleon was stopped by the forces of his two most persistent enemies, Britain and Prussia, and suffered his final defeat. This time, the allies took no chances and shipped their prisoner off to the bleak island of St. Helena in the South Atlantic. The once-mighty emperor, now the exile Bonaparte, lived out a dreary existence writing self-serving memoirs until his death in 1821.

Circular Letter to the Sovereigns of Europe, April 4, 1815

Monsieur, My Brother,

You will have learnt, during the course of last month, of my landing again in France, of my entry into Paris, and of the departure of the Bourbon family. Your Majesty must by now be aware of the real nature of these events. They are the work of an irresistible power, of the unanimous will of a great nation conscious of its duties and of its rights. A dynasty forcibly reimposed upon the French people was no longer suitable for it: the Bourbons refused to associate themselves with the natural feelings or the national customs; and France was forced to abandon them. The popular voice called for a liberator. The expectation which had decided me to make the supreme sacrifice was in vain. I returned; and from the place where my foot first touched the shore I was carried by the affection of my subjects into the bosom of my capital.

My first and heartfelt anxiety is to repay so much affection by the maintenance of an honourable peace. The re-establishment of the Imperial throne was necessary for the happiness of Frenchmen: my dearest hope is that it may also secure repose for the whole of Europe. Each national flag in turn has had its gleam of glory: often enough, by some turn of fortune, great victories have been followed by great defeats.... I have provided the world in the past with a programme of great contests; it will please me better in future to acknowledge no rivalry but that of the advocates of peace, and no combat but a crusade for the felicity of mankind. It is France's pleasure to make a frank avowal of this noble ideal. Jealous of her independence, she will always base her policy upon an unqualified respect for the independence of other peoples....

Monsieur my Brother,
Your good Brother,
Napoleon

Source: K. M. Baker, ed., *The Old Regime and the French Revolution* (Chicago: 1987), pp. 419–420, 426–427.

Questions for Analysis

1. Who in the Caribbean colonies did Napoleon intend to send back into slavery in 1802? Who was to remain free? What did Napoleon hope to accomplish by returning to the prerevolutionary legislation that authorized slavery?
2. In his 1815 address to the monarchs of Europe, can one still detect certain aspects of revolutionary rhetoric in Napoleon's words, even as he harnessed this rhetoric to his project of reestablishing the empire after his 1814 defeat?
3. Looking back on his career of ambitious conquests, what can Napoleon have hoped to accomplish in 1815 by boasting that France's "jealous" protection of her own independence gave her an "unqualified respect for the independence of other peoples"? Do his statements reveal a contradiction between the French revolution's commitment to the "universal" rights of man and the pursuit of national self-interests?

Liberty, Politics, and Slavery: The Haitian Revolution

In the French colonies across the Atlantic, the revolution took a different course, with wide-ranging ramifications. The Caribbean islands of Guadeloupe, Martinique, and Saint-Domingue occupied a central role in the eighteenth-century French economy because of the sugar trade. Their planter elites had powerful influence in Paris. The French National Assembly (like its American counterpart) declined to discuss the matter of slavery in the colonies, unwilling to encroach on the property rights of slave owners and fearful of losing the lucrative sugar islands to their British or Spanish rivals should discontented slave owners talk of independence from France. (Competition between the European powers for the islands of the Caribbean was intense; that islands would change hands was a real possibility.) French men in the National Assembly also had to consider the question of

Past and Present

The Atlantic Revolutions and Human Rights

The eighteenth-century revolutions in the Atlantic world, such as the slave revolt in Saint Domingue (left), were based on the idea that individual rights were universal—they applied to everybody. Since the world is divided into autonomous nation-states, however, it has been challenging for defenders of universal human rights, like the organization Amnesty International (right), to ensure their enforcement globally.

Watch related author interview on StudySpace wwnorton.com/web/westernciv18

rights for free men of color, a group that included a significant number of wealthy owners of property (and slaves).

Saint-Domingue had about 40,000 whites of different social classes, 30,000 free people of color, and 500,000 slaves, most of them recently enslaved in West Africa. In 1790, free people of color from Saint-Domingue sent a delegation to Paris, asking to be seated by the assembly, underscoring that they were men of property and, in many cases, of European ancestry. The assembly refused. Their refusal sparked a rebellion among free people of color in Saint-Domingue. The French colonial authorities repressed the movement quickly—and brutally. They captured Vincent Ogé, a member of the delegation to Paris and one of the leaders of the rebellion, and publicly executed him and his allies by breaking on the wheel and decapitation. Radical deputies in Paris, including Robespierre, expressed outrage but could do little to change the assembly's policy.

In August 1791, the largest slave rebellion in history broke out in Saint-Domingue. How much that rebellion owed to revolutionary propaganda is unclear; like many rebellions during the period, it had its own roots. The British and the Spanish invaded, confident they could crush the rebellion and take the island. In the spring of 1792, the French government, on the verge of collapse and war with Europe, scrambled to win allies in Saint-Domingue by making free men of color citizens. A few months later (after the revolution of August 1792), the new French Republic dispatched commissioners to Saint-Domingue with troops and instructions to hold the island. There they faced a combination of different forces: Spanish and British troops, defiant Saint-Domingue planters, and slaves in rebellion. In this context, the local French commissioners reconsidered their commitment to slavery; in 1793, they promised freedom to slaves who would join the French. A year later, the assembly in Paris extended to slaves in all the colonies a liberty that had already been accomplished in Saint-Domingue, by the slave rebellion.

Emancipation and war brought new leaders to the fore, chief among them a former slave, Toussaint Bréda, later Toussaint L'Ouverture (*too-SAN LOO-vehr-tur*), meaning "the one who opened the way." Over the course of the next five years, Toussaint and his soldiers, now allied with the French army, emerged victorious over the French planters, the British (in 1798), and the Spanish (in 1801). Toussaint also broke the power of his rival generals in both the mulatto and former slave armies, becoming the statesman of the revolution. In 1801, Toussaint set up a constitution, swearing allegiance to France but denying France any right to interfere in Saint-Domingue affairs. The constitution abolished slavery, reorganized the military, established Christianity as the state religion (this entailed a rejection of vodoun, a blend of Christian and various West and Central African traditions), and made Toussaint governor for life. It was an extraordinary moment in the revolutionary period: the formation of an authoritarian society but also an utterly unexpected symbol of the universal potential of revolutionary ideas.

TOUSSAINT L'OUVERTURE. A portrait of L'Ouverture, leader of what would become the Haitian Revolution, as a general.

Toussaint's accomplishments, however, put him on a collision course with the other French general he admired and whose career was remarkably like his own: Napoleon Bonaparte. Saint-Domingue stood at the center of Bonaparte's vision of an expanded empire in the New World, an empire that would recoup North American territories France had lost under the Old Regime and pivot around the lucrative combination of the Mississippi, French Louisiana, and the sugar and slave colonies of the Caribbean. In January 1802, Bonaparte dispatched 20,000 troops to bring the island under control. Toussaint, captured when he arrived for discussions with the French, was shipped under heavy guard to a prison in the mountains of eastern France, where he died in 1803. Fighting continued in Saint-Domingue, however, with fires now fueled by Bonaparte's decree reestablishing slavery where the convention had abolished it. The war turned into a nightmare for the French. Yellow fever killed thousands of French troops, including one of Napoleon's best generals and brother-in-law. Armies on both sides committed atrocities. By December 1803, the French army had collapsed. Napoleon scaled back his vision of an American empire and sold the Louisiana territories to Thomas Jefferson. "I know the value of what I abandon . . . I renounce it with the greatest regret," he told an aide. In Saint-Domingue, a general in the army of former slaves, Jean-Jacques Dessalines, declared the independent state of Haiti in 1804.

The Haitian Revolution remained, in significant ways, an anomaly. It was the only successful slave revolution in history and by far the most radical of the revolutions that occurred in this age. It suggested that the emancipatory ideas of the revolution and Enlightenment might apply to non-Europeans and enslaved peoples—a suggestion that residents of Europe attempted to ignore but one that struck home with planter elites in North and South America. Combined with later rebellions in the British colonies, it contributed to the British decision to end slavery in 1838. And it cast a long shadow over nineteenth-century slave societies from the southern United States to Brazil. The Napoleonic episode, then, had wide-ranging effects across the Atlantic: in North America, the Louisiana purchase; in the Caribbean, the Haitian Revolution; in Latin America, the weakening of Spain and Portugal's colonial empires.

CONCLUSION

The tumultuous events in France formed part of a broad pattern of late-eighteenth-century democratic upheaval. The French Revolution was the most violent, protracted, and contentious of the revolutions of the era; but the dynamics of revolution were much the same everywhere. One of the most important developments of the French Revolution was the emergence of a popular movement, which included political clubs representing people previously excluded from politics, newspapers read by and to the common people, and political leaders who spoke for the sans-culottes. In the French Revolution, as in other revolutions, the popular movement challenged the early and moderate revolutionary leadership, pressing for more radical and democratic measures. And, as in other revolutions, the popular movement in France was defeated, and authority was reestablished by a quasi-military figure. Likewise, the revolutionary ideas of liberty, equality, and fraternity were not specifically French; their roots lay in the social structures of the eighteenth century and in the ideas and culture of the Enlightenment. Yet French armies brought them, literally, to the doorsteps of many Europeans.

What was the larger impact of the revolution and the Napoleonic era? Its legacy is partly summed up in three key concepts: liberty, equality, and nation. Liberty meant individual rights and responsibilities and, more

After You Read This Chapter

Visit StudySpace for quizzes, additional review materials, and multi-media documents. **wwnorton.com/web/westernciv18**

REVIEWING THE OBJECTIVES

- The French Revolution resulted both from an immediate political crisis and long-term social tensions. What was this crisis, and how did it lead to popular revolt against the monarchy?
- The revolutionaries in the National Assembly in 1789 set out to produce a constitution for France. What were their political goals, and what was the reaction of monarchs and peoples elsewhere in Europe?
- After 1792, a more radical group of revolutionaries seized control of the French state. How did they come to power, and how were their political goals different from their predecessors?
- Napoleon's career began during the revolution. What did he owe to the revolution, and what was different about his regime?
- Three major revolutions took place in the Atlantic world at the end of the eighteenth century: the American Revolution, the French Revolution, and the Haitian Revolution. What was similar about these revolutions? What was different?

specifically, freedom from arbitrary authority. By equality, as we have seen, the revolutionaries meant the abolition of legal distinctions of rank among European men. Though their concept of equality was limited, it became a powerful mobilizing force in the nineteenth century. The most important legacy of the revolution may have been the new term *nation*. Nationhood was a political concept. A nation was formed of citizens, not a king's subjects; it was ruled by law and treated citizens as equal before the law; sovereignty did not lie in dynasties or historic fiefdoms but in the nation of citizens. This new form of nation gained legitimacy when citizen armies repelled attacks against their newly won freedoms; the victories of "citizens in arms" lived on in myth and history and provided the most powerful images of the period. As the war continued, military nationhood began to overshadow its political cousin. By the Napoleonic period, this shift became decisive; a new political body of freely associated citizens was most powerfully embodied in a centralized state, its army and a kind of citizenship defined by individual commitment to the needs of the nation at war. This understanding of national identity spread throughout Europe in the coming decades.

PEOPLE, IDEAS, AND EVENTS IN CONTEXT

- Why was **LOUIS XVI** forced to convene the **ESTATES GENERAL** in 1789?
- What argument did **ABBÉ SIEYÈS** make about the role of the **THIRD ESTATE**?
- What made the **TENNIS COURT OATH** a revolutionary act?
- What was the role of popular revolt (the attack on the **BASTILLE**, the **GREAT FEAR**, the **OCTOBER DAYS**) in the revolutionary movements of 1789?
- What was the connection between the French Revolution with the **SLAVE REVOLT IN SAINT-DOMINGUE** that began in 1791?
- What was the **DECLARATION OF THE RIGHTS OF MAN AND OF THE CITIZEN**?
- What was the **CIVIL CONSTITUTION OF THE CLERGY**?
- What circumstances led to the abolition of the monarchy in 1792?
- Why did the **JACOBINS** in the **NATIONAL CONVENTION** support a policy of the **TERROR**?
- What were **NAPOLEON**'s most significant domestic accomplishments in France? What significance did Napoleon's military campaigns have for other parts of Europe and for the French Empire?
- What was the significance of the **HAITIAN REVOLUTION** of 1804?

THINKING ABOUT CONNECTIONS

- Popular movements in favor of democracy, social justice, or national self-determination in the more than two centuries since 1789 have often used the French Revolution as a point of reference or comparison. Obvious comparisons are those movements that saw themselves as "revolutionary," such as the Russian Revolution of 1917 or the Chinese Revolution of 1949. More recent comparisons might be the popular movements for democratic change in eastern Europe that resulted in the end of the Cold War in 1989 or the Arab Spring of 2011.
- Make a list of factors or circumstances that one might want to compare in considering the outcome of such movements. You might consider the degree to which elites support the current regime, the degree of consensus, and the goals of those who are protesting the status quo, economic circumstances, or international support for either the regime or for revolutionaries. What other factors might determine the outcome of revolutionary situations?

Before You Read This Chapter

STORY LINES

- Industrialization put Europe on the path to a new form of economic development, based on the concentration of labor and production in areas with easy access to new sources of energy. This led to rapid growth of new industrial cities and to the development of new transportation to connect industrial centers to growing markets.
- Industrialization created new social groups in society, defined less by their status at birth than by their place in the new economy. Workers faced new kinds of discipline in the workplace, and women and children entered the new industrial workforce in large numbers. A new elite, made up of businessmen, entrepreneurs, bankers, engineers, and merchants, emerged as the primary beneficiaries of industrialization.
- Population growth in rural areas spurred migration to cities where laborers and the middle classes did not mix socially. They adopted different dress, speech, and leisure activities and had significantly different opportunities when it came to marriage, sex, and children.

CHRONOLOGY

1780s	Industrialization begins in Britain
1825	First railroad in Britain
1830s	Industrialization begins in France and Belgium
1845–1849	Irish potato famine
1850s	Industrialization begins in Prussia and German states of central Europe
1861	Russian tsar emancipates the serfs

19

The Industrial Revolution and Nineteenth-Century Society

CORE OBJECTIVES

- **UNDERSTAND** the circumstances that allowed for industrialization to begin in Great Britain.
- **IDENTIFY** the industries that were the first to adopt new systems for mechanical production and the regions in Europe in which they thrived.
- **DESCRIBE** the changes in the nature of work, production, and employment that occurred as a result of the mechanization of industry.
- **EXPLAIN** the effects of industrialization on social life in Europe, especially in the new urban centers associated with industrial development.
- **IDENTIFY** the essential characteristics of the new "middle classes" in nineteenth-century Europe and their differences from property-owning groups prior to the Industrial Revolution.

James Watt, a Scottish mechanic and instrument maker, changed the course of human history when he took the primitive steam engine designed by Thomas Newcomen around 1712 and added a separate condenser, which allowed it to generate more power using less coal as fuel. Newcomen's engine used repeated heating and cooling of a steam container to generate a vacuum that could be used to pump water. Watt's engine, which he marketed after 1775 in a partnership with Matthew Boulton, was soon adapted to produce a rotary motion that could be used industrially in a multitude of ways, including grinding, milling, sawing, and weaving. The spread of Watt's steam technology throughout the north of England at the end of the eighteenth century transformed the manufacturing world, reshaped the landscape of the English countryside, and began a revolution in the way that people lived and worked.

The condensing steam engine also made Watt a very wealthy man—and he was well aware that wealth like his was different from that possessed by Britain's traditional elites. He distinguished this wealth from that of the landed aristocrat by linking it to his own efforts as an inventor and entrepreneur: "The Squire's land has not been so much of his own making as the condensing engine has been of mine. He has only passively inherited his property, while this invention has been the product of my own labour and of God knows how much anguish of mind and body."

Watt was correct in his claim that his wealth and status were different from the status claimed by the landed aristocracy, but this wealth was not the product of his labor alone. In addition to his engineering predecessors, like Newcomen, Watt's engine could only be profitable in a world in which foresters, cotton merchants, and landowners could see profits in the purchase of expensive industrial sawmills, mechanical looms, and steam-driven threshers. Watt's invention also depended on the labor of men and women who dug coal from the ground and who smelted the iron and copper that he used to produce his machines. The profits of industrial entrepreneurs, meanwhile, depended on their ability to find sawyers, weavers, and fieldworkers who were willing to accept a new way of working, where they no longer owned their own tools but rather worked as wage laborers for men of business seeking returns on their investment. Business owners also required customers for the larger amounts of finished timber, woven cloth, and grain that they were now bringing to market. Technology such as Watt's was an important part of the changes that historians call the "Industrial Revolution," but technology alone cannot explain the complicated social and economic transformation contained in the phrase.

The Industrial Revolution led to the proliferation of more capital-intensive enterprises, new ways of organizing human labor, and the rapid growth of cities. It was made possible by new sources of energy and power, which led to faster forms of mechanized transportation, higher productivity, and the emergence of large consumer markets for manufactured goods. In turn, these interrelated developments triggered social and cultural changes with revolutionary consequences for Europeans and their relationship to the rest of the world.

Of all the changes, perhaps the most revolutionary came at the very root of human endeavor: new forms of energy. Over the space of two or three generations, a society and an economy that had drawn on water, wind, and wood for most of its energy needs came to depend on machines driven by steam engines and coal. In 1800, the world produced 10 million tons of coal. In 1900, it produced 1 billion—a hundred times more. The Industrial Revolution brought the beginning of the fossil-fuel age, altering as it did so the balance of humanity and the environment.

Mechanization made possible enormous gains in productivity in some sectors of the economy, but the new machines were limited to a few sectors of the economy, especially at the outset, and did not always lead to a dramatic break with older techniques. Above all, technology did not dispense with human toil. Historians emphasize that the Industrial Revolution intensified human labor—carrying water on iron rails, digging trenches, harvesting cotton, sewing by hand, or pounding hides—much more often than it eased it. One historian has suggested that we would do better to speak of the "industrious revolution." This revolution did not lie solely in machines but in a new economic system based on mobilizing capital and labor on a much larger scale. The industrious economy redistributed wealth and power, creating new social classes and producing new social tensions.

It also prompted deep-seated cultural shifts. The English critic Raymond Williams has pointed out that in the eighteenth century, *industry* referred to a human quality: a hardworking woman was "industrious," an ambitious clerk showed "industry." By the middle of the nineteenth century, industry had come to mean an economic system, one that followed its own logic and worked on its own—seemingly independent of humans. This is our modern understanding of the term, and it was born in the early nineteenth century. As the Industrial Revolution altered the foundations of the economy, it also changed the very assumptions with which people approached economics and the ways in which they regarded the role of human beings in the economy. These new assumptions could foster a sense of power but also anxieties about powerlessness.

The dramatic changes of the late eighteenth and early nineteenth centuries emerged out of earlier developments. Overseas commercial exploration opened new territories to European trade. India, Africa, and the Americas had already been brought into the web of the European economy. Expanding trade networks created new markets for goods and sources for raw materials, and the need to organize commerce over long distances fostered financial innovations and sophisticated credit schemes for managing risk. These developments paved the way for industrialization. Within Europe, the commercialization of agriculture and the spread of handicraft manufacturing in rural areas also changed the economy in ways that anticipated later industrial developments. A final factor seems to have been population growth, which began to accelerate in the eighteenth century. Because these earlier developments did not affect all areas in Europe the same way, industrialization did not always follow the same pattern across the Continent. It happened first in Great Britain, and that is where we will begin.

THE INDUSTRIAL REVOLUTION IN BRITAIN, 1760–1850

Great Britain in the eighteenth century had a fortunate combination of natural, economic, and cultural resources. It was a small and secure island nation with a robust empire and control over crucial lanes across the oceans. It had ample supplies of coal, rivers, and a well-developed network of canals.

In addition, agriculture in Britain was already more thoroughly commercialized than elsewhere. British agriculture had been transformed by a combination of new techniques, new crops, and by the "enclosure" of fields and pastures, which turned small holdings, and in many cases commonly held lands, into large fenced tracts that were privately owned and individually managed by commercial landlords. The British Parliament encouraged enclosure with a series of bills in the second half of the eighteenth century. Commercialized agriculture was more productive and yielded more food for a growing and increasingly urban population. The concentration of property in fewer hands drove small farmers off the land, sending them to look for work in other sectors of the economy. Last, commercialized agriculture produced higher profits, wealth that would be invested in industry.

A key precondition for industrialization, therefore, was Britain's growing supply of available capital, in the forms of private wealth and well-developed banking and credit institutions. London had become the leading center for international trade, and the city was a headquarters for the transfer of raw material, capital, and manufactured products throughout the world. This capital was readily available to underwrite new economic enterprises and eased the transfer of money and goods—importing, for instance, silks from the East or Egyptian and North American cottons.

Social and cultural conditions also encouraged investment in enterprises. In Britain far more than on the Continent, the pursuit of wealth was perceived to be a worthy goal. European nobility cultivated the notion of gentlemanly conduct, in part to hold the line against those moving up from below. British aristocrats respected commoners with a talent for making money and did not hesitate to invest themselves. Their scramble to enclose their

ENCLOSED FIELDS IN CENTRAL BRITAIN. The large, uniform square fields in the background of this photograph are fields that were enclosed from smaller holdings and common lands in the 1830s. They contrast with the smaller and older strip fields in the foreground. The larger enclosed fields were more profitable for their owners, who benefited from legislation that encouraged enclosure, but the process created hardship for the village communities that depended on the use of these lands for their survival. ▪ ***What circumstances made enclosure possible?*** ▪ ***What connection have historians made between enclosure and early industrialization?***

lands reflected a keen interest in commercialization and investment. Outside the aristocracy, an even lower barrier separated merchants from the rural gentry. Many of the entrepreneurs of the early Industrial Revolution came from the small gentry or independent farmer class. Eighteenth-century Britain was not by any means free of social snobbery: lords looked down on bankers and bankers looked down on craft workers. But a lord's disdain might well be tempered by the fact that his own grandfather had worked in the counting house.

Growing domestic and international markets made eighteenth-century Britain prosperous. The British were voracious consumers. The court elite followed and bought up yearly fashions, and so did most of Britain's landed and professional society. "Nature may be satisfied with little," one London entrepreneur declared. "But it is the wants of fashion and the desire of novelties that causes trade." The country's small size and the fact that it was an island encouraged the development of a well-integrated domestic market. Unlike continental Europe, Britain did not have a system of internal tolls and tariffs, so goods could be moved freely to wherever they might fetch the best price. A constantly improving transportation system boosted that freedom of movement. So did a favorable political climate. Some members of Parliament were businessmen themselves; others were investors. And both groups were eager to encourage by legislation the construction of canals, the establishment of banks, and the enclosure of common lands.

THE FIRST INDUSTRIAL NATION. Large-scale mechanization of industry developed first in Britain. ▪ ***The accumulation of large deposits of what two natural resources caused urban growth outside of London?*** ▪ ***What new forms of transportation were critical for moving natural resources to market?*** ▪ ***What else was necessary for industrialization to develop as it did?***

Foreign markets promised even greater returns than domestic ones, though with greater risks. British foreign policy responded to its commercial needs. At the end of every major eighteenth-century war, Britain wrested overseas territories from its enemies. At the same time, Britain penetrated hitherto unexploited territories, such as India and South America. In 1759, over one-third of all British exports went to the colonies; by 1784, if we include the former colonies in North America, that figure had increased to one-half. Production for export rose by 80 percent between 1750 and 1770; production for domestic consumption gained just 7 percent over the same period. The British possessed a merchant marine capable of transporting goods around the world and a navy practiced in the art of protecting its commercial fleets. By the 1780s, Britain's markets, together with its fleet and its established position at the center of world commerce, gave its entrepreneurs unrivaled opportunities for trade and profit.

Innovation in the Textile Industries

The Industrial Revolution began with dramatic technological leaps in a few industries, the first of which was cotton textiles. The industry was already long established. Tariffs prohibiting imports of East Indian cottons, which Parliament had imposed to protect British woolen goods, had spurred the manufacture of British cotton. British textile manufacturers imported raw materials from India and the American South and borrowed patterns from Indian spinners and weavers. What, then, were the revolutionary breakthroughs?

In 1733, John Kay's invention of the flying shuttle speeded the process of weaving. The task of spinning thread, however, had not kept up. A series of comparatively simple mechanical devices eliminated this spinning-to-weaving bottleneck. The most important device was the spinning jenny, invented by James Hargreaves, a handloom weaver, in 1764. The spinning jenny was a compound spinning wheel capable of producing sixteen threads at once—though the threads were not strong enough to be used for the longitudinal fibers, or warp, of cotton cloth. The invention of the water frame by Richard Arkwright, a barber, in 1769, made it possible to produce both warp and woof (latitudinal fibers) in great quantity. In 1799, Samuel Compton invented the spinning mule, which combined the features of both the jenny and the frame. All of these important technological changes were accomplished by the end of the eighteenth century.

COTTON SPINNING, 1861. An illustration from a series showing spinning at Walter Evans and Company, cotton manufacturers in Derby, England. ▪ ***Why did textile factories prefer female employees?***

A jenny could spin from six to twenty-four times more yarn than a hand spinner. By the end of the eighteenth century, a mule could produce 200 to 300 times more. Just as important, the new machines made better-quality—stronger and finer—thread. These machines revolutionized production across the textile industry. Last, the cotton gin, invented by the American Eli Whitney in 1793, mechanized the process of separating cotton seeds from the fiber, thereby speeding up the production of cotton and reducing its price. The supply of cotton fibers could now expand to keep pace with rising demand from cotton cloth manufacturers. This cotton gin had many effects, including, paradoxically, making slavery more profitable in the United States. The cotton-producing slave plantations in the American South became enmeshed in the lucrative trade with manufacturers who produced cotton textiles in the northern United States and England.

The first textile machines were inexpensive enough to be used by spinners in their own cottages. But as machines

JAMES HARGREAVES'S SPINNING JENNY, 1764. Earlier innovations in textile looms allowed weavers to produce cloth more quickly, but the industry was stymied by the slowness of traditional spinning methods. Thread production simply could not keep up with the demand created by new weaving methods. Hargreaves found a solution in a spinning jenny, which allowed spinners to spin thread and yarns on multiple spindles simultaneously—this image from Germany shows a jenny with sixteen spindles. The spinning jenny was capable of producing thread so quickly that it flooded the market, driving down the price of cotton thread. Local spinners were so outraged at this affront to their livelihood that they broke into Hargreaves's workshop and destroyed his machines, forcing him to flee and set up a new manufacture elsewhere in secret. (See also "Ned Ludd and the Luddites" on page 623.)

grew in size and complexity, they were housed instead in workshops or mills located near water that could be used to power the machines. Eventually, the further development of steam-driven equipment allowed manufacturers to build mills wherever they could be used. Frequently, those mills went up in towns and cities in the north of England, away from the older commercial and seafaring centers but nearer to the coal fields that provided fuel for new machines. From 1780 on, British cotton textiles flooded the world market. In 1760, Britain imported 2.5 million pounds of raw cotton; in 1787, 22 million pounds; in 1837, 366 million pounds. By 1815, the export of cotton textiles amounted to 40 percent of the value of all domestic goods exported from Great Britain. Although the price of manufactured cotton goods fell dramatically, the market expanded so rapidly that profits continued to increase.

Behind these statistics lay a revolution in clothing and consumption. Cotton in the form of muslins and calicos was fine enough to appeal to wealthy consumers. Cotton was also light and washable. For the first time, ordinary people could have sheets, table linens, curtains, and underwear. (Wool was too scratchy.) As one writer commented in 1846, the revolution in textiles had ushered in a "brilliant transformation" in dress. "Every woman used to wear a blue or black dress that she kept ten years without washing it for fear that it would fall to pieces. Today her husband can cover her in flower-printed cotton for the price of a day's wages."

The explosive growth of textiles also prompted a debate about the benefits and tyranny of the new industries. The British Romantic poet William Blake famously wrote in biblical terms of the textile mills' blight on the English countryside:

> And did the Countenance Divine
> Shine forth upon our clouded hills?
> And was Jerusalem builded here
> Among these dark Satanic mills?

By the 1830s, the British House of Commons was holding hearings on employment and working conditions in factories, recording testimony about working days that stretched from 3:00 A.M. to 10:00 P.M., the employment of very young children, and workers who lost hair and fingers in the mills' machinery. Women and children counted for roughly two-thirds of the labor force in textiles. The principle of regulating any labor (and emphatically that of adult men), however, was controversial. Only gradually did a series of factory acts prohibit hiring children under age nine and limit the labor of workers under age eighteen to ten hours a day.

Coal and Iron

Meanwhile, decisive changes were transforming the production of iron. As in the textile industry, many important technological changes came during the eighteenth century. A series of innovations (coke smelting, rolling, and puddling) enabled the British to substitute coal (which they had in abundance) for wood (which was scarce and inefficient) to heat molten metal and make iron. The new "pig iron" was higher quality and could be used in building an enormous variety of iron products: machines, engines, railway tracks, agricultural implements, and hardware. Those iron products became, literally, the infrastructure of industrialization. Britain found itself able to export both coal and iron to rapidly expanding markets around the industrializing regions of the world. Between 1814 and 1852, exports of British iron doubled, rising to over 1 million tons of iron, more than half of the world's total production.

Rising demand for coal required mining deeper veins. In 1711, Thomas Newcomen's cumbersome but remarkably effective steam engine was immensely useful to the

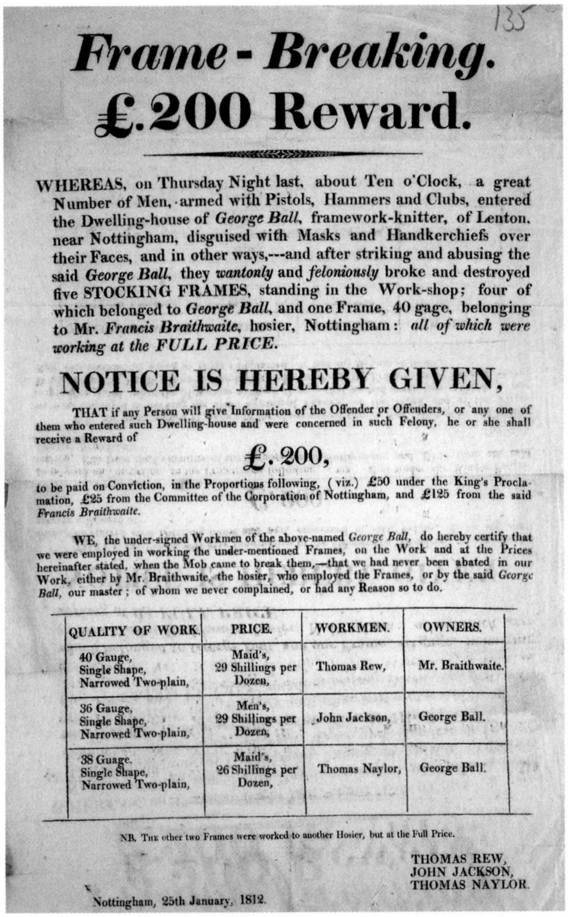

135

Frame - Breaking.

£.200 Reward.

WHEREAS, on Thursday Night last, about Ten o'Clock, a great Number of Men, armed with Pistols, Hammers and Clubs, entered the Dwelling-house of *George Ball*, framework-knitter, of Lenton, near Nottingham, disguised with Masks and Handkerchiefs over their Faces, and in other ways,---and after striking and abusing the said *George Ball*, they *wantonly* and *feloniously* broke and destroyed five STOCKING FRAMES, standing in the Work-shop; four of which belonged to *George Ball*, and one Frame, 40 gage, belonging to Mr. *Francis Braithwaite*, hosier, Nottingham: *all of which were working at the FULL PRICE.*

NOTICE IS HEREBY GIVEN,

THAT if any Person will give Information of the Offender or Offenders, or any one of them who entered such Dwelling-house and were concerned in such Felony, he or she shall receive a Reward of

£. 200,

to be paid on Conviction, in the Proportions following, (viz.) £50 under the King's Proclamation, £25 from the Committee of the Corporation of Nottingham, and £125 from the said *Francis Braithwaite.*

WE, the under-signed Workmen of the above-named *George Ball*, do hereby certify that we were employed in working the under-mentioned Frames, on the Work and at the Prices hereinafter stated, when the Mob came to break them,—that we had never been abated in our Work, either by Mr. Braithwaite, the hosier, who employed the Frames, or by the said *George Ball*, our master; of whom we never complained, or had any Reason so to do.

QUALITY OF WORK.	PRICE.	WORKMEN.	OWNERS.
40 Gauge, Single Shape, Narrowed Two-plain,	Maid's, 29 Shillings per Dozen,	Thomas Rew,	Mr. Braithwaite.
36 Gauge, Single Shape, Narrowed Two-plain,	Men's, 29 Shillings per Dozen,	John Jackson,	George Ball.
38 Guage, Single Shape, Narrowed Two-plain,	Maid's, 26 Shillings per Dozen,	Thomas Naylor,	George Ball.

NB. The other two Frames were worked to another Hosier, but at the Full Price.

THOMAS REW,
JOHN JACKSON,
THOMAS NAYLOR.

Nottingham, 25th January, 1812.

NED LUDD AND THE LUDDITES. In 1811 and 1812, in northern England, bands of working men who resented the adoption of new mechanical devices in the weaving industries attacked several establishments and destroyed the frames used to weave cloth. The movement took the name Luddites from Ned Ludd, a man who had broken the frames belonging to his employer in 1779. His mythological presence in the movement is depicted in the illustration at the right. Although their anger was directed at the machines, the real target of their resentment may have been a new pricing scheme imposed on them by the merchants who bought finished work. The debate about prices is a central part of the poster on the left, which offers a reward for information leading to the conviction of frame breakers. The poster is signed by several workers of the establishment, who published the price they received for each piece of clothing and their lack of complaints about their employer. ▪ ***How might the need to adjust to the price fluctuations of a market economy have been perceived by weavers accustomed to getting fixed prices for their goods?***

coal industry for pumping water from mines. After 1763, as we have seen, James Watt improved on Newcomen's machine, and by 1800 Watt and his partner, Matthew Boulton, had sold 289 engines for use in factories and mines. Watt and Boulton made their fortune from their invention's efficiency; they earned a regular percentage of the increased profits from each mine that operated an engine.

Steam power was still energy consuming and expensive and so only slowly replaced traditional water power. Even in its early form, however, the steam engine decisively transformed the nineteenth-century world with one application: the steam-driven locomotive. Railroads revolutionized industry, markets, public and private financing, and ordinary people's conceptions of space and time.

THE COMING OF RAILWAYS

Transportation had improved during the years before 1830, but moving heavy materials, particularly coal, remained a problem. It is significant that the first modern railway, built in England in 1825, ran from the Durham coal field of Stockton to Darlington, near the coast. Coal had traditionally been hauled short distances via tramways, or tracks along which horses pulled coal carts. The locomotives on the Stockton-Darlington line traveled at fifteen miles per hour, the fastest rate at which machines had yet moved goods overland. Soon they would move people as well, transforming transportation in the process.

Building railways became a massive enterprise and a risky but potentially profitable opportunity for investment. No sooner did the first combined passenger and goods service open in 1830, operating between Liverpool and Manchester, England, than plans were formulated and money pledged to extend rail systems throughout Europe, the Americas, and beyond. In 1830, there were no more than a few dozen miles of railway in the world. By 1840, there were over 4,500 miles; by 1850, over 23,000. British engineers, industrialists, and investors were quick to realize the global opportunities available in constructing railways overseas; a large part of Britain's industrial success in the later nineteenth century came through building other nations' infrastructures. The English contractor Thomas Brassey, for instance, built railways in Italy, Canada, Argentina, India, and Australia.

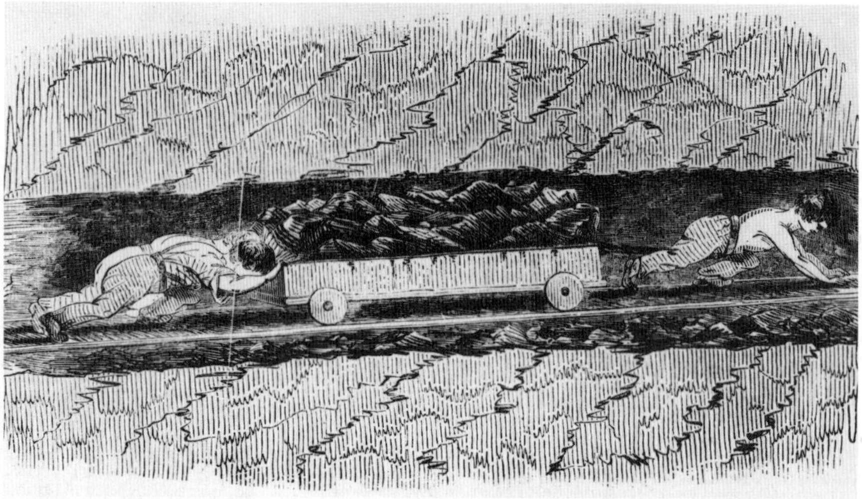

CHILD LABOR IN THE MINES. This engraving of a young worker pulling a coal cart up through the narrow shaft of a mine accompanied a British Parliamentary report on child labor. ▪ ***What attitudes about government and the economy made it difficult for legislatures to regulate working conditions in the new industries?***

Throughout the world, a veritable army of construction workers built the railways. In Britain, they were called "navvies," derived from *navigator,* a term first used for the construction workers on Britain's eighteenth-century canals. Navvies were a rough lot, living with a few women in temporary encampments as they migrated across the countryside. Often they were immigrant workers and faced local hostility. A sign posted by local residents outside a mine in Scotland in 1845 warned the Irish navvies to get "off the ground and out of the country" in a week or else be driven out "by the strength of our armes and a good pick shaft." Later in the century railway building projects in Africa and the Americas were lined with camps of immigrant Indian and Chinese laborers, who also became targets of nativist (a term that means "opposed to foreigners") anger.

The magnitude of the navvies' accomplishment was extraordinary. In Britain and in much of the rest of the world, mid-nineteenth-century railways were constructed almost entirely without the aid of machinery. An assistant engineer on the London-to-Birmingham line calculated that the labor involved was the equivalent of lifting 25 billion cubic feet of earth and stone 1 foot high. He compared this feat with building the Great Pyramid, a task he estimated had involved the hoisting of some 16 billion tons. The building of the pyramid, however, had required over 200,000 men and had taken twenty years. The construction of the London-to-Birmingham railway was accomplished by 20,000 men in less than five years. If we translated this into individual terms, a navvy was expected to move an average of 20 tons of earth per day. Railways were produced by toil as much as by technology, by human labor as much as by engineering; they illustrate why some historians prefer to use the term *industrious revolution*.

Steam engines, textile machines, new ways of making iron, and railways—all these were interconnected. Changes in one area endorsed changes in another. Pumps run by steam engines made it possible to mine deeper veins of coal; steam-powered railways made it possible to trans-

MANCHESTER TO LIVERPOOL, LATE NINETEENTH CENTURY. Lower-class passengers, physically separated from their social superiors, are packed into the rear of the train.

BARRY DOCK AND ISLAND, WALES, 1895. The convergence of coal, steam power, railways, and maritime shipping were at the center of industrialization in Britain. ▪ ***In what way did the circular relationship between coal and iron production and the larger transportation revolution associated with the construction of railroads and, later, steamships help sustain the initial growth associated with industrial development?***

port coal. Mechanization fueled the production of iron for machines and the mining of coal to run steam engines. The railway boom multiplied the demand for iron products: rails, locomotives, carriages, signals, switches, and the iron to make all of these. Building railroads called for engineering expertise: scaling mountains, designing bridges and tunnels. Railway construction, which required capital investment beyond the capacity of any single individual, forged new kinds of public and private financing. The scale of production expanded and the tempo of economic activity quickened, spurring the search for more coal, the production of more iron, the mobilization of more capital, and the recruitment of more labor. Steam and speed were becoming the foundation of the economy and of a new way of life.

THE INDUSTRIAL REVOLUTION ON THE CONTINENT

Continental Europe followed a different path. Eighteenth-century France, Belgium, and Germany did have manufacturing districts in regions with raw materials, access to markets, and long-standing traditions of craft and skill. Yet for a variety of reasons, changes along the lines seen in Britain did not occur until the 1830s. Britain's transportation system was highly developed; those of France and Germany were not. France was far larger than England: its rivers more difficult to navigate; its seaports, cities, and coal deposits farther apart. Much of central Europe was divided into small principalities, each with its own tolls and tariffs, which complicated the transportation of goods over any considerable distance. The Continent had fewer raw materials, coal in particular, than Britain. The abundance and cheapness of wood discouraged exploration that might have resulted in new discoveries of coal. It also meant that coal-run steam engines were less economical on the Continent. Capital, too, was less readily available. Early British industrialization was underwritten by private wealth; this was less feasible elsewhere. Different patterns of landholding formed obstacles to the commercialization of agriculture. In the East, serfdom was a powerful disincentive to labor-saving innovations. In the West, especially in France, the large number of small peasants, or farmers, stayed put on the land.

The wars of the French Revolution and Napoleon disrupted economies. During the eighteenth century, the population had grown and mechanization had begun in a few key industries. The ensuing political upheaval and the

Competing Viewpoints

The Factory System, Science, and Morality: Two Views

Reactions to the Industrial Revolution and the factory system it produced ranged from celebration to horror. Dr. Andrew Ure, a Scottish professor of chemistry, was fascinated with these nineteenth-century applications of Enlightenment science. He believed that the new machinery and its products would create a new society of wealth, abundance, and, ultimately, stability through the useful regimentation of production.

Friedrich Engels (1820–1895) was one of the many socialists to criticize Dr. Ure as shortsighted and complacent in his outlook. Engels was himself part of a factory-owning family and so was able to examine the new industrial cities at close range. He provides a classic nineteenth-century analysis of industrialization. The Condition of the Working Class in England *is compellingly written, angry, and revealing about middle-class concerns of the time, including female labor.*

Dr. Andrew Ure (1835)

This island [Britain] is preeminent among civilized nations for the prodigious development of its factory wealth, and has been therefore long viewed with a jealous admiration by foreign powers. This very pre-eminence, however, has been contemplated in a very different light by many influential members of our own community, and has even been denounced by them as the certain origin of innumerable evils to the people, and of revolutionary convulsions to the state. . . .

The blessings which physico-mechanical science has bestowed on society, and the means it has still in store for ameliorating the lot of mankind, has been too little dwelt upon; while, on the other hand, it has been accused of lending itself to the rich capitalists as an instrument for harassing the poor, and of exacting from the operative an accelerated rate of work. It has been said, for example, that the steam-engine now drives the power-looms with such velocity as to urge on their attendant weavers at the same rapid pace; but that the hand-weaver, not being subjected to this restless agent, can throw his shuttle and move his treddles at his convenience. There is, however, this difference in the two cases, that in the factory, every member of the loom is so adjusted, that the driving force leaves the attendant nearly nothing at all to do, certainly no muscular fatigue to sustain, while it produces for him good, unfailing wages, besides a healthy workshop *gratis:* whereas the non-factory weaver, having everything to execute by muscular exertion, finds the labour irksome, makes in consequence innumerable short pauses, separately of little account, but great when added together; earns therefore proportionally low wages, while he loses his health by poor diet and the dampness of his hovel.

Source: Andrew Ure, *The Philosophy of Manufacturers: Or, An Exposition of the Scientific, Moral, and Commercial Economy of the Factory System of Great Britain, 1835,* as cited in J. T. Ward, *The Factory System,* vol. 1 (New York: 1970), pp. 140–41.

financial strains of warfare did virtually nothing to help economic development. Napoleon's Continental System and British destruction of French merchant shipping hurt commerce badly. The ban on British-shipped cotton stalled the growth of cotton textiles for decades, though the armies' greater demand for woolen cloth kept that sector of textiles humming. Iron processing increased to satisfy the military's rising needs, but techniques for making iron remained largely unchanged. Probably the revolutionary change most beneficial to industrial advance in Europe was the removal of previous restraints on the movement of capital and labor—for example, the abolition of craft guilds and the reduction of tariff barriers across the Continent.

After 1815, a number of factors combined to change the economic climate. In those regions with a well-established commercial and industrial base—the northeast of France, Belgium, and swaths of territory across the Rhineland, Saxony, Silesia, and northern Bohemia (see map on page 000)—population growth further boosted economic development. Rising population did not by itself produce industrialization, however: in Ireland, where other necessary factors were absent, more people meant less food.

Friedrich Engels (1844)

Histories of the modern development of the cotton industry, such as those of Ure, Baines, and others, tell on every page of technical innovations. . . . In a well-ordered society such improvements would indeed be welcome, but social war rages unchecked and the benefits derived from these improvements are ruthlessly monopolized by a few persons. . . . Every improvement in machinery leads to unemployment, and the greater the technical improvement the greater the unemployment. Every improvement in machinery affects a number of workers in the same way as a commercial crisis and leads to want, distress, and crime. . . .

Let us examine a little more closely the process whereby machine-labour continually supersedes hand-labour. When spinning or weaving machinery is installed practically all that is left to be done by the hand is the piecing together of broken threads, and the machine does the rest. This task calls for nimble fingers rather than muscular strength. The labour of grown men is not merely unnecessary but actually unsuitable. . . . The greater the degree to which physical labour is displaced by the introduction of machines worked by water- or steam-power, the fewer grown men need be employed. In any case women and children will work for lower wages than men and, as has already been observed, they are more skillful at piecing than grown men. Consequently it is women and children who are employed to do this work. . . . When women work in factories, the most important result is the dissolution of family ties. If a woman works for twelve or thirteen hours a day in a factory and her husband is employed either in the same establishment or in some other works, what is the fate of the children? They lack parental care and control. . . . It is not difficult to imagine that they are left to run wild.

Source: Friedrich Engels, *The Condition of the Working Class in England in 1844,* ed. and trans. W. O. Henderson and W. H. Chaloner (New York: 1958), pp. 150–151, 158, 160.

Questions for Analysis

1. According to Andrew Ure, why was industrialization good for Britain? How can the blessings of "physico-mechanical science" lead to the improvement of humanity?
2. What criticism did Engels level at Ure and other optimists on industrialization? Why did Engels think conditions for workers were getting worse instead of better?
3. What consequences do these two writers see for society in the wake of technological change? What assumptions do they make about the relationship between economic development and the social order?

Transportation improved. The Austrian Empire added over 30,000 miles of roads between 1830 and 1847; Belgium almost doubled its road network in the same period; France built not only new roads but also 2,000 miles of canals. These improvements, combined with the construction of railroads in the 1830s and 1840s, opened up new markets and encouraged new methods of manufacturing. In many of the Continent's manufacturing regions, however, industrialists continued to tap large pools of skilled but inexpensive labor. Thus, older methods of putting out industry and handwork persisted alongside new-model factories longer than in Britain.

In what other ways was the continental model of industrialization different? Governments played a considerably more direct role in industrialization. France and Prussia granted subsidies to private companies that built railroads. After 1849, the Prussian state took on the task itself, as did Belgium and, later, Russia. In Prussia, the state also operated a large proportion of that country's mines. Governments on the Continent provided incentives for industrialization. Limited-liability laws, to take the most important example, allowed investors to own shares in a corporation or company without becoming liable for the company's debts—and they enabled enterprises to recruit investors to put together the capital for railroads, other forms of industry, and commerce.

Mobilizing capital for industry was one of the challenges of the century. In Great Britain, overseas trade had created well-organized financial markets; on the Continent, capital was dispersed and in short supply. New joint-stock investment banks, unlike private banks, could sell bonds to and take deposits from individuals and smaller companies. They could offer start-up capital in the form of long-term, low-interest commercial loans to aspiring entrepreneurs. The French Crédit Mobilier, for instance, founded in 1852 by the wealthy and well-connected Périere brothers, assembled enough capital to finance insurance companies; the Parisian bus system; six municipal gas companies; transatlantic shipping; enterprises in other European countries; and, with the patronage of the state, the massive railroad-building spree of the 1850s. The Crédit Mobilier collapsed in scandal, but the revolution in banking was well under way.

Finally, continental Europeans actively promoted invention and technological development. They were willing for the state to establish educational systems whose aim, among others, was to produce a well-trained elite capable of assisting in the development of industrial technology. In sum, what Britain had produced almost by chance, the Europeans began to reproduce by design.

Industrialization after 1850

Until 1850, Britain remained the preeminent industrial power. Between 1850 and 1870, however, France, Germany, Belgium, and the United States emerged as challengers to the power and place of British manufacturers. The British iron industry remained the largest in the world (in 1870 Britain still produced half the world's pig iron), but it grew more slowly than did its counterparts in France or Germany. Most of continental Europe's gains came as a result of continuing changes in those areas we recognize as important for sustained industrial growth: transport, commerce, and government policy. The spread of railways encouraged the free movement of goods. International monetary unions were established and restrictions removed on international waterways such as the Danube. Free trade went hand in hand with removing guild barriers to entering trades and ending restrictions on practicing business. Guild control over artisanal production was abolished in Austria in 1859 and in most of Germany by the mid-1860s. Laws against usury, most of which had ceased to be enforced, were officially abandoned in Britain, Holland, Belgium, and in many parts of Germany. Governmental regulation of mining was surrendered by the Prussian state in the 1850s, freeing entrepreneurs to develop resources as they saw fit. Investment banks continued to form, encouraged by an increase in the money supply and an easing of credit after the California gold fields opened in 1849.

The first phase of the Industrial Revolution, one economic historian reminds us, was confined to a narrow set of industries and can be summed up rather simply: "cheaper and better clothes (mainly made of cotton), cheaper and better metals (pig iron, wrought iron, and steel) and faster travel (mainly by rail)." The second half of the century brought changes farther afield and in areas where Great Britain's early advantages were no longer decisive. Transatlantic cable

INTERIOR OF A CANUT HOUSEHOLD IN LYON C. 1830. The growth of the silk industry in Lyon in eighteenth-century France attracted many weavers and their families to the city's central neighborhoods: by the mid-1800s, there were 80,000 master artisans with their own shops in the trade and a further 40,000 *compagnons*, trained weavers who had not yet set up their own establishment and who worked as employees in the shops of others. The Canuts, as these weavers were called, worked as many as eighteen hours a day, and they were known for their militancy and their activism. They rose up in revolt in 1831, 1834, and 1848, and they were among the first examples of workers' insurrections in the nineteenth century. In the above image of a Canut household, the labor of nearly all the members of the family—weaving, spinning, and preparing the thread—can be identified.

(starting in 1865) and the telephone (invented in 1876) laid the ground for a revolution in communications. New chemical processes, dyestuffs, and pharmaceuticals emerged. So did new sources of energy: electricity, in which the United States and Germany led both invention and commercial development; and oil, which was being refined in the 1850s and widely used by 1900. Among the early exploiters of Russian oil discoveries were the Swedish Nobel brothers and the French Rothschilds. The developments that eventually converged to make the automobile came primarily from Germany and France. The internal combustion engine, important because it was small, efficient, and could be used in a very wide variety of situations, was developed by Carl Benz and Gottlieb Daimler in the 1880s. The removable pneumatic tire was patented in 1891 by Edouard Michelin, a painter who had joined with his engineer brother in running the family's small agricultural-equipment business. These developments are discussed fully in Chapter 23, but their pioneers' familiar names illustrate how industry and invention had diversified over the course of the century.

In eastern Europe, the nineteenth century brought different patterns of economic development. Spurred by the ever-growing demand for food and grain, large sections of eastern Europe developed into concentrated, commercialized agriculture regions that played the specific role of exporting food to the West. Many of those large agricultural enterprises were based on serfdom and remained so, in the face of increasing pressure for reform, until 1850. Peasant protest and liberal demands for reform only gradually chipped away at the nobility's determination to hold on to its privilege and system of labor. Serfdom was abolished in most parts of eastern and southern Europe by 1850 and in Poland and Russia in the 1860s.

Although industry continued to take a backseat to agriculture, eastern Europe had several important manufacturing regions. In the Czech region of Bohemia, textile industries, developed in the eighteenth century, continued to thrive. By the 1830s, there were machine-powered Czech cotton mills and iron works. In Russia, a factory industry producing coarse textiles—mostly linens—had grown up around Moscow. At mid-century, Russia was purchasing 24 percent of the total British machinery exports to mechanize its own mills. Many who labored in Russian industry actually remained serfs until the 1860s—about 40 percent of them employed in mines. Of the over 800,000 Russians engaged in manufacturing by 1860, however, most were employed in small workshops of about 40 persons.

By 1870, then, the core industrial nations of Europe included Great Britain, France, Germany, Italy, the Netherlands, and Switzerland. Austria stood at the margins. Russia, Spain, Bulgaria, Greece, Hungary, Romania, and Serbia formed the industrial periphery—and some regions of these nations seemed virtually untouched by the advance of industry. What was more, even in Great Britain, the most fully industrialized nation, agricultural laborers still constituted the single largest occupational category in 1860 (although they formed only 9 percent of the overall population). In Belgium, the Netherlands, Switzerland, Germany, France, Scandinavia, and Ireland, 25 to 50 percent of the population still worked on the land. In Russia, the number was 80 percent. *Industrial,* moreover, did not mean automation or machine production, which long remained confined to a few sectors of the economy. As machines were introduced in some sectors to do specific tasks, they usually intensified the tempo of handwork in other sectors. Thus even in the industrialized regions, much work was still accomplished in tiny workshops—or at home.

Industry and Empire

From an international perspective, nineteenth-century Europe was the most industrial region of the world. Europeans, particularly the British, jealously guarded their international advantages. They preferred to do so through financial leverage. Britain, France, and other European nations gained control of the national debts of China, the Ottoman Empire, Egypt, Brazil, Argentina, and other non-European powers. They also supplied large loans to other states, which bound those nations to their European investors. If the debtor nations expressed discontent, as Egypt did in the 1830s when it attempted to establish its own cotton textile industry, they confronted financial pressure and shows of force. Coercion, however, was not always necessary or even one-sided. Social change in other empires—China, Persia, and the Mughal Empire of India, for example—made those empires newly vulnerable and created new opportunities for the European powers and their local partners. Ambitious local elites often reached agreements with Western governments or groups such as the British East India Company. These trade agreements transformed regional economies on terms that sent the greatest profits to Europe after a substantial gratuity to the Europeans' local partners. Where agreements could not be made, force prevailed, and Europe took territory and trade by conquest (see Chapter 22).

Industrialization tightened global links between Europe and the rest of the world, creating new networks of trade and interdependence. To a certain extent, the world economy divided between the producers of manufactured goods—Europe itself—and suppliers of the necessary

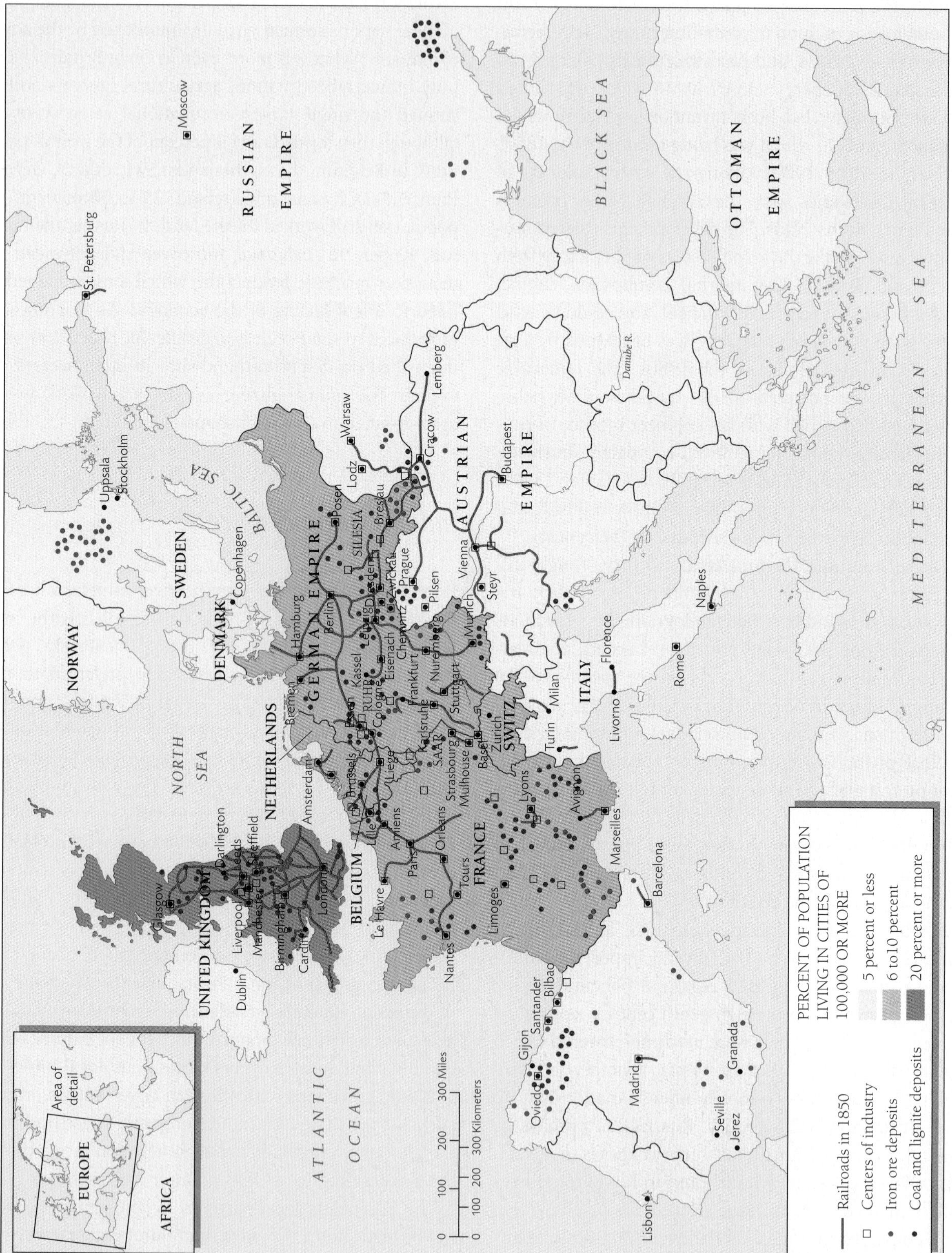

THE INDUSTRIAL REVOLUTION. Rapid industrial growth depended on a circular network of relationships. ▪ ***According to the map key, what elements made up the circular networks of relationships?*** ▪ ***How were these elements connected, and how might they have reinforced one another, contributing to rapid growth?*** ▪ ***Why do you think the percentage of populations living in cities was so much greater in the United Kingdom?***

raw materials and buyers of finished goods—everyone else. Cotton growers in the southern United States, sugar growers in the Caribbean, and wheat growers in Ukraine accepted their arrangements with the industrialized West and typically profited by them. If there were disputes, however, those suppliers often found that Europe could look elsewhere for the same goods or dictate the terms of trade down the business end of a bank ledger or a cannon barrel.

In 1811, Britain imported 3 percent of the wheat it consumed. By 1891, that portion had risen to 79 percent. Why? In an increasingly urban society, fewer people lived off the land. The commercialization of agriculture, which began early in Britain, had taken even firmer hold elsewhere, turning new regions—Australia, Argentina, and North America (Canada and the United States)—into centers of grain and wheat production. New forms of transportation, finance, and communication made it easier to shuttle commodities and capital through international networks. Those simple percentages, in other words, dramatize the new interdependence of the nineteenth century; they illustrate as well as any statistics can how ordinary Britons' lives—like their counterparts' in other nations—were embedded in an increasingly global economy.

BRITISH CLIPPER SHIPS IN CALCUTTA HARBOR, 1860. Calcutta, a long-established city on the eastern coast of India, was one of the hubs of the British Empire—a center for trade in cotton, jute, opium, and tea. The dazzling new clipper ships, first built in the 1830s and 1840s, were very fast and central to the global economy of the nineteenth century. ▪ ***What was the significance of this trade for the Indian economy?*** ▪ ***Could Indian merchants compete on equal terms with U.S. cotton producers in 1860?***

THE SOCIAL CONSEQUENCES OF INDUSTRIALIZATION

We have mentioned population growth as one factor in industrial development, but it deserves treatment on its own terms. By any measure, the nineteenth century constituted a turning point in European demographic history. In 1800, the population of Europe as a whole was estimated roughly at 205 million. By 1850, it had risen to 274 million; by 1900, 414 million; on the eve of the First World War, it was 480 million. (Over the same span of time, the world population went from about 900 million to 1.6 billion.) Britain, with its comparatively high standard of living, saw its population rise from 16 to 27 million. Increases, however, came in the largely rural regions as well. In Russia, the population rose from 39 million to 60 million during the same period.

Population

This population explosion did not occur because people were living longer—declines in mortality were not observable on a large scale until late in the nineteenth century, when improvements in hygiene and medicine had significant impact on the number of people who survived childhood to reach adulthood. Even in 1880, the average male life expectancy at birth in Berlin was no more than thirty years (in rural districts nearby, it was forty-three). Population growth in the nineteenth century resulted from increasing fertility—there were simply more babies being born. Men and women married earlier, which raised the average number of children born to each woman and increased the size of families. Peasants tended to set up households at a younger age. The spread of rural manufacturing allowed couples in the countryside to marry and set up households—even before they inherited any land. Not only did the age of marriage fall, but more people married. And because population growth increased the proportion of young and fertile people, the process reinforced itself in the next generation, setting the stage for a period of prolonged growth.

Interpreting Visual Evidence

Learning to Live in a Global Economy

The commercial networks of the Atlantic world were already well established before the Industrial Revolution, and Europeans were also trading widely with South and East Asia before the end of the eighteenth century. Nevertheless, the advent of an industrial economy in Europe at the beginning of the nineteenth century created such a demand for raw materials and such a need for new markets abroad that it became profitable for manufacturers and merchants to ship much larger amounts of goods over long distances than ever before. As different industrialized regions in Europe became more and more dependent on overseas markets, people in Europe came to be aware of the extent to which their own activities were linked to other parts of the world. Awareness of these linkages did not always mean that they possessed complete or accurate information about the people who produced the cotton that they wore, or who purchased the manufactured goods that they made, but the linkages stimulated their imagination and changed their consciousness of their place in the world.

This awareness is well illustrated in the cartoons shown here, which come from the British illustrated news in the 1850s and 1860s. The first (image A) depicts John Bull (representing British textile manufacturers) looking on as U.S. cotton suppliers fight one another during the Civil War in the United States. He states, "Oh! If you two like fighting better than business, I shall deal at the other shop." In the background, an Indian cotton merchant is happy to have him as a customer.

The second cartoon (image B) depicts the ways that the increasingly interconnected global economy might

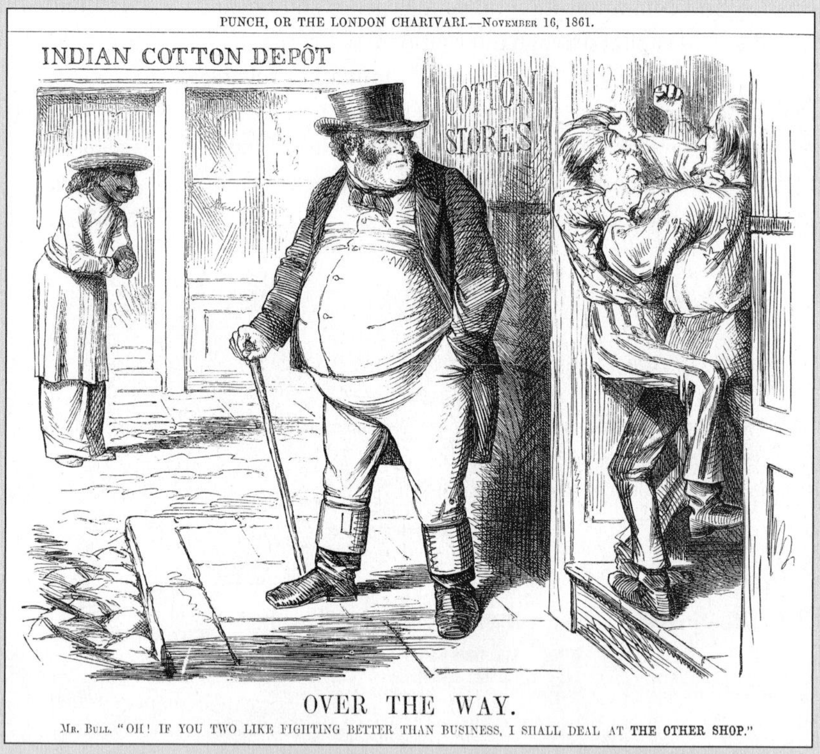

A. John Bull and cotton merchants.

Life on the Land: The Peasantry

Even as the West grew more industrial, the majority of people continued to live on the land. Conditions in the countryside were harsh. Peasants—as farmers of humble origin were called in Europe—still did most of their sowing and harvesting by hand. Millions of tiny farms produced, at most, a bare subsistence living, and families wove, spun, made knives, and sold butter to make ends meet. The average daily diet for an entire family in a good year might amount to no more than two or three pounds of bread—a total of about 3,000 calories daily. By many measures,

stimulate a new kind of political awareness. Emperor Napoleon III has placed a French worker in irons for participating in a revolutionary movement. The worker compares his situation to that of an African slave seated next to him, saying, "Courage, my friend! Am I not a man and a brother?" On the wall behind the two men a poster refers to the Portuguese slave trade—Napoleon III himself came to power by overthrowing the Second Republic in France, a government that had abolished the slave trade in French territories.

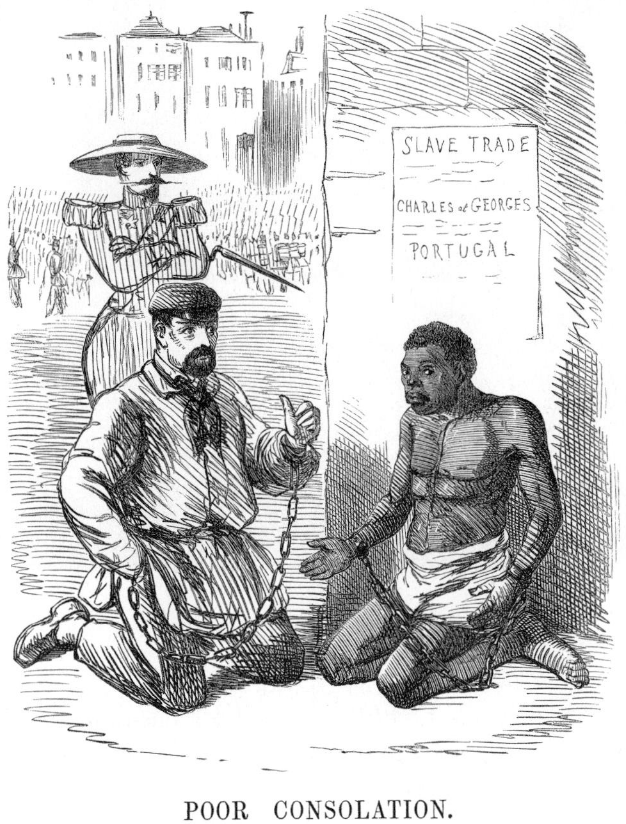

POOR CONSOLATION.

PARISIAN. "COURAGE, MON AMI; 'AM I NOT A MAN AND A BROTHER?'"

B. Increasing global awareness in France.

Questions for Analysis

1. What constellation of private and national interests were at play in the relationships portrayed in image A? What significance might contemporaries have attached to the possibility that the British may have chosen to buy their cotton from an Asian source "over the way" rather than from North America?

2. In image B, what is the message of the cartoon's suggestion that the slave and the worker might discover their equality only in the fact that they are both in chains? What was at stake in comparing a worker to a slave in mid-nineteenth-century Europe? Why does the caption read "Poor Consolation?"

3. How does the racial imagery of these images relate to their intended message?

living conditions for rural inhabitants of many areas in Europe grew worse in the first half of the nineteenth century, a fact of considerable political importance in the 1840s. Rising population put more pressure on the land. Small holdings and indebtedness were chronic problems in regions where peasants scraped by on their own lands. Over the course of the century, some 37 million people—most of them peasants—left Europe, eloquent testimony to the bleakness of rural life. They settled in the United States, South America, northern Africa, New Zealand, Australia, and Siberia. In many cases, governments encouraged emigration to ease overcrowding.

Past and Present

Are there Limits to Economic Growth?

Even in its infancy, industrial society had its critics—those who regretted the changes that the new forms of manufacture brought to work, to the social order, and to the environment (left). The current concern about climate change caused by the burning of fossil fuels (right) is thus the latest chapter in a long history of debate and controversy over the consequences of industrialization.

Watch related author interview on StudySpace
wwnorton.com/web/westernciv18

The most tragic combination of famine, poverty, and population in the nineteenth century came to Ireland in the Great Famine of 1845–1849. Potatoes, which had come to Europe from the New World, fundamentally transformed the diets of European peasants, providing much more nutrition for less money than corn and grain. They also grew more densely, an enormous advantage for peasants scraping a living from small plots of land. Nowhere did they become more important than in Ireland, where the climate and soil made growing grain difficult and both overpopulation and poverty were rising. When a fungus hit the potato crop—first in 1845 and again, fatally, in 1846 and 1847—no alternative foods were at hand. At least 1 million Irish died of starvation; of dysentery from spoiled foods; or of fever, which spread through villages and the overcrowded poorhouses. Before the famine, tens of thousands of Irish were already crossing the Atlantic to North America; they accounted for one-third of all voluntary migration to the New World. In the ten years after 1845, 1.5 million people left Ireland for good. The potato blight also struck in Germany, Scotland, and the Netherlands but with less catastrophic results. Europe had known deadly famines for centuries. The tragic Irish famine came late, however, at a time when many thought that starvation was receding into the past, and it illustrated just how vulnerable the nineteenth-century countryside remained to bad harvests and shortages.

Changes in the land depended partly on particular governments. States sympathetic to commercial agriculture made it easier to transfer land, eliminate small farms, and create larger estates. In Britain, over half the total area of the country, excluding wasteland, was composed of estates of a thousand acres or more. In Spain, the fortunes of large-scale commercial agriculture fluctuated with changes in

Analyzing Primary Sources

Thomas Malthus on Population and Poverty

Thomas Malthus's enormously influential Essay on the Principle of Population *(1798) marked a shift away from Enlightenment optimism about the "perfectibility of society" and a break with a long tradition of considering a large population to be a sign of economic strength. The English cleric (1766–1834) argued that hopes for prosperity ran up against a simple and grim law of nature: population grew more rapidly than food supply. Famine, disease, poverty, infant malnutrition—Malthus considered all of these inevitable, indeed "positive," checks on population. Governments could do nothing to alleviate poverty, he argued; instead, the poor had to exercise "moral restraint," postpone marriage, and have fewer children.*

I say that the power of population is indefinitely greater than the power in the earth to produce subsistence for man.

Population, when unchecked, increases in a geometrical ratio. Subsistence increases only in an arithmetical ratio. A slight acquaintance with numbers will shew the immensity of the first power in comparison of the second.

By that law of our nature which makes food necessary to the life of man, the effects of these two unequal powers must be kept equal.

This implies a strong and constantly operating check on population from the difficulty of subsistence. This difficulty must fall somewhere and must necessarily be severely felt by a large portion of mankind.

Through the animal and vegetable kingdoms, nature has scattered the seeds of life abroad with the most profuse and liberal hand. She has been comparatively sparing in the room and the nourishment necessary to rear them. The germs of existence contained in this spot of earth, with ample food, and ample room to expand in, would fill millions of worlds in the course of a few thousand years. Necessity, that imperious all pervading law of nature, restrains them within the prescribed bounds. The race of plants and the race of animals shrink under this great restrictive law. And the race of man cannot, by any efforts of reason, escape from it. Among plants and animals its effects are waste of seed, sickness, and premature death. Among mankind, misery and vice. The former, misery, is an absolutely necessary consequence of it. Vice is a highly probable consequence, and we therefore see it abundantly prevail, but it ought not, perhaps, to be called an absolutely necessary consequence. The ordeal of virtue is to resist all temptation to evil.

This natural inequality of the two powers of population and of production in the earth, and that great law of our nature which must constantly keep their effects equal, form the great difficulty that to me appears insurmountable in the way to the perfectibility of society. All other arguments are of slight and subordinate consideration in comparison of this. I see no way by which man can escape from the weight of this law which pervades all animated nature. No fancied equality, no agrarian regulations in their utmost extent, could remove the pressure of it even for a single century. And it appears, therefore, to be decisive against the possible existence of a society, all the members of which should live in ease, happiness, and comparative leisure; and feel no anxiety about providing the means of subsistence for themselves and families.

Consequently, if the premises are just, the argument is conclusive against the perfectibility of the mass of mankind.

Source: Thomas Malthus, *An Essay on the Principle of Population*, ed. Philip Appleman, *Norton Critical Edition*, 2nd ed. (New York: 2004), pp. 19–20.

Questions for Analysis

1. What assumptions about human behavior are contained in Malthus's argument that population will always increase more quickly than the available food supply? What are the possible checks on population growth that he considers? Why does he say that "misery" is "a necessary consequence" and "vice" only "highly probable"? Why does he conclude from this that society will never be "perfectible"?

2. The history of the Industrial Revolution and population growth in Europe in the nineteenth century seemed to prove that Malthus's belief in the ecological constraints on population growth were ill founded. What events that he could not have predicted changed the equilibrium between subsistence and population during this period?

3. Compare Malthus's views expressed here with the documents on pages 638–39 concerning the 1846 potato famine. Can one see the influence of his ideas in those documents?

IRISH POTATO FAMINE, 1845–1849. The Irish potato famine was widely held by many in Ireland to have human as well as natural causes. Historians have noted that food exports from Ireland continued and may have even increased for some products during the famine, as merchants sought higher prices abroad. The cartoon at left depicts armed soldiers keeping starving Irish Catholic families at bay as sacks of potatoes are loaded onto a ship owned by a prosperous Irish Protestant trader. At right, an 1848 engraving from the *Illustrated London News* depicts an impoverished tenant family being evicted from their cottage by their landlord for nonpayment of rent. Thousands of such evictions took place, adding to the misery of the tenant farmers, who were thus unable to plant new crops after losing the potato harvest to blight.

the political regime: in 1820, the liberal regime passed legislation encouraging the free transfer of land; when absolutism was restored in 1823, the law was repealed. In Russia some of the largest landowners possessed over half a million acres. Until the emancipation of the serfs in the 1860s, landowners claimed the labor of dependent peasant populations for as much as several days per week. But the system of serfdom gave neither landowners nor serfs much incentive to improve farming techniques.

European serfdom, which bound hundreds of thousands of men, women, and children to particular estates for generations, made it difficult to buy and sell land freely and created an obstacle to the commercialization of agriculture. Yet the opposite was also the case. In France, peasant landholders who had benefited from the French Revolution's sale of lands and laws on inheritance stayed in the countryside, continuing to work their small farms. Although French peasants were poor, they could sustain themselves on the land. This had important consequences. France suffered less agricultural distress, even in the 1840s, than did other European countries; migration from country to city was slower than in the other nations; far fewer peasants left France for other countries.

Industrialization came to the countryside in other forms. Improved communication networks not only afforded rural populations a keener sense of events and opportunities elsewhere but also made it possible for governments to intrude into the lives of these men and women to a degree previously impossible. Central bureaucracies now found it easier to collect taxes from the peasantry and to conscript sons of peasant families into armies. Some rural cottage industries faced direct competition from factory-produced goods, which meant less work or lower piece rates and falling incomes for families, especially during winter months. In other sectors of the economy, industry spread out into the countryside, making whole regions producers of shoes, shirts, ribbons, cutlery, and so on in small shops and workers' homes. Changes in the market could usher in prosperity, or they could bring entire regions to the verge of starvation.

Vulnerability often led to political violence. Rural rebellions were common in the early nineteenth century. In southern England in the late 1820s, small farmers and day laborers joined forces to burn barns and haystacks, protesting the introduction of threshing machines, a symbol of the new agricultural capitalism. They masked and otherwise disguised themselves, riding out at night under the banner of their mythical leader, "Captain Swing." Their raids were preceded by anonymous threats, such as the one received by a large-scale farmer in the county of Kent: "Pull down your threshing machine or else [expect] fire without delay. We are five thousand men [a highly inflated figure] and will not be stopped." In the southwest of France, peasants, at night and in disguise, attacked local authorities who had barred them from collecting wood in the forests. Since forest wood was in demand for new furnaces, the peasants' traditional gleaning rights had come to an end. Similar rural disturbances broke out across Europe in the 1830s and 1840s: insurrections against landlords; against tithes, or taxes to the church; against laws curtailing customary rights; against unresponsive governments. In Russia, serf uprisings were a reaction to continued bad harvests and exploitation.

Many onlookers considered the nineteenth-century cities dangerous seedbeds of sedition. Yet conditions in the countryside and frequent flare-ups of rural protest remained the greatest source of trouble for governments, and rural politics exploded, as we will see, in the 1840s. Peasants were land poor, deep in debt, and precariously dependent on markets. More important, however, a government's inability to contend with rural misery made it look autocratic, indifferent, or inept—all political failings.

The Urban Landscape

The growth of cities was one of the most important facts of nineteenth-century social history, and one with significant cultural reverberations. Over the course of the nineteenth century, as we have seen, the overall population of Europe doubled. The percentage of that population living in cities tripled—that is, urban populations rose sixfold. In mining and manufacturing areas or along newly built railway lines, it sometimes seemed that cities (like Manchester, Birmingham, and Essen) sprang up from nowhere. Sometimes the rates of growth were dizzying. Between 1750 and 1850, London (Europe's largest city) grew from 676,000 to 2.3 million. The population of Paris went from 560,000 to 1.3 million, adding 120,000 new residents between 1841 and 1846 alone! Berlin, which like Paris became the hub of a rapidly expanding railway system, nearly tripled in size during the first half of the century. Such rapid expansion was almost necessarily unplanned and brought in its wake new social problems.

Almost all nineteenth-century cities were overcrowded and unhealthy, their largely medieval infrastructures strained by the burden of new population and the demands of industry. Construction lagged far behind population growth, and working men and women who had left families behind in the country often lived in temporary lodging houses. The poorest workers dwelled in wretched basement or attic rooms, often without any light or drainage. A local committee appointed to investigate conditions in the British manufacturing town of Huddersfield—by no means the worst of that country's urban centers—reported that there were large areas without paving, sewers, or drains, "where garbage and filth of every description are left on the surface to ferment

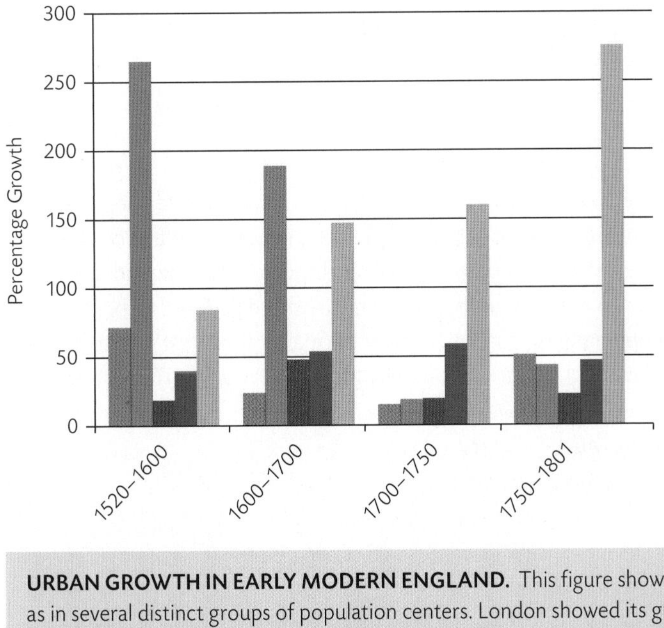

*Norwich, York, Salisbury, Chester, Worcester, Exeter, Cambridge, Coventry, Shrewsbury, Gloucester
**Bristol, Hull, Colchester, Newcastle, Ipswich, Great Yarmouth, King's Lynn, Southampton
***Birmingham, Manchester, Leeds, Sheffield
Source: E. A. Wrigley, *People, Cities, and Wealth* (New York: 1987), p. 166.

URBAN GROWTH IN EARLY MODERN ENGLAND. This figure shows the percentage increases in population in England as a whole, as well as in several distinct groups of population centers. London showed its greatest percentage increases in the periods 1520–1600 and 1600–1700, *before* the period of industrial expansion. The historic regional centers—cathedral and market towns—showed steady but unspectacular growth across these years, as did English port cities. The most remarkable growth, however, was observed in the new industrial areas of the north in the last half of the eighteenth century. ***What can one conclude about the nature of population growth in England from this figure? What other sorts of information would allow you to draw more certain conclusions about the nature of these demographic shifts?***

Competing Viewpoints

The Irish Famine: Interpretations and Responses

When the potato blight appeared for the second year in a row in 1846, famine came to Ireland. The first letter excerpted here is from Father Theobald Mathew, a local priest, to Charles Edward Trevelyan, the English official in charge of Irish relief. While Father Mathew attributes the potato blight to "divine providence," he also worries that businessmen opposed to government intervention in a free market will let the Irish starve.

The second and third excerpts are from letters that Trevelyan wrote to other British officials concerned with the crisis. Trevelyan makes clear that although he does not want the government to bear responsibility for starving its people, he believes that the famine will work to correct "social evils" in Ireland, by which he means everything from families having too many children to farmers failing to plant the right crops. In the nineteenth century, reactions to food crises were reshaped by the rise of new economic doctrines, changing social assumptions, and the shifting relationship between religion and government. These letters provide good examples of those changes and how they affected government officials.

The Reverend Theobald Mathew to Trevelyan

Cork, 7 August 1846.

Divine providence, in its inscrutable ways, has again poured out upon us the viol [*sic*] of its wrath. A blot more destructive than the simoom of the desert has passed over the land, and the hopes of the poor potato-cultivators are totally blighted, and the food of a whole nation has perished. On the 27th of last month I passed from Cork to Dublin, and this doomed plant bloomed in all the luxuriance of an abundant harvest. Returning on the 3rd instant, I beheld, with sorrow, one wide waste of putrefying vegetation. In many places the wretched people were seated on the fences of their decaying gardens, wringing their hands and wailing bitterly the destruction that had left them foodless.

It is not to harrow your benevolent feelings, dear Mr. Trevelyan, I tell this tale of woe. No, but to excite your sympathy in behalf of our miserable peasantry. It is rumoured that the capitalists in the corn and flour trade are endeavoring to induce government not to protect the people from famine, but to leave them at their mercy. I consider this a cruel and unjustifiable interference.

Trevelyan to Routh

Treasury, 3 February 1846.

That indirect permanent advantages will accrue to Ireland from the scarcity and the measures taken for its relief, I entertain no doubt; but if we were to pursue these incidental objects to the neglect of any of the precautions immediately required to save the people from actual starvation, our responsibility would be fearful indeed. Besides, the greatest improvement of all which could take place in Ireland would be to teach the people to depend upon themselves for developing the resources of their country, instead of having recourse to the assistance of the government on every occasion. Much has been done of late years to put this important matter on its proper footing; but if a firm stand is not made against the prevailing disposition to take advantage of this crisis to break down all barriers, the true permanent interest of the country will, I am convinced, suffer in a manner which will be irreparable in our time.

Trevelyan to Lord Monteagle

To the Right Hon. Lord Monteagle.

My Dear Lord,

I need not remind your lordship that the ability even of the most powerful government is extremely limited in dealing with a social evil of this description. It forms no part of the functions of government to provide supplies of food or to increase the productive powers of the land. In the great institution of the business of society, it falls to the share of government to protect the merchant and the agriculturist in the free exercise of their respective employments; but

not itself to carry on those employments; and the condition of a community depends upon the result of the efforts which each member of it makes in his private and individual capacity. . . .

I must give expression to my feelings by saying that I think I see a bright light shining in the distance through the dark cloud which at present hangs over Ireland. A remedy has been already applied to that portion of the maladies of Ireland which was traceable to political causes, and the morbid habits which still to a certain extent survive are gradually giving way to a more healthy action. The deep and inveterate root of social evil remains, and I hope I am not guilty of irreverence in thinking that, this being altogether beyond the power of man, the cure has been applied by the direct stroke of an all-wise providence in a manner as unexpected and unthought of as it is likely to be effectual. God grant that we may rightly perform our part and not turn into a curse what was intended for a blessing. The ministers of religion and especially the pastors of the Roman Catholic Church, who possess the largest share of influence over the people of Ireland, have well performed their part; and although few indications appear from any proceedings which have yet come before the public that the landed proprietors have even taken the first step of preparing for the conversion of the land now laid down to potatoes to grain cultivation, I do not despair of seeing this class in society still taking the lead which their position requires of them, and preventing the social revolution from being so extensive as it otherwise must become.

Believe me, my dear lord,
yours very sincerely,
C. E. Trevelyan.
Treasury, 9 October 1846.

Source: Noel Kissane, *The Irish Famine: A Documentary History* (Dublin: 1995), pp. 17, 47, 50–51.

Questions for Analysis

1. Reverend Mathew's letter suggests that although the potato blight seems to be an act of God, the response to the crisis by those in government and in commerce plays a role in determining who has enough to eat. What relationship between hunger and the market does Mathew fear most?
2. What are the stakes in the crisis for Trevelyan, as the English official responsible for relief of the food shortage? What interests does he appear to serve and in what order of preference? What exactly is the responsibility of the government in the face of such an emergency, according to his view?
3. Do Mathew and Trevelyan agree on the relationship that should exist between the government and the economy? What accounts for their difference of opinion? Are the religious values of the reverend and the economic calculations of the official compatible with one another?

and rot; where pools of stagnant water are almost constant; where dwellings adjoining are thus necessarily caused to be of an inferior and even filthy description; thus where disease is engendered, and the health of the whole town perilled."

Governments gradually adopted measures in an attempt to cure the worst of these ills, if only to prevent the spread of catastrophic epidemics. Legislation was designed to rid cities of their worst slums by tearing them down and to improve sanitary conditions by supplying both water and drainage. Yet by 1850, these projects had only just begun. Paris, perhaps better supplied with water than any other European city, had enough for no more than two baths per person per year; in London, human waste remained uncollected in 250,000 domestic cesspools; in Manchester, fewer than one-third of the dwellings were equipped with toilets of any sort.

Industry and Environment in the Nineteenth Century

The Industrial Revolution began many of the environmental changes of the modern period. Nowhere were those changes more visible than in the burgeoning cities. Dickens's description of the choking air and polluted water of "Coketown," the fictional city in *Hard Times* (1854) is deservedly well known:

> It was a town of red brick, or of brick that would have been red if the smoke and ashes had allowed it. . . . It was a town of machines and tall chimneys, out of which interminable serpents of smoke

> trailed themselves forever and ever, and never got uncoiled. It had a black canal in it, and a river that ran purple with ill-smelling dye, and vast piles of building full of windows where there was a rattling and a trembling all day long.

***VIEW OF LONDON WITH SAINT PAUL'S CATHEDRAL IN THE DISTANCE* BY WILLIAM HENRY CROME.** Despite the smog-filled skies and intense pollution, many entrepreneurs and politicians celebrated the new prosperity of the Industrial Revolution. As W. P. Rend, a Chicago businessman, wrote in 1892, "Smoke is the incense burning on the altars of industry. It is beautiful to me. It shows that men are changing the merely potential forces of nature into articles of comfort for humanity."

Wood-fired manufacturing and heating for homes had long spewed smoke across the skies, but the new concentration of industrial activity and the transition to coal made the air measurably worse. In London especially, where even homes switched to coal early, smoke from factories, railroads, and domestic chimneys hung heavily over the city; and the last third of the century brought the most intense pollution in its history. Over all of England, air pollution took an enormous toll on health, contributing to the bronchitis and tuberculosis that accounted for 25 percent of British deaths. The coal-rich and industrial regions of North America (especially Pittsburgh) and central Europe were other concentrations of pollution; the Ruhr, in particular, by the end of the century had the most polluted air in Europe.

Toxic water—produced by industrial pollution and human waste—posed the second critical environmental hazard in urban areas. London and Paris led the way in building municipal sewage systems, though those emptied into the Thames and the Seine. Cholera, typhus, and tuberculosis were natural predators in areas without adequate sewage facilities or fresh water. The Rhine River, which flowed through central Europe's industrial heartland and intersected with the Ruhr, was thick with detritus from coal mining, iron processing, and the chemical industry. Spurred by several epidemics of cholera, in the late nineteenth century the major cities began to purify their water supplies; but conditions in the air, rivers, and land continued to worsen until at least the mid-twentieth century.

The Social Question

Against the backdrop of the French Revolution of 1789 and subsequent revolutions in the nineteenth century (as we will see in the following chapters), the new "shock" cities of the nineteenth century and their swelling multitudes posed urgent questions. Political leaders, social scientists, and public health officials across all of Europe issued thousands of reports—many of them several volumes long—on criminality, water supply, sewers, prostitution, tuberculosis and cholera, alcoholism, wet nursing, wages, and unemployment. Radicals and reformers grouped all these issues under a broad heading known as "the social question." Governments, pressed by reformers and by the omnipresent rumblings of unrest, felt they had to address these issues before complaints swelled into revolution. They did so, in the first social engineering: police forces, public health, sewers and new water supplies, inoculations, elementary schools, Factory Acts (regulating work hours), poor laws (outlining the conditions of receiving relief), and new urban regulation and city planning. Central Paris, for instance, would be almost entirely redesigned in the nineteenth century—the crowded, medieval, and revolutionary poor neighborhoods gutted; markets rebuilt; streets widened and lit (see Chapter 21). From the 1820s on, the social question hung over Europe like a cloud, and it formed part of the backdrop to the revolutions of 1848 (discussed in Chapter 21). Surveys and studies, early social science, provided direct inspiration for novelists such as Honoré de Balzac, Charles Dickens, and Victor Hugo. In his novel *Les Misérables* (1862), Hugo even used the sewers of Paris as a central metaphor for the general condition of urban existence. Both Hugo and Dickens wrote sympathetically of the poor, of juvenile delinquency, and of child labor; revolution was never far from their minds. The French writer

Balzac had little sympathy for the poor, but he shared his fellow writers' views on the corruption of modern life. His *Human Comedy* (1829–55) was a series of ninety-five novels and stories, including *Eugenie Grandet, Old Goriot, Lost Illusions,* and *A Harlot High and Low.* Balzac was biting in his observations about ruthless and self-promoting young men and about the cold calculations behind romantic liaisons. And he was but one of many writers to use prostitution as a metaphor for what he considered the deplorable materialism and desperation of his time.

Sex in the City

Prostitution flourished in nineteenth-century cities; in fact, it offers a microcosm of the nineteenth-century urban economy. At mid-century, the number of prostitutes in Vienna was estimated to be 15,600; in Paris, where prostitution was a licensed trade, 50,000; in London, 80,000. London newspaper reports of the 1850s cataloged the elaborate hierarchies of the vast underworld of prostitutes and their customers. Those included entrepreneurs with names like Swindling Sal who ran lodging houses; the pimps and "fancy men" who managed the trade of prostitutes on the street; and the relatively few "prima donnas" or courtesans who enjoyed the protection of rich, upper-middle-class lovers, who entertained lavishly and whose wealth allowed them to move on the fringes of more respectable high society. The heroines of Alexandre Dumas's novel *La Dame aux Camélias* (*"The Lady of the Camellias"*) and of Giuseppe Verdi's opera *La Traviata* (*"The Fallen Woman"*) were modeled on these women. Yet the vast majority of prostitutes were not courtesans but rather women (and some men) who worked long and dangerous hours in port districts of cities or at lodging houses in the overwhelmingly male working-class neighborhoods. Most prostitutes were young women who had just arrived in the city or working women trying to manage during a period of unemployment. Single women in the cities were very vulnerable to sexual exploitation. Many were abandoned by their partners if they became pregnant; others faced the danger of rape by their employers. Such experiences—abandonment and rape—could lead to prostitution since women in these circumstances were unlikely to secure "respectable" employment.

PROSTITUTION IN NINETEENTH-CENTURY EUROPEAN CITIES. This sketch by Constantin Guys (1802–1892) captures the moment when two *grisettes* (slang for flirtatious working-class women) entertain a proposition from two soldiers in the street. Guys's portrayal of the men's indistinct facial features and the saucy posture of the women captured the impersonal nature of the exchange as well as the mercenary intentions of all parties. ▪ ***How did the construction of new cities, with expanded streets designed to facilitate the efficient mixing and movement of peoples, change the way that individuals interacted with one another in modern cities?***

THE MIDDLE CLASSES

Nineteenth-century novelists such as Charles Dickens and William Thackeray in Britain, Victor Hugo and Honoré Balzac in France, and Theodor Fontane in Germany painted a sweeping portrait of middle-class society in the nineteenth century. Their novels are peopled with characters from all walks of life—journalists, courtesans, small-town mayors, mill owners, shopkeepers, aristocrats, farmers, laborers, and students. The plots of these stories explore the ways that older hierarchies of rank, status, and privilege were gradually giving way to a new set of gradations based on wealth and social class. In this new world, money trumped birth, and social mobility was an accepted fact rather than something to be hidden. One of Thackeray's characters observes caustically that "[o]urs is a ready-money society. We live among bankers and city big-wigs . . . and every man, as he talks to you, is jingling his guineas in his pocket." Works of literature need to be approached cautiously, for their characters express their authors' points of view. Still, literature and art offer an extraordinary source of social historical detail and insight. And we can safely say that the rising visibility of the middle classes and their new political and social power—lamented by some writers but hailed by others—were central facts of nineteenth-century society.

Who were the middle classes? (Another common term for this social group, the *bourgeoisie,* originally meant "city [*bourg*] dweller.") Its ranks included shopkeepers and their households, the families of lawyers, doctors, and other professionals, as well as well-off factory owners who might aspire to marry their daughters to titled aristocrats. At the lower end of the social scale the middle classes included the families of salaried clerks and office workers for whom white-collar employment offered hope of a rise in status.

***THE LEGISLATIVE BELLY* BY HONORE DAUMIER, 1834.** Daumier's caricatures of bourgeois politicians mock the close link between politics and a prosperous elite made up of men of property.

Movement within middle-class ranks was often possible in the course of one or two generations. Very few, however, moved from the working class into the middle class. Most middle-class success stories began in the middle class itself, with the children of relatively well-off farmers, skilled artisans, or professionals. Upward mobility was almost impossible without education, and education was a rare, though not unattainable, luxury for working-class children. Careers open to talents, that goal achieved by the French Revolution, frequently meant opening jobs to middle-class young men who could pass exams. The examination system was an important path upward within government bureaucracies.

The journey from middle class to aristocratic, landed society was equally difficult. In Britain, mobility of this sort was easier to achieve than on the Continent. Sons from wealthy upper-middle-class families, if they were sent to elite schools and universities and if they left the commercial or industrial world for a career in politics, might actually move up. William Gladstone, son of a Liverpool merchant, attended the exclusive educational preserves of Eton (a private boarding school) and Oxford University, married into the aristocratic Grenville family, and became prime minister of England. Yet Gladstone was an exception to the rule, even in Britain, and most upward mobility was much less spectacular.

Nevertheless, the European middle class helped sustain itself with the belief that it was possible to get ahead by means of intelligence, pluck, and serious devotion to work. The Englishman Samuel Smiles, in his extraordinarily successful how-to-succeed book *Self-Help* (1859), preached a gospel dear to the middle class: "The spirit of self-help is the root of all genuine growth in the individual." As Smiles also suggested, those who succeeded were obliged to follow middle-class notions of respectability. The middle-class's claim to political power and cultural influence rested on arguments that they constituted a new and deserving social elite, superior to the common people yet sharply different from the older aristocracy, and the rightful custodians of the nation's future. Thus, middle-class respectability, like a code, stood for many values. It meant financial independence, providing responsibly for one's family, avoiding gambling and debt. It suggested merit and character as opposed to aristocratic privilege and hard work as opposed to living off noble estates. Respectable middle-class gentlemen might be wealthy, but they should live modestly and soberly, avoiding conspicuous consumption, lavish dress, womanizing, and other forms of dandyish behavior associated with the aristocracy. Of course, these were aspirations and codes, not social realities. They nonetheless remained key to the middle-class sense of self and understanding of the world.

Private Life and Middle-Class Identity

Family and home played a central role in forming middle-class identity. Few themes were more common in nineteenth-century fiction than men and women pursuing mobility and status by or through marriage. Families served intensely practical purposes: sons, nephews, and cousins were expected to assume responsibility in family firms when it came their turn; wives managed accounts; and parents-in-law provided business connections, credit, inheritance, and so on. The family's role in middle-class thought, however, did not arise only from these practical considerations; family was part of a larger worldview.

A well-governed household offered a counterpoint to the business and confusion of the world, and families offered continuity and tradition in a time of rapid change.

Gender and the Cult of Domesticity

There was no single type of middle-class family or home. Yet many people held powerful convictions about how a respectable home should be run. According to advice manuals, poetry, and middle-class journals, wives and mothers were supposed to occupy a "separate sphere" of life, in which they lived in subordination to their spouses. "Man for the field and woman for the hearth; man for the sword and for the needle she. . . . All else confusion," wrote the British poet Alfred, Lord Tennyson in 1847. These prescriptions were directly applied to young people. Boys were educated in secondary schools; girls at home. This nineteenth-century conception of separate spheres needs to be understood in relation to much longer-standing traditions of paternal authority, which were codified in law. Throughout Europe, laws subjected women to their husbands' authority. The Napoleonic Code, a model for other countries after 1815, classified women, children, and the mentally ill together as legally incompetent. In Britain, a woman transferred all her property rights to her husband on marriage. Although unmarried women did enjoy a degree of legal independence in France and Austria, laws generally assigned them to the "protection" of their fathers. Gender relations in the nineteenth century rested on this foundation of legal inequality. Yet the idea or doctrine of separate spheres was meant to underscore that men's and women's spheres complemented each other. Thus, for instance, middle-class writings were full of references to spiritual equality between men and women; and middle-class people wrote, proudly, of marriages in which the wife was a "companion" and "helpmate."

It is helpful to recall that members of the middle class articulated their values in opposition to aristocratic customs, on the one hand, and the lives of the common people, on the other. They argued, for instance, that middle-class marriages did not aim to found aristocratic dynasties and were not arranged to accumulate power and privilege; instead they were to be based on mutual respect and division of responsibilities. A respectable middle-class woman should be free from the unrelenting toil that was the lot of a woman of the people. Called in Victorian Britain the "angel in the house," the middle-class woman was responsible for the moral education of her children. It was understood that being a good wife and mother was a demanding task, requiring an elevated character. This belief, sometimes called the "cult of domesticity," was central to middle-class Victorian thinking about women. Home life and, by extension, the woman's role in that life were infused with new meaning. As one young woman put it after reading a popular book on female education, "What an important sphere a woman fills! How thoroughly she ought to be qualified for it—I think hers the more honourable employment than a man's." In sum, the early nineteenth century brought a general reassessment of femininity. The roots of this reassessment lay in early-nineteenth-century religion and efforts to moralize society, largely to guard against the disorders of the French and Industrial Revolutions.

As a housewife, a middle-class woman had the task of keeping the household functioning smoothly and harmoniously. She maintained the accounts and directed the activities of the servants. Having at least one servant was a mark of middle-class status; and in wealthier families governesses and nannies cared for children, idealized views of motherhood notwithstanding. The middle classes, however, included many gradations of wealth, from a well-housed banker with a governess and five servants to a village preacher with one. Moreover, the work of running and maintaining a home was enormous. Linens and clothes had to be made and mended. Only the wealthy had the luxury of running water, and others had to carry and heat water for cooking, laundry, and cleaning. Heating with coal and lighting with kerosene involved hours of cleaning. If the "angel in the house" was a cultural ideal, it was partly because she had real economic value.

ILLUSTRATION FROM A VICTORIAN BOOK ON MANNERS. Advice books such as this were very popular in the nineteenth century—a mark, perhaps, of preoccupation with status and the emergence of new social groups. ▪ ***Why would people be concerned about "respectability" in an age of greater social mobility?***

Analyzing Primary Sources

Marriage, Sexuality, and the Facts of Life

In the nineteenth century, sexuality became the subject of much anxious debate, largely because it raised other issues: the roles of men and women, morality, and social respectability. Doctors threw themselves into the discussion, offering their expert opinions on the health (including the sexual lives) of the population. Yet doctors did not dictate people's private lives. Nineteenth-century men and women responded to what they experienced as the facts of life more than to expert advice. The first document provides an example of medical knowledge and opinion in 1870. The second offers a glimpse of the daily realities of family life in 1830.

A French Doctor Denounces Contraception (1870)

One of the most powerful instincts nature has placed in the heart of man is that which has for its object the perpetuation of the human race. But this instinct, this inclination, so active, which attracts one sex towards the other, is liable to be perverted, to deviate from the path nature has laid out. From this arises a number of fatal aberrations which exercise a deplorable influence upon the individual, upon the family and upon society. . . .

We hear constantly that marriages are less fruitful, that the increase of population does not follow its former ratio. I believe that this is mainly attributable to genesiac frauds. It might naturally be supposed that these odious calculations of egotism, these shameful refinements of debauchery, are met with almost entirely in large cities, and among the luxurious classes, and that small towns and country places yet preserve that simplicity of manners attributed to primitive society, when the *pater familias* was proud of exhibiting his numerous offspring. Such, however, is not the case, and I shall show that those who have an unlimited confidence in the patriarchal habits of our country people are deeply in error. At the present time frauds are practiced by all classes. . . .

The laboring classes are generally satisfied with the practice of Onan [withdrawal]. . . . They are seldom familiar with the sheath invented by Dr. Condom, and bearing his name.

Among the wealthy, on the other hand, the use of this preservative is generally known. It favors frauds by rendering them easier; but it does not afford complete security. . . .

Case X.–This couple belongs to two respectable families of vintners. They are both pale, emaciated, downcast, sickly. . . .

They have been married for ten years; they first had two children, one immediately after the other, but in order to avoid an increase of family, they have had recourse to conjugal frauds. Being both very amorous, they have found this practice very convenient to satisfy their inclinations. They have employed it to such an extent, that up to a few months ago, when their health began to fail, the husband had intercourse with his wife habitually two and three times in twenty-four hours.

The following is the condition of the woman: She complains of continual pains in the lower part of the abdomen and kidneys. These pains disturb the functions of the stomach and render her nervous. . . . By the touch we find a very intense heat, great sensibility to pressure, and all the signs of a chronic metritis. The patient attributes positively her present state to the too frequent approaches of her husband.

Outside the home, women had very few respectable options for earning a living. Unmarried women might act as companions or governesses—the British novelist Charlotte Brontë's heroine Jane Eyre did so and led a generally miserable life until "rescued" by marriage to her difficult employer. But nineteenth-century convictions about women's moral nature, combined as they were with middle-class aspirations to political leadership, encouraged middle-class wives to undertake voluntary charitable work or to campaign for social reform. In Britain and the United States, women played an important role in the struggle to abolish the slave trade and slavery in the British Empire. Many of these movements also drew on the energies of religious, especially Protestant, organizations, committed to the eradication of social evils

The husband does not attempt to exculpate himself, as he also is in a state of extreme suffering. It is not in the genital organs, however, that we find his disorder, but in the whole general nervous system; his history will find its place in the part of this work relative to general disturbances. . . .

Source: Louis-François-Etienne Bergeret, *The Preventive Obstacle, or Conjugal Onanism*, trans. P. de Marmon (New York: 1870), pp. 3–4, 12, 20–22, 25, 56–57, 100–101, 111–113. Originally published in Paris in 1868.

Death in Childbirth (1830)

Mrs. Ann B. Pettigrew was taken in Labour after returning from a walk in the garden, at 7 o'clock in the evening of June 30, 1830. At 40 minutes after 11 o'clock, she was delivered of a daughter. A short time after, I was informed that the Placenta was not removed, and, at 10 minutes after 12 was asked into the room. I advanced to my dear wife, and kissing her, asked her how she was, to which she replied, I feel very badly. I went out of the room, and sent for Dr. Warren.

I then returned, and inquired if there was much hemorrhage, and was answered that there was. I then asked the midwife (Mrs. Brickhouse) if she ever used manual exertion to remove the placenta. She said she had more than fifty times. I then, fearing the consequences of hemorrhage, observed, Do, my dear sweet wife, permit Mrs. Brickhouse to remove it: To which she assented. . . . After the second unsuccessful attempt, I desired the midwife to desist. In these two efforts, my dear Nancy suffered exceedingly and frequently exclaimed: "O Mrs. Brickhouse you will kill me," and to me, "O I shall die, send for the Doctor." To which I replied, "I have sent."

After this, my feelings were so agonizing that I had to retire from the room and lay down, or fall. Shortly after which, the midwife came to me and, falling upon her knees, prayed most fervently to God and to me to forgive her for saying that she could do what she could not. . . .

The placenta did not come away, and the hemorrhage continued with unabated violence until five o'clock in the morning, when the dear woman breathed her last 20 minutes before the Doctor arrived.

So agonizing a scene as that from one o'clock, I have no words to describe. O My God, My God! have mercy on me. I am undone forever. . . .

Source: Cited in Erna Olafson Hellerstein, Leslie Parker Hume, and Karen M. Offen, eds., *Victorian Women: A Documentary Account of Women's Lives in Nineteenth-Century England, France, and the United States.* (Stanford, CA: 1981) pp. 193–94, 219–20.

Questions for Analysis

1. The French doctor states that the impulse to have sexual relations is "one of the most powerful instincts" given to humans by nature, while simultaneously claiming that this natural instinct is "liable to be perverted." What does this reveal about his attitude toward "nature"?

2. What does he mean by "genesiac frauds"? Who is being deceived by this fraud? What consequences for individuals and for society as a whole does the doctor fear from this deception?

3. What does the story of Mrs. Pettigrew's death reveal about the dangers of childbirth and the state of obstetric medicine in the nineteenth century?

and moral improvement. Throughout Europe, a wide range of movements to improve conditions for the poor in schools and hospitals, for temperance, against prostitution, or for legislation on factory hours were often run by women. Florence Nightingale, who went to the Crimean Peninsula in Russia to nurse British soldiers fighting there in the 1850s, remains the most famous of those women, whose determination to right social wrongs compelled them to defy conventional notions of woman's "proper" sphere. Equally famous—or infamous, at the time—was the French female novelist George Sand (1804–1876), whose real name was Amandine Aurore Dupin Dudevant. Sand dressed like a man and smoked cigars, and her novels often told the tales of independent women thwarted by convention and unhappy marriage.

Queen Victoria, who came to the British throne in 1837, labored to make her solemn public image reflect contemporary feminine virtues of moral probity and dutiful domesticity. Her court was eminently proper, a marked contrast to that of her uncle George IV, whose cavalier ways had set the style for high life a generation before. Though possessing a bad temper, Victoria trained herself to curb it in deference to her ministers and her public-spirited, ultrarespectable husband, Prince Albert of Saxe-Coburg. She was a successful queen because she embodied the traits important to the middle class, whose triumph she seemed to epitomize and whose habits of mind we have come to call Victorian. Nineteenth-century ideas about gender had an impact on masculinity as well as femininity. Soon after the revolutionary and Napoleonic period, men began to dress in sober, practical clothing—and to see as effeminate or dandyish the wigs, ruffled collars, and tight breeches that had earlier been the pride of aristocratic masculinity.

"Passionlessness": Gender and Sexuality

Victorian ideas about sexuality are among the most remarked-on features of nineteenth-century culture. They have become virtually synonymous with anxiety, prudishness, and ignorance. An English mother counseling her daughter about her wedding night is said to have told her to "lie back and think of the empire." Etiquette apparently required that piano legs be covered. Many of these anxieties and prohibitions, however, have been caricatured. More recently, historians have tried to disentangle the teachings or prescriptions of etiquette books and marriage manuals from the actual beliefs of men and women. Equally important, they have sought to understand each on its own terms. Beliefs about sexuality followed from convictions, described earlier, concerning separate spheres. Indeed, one of the defining aspects of nineteenth-century ideas about men and women is the extent to which they rested on scientific arguments about nature. Codes of morality and methods of science combined to reinforce the certainty that specific characteristics were inherent to each sex. Men and women had different social roles, and those differences were rooted in their bodies. The French social thinker Auguste Comte provides a good example: "Biological philosophy teaches us that, through the whole animal scale, and while the specific type is preserved, radical differences, physical and moral, distinguish the sexes." Comte also spelled out the implications of biological difference: "[T]he equality of the sexes, of which so much is said, is incompatible with all social existence. . . . The economy of the human family could never be inverted without an entire change in our cerebral organism." Women were unsuited for higher education because their brains were smaller or because their bodies were fragile. "Fifteen or 20 days of 28 (we may say nearly always) a woman is not only an invalid, but a wounded one. She ceaselessly suffers from love's eternal wound," wrote the well-known French author Jules Michelet about menstruation.

Finally, scientists and doctors considered women's alleged moral superiority to be literally embodied in an absence of sexual feeling, or "passionlessness." Scientists and doctors considered male sexual desire natural, if not admirable—an unruly force that had to be channeled. Many governments legalized and regulated prostitution—which included the compulsory examination of women for venereal disease—precisely because it provided an outlet for male sexual desire. Doctors disagreed about female sexuality, but the British doctor William Acton stood among those who asserted that women functioned differently:

> I have taken pains to obtain and compare abundant evidence on this subject, and the result of my inquiries I may briefly epitomize as follows:—I should say that the majority of women (happily for society) are not very much troubled with sexual feeling of any kind. What men are habitually, women are only exceptionally.

Like other nineteenth-century men and women, Acton also believed that more open expressions of sexuality were disreputable and, also, that working-class women were less "feminine."

Convictions like these reveal a great deal about Victorian science and medicine, but they did not necessarily dictate people's intimate lives. As far as sexuality was concerned, the absence of any reliable contraception mattered more in people's experiences and feelings than sociologists' or doctors' opinions. Abstinence and withdrawal were the only common techniques for preventing pregnancy. Their effectiveness was limited, since until the 1880s doctors continued to believe that a woman was most fertile during and around her menstrual period. Midwives and prostitutes knew of other forms of contraception and abortifacients (all of them dangerous and most ineffective), and surely some middle-class women did as well, but such information was not respectable middle-class fare. Concretely, then, sexual intercourse was directly related to the very real dangers of frequent pregnancies. In England, 1 in 100 childbirths ended in the death of the mother; at a time when a woman might become pregnant eight or nine times in her life, this was a sobering prospect. Those dangers varied with social class, but even among wealthy and better-cared-for women, they took a real toll. It is not surprising that middle-class women's diaries and letters are full of their anticipations of childbirth, both joyful and anxious. Queen Victoria, who bore nine children, declared that childbirth was the "shadow side" of marriage—and she was a pioneer in using anesthesia!

Middle-Class Life in Public

The public life of middle-class families literally reshaped the nineteenth-century landscape. Houses and their furnishings were powerful symbols of material security. Solidly built, heavily decorated, they proclaimed the financial worth and social respectability of those who dwelt within. In provincial cities they were often freestanding villas. In London, Paris, Berlin, and Vienna, they might be in rows of five- or six-story townhouses or large apartments. Whatever particular shape they took, they were built to last a long time. The rooms were certain to be crowded with furniture, art objects, carpets, and wall hangings. The size of the rooms, the elegance of the furniture, the number of servants—all depended, of course, on the extent of one's income. A bank clerk did not live as elegantly as a bank director. Yet they shared many standards and aspirations, and those common values helped bind them to the same class, despite the differences in their material way of life.

As cities grew, they became increasingly segregated. Middle-class people lived far from the unpleasant sights and smells of industrialization. Their residential areas, usually built to the west of the cities, out of the path of the prevailing breeze and therefore of industrial pollution, were havens from congestion. The public buildings in the center, many constructed during the nineteenth century, were celebrated as signs of development and prosperity. The middle classes increasingly managed their cities' affairs, although members of the aristocracy retained considerable power, especially in central Europe. And it was these new middle-class civic leaders who provided new industrial cities with many of their architectural landmarks: city halls, stock exchanges, museums, opera houses, outdoor concert halls, and department stores. One historian has called these buildings the new cathedrals of the industrial age; projects intended to express the community's values and represent public culture, they were monuments to social change.

The suburbs changed as well. The advent of the railways made outings to concerts, parks, and bathing spots popular. They made it possible for families of relatively moderate means to take one- or two-week-long trips to the mountains or to the seashore. New resorts opened, offering racetracks, mineral springs baths, and cabanas on the beach. Mass tourism would not come until the twentieth century. But the now-familiar impressionist paintings of the 1870s and 1880s testify to something that was dramatically new in the nineteenth century: a new range of middle-class leisures.

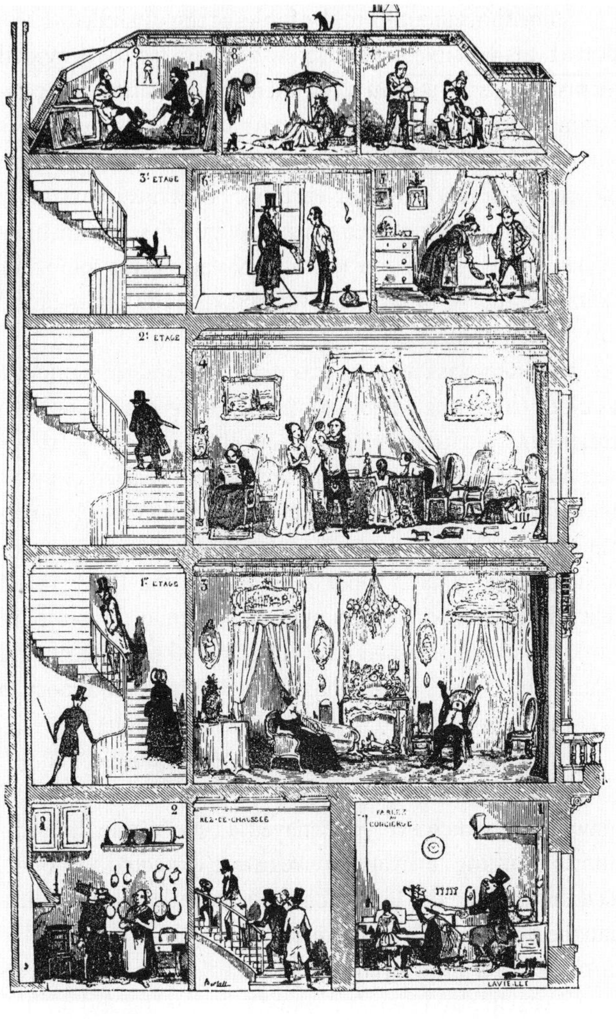

APARTMENT LIVING IN PARIS. This print shows that on the Continent, rich and poor often lived in the same buildings—the rich on the lower floors, the poor at the top. This sort of residential mixing was less common in Britain.

Working-Class Life

Like the middle class, the working class was divided into various subgroups and categories, determined in this case by skill, wages, gender, and workplace. Workers' experiences varied, depending on where they worked, where they lived, and, above all, how much they earned. A skilled textile worker lived a life far different from that of a ditch digger, the former able to afford the food, shelter, and clothing necessary for a decent existence, the latter barely able to scrape by.

Some movement from the ranks of the unskilled to the skilled was possible, if children were provided, or provided themselves, with at least a rudimentary education. Yet education was considered by many parents a luxury, especially since children could be put to work at an early age to supplement a family's meager earnings. Downward mobility from skilled to unskilled was also possible, as technological change—the introduction of the power loom, for example—drove highly paid workers into the ranks of the unskilled and destitute.

Working-class housing was unhealthy and unregulated. In older cities single-family dwellings were broken up into apartments, often of no more than one room per family. In new manufacturing centers, rows of tiny houses, located close by smoking factories, were built back to back, thereby eliminating any cross-ventilation or space for gardens. Crowding was commonplace. A newspaper account from the 1840s noted that in Leeds, a textile center in northern Britain, an ordinary worker's house contained no more than 150 square feet, and that in most cases those houses were "crammed almost to suffocation with human beings both day and night."

Household routines, demanding in the middle classes, were grinding for the poor. The family remained a survival network, in which everyone played a crucial role. In addition to working for wages, wives were expected to house, feed, and clothe the family on the very little money different members of the family earned. A good wife was able to make ends meet even in bad times. Working women's daily lives involved constant rounds of carrying and boiling water, cleaning, cooking, and doing laundry—in one- and two-room crowded, unventilated, poorly lit apartments. Families could not rely on their own gardens to help supply them with food. City markets catered to their needs for cheap goods, but these were regularly stale, nearly rotten, or dangerously adulterated. Formaldehyde was added to milk to prevent spoilage. Pounded rice was mixed into sugar. Fine brown earth was introduced into cocoa.

WORKING WOMEN IN THE INDUSTRIAL LANDSCAPE

Few figures raised more public anxiety and outcry in the nineteenth century than the working woman. Contemporaries worried out loud about the "promiscuous mixing of the sexes" in crowded and humid workshops. Nineteenth-century writers, starting in England and France, chronicled what they considered to be the economic and moral horrors of female labor: unattended children running in the streets, small children caught in accidents at the mills or the mines, pregnant women hauling coal, or women laboring alongside men in shops.

Women's work was not new, but industrialization made it more visible. Both before and after the Industrial Revolution labor was divided by gender, but as employers implemented new manufacturing processes, ideas about which jobs were appropriate for women shifted. In traditional textile production, for example, women spun and men operated the looms. In industrial textile factories, on the other hand, employers preferred women and children, both because they were considered more docile and less likely to make trouble and because it was believed that their smaller hands were better suited to the intricate job of tying threads on the power looms. Manufacturers sought to recruit women mill hands from neighboring villages, paying good wages by comparison with other jobs open to women. Most began to work at the age of ten or eleven, and when they had children they either put their children out to a wet nurse, brought them to the mills, or continued to work doing piecework at home. This transformation of the gendered structure of work caused intense anxiety in the first half of the nineteenth century and is one of the reasons that the emerging labor movement began to include calls for excluding women from the workplace in their programs.

Most women did not work in factories, however, and continued to labor at home or in small workshops—"sweatshops," as they came to be called—for notoriously low wages paid not by the hour but by the piece for each shirt stitched or each matchbox glued. The greatest number of unmarried working-class women worked less visibly in domestic service, a job that brought low wages and, to judge by the testimony of many women, coercive sexual relationships with male employers or their sons. Domestic service, however, provided room and board. In a time when a single woman simply could not survive on her own wages, a young woman who had just arrived in the city had few choices: marriage, which was unlikely to happen right away; renting a room in a boardinghouse, many of which were often centers of prostitution; domestic service; or living with someone. How women balanced the demands for money and the time for household work varied with the number and age of their children. Mothers were actually more likely to work when their children were very small, for there were more mouths to feed and the children were not yet old enough to earn wages.

Poverty, the absence of privacy, and the particular vulnerabilities of working-class women made working-class sexuality very different from its middle-class counterpart. Illegitimacy rose dramatically between 1750 and 1850. In Frankfurt, Germany, for example, where the illegitimacy rate had been a mere 2 percent in the early 1700s, it reached 25 percent in 1850. In Bordeaux, France, in 1840, one-third of the recorded births were illegitimate. Reasons for

CAPITAL AND LABOUR. In its earliest years, the British magazine *Punch*, though primarily a humorous weekly, manifested a strong social conscience. This 1843 cartoon shows the capitalists enjoying the rewards of their investments while the hungry workers shiver in cold. ▪ ***How would a defender of the new industrial order respond to this cartoon?***

this increase are difficult to establish. Greater mobility and urbanization meant weaker family ties, more opportunities for young men and women, and more vulnerabilities. Premarital sex was an accepted practice in preindustrial villages, but because of the social controls that dominated village life, it was almost always followed by marriage. These controls were weaker in the far more anonymous setting of a factory town or commercial city. The economic uncertainties of the early industrial age meant that a young workingman's promise of marriage based on his expectation of a job might frequently be difficult to fulfill. Economic vulnerability drove many single women into temporary relationships that produced children and a continuing cycle of poverty and abandonment. Historians have shown, however, that in the city as in the countryside, many of these temporary relationships became enduring ones: the parents of illegitimate children would marry later. Again, nineteenth-century writers dramatized what they considered the disreputable sexuality of the "dangerous classes" in the cities. Some of them attributed illegitimacy, prostitution, and so on to the moral weakness of working-class people, others to the systematic changes wrought by industrialization. Both sides, however, overstated the collapse of the family and the destruction of traditional morality. Working-class families transmitted expectations about gender roles and sexual behavior: girls should expect to work, daughters were responsible for caring for their younger siblings as well as for earning wages, sexuality was a fact of life, midwives could help desperate pregnant girls, marriage was an avenue to respectability, and so on. The gulf that separated these expectations and codes from those of middle-class women was one of the most important factors in the development of nineteenth-century class identity.

A Life Apart: "Class Consciousness"

The new demands of life in an industrial economy created common experiences and difficulties. The factory system denied skilled workers the pride in craft they had previously enjoyed. Stripped of the protections of guilds and apprenticeships and prevented from organizing by legislation in France, Germany, and Britain in the first half of the nineteenth century, workers felt vulnerable in the face of their socially and politically powerful employers. Factory hours were long—usually twelve to fourteen hours. Textile mills were unventilated, and minute particles of lint lodged in workers' lungs. Machines were unfenced and posed dangers to child workers. British physicians cataloged the toll that long hours tending machines took on children, including spinal curvature and bone malformations. Children were also employed in large numbers in mines—over 50,000 worked in British mines in 1841.

Factories also imposed new routines and disciplines. Artisans in earlier times worked long hours for little pay, but they set their own schedules and controlled the pace of work, moving from their home workshops to their small garden plots as they wished. In a factory, all hands learned the discipline of the clock. To increase production, the factory system encouraged the breaking down of the manufacturing process into specialized steps, each with its own time. Workers began to see machinery itself as the tyrant that changed their lives and bound them to industrial slavery. A radical working-class song written in Britain in the 1840s expressed the feeling:

> There is a king and a ruthless king;
> Not a king of the poet's dream;
> But a tyrant fell, white slaves know well,
> And that ruthless king is steam.

Yet the defining feature of working-class life was vulnerability—to unemployment, sickness, accidents in dangerous jobs, family problems, and spikes in the prices of food. Seasonal unemployment, high in almost all trades, made it impossible to collect regular wages. Markets for manufactured goods were small and unstable, producing cyclical economic depressions; when those came, thousands of workers found themselves laid off with no system of unemployment insurance to sustain them. The early decades of industrialization were also marked by several severe agricultural depressions and economic crises. During the crisis years of the 1840s, half the working population of Britain's industrial cities was unemployed. In Paris, 85,000 went on relief in 1840. Families survived by working several small jobs, pawning their possessions, and getting credit from local wineshops and grocery stores. The chronic insecurity of working-class life helped fuel the creation of workers' self-help societies, fraternal associations, and early socialist organizations. It also meant that economic crises could have explosive consequences (see Chapter 21).

By mid-century, various experiences were beginning to make working people conscious of themselves as different from and in opposition to the middle classes. Changes in the workplace—whether the introduction of machines and factory labor, speedups, subcontracting to cheap labor, or the loss of guild protections—were part of the picture. The social segregation of the rapidly expanding nineteenth-century cities also contributed to the sense that working people lived a life apart. Class differences seemed embedded in a very wide array of everyday experiences and beliefs: work, private life, expectations for children, the roles of men and women, and definitions of respectability. Over the course of the nineteenth century all of these different experiences gave concrete, specific meaning to the word *class*.

CONCLUSION

Why did the Industrial Revolution occur at this moment in human history? Why did it begin in Europe? Why did it not occur in other regions in the world with large populations and advanced technologies, such as China or India? These fundamental questions remain subject to serious debate among historians. One school of explanations focuses on the fact that the mechanization of industry occurred first in northern Europe and seeks to explain the Industrial Revolution's origins in terms of this region's vibrant towns,

After You Read This Chapter

Visit StudySpace for quizzes, additional review materials, and multimedia documents. **wwnorton.com/web/westernciv18**

REVIEWING THE OBJECTIVES

- The Industrial Revolution in Europe began in northern Great Britain. What circumstances made this process of economic development begin there?
- Certain industries were particularly suitable for the kinds of technological developments that encouraged industrialization. What were these industries, and where did they exist in Europe?
- Industrial development changed the nature of work and production in significant ways. What were these changes, and how did they change the relations between laborers and their employers, or local producers and wider markets?
- Industrialization had social effects far beyond the factories. What larger changes in European society were associated with the Industrial Revolution?
- A large and diverse group of middle-class people emerged in Europe as a result of the social changes brought on by industrialization. What kinds of people qualified as middle class during the nineteenth century, and how were they different from other social groups?

its well-developed commercial markets, and the presence of a prosperous land-owning elite that had few prejudices against entrepreneurial activity. These historians have suggested that industrialization is best understood as a process rooted in European culture and history.

More recently, however, historians with a more global approach have argued that it may be incorrect to assert that industrialization developed as it did because of the advantages enjoyed by a central, European, core. Instead, they have explored the possibility that the world's economies constituted a larger interlocking system that had no definitive center until *after* the takeoff of European industrialization. Before that period, when it came to agricultural practices, ecological constraints, population densities, urbanization, and technological development, *many* global regions were not so different from the western European model. In the end, suggest these historians, Europe was able to move more quickly to industrial production because its economies were better positioned to mobilize the resources available to them on the periphery of their trading sphere. The access enjoyed by European traders to agricultural products from slave-owning societies in the Americas helped them escape the ecological constraints imposed by their own intensely farmed lands and made the move to an industrial economy possible. Contingent factors—such as patterns of disease and epidemic or the location of coal fields—may have also played a role.

There is less debate about the consequences of the Industrial Revolution within Europe. New forms of industrial production created a new economy and changed the nature of work for both men and women. Industrialization changed the landscape of Europe and changed the structures of families and the private lives of people in both the cities and the countryside. Industrialization created new forms of wealth along with new kinds of poverty. It also fostered an acute awareness of the disparity between social groups. In the eighteenth century, that disparity would have been described in terms of birth, rank, or privilege. In the nineteenth century, it was increasingly seen in terms of class. Both champions and critics of the new industrial order spoke of a "class society." The identities associated with class were formed in the crowded working-class districts of the new cities, in experiences of work, and in the new conditions of respectability that determined life in middle-class homes. These new identities would be sharpened in the political events to which we now turn.

PEOPLE, IDEAS, AND EVENTS IN CONTEXT

- Why was **ENCLOSURE** an important factor in the Industrial Revolution?
- What was the **SPINNING JENNY**? What was the **COTTON GIN**? What effect did these machines have on industrial development?
- What was the significance of **EUROPEAN EMPIRE** and overseas expansion for industrialization?
- How did industrialization affect **POPULATION GROWTH** in Europe? What effects did it have on the **PEASANTRY**? On **URBAN POPULATIONS**?
- What environmental changes were associated with the use of new sources of fuel such as coal or the construction of large and concentrated centers of industrial manufacture?
- What was the **IRISH POTATO FAMINE**, and how was it related to the economic developments of nineteenth-century Europe? What might **THOMAS MALTHUS** have thought about the potato famine?

THINKING ABOUT CONNECTIONS

- What might the changes associated with the Industrial Revolution have done to people's conceptions of time and space? How might they have perceived their lives against what they knew of the experience of their parents' generation or what they anticipated for their children?
- Awareness that these changes made the present radically different from the recent past gave many people the sensation that time was hurtling ever faster into a future whose outlines could only dimly be perceived.
- In the early twenty-first century, innovations in information technology have created a similar sensation of accelerated change and diminishing distances in a more interconnected globe. What are the similarities between our own period and the period between the 1780s and 1830s, when large numbers of people first began to think of the power of technology to change the way that society was organized and to conceive of history as a headlong rush into the future? What are the differences?

Before You Read This Chapter

STORY LINES

- The conservative regimes that defeated Napoleon in 1815 set out to reverse the changes in Europe caused by the French Revolution. They aimed for a balance of forces between European powers so that no single ruler could dominate Europe.
- Conservative rulers in Europe remained on the defensive. Liberalism, republicanism, and nationalism continued to fuel resistance to the conservative order. Socialism provided Europe's laborers with a new vocabulary to express their unhappiness with industrialization.
- The conservative political reaction after 1815 found its cultural counterpart in Romanticism. This movement rejected the Enlightenment's rationalism and emphasized instead the power of nature and human emotions.

CHRONOLOGY

1808	Slave trade prohibited by Britain and United States but not slavery itself
1810–1825	South American revolutions
1814–1815	Congress of Vienna
1821–1827	Greek war for independence
1823	France restores King Ferdinand of Spain
1825	Decembrist Revolt in Russia
1830	Revolutions in France and Belgium
1832	British Reform Bill
1833	British Empire abolishes slavery
1840s	Chartist movement in Britain
1846	Corn Laws repealed
1848	Karl Marx's *Communist Manifesto* published

20

The Age of Ideologies: Europe in the Aftermath of Revolution, 1815–1848

CORE OBJECTIVES

- **UNDERSTAND** the political goals of the European leaders who met at the Congress of Vienna in 1815 and the challenges to the Concert of Europe in the decades between 1815 and 1848.
- **TRACE** the evolution of the debate about slavery after the French Revolution, and understand the reasons why an abolition movement developed even as slavery persisted in the United States, Latin America, and Cuba.
- **IDENTIFY** the core principles of conservatism, liberalism, republicanism, and socialism in Europe after 1815.
- **DEFINE** *nationalism* and understand how conservatives, liberals, republicans, and socialists were forced to grapple with this powerful political idea.
- **EXPLAIN** the ideas contained in the cultural movement known as Romanticism and its relationship to the Enlightenment.

When the defeated Napoleon left the field of battle at Waterloo on June 18, 1815, headed eventually to exile on the rocky island of St. Helena in the South Atlantic, his victorious opponents hoped the age of revolution had ended. The Austrian foreign minister, Klemens von Metternich, perhaps the most influential conservative diplomat of the early nineteenth century, called revolution a "sickness," "plague," and "cancer" and with his allies set out to inoculate Europe against any outbreak. In their view, revolution produced war and disorder. Peace depended on avoiding political turmoil and reinforcing the power of conservative monarchies in all corners of Europe. Bolstering the legitimacy of such monarchies was Metternich's primary goal in the post-Napoleonic decades.

The decades between 1815 and 1848 saw the legitimacy of these monarchies challenged on multiple fronts. Conservative efforts to restore the old order succeeded only in part. Why? To begin with, the developments of the eighteenth century proved impossible to reverse. The expansion of an informed public, begun in the Enlightenment, continued. The word *citizen* (and the liberal political ideas contained within it) was controversial in the aftermath of the French Revolution, but it was difficult to banish the term from political debates. Liberalism's fundamental principles—equality before the law, freedom of expression, and the consent of the governed—were still a potent threat to Europe's dynastic rulers, especially when coupled with the emotions stirred up by popular nationalism. Liberal nationalists believed that legitimate sovereignty could only be exercised by citizens acting collectively as a nation. Such a conception of sovereignty was diametrically opposed to conservative monarchs who believed their authority came not from the people but from God.

At the same time, the political opposition to the conservative order in Europe began to be infused with new and more radical political ideologies. Some liberals were comfortable living under a constitutional monarch—one who agreed to rule in accordance with the law. Others accepted the idea of representation but believed that voting was a privilege that should be extended only to wealthy property owners. Much more radical were republicans who called for universal (male) suffrage and an end to monarchy altogether. Socialists, disturbed by the inequalities produced in the new market economy of industrial society, went even further and argued that political reform was not enough to free the people from want and exploitation. To socialists, justice was possible only with a radical reordering of society that redistributed property equitably. Between 1815 and 1848, none of these more radical oppositional movements succeeded in carrying the day, but their ideas circulated widely and occupied the attention of conservative monarchs (and their police spies) throughout Europe.

In culture as well as in politics, imagination and a sense of possibility were among the defining characteristics of the first half of the century. Romanticism broke with what many artists considered the cold Classicism and formality of eighteenth-century art. The Enlightenment had championed reason; the Romantics prized subjectivity, feeling, and spontaneity. Their revolt against eighteenth-century conventions had ramifications far beyond literature and painting. The Romantics had no single political creed: some were fervent revolutionaries and others fervent traditionalists who looked to the past, to religion or history, for inspiration. Their sensibility, however, infused politics and culture. And to look ahead, their collective search for new means of expression sent nineteenth-century art off in a new direction.

THE SEARCH FOR ORDER IN EUROPE, 1815–1830

In 1814, the European powers—including the France of the restored king, Louis XVIII—met at the Congress of Vienna to settle pressing questions about the post-Napoleonic political order and to determine the territorial spoils of their victory over the French emperor. An observer of the lavish balls and celebrations that accompanied the Congress's diplomatic negotiations might well have assumed that the calendar had been turned back several decades, to a time when the European nobility had not yet been humiliated and terrorized by violent revolutionaries. But the celebrations of Louis XVIII's return to the throne and the glittering display of aristocratic men in wigs and fine clothes, accompanied by their bejeweled wives (and mistresses), could not hide the fact that twenty years of war, revolution, and political experimentation had changed Europe in fundamental ways. The task of the Congress of Vienna was to reinforce Europe's monarchical regimes against the powerful social and political forces that had been unleashed in the years since 1789.

The Congress of Vienna and the Restoration

The Russian tsar Alexander I (r. 1801–25) and the Austrian diplomat Klemens von Metternich (1773–1859) dominated the Congress of Vienna. After Napoleon's fall, Russia became the most powerful continental state. Alexander I presented himself during the Napoleonic Wars as the "liberator" of Europe, and many feared that he would substitute an all-powerful Russia for an all-powerful France. The French prince Charles Maurice de Talleyrand (1754–1838) had a surprisingly strong supporting role. Talleyrand had been a bishop and a revolutionary and survived the Terror in exile in the United States before becoming first Napoleon's foreign minister and then occupying the same post under Louis XVIII. That he was present at Vienna testified to his diplomatic skill—or opportunism.

Metternich, the architect of the peace, had witnessed the popular violence connected with the French Revolution while a student at the University of Strasbourg in 1789. It left him with a lifelong hatred of revolutionary movements. At the Congress of Vienna, his central concerns were checking Russian expansionism and preventing political

THE CONGRESS OF VIENNA. Note how the borders of European nations were established after the final defeat of Napoleon in 1815, and compare these boundaries to Europe in 1713 after the Peace of Utrecht (page 508). ▪ ***What major changes had occurred in the intervening years in central Europe?*** ▪ ***Which territorial powers played an active role in determining the balance of power at the Congress of Vienna?*** ▪ ***What social or political developments might disrupt this balance?***

and social change. He favored treating the defeated French with moderation. Nevertheless, he remained an archconservative who readily resorted to harsh repressive tactics, including secret police and spying. But the peace he crafted was enormously significant and helped prevent a major European war until 1914.

The Congress sought to restore order by insisting that Europe's dynastic rulers were the only legitimate political authority. It recognized Louis XVIII as the legitimate sovereign of France and confirmed the restoration of Bourbon rulers in Spain and the Two Sicilies. Other European monarchs had no interest in undermining the French restoration: Louis XVIII was a bulwark against revolution. But after Napoleon's Hundred Days, the allies imposed an indemnity of 700 million francs and an occupying army for five years. France's borders remained the same as in 1789—less than the revolution's "greater France" but not as punitive as they might have been.

The guiding principle of the peace was the balance of power, according to which no country should be powerful enough to destabilize international relations. Metternich's immediate goal, therefore, was to build a barrier against renewed French expansion. The Dutch Republic, conquered by the French in 1795, was restored as the kingdom of the Netherlands, securing France's northern border. The Congress also ceded the left bank of the Rhine to Prussia, and Austria expanded into northern Italy.

In central Europe, the allied powers reorganized the German states, reducing them from over 300 in number to 39. Prussia and Habsburg Austria joined these German states in a loosely structured German Confederation, with Austria careful to reserve for itself the presidency of this new body, as a check against attempts by the Prussians to increase their regional influence. Eventually, this confederation became the basis for German unification, but this was not the intention in Vienna in 1815. Bavaria, Württemburg, and Saxony remained independent kingdoms. Poland became a particular bone of contention, and the final compromise saw a nominally independent kingdom of Poland placed under the control of Tsar Alexander, with large slices of formerly Polish territory being handed over to Austria and Prussia. Meanwhile, Britain demanded compensation for its long war with Napoleon and received formerly French territories in South Africa and South America, as well as the island of Ceylon.

The Congress of Vienna also called for a Concert of Europe to secure the peace. Britain, Austria, Prussia, and Russia pledged to cooperate in the suppression of any disturbances—and France officially joined this conservative alliance in 1818. Alexander I pushed for what he called a Holy Alliance, dedicated to justice, Christian charity, and peace. The British foreign minister remained skeptical—calling the Holy Alliance "a piece of sublime mysticism and nonsense"—but agreed that the European powers should defend their conception of authority, centered on legitimacy. A ruler was legitimate if his power was guaranteed not only by claims of divine right but also by international treaties and support by his recognized peers. The Concert of Europe's opposition to liberal notions of political representation and national self-determination could not have been clearer. King Leopold of Belgium, himself placed on the throne by the allied powers in 1831, observed that war now threatened to become "a conflict of principles," sparked by revolutionary ideas, setting "peoples" against emperors. "From what I know of Europe," he continued, "such a conflict would change her form and overthrow her whole structure." Metternich and his fellow diplomats at Vienna dedicated their lives to seeing that such a conflict would never take place.

Revolt against Restoration

Much of the resistance to the Restoration was clandestine. On the Italian peninsula, the Carbonari (the name came from the charcoal they used to blacken their faces) vowed to oppose the government in Vienna and its conservative allies. Their political views varied: some called for constitutions and representative government and others praised Bonaparte. The Carbonari's influence spread through southern Europe and France in the 1820s, with members meeting in secret and identifying one another with closely guarded rituals. Veterans of Napoleon's armies and military officers were prominent in their ranks.

In Naples and Piedmont, and especially in Spain and the Spanish Empire, opposition to Metternich's Concert of Europe turned to revolt when monarchs restored by the Congress of Vienna betrayed their promises of reform. Metternich responded by spurring Austria, Prussia, and Russia to take a strong stand against revolution. In the Troppau Memorandum (1820), the conservative regimes pledged to assist one another in suppressing revolt. Austria dealt firmly with the Italian revolts, and France sent 200,000 troops to the Iberian Peninsula in 1823, crushing the Spanish revolutionaries and restoring King Ferdinand's authority.

Revolution in Latin America

King Ferdinand's empire in Latin America, however, would not be restored. Napoleon's conquest of Spain (1807) had shaken Spain's once vast empire. Local elites in the colonies who resented Spanish imperial control took advantage of the crown's weakness to push for independence. Rio de la Plata (now Argentina) was the first to succeed, declaring independence in 1816. Soon after, a monarchist general from Rio de la Plata, José de San Martin (1778–1850), led an expedition to liberate Chile and Peru. At the same time, Simón Bolívar (1783–1830), a republican leader, sparked a series of uprisings from Venezuela to Bolivia. Bolívar and Martin joined forces, though Bolívar's plans were more radical—he envisioned mobilizing free people of color and slaves (who made up roughly a quarter of those fighting the Spanish) as well as Indians to fight against Spanish rule. Bolívar's goal was to create a pan-American republic on the continent, along the lines of the United States. These political revolts unleashed violent social conflicts and, in some cases, civil

SECRET MEETING OF THE CARBONARI. Not all resistance took the form of open protest. The Carbonari, an Italian organization named for the charcoal that obscured the faces of its members, was an underground expression of opposition to the Restoration.

war. Elite landowners who wanted only to free themselves from Spain opposed groups who wanted land reform and an end to slavery. In the end, the radical movements were suppressed, and the newly independent Latin American nations were dominated by an alliance of conservative landowners and military officers.

Britain and the newly ambitious United States prevented the European powers from intervening in the Latin American revolutions. In 1823, U.S. president James Monroe issued the Monroe Doctrine, declaring that European meddling in the Americas would be seen as a hostile act, a declaration that signaled a new willingness on the part of the United States to play a role on the world stage. Without British support, however, the Monroe Doctrine was unenforceable. Britain saw the new South American republics as potential trading partners and used its navy to prevent Spain from intervening. By the 1820s, the Spanish Empire had vanished, ending an age that had begun in 1492. Brazil's independence in 1823 similarly ended the era of Portuguese colonialism in South America. Together, these revolutions demonstrated the circular relationships that bound the Atlantic world together. Encouraged by political movements associated with the French Revolution and Napoleon, the Latin American revolutionaries would in turn inspire nationalists in Europe who sought to overthrow Metternich's conservative Concert of Europe.

Russia: The Decembrists

Revolt also broke out in conservative Russia. In 1825, Tsar Alexander died, and a group of army officers known as the Decembrists led an uprising to push the pace of reform. Many were veterans of the Napoleonic Wars, and they feared that Russia could not live up to its promise to be the "liberator of Europe" without change in its social and political order. Serfdom contradicted the promise of liberation. So did the tsar's monopoly on power. Not only were Russian peasants enslaved, argued the Decembrists, the nobles were "slaves to the tsar."

The officers failed to gain support from the rank-and-file soldiers, and without that support they could not succeed. The new tsar, Nicholas I (r. 1825–55), interrogated hundreds of mutinous soldiers, sentencing many to hard labor and exile. The five leaders—all young and leading members of the aristocratic elite—were sentenced to death. Fearing they would be seen as martyrs, the tsar had them hung at dawn behind the walls of a fortress in St. Petersburg and buried in secret graves.

Nicholas went on to rule in the manner of his predecessor, becoming Europe's most uncompromising conservative. He created a powerful political police force, the Third Section, to prevent further domestic disorder. Still, Russia was not immune to change. Bureaucracy became more centralized, more efficient, and less dependent on the nobility. Accomplishing this task required making Russia's complex legal system more systematic and uniform. To accomplish this task Nicholas oversaw the publication of a new Code of Law, which recategorized every law passed since 1648 and published them in forty-eight volumes, a measure comparable to Napoleon's Civil Code of 1804. Meanwhile, landowners responded to increased demand for Russian grain by reorganizing their estates to increase productivity, and the state began to build railroads to transport the grain to Western markets. At the same time, opponents of the regime, such as the writer Alexander Herzen, carried on the Decembrists' unresolved political legacy.

NEW NATIONS OF LATIN AMERICA. After Haiti became the Western Hemisphere's second independent nation, many areas of Central and South America also broke away from colonial rule. ▪ ***When did the nations of Latin America gain their independence?*** ▪ ***What major events in Europe contributed to this move to independence?*** ▪ ***What is their relation to the Atlantic revolutions established in the late eighteenth century?***

Southeastern Europe: Greece and Serbia

When the Greeks and Serbians revolted against the once powerful Ottoman Empire, the conservative European powers showed themselves to be more tolerant of rebellion. Although the Ottoman Empire had defeated Napoleon Bonaparte's attempt to invade Egypt in 1798 (with British help), the episode strained the Ottoman hold on the eastern Mediterranean. Serbs in the Balkans rebelled against the Ottomans as early as 1804 and, with the help of the Russians, succeeded in establishing hereditary rule by a Serbian prince in 1817. This Serbian quasi-state persisted as an Orthodox Christian principality with a significant minority Muslim population until finally achieving formal independence from the Ottoman Empire in 1878.

The Serb revolt and the subsequent Greek war for independence (1821–27), were part of a new pattern in Ottoman history beginning in the early nineteenth century in which groups within the empire's border regions began to seek independence from Ottoman rule. Eighteenth-century revolts against Ottoman control in these regions had usually not sought outright separation and had generally been resolved within the imperial system, by redistributing tax burdens or instituting legal reforms. After 1800, European powers were more likely to get involved and the result was the establishment of new independent states and a weakening of Ottoman power. The French and the British viewed the eastern Mediterranean as an important arena of commercial competition while Russians viewed their frontiers with the Ottoman Empire's Balkan holdings as a natural place to exert foreign influence.

The Greek revolt immediately gained support from the British government, and sympathy for the Greeks was widespread in Europe. Christians in Europe cast the rebellion as part of an ongoing struggle between Christianity and Islam, whereas secular observers sought to interpret the struggle as one between an ancient pre-Christian European heritage and the Ottoman Empire. "We are all Greeks," wrote Percy Shelley, the Romantic poet. "Our laws, our literature, our religion, our arts have their roots in Greece." George Gordon, better known as Lord Byron (1788–1824), another Romantic poet, fought in Greece along with other volunteers, before dying there from fever. Celebrating the Greeks went hand in hand with demonizing the Ottomans, in spite of the fact that the Ottoman Empire's adaptable imperial system had frequently done better than Europeans in preserving the peace between diverse peoples and different religions over the many centuries of their rule.

THE MASSACRE AT CHIOS* BY EUGÈNE DELACROIX (1789–1863).** Delacroix was a Romantic painter of dramatic and emotional scenes. Here, he put his brush to work for the cause of Greek nationalism, eulogizing the victims of killings on the island of Chios during the Greek war for independence against the Ottoman Empire. ▪ ***How did the choices that Delacroix made in his depiction of the massacre's victims shape the vision of the conflict for his European audience?

On the ground in Greece, the struggle was brutal and massacres of civilians occurred on both sides. In March 1822, the Greeks invaded the island of Chios and proclaimed its independence. When Ottoman troops arrived to retake the island, the Greek invaders killed their prisoners and fled. The Ottoman armies took revenge by slaughtering thousands of Greeks and selling 40,000 more into slavery. The French Romantic painter Eugène Delacroix memorialized the event in a painting that characteristically depicted only Ottoman brutality (see above).

In the end, Greek independence depended on great-power politics, as it did in Serbia. In 1827, British, French, and Russian troops sided with the Greeks against the Ottomans, who were forced to concede and grant Greek independence. The new nations of Serbia and Greece were small and fragile. Only 800,000 Greeks actually lived in the new Greek state. Serbia, meanwhile, could not survive without Russian protection. Moreover, neither of the new nations broke their close links with the Ottomans, and

Greek and Serbian merchants, bankers, and administrators were still very present in the Ottoman Empire. The region remained a borderland of Europe, a region where peoples alternated between tolerant coexistence and bitter conflict.

As Ottoman control in southeastern Europe waned, the European powers often played a double game. On the one hand, they recognized that regional stability depended on the continued existence of the Ottoman Empire and that its collapse would constitute a serious threat to European peace. By continuing to pursue their own self-interests, however, and by meddling in the affairs of the Ottoman Empire's rebellious subjects, they contributed to the weakening of Ottoman authority.

Leaders of independence movements were likely to succeed when they could take advantage of conflict between great powers, as in Latin America, or when those movements aligned with Europe's competition with the Ottoman Empire, as in Greece and Serbia. Meanwhile, Metternich's ability to prevent the spread of nationalism and liberalism—both ideologies associated with the French Revolution—increasingly depended on repressive political regimes that could not tolerate open expressions of dissent. Containing these movements for political and social change would eventually become impossible.

CITIZENSHIP AND SOVEREIGNTY, 1830–1848

In the aftermath of the French Revolution, then, debates about citizenship, sovereignty, and social inequality remained divisive in many parts of Europe, even in those kingdoms with conservative monarchies that supported the Concert of Europe. In France, Belgium, and Poland, political movements challenging the post-Napoleonic settlement led to open revolt in the years 1830–32. A similar threat developed in the 1840s. During these same decades, many in Britain feared that conflicts over voting rights and the treatment of the poor might lead to a similar crisis. In the end, political leaders in Britain succeeded in negotiating reforms that prevented open rebellion during these years, whereas the revolutionary movements of the 1830s and 1840s on the Continent proved to be a prelude to a wave of revolutions in 1848 that swept across Europe (see Chapter 21).

The 1830 Revolution in France

The first decisive blow against the Concert of Europe came in 1830 in France. In 1815, the Congress of Vienna returned a Bourbon monarch to the throne. Louis XVIII was the oldest of the former king's surviving brothers. Louis claimed absolute power, but in the name of reconciliation he granted a "charter" and conceded some important rights: legal equality, careers open to talent, and a two-chamber parliamentary government. Voting rights excluded most citizens from government. Louis XVIII's narrow base of support, combined with the sting of military defeat, nostalgia for a glorious Napoleonic past, and memories of the revolution undermined the Restoration in France.

In 1824, Louis XVIII succeeded his far more conservative brother, Charles X (r. 1824–30). Charles pleased the ultra-royalists by pushing the assembly to compensate nobles whose land had been confiscated and sold during the revolution, but the measure antagonized property holders. He restored the Catholic Church to its traditional place in French schools, provoking discontent among French liberals, who began to organize an oppositional movement in Parliament. Economic troubles encouraged the opposition, and in Paris and the provinces worried police reports documented widespread unemployment, hunger, and anger. Confronted with alarming evidence of the regime's unpopularity, Charles called for new elections; when they went against him, he tried to overthrow the parliament with his so-called July Ordinances of 1830: he dissolved the new assembly before it had met, restricted suffrage even further, and announced strict press censorship.

In return, Charles got revolution. Parisian workers, artisans, and students took to the streets in three days of intense street battles. Crucial to the spread of the movement was the press, which defied the censors and quickly spread the news of the initial confrontations between protesters and the forces of order. In the end, the army was unwilling to fire into the crowd, and Charles was forced to abdicate, his support evaporating. Although many revolutionaries who had fought in the streets wanted another republic, the leaders of the movement opted for stability by crowning the former king's cousin, the Duke of Orléans, Louis-Philippe (r. 1830–48), as a constitutional monarch. The July Monarchy, as it was called, doubled the number of voters, though voting was still based on steep property requirements. The propertied classes benefited most from the revolution of 1830, but it also brought the common people back into politics, revived memories of 1789, and spurred movements elsewhere in Europe. For opponents of the Restoration, the year 1830 suggested that history was moving in a new direction and that the political landscape had changed since the Congress of Vienna.

LIBERTY LEADING THE PEOPLE* BY EUGÈNE DELACROIX.** This painting is among the best-known images of the revolutions of 1830. Delacroix is the same artist who had mourned the extinction of liberty in his painting of the *Massacre at Chios* in Greece (see page 659). The allegorical female figure of liberty leads representatives of the united people: a middle-class man (identified by his top hat), a worker, and a boy of the streets wielding a pistol. Neither middle-class people nor children fought on the barricades, and the image of revolutionary unity was romanticized. ▪ ***What made this mix of social classes important for Delacroix's image of the French people in revolt? ▪ ***And why this particular image of liberty, carrying a rifle, with exposed breasts?***

Belgium and Poland in 1830

In 1815, the Congress of Vienna joined Belgium (then called the Austrian Netherlands) to Holland to form a buffer against France known as the United Provinces. The Belgians had never accepted this arrangement, and the 1830 revolution in France energized the Belgian opposition. The city of Brussels rebelled and forced Dutch troops to withdraw. Unwilling to intervene, the great powers agreed to guarantee Belgian independence and neutrality—a provision that remained in force until 1914. Although the economy of Belgian cities suffered by being separated from the Atlantic trade of the Dutch ports, religious divisions between the largely Catholic provinces of Belgium and Protestant Holland reinforced the division. French-speaking elites in Belgium also supported independence, though Flemish-speaking Belgians continue to cultivate a sense of cultural distinctiveness even today.

The years 1830–32 thus became full-fledged crisis for the Concert of Europe. After France and Belgium, revolt also spread to Poland, governed by the Russian tsar's brother, Constantine. Poland had its own parliament (or *diet*), a relatively broad electorate, a constitution, and basic liberties of speech and the press. The Russian head of state increasingly ignored these liberties, however, and news of the French Revolution of 1830 tipped Poland into revolt. The revolutionaries—including aristocrats, students, military officers, and middle-class people—drove out Constantine. Within less than a year, Russian forces retook Warsaw, and the conservative tsar Nicholas crushed the revolt and put Poland under military rule.

Reform in Great Britain

Why was there no revolution in England between 1815 and 1848? One answer is that there almost was. After an era of political conservatism comparable to that of the Continent's, however, Britain became one of the most liberal nations in Europe.

The end of the Napoleonic Wars brought a major agricultural depression to Britain. Low wages, unemployment, and bad harvests provoked regular social unrest. In the new industrial towns of the north, radical members of the middle class joined with workers to demand increased representation in Parliament. When 60,000 people gathered in 1819 to demonstrate for political reform at St. Peter's Field in Manchester, the militia and soldiers on horseback charged the crowd, killing 11 and injuring 400. Radicals condemned "Peterloo," a domestic Waterloo, and criticized the nation's army for turning against its own citizens. Parliament quickly passed the Six Acts (1819), outlawing "seditious" literature, increasing the stamp tax on newspapers, allowing house searches, and restricting rights of assembly.

British political leaders reversed their opposition to reform in response to pressure from below. The reforms actually began under the conservative Tory Party, when Catholics and non-Anglican Protestants were allowed to participate in public life. The Tories nevertheless refused to reform representation in the House of Commons. About two-thirds of the members of the House of Commons owed their seats to the patronage of the richest titled landowners in the country. In districts known as "rotten" or "pocket" boroughs, landowners used their power to return members of Parliament who would serve their interests. Defenders of this system argued that the interests of landed property coincided with the nation at large.

Liberals in the Whig Party, the new industrial middle class, and radical artisans argued passionately for reform. They were not necessarily democrats—liberals in particular wanted only to enfranchise responsible citizens—but they made common cause with organized middle-class and working-class radicals to push for reform. A Birmingham banker named Thomas Atwood, for example, organized the Political Union of the Lower and Middle Classes of the People. By July 1830, similar organizations arose in several cities, and some clashed with the army and police. Middle-class shopkeepers announced they would withhold taxes and form a national guard. The country appeared to be on the verge of serious general disorder, if not outright revolution. Lord Grey, head of the Whig Party, seized the opportunity to push through reform.

The Reform Bill of 1832 eliminated the rotten boroughs and reallocated 143 parliamentary seats, mostly from the rural south, to the industrial north. The bill expanded the franchise, but only one in six men could vote. Landed aristocrats had their influence reduced but not destroyed. This modest reform nevertheless brought British liberals and members of the middle class into a junior partnership with a landed elite that had ruled Britain for centuries.

What changes did this more liberal parliament produce? It abolished slavery in the British colonies in 1838 (see Chapter 21). The most significant example of middle-class power came in the repeal of the Corn Laws in 1846. The Corn Laws (the British term for grain is *corn*) protected British landowners and farmers from foreign competition by establishing tariffs for imports, and they kept bread prices high. The middle class increasingly saw this as an unfair protection of the aristocracy and pushed for their repeal in the name of free trade. The Anti-Corn Law League held meetings throughout the north of England and lobbied Parliament, eventually resulting in a repeal of the law and a free-trade policy that lasted until the 1920s.

British Radicalism and the Chartist Movement

Reformers disappointed with the narrow gains of 1832 pushed for expanded political reforms. Their attention focused on a petition known as the "People's Charter," which contained six demands: universal white male suffrage, a secret ballot, an end to property qualifications as a condition of public office, annual parliamentary elections, salaries for members of the House of Commons, and equal electoral districts. The Chartists organized committees across the country, and the charter was eventually signed by millions.

Chartism spread in a climate of economic hardship during the 1840s. The movement tapped into local traditions of worker self-help, but the Chartists often disagreed about tactics and goals. Should Irish Catholics be included in the movement or excluded as dangerous competitors? Should women be included in the franchise?

THE GREAT CHARTIST RALLY OF APRIL 10, 1848. The year 1848 brought revolution to continental Europe and militant protest to England. This photo shows the April rally in support of the Chartists' six points, which included expanding the franchise, abolishing property qualifications for representatives, and instituting a secret ballot.

Analyzing Primary Sources

Women in the Anti-Corn Law League, 1842

Members of the Anti-Corn Law League sought to repeal the protectionist laws that prohibited foreign grain from entering the British market. The laws were seen as an interference with trade that kept bread prices artificially high, benefiting British landowners and grain producers at the expense of the working population. The campaign to repeal the Corn Laws enlisted many middle-class women in its ranks, and some later campaigned for woman suffrage. This article, hostile to the reform, deplored women's participation in the reform movement.

We find that the council of the Manchester Anti-Corn Law Association had invited the inhabitants to "an *anti-Corn-law tea-party,* to be held on the 20th of May, 1841—gentlemen's tickets, 2s.; ladies 1s. 6d." . . . [L]adies were advertised as *stewardesses* of this assembly. So now the names of about 300 Ladies were pompously advertised as the *Patroness* and *Committee* of the *National Bazaar.* We exceedingly wonder and regret that the members of the Association . . . and still more that anybody else, should have chosen to exhibit their wives and daughters in the character of political agitators; and we most regret that so many ladies—modest, excellent, and amiable persons we have no doubt in their domestic circles—should have been persuaded to allow their names to be *placarded* on such occasions—for be it remembered, this Bazaar and these *Tea-parties* did not even pretend to be for any *charitable* object, but entirely for the purposes of *political agitation*. . . .

We have before us a letter from Mrs. Secretary Woolley to one body of workmen. . . . She "appeals to them to stand forth and denounce as *unholy,* unjust, and cruel all restrictions on the food of the people." She acquaints them that "the ladies are resolved to perform *their* arduous part in the attempt to *destroy a monopoly* which, for *selfishness* and its *deadly* effects, has no parallel in the history of the world." "We therefore," she adds, "ask you for contributions. . . ." Now surely . . . not only should the *poorer classes* have been exempt from such unreasonable solicitations, but whatever subscriptions might be obtainable from the wealthier orders should have been applied, not to *political agitation* throughout England, but to charitable relief at home.

Source: J. Croker, "Anti-Corn Law Legislation," *Quarterly Review* (December 1842), as cited in Patricia Hollis, ed., *Women in Public: The Women's Movement 1850–1900* (London: 1979), p. 287.

Questions for Analysis

1. Why does the article highlight the participation of women in the Anti-Corn Law Association? What does this argument tell us about attitudes toward women's political activity?

2. Does the article actually mention any of the arguments in favor of repealing the Corn Laws? What alternative to repeal does the article appear to support?

The Chartist William Lovett, a cabinetmaker, was a fervent believer in self-improvement and advocated a union of educated workers that could claim its fair share of the nation's increasing industrial wealth. The Chartist Feargus O'Connor appealed to the more impoverished and desperate class of workers by attacking industrialization and the resettlement of the poor on agricultural allotments. Chartist James Bronterre O'Brien shocked the crowds by openly expressing his admiration for Robespierre and attacking "the big-bellied, little-brained, numbskull aristocracy." Chartism had many faces, but the movement's common goal was social justice through political democracy.

In spite of the Chartists' efforts to present massive petitions to the Parliament in 1839 and 1842, the Parliament rejected them both times. Members of the movement resorted to strikes, trade union demonstrations, and attacks on factories and manufacturers who imposed low wages and long hours or who harassed unionists. The movement peaked in April 1848. Inspired by revolutions in continental Europe (see Chapter 21), the Chartists' leaders planned a major demonstration in London. Twenty-five thousand workers carried to Parliament a petition with 6 million signatures. Confronted with the specter of class conflict, special constables and regular army units were marshaled by the aged Duke of Wellington to resist any threat to public order. In the end, only a small delegation presented the petition, and rain and an unwillingness to do battle with the constabulary put an end to the Chartist movement. A relieved liberal observer, Harriet Martineau, observed, "From that day it was a settled matter that England was safe from revolution."

THE POLITICS OF SLAVERY AFTER 1815

These political conflicts within nations about citizenship, sovereignty, and equality were also linked to a transnational debate about slavery and its legitimacy, which was taking place at the same time. When the age of revolution opened in the 1770s, slavery was legal everywhere in the Atlantic world. By 1848, slavery remained legal only in the southern United States, Brazil, and Cuba. (It endured, too, in most of Africa and parts of India and the Islamic world.) Given the importance of slavery to the Atlantic economy, this was a remarkable shift. The debate about slavery was fundamental, because it challenged the defenders of citizenship rights to live up to the claims of universality that had been a central part of Enlightenment political thought. If "all men" were "created equal," how could some be enslaved?

Slavery, Enlightenment, and Revolution

In fact, the revolutions of the eighteenth century by no means brought emancipation in their wake. Eighteenth-century Enlightenment thinkers had persuaded many Europeans that slavery contradicted natural law and natural freedom (see Chapter 17). As one historian trenchantly puts it, however, "Slavery became a metaphor for everything that was bad—except the institution of slavery itself." Thus, Virginia planters who helped lead the American Revolution angrily refused to be "slaves" to the English king while at the same time defending plantation slavery. The planters' success in throwing off the British king expanded their power and strengthened slavery.

Likewise, the French revolutionaries denounced the tyranny of a king who would "enslave" them but refused to admit free people of color to the revolutionary assembly for fear of alienating the planters in the lucrative colonies of Martinique, Guadeloupe, and Saint-Domingue. Only a slave rebellion in Saint-Domingue in 1791 forced the French revolutionaries, eventually, to contend with the contradictions of revolutionary policy. Napoleon's failure to repress that rebellion allowed for the emergence of Haiti in 1804 (see Chapter 18). The Haitian Revolution sent shock waves through the Americas, alarming slave owners and offering hope to slaves and former slaves. In the words of a free black sailmaker in Philadelphia, the Haitian nation signaled that black people "could not always be detained in their present bondage."

Yet the revolution in Haiti had other, contradictory consequences. The "loss" of slave-based sugar production in the former Saint-Domingue created an opportunity for its expansion elsewhere, in Brazil, where slavery expanded in the production of sugar, gold, and coffee, and in the American South. Slavery remained intact in the French, British, and Spanish colonial islands in the Caribbean, backed by the Congress of Vienna in 1815.

The Slow Path to Abolition

An abolitionist movement did emerge, in England. The country that ruled the seas was "the world's leading purchaser and transporter of African slaves," and the movement aimed to abolish that trade. From the 1780s on, pamphlets and books (the best known is *The Interesting Narrative of the Life of Olaudah Equiano,* 1789) detailed the horrors of the slave ships to an increasingly sympathetic audience. Abolitionist leaders like William Wilberforce believed that the slave trade was immoral and hoped that banning it would improve conditions for the enslaved, though like most abolitionists Wilberforce did not want to foment revolt. In 1807, the reform movement compelled Parliament to pass a bill declaring the "African Slave Trade to be contrary to the principles of justice, humanity and sound policy" and prohibiting British ships from participating in it, effective 1808. The United States joined in the agreement; ten years later the Portuguese agreed to a limited ban on traffic north of the equator. More treaties followed, which slowed but did not stop the trade.

What roots did abolitionism tap? Some historians argue that slavery was becoming less profitable and that its decline made humanitarian concern easier to accept. Others argue that slavery was expanding: among other things, ships carried 2.5 million slaves to markets in the Americas in the four decades *after* the abolition of the slave trade.

Some historians believe economic factors undermined slavery. Adam Smith and his followers argued that free labor, like free trade, was more efficient. This was not necessarily the case, but such arguments still had an effect. Critics claimed slavery was wasteful as well as cruel. Economic calculations, however, did less to activate abolitionism than did a belief that the slave trade and slavery itself represented the arrogance and callousness of wealthy British traders, their planter allies, and the British elite in general. In a culture with high literacy and political traditions of activism, calls for "British liberty" mobilized many.

In England, and especially in the United States, religious revivals supplied much of the energy for the abolitionist movement. The hymn "Amazing Grace" was written by a former slave trader turned minister, John Newton, to describe his conversion experience and salvation. The moral and religious dimensions of the struggle made it acceptable for women, who would move from antislavery to the Anti-Corn Law League and, later, to woman suffrage. Finally, the issue spoke to laborers whose sometimes brutal working conditions and sharply limited political rights we have discussed in the previous chapters. To oppose slavery and to insist that labor should be dignified, honorable, and minimally free resonated broadly in the social classes accustomed to being treated as "servile." The issue, then, cut across material interests and class politics, and antislavery petitions were signed by millions in the 1820s and 1830s.

Slave rebellions and conspiracies to rebel also shook opinion, especially after the success of the Haitian Revolution (see Chapter 19). In 1800, slaves rebelled in Virginia; in 1811, there was an uprising in Louisiana; and in 1822, an alleged conspiracy took hold in South Carolina. The British colonies saw significant rebellions in the Barbados (1816); Demerara, just east of Venezuela (1823); and, most important, the monthlong insurrection in Jamaica (1831). All of these were ferociously repressed. Slave rebellions had virtually no chance of succeeding and usually erupted only when some crack in the system opened up: divisions within the white elite or the (perceived) presence of a sympathetic outsider. Still, these rebellions had important consequences. They increased slaveholders' sense of vulnerability and isolation. They polarized debate. Outsiders (in England or New England) often recoiled at the brutality of repression. Slave owners responded to antislavery sentiment much as Russian serf owners had responded to their critics, by insisting that slavery was vital to their survival, that emancipation of inferior peoples would sow chaos, and that abolitionists were dangerously playing with fire.

In Great Britain, the force of abolitionism wore down the defense of slavery. In the aftermath of the Great Reform Bill of 1832, Great Britain emancipated 800,000 slaves in its colonies—effective in 1838, after four years of "apprenticeship." In France, republicans took the strongest antislavery stance, and emancipation came to the French colonies when the revolution of 1848 brought republicans, however briefly, to power (see Chapter 21).

In Latin America, slavery's fate was determined by demographics, economics, and the politics of breaking away from the Spanish and Portuguese empires. In most of mainland Spanish America (in other words, not Cuba or Brazil), slavery had been of secondary importance, owing to the relative ease of escape and the presence of other sources of labor. As the struggles for independence escalated, nationalist leaders recruited slaves and free people of

FEAR OF SLAVE VIOLENCE. This cartoon, published in Britain in 1789 in opposition to the movement to end slavery, played on public fears of the consequences of abolition. The former slaves, dressed in the fashionable attire of the landed gentry, dine at their former master's table, and beat the master in retaliation for what they have suffered. In the background, other former slave owners are stooped in labor in the cane fields. By the logic of this cartoon, such a reversal was intolerable, and given the choice between "Abolition" and "Regulation" (the two heads at the bottom) the cartoonist chose "Regulation" as the wiser course.

color to fight against the Spanish, promising emancipation in return. Simón Bolívar's 1817 campaign to liberate Venezuela was fought in part by slaves, ex-slaves, and 6,000 troops from Haiti. The new nations in Spanish America passed emancipation measures in stages but had eliminated slavery by the middle of the century.

Cuba was starkly different: with 40 percent of its population enslaved, the Spanish island colony had almost as many slaves as all of mainland Spanish America together. A Cuban independence movement would have detonated a slave revolution, a fact that provided a powerful incentive for Cuba to remain under the Spanish crown. Spain, for its part, needed the immensely profitable sugar industry and could not afford to alienate Cuban planters pushing for an end to slavery. Only a combination of slave rebellion in Cuba and liberal revolution in Spain brought abolition, beginning in the 1870s. Brazil too was 40 percent enslaved and, like Cuba, had a large population of free people of color. Unlike Cuba, Brazil won national independence, breaking away from Portugal with relative ease (1822). Like the American South, Brazil came through the revolution for independence with slavery not only intact but expanding, and slavery endured in Brazil until 1888.

TAKING SIDES: NEW IDEOLOGIES IN POLITICS

Debates about citizenship, sovereignty, and slavery made it clear that issues raised by the French Revolution were very much alive in Europe after 1815. The Congress of Vienna was able to place the Bourbon family back on the throne in France, but it could not make debates about popular sovereignty, national independence, or the authority of conservative dynastic regimes go away. Throughout Europe, political actors increasingly understood themselves to be facing a choice. If the debate about political change after the French Revolution was one between groups holding incompatible worldviews, then winning meant imposing your vision of the world on your opponents by any means necessary. Such assumptions naturally encouraged extremists on all sides of the debate. On the other hand, if disputing groups could come to some kind of mutual understanding about the goals of political association, then some compromise or middle way might be possible. It was within this context that modern political ideologies of conservatism, liberalism, socialism, and nationalism began to come into clearer focus.

Early nineteenth-century politics did not have parties as we know them today. But more clearly defined groups and competing doctrines, or ideologies, took shape during this time. An ideology may be defined as a coherent system of thought that claims to represent the workings and structure of the social order and its relationship to political powers and institutions. Ideologies consciously compete with other views of how the world is or should be, and their defenders seek to establish their views as dominant. The roots of conservatism, liberalism, and nationalism lay in earlier times, but ongoing political battles about the legacy of the French Revolution brought them to the fore. The Industrial Revolution (see Chapter 19) and the social changes that accompanied it proved a tremendous spur to political and social thought and led to the development of socialism as a political and social project. Would the advance of industry yield progress or misery? What were the "rights of man," and who would enjoy them? Did equality necessarily go hand in hand with liberty? A brief survey of the political horizon will show how different groups formulated their responses to these questions and will dramatize how the ground had shifted since the eighteenth century.

Principles of Conservatism

At the Congress of Vienna and in the Restoration generally, the most important guiding concept was legitimacy. Legitimacy had broad appeal as a general antirevolutionary policy. It might be best understood as a code word for a new political order that the Congress sought to impose. Conservatives aimed to make legitimate—and thus to solidify—both the monarchy's authority and the hierarchical social order undermined by the French Revolution. The most thoughtful conservatives of the period did not believe that the old order would survive completely intact or that time could be reversed, especially after the events of the 1820s made it clear that the Restoration would be challenged. They did believe, however, that the monarchy guaranteed political stability, that the nobility were the rightful leaders of the nation, and that both needed to play active and effective roles in public life. They insisted that, as a matter of strategy, the nobility and the crown shared a common interest, despite their disagreements in the past. Conservatives believed that change had to be slow, incremental, and managed so as to strengthen rather than weaken the structures of authority. Conserving the past and cultivating tradition would ensure an orderly future.

Edmund Burke's writings became a point of reference for nineteenth-century conservatives. His *Reflections on the*

Analyzing Primary Sources

Edmund Burke, *Reflections on the Revolution in France*

Edmund Burke's Reflections on the Revolution in France *was first published in 1790, while the French Revolution was still under way. Burke's opposition to revolutionary change had a profound influence on conservatives in the decades after the Congress of Vienna in 1815. The following passages contain Burke's defense of hereditary elites, his insistence on the power of tradition—here referred to as "convention"—and his criticism of the doctrine of natural rights.*

The power of perpetuating our property in our families is one of the most valuable and interesting circumstances belonging to it, and that which tends the most to the perpetuation of society itself. It makes our weakness subservient to our virtue; it grafts benevolence even upon avarice. The possessors of family wealth, and of the distinction which attends hereditary possession . . . are the natural securities for this transmission. With us, the house of peers is formed upon this principle. It is wholly composed of hereditary property and hereditary distinction; and made therefore the third of the legislature; and in the last event, the sole judge of all property in all its subdivisions. The house of commons too, though not necessarily, yet in fact, is always so composed in the far greater part. Let those large proprietors be what they will, and they have their chance of being amongst the best, they are at the very worst, the ballast in the vessel of the commonwealth. [. . .]

If civil society be the offspring of convention, that convention must be its law. That convention must limit and modify the descriptions of constitution which are formed under it. Every sort of legislative, judicial, or executor power are its creatures. They can have no being in any other state of things; and how can any man claim, under the conventions of civil society, rights which do not so much as suppose its existence? Rights which are absolutely repugnant to it? One of the first motives to civil society, and which becomes one of its fundamental rules, is *that no man should be judge in his own cause.* By this each person has at once divested himself of the first fundamental right of uncovenanted man, that is, to judge for himself, and to assert his own cause. He abdicates all right to be his own governor. He inclusively, in a great measure, abandons the right of self-defense, the first law of nature. Men cannot enjoy the rights of an uncivil and of a civil state together. That he may obtain justice he gives up his right of determining what it is in points the most essential to him. That he may secure some liberty, he makes a surrender in trust of the whole of it. [. . .]

Government is not made in virtue of natural rights, which may and do exist in total independence of it; and in a much greater degree of abstract perfection; but their abstract perfection is their practical defect. . . . The moment you abate anything from the full rights of men, each to govern himself, and suffer any artificial positive limitation upon those rights, from that moment the whole organization of government becomes a consideration of convenience. That is which makes the constitution of a state, and the due distribution of its powers, a matter of the most delicate and complicated skill. It requires a deep knowledge of human nature and human necessities, and of the things which facilitate or obstruct the various ends which are to be pursued by the mechanism of civil institutions. The state is to have recruits to its strength and remedies to its distempers. What is the use of discussing a man's abstract right to food or to medicine? The question is upon the method of procuring and administering them. In that deliberation I shall always advise to call in the aid of the farmer and the physician, rather than the professor of metaphysics.

Source: Edmund Burke, *Reflections on the Revolution in France* (London: J. Dodsley, 1791, 9th edition), pp. 75–76, 86–88, 89–90.

Questions for Analysis

1. Note that Burke does not defend hereditary elites with reference to God or a divinely inspired order. How does he justify the authority of the hereditary aristocracy?
2. What power does Burke grant to "convention" in the construction of the state and its laws?
3. What is Burke's principal complaint about revolutionaries who base their programs on "natural rights"?

Revolution in France was more influential in this new context than it had been during the 1790s, when it was first published. Burke did not oppose all change; he had argued, for instance, that the British should let the North American colonies go. But he opposed talk of natural rights, which he considered dangerous abstractions. He believed enthusiasm for constitutions to be misguided and the Enlightenment's emphasis on what he called the "conquering power of reason" to be dangerous. Instead, Burke counseled deference to experience, tradition, and history. Other conservatives, such as the French writers Joseph de Maistre (1753–1821) and Louis-Gabriel-Ambroise Bonald (1754–1840), penned carefully elaborated defenses of absolute monarchy and its main pillar of support, the Catholic Church. De Maistre, for instance, blamed the Enlightenment's critique of the Catholic Church for the French Revolution, and he assailed Enlightenment individualism for ignoring the bonds and collective institutions (the Church, for instance, or family) that he believed held society together. As conservatives saw it, monarchy, aristocracy, and the Church were the mainstays of the social and political order. Those institutions needed to stand together in face of the challenges of the new century.

Conservatism was not simply the province of intellectuals. A more broadly based revival of religion in the early nineteenth century also expressed a popular reaction against revolution and an emphasis on order, discipline, and tradition. What was more, conservative thinkers also exercised influence well beyond their immediate circle. Their emphasis on history, on the untidy and unpredictable ways in which history unfolded, and their awareness of the past became increasingly central to social thought and artistic visions of the first half of the century.

Liberalism

Liberalism's core was a commitment to individual liberties, or rights. Liberals believed that the most important function of government was to protect liberties and that doing so would benefit all, promoting justice, knowledge, progress, and prosperity. Liberalism had three components. First, liberalism called for equality before the law, which meant ending traditional privileges and the restrictive power of rank and hereditary authority. Second, liberalism held that government needed to be based on political rights and the consent of the governed. Third, with respect to economics, liberals believed that individuals should be free to engage in economic activities without interference from the state or their community.

The roots of legal and political liberalism lay in the late seventeenth century, in the work of John Locke, who had defended the English Parliament's rebellion against absolutism and the "inalienable" rights of the British people (see Chapter 15). Liberalism had been developed by the Enlightenment writers of the eighteenth century and was especially influenced by the founding texts of the American and French Revolutions (the Declaration of Independence and the Declaration of the Rights of Man). Freedom from arbitrary authority, imprisonment, and censorship; freedom of the press; the right to assemble and deliberate—these principles were the starting points for nineteenth-century liberalism. Liberals believed in individual rights, that those rights were inalienable, and that they should be guaranteed in written constitutions. (Conservatives, as we saw earlier, considered constitutions abstract and dangerous.) Most liberals called for constitutional as opposed to hereditary monarchy; all agreed that a monarch who abused power could legitimately be overthrown.

Liberals advocated direct representation in government—at least for those who had the property and public standing to be trusted with the responsibilities of power. Liberalism by no means required democracy. In the July Monarchy in France, established after the 1830 revolution, the property qualifications were so high that only 2 percent of the population could vote. Even after the Reform Bill of 1832 in England, only 18 percent of the population could vote for parliamentary representatives. Nineteenth-century liberals, with fresh memories of the French Revolution of 1789, were torn between their belief in rights and their fears of political turmoil. They considered property and education essential prerequisites for participation in politics. Wealthy liberals opposed extending the vote to the common people. To demand universal male suffrage was too radical, and to speak of enfranchising women or people of color even more so. As far as slavery was concerned, nineteenth-century liberalism inherited the contradictions of the Enlightenment. Belief in individual liberty collided with vested economic interests, determination to preserve order and property, and increasingly "scientific" theories of racial inequality (see Chapter 23).

Economic liberalism was newer. Its founding text was Adam Smith's *Wealth of Nations* (1776), which attacked mercantilism (the government practice of regulating manufacturing and trade to raise revenues) in the name of free markets. Smith's argument that the economy should be based on a "system of natural liberty" was reinforced by a second generation of economists and popularized in journals such as the *Economist,* founded in 1838. The economists (or political economists, as they were called) sought to identify basic economic laws: the law of supply and demand, the balance of trade, the law of diminishing returns, and so on. They argued that economic policy had to begin by recognizing these laws. David Ricardo (1772–1823) of Britain, for example, set out laws of wages and of rents, trying to determine the long-run outcomes of fluctuations in each.

Liberal political economists such as Smith and Ricardo believed that economic activity should be unregulated. Labor should be contracted freely, unhampered by guilds or unions, or state interference. Property should be unencumbered by feudal restrictions. Goods should circulate freely, which meant, concretely, an end to government-granted monopolies, trade barriers, import tariffs, and traditional practices of regulating markets, especially in valuable commodities such as grain, flour, or corn. At the time of the Irish famine, for instance, their writings played a role in hardening opposition to government intervention or relief (see Chapter 19). Liberal economists believed that the functions of the state should be kept to a minimum, though they also argued that markets could not function without states to preserve the rule of law and government's role was to preserve order and protect property but not to interfere with the natural play of economic forces, a doctrine known as *laissez-faire,* which translates, roughly, as "leave things to go on their own." This strict opposition to government intervention makes nineteenth-century liberalism different from common understandings of "liberalism" in the United States today.

ADAM SMITH POINTING TO HIS BOOK *THE WEALTH OF NATIONS* (1776). Smith was an Enlightenment thinker whose work was popularized in the nineteenth century, and he helped to establish "political economy," or economics.

Liberty and freedom meant different things in different countries. In lands occupied by other powers, liberal parties demanded freedom from foreign rule. The colonies of Latin America demanded liberty from Spain, and similar struggles set Greece and Serbia against the Ottoman Empire, northern Italy against the Austrians, Poland against Russian rule, and so on. In central and southeastern Europe, liberty meant eliminating feudal privilege and allowing at least the educated elite access to political power, more rights for local parliaments, and creating representative national political institutions. Some cited the British system of government as a model; others pointed to the French Declaration of the Rights of Man. Most shied away from the radicalism of the French Revolution. The issue was constitutional, representative government. In such countries as Russia, Prussia, and France under the restored Bourbon monarchy, liberty meant political freedoms, such as the right to vote, assemble, and print political opinions without censorship.

In Great Britain, where political freedoms were relatively well established, liberals focused on expanding the franchise, on laissez-faire economics and free trade, and on reforms aimed at creating limited and efficient government. In this respect, one of the most influential British liberals was Jeremy Bentham (1748–1832). Bentham's major work, *The Principles of Morals and Legislation* (1789), illustrates how nineteenth-century liberalism continued the Enlightenment legacy and also transformed it. Unlike, for instance, Smith, Bentham did not believe that human interests were naturally harmonious or that a stable social order could emerge naturally from a body of self-interested individuals. Instead he proposed that society adopt the organizing principle of utilitarianism. Social institutions and laws (an electoral system, for instance, or a tariff) should be measured according to their social usefulness—according to whether they produced the "greatest happiness of the greatest number." If a law passed this test, it could remain on the books; if it failed, it should be jettisoned. Utilitarians acknowledged the importance of the individual. Each individual best understood his or her own interests and was, therefore, best left free, whenever possible, to pursue those interests as he or she saw fit. Only when an individual's interests conflicted with the interests—the happiness—of the greatest number was individual freedom to be curtailed. The intensely practical spirit of utilitarianism enhanced its influence as a creed for reform. In his personal political views, Bentham went further than many liberals—he befriended Jacobins and believed in granting equal rights for women. Nevertheless, his rationalist approach to measuring the "utility" of laws and reforms nevertheless was an essential contribution to the liberal tradition.

Radicalism, Republicanism, and Early Socialism

The liberals were flanked on their left by two radical groups: republicans and socialists. Whereas liberals advocated a constitutional monarchy (in the name of stability and keeping power in the hands of men of property), republicans, as their name implies, pressed further, demanding a government by the people, an expanded franchise, and democratic participation in politics. The crucial distinction between the more moderate liberals and radical republicans, therefore, depended on the criteria they used for defining citizenship. Both groups believed that government should have the consent of citizens, but liberals were more likely to support restricted qualifications for citizenship, such as property ownership or the amount of taxes paid. Republicans were more committed to political equality and advocated more open definitions of citizenship, regardless of wealth or social standing. In thinking about the legacy of the French Revolution, therefore, liberals were likely to look favorably on the attempts by the National Assembly to create a constitution between 1789 and 1791. Republicans sympathized more openly with the Jacobins of the French Republic after 1792. Likewise, liberals remained suspicious of direct democracy and "mob rule" and sought constitutional measures that would allow propertied elites to exert their control over the political process and maintain social order. Radical republicans, on the other hand, were more likely to support civil militias, free public education, and civic liberties such as a free press and the right to assemble. In the debates between liberals and republicans, however, a general consensus about gender remained uncontroversial: only a very few liberals or republicans supported allowing women to vote. The virtues necessary for citizenship—rationality, sobriety, and independence of mind—were assumed by nearly all political thinkers of the period to be essentially masculine traits.

Where liberals called for individualism and laissez-faire, and republicans emphasized direct democracy and political equality, socialists pointed out that giving men the

QUADRILLE DANCING AT NEW LANARK, ROBERT OWEN'S MODEL COMMUNITY. Owen's Scottish experiment with cooperative production and community building, including schooling for infants, was only one of many utopian ventures in early-nineteenth-century Europe and North America.

Past and Present

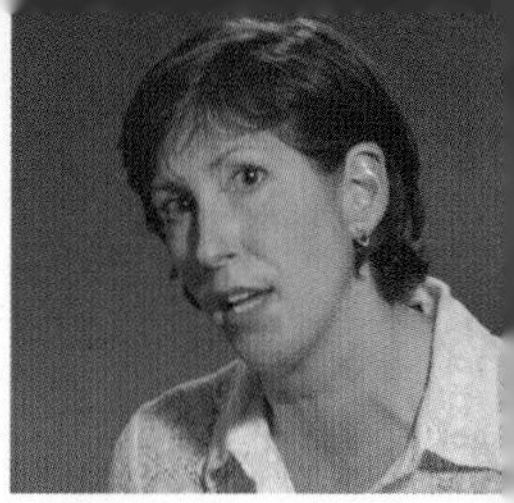

Revolts Against Reason

After the French Revolution, confidence in the power of reason and social progress was diminished in some quarters: many conservatives were skeptical about human improvement and some radicals, including the Saint-Simonians in France (left), sought a different kind of community and a different future than one solely based on rationality. Some of these cultural movements proved enduring and persist today in novel but recognizable forms, such as the "back-to-nature" movement of the 1960s (right).

Watch related author interview on StudySpace
wwnorton.com/web/westernciv18

vote would not necessarily eradicate other persistent forms of injustice and inequality. To put it in the terms that were used at the time, socialists raised the "social question." How could the growing economic inequalities produced by industrialization and the miseries of working people be remedied? This "social" question, socialists insisted, was an urgent political matter. Socialists offered varied responses to this question and different ways of redistributing economic and social power. These solutions ranged from cooperation and new ways of organizing everyday life to collective ownership of the means of production; some were speculative, others very concrete.

Socialism was a nineteenth-century system of thought and a response in large measure to the visible problems ushered in by industrialization: the intensification of labor, the poverty of working-class neighborhoods in industrial cities, and the widespread perception that a hierarchy based on rank and privilege had been replaced by one based on social class. For the socialists, the problems of industrial society were not incidental; they arose from the core principles of competition, individualism, and private property. The socialists did not oppose industry and economic development. On the contrary, what they took from the Enlightenment was a commitment to reason and human progress. They believed society could be both industrial and humane.

These radical thinkers were often explicitly utopian. Robert Owen, a wealthy industrialist turned reformer, bought a large cotton factory at New Lanark in Scotland and proceeded to organize the mill and the surrounding town according to the principles of cooperation rather than those of profitability. New Lanark organized decent housing and sanitation, good working conditions, child care, free schooling, and a system of social security for the factory's workers. Owen advocated a general reorganization of society on the basis of cooperation and mutual respect, and he tried to persuade other manufacturers of the rightness of his cause. The Frenchman Charles Fourier, too, tried to organize utopian communities based on the abolition of the wage system, the division of work according to people's natural inclinations, the complete equality of the sexes, and collectively organized child care and household labor. The charismatic socialist Flora Tristan (1803–1844) toured France speaking to workers about the principles of cooperation and the equality of men and women. Numerous men and women followed like-minded leaders into experimental communities. That so many took utopian visions seriously is a measure of people's unhappiness with early industrialization and of their conviction that society could be organized along radically different lines.

Other socialists proposed simpler, practical reforms. Louis Blanc, a French politician and journalist, campaigned for universal male suffrage with an eye to giving working-class men control of the state. Instead of protecting private property and the manufacturing class, the transformed state would become "banker of the poor," extending credit to those who needed it and establishing "associations of production," a series of workshops governed by laborers that would guarantee jobs and security for all. Such workshops were established, fleetingly, during the French Revolution of 1848. So were clubs promoting women's rights. Pierre-Joseph Proudhon (1809–1865) also proposed establishing producers' cooperatives, which would sell goods at a price workers could afford; working-class credit unions; and so on. Proudhon's "What Is Property?"—to which the famous answer was "Property is theft"—became one of the most widely read socialist pamphlets, familiar to artisans, laborers, and middle-class intellectuals, including Karl Marx. As we will see, a period of economic depression and widespread impoverishment in the 1840s brought the socialists many more working-class followers.

KARL MARX, 1882. Despite the unusual smile in this portrait, Marx was near the end of his life, attempting to recuperate in Algeria from sickness and the deaths of his wife and daughter.

Karl Marx's Socialism

The father of modern socialism, Karl Marx (1818–1883), was barely known in the early nineteenth century. His reputation rose later, after 1848, when a wave of revolutions and violent confrontation seemed to confirm his distinctive theory of history and make earlier socialists' emphasis on cooperation, setting up experimental communities, and peaceful reorganization of industrial society seem naive.

Marx grew up in Trier, a city in the Rhineland close to the French border, in a region and a family keenly interested in the political debates and movements of the revolutionary era. His family was Jewish, but his father had converted to Protestantism to be able to work as a lawyer. Marx studied law briefly at the University of Berlin before turning instead to philosophy and particularly the ideas of Georg Wilhelm Friedrich Hegel. With the so-called Young Hegelians, a group of rebellious students who chafed under the narrow thinking of a deeply conservative Prussian university system, Marx appropriated some of Hegel's concepts for his radical politics. His radicalism (and atheism, for he repudiated all his family's religious affiliations) made it impossible for him to get a post in the university. He became a journalist, writing now-famous articles on, for instance, peasants "stealing" wood from forests that used to be common land. From 1842 to 1843 he edited the liberal *Rhineland Gazette* (*"Rheinische Zeitung"*). The paper's criticism of legal privilege and political repression put it on a collision course with the Prussian government, which closed it down and sent Marx into exile—first in Paris, then Brussels, and eventually London.

While in Paris, Marx studied early socialist theory, economics, and the history of the French Revolution. He also began a lifelong intellectual and political partnership with Friedrich Engels (1820–1895). Engels was the son of a textile manufacturer from the German Rhineland and had been sent to learn business with a merchant firm in Manchester, one of the heartlands of England's Industrial Revolution (see Chapter 19). Engels worked in the family business until 1870, but this did not prevent him from taking up his pen to denounce the miserable working and living conditions in Manchester and what he saw as the systematic inequalities of capitalism (*The Condition of the Working Classes in England,* 1844). Marx and Engels joined a small international group of radical artisans called the League of the Just, in 1847 renamed the Communist League. The league asked Marx to draft a statement of its principles, published in 1848 as *The Communist Manifesto,* with Engels listed as a coauthor.

The Communist Manifesto laid out Marx's theory of history in short form. From Hegel, Marx imported the view of history as a dynamic process, with an inner logic, moving toward human freedom. (This is a good example of the larger influence of conservative historical thinking.) In Hegel's view, the historical process did not unfold in any simple and predictable way. Instead history proceeded "dialectically," or through conflict. Hegel saw the conflict as one between ideas: a "thesis" produced an "antithesis," and the clash between the two created a distinctive and new "synthesis." In a classic example, Hegel posited that the natural but limited freedom of the savage (thesis) encountered its opposite (antithesis) in the constraints imposed on the individual by the family and by the developing institutions of civil society. The result of this clash was a new and superior freedom (synthesis), the freedom of individuals in society, protected by moral customs, law and the state.

Marx applied Hegel's dialectic, or theory of conflict, to history in a different way. He did not begin with ideas, as Hegel had, but rather with the material social and economic forces. According to this materialist vision, world history had passed through three major stages, each characterized by conflict between social groups or "classes" whose divisions were linked to the underlying economic order: master versus slave in ancient slavery, lord versus serf in feudalism, and bourgeois capitalist versus proletariat (industrial laborer) in capitalism. For Marx, this "class struggle" was the motor of human history. He believed that the feudal stage of history, where an aristocratic class dominated the enserfed peasantry, had ended in 1789, with the French Revolution. What followed was a new order, dominated by an entrepreneurial middle class—he called them "bourgeois"—who built the world of industrial capitalism.

In *The Communist Manifesto,* Marx and Engels admired the revolutionary accomplishments of capitalism, saying that the bourgeoisie had "created more impressive and more colossal productive forces than had all preceding generations together." But, they argued, the revolutionary character of capitalism would also undermine the bourgeois economic order. As capital became more concentrated in the hands of the few, a growing army of wageworkers would become increasingly aware of its economic and political disenfranchisement. This struggle between competing classes was central to industrial capitalism itself. Eventually, *The Communist Manifesto* predicted, recurring economic crises, caused by capitalism's unending need for new markets and the cyclical instability of overproduction, would bring capitalism to collapse. Workers would seize the state, reorganize the means of production, abolish private property, and eventually create a communist society based on egalitarian principles. In other words, this ultimate revolution would abolish the division of labor altogether, ending the class conflict that had been the motor of history and ushering in a future whose outlines Marx could only hesitantly describe.

What was distinctive about Marx's version of socialism? It took up the disparity between public proclamations of progress and workers' daily experiences in a systematic, scholarly manner. Marx was an inexhaustible reader and thinker, with an extraordinarily broad range. He took insights where he found them: in British economics, French history, and German philosophy. He wove others' ideas that labor was the source of value and that property was expropriation into a new theory of history that was also a thoroughgoing critique of nineteenth-century liberalism. Most important, he differed from his utopian socialist predecessors by identifying industrial laborers as a revolutionary class and by linking revolution to a vision of human history as a whole. Because the Marxist view of history began with assumptions about the economic or material base of society, and because he borrowed the idea of the dialectic from Hegel, his theory of history is sometimes referred to as *dialectical materialism*.

Citizenship and Community: Nationalism

Of all the political ideologies of the early nineteenth century, nationalism is most difficult to grasp. What, exactly, counted as a nation? Who demanded a nation, and what did their demand mean? In the early nineteenth century, nationalism was usually aligned with liberalism against the conservative states that dominated Europe after Napoleon's fall. As the century progressed, however, it became increasingly clear that nationalism could be molded to fit any doctrine.

The meaning of *nation* has changed over time. The term comes from the Latin verb *nasci,* "to be born," and suggests "common birth." In sixteenth-century England,

Competing Viewpoints

Karl Marx and Pierre-Joseph Proudhon, *Correspondence*

Karl Marx was both a prolific political and economic theorist and a political militant who corresponded with socialists and other political radicals throughout Europe. Along with Friedrich Engels, Marx was the author of The Communist Manifesto *(1848), a widely circulated polemical critique of the capitalist economic system, which predicted the emergence of a revolutionary movement led by Europe's industrial working classes. This exchange of letters with a prominent French socialist thinker, Pierre-Joseph Proudhon, reveals disagreements among socialists in Europe about the desirability of revolution, as well as Marx's ideas about how intellectuals such as himself might participate in the revolutionary movement.*

Brussels, 5 May 1846

My dear Proudhon,

. . . I have made arrangements with the German communists and socialists for a constant interchange of letters which will be devoted to discussing scientific questions, and to keeping an eye on popular writings, and the socialist propaganda that can be carried on in Germany by this means. The chief aim of our correspondence, however, will be to put the German socialists in touch with the French and English socialists; to keep foreigners constantly informed of the socialist movements that occur in Germany and to inform the Germans in Germany of the progress of socialism in France and England. In this way differences of opinion can be brought to light and an exchange of ideas and impartial criticism can take place. It will be a step made by the social movement in its *literary* manifestation to rid itself of the barriers of *nationality*. And when the moment for action comes, it will clearly be much to everyone's advantage to be acquainted with the state of affairs abroad as well as at home.

Our correspondence will embrace not only the communists in Germany, but also the German socialists in Paris and London. Our relations with England have already been established. So far as France is concerned, we all of us believe that we could find no better correspondent than yourself. As you know, the English and Germans have hitherto estimated you more highly than have your own compatriots.

So it is, you see, simply a question of establishing a regular correspondence and ensuring that it has the means to keep abreast of the social movement in the different countries, and to acquire a rich and varied interest, such as could never be achieved by the work of one single person. . . .

Yours most sincerely

Karl Marx

the nation designated the aristocracy, or those who shared noble birthright. The French nobility also referred to itself as a nation. Those earlier and unfamiliar usages are important. They highlight the most significant development of the late eighteenth and early nineteenth centuries: the French Revolution redefined *nation* to mean "the sovereign people." The revolutionaries of 1789 boldly claimed that the nation, and no longer the king, was the sovereign power. *Vive la nation,* or "long live the nation"—a phrase found everywhere, from government decrees to revolutionary festivals, engravings, and memorabilia—celebrated a new political community, not a territory or

Lyon, 17 May 1846

My dear Monsieur Marx,

I am happy to become a recipient of your correspondence, whose goal and organization seem to me to be very useful. I cannot promise to write you at length or often, however, as my many occupations and my natural laziness will not permit such epistolary efforts. I would also like to take the liberty of expressing several reservations about a few of the passages in your letter.

First, [. . .] I believe that it is my duty, and the duty of all socialists, to maintain for the time being a skeptical or critical perspective, in a word, I claim [in matters of economics] an almost absolute anti-dogmatism.

Let us search together, if you wish, the laws of society, and the ways that these laws make themselves felt, and the process of development that allows us to discover them; but by God, after having demolished all the *a priori* dogmatisms, let us not dream of then indoctrinating the people ourselves, do not fall into the same contradiction faced by your compatriot Martin Luther, who after having overthrown Catholic theology, set about at once excommunicating others, in order to found a Protestant theology. [. . .] I applaud with all my heart your idea of bringing forth all possible opinions; let us therefore pursue a good and loyal argument; let us offer the world an example of a wise and perceptive toleration, but we should not, simply because we are the leaders of a movement, seek to pose as the apostles of a new religion, even if this religion is that of logic, of reason. Under these terms, I am happy to join your association, but if not—then No!

I would also like to comment on these words in your letter: *At the moment of action.* You may still think that no reform is possible at present without a bold stroke, without what was formerly called a revolution [. . .] Having myself held this opinion for a long time, I confess now that my more recent works have made me revisit this idea completely. I believe that we do not need [a revolution] to succeed, because this alleged solution would simply be an appeal to force, to something arbitrary, in short, a contradiction. I see the problem like this: *to find a form of economic combination that would restore to society the wealth that has been taken from it by another form of economic combination.* In other words, [. . .] to turn Property against Property, in such a way as to establish what you German socialists call *community*, and which I limit myself to calling *liberty, equality*. [. . .] I prefer to burn Property with a slow fuse, rather than to give it new energy by massacring the property owners.

Your very devoted
Pierre-Joseph Proudhon

Source: Karl Marx, Frederick Engels, *Collected Works*, vol. 38 (New York: International Publishers, 1982), pp. 38–40. P.-J. Proudhon, Amédée Jérôme, *Correspondance de P.-J. Proudhon* (Paris: A. Lacroix, 1875), pp. 198–200.

Questions for Analysis

1. What is the purpose of the network of correspondents that Marx was inviting Proudhon to join, and why did he believe it necessary to overcome "the barriers of nationality"?
2. Why does Proudhon compare Marx's analysis of "scientific questions" or "the laws of society" to religious dogmas?
3. Why does Proudhon reject Marx's assumption that a revolution is necessary, and what alternative does he propose?

an ethnicity. Philosophically, the French revolutionaries and the others who developed their views took from Jean-Jacques Rousseau the argument that a regenerated nation, based on the equality of its members (or on the limits of that equality; see Chapter 18), was not only more just but also more powerful. On a more concrete level, the revolutionaries built a national state, a national army, and a national legal system whose jurisdiction trumped the older regional powers of the nobility and local courts. In the aftermath of the French Revolution of 1789, the nation became what one historian calls "the collective image of modern citizenry."

MAJOR EUROPEAN LANGUAGE GROUPS, c. 1850. Compare the distribution of language groups in Europe with the political boundaries of European nations in 1848. ▪ ***Do they line up?*** ▪ ***Which political units were forced to deal with a multitude of languages within their borders?*** ▪ ***How might this distribution of language groups be related to the history of European nationalisms?***

In the early nineteenth century, then, *nation* symbolized legal equality, constitutional government, and unity, or an end to feudal privileges and divisions. Conservatives disliked the term. National unity and the creation of national political institutions threatened to erode the local power of aristocratic elites. New nations rested on constitutions, which, as we have seen, conservatives considered dangerous abstractions. Nationalism became an important rallying cry for liberals across Europe in the early nineteenth century precisely because it was associated with political transformation. It celebrated the achievements and political awakening of the common people.

Nationalism also went hand in hand with liberal demands for economic modernity. Economists, such as the influential German Friedrich List (1789–1846), sought to develop national economies and national infrastructures:

larger, stronger, better integrated, and more effective systems of banking, trade, transportation, production, and distribution. List linked ending the territorial fragmentation of the German states and the development of manufacturing to "culture, prosperity, and liberty."

Nationalism, however, could easily undermine other liberal values. When liberals insisted on the value and importance of individual liberties, those committed to building nations replied that their vital task might require the sacrifice of some measure of each citizen's freedom. The Napoleonic army, a particularly powerful symbol of nationhood, appealed to conservative proponents of military strength and authority as well as to liberals who wanted an army of citizens.

Nineteenth-century nationalists wrote as if national feeling were natural, inscribed in the movement of history. They waxed poetic about the sudden awakening of feelings slumbering within the collective consciousness of a "German," an "Italian," a "French," or a "British" people. This is misleading. National identity (like religious, gender, or ethnic identities) developed and changed historically. It rested on specific nineteenth-century political and economic developments; on rising literacy; on the creation of national institutions such as schools or the military; and on the new importance of national rituals, from voting to holidays, village festivals, and the singing of anthems. Nineteenth-century governments sought to develop national feeling, to link their peoples more closely to their states. State-supported educational systems taught a "national" language, fighting the centrifugal forces of traditional dialects. Italian became the official language of the Italian nation, despite the fact that only 2.5 percent of the population spoke it. In other words, even a minority could define a national culture. Textbooks and self-consciously nationalist theater, poetry, and painting helped elaborate and sometimes "invent" a national heritage.

Political leaders associated the nation with specific causes. But ordinary activities, such as reading a daily newspaper in the morning, helped people imagine and identify with their fellow citizens. As one influential historian puts it, "All communities larger than primordial villages of face-to-face contact (and perhaps even these) are imagined." The nation is imagined as "limited," "sovereign," and "finally, it is imagined as a community, because regardless of the actual inequality and exploitation that may prevail . . . , the nation is always conceived as a deep, horizontal comradeship." The different meanings of *nationhood,* the various political beliefs it evoked, and the powerful emotions it tapped made nationalism exceptionally unpredictable.

Eventually, conservatives, liberals, and republicans all implicitly recognized the power of nationalism by attempting to describe a vision of the nation that was compatible with their core principles. Conservatives linked dynastic ruling families and aristocratic elites to "national" traditions embodied in the history of territorially rooted peasant cultures and their traditional rulers. Liberals and republicans praised the nation as a body of free citizens. Marxist socialists, on the other hand, rejected the claims of nationalists, saying that the interest of social classes trumped national identity. The resolutely internationalist message of *The Communist Manifesto* was embodied in its concluding motto: "Workers of the world unite!"

Conservatism, liberalism, republicanism, socialism, and nationalism were the principal political ideologies of the early nineteenth century. They were rooted in the eighteenth century but brought to the forefront by the political turmoil of the early nineteenth century. Some nineteenth-century ideologies were continuations of the French revolutionary trio: liberty (from arbitrary authority), equality (or the end of legal privilege), and fraternity (the creation of new communities of citizens). Others, like conservatism, were reactions against the French Revolution. All could be reinterpreted. All became increasingly common points of reference as the century unfolded.

CULTURAL REVOLT: ROMANTICISM

Romanticism, the most significant cultural movement in the early nineteenth century, touched all the arts and permeated politics as well. It marked a reaction against the Classicism of the eighteenth century and the Enlightenment. Whereas Classicism aspired to reason, discipline, and harmony, Romanticism stressed emotion, freedom, and imagination. Romantic artists prized intense individual experiences and considered intuition and emotion to be better guides to truth and human happiness than reason and logic.

British Romantic Poetry

Romanticism developed first in England and Germany as a reaction against the Enlightenment. Early Romantics developed ideas originating from some of the Enlightenment's dissenters, such as Jean-Jacques Rousseau (see Chapter 17). The poet William Wordsworth (1770–1834) took up Rousseau's central themes—nature, simplicity, and feeling—in his *Lyrical Ballads* (1798). For Wordsworth, poetry was "the spontaneous overflow of powerful feelings," and like Rousseau, he also emphasized the ties of compassion that bind all humankind, regardless of social class. "We have all of us one human heart," he wrote, "men who do not wear fine cloths can feel deeply." Wordsworth considered nature to be humanity's most trustworthy teacher and the source of true feeling. His poems were inspired by the wild hills and tumbledown cottages of England's Lake District. In "The Ruined Cottage," he quoted from the Scottish Romantic poet Robert Burns:

> Give me a spark of Nature's fire,
> 'Tis the best learning I desire . . .
> My muse, though homely in attire,
> May touch the heart.

Wordsworth's poetry, along with that of his colleague Samuel Taylor Coleridge (1772–1834), offered a key theme of nineteenth-century Romanticism: a view of nature that rejected the abstract mechanism of eighteenth-century Enlightenment thought. Nature was not a system to be dissected by science but the source of a sublime power that nourished the human soul.

The poet William Blake (1757–1827) sounded similar themes in his fierce critique of industrial society and the factories (which he called "dark satanic mills") that blighted the English landscape. Blake championed the individual imagination and poetic vision, seeing both as transcending the limits of the material world. Imagination could awaken human sensibilities and sustain belief in different values, breaking humanity's "mind-forged manacles." Blake's poetry paralleled early socialist efforts to imagine a better world. And like many Romantics, Blake looked back to a past in which he thought society had been more organic and humane.

English Romanticism peaked with the next generation of poets—Lord Byron (1788–1824); Percy Bysshe Shelley (1792–1822); and John Keats (1795–1821). Their lives and loves often appealed to readers as much as their writings. Byron was an aristocrat, rich, handsome, and defiant of convention. Poetry, he wrote, was the "lava of the imagination, whose eruption prevents an earthquake." His love affairs helped give Romantics their reputation as rebels against conformity, but they were hardly carefree. Byron treated his wife cruelly and drove her away after a year. Byron also rebelled against Britain's political leaders, labeling them corrupt and repressive. A Romantic hero, he defended working-class movements and fought in the war for Greek independence, during which he died of tuberculosis. Byron's friend Percy Shelley emphasized similar themes of individual audacity in his poem, *Prometheus*

***NEWTON* BY WILLIAM BLAKE, 1795.** Blake was also a brilliant graphic artist. Here, he depicts Sir Isaac Newton shrouded in darkness, distracted by his scientific calculations from the higher sphere of the imagination. Blake's image is a Romantic critique of Enlightenment science, for which Newton had become a hero.

Unbound (1820). Prometheus defied an all-powerful god, Zeus, by stealing fire for humanity and was punished by being chained to a rock while an eagle tore out his heart. The poem celebrated the title character as a selfless mythic hero, comparable to Christ in his willingness to sacrifice himself for others. Shelley himself in his correspondence described the play as a parable about revolutionary change, and the need to overthrow tyranny in the name of a new political ideal of struggle and hope, a sentiment captured in the play's closing lines:

> To suffer woes which Hope thinks infinite;
> To forgive wrongs darker than Death or Night;
> To defy Power, which seems omnipotent;
> To love, and bear; to hope till Hope creates
> From its own wreck the thing it contemplates;
> Neither to change nor falter nor repent
> This, like thy glory, Titan! is to be
> Good, great, and joyous, beautiful and free;
> This is alone Life, Joy, Empire, and Victory.

Women Writers, Gender, and Romanticism

No romantic work was more popular than Mary Shelley's *Frankenstein* (1818). Shelley was the daughter of radical celebrities—the philosopher William Godwin and the feminist Mary Wollstonecraft (see Chapter 17), who died as her daughter was born. Mary Godwin met Percy Shelley when she was sixteen, had three children by him before they were married, and published *Frankenstein* at twenty. The novel captured the Romantic critique of science and Enlightenment reason and tells the story of an eccentric doctor determined to find the secret of human life. Conducting his research on corpses and body parts retrieved from charnel houses, Dr. Frankenstein produced life in the form of a monster. The monster had human feelings but was overwhelmed by loneliness and self-hatred when his creator cast him out. Shelley told the story as a twisted creation myth, a study of individual genius gone wrong. The novel remains one of the most memorable characterizations in literature of the limits of reason and the impossibility of controlling nature.

The Romantic's belief in individuality and creativity led in several directions. It became a cult of artistic genius—of the "inexplicably and uniquely creative individual" who could see things others could not. It also led people to seek out experiences that would elicit intense emotions and spark their imagination and creativity, ranging from foreign travel to using opium. The Romantic style encouraged the daring to defy convention as did Lord Byron, the Shelleys, and the French writer George Sand (1804–1876). Sand, like Byron, cultivated a persona—in her case, by living as a woman writer, taking lovers at her pleasure, and wearing men's clothing.

Women played an important role in Romantic writing, and Romanticism stimulated new thinking about gender and creativity. It was common at the time to assert that men were rational and women emotional or intuitive. Many Romantics, like their contemporaries, accepted such gender differences as natural, and some exalted the superior moral virtues of women. Since Romanticism placed such value on the emotions as an essential part of artistic creation, however, some female writers or painters were able to use these ideas to claim a place for themselves in the world of letters

MARY SHELLEY'S *FRANKENSTEIN*. Perhaps the best-known work of Romantic fiction, *Frankenstein* joined the Romantic critique of Enlightenment reason with early-nineteenth-century ambivalence about science to create a striking horror story. Shelley (pictured at left, around the time she published *Frankenstein*) was the daughter of the philosopher William Godwin and the feminist Mary Wollstonecraft; she married the poet Percy Shelley. On the right is an engraving from the first illustrated edition (1831) by Theodore von Holst.

and the arts. Germaine de Staël (1766–1817), for example, emigrated from revolutionary France to Germany and played a key part in popularizing German Romanticism in France. The language of Romanticism allowed Madame de Staël to describe herself as a genius, by way of explaining her own subversion of social norms. Romantics such as Madame de Staël suggested that men too could be emotional and that feelings were a part of a common human nature shared by both sexes. For many literate middle-class people, the language of Romanticism gave them a way to express their own search for individual expression and feeling in writing—and in thinking—about love. In this way, Romanticism reached well beyond small circles of artists and writers into the everyday writing and thoughts of European men and women.

Romantic Painting

Painters carried the Romantic themes of nature and imagination onto their canvases (see ***Interpreting Visual Evidence*** on pages 682–83). In Great Britain, John Constable (1776–1837) and J. M. W. Turner (1775–1851) developed more emotional and poetic approaches to depicting nature. "It is the soul that sees," wrote Constable, echoing Wordsworth. Constable studied Isaac Newton and the properties of light but aimed to capture the "poetry" of a rainbow. Turner's intensely subjective paintings were even more unconventional. His experiments with brushstroke and color produced remarkable images. Critics assailed the paintings, calling them incomprehensible, but Turner merely responded, "I did not paint it to be understood." In France, Théodore Géricault (1791–1824) and Eugène Delacroix (1799–1863) produced very different paintings from Turner's, but like the English painter they too were preoccupied by subjectivity and the creative process. The poet Charles Baudelaire credited Delacroix with showing him new ways to see: "The whole visible universe is but a storehouse of images and signs. . . . All the faculties of the human soul must be subordinated to the imagination." These Romantic experiments prepared the way for the later development of modernism in the arts.

Romantic Politics: Liberty, History, and Nation

Victor Hugo (1802–1885) wrote that "Romanticism is only . . . liberalism in literature." Hugo's plays, poetry, and historical novels focused sympathetically on the experience of common people, especially *Notre Dame de Paris* (1831) and *Les Misérables* (1862). Delacroix's painting *Liberty Leading the People* gave a revolutionary face to Romanticism, as did Shelley's and Byron's poetry. In works such as these, political life was no longer the preserve of social elites, and the commoners in the street could embrace new freedoms with a violent passion that would have surprised the *philosophes,* with their emphasis on reasoned debate.

Yet Romantics could also be ardently conservative. French conservative François Chateaubriand's *Genius of Christianity* (1802) emphasized the primacy of religious emotions and feeling in his claim that religion was woven into the national past and could not be ignored without threatening the culture as a whole. The period, in fact, witnessed a broad and popular religious revival and a renewed interest in medieval literature, art, and architecture, all of which drew heavily on religious themes.

Early nineteenth-century nationalism took the Romantic emphasis on individuality and turned it into a faith in the uniqueness of individual cultures. Johann von Herder, among the most influential of nationalist thinkers, argued that civilization sprang from the culture of the common people, not from a learned or cultivated elite, as the *philosophes* had argued in the Enlightenment. Herder extolled the special creative genius of the German people, the *Volk*, and insisted that each nation must be true to its own particular heritage and history.

The Romantic's keen interest in history and the lives of ordinary people led to new kinds of literary and historical works. The brothers Grimm, editors of the famous collection of fairy tales (1812–1815), traveled across Germany to study native dialects and folktales. The poet Friedrich Schiller retold the story of William Tell (1804) to promote German national consciousness, but the Italian composer Gioacchino Rossini turned Schiller's poem into an opera that promoted Italian nationalism. In Britain, Sir Walter Scott retold the popular history of Scotland and the Pole Adam Mickiewicz wrote a national epic *Pan Tadeusz ("Lord Thaddeus")* as a vision of a Polish past that had been lost. After 1848, these nationalist enthusiasms would overwhelm the political debates that divided conservatives from liberals and socialists in the first half of the nineteenth century (see Chapter 21).

Orientalism

This passion for theories and histories of distinctive cultures also created broad interest in what contemporary Europeans called the "Orient"—a catch-all term used rather indiscriminately and confusedly to refer to the non-European cultures of North Africa, the eastern Mediterranean, the

Arabian Peninsula, and eventually to the vast and densely populated lands of southern and eastern Asia. Napoleon wrote, "This Europe of ours is a molehill. Only in the East, where 600 million human beings live, is it possible to found great empires and realize great revolutions." The dozens of scholars who accompanied Napoleon on his invasion of Egypt in 1798 collected information on Egyptian history and culture. Among the artifacts the French took from Egypt was the Rosetta Stone, with versions of the same text in three different languages: hieroglyphic writing (pictorial script), demotic (an early alphabetic writing), and Greek, which scholars used to decode and translate the first two. The twenty-three volume, lavishly illustrated *Description of Egypt*, published in French between 1809 and 1828, was a major event, heightening the soaring interest in Eastern languages and history. "We are now all orientalists," wrote Victor Hugo in 1829. The political echoes to this cultural fascination with the East could be seen in great power rivalries that surfaced in the British incursion into India, in the Greek war for independence, and in the French invasion of Algeria in 1830.

Nineteenth-century Europeans cast the "Orient" as a contrasting mirror for their own civilization, a process that did more to create a sense of their own identity as Europeans than it did to promote an accurate understanding of the diversity of cultures that lay beyond Europe's uncertain eastern and southern frontiers. During the Greek war for independence, Europeans identified with Greek heritage against Oriental despotism. Romantic painters such as Delacroix depicted the landscapes of the East in bold and sensuous colors and emphasized the sensuality, mystery, and irrationality of Eastern peoples. The fascination with medieval history and religion shared by many Romantic writers also bred interest in the medieval crusades in the Holy Lands of the Middle East—important subjects for Romantics such as Scott and Chateaubriand. These habits of mind, encouraged by Romantic literature and art, helped to crystallize a sense of what were felt to be essential differences between the East and the West.

***WOMEN OF ALGIERS* BY EUGÈNE DELACROIX.** This is one of many paintings done during Delacroix's trips through North Africa and a good example of the Romantics' Orientalism.

Goethe and Beethoven

Two important artists of the period are especially difficult to classify. Johann Wolfgang von Goethe (1749–1832) had an enormous influence on the Romantic movement with his early novel *The Passions of Young Werther* (1774), which told the story of a young man's failure in love and eventual suicide. The novel brought international fame to its young author, though many who sympathized with the main character perhaps missed the point about the self-destructiveness of the "cult of feeling." Rumors spread that some in his audience identified so strongly with Werther's alienation that they killed themselves in imitation. Though scholars now doubt that such suicides occurred, the rumor itself indicates the fascination that Goethe's emotionally complex character exerted over the reading public. The significance of the novel lay in Goethe's ability to capture in prose the longing that many middle-class readers felt for something more meaningful than a life lived in strict conformity with social expectations. It also revealed that a new sense of self and aspirations for self-fulfillment might be emerging in Europe alongside the narrower definitions of individualism that one might find in liberal political or economic theory. In his masterpiece, *Faust*, published in part in 1790 and finished just before his death in 1832, Goethe retold the German story of a man who sold his soul to the devil for eternal youth and universal knowledge. *Faust*, written in dramatic verse, was more Classical in its tone, though it still expressed a Romantic concern with spiritual freedom and humanity's daring in probing life's divine mysteries.

The composer Ludwig van Beethoven (1770–1827) was steeped in the principles of Classical music composition, but his insistence that instrumental music without vocal

Interpreting Visual Evidence

Romantic Painting

Romantic painters shared with Romantic poets a fascination with the power of nature. To convey this vision of nature as both an overwhelming power and source of creative energy, Romantic painters created new and poetic visions of the natural world, where human beings and their activities were reduced in significance, sometimes nearly disappearing altogether. At times, these visions also were linked to a backward-looking perspective, as if the dramatic changes associated with industrialization provoked a longing for a premodern past, where Europeans sought and found their sense of place in the world from an awareness of a quasi-divine natural setting invested with powerful mysteries. John Martin's *The Bard* (image A) shows a highly romanticized vision of a medieval subject: a single Welsh bard strides across rocky peaks above a mountain river, after escaping a massacre ordered by the English king Edward I. Across the river, Edward's troops can barely be seen leaving the scene of the crime, which still glows with destructive fires. The emotional qualities of this early expression of Romantic nationalism are reinforced by the forbidding and dynamic sky above, where the clouds merge into the Welsh mountaintops as if they were stirred by the hand of God himself.

A. John Martin, *The Bard*, 1817.

Other Romantic painters minimized the significance of human activity in their landscapes, though without reference to history. John Constable's *Weymouth Bay* (image B) contains a tiny, almost imperceptible human figure in the middle ground, a man walking on the beach, near a thin stone wall that snakes up a hill in the background. These passing references to human lives are completely dominated, however, by Constable's sky and the movement of the clouds in particular, which seem to be the real subject of the painting.

Of all the Romantic painters, J. M. W. Turner (image C) may have tackled the tricky subject of the new industrialized landscape in the most novel way. His painting *Rain, Steam, Speed–The Great Western Railway* (1844) boldly places the most modern technology of the period,

B. John Constable, *Weymouth Bay*, 1816.

C. J. M. W. Turner, *Rain, Steam, Speed–The Great Western Railway*, 1844.

the steam train on an arched bridge, into a glowing and radiant painting where both nature's forces and the tremendous new power unleashed by human activity seem to merge into one continuous burst of energy. To the left of the train, on the river's edge, a fire of indeterminate but evidently industrial origin burns, illuminating several small but ecstatic figures with its light. Most enigmatic of all, a tiny rabbit sprints ahead of the train between the rails (unfortunately invisible in this reproduction), highlighting the painting's complex message about nature and human creation. Are they heading in the same direction? Will one overtake the other and destroy it in the process?

Questions for Analysis

1. In Martin's *Bard*, what vision of the individual emerges from this painting, and how is it different from the rational, rights-bearing individual that political liberalism sought to protect?
2. Is Constable's painting concerned with nature as a source of nourishment for humans, or is it presented as a value in itself?
3. How is one to interpret Turner's explicit connection between the power of nature and the new force of industrial societies? Is he suggesting that contemplating the industrial landscape can be just as moving to a human observer as is the sight of nature's magnificence?

accompaniment could be more expressive of emotion made him a key figure for later Romantic composers. The glorification of nature and Romantic individuality rang clearly throughout his work. Like many of his contemporaries, Beethoven was enthusiastic about the French Revolution in 1789, but he became disillusioned with Napoleon. At the age of thirty-two he began to lose his hearing, and by 1819 he was completely deaf—the intensely personal crisis that this catastrophe produced in the young musician drove him to retreat into the interior of his own musical imagination, and the compositions of his later life expressed both his powerfully felt alienation as well as his extraordinary and heroic creativity in the face of enormous hardship.

Beethoven and Goethe marked the transition between eighteenth-century artistic movements that prized order and harmony to the turbulent and disruptive emotions of the nineteenth-century artists and writers. Their work embraced the cult of individual heroism, sympathized with the Romantic's quasi-mystical view of nature, and represented different aspects of a shared search for new ways of seeing and hearing. The many shapes of Romanticism make a simple definition of the movement elusive, but at the core, the Romantics sought to find a new way of expressing emotion, and in doing so, they sent nineteenth-century art in a new direction.

CONCLUSION

With the fizzling of the Chartist movement, the British monarchy avoided an outbreak of revolution in 1848. Monarchs on the Continent were not so lucky. As we will see in the next chapter, a wave of revolutionary activity unprecedented since the 1790s spread to nearly every capital in Europe in 1848. This resurgence of rebellion and revolt pointed to the powerful ways that the French Revolution of 1789 polarized Europe in the first half of the nineteenth century. In its aftermath, the Congress of Vienna aimed to establish a new conservative, international system and to prevent further revolutions. It succeeded in the first aim but only partially in the second. A combination of new political movements and economic hardship undermined the conservative order. Social grievances and political disappointments created powerful movements for change, first in Latin America and the Balkans and then in western Europe and Great Britain.

All of the contesting ideologies of these postrevolutionary decades could point to a longer history: conservatives could point to traditional religious justifications for royal authority and the absolutist's conception of indivisible monarchical power; liberals could point to the debates

After You Read This Chapter

Visit StudySpace for quizzes, additional review materials, and multimedia documents. **wwnorton.com/web/westernciv18**

REVIEWING THE OBJECTIVES

- The European leaders who met at the Congress of Vienna possessed a conservative vision for post–Napoleonic Europe. What were their goals and what challenges did their political system face between 1815 and 1848?
- Slavery persisted long after the French Revolution. What accounts for the development of an abolition movement, and why did it persist in the United States, Latin America, and Cuba?
- Conservatives, liberals, and republicans differed from one another about the lessons to be learned from the French Revolution, while socialists sought to address the inequalities produced by the Industrial Revolution. What were the core principles of conservatism, liberalism, republicanism, and socialism?
- Nationalism reshaped the political landscape in Europe between 1815 and 1848. How did conservatives, liberals, republicans, and socialists view the claims of nationalists?
- Romanticism was a cultural movement defined in opposition to the Enlightenment. Who were the Romantics and what did they believe?

about the rule of law in the English revolution of the seventeenth century; even socialists could point to age-old collective traditions among rural communities as precedents for their defense of communal property and egalitarianism. Nevertheless, all of these ideologies were shaped and brought into clearer focus during these decades by the combined effects of the French Revolution and industrialization. Conservatives may have differed among themselves as to why they preferred a government of monarchs and landed aristocrats, but they were united by their horror of revolutionary violence and dismayed by the social disruptions that attended industrialization. Liberals may have disagreed with each other about who qualified for citizenship, but they defended the revolutionary's insistence that the only legitimate government was one whose institutions and laws reflected the consent of at least some, if not all, of the governed. Many socialists, Marx included, celebrated the insurrectionary tradition of the French revolutionaries, even as they demanded a reordering of society that went far beyond the granting of new political rights to include a redistribution of society's wealth. Meanwhile, nationalists throughout Europe remained inspired by the collective achievements of the French nation that was forged in revolution in the 1790s.

The reemergence of social and political conflict in 1848 pit the defenders of these ideologies against one another under the most dramatic of circumstances, making the revolutions of 1848 the opening act of a much larger drama. In France, as in 1792 and 1830, revolutionaries rallied around an expanded notion of representative government and the question of suffrage, though they were divided on how much responsibility their new government had for remedying social problems. In southern and central Europe, as we will see in the next chapter, the issues were framed differently, around new struggles for national identity. The eventual failure of these revolutions set a pattern that was also observed elsewhere: exhilarating revolutionary successes were followed by a breakdown of revolutionary unity and the emergence of new forms of conservative government. The crisis of 1848 became a turning point for all of Europe. The broad revolutionary alliances that had pushed for revolutionary change since 1789 were broken apart by class politics, and earlier forms of utopian socialism gave way to Marxism. In culture as in politics, Romanticism lost its appeal, its expansive sense of possibility replaced by the more biting viewpoint of realism. No nationalist, conservative, liberal, or socialist was exempt from this bitter truth after the violent conflicts of 1848.

PEOPLE, IDEAS, AND EVENTS IN CONTEXT

- Who was **KLEMENS VON METTERNICH** and what was the **CONCERT OF EUROPE**?
- How did the **CARBONARI** in Italy, the **DECEMBRISTS** in Russia, and **GREEK NATIONALISTS** in the Balkans in the 1820s disturb the conservative order in Europe after Napoleon's defeat?
- Where did revolutions occur in 1830–1832, and what was their outcome?
- What political changes did movements such as the **CHARTISTS** or the **ANTI-CORN LAW LEAGUE** accomplish in Britain? Why was there no revolution in Britain?
- What beliefs made **EDMUND BURKE** a conservative?
- What beliefs made **ADAM SMITH** and **JEREMY BENTHAM** liberals? What was **UTILITARIANISM**?
- What beliefs did **UTOPIAN SOCIALISTS** such as **ROBERT OWEN** and **CHARLES FOURIER** share? What made **KARL MARX**'s brand of socialism different from his predecessors'?
- How did the values of **ROMANTICISM** challenge Europeans to reconsider their assumptions about the differences between men and women?
- What beliefs led romantic writers such as **WILLIAM WORDSWORTH**, **WILLIAM BLAKE**, and **LORD BYRON** to reject the rationalism of the Enlightenment and embrace emotion and imagination as the most essential and vital aspects of human experience?

THINKING ABOUT CONNECTIONS

- What new ideas about historical change made it possible to think in terms of a political conflict between "conservatives" and "revolutionaries" during the decades immediately before and after 1800? Would such an opposition have been conceivable in earlier periods of history?
- Terms such as *conservative*, *liberal*, and *socialist* are still used today in contemporary political debates. Do they still mean the same thing as they did between 1815 and 1848?

Before You Read This Chapter

STORY LINES

- In 1848, a wave of liberal and national revolutions demanded but failed to achieve lasting constitutions and elected parliaments in many European kingdoms. Instead, Europe's conservative monarchs found ways to harness the popular nationalism expressed in the 1848 revolutions to their own ends.
- The emergence of Germany and Italy as unified nation-states upset the European balance of power, as did the increasing weakness of the Ottoman Empire. The resulting wars benefited Germany and diminished the power of Austria-Hungary in central Europe.
- Russia, the United States, and Canada also went through an intense phase of nation building after 1850. Common to all three were the conquest of native peoples, the acquisition of new territories, and economic development. As in Europe, the process of nation building unleashed sectional conflicts and intense debates about citizenship, slavery (or serfdom, in Russia), and the power of the nation-state.

CHRONOLOGY

1834–1870	Unification of Germany
1848	Revolutions of 1848
1848	France and Denmark abolish slavery
1848	Treaty of Guadalupe Hidalgo
1848–1870	Unification of Italy
1853–1856	Crimean War
1861	Emancipation of the serfs, Russia
1861–1865	American Civil War
1871–1888	Brazilian emancipation

21

Revolutions and Nation Building, 1848–1871

CORE OBJECTIVES

- **EXPLAIN** why so many revolutions occurred nearly simultaneously in Europe in 1848.
- **UNDERSTAND** the causes and failure of the revolutions of 1848 in France.
- **DESCRIBE** the goals of revolutionaries in the German-speaking lands of central Europe and their relationship to the monarchies of Prussia and Austria.
- **IDENTIFY** the social groups that supported a process of national unification from below, by the people, in Italy and Germany and those that favored a process of national unification directed from the top, by the state.
- **DESCRIBE** the process of nation building in Russia and the United States in the nineteenth century and the ensuing debates about slavery.
- **IDENTIFY** the powers involved in the Crimean War, the Austro-Prussian War, and the Franco-Prussian War, and understand how these wars changed the balance of power in Europe.

The year 1848 was a tumultuous one. From Paris to Berlin, and Budapest to Rome, insurgents rushed to hastily built barricades, forcing kings and princes to beat an equally hasty—though only temporary—retreat. Perhaps the most highly symbolic moment came on March 13, 1848, when Klemens von Metternich, the primary architect of the Concert of Europe, was forced to resign as minister of state in the Austrian capital of Vienna while a revolutionary crowd outside celebrated his departure. Metternich's balanced system of international relations, where stability was guaranteed by reinforcing the legitimacy of traditional dynastic rulers against movements for reform, was swept aside in a wave of enthusiasm for liberal political ideals and popular anger. Metternich himself was forced to flee to England, which less than one month earlier had also welcomed King Louis-Philippe of France, after another revolution in France.

Metternich's downfall and the collapse of the French monarchy made clear that the 1848 revolutions were strongly linked to powerful forces for change unleashed earlier by the French Revolution. At the same time, however, this was also the year that Karl Marx and Friedrich Engels published *The Communist Manifesto*, which announced as its goal an even more sweeping remaking of society than that imagined by the French revolutionaries of 1789. If 1848 was the last wave of the revolutionary movements that began in Europe and the Atlantic world at the end of the eighteenth century, it was also the first chapter in a new revolutionary movement that would have enormous consequences in the twentieth century.

Revolutionary regime change, territorial expansion, economic development, and debates about who deserved citizenship: all of these were issues in 1848, and all were related to the spread of nationalism and nation building in Europe and the Americas. As we saw in the last chapter, the term *nation* had taken on a new meaning at the end of the eighteenth century and had come to mean "a sovereign people." *Nationalism* was a related political ideal, based on the assumption that governments could be legitimate only if they reflected the character, history, and customs of the nation—that is, the common people. This idea undermined the assumptions of Europe's dynastic rulers, as hereditary monarchs had emphasized the differences between themselves and the people they ruled. Kings and aristocrats often did not even speak the same language as their subjects. Nobody would have thought this odd before 1789, since peasants often spoke regional dialects that were different from the language spoken in cities. But once the notion of national sovereignty emanating from the people became widespread, such discrepancies between the language and culture of elites and of the common people loomed larger as political questions that needed to be solved. Intellectuals, revolutionaries, and governments all propagated the radical new idea that nations of like peoples and the states that ruled over them should be congruent with one another. This simple idea lay at the heart of all forms of nationalism, but there was often bitter debate about who best represented the nation and what the goals of a unified nationalist government should be.

Between 1789 and 1848, Europeans commonly associated nationalism with liberalism. Liberals saw constitutions, the rule of law, and elected assemblies as necessary expressions of the people's will, and they sought to use popular enthusiasm for liberal forms of nationalism against the conservative monarchs of Europe. The upheavals of 1848 marked the high point of this period of liberal revolution, and their failure marked the end of that age. By the end of the nineteenth century, conservative governments also found ways to mobilize popular support by invoking nationalist themes. The only political movement to swim against the tide of nationalism was that of the socialists, who stressed the importance of class unity across national boundaries: Marx and his followers believed that German, French, and British workers had more in common with each other than with their middle-class employers. Even so, however, socialist movements in Europe developed in distinctly different nationalist political contexts, making traditions of French socialism different from German socialism, or from Italian socialism, for example.

The years following the 1848 revolutions witnessed a shift in the connections between liberalism, nationalism, and nation building. In the United States, territorial changes such as the treaty of Guadalupe Hidalgo transformed the boundaries of nations; equally significant was the American Civil War, which resulted in wrenching political change. The unification of Germany and Italy in the years after 1848 also involved the conquest of territory, but the process could not have been completed without political reforms and new state structures that changed how governments worked and how they related to their citizens. The governments of France, Britain, Russia, and Austria undertook vast projects of administrative reform during this period: they overhauled their bureaucracies, expanded their electorates, and reorganized relations among ethnic groups. The Russian tsar abolished serfdom, and Abraham Lincoln, an American president, abolished slavery, decades after the French and British had prohibited slavery in their territories.

As the process of nation building continued, the balance of power in Europe shifted toward the states that were the earliest to industrialize and most successful in building strong, centralized states. Older imperial powers such as the Habsburg Empire in Austria-Hungary or the Ottoman Empire found their influence waning, in spite of their long history of successful rule over vast territories with diverse populations. At the heart of this nineteenth-century period of nation building lay changing relations between states and those they governed, and these changes were hastened by reactions to the revolutionary upheavals of 1848.

THE REVOLUTIONS OF 1848

Throughout Europe, the spring of 1848 brought a dizzying sequence of revolution and repression. The roots of revolution lay in economic crisis, social antagonisms, and political grievances. But these revolutions were also shaped decisively by nationalism, especially in southern, central, and eastern Europe. To be sure, reformers and revolutionaries had liberal goals: representative government, an end to privilege, economic development, and so on. They also sought some form of national unity. Indeed, reformers in Germany, Italy, Poland, and the Austrian Empire believed that their liberal goals might be realized only in a vigorous, "modern" nation-state. The fate of the 1848 revolutions in these regions demonstrated nationalism's power to mobilize opponents of the regime and also its potential to splinter revolutionary alliances and to override other allegiances and values entirely.

The Hungry Forties

A deteriorating economic climate in Europe was an important contributing factor to the outbreak of revolution in 1848, one that helps to explain why revolutions occurred in so many places nearly simultaneously. Poor harvests in the early 1840s were followed by two years in 1845–46 when the grain harvest failed completely. A potato blight brought starvation in Ireland and hunger in Germany (see ***Competing Viewpoints*** on pages 690–91). Food prices doubled in 1846–47, and bread riots broke out across Europe. Villagers attacked carts carrying grain, refusing to let merchants take it to other markets. At times, hungry people seized the grain and forced the merchants to sell it at what they thought was a "just" price. Compounding the problem was a cyclical industrial slowdown that spread across Europe, throwing thousands into unemployment. Starving peasants and unemployed laborers swamped public-relief organizations in many European cities. The years 1846 and 1847 were "probably the worst of the entire century in terms of want and human suffering," and the decade has earned the name the "Hungry Forties."

GERMAN CONFEDERATION, 1815. Compare this map with the one on page 714. ▪ ***What major areas were left out of the German Confederation?*** ▪ ***Why do you think they were left out?*** ▪ ***What obstacles made it difficult to establish a unified German nation during this period?***

Competing Viewpoints

Two Views of the June Days, France, 1848

These two passages make for an interesting comparison. The socialist Karl Marx reported on the events of 1848 in France as a journalist for a German newspaper. For Marx, the bloodshed of the June Days shattered the "fraternal illusions" of February 1848, when the king had been overthrown and the provisional government established. That bloodshed also symbolized a new stage in history: one of acute class conflict.

The French liberal politician Alexis de Tocqueville also wrote about his impressions of the revolution. (Tocqueville's account, however, is retrospective, for he wrote his memoirs well after 1848.) For Marx, a socialist observer, the June Days represented a turning point: "The working class was knocking on the gates of history." For Tocqueville, a member of the government, the actions of the crowd sparked fear and conservative reaction.

Karl Marx's Journalism

The last official remnant of the February Revolution, the Executive Commission, has melted away, like an apparition, before the seriousness of events. The fireworks of Lamartine [French Romantic poet and member of the provisional government] have turned into the war rockets of Cavaignac [French general, in charge of putting down the workers' insurrection]. *Fraternité,* the fraternity of antagonistic classes of which one exploits the other, this *fraternité,* proclaimed in February, on every prison, on every barracks—its true, unadulterated, its prosaic expression is civil war, civil war in its most fearful form, the war of labor and capital. This fraternity flamed in front of all the windows of Paris on the evening of June 25, when the Paris of the bourgeoisie was illuminated, whilst the Paris of the proletariat [Marxist term for the working people] burnt, bled, moaned. . . . The February Revolution was the beautiful revolution, the revolution of universal sympathy, because the antagonisms, which had flared up in it against the monarchy, slumbered peacefully side by side, still undeveloped, because the social struggle which formed its background had won only a joyous existence, an existence of phrases, of words. The June revolution is the ugly revolution, the repulsive revolution, because things have taken the place of phrases, because the republic uncovered the head of the monster itself, by striking off the crown that shielded and concealed it.—Order! was the battle cry of Guizot . . . Order! shouts Cavaignac, the brutal echo of the French National Assembly and of the republican bourgeoisie. Order! thundered his grape-shot, as it ripped up the body of the proletariat. None of the numerous revolutions of the French bourgeoisie since 1789 was an attack on order; for they allowed the rule of

Hunger itself cannot cause revolution. It does, however, test governments' abilities to manage a crisis, and failure can make a ruler seem illegitimate. When public relief foundered in France and troops repressed potato riots in Berlin, when regimes armed middle-class citizens to protect themselves against the poor, governments looked both authoritarian and inept. In the 1840s, European states already faced a host of political challenges: from liberals who sought constitutional government and limits on royal power, from republicans who campaigned for universal manhood suffrage, from nationalists who challenged the legitimacy of their hereditary rulers, and from socialists whose appeal lay in their claim to speak for the most economically vulnerable among the population. These political challenges were reinforced by the economic crisis of the 1840s, and the result was a wave of revolution that swept across Europe as one government after another lost the confidence of its people. The first of these revolutions came in France, and as elsewhere in 1848, it did not have the outcome that revolutionaries had hoped for.

the class, they allowed the slavery of the workers, they allowed the bourgeois order to endure, however often the political form of this rule and of this slavery changed. June has attacked this order. Woe to June!"

Source: *Neue Rheinische Zeitung* (New Rhineland Gazette), June 29, 1848, as cited in Karl Marx, *The Class Struggles in France* (New York: 1964), pp. 57–58.

Alexis de Tocqueville Remembers the June Days (1893)

Now at last I have come to that insurrection in June which was the greatest and the strangest that had ever taken place in our history, or perhaps in that of any other nation: the greatest because for four days more than a hundred thousand men took part in it, and there were five generals killed; the strangest, because the insurgents were fighting without a battle cry, leaders, or flag, and yet they showed wonderful powers of coordination and a military expertise that astonished the most experienced officers.

Another point that distinguished it from all other events of the same type during the last sixty years was that its object was not to change the form of government, but to alter the organization of society. In truth it was not a political struggle (in the sense in which we have used the word "political" up to now), but a class struggle, a sort of "Servile War." . . . One should not see it only as a brutal and a blind, but as a powerful effort of the workers to escape from the necessities of their condition, which had been depicted to them as an illegitimate depression, and by the sword to open up a road towards that imaginary well-being that had been shown to them in the distance as a right. It was this mixture of greedy desires and false theories that engendered the insurrection and made it so formidable. These poor people had been assured that the goods of the wealthy were in some way the result of a theft committed against themselves. They had been assured that inequalities of fortune were as much opposed to morality and the interests of society as to nature. This obscure and mistaken conception of right, combined with brute force, imparted to it an energy, tenacity and strength it would never have had on its own.

Source: From Alexis de Tocqueville, *Recollections: The French Revolution of 1848*, ed. J. P. Mayer and A. P. Kerr, trans. George Lawrence (New Brunswick, NJ: 1987), pp. 436–37.

Questions for Analysis

1. Was Tocqueville sympathetic to the revolutionaries of June?
2. Did Tocqueville think the events were historically significant?
3. Where did Tocqueville agree and disagree with Marx?

The French Revolution of 1848: A Republican Experiment

The French monarchy after the revolution of 1830 (see Chapter 20) seemed little different from its predecessor. King Louis Philippe gathered around him members of the banking and industrial elite. Confronted with demands to enlarge the franchise, the prime minister quipped that everyone was free to acquire enough property to qualify for the vote: "Enrich yourselves!" Building projects, especially the railway, presented ample opportunities for graft, and the reputation of the government suffered. Protest movements, in the form of republican societies, proliferated in French cities. In 1834, the government declared these organizations illegal. Rebellions broke out in Paris and Lyon, bringing a harsh repression that resulted in deaths and arrests. The government's refusal to compromise drove even moderates into opposition. In 1847, the opposition organized a campaign for electoral reform around repeated political "banquets"—an attempt to get around the laws against assembly. When they called for a giant banquet on February 22, 1848, the king responded by banning the meeting. A sudden and surprising popular revolution in the streets caused Louis Philippe to abdicate his throne only days later. A hastily assembled group of French political figures declared France a republic, for the first time since 1792.

The provisional government of the new republic consisted of liberals, republicans, and—for the first time—socialists. They produced a new constitution, with elections based on universal male suffrage. Among their first acts was the abolition of slavery in France and French colonies (slavery had been abolished in 1794 during the revolution but reestablished by Napoleon in 1802). In spite of these accomplishments, tensions between propertied republicans and socialists shattered the unity of the coalition that toppled Louis Philippe. Suffering because of the economic crisis, working men and women demanded the "right to work," the right to earn a living wage. The provisional government responded by creating the National Workshops, a program of public works, to give jobs to the unemployed, headed by the socialist Louis Blanc. Initial plans were made to employ 10,000–12,000 workers, but unemployment was so high that 120,000 job-seekers had gathered in the city by June 1848. Meanwhile, voters in rural areas resented the increase in taxation that was required to pay for the public works program.

***THE BURNING OF THE THRONE* (1848).** A contemporary print shows revolutionaries burning the king's throne. Note the man with a top hat standing next to a man in a worker's smock. Delacroix used similar images to depict cooperation between workers and middle-class revolutionaries (see page 661).

Popular politics flourished in Paris in 1848. The provisional government lifted restrictions on speech and assembly. One hundred seventy new journals and more than 200 clubs formed within weeks. Delegations claiming to represent the oppressed of Europe—Chartists, Hungarians, Poles—moved freely about the city. Women's clubs and newspapers appeared, demanding universal suffrage and living wages. Many middle-class Parisians were alarmed, and more conservative rural populations also looked for stern measures to restore order. When elections for parliament were held—the first elections ever in France under a regime of universal male suffrage—the conservative voices won out, and a majority of moderate republicans and monarchists were elected.

A majority in the new assembly believed the National Workshops were a financial drain and a threat to order. In May, they closed the workshops to new enrollment, excluded recent arrivals to Paris, and sent members between the ages of eighteen and twenty-five into the army. On June 21, they abolished the workshops altogether. In defense of this social program, the workers of Paris—laborers, journeymen, the unemployed—rose in revolt, building barricades across Paris. For four days, June 23–26, they fought a hopeless battle against armed forces recruited from the provinces. The repression of the June Days shocked many observers. About 3,000 were killed and 12,000 arrested. Many of the prisoners were deported to Algerian labor camps. After this repression, support for the republic among the workers in Paris declined rapidly.

In the aftermath, the government moved quickly to restore order. The parliament hoped for a strong leader in the presidential election. Four candidates ran: Alphonse de Lamartine, the moderate republican and poet; General Louis Eugène de Cavaignac, who had perfected the art of urban warfare in the conquest of Algeria and who used these skills in repressing the workers' revolt in Paris; Alexandre Ledru-Rollin, a socialist; and Louis Napoleon Bonaparte, the nephew of the former emperor, who had spent his life in exile. Buoyed by enthusiastic support from rural voters, the upstart Louis Napoleon polled more than twice as many votes as the other three candidates combined.

"All facts and personages of great importance in world history occur twice . . . the first time as tragedy, the second as farce." Karl Marx's judgment on Louis Napoleon's relationship to his famous uncle was shared by many, but his name gave him wide appeal. Conservatives believed

***BARRICADE IN THE RUE DE LA MORTELLERIE, JUNE, 1848* BY ERNEST MEISSONIER (1815–1891).** A very different view of 1848, a depiction of the June Days.

he would protect property and order. Some on the left had read his book *The Extinction of Pauperism* and noted his correspondence with important socialists. One old peasant put it succinctly, "How could I help voting for this gentleman—I whose nose was frozen at Moscow?"

Louis Napoleon used his position to consolidate his power. He rallied the Catholics by restoring the Church to its former role in education and by sending an expedition to Rome to rescue the pope from revolutionaries (see Chapter 4). He banned radical activities, workers' associations, and suspended press freedoms. In 1851, he called for a plebiscite to give him the authority to change the constitution, and one year later another plebiscite allowed him to establish the Second Empire, ending the Republican experiment. He assumed the title of Napoleon III (r. 1852–70), emperor of the French.

The dynamics of the French Revolution of 1848—initial success, followed by divisions among the supporters of revolution, followed by a reassertion of authoritarian control—would be repeated elsewhere, especially evidenced in the pivotal role of the propertied middle classes. Louis Philippe's reign had been proudly bourgeois but alienated many of its supporters. Key groups in the middle class joined the opposition, allying with radicals who could not topple the regime alone. Yet demands for reform soon led to fears of disorder and the desire for a strong state. This dynamic led to the collapse of the republic and to the rule of Napoleon III. The abandonment of the revolution's social goals—most visibly evident in the National Workshops—led to a stark polarization along class lines, with middle-class and working-class people demanding different things from the state. This political conflict would grow even more intense as socialism came into its own as an independent political force.

Nationalism, Revolution, and the German Question in 1848

The revolutions of 1848 in the German-speaking lands of Europe shared some similarities with the revolutions in France. Like liberals in France, liberal Germans wanted a ruler who would abide by a constitution, allow for greater press freedoms, and accept some form of representative government, though not necessarily universal suffrage. As in France, artisans and urban laborers in German cities gravitated toward more radical ideologies of republicanism and socialism, and protested against new methods of industrial production. More so than in France, German peasants still faced the burden of feudal obligations owed to an entrenched and powerful aristocracy. The great difference between France and Germany in 1848, however, was that France already had a centralized state and a unified territory. In central Europe, a unified Germany did not exist in 1848. In 1815, the Congress of Vienna had created the German Confederation, a loose organization of thirty-nine states, including Habsburg Austria with its Catholic monarchy, and Prussia, ruled by a Protestant king. The German Confederation did not include Prussian and Austrian territories in Poland and Hungary with large non-German populations. This confederation was intended to provide only common defense. It had no real executive power. As a practical matter, Prussia and Austria competed with one another to occupy the dominant position in German politics, and as a result revolutionaries in the German states were forced to reckon with these two powers as they struggled to achieve the national unity that they hoped would allow them to achieve their political goals.

In 1806, Prussia had been defeated by the French under Napoleon. Many Prussians considered the defeat an indictment of the country's inertia since the reign of Frederick the Great (r. 1740–86). Aiming to revive "patriotism and a national honor and independence," they passed a series of aggressive reforms, imposed from above. Prussian reformers reconstituted the army, following the Napoleonic example. Officers were recruited and promoted on the basis of merit rather than birth, although the large majority continued to come from the Junker class. Other reforms modernized training at the royal cadet school in Berlin and encouraged the middle class to take a more active role in the civil service. In 1807, serfdom and the estate system were abolished. A year later, in a conscious attempt to increase middle-class Germans' sense of themselves as citizens, cities and towns were allowed to elect their councilmen and handle their own finances. (Justice and security continued to be administered by the central government in Berlin.) The Prussian reformers expanded facilities for both primary and secondary education and founded the University of Berlin, which numbered among its faculty several ardent nationalists.

Prussia aimed to establish itself as the leading German state and a counter to Austrian power in the region. Prussia's most significant victory in this respect came with the *Zollverein*, or customs union, in 1834, which established free trade among the German states and a uniform tariff against the rest of the world—an openly protectionist policy advocated by the economist Friedrich List. By the 1840s, the union included almost all of the German states except German Austria and offered manufacturers a market of almost 34 million people. The spread of the railways after 1835 accelerated exchange within this expanded internal market.

During the 1840s, in both Prussia and the smaller German states, political clubs of students and other radicals joined with middle-class groups of lawyers, doctors, and businessmen to press new demands for representative government and reform. Newspapers multiplied, defying censorship. Liberal reformers resented both Prussian domination of the German Confederation and the conservatism of the Habsburgs, who ruled the Austrian Empire. They attacked the combination of autocracy and bureaucratic authority that stifled political life in Prussia and Austria. German nationhood, they reasoned, would break Austrian or Prussian domination and end the sectional fragmentation that made reform so difficult.

When Frederick William IV (r. 1840–61) succeeded to the Prussian throne in 1840, hopes ran high. The new king did gesture toward liberalizing reforms. When economic troubles hit in the 1840s, however, Frederick William asserted firmly that his authority could not be questioned by his subjects. He sent the army to crush a revolt among the textile weavers of Silesia, who were protesting British imports and, more generally, unemployment, falling wages, and hunger. The brutality of the regime's response shocked many. The king also opposed constitutionalism and any representative participation in issues of legislation and budgets—like the "enlightened" absolutists who preceded him, the Prussian king firmly believed that his leadership did not need assistance from elected legislatures or from civil society as a whole.

As in France, liberals and radicals in Prussia and the German states continued their reform campaigns. And when revolution came to France in the spring of 1848, unrest spread across the Rhine. In the Catholic south German state of Bavaria, a student protest forced King Ludwig I to grant greater press freedoms, and when revolutionary movements appeared elsewhere in the smaller German states, kings and princes yielded surprisingly quickly. The governments promised elections, expanded suffrage, jury

"EYES OPEN!" (c. 1845). This German cartoon from just before the 1848 revolution warns that aristocrats and clergy are conspiring to deny the German people their rights. The caption reads "Eyes Open! Neither the nobility nor the clergy shall oppress us any longer. For too long they have broken the backs of the people." ■ ***Did supporters of the revolution consider the aristocracy or the clergy to be legitimate members of the nation? Compare the cartoon with the pamphlet of Abbé Sieyès in the French Revolution (see page 586).***

Past and Present

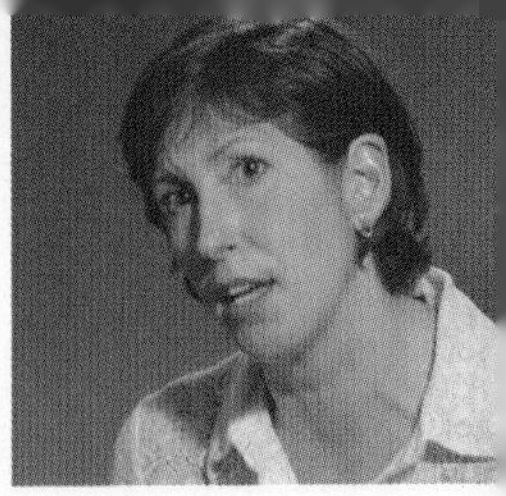

Germany's Place in Europe

The unification of Germany under Prussian leadership in 1870 (left) destabilized the balance of power in Europe. World War I and World War II confirmed for many people the dangers of a strong German state. The history of European integration after 1945 nevertheless depended on rebuilding Germany and binding it more closely to its European neighbors. In spite of recent troubles in the European Union, including a financial crisis that threatened the euro currency (right), this history remains one of the great success stories of late-twentieth-century Europe.

Watch related author interview on StudySpace
wwnorton.com/web/westernciv18

trials, and other liberal reforms. In Prussia, Frederick William, shaken by unrest in the countryside and stunned by a showdown in Berlin between the army and revolutionaries in which 250 were killed, promised to grant a constitution and met with representatives of the protest movement.

The Frankfurt Assembly and German Nationhood

The second and most idealistic stage of the revolution began with the election of 800 delegates to an all-German assembly in Frankfurt, where representatives from Prussia, Austria, and the small German states met to discuss creating a unified German nation. Most of the delegates came from the professional classes—lawyers, professors, administrators—and most were moderate liberals. Their views were not as radical as those of the workers and artisans who had led the street protests against the king. The delegates assumed that the Frankfurt Assembly would draft a constitution for a liberal, unified Germany, much as an assembly of Frenchmen had done for their country in 1789. The comparison was mistaken. In 1789, a French nation-state and a centralized sovereign power already existed, to be reformed and redirected by the assembled French delegates. By contrast, the Frankfurt Assembly had no resources, no sovereign power to take, no single legal code, and, of course, no army.

On the assembly floor, questions of nationality proved contentious and destructive. Which Germans would be in the new state? A majority of the assembly's delegates argued that Germans were all those who, by language, culture, or geography, felt themselves bound to the enterprise of unification. They believed the German nation should include as many Germans as possible—a position encouraged by the

Analyzing Primary Sources

Frederick William IV Refuses the Throne

In March 1849, after months of deliberation and constitution making, the Frankfurt Assembly offered the throne of its proposed German state to the Prussian monarch Frederick William IV, who quickly turned it down. He had already reflected on the matter. In an earlier (December 1848) letter to one of his advisers, the diplomat Christian von Bunsen, he had set out his reasoning as follows.

I want the princes' approval of neither *this* election nor *this* crown. Do you understand the words emphasized here? For you I want to shed light on this as briefly and brightly as possible. First, *this* crown is no crown. The crown which a Hohenzoller [the Prussian royal house] could accept, *if* circumstances *permitted,* is not one *made* by an assembly sprung from a revolutionary seed in the genre of the crown of cobble stones of Louis Philippe—even if this assembly was established with the sanction of princes . . . but one which bears the stamp of God, one which makes [the individual] on whom it [the crown] is placed, after his anointment, a "divine right" monarch—just as it has elevated more than 34 princes to Kings of the Germans by divine right and just as it bonds the last of these to his predecessors. The crown worn by Ottonians, Staufens [earlier German royal houses], Habsburgs can of course also be worn by a Hohenzoller; it honors him overwhelmingly with the luster of a thousand years. But *this* one, to which you regrettably refer, overwhelmingly dishonors [its bearer] with its smell of the gunpowder of the 1848 revolution—the silliest, dumbest, worst, though—thank God!—not the most evil of this century. Such an imaginary headband, baked out of dirt and the letters of the alphabet, is supposed to be welcome to a legitimate divine right king: to put it more precisely, to the King of Prussia who is blessed with a crown which may not be the oldest but, of all those which have never been stolen, is the most noble? . . . I will tell you outright: if the thousand-year-old crown of the German nation . . . should be bestowed again, it will be *I* and my equals who will bestow it. And woe to those who assume [powers] to which they have no title.

Source: Ralph Menning, *The Art of the Possible: Documents on Great Power Diplomacy, 1814–1914* (New York: 1996), p. 82.

Questions for Analysis

1. For Frederick William IV, what was the only legitimate source of a monarch's authority?
2. Why did he call the crown offered to him by the Frankfurt Assembly a "crown of cobble stones . . . with its smell of gunpowder of the 1848 revolution"?
3. Frederick William referred to himself by his family name, Hohenzollern, and to his title, king of Prussia, but he also used the expression "German nation" once in his letter. What relationship did he see among his family, the kingdom of Prussia, and the possibility of a unified German nation?

spectacle of disintegration in the Habsburg Empire. This was the "Great German" position. It was countered by a minority who called for a "Small Germany," one that left out all lands of the Habsburg Empire, including German Austria. Great Germans had a majority but were stymied by other nationalities unwilling to be included in their fold. Many Czechs in Bohemia, for instance, wanted no part of Great Germany, believing that they needed the protection of the Habsburg monarchy to avoid being swallowed up by a new German state on one side and the Russian monarchy on the other. After a long and difficult debate, the Austrian emperor withdrew his support, and the assembly retreated to the Small German solution. In April 1849, the Frankfurt Assembly offered the crown of a new German nation to the Prussian king, Frederick William IV.

By this time, however, Frederick William was negotiating from a position of greater strength. Already in the fall of 1848, he had used the military to repress the radical revolutionaries in Berlin while the delegates debated the constitutional question in Frankfurt. He was also encouraged by a backlash against revolutionary movements in Europe after the bloody repression during the June Days

THE FRANKFURT PREPARLIAMENT MEETS AT ST. PAUL'S CHURCH, 1848. This assembly brought together 500 delegates from the various German states to establish a constitution for a new German nation. An armed militia lined the square, and lines of student gymnasts (dressed in white with wide-brimmed hats) escorted the delegates. Their presence was a sign that the organizers of the preparliament feared violence. The black, red, and gold banners were also associated with republicanism. ▪ ***What image did the organizers mean to convey with this pageantry, the disciplined lines of students and delegates, their forms of dress, and their use of republican symbols?***

in Paris. He therefore refused to become a constitutional monarch on the terms offered by the Frankfurt Assembly. The proposed constitution, he said, was too liberal and receiving his crown from a parliament would be demeaning. The Prussian monarch wanted both the crown and a larger German state, but on his own terms, and he therefore dissolved the assembly before they could approve it with an official vote. After brief protests, summarily suppressed by the military, the Frankfurt delegates went home, disillusioned by their experience and convinced that their liberal and nationalist goals were incompatible. Some fled repression by immigrating to the United States. Others convinced themselves to sacrifice their liberal views for the seemingly realistic goal of nationhood. In Prussia itself, the army dispatched what remained of the revolutionary forces.

Elsewhere in the German-speaking states as popular revolution was taking its own course, many moderate liberals began to have second thoughts about the pace of change. Peasants ransacked tax offices and burned castles; workers smashed machines in protests against industrialization. In towns and cities, citizen militias formed, threatening the power of established elites. New daily newspapers multiplied. So did political clubs. For the first time, many of these clubs admitted women (although they denied them the right to speak), and newly founded women's clubs demanded political rights. This torrent of popular unrest made moderate reformers uneasy; they considered universal manhood suffrage too radical. While peasant and worker protests had forced the king to make concessions in the early spring of 1848, moderate reformers now found those protests threatening. Throughout the German states, rulers took advantage of this shift in middle-class opinion to undo the concessions that they had granted in 1848 and to push through counterrevolutionary measures in the name of order.

For German liberals, national unification was now seen as necessary to maintain political stability. "In order to realize our ideas of freedom and equality, we want above all a strong and powerful government," claimed one candidate during the election campaigns for the Frankfurt Assembly. Popular sovereignty, he continued, "strengthened by the authority of a hereditary monarchy, will be able to repress with an iron hand any disorder and any violation of the law." In this context, nationhood stood for a new constitution and political community but also for a sternly enforced rule of law. After the failure of the Frankfurt Assembly, therefore, German liberals increasingly looked to a strong Prussian state as the only possible route toward national unification.

Peoples against Empire: The Habsburg Lands

In the sprawling Habsburg (Austrian) Empire, nationalism played a different role. On the one hand, the Habsburg emperors could point to a remarkable record of political success: as

"NO PIECE OF PAPER WILL COME BETWEEN MYSELF AND MY PEOPLE" (1848). In this cartoon, Frederick William IV and a military officer refuse to accept the constitution for a new Germany offered to him by the Frankfurt Assembly. Note that the caption refers to a conservative definition of the relationship between a monarch and "his people." Compare this autocratic vision of the nation-state with the liberal nationalist's demand for a government that reflects the people's will. ▪ ***What contrasting visions of the nation and its relation to the state are contained in this cartoon?***

HUNGARIAN REVOLUTIONARY LAJOS KOSSUTH, 1851. A leader of the Hungarian nationalist movement who combined aristocratic style with rabble-rousing politics, Kossuth almost succeeded in an attempt to separate Hungary from Austria in 1849.

heir to the medieval Holy Roman Empire, Habsburg kings had ruled for centuries over a diverse array of ethnicities and language groups in central Europe that included Germans, Czechs, Magyars, Poles, Slovaks, Serbs, and Italians, to name only the most prominent. In the sixteenth century, under Charles V, the empire had included Spain, parts of Burgundy, and the Netherlands. In the nineteenth century, however, the Habsburgs found it increasingly difficult to hold their empire together as the national demands of the different peoples in the realm escalated after 1815. Whereas the greater ethnic and linguistic homogeneity of the German-speaking lands allowed for a convergence between liberal ideas of popular sovereignty and national unification, no such program was possible in the Habsburg Empire. Popular sovereignty for peoples defined in terms of their ethnic identity implied a breakup of the Habsburg lands.

At the same time, however, the existence of nationalist movements did not imply unity, even within territories that spoke the same language. In the Polish territories of the empire, nationalist sentiment was strongest among aristocrats, who were especially conscious of their historic role as leaders of the Polish nation. Here, the Habsburg Empire successfully set Polish serfs against Polish lords, ensuring that social grievances dampened ethnic nationalism. In the Hungarian region, national claims were likewise advanced by the relatively small Magyar aristocracy. (*Hungarian* is a political term; *Magyar,* which was often used, refers to the Hungarians' non-Slavic language.) Yet they gained an audience under the gifted and influential leadership of Lajos (Louis) Kossuth (*KAW-shut*). A member of the lower nobility, Kossuth was by turns a lawyer, publicist, newspaper editor, and political leader. To protest the closed-door policy of the empire's barely representative Diet (parliament), Kossuth published transcripts of parliamentary debates and distributed them to a broader public. He campaigned for independence and a separate Hungarian parliament, but he also (and more influentially) brought politics to the people. Kossuth staged political "banquets" like those in France, at which local and national personalities made speeches in the form of toasts and interested citizens could eat, drink, and participate in politics. The Hungarian political leader combined aristocratic style with rabble-rousing politics: a delicate balancing act but one that, when it worked, catapulted him to the center of Habsburg politics. He was as well known in the Habsburg capital of Vienna as he was in Pressburg and Budapest.

The other major nationalist movement that troubled the Habsburg Empire was pan-Slavism. Slavs included Russians, Poles, Ukrainians, Czechs, Slovaks, Slovenes, Croats, Serbs, Macedonians, and Bulgarians. Before 1848, pan-Slavism was primarily a cultural movement united by a general pro-Slavic sentiment. It was internally divided, however, by the competing claims of different Slavic languages and traditions. Pan-Slavism inspired the works of the Czech historian and political leader, František Palacký, author of the *History of the Bohemian People*, and the Slovak Jan Kollár, whose book *Salvy Dcera* (*"Slava's Daughter"*) mourned the loss of identity among Slavs in the Germanic world. The movement also influenced the Polish Romantic poet Adam Mickiewicz (*mihtz-KYAY-vihch*), who sought to rekindle Polish nationhood against foreign oppression.

The fact that Russia and Austria were rivals in eastern Europe made pan-Slavism a volatile and unpredictable political force in the regions of eastern Europe where the two nations vied for power and influence. Tsar Nicholas of Russia sought to use pan-Slavism to his advantage, making arguments about "Slavic" uniqueness part of his "autocracy, orthodoxy, nationality" ideology after 1825. Yet the tsar's Russian-sponsored pan-Slavism alienated Western-oriented Slavs who resented Russia's ambitions. Here, as elsewhere, nationalism created a tangled web of alliances and antagonisms.

Austria and Hungary in 1848: Springtime of Peoples and the Autumn of Empire

The empire's combination of political, social, and ethnic tensions came to the point of explosion in 1848. The opening salvo came from the Hungarians. Emboldened by uprisings in France and Germany, Kossuth stepped up his reform campaigns, pillorying the "Metternich system" of Habsburg autocracy and control, demanding representative institutions throughout the empire and autonomy for the Hungarian Magyar nation. The Hungarian Diet prepared to draft its own constitution. In Vienna, the seat of Habsburg power, a popular movement of students and artisans demanding political and social reforms built barricades and attacked the imperial palace. A Central Committee of Citizens took shape, as did a middle-class militia, or national guard, determined at once to maintain order and to press demands for reform. The Habsburg regime tried to shut the movement down by closing the university, but that only unleashed more popular anger. The regime found itself forced to retreat almost entirely. Metternich, whose political system had weathered so many storms, fled to Britain in disguise—a good indication of the political turmoil—leaving the emperor Ferdinand I in Vienna. The government conceded to radical demands for male suffrage and a single house of representatives. It agreed to withdraw troops from Vienna and to put forced labor and serfdom on a path to abolition. The government also yielded to Czech demands in Bohemia, granting that kingdom its own constitution. To the south, Italian liberals and nationalists attacked the empire's territories in Naples and Venice. In Milan, the forces of King Charles Albert of Piedmont routed the Austrians, raising hopes of victory. As what would be called "the springtime of peoples" unfolded, Habsburg control of its various provinces seemed to be coming apart.

Yet the explosion of national sentiment that shook the empire later allowed it to recoup its fortunes. The paradox of nationalism in central Europe was that no cultural or ethnic majority could declare independence in a given region without prompting rebellion from other minority groups that inhabited the same area. In Bohemia, for instance, Czechs and Germans who lived side by side had worked together to pass reforms scuttling feudalism. Within a month, however, nationalism began to fracture their alliance. German Bohemians set off to attend the all-important Frankfurt Assembly, but the Czech majority refused to send representatives and countered by convening a confederation of Slavs in Prague. What did the delegates at the Slav confederation want? Some were hostile to what the Russian anarchist Mikhail Bakunin called the "monstrous Austrian Empire." But the majority of delegates preferred to be ruled by the Habsburgs (though with some autonomy) than to be dominated by either the Germans or the Russians.

This bundle of animosities allowed the Austrians to divide and conquer. In May 1848, during the Slav Congress, a student- and worker-led insurrection broke out in Prague. On the orders of the newly installed liberal government, Austrian troops entered the city to restore order, sent the Slav Congress packing, and reasserted control in Bohemia. For economic as well as political reasons, the new government was determined to keep the empire intact. The regime also sent troops to regain control in the Italian provinces of Lombardy and Venetia, and quarrels among the Italians helped the Austrians succeed.

Nationalism and counternationalism in Hungary set the stage for the final act of the drama. The Hungarian parliament had passed a series of laws including new provisions for the union of Hungary and Austria. In the heat of 1848, Ferdinand I had little choice but to accept them. The Hungarian parliament abolished serfdom and ended noble privilege to prevent a peasant insurrection. It also established freedom

THE FIRST UNCENSORED NEWSPAPER AFTER THE REVOLUTION IN VIENNA, JANUARY 1848. This watercolor illustrates the power of public information during the 1848 revolution in the Austrian capital. An uncensored newspaper, wall posters, caps with political insignia and slogans, and an armed citizenry all are evidence of a vibrant and impassioned public discussion on the events of the day. Note, too, the modest dress of the woman selling the papers, the top hat and fashionable dress of the middle-class man smoking a pipe, and the presence of military uniforms, all of which illustrate support for the revolution among a broad portion of the population. ▪ ***How does this vision of the public sphere in action compare with previous depictions of public debate in the Enlightenment (see page 571) or in the French Revolution (see page 599, or elsewhere in Europe in 1848 (see page 704)?***

of the press and of religion and changed the suffrage requirements, enfranchising small property holders. Many of these measures (called the March laws) were hailed by Hungarian peasants, Jewish communities, and liberals. But other provisions—particularly the extension of Magyar control—provoked opposition from the Croats, Serbs, and Romanians within Hungary. On April 14, 1848, Kossuth upped the ante, severing all ties between Hungary and Austria. The new Austrian emperor, Franz Josef, now played his last card: he asked for military support from Nicholas I of Russia. The Habsburgs were unable to win their "holy struggle against anarchy," but the Russian army of over 300,000 found it an easier task. By mid-August 1849, the Hungarian revolt was crushed.

In the city of Vienna itself, the revolutionary movement had lost ground. When economic crisis and unemployment helped spark a second popular uprising, the emperor's forces, with Russian support, descended on the capital. On October 31, the liberal government capitulated. The regime reestablished censorship, disbanded the national guard and student organizations, and put twenty-five revolutionary leaders to death in front of a firing squad. Kossuth went into hiding and lived the rest of his life in exile.

Paradoxically, then, the Habsburg Empire of Austria was in part saved during the revolutions of 1848 by the very nationalist movements that threatened to tear it apart. Although nationalists in Habsburg lands, especially in Hungary, gained the support of significant numbers of people, the fact that different nationalist movements found it impossible to cooperate with one another allowed the new emperor, Franz Josef, to defeat the most significant challenges to his authority one by one and consolidate his rule (with Russian help), ultimately gaining popular support from many quarters, especially from middle-class populations that came to express a certain civic pride in the spirit of toleration that allowed so many peoples to live together within such a patchwork of peoples and tongues. Franz Josef would survive these crises, and many others, until his death in 1916 during World War I, a much larger conflict that would finally overwhelm and destroy the Habsburg Empire for good.

The Early Stages of Italian Unification in 1848

The Italian peninsula had not been united since the Roman Empire. At the beginning of the nineteenth century, like the German-speaking lands of central Europe, the area that is now Italy was a patchwork of small states (see map on page 655). Austria occupied the northernmost states of Lombardy and Venetia, which were also the most urban and industrial. Habsburg dependents also ruled Tuscany, Parma, and Modena, extending Austria's influence over the north of the peninsula. The independent Italian states included the southern kingdom of the Two Sicilies, governed by members of the Bourbon family; the Papal States, ruled by Pope Gregory XVI (1831–46); and most important, Piedmont-Sardinia, ruled by the reform-minded monarch Charles Albert (r. 1831–49) of the House of Savoy. Charles Albert had no particular commitment to creating an Italian

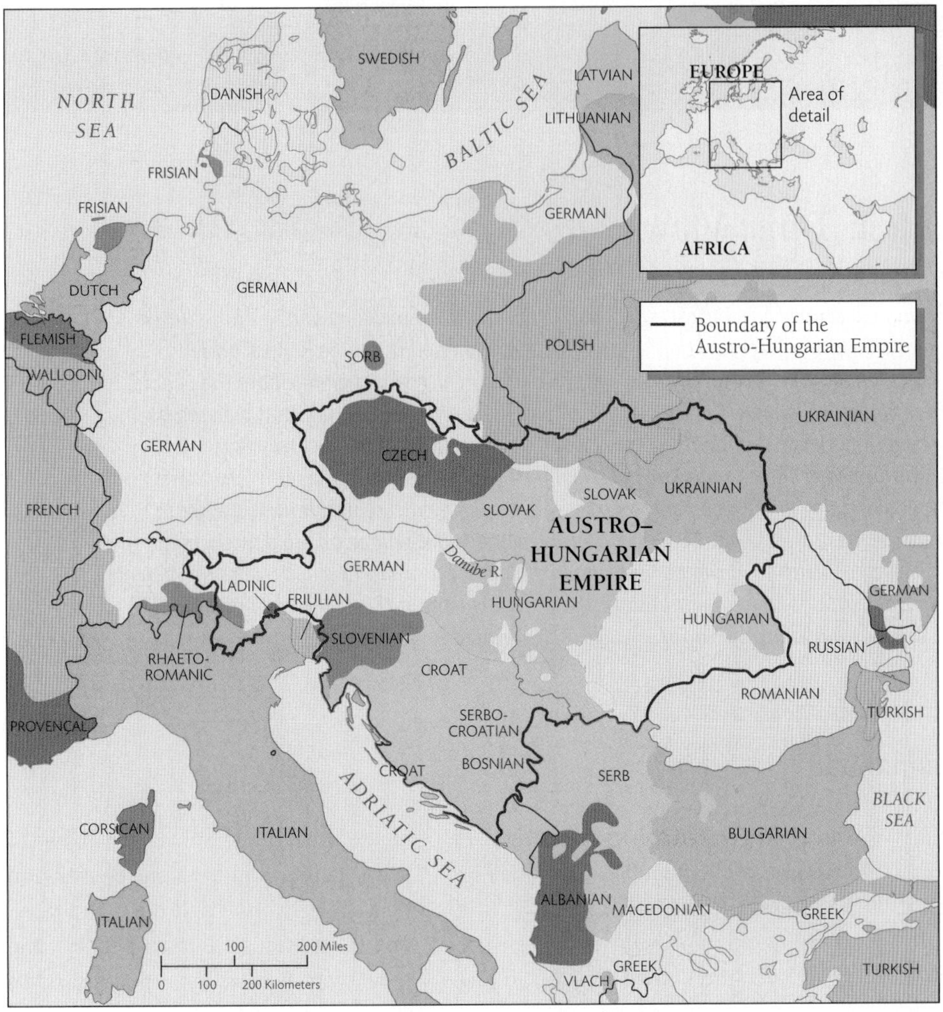

LANGUAGES OF CENTRAL AND EASTERN EUROPE. In Habsburg Austria-Hungary, ethnic/linguistic boundaries did not conform to political boundaries between states. ▪ ***How many different language groups can you count in the Austrian Empire?*** ▪ ***Why was it ultimately easier for the German states to unify when looking at this map?*** ▪ ***How did the diversity of peoples in the Habsburg Empire make a convergence between liberal revolution and nationalism more difficult to achieve?***

national state, but by virtue of Piedmont-Sardinia's economic power, geographical location, and long tradition of opposition to the Habsburgs, Charles Albert's state played a central role in nationalist and anti-Austrian politics.

The leading Italian nationalist in this period—one whose republican politics Charles Albert disliked—was Giuseppe Mazzini (1805–1872) from the city of Genoa, in Piedmont. Mazzini began his political career as a member of the Carbonari (see Chapter 20), an underground society pledged to resisting Austrian control of the region and establishing constitutional rule. In 1831, Mazzini founded his own society, Young Italy, which was anti-Austrian and in favor of constitutional reforms but also dedicated to Italian unification. Charismatic and persuasive, Mazzini was one of the best-known nationalists of his time. He spoke in characteristically Romantic tones of the awakening of the Italian people and of the common people's mission to bring republicanism to the world. Under his leadership, Young Italy clubs multiplied. Yet the organization's favored tactics, plotting mutinies and armed rebellions, proved ineffective. In 1834, Mazzini launched an invasion of the kingdom of Sardinia. Without sufficient support, it fizzled, driving Mazzini into exile in England.

Mazzini's republican vision of a united Italy clashed with the goals of his potential allies. Many liberals shared his commitment to creating a single Italian state but not his enthusiasm for the people and popular movements. They hoped instead to merge existing governments into some form of constitutional monarchy or, in a few cases, for a government under the pope. Mazzini's insistence on a democratic republic committed to social and political transformation struck pragmatic liberals as utopian and well-to-do members of the middle classes as dangerous.

The turmoil that swept across Europe in 1848 raised hopes for political and social change and put Italian unification on the agenda. As in Germany, those who hoped for change were divided in their goals, but they shared a common hope that national unification might allow them to achieve the reforms they sought, whether it was a constitution, civil liberties, universal suffrage, or revolutionary social change that would benefit the working poor. In March

Competing Viewpoints

Building the Italian Nation: Three Views

The charismatic revolutionary Giuseppe Mazzini left more than fifty volumes of memoirs and writings. In the first excerpt, he sets out his vision of the "regeneration" of the Italian nation and the three Romes: ancient Rome, the Rome of the popes, and (in the future) the Rome of the people, which would emancipate the peoples of Europe. Mazzini's conception of Italian nationalism was Romantic in its interpretation of Italy's distinctive history and destiny and revolutionary in its emphasis on the Italian people rather than on statesmen.

The National Society was formed in 1857 to support Italian unification. By the 1860s, the society had over 5,000 members. It was especially strong in the Piedmont, where it was formed, and in central Italy. Giuseppe la Farina was a tenacious organizer; he drafted the society's political creed and had it printed and sold throughout Italy.

The unification of Italy owed as much to Cavour's hard-nosed diplomacy as it did to middle-class movements for unification. In 1862, one of Cavour's contemporaries offered an assessment of the count and how he had found "an opening in the complicated fabric of European politics," reprinted in the third piece here.

Mazzini and Romantic Nationalism

I saw regenerate Italy becoming at one bound the missionary of a religion of progress and fraternity. . . .

The worship of Rome was a part of my being. The great Unity, the One Life of the world, had twice been elaborated within her walls. Other peoples—their brief mission fulfilled—disappeared for ever. To none save to her had it been given twice to guide and direct the world. . . . There, upon the vestiges of an epoch of civilization anterior to the Grecian, which had had its seat in Italy . . . the Rome of the Republic, concluded by the Caesars, had arisen to consign the former world to oblivion, and borne her eagles over the known world, carrying with them the idea of right, the source of liberty.

In later days . . . she had again arisen, greater than before, and at once constituted herself, through her Popes—the accepted center of a new Unity. . . .

Why should not a new Rome, the Rome of the Italian people . . . arise to create a third and still vaster Unity; to link together and harmonize earth and heaven, right [law] and duty; and utter, not to individuals but to peoples, the great word Association—to make known to free men and equal their mission here below?

Source: Giuseppe Mazzini, *The Life and Writings of Joseph Mazzini* (London: 1964), as cited in Denis Mack Smith, *The Making of Italy, 1796–1870* (New York: 1968), pp. 48–49.

The Political Creed of the National Society, February 1858

Italian independence should be the aim of every man of spirit and intelligence. Neither our educational system in Italy, nor our commerce and industry, can ever be flourishing or properly modernized while Austria keeps one foot on our neck. . . . What good is it to be born in the most fertile and beautiful country in the world, to lie midway between East and West with magnificent ports in both the Adriatic and Mediterranean, to be descended from the Genoese, the Pisans, the men of Amalfi, Sicily and Venice? What use is it to have invented the compass, to have discovered the New World and been the progenitor of two civilizations? . . .

To obtain political liberty we must expel the Austrians who keep us enslaved. To win freedom of conscience

we must expel the Austrians who keep us slaves of the Pope. To create a national literature we must chase away the Austrians who keep us uneducated. . . .

Italy must become not only independent but politically united. Political unity alone can reconcile various interests and laws, can mobilize credit and put out collective energies to speeding up communications. Only thus will we find sufficient capital for large-scale industry. Only thus will we create new markets, suppress internal obstacles to the free flow of commerce, and find the strength and reputation needed for traffic in distant lands. . . .

Everything points irresistibly to political unification. Science, industry, commerce, and the arts all need it. No great enterprise is possible any longer if we do not first put together the skill, knowledge, capital and labor of the whole of our great nation. The spirit of the age is moving toward concentration, and woe betide any nation that holds back!

Source: A. Franchi, ed., *Scritti politici di Giuseppe La Farina*, vol. 2 (Milan: 1870), as cited in Denis Mack Smith, *The Making of Italy, 1796–1870* (New York: 1968), pp. 224–25.

Count Cavour as a Leader

Count Cavour undeniably ranks as third among European statesmen after Lord Palmerston [British prime minister 1855–1858, 1859–1865] and the Emperor Napoleon. . . . Count Cavour's strength does not lie in his principles; for he has none that are altogether inflexible. But he has a clear, precise aim, one whose greatness would—ten years ago—have made any other man reel: that of creating a unified and independent Italy. Men, means, circumstances were and still are matters of indifference to him. He walks straight ahead, always firm, often alone, sacrificing his friends, his sympathies, sometimes his heart, and often his conscience. Nothing is too difficult for him. . . .

Count Cavour . . . always has the talent to assess a situation and the possibilities of exploiting it. And it is this wonderful faculty that has contributed to form the Italy of today. As minister of a fourth-rate power, he could not create situations like Napoleon III, nor has he possessed the support of a great nation like Palmerston.

Count Cavour had to seek out an opening in the complicated fabric of European politics; he had to wriggle his way in, conceal himself, lay a mine, and cause an explosion. And it was by these means that he defeated Austria and won the help of France and England. Where other statesmen would have drawn back, Cavour plunged in headlong—as soon as he had sounded the precipice and calculated the possible profit and loss. The Crimean expeditionary force . . . the cession of Nice, the invasion of the Papal States last autumn [i.e., in 1860], were all the outcome of his vigorous stamina of mind.

There in brief you have the man of foreign affairs. He is strong; he is a match for the situation, for the politicians of his time or indeed of any time.

Source: F. Petruccelli della Gattina, *I moribundi del Palazzo Carignano* (Milan: 1862), as cited in Denis Mack Smith, *The Making of Italy, 1796–1870* (New York: 1968), pp. 181–82.

Questions for Analysis

1. Compare Mazzini's romantic vision of Italian history with the more pragmatic arguments for political unity coming from the liberal supporters of the National Society. Are there any points of overlap?
2. How would a supporter of Mazzini or a member of the National Society react to the third document's claim that an individual, Cavour, deserved primary credit for Italian unification?
3. Why should history and claims about "the spirit of the age" be so important to Italian nationalists?

SIEGE OF VENICE, 1848. This image, designed to provoke an anti-Austrian and nationalist sentiment among Italians, shows Venetian women and children donating their jewels to support their city while it was besieged by the Austrian army in 1848. ▪ ***What makes the image of women and children sacrificing their possessions for the larger good so powerful?*** ▪ ***What does it say about the connections between nationalism and social obligations associated with gender?*** ▪ ***Did nationalism depend on a vision of the family as well as a vision of the nation?***

1848, only a few weeks after revolution had toppled the French monarchy, popular revolts broke out in the northern provinces of Venetia and Lombardy, fueled by anger at the Austrian occupation. In Milan, the capital of Lombardy, thousands of people marched on the palace of the Austrian governor general calling for reforms, leading to pitched battles in the streets. In Venice, the revolutionaries forced the Austrian troops out of the city and declared a republic. Charles Albert of Piedmont-Sardinia provided the rebels with military support and took up the banner of Italian nationalism, although many charged that he was primarily interested in expanding his own power. At the same time, Charles Albert pleased Italian liberals by creating an elected legislature and relaxing press censorship in his kingdom.

In August 1848, an insurrection of laborers broke out in Bologna, challenging the authority of the pope in the Papal States. Soon after, a popular uprising in Rome confronted the pope directly, and by February 1849 a new government in Rome had declared itself a republic. The next month, Mazzini arrived from exile to join the revolutionary movement in Rome.. These movements were neither coordinated nor ultimately successful. Charles Albert hesitated to confront the Austrians directly, and over the next few months the Austrians regained the upper hand in the north. French forces under Louis Napoleon intervened in Rome and the Papal States; and although they met fierce resistance from the Roman republicans joined by Giuseppe Garibaldi (see below), they nonetheless restored the pope's power and defeated the Roman Republic. The Venetian Republic was the last of the Italian revolutions to fall after a blockade and

GIUSEPPE MAZZINI (1805–1872). Born in Genoa when it was ruled by Napoleon's France, Mazzini devoted his life to the cause of Italian unification and independence. As a young man, Mazzini was a member of the underground revolutionary organization known as the Carbonari, and in 1831 he founded a new group, Young Italy, which soon attracted many adherents. Early attempts at insurrection resulted in political exile, but he returned during the 1848 revolutions to help lead the Roman Republic. Although his hopes for a Republican Italy were blocked by Cavour's plans for unification under the leadership of Piedmont-Sardinia, Mazzini remained a hero to many Italians, and his description of a "United States of Europe" anticipated the European Union.

an artillery bombardment from the Austrian army in August 1849. Like most of the radical movements of 1848, these Italian uprisings all failed. Still, they raised the hopes of nationalists who spoke of a *risorgimento*, or Italian resurgence, that would restore the nation to the position of leadership it had held in Roman times and during the Renaissance.

BUILDING THE NATION-STATE

In the wake of the revolutions of 1848, new nation-states were built or consolidated—often by former critics of nationalism. Since the French Revolution of 1789, conservative politicians had associated nationhood with liberalism: constitutions, reforms, new political communities. During the second half of the century, however, the political ground shifted dramatically. States and governments took the national initiative. Alarmed by revolutionary ferment, they promoted economic development, pressed social and political reforms, and sought to shore up their base of support. Rather than allow popular nationalist movements to emerge from below, statesmen consolidated their governments' powers and built nations from above.

France under Napoleon III

Napoleon III, like his uncle, believed in personal rule and a centralized state. As emperor, he controlled the nation's finances, the army, and foreign affairs. The assembly, elected by universal male suffrage, could approve only legislation drafted at the emperor's direction. Napoleon's regime aimed to undermine France's traditional elites by expanding the bureaucracy and cultivating a new relationship with the people. "The confidence of our rough peasants can be won by an energetic authority," asserted one of the emperor's representatives.

Napoleon III also took steps to develop the economy. He harbored a near-utopian faith in the power of industrial expansion to bring prosperity, political support, and national glory. An adviser to the emperor put it this way: "I see in industry, machinery, and credit the indispensable auxiliaries of humanity's moral and material progress." His government encouraged credit and new forms of financing, passed new limited-liability laws, and signed a free-trade treaty with Britain in 1860. The government also supported the creation of the Crédit Mobilier, an investment banking institution that sold shares and financed railroads, insurance and gas companies, coal and construction companies, and the building of the Suez Canal (see Chapter 22). Napoleon also reluctantly permitted the existence of trade unions and legalized strikes. By appealing to both workers and the middle class, he sought to gain support for his goal of reestablishing France as a leading world power.

Most emblematic of the emperor's ambition was his transformation of the nation's capital. Paris's medieval infrastructure was buckling under the weight of population growth and industrial development. Cholera epidemics in 1832 and 1849 killed tens of thousands. In 1850, only one house in five had running water. Official concerns about public health were reinforced by political fears of crime and revolutionary militancy in working-class neighborhoods. A massive rebuilding project razed much of the medieval center of the city and erected 34,000 new buildings, including elegant hotels with the first elevators. The construction installed new water pipes and sewer lines, laid out 200 kilometers of new streets, and rationalized the traffic flow. Wide new boulevards, many named for Napoleon I's most famous generals, radiated from the Arc de Triomphe. The renovation did not benefit everyone. Although the regime built model worker residences, rising rents drove working people from the city's center into increasingly segregated suburbs. Baron Haussmann, the prefect of Paris who presided over the project, considered the city a monument to "cleanliness and order." Others called Haussmann an "artist of demolition."

Victorian Britain and the Second Reform Bill (1867)

Less affected by the revolutionary wave of 1848, Great Britain was able to chart a course of significant social and political reform, continuing a process that had begun in 1832 with the First Reform Bill. The government faced mounting demands to extend the franchise beyond the middle classes. Industrial expansion sustained a growing stratum of highly skilled and relatively well-paid workers (almost exclusively male). These workers, concentrated for the most part within the building, engineering, and textile industries, turned away from the tradition of militant radicalism that had characterized the Hungry Forties. Instead, they favored collective self-help through cooperative societies or trade unions, whose major role was to accumulate funds for insurance against old age and unemployment. They saw education as a tool for advancement and patronized the mechanics' institutes and similar institutions founded by them or on their behalf. These prosperous workers created real pressure for electoral reform.

Some argued for the vote in the name of democracy. Others borrowed arguments from earlier middle-class campaigns for electoral reform: they were responsible workers, respectable and upstanding members of society, with strong religious convictions and patriotic feelings. Unquestionably loyal to the state, they deserved the vote and direct representation just as much as the middle class. These workers were joined in their campaign by many middle-class dissenting reformers in the Liberal party, whose religious beliefs (as dissenters from the Church of England) linked them to the workers' campaigns for reform. Dissenters had long faced discrimination. They were denied posts in the civil service and the military, which liberals felt should be open to talent, and for centuries had been excluded from the nation's premier universities, Oxford and Cambridge, unless they renounced their faith and subscribed to the articles of the Anglican church. Moreover, they resented paying taxes to support the Church of England, which was largely staffed by sons of the gentry and run in the interests of landed society. The fact that the community of dissent crossed class lines was vital to Liberal party politics and the campaign for reforming the vote.

PARIS REBUILT. Baron Haussmann, prefect of Paris under Napoleon III, presided over the wholesale rebuilding of the city, with effects we still see today. The Arc de Triomphe, seen here in a photograph from the 1960s, became the center of an *étoile* (star) pattern, with the wide boulevards named after Napoleon I's famous generals.

Working-class leaders and middle-class dissidents joined in a countrywide campaign for a new reform bill and a House of Commons responsive to their interests. They were backed by some shrewd Conservatives, such as Benjamin Disraeli (1804–1881), who argued that political life would be improved, not disrupted, by including the "aristocrats of labor." In actuality, Disraeli was betting that the newly enfranchised demographic would vote Conservative; and in 1867, he steered through Parliament a bill that reached further than anything proposed by his political opponents. The 1867 Reform Bill doubled the franchise by extending the vote to any men who paid poor rates or rent of £10 or more a year in urban areas (this meant, in general, skilled workers) and to rural tenants paying rent of £12 or more. As in 1832, the bill redistributed seats, with large northern cities gaining representation at the expense of the rural south. The success of the 1867 Reform Bill also points to the lingering influence of the Chartist movement of the 1840s (see Chapter 20). Although the Chartists' goal of universal manhood suffrage remained unfulfilled, the 1867 law allowed the responsible working class to participate in the affairs of state.

The reform bill was silent on women, but an important minority insisted that liberalism should include women's enfranchisement. These advocates mobilized a woman suffrage movement, building on women's remarkable participation in earlier reform campaigns, especially the Anti-Corn Law League and the movement to abolish slavery. Their cause found a passionate supporter in John Stuart Mill, perhaps the century's most brilliant, committed, and influential defender of personal liberty. Mill's father had worked closely with the utilitarian philosopher Jeremy Bentham, and the young Mill had been a convinced utilitarian himself (see Chapter 20). He went on, however, to develop much more expansive notions of human freedom. In 1859, Mill wrote *On Liberty,* which many consider the classic defense of individual freedom in the face of the state and the "tyranny of the majority." During the same period he coauthored—with his lover and eventual wife, Harriet Taylor—essays on women's political rights, the law of marriage, and divorce. At the time, Taylor was trapped in an unhappy marriage and divorce required an act of Parliament. Taylor's relationship with Mill thus added a measure of personal scandal to their political views, which contemporaries considered scandalous enough. His *Subjection of Women* (1869), published after Harriet died, argued what few could even contemplate: that women had to be considered individuals on the same plane as men and that women's freedom was a measure of social progress. *Subjection* was an international success and with *On Liberty* became one of the defining texts of Western liberalism. Mill's arguments, however, did not carry the day. Only militant suffrage movements and the crisis of the First World War brought women the vote.

The decade or so following the passage of the Reform Bill of 1867 marked the high point of British liberalism. By opening the doors to political participation, liberalism had accomplished a peaceful restructuring of political institutions and social life. It did so under considerable pressure from below, however, and in Britain, as elsewhere, liberal leaders made it clear that these doors were unquestionably not open to everyone. Their opposition to woman's suffrage is interesting for what it reveals about their views on male and female nature. They insisted that female individuality (expressed in voting, education, or wage earning) would destabilize family life. Yet their opposition to woman's suffrage also reflected conception of the vote: casting a ballot was a privilege granted only to specific social groups in return for their contributions to and vested interest in society. Men of property might champion the rule of law and representative government, but they balked at the prospect of a truly democratic politics and did not shy from heavy-handed law-and-order politics. Expanding the franchise created new constituencies with new ambitions and paved the way for socialist and labor politics in the last quarter of the century. Tensions within liberalism remained and forecast conflicts in the future.

Italian Unification: Cavour and Garibaldi

After the failure of Italian unification in 1848, nationalists in Italy faced a choice between two strategies for achieving statehood. One group, supported by Mazzini and his follower Giuseppe Garibaldi, envisioned a republican Italy built from below by a popular uprising. A second group of more moderate nationalists sought to unify Italy as a constitutional monarchy under the leadership of the kingdom of Piedmont-Sardinia. Giuseppe Garibaldi was a guerrilla fighter who had been exiled twice: first in Latin America, where he fought along with independence movements, and again in the United States. Like Mazzini, Garibaldi was committed to achieving national unification through a popular movement.

The more conservative supporters of Piedmont-Sardinia, on the other hand, sought to steer clear of democracy and the destabilizing forces that it might unleash. The king of Piedmont-Sardinia, Charles Albert, had drawn the attention of Italian nationalists in 1848 when he took up the anti-Austrian cause. Though he later died in exile, his son Victor Emmanuel II (r. 1849–1861) brought a man into his government who would embody the conservative vision of nationhood: the shrewd Sardinian nobleman Count Camillo Benso di Cavour (1810–1861). "In Italy a democratic movement has almost no chance of success," Cavour declared. He instead pursued ambitious but pragmatic reforms guided by the state. As prime minister, he promoted economic expansion, encouraged the construction of a modern transportation infrastructure, reformed the currency, and sought to raise Piedmont-Sardinia's profile in international relations. Garibaldi and Cavour thus represented two different routes to Italian unification: Garibaldi stood for unification from below, Cavour for unification guided from above.

MILL'S LOGIC, OR FRANCHISE FOR FEMALES
"Pray clear the way, there, for these—ah—persons."

JOHN STUART MILL AND SUFFRAGETTES. By 1860, when this cartoon was published, Mill had established a reputation as a liberal political philosopher and a supporter of women's right to vote. Mill argued that women's enfranchisement was essential both from the standpoint of individual liberty and for the good of society as a whole. ▪ ***What was amusing about Mill's assertion that women be considered persons in their own right?***

GIUSEPPE GARIBALDI. Note the simple uniform Garibaldi wears in this commemorative portrait, with its iconic symbols of his nationalist movement: the red shirt and the flag of Italy in the background. Compare this with the official portraits of absolutist rulers in previous chapters. ▪ ***What was significant about the absence of finery and precious materials in this painting?*** ▪ ***What does it say about images of masculine leadership in mid-nineteenth-century nationalist imagination? (Compare this with the drawing of Garibaldi and Victor Emmanuel on page 710.)***

Cavour's plan depended on diplomacy. Since Piedmont-Sardinia did not have the military capacity to counter the Austrians in northern Italy, Cavour skillfully cultivated an alliance with one of Austria's traditional rivals: Napoleonic France. In 1858, Cavour held a secret meeting with Napoleon III, who agreed to cooperate in driving the Austrians from Italy if Piedmont would cede Savoy and Nice to France. A war with Austria was duly provoked in 1859, and for a time all went well for the Franco-Italian allies. After the conquest of Lombardy, however, Napoleon III suddenly withdrew, concerned that he might either lose the battle or antagonize French Catholics, who were alienated by Cavour's hostility to the pope. Deserted by the French, Piedmont could not expel the Austrians from Venetia. Yet the campaign made extensive gains. Piedmont-Sardinia annexed Lombardy. The duchies of Tuscany, Parma, and Modena agreed by plebiscite to join the new state. By the end of this process in 1860, Piedmont-Sardinia had grown to more than twice its original size and was by far the most powerful state in Italy.

As Cavour consolidated the northern and central states, events in the southern states seemed to put those areas up for grabs as well. The unpopular Bourbon king of the Two Sicilies, Francis II (r. 1859–60), faced a fast-spreading peasant revolt that rekindled the hopes of earlier insurrections of the 1820s and 1840s. That revolt, in turn, got a much needed boost from Garibaldi, who landed in Sicily in May of 1860. "The Thousand," as Garibaldi's volunteer fighters called themselves, embodied the widespread support for Italian unification: they came from the north as well as from the south and counted among them members of the middle class as well as workers and artisans. Garibaldi's troops took Sicily and continued on to the mainland. By November 1860, Garibaldi's forces, alongside local insurgents, had taken Naples and toppled the kingdom of Francis II. Emboldened by success, Garibaldi looked to Rome, where French troops guarded the pope.

Garibaldi's rising popularity put him on a collision course with Cavour. Cavour worried that Garibaldi's forces would bring French or Austrian intervention, with unknown consequences. He feared Garibaldi's "irresistible" prestige. Above all, Cavour preferred that Italian unification happen quickly, under Piedmont-Sardinia's stewardship, without domestic turmoil or messy, unpredictable negotiations with other Italian states. "As long as he [Garibaldi] is faithful to his flag, one has to march along with him," Cavour wrote. "This does not alter the fact that it would be eminently desirable for the revolution . . . to be accomplished without him." Determined to recoup the initiative, Cavour dispatched Victor Emmanuel and his army to Rome. Flush with success, the king ordered Garibaldi to cede him military authority, and Garibaldi obeyed. Most of the peninsula was united under a single rule, and Victor Emmanuel assumed the title of king of Italy (r. 1861–78). Cavour's vision of Italian nationhood had won the day.

The final steps of Italy's territorial nation building came indirectly. Venetia remained in the hands of the Austrians until 1866, when Austria was defeated by Prussia and forced to relinquish their last Italian stronghold. Rome had resisted conquest largely because of the military protection that Napoleon III accorded the pope. But in 1870, the

THE UNIFICATION OF ITALY.
- ***How many phases were involved in Italian unification, according to the map key?***
- ***Why did it take an extra decade to incorporate Rome and Venetia into the Italian state?***
- ***Why was Italian unification incomplete until the early twentieth century?***

outbreak of the Franco-Prussian War compelled Napoleon to withdraw his troops. That September, Italian soldiers occupied Rome, and in July 1871 Rome became capital of the united Italian kingdom.

What of the pope's authority? The Italian parliament passed the Law of Papal Guarantees to define and limit the pope's status—an act promptly defied by the reigning pontiff, Pius IX, who refused to have anything to do with a disrespectful secular government. His successors continued to close themselves off in the Vatican until 1929, when a series of agreements between the Italian government and Pius XI settled the dispute.

In 1871, Italy was a state, but nation building was hardly over. A minority of the "Italian" population spoke Italian; the rest used local and regional dialects so diverse that schoolteachers sent from Rome to Sicily were mistaken for foreigners. As one politician remarked, "We have made Italy; now we must make Italians." The task did not prove easy. The gap between an increasingly industrialized north and a poor and rural south remained wide. Cavour and those who succeeded him as prime minister had to contend with those economic and social inequalities, with rising tensions beween landlords and agricultural workers in rural regions and with lingering resentments of the centralized northern-oriented state. Banditry in the territory of the former kingdom of the Two Sicilies compelled the central administration to dispatch troops to quell serious uprisings, killing more people than in the war of unification. Regional differences and social tensions, then, made building the Italian nation an ongoing process.

"RIGHT LEG IN THE BOOT AT LAST." This image shows Garibaldi helping Victor Emmanuel, former king of Piedmont-Sardinia and the newly crowned king of Italy, get his foot in the Italian boot. What is the significance of their different forms of dress and postures? (Compare this with the portrait of Garibaldi on page 708.) ▪ ***How does this image portray the outcome of the contest between the conservative nationalism of Cavour and the more romantic and democratic nationalism of Garibaldi?***

The Unification of Germany: Realpolitik

In 1853, the former revolutionary August Ludwig von Rochau wrote a short book with a long title: *The Principles of Realpolitik Applied to the Conditions of Germany.* Rochau banished the idealism and revolutionary fervor of his youth. "The question of who ought to rule . . . belongs in the realm of philosophical speculation," he wrote. "Practical politics has to do with the simple fact that it is power alone that can rule." Rochau's vision of *Realpolitik*—practical, realistic politics—held that finding ways to achieve and maintain power were more important than moral or ideological goals such as justice or freedom. This view rejected the aspirations of earlier generations of liberal reformers in Germany who believed that progress depended on constitutions and Enlightenment conceptions of rights. In several important ways, Rochau's views captured the changing outlook of broad sections of the German middle classes. Realpolitik became the watchword of the 1850s and 1860s and was most closely associated with the deeply conservative and pragmatic Otto von Bismarck, whose skillful diplomacy and power politics played an important role in German unification.

Despite its decisive defeat in 1848, German liberalism revived within a decade, against considerable opposition. King Frederick William granted a Prussian constitution in 1850 that established a two-house parliament, with the lower house elected by universal male suffrage. A series of edicts modified the electoral system, however, to preserve the power of traditional elites. The king's edicts divided voters into three classes based on the amount of taxes they paid, and their votes were apportioned accordingly. Thus the relatively small number of wealthy voters who paid one-third of Prussia's taxes elected one-third of the legislators in Parliament. In this way, a large landowner or a wealthy industrialist exercised perhaps seventeen times the voting power of a working man. Furthermore, voting took place in public, orally, so a secret ballot was impossible.

In 1858, William I became prince regent of Prussia. William, who had led troops against the revolutionaries of 1848 in his youth, became king in 1861 and ruled until 1888. Under his rule, Prussia remained a notoriously conservative state, but a decade of industrial growth had also expanded the size and confidence of the middle classes. By the late 1850s, Prussia had an active liberal intelligentsia, a thoughtful and engaged press, and a liberal civil service dedicated to political and economic modernization. These changes helped forge a liberal political movement that won a majority in elections to the lower house and could confidently confront the king.

Liberals in Prussia were especially opposed to the king's high levels of military spending. William wanted to expand the standing army, reduce the role of reserve forces (a more middle-class group), and ensure that military matters were not subject to parliamentary control. Opponents in Parliament suspected the king of making the military his own private force or a state within a state. Between 1859 and 1862, relations deteriorated; and when liberals' protests went unanswered, they refused to approve the regular budget. Faced with a crisis, in 1862 William named Otto von Bismarck minister-president of Prussia. (A prime minister answers to Parliament; Bismarck did not.) This crucial moment in Prussian domestic politics became a decisive turning point in the history of German nationhood.

Born into the Junker class of conservative, land-owning aristocrats, Bismarck had fiercely opposed the liberal movement of 1848–49. He was not a nationalist. He was before all else a Prussian. He did not institute domestic reforms because he favored the rights of a particular group but because he thought that these policies would unify and strengthen Prussia. When he maneuvered to bring other German states under Prussian domination, he did so not in pursuit of a grand German design but because he believed that union in some form was inevitable and that Prussia had to seize the initiative. Bismarck happily acknowledged that he admired power and that he considered himself destined for greatness. He had a reputation for cynicism, arrogance, and uninhibited frankness in expressing his views. Yet a Latin phrase he frequently quoted distilled a more careful assessment of the relationship between individuals and history: "Man cannot create or control the tide of time, he can only move in the same direction and try to direct it."

In Prussia, Bismarck defied parliamentary opposition. When the liberal majority refused to pass a budget because of disagreements about spending for the army, he dissolved Parliament, claiming that the constitution, whatever its purposes, had not been designed to subvert the state. His most decisive actions, however, were in foreign policy. Once opposed to nationalism, Bismarck skillfully played the national card to preempt his liberal opponents at home and to make German nation building an accomplishment—and an extension—of Prussian authority.

The other "German" power was Austria, which wielded considerable influence within the German Confederation and especially over the largely Catholic regions in the south. Bismarck saw a stark contrast between Austrian and Prussian interests and skillfully exploited Austria's economic disadvantages and the Habsburgs' internal ethnic struggles. He inflamed a long-smoldering dispute with Denmark over Schleswig (*SHLAYS-vihg*) and Holstein, two provinces peopled by Germans and Danes and claimed by both the German Confederation and Denmark. In 1864, the Danish king attempted to annex the provinces, prompting a German nationalist outcry. Bismarck cast the conflict as a Prussian matter and persuaded Austria to join Prussia in a war against Denmark. The war was short, and it forced the Danish ruler to cede the two provinces to Austria and Prussia. As Bismarck hoped, the victorious alliance promptly fell apart. In 1866, casting Prussia as the defender of larger German interests, he declared war on Austria. The conflict, known as the Seven Weeks' War, ended in Prussian victory. Austria gave up all claims to Schleswig and Holstein, surrendered Venetia to the Italians, and agreed to dissolve the German Confederation. In its place, Bismarck created the North German Confederation, a union of all the German states north of the Main River.

Bismarck "played power politics with an eye to public opinion." Both wars had strong public support, and Prussian victories weakened liberal opposition to the king and his president-minister. In the aftermath of the Austrian defeat, Prussian liberals gave up their battle over budgets, the military, and constitutional provisions. Bismarck also sought support among the masses. He understood that Germans did not necessarily support business elites, the bureaucracies of their own small states, or the Austrian Habsburgs. The constitution of the North German Confederation gave the appearance of a more liberal political body, with a bicameral legislature, freedom of the press, and universal male suffrage in the lower house. Its structure, however, gave Prussia and the conservative emperor a decisive advantage in the North German Confederation—and in the soon to be expanded empire.

The final step in the completion of German unity was the Franco-Prussian War of 1870–71. Bismarck hoped that a conflict with France would arouse German nationalism in Bavaria, Württemberg, and other southern states still outside the confederation and overcome their historic wariness of Prussia. A diplomatic tempest concerning the right of the Hohenzollerns (Prussia's ruling family) to occupy the Spanish throne created an opportunity to foment a Franco-German misunderstanding. King William agreed to meet with the French ambassador at the resort spa of Ems in Prussia to discuss the Spanish succession. William initially acquiesced to French demands, but when the French blundered by asking for "perpetual exclusion" of the Hohenzollern family from the Spanish throne, Bismarck seized his opportunity. He edited a telegraph from King William so as to make it appear that the Prussian king had rebuffed the French ambassador. Once the redacted report reached France, the nation reacted with calls for war. Prussia echoed the call, and Bismarck published evidence that he claimed proved French designs on the Rhineland.

As soon as war was declared, the south German states rallied to Prussia's side. The conflict was quickly over. No European powers came to France's aid. Austria, the most likely candidate, remained weakened by its recent war with Prussia. The Hungarians welcomed a strengthened Prussia, for the weaker Austria was as a German power, the stronger would be the Magyar claims to power sharing in the empire. On the battlefield, France could not match Prussia's professionally trained and superbly equipped forces. The war began in July and ended in September with the defeat of the French and the capture of Napoleon III at Sedan in France. Insurrectionary forces in Paris continued to hold out against the Germans through the winter of 1870–71, but the French imperial government collapsed.

On January 18, 1871, in the Hall of Mirrors at Versailles, symbol of the powerful past of French absolutism, the German Empire was proclaimed. All the German

Interpreting Visual Evidence

The New German Nation

In order to silence their critics at home and abroad, nationalists in Germany sought to create a vision of German history that made unification the natural outcome of a deep historical process that had begun hundreds of years before. In image A, the family of a cavalry officer prepares to hang a portrait of King William on the wall, next to portraits of Martin Luther, Frederick the Great, and Field Marshal von Blücher, who commanded the Prussian forces at Waterloo. In the lower left corner, two boys roll up a portrait of the defeated French emperor, Napoleon III. The implication, of course, was that the unification of Germany was the inevitable culmination of generations of German heroes who all worked toward the same goal.

This unity was itself controversial among German people. Image B, a pro-Bismarck cartoon, shows the German minister-president dragging the unwilling liberal members of the Prussian parliament along with him as he pulls a triumphal chariot toward his military confrontation with Austria in 1866. The caption reads: "And in this sense, too, we are in agreement with Count Bismarck, and we have pulled the same rope as him." Image C, on the other hand, expresses reservations about Prussian dominance in the new empire. The title "Germany's Future" and the caption:

A. *Homage to Kaiser Wilhelm I* by Paul Bürde, 1871.

states that had not already been absorbed into the Prussian fold, except Austria, declared their allegiance to William I, henceforth emperor or kaiser. Four months later, at Frankfurt, a treaty between the French and the Germans ceded the border region of Alsace to the new German Empire and forced the French to pay an indemnity of 5 billion francs. Prussia accounted for 60 percent of the new state's territory and population. The Prussian kaiser, prime minister, army, and most of the bureaucracy remained intact, now reconfigured as the German nation-state. This was not the new nation for which Prussian liberals had hoped. It marked a "revolution from above" rather than from below. Still, the more optimistic believed that the German Empire would evolve in a different political direction and that they could eventually "extend freedom through unity."

The State and Nationality: Centrifugal Forces in the Austrian Empire

Germany emerged from the 1860s a stronger, unified nation. The Habsburg Empire faced a very different situation, with different resources, and emerged a weakened,

"Will it fit under one hat? I think it will only fit under a [Prussian] Pickelhaube." The *Pickelhaube*—the characteristic pointed helmet of the Prussian army—had already become a much-feared symbol of Prussian military force. Such an image may well have struck a chord with residents of the non-Prussian German states who now paid taxes to the Prussian monarchy and served in an army dominated by Prussian officers.

Questions for Analysis

1. What is the significance of the familial setting in image A? Why was it important for nationalists to emphasize a multigenerational family as the repository of German national spirit?
2. How do images B and C treat the question of Prussia's role within the new German nation? Was German national identity seen as something built from below or defined from above by a strong monarchy?
3. What is the place of the individual citizen in these representations of the German nation?

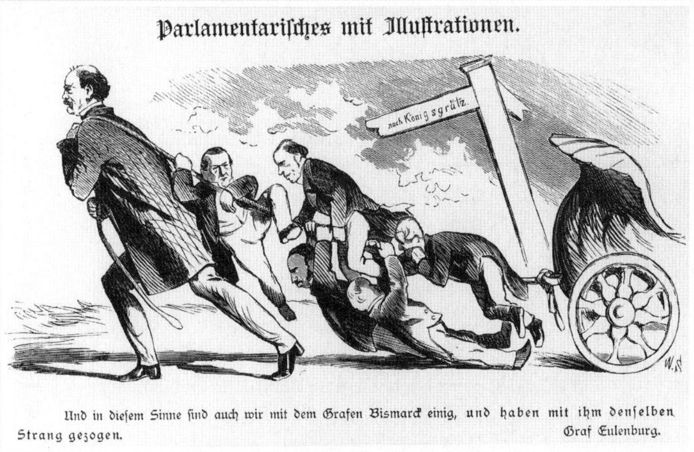

B. Prussian liberals and Bismarck after Königgrätz (1866).

C. "Germany's Future" (1870).

precariously balanced, multiethnic dual monarchy, also called Austria-Hungary.

As we have seen, ethnic nationalism was a powerful force in the Habsburg monarchy in 1848. Yet the Habsburg state, with a combination of military repression and tactics that divided its enemies, had proved more powerful. It abolished serfdom but made few other concessions to its opponents. The Hungarians, who had nearly won independence in the spring of 1848, were essentially reconquered. Administrative reforms created a new and more uniform legal system, rationalized taxation, and imposed a single-language policy that favored German. The issue of managing ethnic relations, however, only grew more difficult. Through the 1850s and 1860s, the subject nationalities, as they were often called, bitterly protested the powerlessness of their local diets, military repression, and cultural disenfranchisement. The Czechs in Bohemia, for instance, grew increasingly alienated by policies that favored the German minority of the province. In response, they became more insistent on their Slavic identity—a movement welcomed by Russia, which became the sponsor of a broad pan-Slavism. The Hungarians, or Magyars, the most powerful of the subject nationalities, sought to reclaim the autonomy they had glimpsed in 1848.

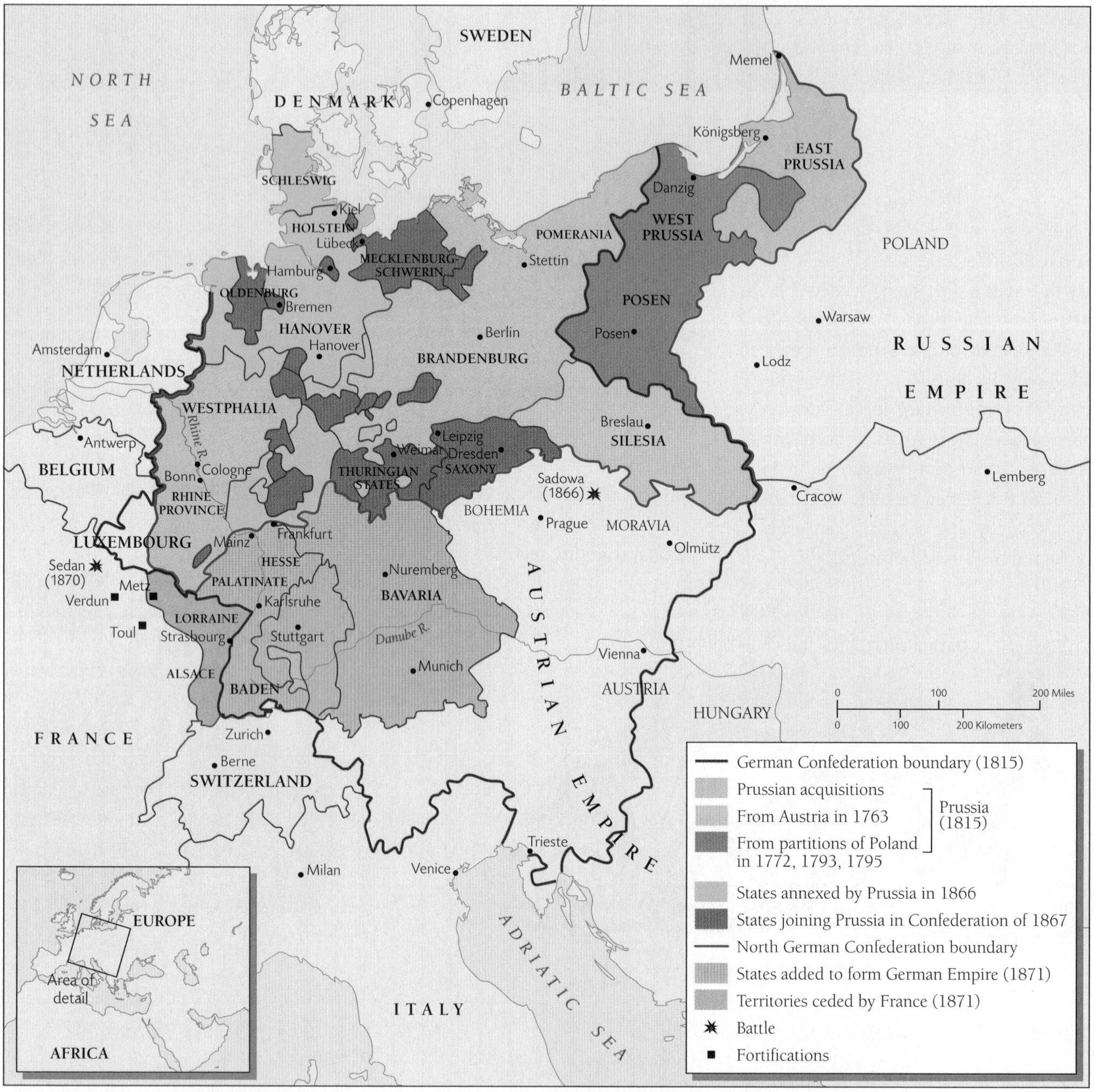

TOWARD THE UNIFICATION OF GERMANY. Note the many elements that made up a unified Germany and the stages that brought them together. ▪ ***Did this new nation have any resemblance to the unified Germany envisioned by the liberal revolutionaries of the Frankfurt Preparliament in 1848? (See page 697.)*** ▪ ***How many stages were involved in the unification of Germany, and how many years did it take?*** ▪ ***What region filled with German-speaking peoples was not included in the new unified Germany and why?***

In this context, Austria's defeats at the hands of Piedmont-Sardinia in 1859 and Prussia in 1866 became especially significant. The 1866 war forced the emperor Franz Josef to renegotiate the very structure of the empire. To stave off a revolution by the Hungarians, Francis Joseph agreed to a new federal structure in the form of the Dual Monarchy. Austria-Hungary had a common system of taxation, a common army, and made foreign and military policy together. Francis Joseph was emperor of Austria and king of Hungary. But internal and constitutional affairs were separated. The Ausgleich, or Settlement, allowed the Hungarians to establish their own constitution; their own legislature; and their own capital, combining the cities of Buda and Pest.

What of the other nationalities? The official policy of the Dual Monarchy stated that they were not to be discriminated against and that they could use their own languages. Official policy was only loosely enforced. More important, elevating the Hungarians and conferring on them alone the benefits of political nationhood could only worsen relations with other groups. On the Austrian side of the Dual Monarchy, minority nationalities such as the Poles, Czechs, and Slovenes resented their second-class status. On the Hungarian side, the regime embarked on a project of Magyarization, attempting to make the state, the civil service, and the schools more thoroughly Hungarian—an effort that did not sit well with Serbs and Croats.

In spite of these divisions, however, the Austro-Hungarian Empire succeeded for a time in creating a different kind of political and culture space within a Europe that was increasingly given over to nation-states who perceived their interests to be irrevocably opposed. The Austrian capital of Vienna developed a reputation for intellectual and cultural refinement that was in part a product of the many different peoples who made up the Habsburg lands, including Germans, Jews, Hungarians, Italians, Czechs, Poles, Serbs, Croats, and Balkan Muslims from lands that formerly belonged to the Ottoman Empire. This polyglot culture produced Béla Bartók (1881–1945), the great Hungarian composer and admirer of folk musical traditions; Gustav Mahler (1860–1911), a German-Austrian composer whose romantic symphonies and conducting prowess made him a global celebrity by the time of his death. From the same intellectual milieu came Sigmund Freud (1856–1939), a German-speaking Jewish doctor from Vienna whose writings helped shape modern psychology; and Gustav Klimt (1862–1918), a painter and founding member of the Viennese Secession movement, which rejected the reigning classicism of the Austrian art world and made the Austrian capital an important center for the birth of modern art.

The Austrian emperor's deep opposition to nationalism was not just geopolitical, therefore, but also a defense of a different relationship between the nation-state and culture. Unlike the governments of France, England, Italy, or Germany, the Habsburgs did not seek to build a nation-state based on a common cultural identity. It tried instead to build a state and administrative structure strong enough to keep the pieces from spinning off, at times playing different minorities off against each other, but also conceding greater autonomy to different groups when it seemed necessary. As the nineteenth century unfolded, however, discontented subject nationalities would appeal to other powers—Serbia, Russia, the Ottomans—and this balancing act would become more difficult.

NATION AND STATE BUILDING IN RUSSIA AND THE UNITED STATES

The challenges of nationalism and nation building also occupied Russia, the United States, and Canada. In all three countries, nation building entailed territorial and economic expansion, the incorporation of new peoples, and—in Russia and the United States—contending with the enormous problems of slavery and serfdom.

Territory, the State, and Serfdom: Russia

Serfdom in Russia, which had been legally formalized in 1649, had begun to draw significant protest from the intelligentsia under the reign of Catherine the Great (r. 1762–96). After 1789, and especially after 1848, the abolition of serfdom elsewhere in Europe made the issue more urgent. Abolishing serfdom became part of the larger project of building Russia as a modern nation. How that should happen was the subject of much debate. Two schools of thought emerged. The "Slavophiles," or Romantic nationalists, sought to preserve Russia's distinctive features. They idealized traditional Russian culture and the peasant commune, rejecting Western secularism, urban commercialism, and bourgeois culture. In contrast, the "westernizers" wished to see Russia adopt European developments in science, technology, and education, which they believed to be the foundation for Western liberalism and the protection of individual rights. Both groups agreed that serfdom must be abolished. The Russian nobility, however, tenaciously opposed emancipation. Tangled debates about how lords would be compensated for the loss of "their" serfs, and how emancipated serfs would survive without full-scale land redistribution, also checked progress on the issue. The Crimean War (see below) broke the impasse. In its aftermath, Alexander II (r. 1855–81) forced the issue. Worried that the persistence of serfdom had sapped Russian strength and contributed to its defeat in the war, and persuaded that serfdom would only continue to prompt violent conflict, he ended serfdom by decree in 1861.

The emancipation decree of 1861 was a reform of massive scope, but paradoxically it produced limited change. It granted legal rights to some 22 million serfs and authorized their title to a portion of the land they had worked. It also required the state to compensate landowners for the properties they relinquished. Large-scale landowners vastly inflated their compensation claims, however, and

Competing Viewpoints

The Abolition of Serfdom in Russia

The abolition of serfdom was central to Tsar Alexander II's program of modernization and reform after the Crimean War. Emancipated serfs were now allowed to own their land, ending centuries of bondage. The decree, however, emphasized the tsar's benevolence and the nobility's generosity—not peasant rights. The government did not want emancipation to bring revolution to the countryside; it sought to reinforce the state's authority, the landowners' power, and the peasants' obligations. After spelling out the detailed provisions for emancipation, the decree added the paragraphs reprinted here.

Emancipation did not solve problems in the Russian countryside. On the contrary, it unleashed a torrent of protest, including complaints from peasants that nobles were undermining attempts to reform. These petitions in the second section detail the struggles that came in the wake of emancipation in two villages.

Tsar Alexander II's Decree Emancipating the Serfs, 1861

And We place Our hope in the good sense of Our people.

When word of the Government's plan to abolish the law of bondage [serfdom] reached peasants unprepared for it, there arose a partial misunderstanding. Some [peasants] thought about freedom and forgot about obligations. But the general good sense [of the people] was not disturbed in the conviction that anyone freely enjoying the goods of society correspondingly owes it to the common good to fulfill certain obligations, [a conviction held] both by natural reason and by Christian law, according to which "every soul must be subject to the governing authorities." . . . Rights legally acquired by the landlords cannot be taken from them without a decent return or [their] voluntary concession; and that it would be contrary to all justice to make use of the lords' land without bearing the corresponding obligation.

And now We hopefully expect that the bonded people, as a new future opens before them, will understand and accept with gratitude the important sacrifice made by the Well-born Nobility for the improvement of their lives.

Source: James Cracraft, ed., *Major Problems in the History of Imperial Russia* (Lexington, MA: 1994), pp. 340–44.

Emancipation: The View from Below

Petition from Peasants in Podosinovka (Voronezh Province) to Alexander II, May 1863

The most merciful manifesto of Your Imperial Majesty from 19 February 1861, with the published rules, put a limit to the enslavement of the people in blessed Russia. But some former serfowners—who desire not to improve the peasants' life, but to oppress and ruin them—apportion land contrary to the laws, choose the best land from all the fields for themselves, and give the poor peasants . . . the worst and least usable lands.

To this group of squires must be counted our own, Anna Mikhailovna Raevskaia. . . . Of our fields and resources, she chose the best places from amidst our strips, and, like a cooking ring in a hearth, carved off 300 desiatines [measures of land] for herself. . . . But our community refused to accept so ruinous an allotment and requested that we be given an allotment in accordance with the local Statute. . . . The peace arbitrator . . . and the police chief . . . slandered us before the governor, alleging that we were rioting and that it is impossible for them to enter our village.

The provincial governor believed this lie and sent 1,200 soldiers of the penal

command to our village. . . . Without any cause, our village priest Father Peter—rather than give an uplifting pastoral exhortation to stop the spilling of innocent blood—joined these reptiles, with the unanimous incitement of the authorities. . . . They summoned nine township heads and their aides from other townships. . . . In their presence, the provincial governor—without making any investigation and without interrogating a single person—ordered that the birch rods be brought and that the punishment commence, which was carried out with cruelty and mercilessness. They punished up to 200 men and women; 80 people were at four levels (with 500, 400, 300 and 200 blows); some received lesser punishment . . . and when the inhuman punishment of these innocent people had ended, the provincial governor said: "If you find the land unsuitable, I do not forbid you to file petitions wherever you please," and then left. . . .

We dare to implore you, Orthodox emperor and our merciful father, not to reject the petition of a community with 600 souls, including wives and children. Order with your tsarist word that our community be allotted land . . . as the law dictates without selecting the best sections of fields and meadows, but in straight lines. . . . [Order that] the meadows and haylands along the river Elan be left to our community without any restriction; these will enable us to feed our cattle and smaller livestock, which are necessary for our existence.

Petition from Peasants in Balashov District to Grand Duke Constantin Nikolaevich, January 25, 1862

Your Imperial Excellency! Most gracious sire! Grand Duke Konstantin Nikolaevich! . . .

After being informed of the Imperial manifesto on the emancipation of peasants from serfdom on 1861 . . . we received this [news] with jubilation. . . . But from this moment, our squire ordered that the land be cut off from the entire township. But this is absolutely intolerable for us: it not only denies us profit, but threatens us with a catastrophic future. He began to hold repeated meetings and [tried to] force us to sign that we agreed to accept the above land allotment. But, upon seeing so unexpected a change, and bearing in mind the gracious manifesto, we refused. . . . After assembling the entire township, they tried to force us into making illegal signatures accepting the land cut-offs. But when they saw that this did not succeed, they had a company of soldiers sent in. . . . Then [Colonel] Globbe came from their midst, threatened us with exile to Siberia, and ordered the soldiers to strip the peasants and to punish seven people by flogging in the most inhuman manner. They still have not regained consciousness.

Source: Gregory L. Freeze, ed., *From Supplication to Revolution: A Documentary Social History of Imperial Russia* (New York: 1988), pp. 170–73.

Questions for Analysis

1. What did Tsar Alexander II fear most in liberating the serfs from bondage? What provisions did he make to ensure that the emancipation would not destabilize his regime?
2. What issues mattered most to the peasantry? What is their attitude toward the tsar?
3. Given the immediate danger to social peace, why did the tsar feel that emancipating the serfs was necessary?

managed to retain much of the most profitable acreage for themselves. As a result, the land granted to peasants was often of poor quality and insufficient to sustain themselves and their families. Moreover, the newly liberated serfs had to pay in installments for their land, which was not granted to them individually but rather to a village commune, which collected their payments. As a result, the pattern of rural life in Russia did not change drastically. The system of payment kept peasants in the villages—not as freestanding farmers but as agricultural laborers for their former masters.

While the Russian state undertook reforms, it also expanded its territory. After midcentury, the Russians pressed east and south. They invaded and conquered several independent Islamic kingdoms along the former Silk Road and expanded into Siberia in search of natural resources. Russian diplomacy wrung various commercial concessions from the Chinese that led to the founding of the Siberian city of Vladivostok in 1860. Racial, ethnic, and religious differences made governing a daunting task. In most cases, the Russian state did not try to assimilate the populations of the new territories: an acceptance of ethnic particularity was a pragmatic response to the difficulties of governing such a heterogeneous population. When the state did attempt to impose Russian culture, the results were disastrous. Whether power was wielded by the nineteenth-century tsars or, later, by the Soviet Union, powerful centrifugal forces pulled against genuine unification. Expansion helped Russia create a vast empire that was geographically of one piece but by no means one nation.

THE EMANCIPATION OF THE SERFS. This engraving depicts officials delivering the formal decree liberating serfs. A massive reform granting legal rights to millions of people, emancipation was undermined by the payments serfs owed to their former owners.

Territory and the Nation: The United States

The American Revolution had bequeathed to the United States a loose union of slave and free states, tied together in part by a commitment to territorial expansion. The so-called Jeffersonian Revolution combined democratic aspirations with a drive to expand the nation's boundaries. Leaders of the movement, under the Democratic-Republican president Thomas Jefferson (1801–1809), campaigned to add the Bill of Rights to the Constitution and were almost exclusively responsible for its success. Though they supported, in principle, the separation of powers, they believed in the supremacy of the people's representatives and viewed with alarm attempts of the executive and judicial branches to increase their power. They supported a political system based on an aristocracy of "virtue and talent," in which respect for personal liberty would be the guiding principle. They opposed the establishment of a national religion and special privilege, whether of birth or of wealth. Yet the Jeffersonian vision of the republic rested on the independence of yeoman farmers, and the independence and prosperity of those farmers depended on the availability of new lands. This made territorial expansion, as exemplified by the Louisiana Purchase in 1803, central to Jeffersonian America. Expansion brought complications. While it did provide land for many yeoman farmers in the north and south, it also added millions of acres of prime cotton land, thus extending the empire of slavery. The purchase of the port of New Orleans made lands in the south well worth developing but led the American republic forcibly to remove Native Americans from the Old South west of the Mississippi River. This process of expansion and expropriation stretched from Jefferson's administration through the age of Jackson, or the 1840s.

Under Andrew Jackson (1829–1837), the Democrats (as some of the Democratic-Republicans were now called) transformed the circumscribed liberalism of the Jeffersonians. They campaigned to extend the suffrage to all white males; they argued that all officeholders

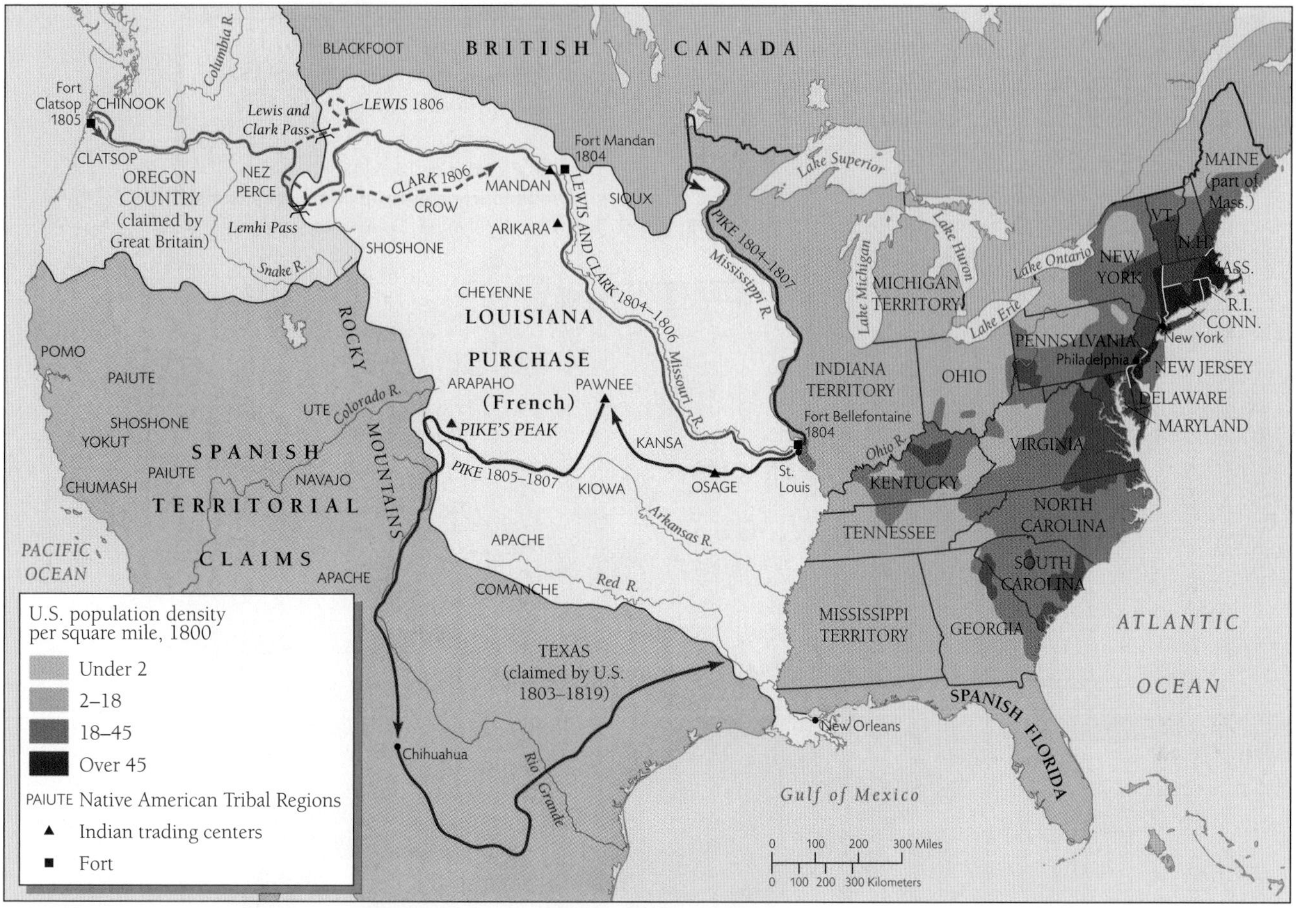

AMERICAN EXPANSION IN THE EARLY NINETEENTH CENTURY. ▪ ***What three European powers had a substantial role to play in American expansion?*** ▪ ***What events enabled the United States to acquire all lands west of the Mississippi River?*** ▪ ***How did the loss of these lands affect European powers?***

should be elected rather than appointed; and they sought the frequent rotation of men in positions of political power—a doctrine that permitted politicians to use patronage to build national political parties. Moreover, the Jacksonian vision of democracy and nationhood carried over into a crusade to incorporate more territories into the republic. It was the United States' "Manifest Destiny," wrote a New York editor, "to overspread the continent allotted by Providence for the free development of our yearly multiplying millions." That "overspreading" brought Oregon and Washington into the Union through a compromise with the British and brought Arizona, Texas, New Mexico, Utah, Nevada, and California through war with Mexico—all of which led to the wholesale expropriation of Native American lands. Territorial expansion was key to nation building, but it was built on increasingly impossible conflict over slavery.

The American Civil War, 1861–1865

The politics of slavery had already led to its abolition in France and Britain (see Chapter 20), but in the United States the combination of a growing abolitionist movement, a slave-owning class that feared the economic power of the north, and territorial expansion created deadlock and crisis. As the country expanded west, the North and South engaged in a protracted tug of war about whether new states were to be "free" or "slave." In the North, territorial expansion heightened calls for free labor; in the South, it deepened whites' commitment to an economy and society based on plantation slavery. Ultimately, the changes pushed southern political leaders toward secession. The failure of a series of elaborate compromises led to the outbreak of the Civil War in 1861.

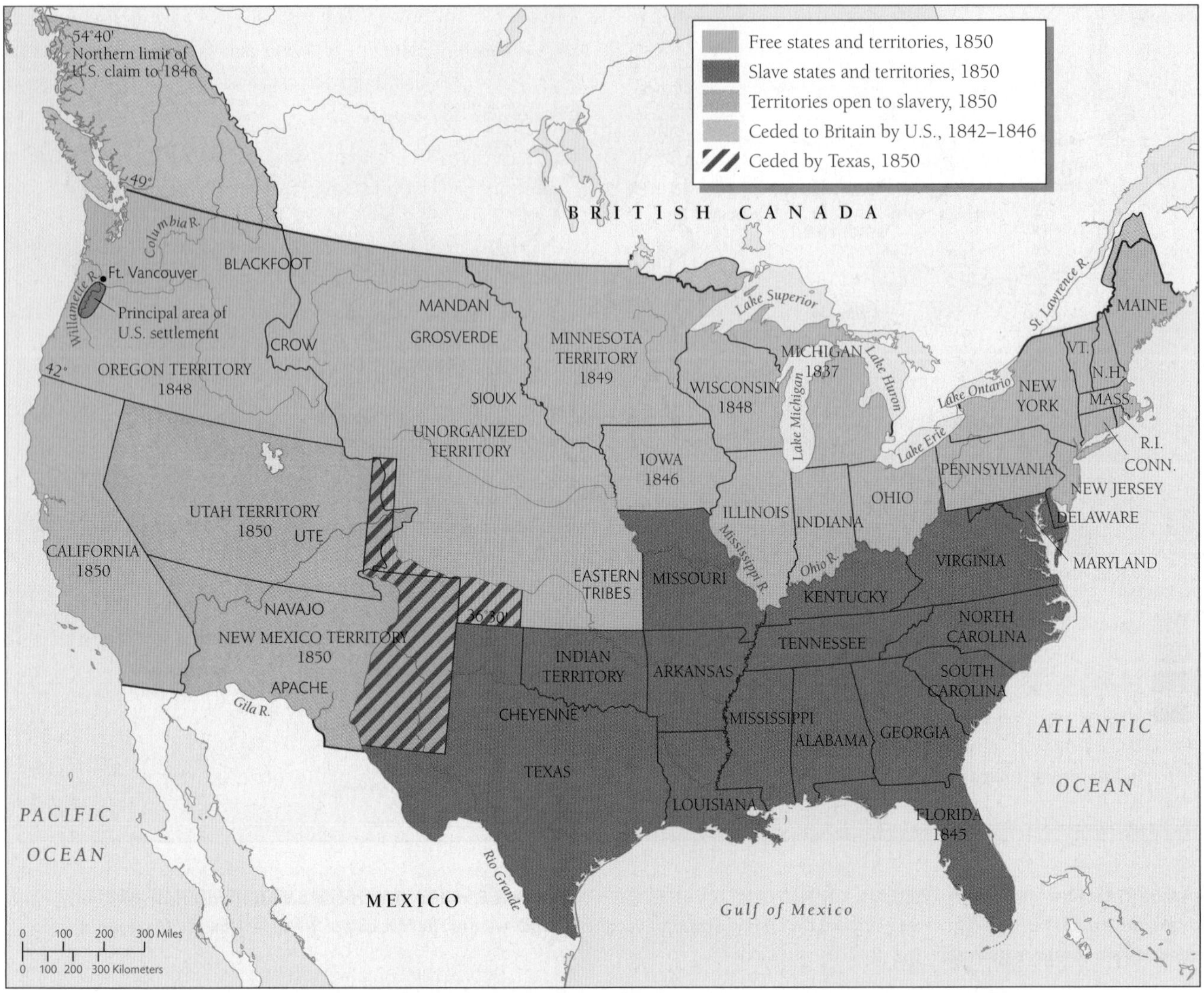

AMERICAN EXPANSION IN THE LATE NINETEENTH CENTURY. Note the stages of American settlement across the North American continent and the dates for the extension of slavery into new territories. ▪ ***How did the question of slavery shape the way that new territories were absorbed into the republic?*** ▪ ***Compare American expansion with European colonialism?***

The protracted and costly struggle proved a first experience of the horrors of modern war and prefigured the First World War. It also decisively transformed the nation. First, it abolished slavery. Second, it established the preeminence of the national government over states' rights. The Fourteenth Amendment to the Constitution stated specifically that all Americans were citizens of the United States and not of an individual state or territory. In declaring that no citizen was to be deprived of life, liberty, or property without due process of law, it established that "due process" was to be defined by the national, not the state or territorial, government. Third, in the aftermath of the Civil War, the U.S. economy expanded with stunning rapidity. In 1865, there were 35,000 miles of railroad track in the United States; by 1900, there were almost 200,000. Industrial and agricultural production rose, putting the United States in a position to compete with Great Britain. As we will see later on, American industrialists, bankers, and retailers introduced innovations in assembly-line manufacturing, corporate organization, and advertising that startled their European counterparts and gave the United States new power in world politics. These developments were all part of the process of nation building. They did not overcome deep racial, regional, or class divides. Though the war brought the South back into the Union, the rise of northern capitalism magnified the backwardness of the South as an underdeveloped agricultural region whose wealth was extracted by northern industrialists. The railroad corporations, which pieced together the national infrastructure, became the classic foe of labor and agrarian reformers. In

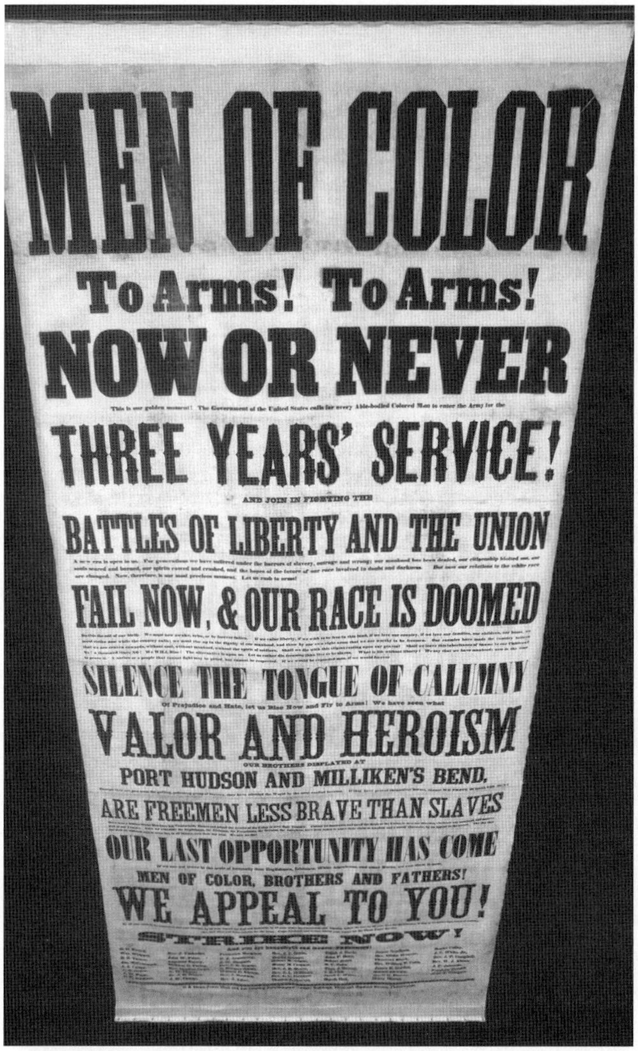

CIVIL WAR RECRUITING POSTER. This poster, created by northern African American abolitionists, exhorts fellow blacks to fight in the American Civil War.

these ways, the Civil War laid the foundations for the modern American nation-state.

"EASTERN QUESTIONS": INTERNATIONAL RELATIONS AND THE DECLINE OF OTTOMAN POWER

During the nineteenth century, questions of national identity and international power were inextricable from contests over territory. War and diplomacy drew and redrew boundaries as European nations groped toward a sustainable balance of power. The rise of new powers, principally the German Empire, posed one set of challenges to continental order. The waning power of older regimes posed another. The Crimean War, which lasted from 1853 to 1856, was a particularly gruesome attempt to cope with the most serious such collapse. As the Ottoman Empire lost its grip on its provinces in southeastern Europe, the "Eastern Question" of who would benefit from Ottoman weakness drew Europe into war. At stake were not only territorial gains but also strategic interests, alliances, and the balance of power in Europe. And though the war occurred before the unification of the German and Italian states, it structured the system of Great Power politics that guided Europe until (and indeed toward) the First World War.

The Crimean War, 1853–1856

The root causes of the war lay in the Eastern Question and the decline of the Ottoman Empire. The crisis that provoked it, however, involved religion—namely French and Russian claims to protect religious minorities and the holy places of Jerusalem within the Muslim Ottoman Empire. In 1853, a three-way quarrel among France (on behalf of Roman Catholics), Russia (representing Eastern Orthodox Christians), and Turkey devolved into a Russian confrontation with the Turkish sultan. Confident that Turkey would be unable to resist, concerned that other powers might take advantage of Turkish weakness, and persuaded (mistakenly) that they had British support, the Russians moved troops into the Ottoman-governed territories of Moldavia and Walachia (see the map on page 722). In October 1853, Turkey, also persuaded they would be supported by the British, declared war on Russia. The war became a disaster for the Turks, who lost their fleet at the battle of Sinope in November. But Russia's success alarmed the British and the French, who considered Russian expansion a threat to their interests in the Balkans, the eastern Mediterranean, and, for the British, the route to India. Determined to check that expansion, France and Britain each declared war on Russia in March 1854. In September, they landed on the Russian peninsula of Crimea and headed for the Russian naval base at Sevastopol, to which they laid siege. France, Britain, and the Ottomans were joined in 1855 by the small but ambitious Italian state of Piedmont-Sardinia, all fighting against the Russians. This was the closest Europe had come to a general war since 1815.

The war was relatively short, but its conduct was devastating. Conditions on the Crimean peninsula were dire, and the disastrous mismanagement of supplies and hygiene by the British and French led to epidemics among the troops.

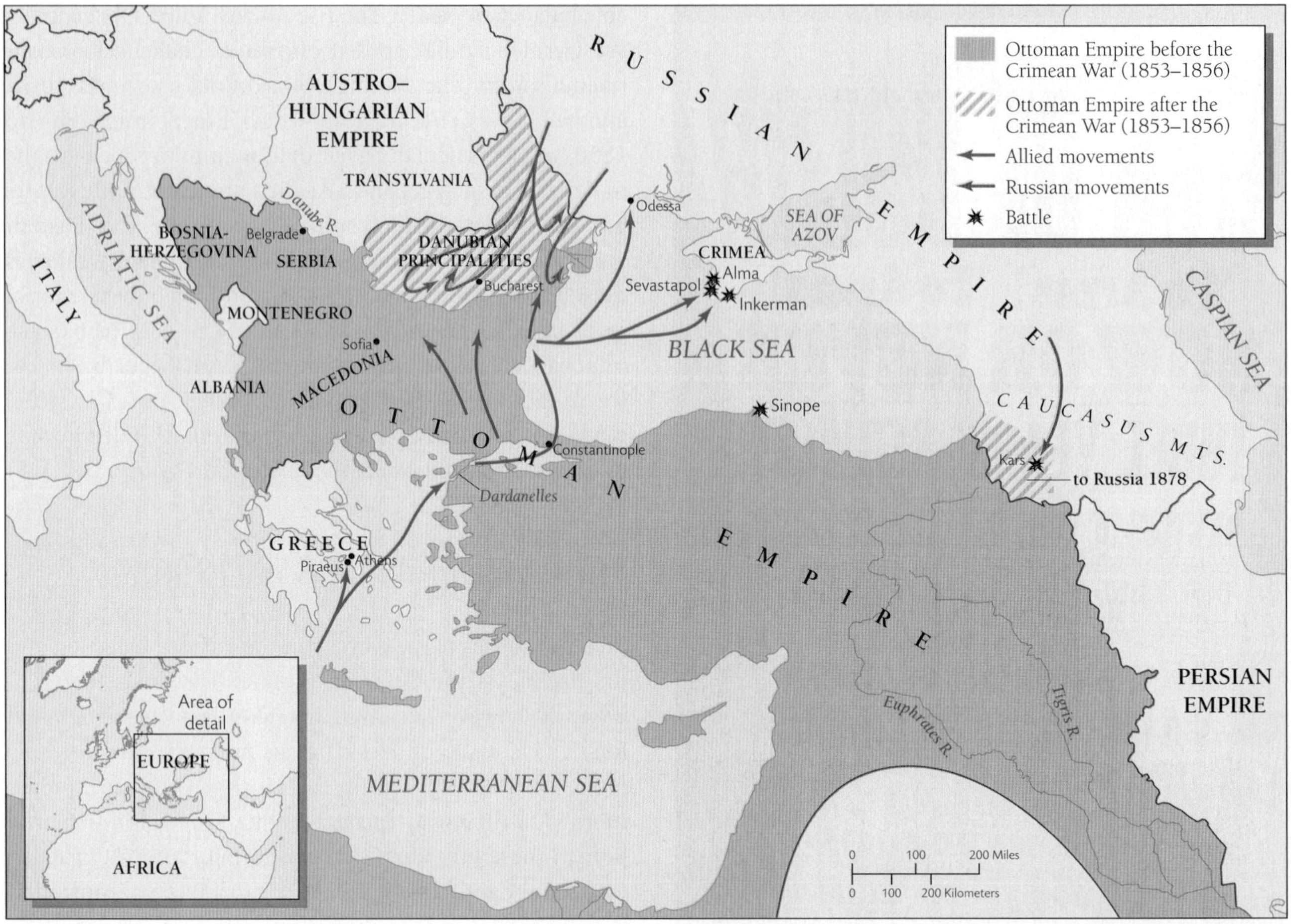

THE CRIMEAN WAR. Note the theater of operations and the major assaults of the Crimean War. ▪ ***Which empires and nations were in a position to take advantage of Ottoman weakness?*** ▪ ***Who benefited from the outcome, and who was most harmed?*** ▪ ***In what ways was the Crimean War the first modern war?***

At least as many soldiers died from typhus or cholera as in combat. The fighting was bitter, marked by such notoriously inept strategies as the British "charge of the Light Brigade," in which a British cavalry unit was slaughtered by massed Russian artillery. Vast battles pitted tens of thousands of British and French troops against Russian formations, combat that was often settled with bayonets. Despite the disciplined toughness of the British and French troops, and despite their nations' dominance of the seas around Crimea, the Russians denied them a clear victory. Sevastopol, under siege for nearly a year, did not fall until September 1855. The bitter, unsatisfying conflict was ended by treaty in 1856.

For the French and Sardinians, the bravery of their soldiers bolstered positive national sentiments at home; for the British and Russians, however, the poorly managed war provoked waves of intense criticism. As far as international relations were concerned, the peace settlement dealt a blow to Russia, whose influence in the Balkans was drastically curbed. The provinces of Moldavia and Walachia were united as Romania and became an independent nation. Austria's refusal to come to the aid of Russia cost Russia the support of its powerful former ally. The Crimean War embarrassed France and left Russia and Austria considerably weaker, opening an advantage for Bismarck in the 1860s, as we saw earlier.

The Crimean War was important in other ways as well. Though fought largely with the same methods and mentalities employed in the Napoleonic Wars forty years earlier, the war brought innovations that forecast the direction of modern warfare. It saw the first significant use of rifled muskets, underwater mines, and trench warfare as well as the first tactical use of railroads and telegraphs.

In addition, the war was covered by the first modern war correspondents and photojournalists, making it the most public war to date. Reports from the theater of war were sent "live" by telegraph to Britain and France with

***CAPTAIN DAMES OF THE ROYAL ARTILLERY,* 1855.** Roger Fenton studied painting in London and then Paris, where he learned about and started to experiment with photography. He developed a mobile darkroom and ventured into the English countryside. In 1855, he went to the Crimea, subsidized by the British government. Photographs of movement and troops in battle were still impossible, and political restraint kept him from photographing the horrors of the increasingly unpopular Crimean War. Still, his were the first war photographs.

objective and sobering detail; the (London) *Times* reporter William Howard Russell, for instance, heaped criticism on the government for the deplorable conditions British soldiers endured. The care and supply of the troops became national scandals in the popular press, prompting dramatic changes in the military's administrative and logistical systems and making heroes of individual doctors and nurses such as Florence Nightingale. The British government and commercial publishers both sent photographers to document the war's progress and perhaps also to counter charges that troops were undersupplied and malnourished. Roger Fenton, the most prominent and prolific of these war photographers, employed the new medium to capture the grim realities of camp life. Technological limitations and political considerations kept him from photographing the more gruesome carnage of the battlefield, but Fenton's photographs introduced a new level of realism and immediacy to the public's conception of war.

CONCLUSION

The decades between 1848 and 1870 brought intense nation building in the Western world. The unification of Germany and Italy changed the map of Europe, with important consequences for the balance of power. The emergence of the United States as a major power also had international ramifications. For old as well as new nation-states, economic development and political transformation—often on a very large scale—were important means of increasing and securing the state's power. Even though the liberal revolutionaries of 1848 had not achieved the goals

***THE STONE BREAKERS* BY GUSTAVE COURBET, 1849.** Courbet was a French realist painter who depicted everyday men and women in an honest and unromantic manner. Considered one of his most important works, this painting of two ordinary peasants building a road was destroyed in Dresden during the Second World War.

AUTHOR LEO TOLSTOY. Although a wealthy landowner, Tolstoy often dressed as a peasant. He became increasingly ascetic, casting off the corruptions of the world, and pacifist. In this picture, he is leaving his home for a hermitage.

they sought, their demands for more representative government, the abolition of privilege, and land reform still had to be reckoned with, as did the systems of slavery and serfdom. Trailing the banner of nationhood was an explosive set of questions about how to balance the power and interests of minorities and majorities, of the wealthy and poor, of the powerful and the dispossessed. Nation building not only changed states, it transformed relations between states and their citizens.

These transformations were anything but predictable. Nationalism showed itself to be a volatile, erratic, and malleable force during the mid-nineteenth century. It provided

After You Read This Chapter

Visit StudySpace for quizzes, additional review materials, and multimedia documents. **wwnorton.com/web/westernciv18**

REVIEWING THE OBJECTIVES

- Revolutions broke out in 1848 in almost every capital of Europe except for London and St. Petersburg. What accounts for this wave of simultaneous revolutionary movements?
- Liberal revolutionaries in France in 1848 did not have the same goals as their socialist allies. What were their goals and why did they fail to achieve them?
- Liberal revolutionaries in the German-speaking lands of central Europe in 1848 were forced to reckon with Austrian and Prussian states in their bid for national unification. What did they want, and why did they fail?
- Nationalists in both Germany and Italy were divided between those who supported the creation of a new nation from below, through popular movements, and those who preferred nation building from above. How did these divisions work themselves out in the process of national unification?
- Creating a modern nation in Russia entailed the end of serfdom, whereas in the United States, political leaders from the North and South debated the place of slavery in the modern nation-state. In what ways were national debates about citizenship in these countries shaped by the widespread practices of bondage?
- The three major European wars of this period were of relatively short duration, but they had profound effects on the international balance of power in Europe. Which countries emerged stronger from these conflicts, and which found their interests most damaged?

much of the fuel for revolutionary movements in 1848, but it also helped tear their movements apart, undermining revolutionary gains. Those who had linked their democratic goals to the rise of new nation-states were sorely disappointed. In the aftermath of the defeated revolutions, most nation building took a conservative tack. Nationalism came to serve the needs of statesmen and bureaucrats who did not seek an "awakening of peoples" and who had serious reservations about popular sovereignty. For them, nations simply represented modern, organized, and stronger states.

The result of these many tensions was an age that seemed a contradictory mix of the old and the new, of monarchies beset with debates about nationality and citizenship, of land-owning aristocratic elites rubbing elbows with newly wealthy industrialists, and of artisan handworkers meeting up with factory laborers in worker's associations that debated the proper path toward realizing their socialist goals. Remarkably, the result of this period of intense nation building was a period of unusual stability on the Continent, which ushered in an era of unprecedented capitalist and imperial expansion. The antagonisms unleashed by German unification and the crumbling of the Ottoman Empire would reemerge, however, in the Great Power politics that precipitated the First World War.

PEOPLE, IDEAS, AND EVENTS IN CONTEXT

- What circumstances led to the downfall of **LOUIS PHILIPPE**'s government in France? What divisions between supporters of the revolution led to the **JUNE DAYS** in Paris in 1848?
- What role did the **ZOLLVEREIN** and the **FRANKFURT PARLIAMENT** play in the creation of a unified Germany?
- How and why did **OTTO VON BISMARCK** aim for a policy of German national unification during his time in office?
- How did **GIUSEPPE GARIBALDI** and **CAMILLO BENSO DI CAVOUR** initially see the process of Italian unification? Whose vision came closest to reality?
- Who was **NAPOLEON III**, and how did his policies contribute to nation building in France?
- What was the contribution of **JOHN STUART MILL** to debates about citizenship in Britain?
- Why were nationalist movements such as **PAN-SLAVISM** or **MAGYAR NATIONALISM** such a danger to the Austro-Hungarian Empire?
- Why did **TSAR ALEXANDER II** decide to **EMANCIPATE THE SERFS**?
- What made the **CRIMEAN WAR** different from previous conflicts and more like the wars of the twentieth century?

THINKING ABOUT CONNECTIONS

- Revolutionaries in 1848, whether they were in Paris, Rome, Berlin, or Vienna, must have been aware of connections between their own struggles and the historical example of the French Revolution of 1789–99. Did revolutionaries in 1848 have goals that were similar to the goals of French revolutionaries at the end of the eighteenth century?
- How might the failure of the 1848 revolutions have shaped the beliefs of European conservatives and liberals or the beliefs of supporters of more radical ideologies such as republicanism and socialism?

Before You Read This Chapter

STORY LINES

- Industrialization, rapid technological development, and the concentration of economic wealth gave western European nations great power during this period, along with the confidence to use this power to extend their control to other parts of the world.
- Colonial expansion occurred simultaneously with the development of mass politics and the spread of consumer culture in Europe, a combination that made colonies and the power to control them an important part of national identity for many people in Europe, especially in Britain, France, and Germany.
- The new imperialism ushered in a new era of conflict: between European powers and newly colonized peoples in Africa and Asia, and between the colonizing nations themselves, as they competed with one another for global influence and resources.

CHRONOLOGY

1788	British establish colony in New South Wales, Australia
1797–1818	British expand foothold in India
1830	France invades Algeria
1839–1842	Opium Wars in China
1840	British establish colony in New Zealand
1857	Sepoy Mutiny in India
1870–1900	European scramble for Africa
1875	Britain gains control of Suez Canal
1882	British occupation of Egypt begins
1883–1893	France moves into Vietnam, Laos, and Cambodia
1884–1885	Berlin West Africa Conference
1896	Italian forces defeated by Ethiopians
1898	Fashoda Crisis
1898	Spanish-American War
1898–1901	Boer War
1900	London Pan-African Conference
1904–1905	Russo-Japanese War

22

Imperialism and Colonialism, 1870–1914

CORE OBJECTIVES

- **DEFINE** *imperialism* and locate the major colonies established by European powers in Africa and Asia in the nineteenth century.
- **UNDERSTAND** the major reasons for European colonial expansion in the nineteenth century.
- **DESCRIBE** the choices faced by colonized peoples in the face of European power.
- **EXPLAIN** how imperialism shaped the culture of European nations at home.
- **UNDERSTAND** the nature of the crisis faced by European imperial powers at the end of the nineteenth century.

In 1869, the Suez Canal opened with a grand celebration. The imperial yacht *Eagle,* with Empress Eugénie of France on board, entered the canal on November 17, followed by sixty-eight steamships carrying the emperor of Austria, the crown prince of Prussia, the grand duke of Russia, and scores of other dignitaries. Flowery speeches flowed freely, as did the champagne. The ceremony cost a staggering £1.3 million (about $121 million today). Even so, the size of the celebration paled in comparison to the canal itself. The largest project of its kind, the canal sliced through a hundred miles of Egyptian desert to link the Mediterranean and Red seas, cutting the trip from London to Bombay in half. The canal dramatically showcased the abilities of Western power and technology to transform the globe, but the human cost was high: 30,000 Egyptians worked on the canal as forced laborers, and thousands died during cholera epidemics in the work camps.

The building of the canal was the result of decades of European involvement in Egypt. French troops under Napoleon led the way, but Britain's bankers soon followed. European financial interests developed a close relationship with those who governed Egypt as a semi-independent state inside the Ottoman Empire. By 1875, the British controlled the canal, after purchasing 44 percent of the canal's shares from the Egyptian khedive (viceroy) when he was threatened with bankruptcy. By the late 1870s, these economic and political relationships had produced debt and instability in Egypt. In a bid for national independence, a group of Egyptian army officers led by 'Urabi Pasha took control of Egypt's government in 1882.

The British government, determined to protect its investments, decided to intervene. The Royal Navy shelled Egyptian forts along the canal into rubble, and a British task force landed near 'Urabi Pasha's central base, overwhelming the Egyptian lines. This striking success rallied popular support at home, and the political consequences lasted for seventy years. Britain took effective control of Egypt. A British lord, Evelyn Baring, assumed the role of proconsul in a power-sharing relationship with Egyptian authorities, but real power rested with Britain. Britain demanded the repayment of loans and regulated the trade in Egyptian cotton that helped supply Britain's textile mills. Most important, the intervention secured the route to India and the markets of the East.

The Suez Canal and the conquest of Egypt was made possible by the convergence of technology, money, politics, and a global strategy of imperial control. A similar interplay between economics and colonialism produced the stunning expansion of European empires in the late nineteenth century. The years 1870 to 1914 brought both rapid industrialization throughout the West and an intense

THE INAUGURATION OF THE SUEZ CANAL. This allegory illustrates the union of the Mediterranean and Red Seas attended by Ismail Pasha, the khedive of Egypt, Abdul Aziz, sultan of the Ottoman Empire, Ferdinand de Lesseps, president of the Suez Canal Company, Empress Eugénie of France, and several mermaids. It also represents the nineteenth-century vision of imperialism as a bearer of global progress, promoting technological advance and breaking down barriers between the Orient and the West. ▪ ***Who was the audience for this image?***

push to expand the power and influence of Western power abroad. The "new imperialism" of the late nineteenth century was distinguished by its scope, intensity, and long-range consequences. It transformed cultures and states in Europe, Africa, and Asia. Projects such as the Suez Canal changed—literally—the landscape and map of the world. They also represented an ideology: the belief in technology and Western superiority. In the minds of imperialists, the elimination of geographic barriers had opened the entire world, its lands and its peoples, to the administrative power of the West.

The new imperialism, however, was not a one-way street. Europeans could not simply conquer vast territories and dictate their terms to the rest of the world. The new political and economic relationships between colonies and dependent states, on the one hand, and the "metropole" (the colonizing power), on the other, ran both ways, bringing changes to both parties. Fierce competition among nations upset the balance of power. The new imperialism was an expression of European strength, but it was also profoundly destabilizing.

IMPERIALISM

Imperialism is the process of extending one state's control over another—a process that takes many forms. Sometimes this control was exercised by *direct rule*, by which the colonizing nation annexed territories outright and subjugated the peoples who lived there. At times, colonialism worked through *indirect rule*, by which conquering European nations reached agreements with local leaders and governed through them. Finally, *informal imperialism* could be a less visible exercise of state power, where stronger states allowed weaker states to maintain their independence while reducing their sovereignty. Informal imperialism took the form of carving out zones of European sovereignty and privilege, such as treaty ports, within other states. There was no single technique of colonial control; as we will see, resistance forced colonial powers to shift strategies frequently.

Both formal and informal imperialism expanded dramatically in the nineteenth century. The "scramble for Africa" was the most startling case of formal imperialism: from 1875 to 1902, Europeans seized up to 90 percent of the continent. The overall picture is no less remarkable: between 1870 and 1900, a small group of states (France, Britain, Germany, the Netherlands, Russia, and the United States) colonized about one quarter of the world's land surface. In addition, these same states extended informal empire in China and Turkey, across South and East Asia, and into Central and South America. So striking was this expansion of European power that contemporaries spoke of the "new imperialism." Nevertheless, imperialism was not new. It is more helpful to think of these nineteenth-century developments as a new stage of European empire building, after the collapse of Europe's early modern empires in North and South America at the end of the eighteenth century.

The nineteenth-century empires rose against the backdrop of industrialization, liberal revolution, and the rise of nation-states. Industrialization produced greater demand for raw materials from distant locations. At the same time, many Europeans became convinced in the nineteenth century that their economic development, science, and technology would inevitably bring progress to the rest of the world. Finally, especially in Britain and France, nineteenth-century imperial powers were in principle democratic nations, where government authority relied on consent and on notions of civic equality. This made conquest difficult to justify and raised thorny questions about the status of colonized peoples. Earlier European conquerors had claimed a missionary zeal to convert people to Christianity as a justification for their actions. Nineteenth-century imperialists justified their projects by saying that their investment in infrastructure—railroads, harbors, and roads—and their social reforms would fulfill Europe's secular mission to bring civilization to the rest of the world. This vision of the "white man's burden"—the phrase is Rudyard Kipling's—became a powerful argument in favor of imperial expansion throughout Europe (see ***Competing Viewpoints*** on pages 756–57).

In spite of these ambitious goals, the resistance of colonized peoples did as much to shape the history of colonialism as did the ambitious plans of the colonizers. The Haitian revolution of 1804 compelled the British and the French to end the slave trade and slavery in their colonies in the 1830s and the 1840s, though new systems of forced labor cropped up to take their places. The American Revolution encouraged the British to grant self-government to white settler states in Canada (1867), Australia (1901), and New Zealand (1912). Rebellion in India in 1857 caused the British to place the colony under the direct control of the crown, rather than the East India Company. In general, nineteenth-century imperialism involved less independent entrepreneurial activity by merchants and traders and more "settlement and discipline." This required legal distinctions made on racial or religious grounds in order to organize relationships between Europeans and different indigenous groups and an administration to enforce such distinctions. (Apartheid in South Africa is but one example.) Defending such empires thus became a vast project, involving legions of government officials, schoolteachers, and engineers. Nineteenth-century imperialism produced new forms of government and management in the colonies, and as it did so, it forged new interactions between Europeans and indigenous peoples.

The New Imperialism and Its Causes

As early as 1902, British author J. A. Hobson charged that the interests of a small group of wealthy financiers had driven the "scramble for Africa." British taxpayers subsidized armies of conquest and occupation, and journalists whipped up the public's enthusiasm for imperialism. Hobson, a reformer and a social critic, argued that international finance and business had distorted conceptions of England's real national interests. He hoped that a genuine democracy would curb the country's imperial policies.

Hobson's analysis inspired an influential Marxist critique of imperialism made by Vladimir Ilyich Lenin. Like Hobson, Lenin believed that imperialism was best understood on economic grounds. Unlike Hobson, however, Lenin believed that imperialism was an integral part of late-nineteenth-century capitalism. With domestic markets saturated and growth limited by competition at home, capitalists were forced to invest and search for new markets overseas, producing an ever more intensive pressure for the expansion of European imperialism. Lenin published *Imperialism: The Highest Stage of Capitalism* (1917) at the height of the First World War, and he used this argument to assert that hopes for a democratic reform of capitalism were misplaced and that the only solution was the replacement of capitalism with a revolutionary new economic order.

Historians now agree that economic pressures were only one of the causes of imperialism. Only half of Britain's £4 billion in foreign investments was at work within its empire, and in France the proportion was even smaller: one fifth of French capital was invested overseas. The French had more capital invested in their ally Russia than in all their colonial possessions. Nevertheless, Europeans expected the colonies to produce profits. French newspapers, for instance, reported that the Congo was "rich, vigorous, and fertile virgin territory" with "fabulous quantities" of gold, copper, ivory, and rubber. Such hopes contributed to expansionism, even if the profits did not meet expectations.

A second interpretation of imperialism emphasized strategic and nationalist motives. International rivalries made European powers more determined to control less-developed nations and territories. French politicians hoped that imperialism would restore the honor France had lost in their defeat by the Prussians in 1870. The British looked with alarm at Germany's industrialization and feared losing their share of world markets. The Germans, recently unified into a modern nation-state, saw overseas empire as the only way to become a great power.

This interpretation suggests a link between imperialism and nineteenth-century state and nation building. Colonies demonstrated military power; they showed the vigor of a nation's economy; the strength of its citizens, the force of its law, the power of its culture. A strong national community could assimilate others, bringing progress to new lands and new peoples. One German proponent of expansion called colonialism the "national continuation of the German desire for unity." Lobby groups such as the German Colonial Society, the French Colonial Party, and the Royal Colonial Institute in Britain argued for empire in similar terms, as did newspapers, which recognized the profits to be made in selling sensational stories of overseas conquest.

Finally, imperialism had important cultural dimensions. A French diplomat once described the British imperial adventurer Cecil Rhodes as a "force cast in an idea"; the same might be said of imperialism itself. Scottish missionary David Livingston believed that the British conquest of Africa would end the East African slave trade and "introduce the Negro family into the body of corporate nations." Taking arms against the slave trade, famine, disorder, and illiteracy seemed to many Europeans not only a reason to invade Africa but also a duty and proof of a somehow superior civilization. These convictions did not cause imperialism, but they illustrate how central empire building became to the West's self-image.

In short, it is difficult to disentangle the economic, political, and strategic causes of imperialism. It is more important to understand how the motives overlapped. Economic interests often helped convince policy makers that strategic interests were at stake. Different constituencies—the military, international financiers, missionaries, colonial lobby groups at home—held different and often clashing visions of the purpose and benefits of imperialism. Imperial policy, therefore, was less a matter of long-range planning than a series of quick responses, often improvised, to particular situations. And of course, Europeans were not the only players on the stage. Their goals and intentions were shaped by social changes in the countries in which they became involved; by the independent interests of local peoples; and by resistance, which, as often as not, Europeans found themselves unable to understand and powerless to stop.

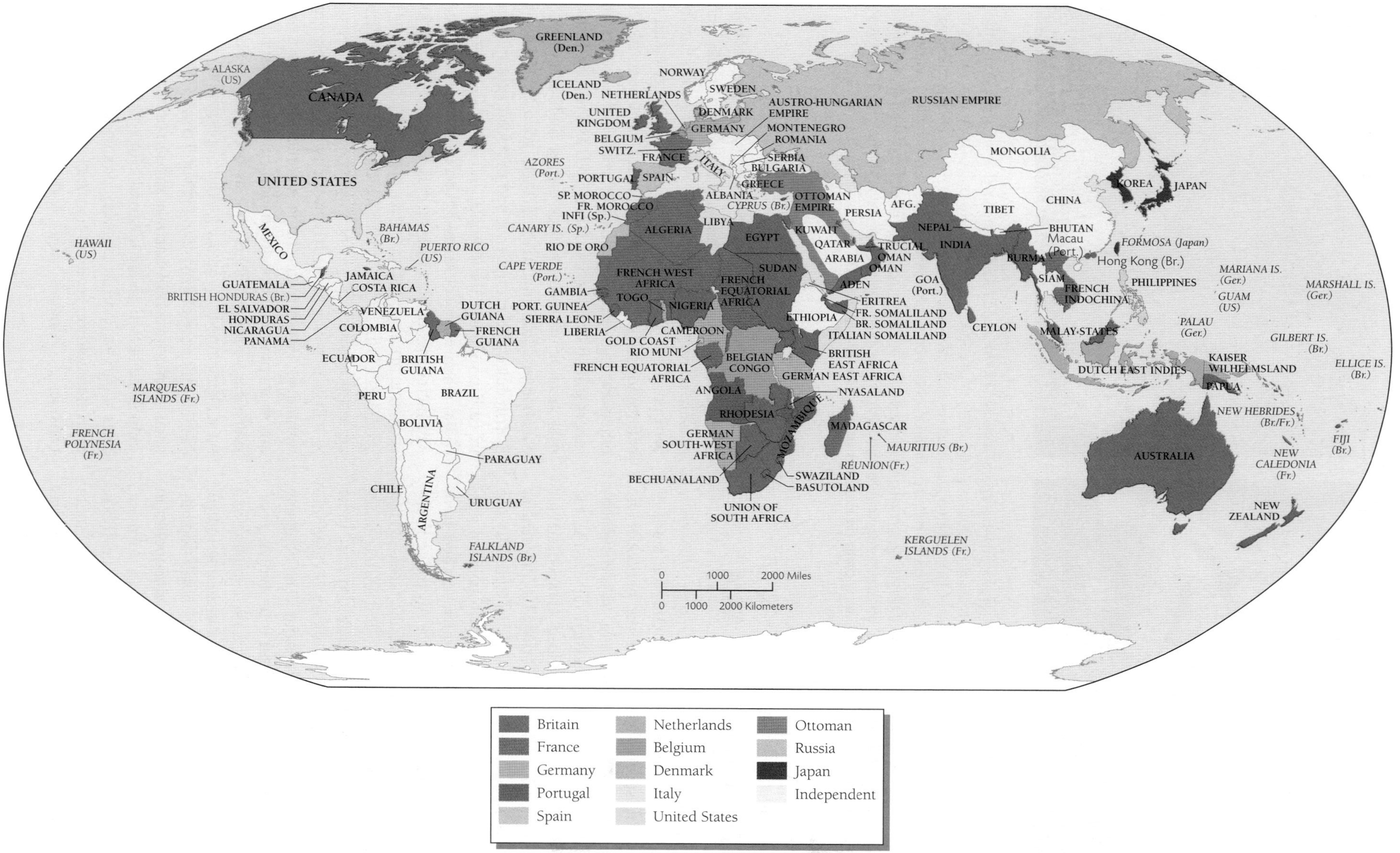

EUROPEAN EMPIRES IN 1900. ▪ *Where were Britain's major imperial interests, and what trade routes did they have most incentive to protect?* ▪ *Where were France's most important imperial holdings and who was their major competitor?* ▪ *How substantial were German, Dutch, Portuguese, or U.S. colonies in comparison to British and French holdings?*

IMAGES OF WOMEN IN THE COLONIES. Photographs and engravings of women in Africa and Asia circulated widely in Europe during the nineteenth century, and these images shaped attitudes toward colonization. Many images—some openly pornographic—portrayed African or Asian women as attractive, exotic, and in postures that invited European fantasies of domination. "Reclining Jewess" (left) is a typical example of such imagery, from French Algeria. Other images portrayed colonial women as victims of barbaric customs, such as sati, a social funeral practice in which a new widow would burn herself during the cremation of her deceased husband (right). This image, which first appeared in a work by a missionary who had been to Calcutta, was widely reproduced later as an illustration of the need for the British to bring "civilization" to India. ▪ ***Could these images have the same impact without the emphasis on the gender of the subject?***

IMPERIALISM IN SOUTH ASIA

India was the center of the British Empire, the jewel of the British crown, secured well before the period of the new imperialism. The conquest of most of the subcontinent began in the 1750s and quickened during the age of revolution. Conquering India helped compensate for "losing" North America. General Cornwallis, defeated at Yorktown, went on to a brilliant career in India. By the mid-nineteenth century, India was the focal point of Britain's newly expanded global power, which reached from southern Africa across South Asia and to Australia. Keeping this region involved changing tactics and forms of rule.

Until the mid-nineteenth century, British territories in India were under the control of the British East India Company. The company had its own military, divided into European and (far larger) Indian divisions. The company held the right to collect taxes on land from Indian peasants. Until the early nineteenth century, the company had legal monopolies over trade in all goods, including indigo, textiles, salt, minerals, and—most lucrative of all—opium. The British government had granted trade monopolies in its northern American colonies. Unlike North America, however, India never became a settler state. In the 1830s, Europeans were a tiny minority, numbering 45,000 in an Indian population of 150 million. The company's rule was repressive and enforced by the military. Soldiers collected taxes; civil servants wore military uniforms; British troops brashly commandeered peasants' oxen and carts for their own purposes. Typically, though, the company could not enforce its rule uniformly. It governed some areas directly, others through making alliances with local leaders, and others still by simply controlling goods and money. Indirect rule, here as in other empires, meant finding indigenous collaborators and maintaining their goodwill. Thus, the British cultivated groups that had provided administrators in earlier regimes: the Rajputs and Bhumihars of North India, whom they considered especially effective soldiers, and merchants of big cities such as Calcutta. They offered economic privileges, state offices, or military posts to either groups or entire nations that agreed to ally with the British against others.

British policy shifted between two poles: one group wanted to "Westernize" India; another believed it safer, and more practical, to defer to local culture. Christian missionaries, whose numbers rose as occupation expanded, were determined to replace "blind superstition" with the "genial influence of Christian light and truth." Indignant at such practices as child marriage and *sati* (in which a widow immolated herself on her husband's funeral pyre), missionaries sought support in England for a wide-ranging assault on Hindu culture. Secular reformers, many of them liberal, considered "Hindoos" and "Mahommedans" susceptible to forms of despotism—both in the family and in the state. They turned their reforming zeal to legal and political change. But other British administrators warned their countrymen not to meddle with Indian institutions. "Englishmen are as great fanatics in politics as Mahommedans in religion. They suppose that no country can be saved without English institutions," said one British administrator. Indirect rule, they argued, would work only with the cooperation of local powers. Conflicts such as these meant that the British never agreed on any single cultural policy.

From Mutiny to Rebellion

The East India Company's rule often met resistance and protest. In 1857–58, it was badly shaken by a revolt of Indian soldiers in the British army, now known in India as the Great Mutiny of 1857. The uprising began near Delhi, when the military disciplined a regiment of *sepoys* (the traditional term for Indian soldiers employed by the British) for refusing to use rifle cartridges greased with pork fat—unacceptable to either Hindus or Muslims. Yet, as the British prime minister Disraeli later observed, "The decline and fall of empires are not affairs of greased cartridges." The causes of the mutiny were deeper and involved social, economic, and political grievances. Indian peasants attacked law courts and burned tax rolls, protesting debt and corruption. In areas that had recently been annexed, rebels defended their traditional leaders, who had been ousted by the British. Army officers from privileged castes resented arbitrary treatment at the hands of the British; they were first promoted as loyal allies and then forced to serve without what they considered titles and honors. The mutiny spread through large areas of northwest India. European troops, which counted for fewer than one-fifth of those in arms, found themselves losing control. Religious leaders, both Hindu and Muslim, seized the occasion to denounce Christian missionaries sent in by the British and their assault on local traditions.

At first, the British were faced with a desperate situation, with areas under British control cut off from one another and pro-British cities under siege. Loyal Indian troops were brought south from the frontiers, and British troops, fresh from the Crimean War, were shipped directly from Britain to suppress the rebellion. The fighting lasted more than a year, and the British matched the rebels' early massacres with a systematic campaign of repression. Whole rebel units were killed rather than being allowed to surrender or tried on the spot and executed. Towns and villages that supported the rebels were burned, just as the rebels had burned European homes and outposts. Yet the defeat of the rebellion caught the British public's imagination. After the bloody, inconclusive mess of Crimea, the terrifying threat to British India and the heroic rescue of European

THE EXECUTION OF INDIANS WHO PARTICIPATED IN THE REBELLION OF 1857. The British were determined to make an example of rebel Indian soldiers after the Great Mutiny. The engraving on the left shows executions in which the condemned were blown apart by cannons. The cartoon on the right, "The Execution of 'John Company,'" shows the same cannons destroying the British East India Company, which was abolished by the British government as a result of the rebellion. ▪ ***What do these images tell us about public awareness of the rebellion's violence and its suppression?***

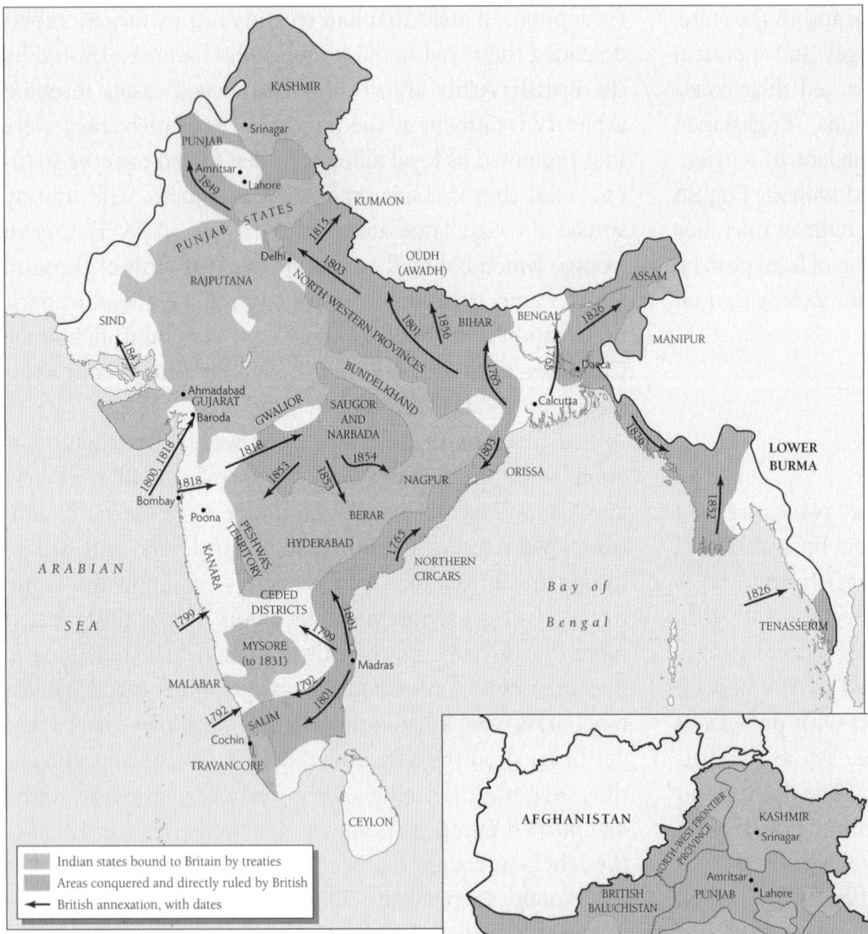

BRITISH INDIA BEFORE AND AFTER 1857. Note the dates of British territorial annexations on the left, and the complexity of colonial India's political boundaries (on the right) even after direct rule by the British crown had been established. ▪ ***According to the first map, what were the three ways the British gained control over various kingdoms and states in India before 1857?*** ▪ ***What is the most important change in British rule before and after 1857?*** ▪ ***How did the British hope to successfully rule over such a large and diverse group of people after 1857?***

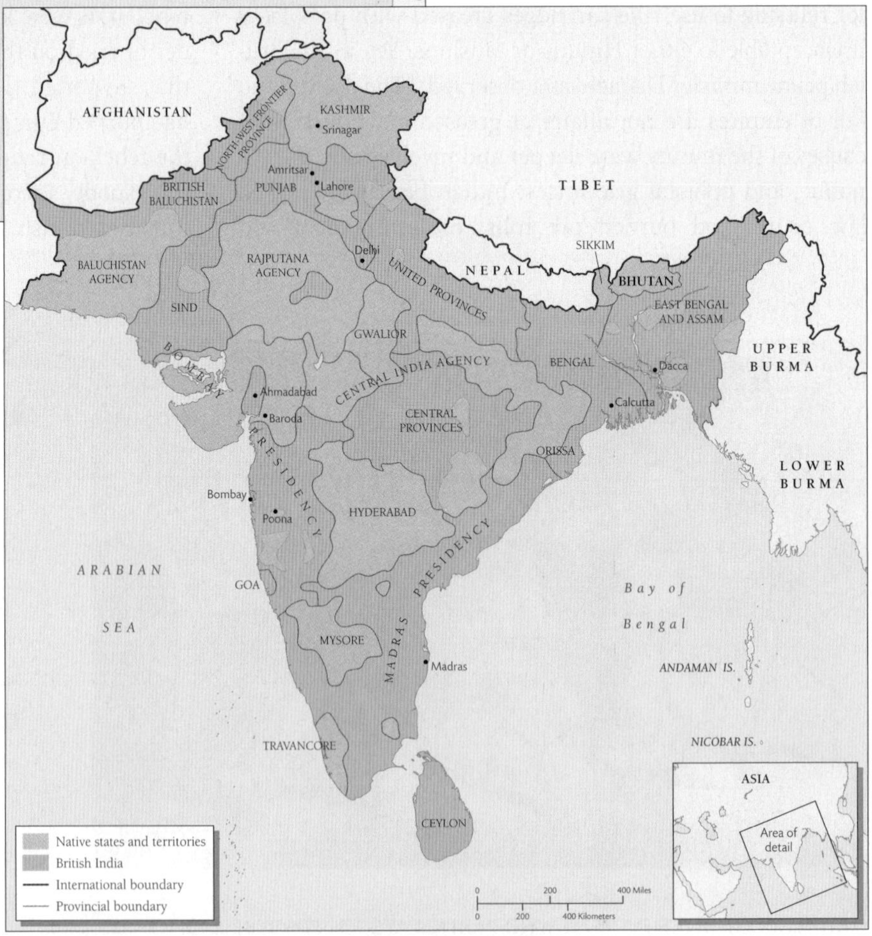

Analyzing Primary Sources

Lord Curzon on the Importance of India and Indians to the British Empire

Lord George Nathaniel Curzon (1859–1925) served as viceroy of India from 1898 to 1905 and as foreign secretary from 1919 to 1924. He made his reputation in India, and as a prominent Tory politician he became among the most vocal proponents of the new imperialism. In this speech, Curzon spells out the benefits of empire and underscores British dependence on India.

If you want to save your Colony of Natal from being over-run by a formidable enemy, you ask India for help, and she gives it; if you want to rescue the white men's legations from massacres at Peking, and the need is urgent, you request the Government of India to despatch an expedition, and they despatch it; if you are fighting the Mad Mullah in Somaliland, you soon discover that Indian troops and an Indian general are best qualified for the task, and you ask the Government of India to send them; if you desire to defend any of your extreme out-posts or coaling stations of the Empire, Aden, Mauritius, Singapore, Hong-Kong, even Tien-tsin or Shan-hai-kwan, it is to the Indian Army that you turn; if you want to build a railway to Uganda or in the Soudan, you apply for Indian labour. When the late Mr. Rhodes was engaged in developing your recent acquisition of Rhodesia, he came to me for assistance. It is with Indian coolie labor that you exploit the plantations equally of Demerara and Natal; with Indian trained officers that you irrigate and dam the Nile; with Indian forest officers that you tap the resources of Central Africa and Siam; with Indian surveyors that you explore all the hidden places of the earth. . . . [Moreover,] India is a country where there will be much larger openings for the investment of capital in the future than has hitherto been the case, and where a great work of industrial and commercial exploitation lies before us.

Source: Andrew Porter, ed., *The Oxford History of the British Empire*, vol. 3, *The Nineteenth Century* (Oxford: 1999), p. 403.

Questions for Analysis

1. Curzon not only served as viceroy of India and foreign minister but also had extensive knowledge of Afghanistan and Persia. Drawing on his expertise, what did he think was the greatest value of India to the British Empire?
2. Was there any risk involved in the British Empire's reliance on colonial troops? What compensation might Indian soldiers have come to expect for their participation in the defense of empire?

hostages and British territory by British troops were electrifying news. Pictures of the Scottish highland regiments (wearing wool kilts in the sweltering heat of India) liberating besieged white women and children went up in homes across the United Kingdom. At a political level, British leaders were stunned by how close the revolt had brought them to disaster and were determined never to repeat the same mistakes.

After the mutiny, the British were compelled to reorganize their Indian empire, developing new strategies of rule. The East India Company was abolished, replaced by the British crown. The British *raj* (or rule) was governed directly, though the British also sought out collaborators and cooperative interest groups. Princely India was left to the local princes, who were subject to British advisers. The British also reorganized the military and tried to change relations among soldiers. Indigenous troops were separated from each other to avoid the kind of fraternization that proved subversive. As one British officer put it, "If one regiment mutinies I should like to have the next so alien that it would fire into it." Even more than before, the British sought to rule through the Indian upper classes rather than in opposition to them. Queen Victoria, now empress of India, set out the principles of indirect rule: "We shall respect the rights, dignity and honour of native princes as our own, and we desire that they, as well as our own subjects, should enjoy that prosperity and that social advancement which can only be secured by internal peace and good government."

Past and Present

The Legacy of Colonialism

Decolonization in the 1950s and 1960s brought an end to the era of European imperialism (left), but the colonial past continues to shape the relations among European nations and former colonies elsewhere in the world. These links are reinforced by the large number of people from former colonies that now live in Europe, including the diverse neighborhood of Southall, London (right).

Watch related author interview on StudySpace
wwnorton.com/web/westernciv18

Civil-service reform opened new positions to members of the Indian upper classes. The British had to reconsider their relationship to Indian cultures. Missionary activity was no longer encouraged, and the British channeled their reforming impulses into the more secular projects of economic development, railways, roads, irrigation, and so on. Still, consensus on effective colonial strategies was lacking. Some administrators counseled more reform; others sought to support the princes. The British tried both policies, in fits and starts, until the end of British rule in 1947.

In India, the most prominent representative of the new imperialism was Lord Curzon, the viceroy of India from 1898 to 1905. Curzon deepened British commitments to the region. Concerned about the British position in the world, he warned of the need to fortify India's borders against Russia. He urged continued economic investment. Curzon worried that the British would be worn down by resistance to the raj and that, confronted with their apparent inability to transform Indian culture, they would become cynical, get "lethargic and think only of home." In the same way that Rudyard Kipling urged the British and the Americans to "take up the white man's burden" (see ***Competing Viewpoints*** on pages 756–57), Curzon pleaded with his countrymen to see how central India was to the greatness of Britain.

What did India do for Great Britain? By the eve of the First World War, India was Britain's largest export market. One tenth of all the British Empire's trade passed through India's port cities of Madras, Bombay, and Calcutta. India mattered enormously to Britain's balance of payments; surpluses earned there compensated for deficits with Europe and the United States. Equally important to Great Britain were the human resources of India. Indian laborers worked on tea plantations in Assam, near Burma, and they built railways and dams in southern Africa and Egypt. Over a million indentured Indian servants left their country in the second half of the century to work elsewhere in the empire.

India also provided the British Empire with highly trained engineers, land surveyors, clerks, bureaucrats, schoolteachers, and merchants. The nationalist leader Mohandas Gandhi, for instance, first came into the public eye as a young lawyer in Pretoria, South Africa, where he worked for an Indian law firm. The British deployed Indian troops across the empire. (They would later call up roughly 1.2 million troops in the First World War.) For all these reasons, men such as Curzon found it impossible to imagine their empire, or even their nation, without India.

How did the British raj shape Indian society? The British practice of indirect rule sought to create an Indian elite that would serve British interests, a group "who may be the interpreters between us and the millions whom we govern—a class of persons Indian in colour and blood, but English in tastes, in opinion, in morals, and in intellect," as one British writer put it. Eventually, this practice created a class of British-educated Indian civil servants and businessmen, well trained for government and skeptical about British claims that they brought progress to the subcontinent. This group provided the leadership for the nationalist movement that challenged British rule in India. At the same time, this group became increasingly distant from the rest of the nation. The overwhelming majority of Indians remained desperately poor peasants struggling to subsist on diminishing plots of land and, in many cases, in debt to British landlords. Meanwhile, villagers working in the textile trade were beaten down by imports of cheap manufactured goods from England.

IMPERIALISM IN CHINA

In China, too, European imperialism began early, well before the period of the new imperialism. Yet there it took a different form. Europeans did not conquer and annex whole regions. Instead, they forced favorable trade agreements at gunpoint, set up treaty ports where Europeans lived and worked under their own jurisdiction, and established outposts of European missionary activity. The Chinese spoke of their country as being "carved up like a melon."

Since the seventeenth century, European trade with China focused on coveted luxuries such as silk, porcelain, art objects, and tea. The Chinese government, however, was determined to keep foreign traders, and foreign influence in general, at bay. By the early nineteenth century, Britain's global ambitions and rising power were setting the stage for a confrontation. Freed from the task of fighting Napoleon, the British set their sights on improving the terms of the China trade, demanding the rights to come into open harbors and to have special trading privileges. The other source of constant friction involved the harsh treatment of British subjects by Chinese law courts—including the summary execution of several Britons convicted of crimes. By the 1830s, these diplomatic conflicts had been intensified by the opium trade.

The Opium Trade

Opium provided a direct link among Britain, British India, and China. Since the sixteenth century, the drug had been produced in India and carried by Dutch and, later, British traders. In fact, opium (derived from the poppy plant) was one of the very few commodities that Europeans could sell in China. For this reason, it became crucial to the balance of East–West trade. When the British conquered northeast India, they also annexed one of the world's richest opium-growing areas and became deeply involved in the trade—so much so that historians have called the East India Company's rule a "narco-military empire." British agencies designated specific poppy-growing regions and gave cash advances to Indian peasants who cultivated the crop. Producing opium was a labor-intensive process: peasant cultivators collected sap from the poppy seeds, and others cleaned the sap and formed it into opium balls that were dried before being weighed and shipped out. In the opium-producing areas northwest of Calcutta, "factories" employed as many as a thousand Indian workers, who formed and cured the opium, as well as young boys, whose job it was to turn the opium balls every four days.

From India, the East India Company sold the opium to "country traders"—small fleets of British, Dutch, and Chinese shippers who carried the drug to Southeast Asia and China. The East India Company used the silver it earned from the sale of opium to buy Chinese goods for the European market. The trade, therefore, was not only profitable, but it was also key to a triangular European-Indian-Chinese economic relationship. Production and export rose dramatically in the early nineteenth century, in spite of the Chinese emperor's attempts to discourage the trade. By the 1830s, when the British-Chinese confrontation was taking shape, opium provided British India with more revenues than any other source except taxes on land.

People all over the world consumed opium, for medicinal reasons as well as for pleasure. The Chinese market was especially lucrative. Eighteenth-century China witnessed a craze for tobacco smoking that taught users how to smoke opium. A large, wealthy Chinese elite of merchants and government officials provided much of the market, but opium smoking also became popular among

AN OPIUM FACTORY IN PATNA, INDIA, c. 1851. Balls of opium dry in a huge warehouse before being shipped to Calcutta for export to China and elsewhere.

soldiers, students, and Chinese laborers. In the nineteenth century, opium imports followed Chinese labor all over the world—to Southeast Asia and San Francisco. In 1799, in an effort to control the problem, the Chinese government banned opium imports, prohibited domestic production, criminalized smoking, and in the 1830s began a full-scale campaign to purge the drug from China. That campaign set the Chinese emperor on a collision course with British opium traders. In one confrontation, the Chinese drug commissioner Lin confiscated 3 million pounds of raw opium from the British and washed it out to sea. In another, the Chinese authorities blockaded British ships in port, and local citizens demonstrated angrily in front of British residences.

THE OPIUM WARS

In 1839, these simmering conflicts broke into what was called the first Opium War. Drugs were not the core of the matter. The dispute over the drug trade highlighted larger issues of sovereignty and economic status. The Europeans claimed the right to trade with whomever they pleased, bypassing Chinese monopolies. They wished to set up zones of European residence in defiance of Chinese sovereignty and to proselytize and open schools. The Chinese government could not accept these challenges to its authority, and war flared up several times over the course of the century. After the first war of 1839–42, in which British steam vessels and guns overpowered the Chinese fleet, the Treaty of Nanking (1842) compelled the Chinese to give the British trading privileges, the right to reside in five cities, and the port of Hong Kong "in perpetuity." After a second war, the British secured yet more treaty ports and privileges, including the right to send in missionaries. In the aftermath of those agreements between the Chinese and the British, other countries demanded similar rights and economic opportunities. By the end of the nineteenth century, the French, Germans, and Russians had claimed mining rights and permission to build railroads, to begin manufacturing with cheap Chinese labor, and to arm and police European communities in Chinese cities. In Shanghai, for instance, 17,000 foreigners lived with their own courts, schools, churches, and utilities. The United States, not wanting to be shouldered aside, demanded its own Open Door Policy. Japan was an equally active imperialist power in the Pacific, and the Sino-Japanese War of 1894–95 was a decisive moment in the history of the region. The Japanese victory forced China to concede trading privileges, the independence of Korea, and the Liaotung Peninsula in Manchuria. It opened a scramble for spheres of influence and for mining and railway concessions. The demand for reparations forced the Chinese government to levy greater taxes. All these measures heightened resentment and destabilized the regime.

Surrendering privileges to Europeans and the Japanese seriously undermined the authority of the Chinese Qing (Ching) emperor at home and heightened popular hostility to foreign intruders. Authority at the imperial center had been eroding for more than a century by 1900, hastened by the Opium Wars and by the vast Taiping Rebellion (1852–64), an enormous, bitter, and deadly conflict in which radical Christian rebels in south-central China challenged the authority of the emperors. On the defensive against the rebels, the dynasty hired foreign generals, including the British commander Charles Gordon, to lead its forces. The war devastated China's agricultural heartland; and the death toll, never confirmed, may have reached 20 million.

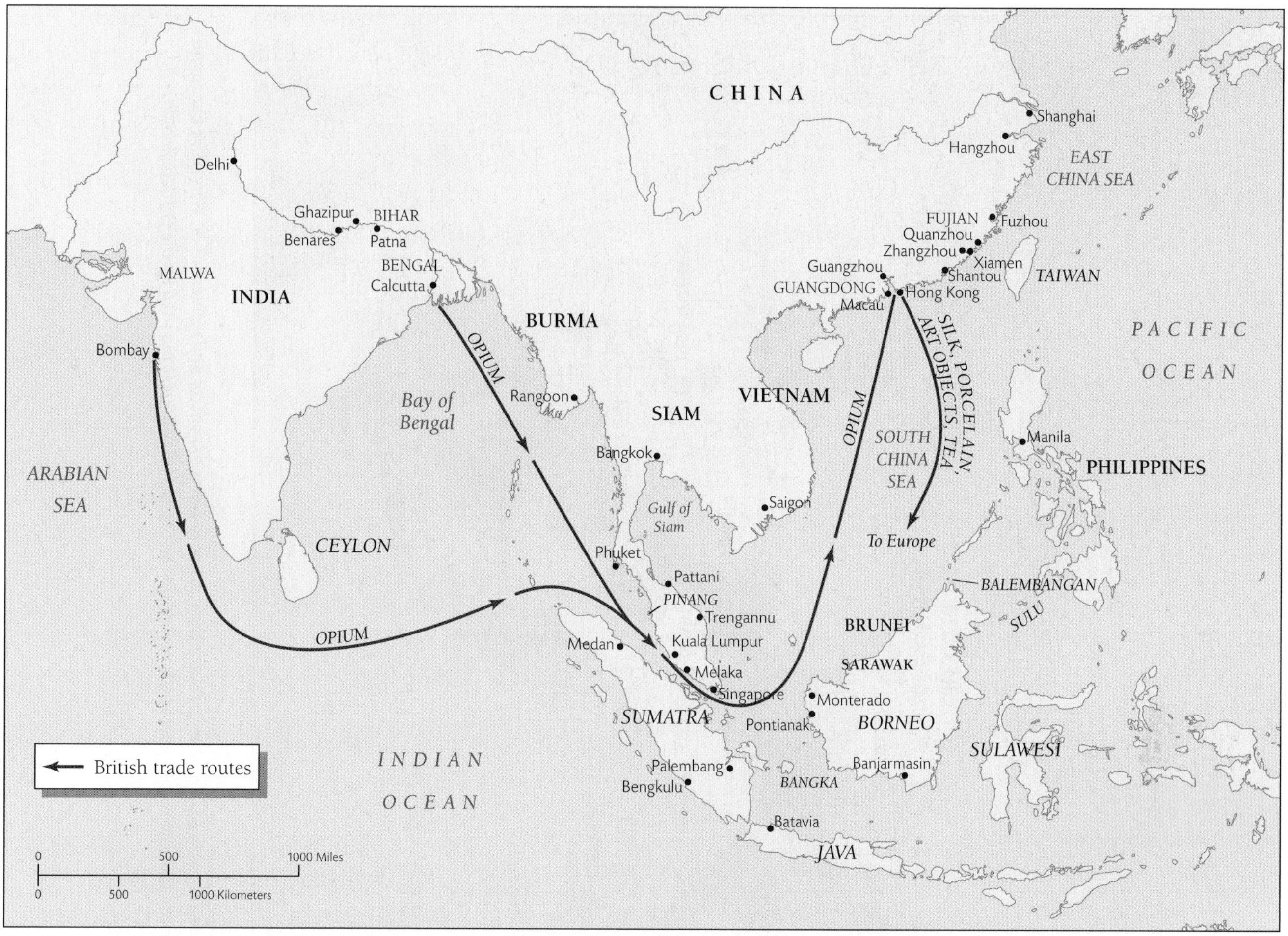

BRITISH OPIUM TRADE. Note the way that the British trade in opium linked the economies of India, China, and Europe. ▪ ***What were the major products involved in trade between East Asia, South Asia, and Europe during this period?*** ▪ ***In what ways did the opium trade destabilize East Asia?*** ▪ ***What efforts did the Chinese government make to restrict the sale of opium?*** ▪ ***What was the response of European nations involved in this trade?***

This ruinous disorder and the increasing inability of the emperor to keep order and collect the taxes necessary to repay foreign loans, led European countries to take more and more direct control of the China trade.

The Boxer Rebellion

From a Western perspective, the most important of the nineteenth-century rebellions against the corruptions of foreign rule was the Boxer Rebellion of 1900. The Boxers were a secret society of young men trained in Chinese martial arts and believed to have spiritual powers. Antiforeign and antimissionary, they provided the spark for a loosely organized but widespread uprising in northern China. Bands of Boxers attacked foreign engineers, tore up railway lines, and in the spring of 1900 marched on Beijing. They laid siege to the foreign legations in the city, home to several thousand Western diplomats and merchants and their families. The legations' small garrison defended their walled compound with little more than rifles, bayonets, and improvised artillery; but they withstood the siege for fifty-five days until a large relief column arrived. The rebellion, particularly the siege at Beijing, mobilized a global response. Europe's Great Powers, rivals everywhere else in the world, drew together in response to this crisis to tear China apart. An expedition numbering 20,000 troops—combining the forces of Britain, France, the United States, Germany, Italy, Japan, and Russia—ferociously repressed the Boxer movement. The outside powers then demanded indemnities, new trading concessions, and reassurances from the Chinese government.

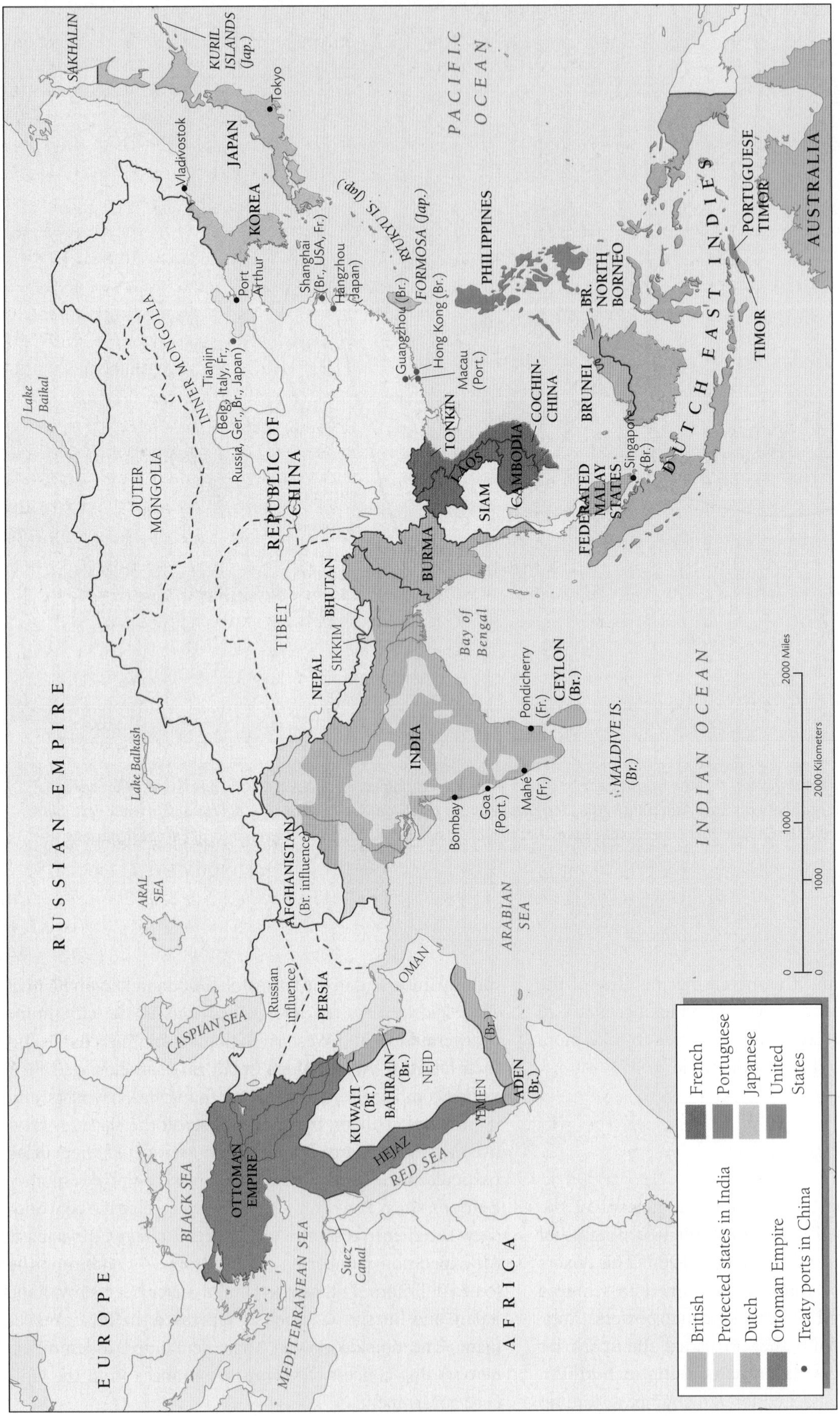

IMPERIALISM IN SOUTH AND EAST ASIA, c. 1914. ▪ *Which imperial powers were most present in Asia and where were their primary zones of control and influence?* ▪ *Why were European nations and the United States interested in establishing treaty ports in China?* ▪ *How were the Chinese treaty ports different from the territorial conquest pursued by the British, French, and Dutch in their respective Asian colonies?*

THE OPIUM TRADE, 1880s. A European merchant examines opium. At first, European traders were forced to carry silver to China to pay for the luxury goods they wanted. The discovery that they could sell this highly addictive narcotic in China allowed them to correct this trade imbalance and increase their profits.

The Boxer Rebellion was one of several anti-imperialist movements at the end of the nineteenth century. The rebellion testified to the vulnerability of Europeans' imperial power. It dramatized the resources Europeans would have to devote to maintaining their far-flung influence. In the process of repression, the Europeans became committed to propping up corrupt and fragile governments to protect their agreements and interests, and they were drawn into putting down popular uprisings against local inequalities and foreign rule.

In China, the age of the new imperialism capped a century of conflict and expansion. By 1900, virtually all of Asia had been divided up among the European powers. Japan, an active imperial power in its own right, maintained its independence. British rule extended from India across Burma, Malaya, Australia, and New Zealand. The Dutch, Britain's long-standing trade rivals, secured Indonesia. Thailand remained independent. During the 1880s, the French moved into Indochina. Imperial rivalries (among Britain, France, and Russia, China and Japan, Russia and Japan) drove European powers to press for influence and economic advantage in Asia; that struggle, in turn, encouraged the development of nationalist feeling among local populations. Imperial expansion was showing its destabilizing effects.

AN AMERICAN CARICATURE OF THE BOXER REBELLION. Uncle Sam (to the obstreperous Boxer), "I occasionally do a little boxing myself."

Russian Imperialism

Russia championed a policy of annexation—by conquest, treaty, or both—of lands bordering on the existing Russian state throughout the nineteenth century. Beginning in 1801, with the acquisition of Georgia after a war with Persia, the tsars continued to pursue their expansionist dream. Bessarabia and Turkestan (taken from the Turks) and Armenia (from the Persians) vastly increased the empire's size. This southward colonization brought large Muslim populations in central Asia into the Russian Empire. It also brought the Russians close to war with the British twice: first in 1881, when Russian troops occupied territories in the trans-Caspian region, and again in 1884–87, when the tsar's forces advanced to the frontier of Afghanistan. In both cases, the British feared incursions into areas they deemed within their sphere of influence in the Middle East. They were concerned, as well, about a possible threat to India. The maneuvering, spying, and support of friendly puppet governments by Russia and Britain became known

BUILDING THE RUSSIAN EMPIRE. ▪ *In what directions did the Russian Empire primarily expand after 1795?* ▪ *What drove Russian expansion?* ▪ *Which areas were most contentious and why?*

as the "Great Game" and foreshadowed Western countries' jockeying for the region's oil resources in the twentieth century.

Russian expansion also moved east. In 1875, the Japanese traded the southern half of Sakhalin Island for the previously Russian Kurile Islands. The tsars' eastward advance was finally halted in 1904, when Russian expansion in Mongolia and Manchuria came up against Japanese expansion. In the Russo-Japanese War of 1904, Russia's huge imperial army more than met its match. Russia's navy was sent halfway around the world to reinforce the beleaguered Russian troops but was ambushed and sunk by the better-trained and -equipped Japanese fleet. This national humiliation helped provoke a revolt in Russia and led to an American-brokered peace treaty in 1905 (see Chapter 23). The defeat shook the already unsteady regime of the tsar and proved that European nations were not the only ones who could play the imperial game successfully.

THE FRENCH EMPIRE AND THE CIVILIZING MISSION

Like British expansion into India, French colonialism in northern Africa began before the new imperialism of the late nineteenth century. By the 1830s, the French had created a general government of their possessions in Algeria, the most important of which were cities along the Mediterranean coast. From the outset, the Algerian conquest was different from most other colonial ventures: Algeria became a settler state, one of the few apart from South Africa. Some of the early settlers were utopian socialists, out to create ideal communities; some were workers the French government deported after the revolution of 1848 to be "resettled" safely as farmers; some were winegrowers whose vines at home had been destroyed by an insect infestation. The settlers were by no means all French; they included Italian, Spanish, and Maltese merchants and shopkeepers of modest means, laborers, and

THE ENTRY OF THE CRUSADERS INTO CONSTANTINOPLE* BY EUGÉNE DELACROIX, 1840.** The invasion of Algeria in 1830 became an occasion for thinking about Europe's long historical relationship with Muslim civilizations in Africa and the Middle East. Delacroix's work, painted while the conquest of Algeria was going on, portrays these civilizations as exotic and subservient, even as it glorifies the figures of conquering Christian armies. ▪ ***How might this long historical view have shaped European attitudes toward conquest in the nineteenth century?

peasants. By the 1870s, in several of the coastal cities, this new creole community outnumbered indigenous Algerians, and within it, other Europeans outnumbered the French. With the French military's help, the settlers appropriated land, and French business concerns took cork forests and established mining in copper, lead, and iron. Economic activity was for European benefit. The first railroads, for instance, did not even carry passengers; they took iron ore to the coast for export to France, where it would be smelted and sold.

The settlers and the French government did not necessarily pursue common goals. In the 1870s, the new and still-fragile Third Republic (founded after Napoleon III was defeated in 1870; see Chapter 21), in an effort to ensure the settlers' loyalty, made the colony a department of France. This gave the French settlers the full rights of republican citizenship. It also gave them the power to pass laws in Algeria that consolidated their privileges and community (naturalizing all Europeans, for instance) and further disenfranchised indigenous Muslim populations, who had no voting rights at all. French politicians in Paris occasionally objected to the settlers' contemptuous treatment of indigenous peoples, arguing that it subverted the project of "lifting up" the natives. The French settlers in Algeria had little interest in such a project; although they paid lip service to republican ideals, they wanted the advantages of Frenchness for themselves. Colonial administrators and social scientists differentiated the "good" mountain-dwelling Berbers, who they believed could be brought into French society, from the "bad" Arabs, whose religion made them supposedly unassimilable. France's divide and rule strategy, which treated European settlers, Arabs, Berbers, and Jews very differently, illustrates the contradictions of "the civilizing mission" in action.

Before the 1870s, colonial activities aroused relatively little interest among the French at home. But after the

SLAVES IN CHAINS, 1896. In Africa, native labor was exploited by Europeans and by other Africans.

humiliating defeat in the Franco-Prussian War (1870–71) and the establishment of the Third Republic, colonial lobby groups and politicians became increasingly adamant about the benefits of colonialism. These benefits were not simply economic. Taking on the "civilizing mission" would reinforce the international influence of the French republic and the prestige of the French people. It was France's duty "to contribute to this work of civilization." Jules Ferry, a republican leader, successfully argued for expanding the French presence in Indochina, saying, "We must believe that if Providence deigned to confer upon us a mission by making us masters of the earth, this mission consists not of attempting an impossible fusion of the races but of simply spreading or awakening among the other races the superior notions of which we are the guardians." Those "superior notions" included a commitment to economic and technological progress and to liberation from slavery, political oppression, poverty, and disease. Ferry argued that "the superior races have a right vis-à-vis the inferior races . . . they have a right to civilize them."

Under Ferry, the French acquired Tunisia (1881), northern and central Vietnam (Tonkin and Annam; 1883), and Laos and Cambodia (1893). They also carried this civilizing mission into their colonies in West Africa. European and Atlantic trade with the west coast of Africa—in slaves, gold, and ivory—had been well established for centuries. In the late nineteenth century, trade gave way to formal administration. The year 1895 saw the establishment of a Federation of French West Africa, a loosely organized administration to govern an area nine times the size of France, including Guinea, Senegal, and the Ivory Coast. Even with reforms and centralization in 1902, French control remained uneven. Despite military campaigns of pacification, resistance remained. The French dealt gingerly with tribal leaders, at times deferring to their authority and at others trying to break their power. They established French courts and law only in cities, leaving Islamic or tribal courts to run other areas. The federation aimed to rationalize the economic exploitation of the area and to replace "booty capitalism" with a more careful management and development of resources. The French called this "enhancing the value" of the region, which was part of the civilizing mission of the modern republic. The federation embarked on an ambitious program of public works. Engineers rebuilt the huge harbor at Dakar, the most important on the coast, to accommodate rising exports. With utopian zeal they redesigned older cities, tried to improve sanitation and health, improved water systems, and built roads and railways. The French republic was justifiably proud of the Pasteur Institute for bacteriological research, which opened in France in 1888; overseas institutes became part of the colonial enterprise. One plan called for a large-scale West African railroad network to lace through the region. A public-school program built free schools in villages not controlled by missionaries. Education, though, was not compulsory and was usually for boys.

Such programs plainly served French interests. "Officially this process is called civilizing, and after all, the term is apt, since the undertaking serves to increase the degree of prosperity of our civilization," remarked one Frenchman who opposed the colonial enterprise. None of these measures aimed to give indigenous peoples political rights. As one historian puts it, "the French Government General was in the business not of making citizens, but of civilizing its subjects." More telling, however, the French project was not often successful. The French government did not have the resources to carry out its plans, which proved much more expensive and complicated than anyone imagined. Transportation costs ran very high. Labor posed the largest problems. Here as elsewhere, Europeans faced massive resistance from the African peasants, whom they wanted to do everything from building railroads to working mines and carrying rubber. The Europeans resorted to forced labor, signing agreements with local tribal leaders to deliver workers, and they turned a blind eye to the continuing use of slave labor in the interior. For all of these reasons, the colonial project did not produce the profits some expected. In important respects, however, the French investment in colonialism was cultural.

Railroads, schools, and projects such as the Dakar harbor were, like the Eiffel Tower (1889), symbols of the French nation's modernity, power, and world leadership.

THE "SCRAMBLE FOR AFRICA" AND THE CONGO

French expansion into West Africa was only one instance of Europe's voracity on the African continent. The scope and speed with which the major European powers conquered and asserted formal control was astonishing. The effects were profound. In 1875, 11 percent of the continent was in European hands. By 1902, the figure was 90 percent. European powers mastered logistical problems of transport and communication; they learned how to keep diseases at bay. They also had new weapons. The Maxim gun, adopted by the British army in 1889 and first used by British colonial troops, pelted out as many as 500 rounds a minute; it turned encounters with indigenous forces into bloodbaths and made armed resistance virtually impossible.

The Congo Free State

In the 1870s, the British had formed new imperial relationships in the north and west of Africa and along the southern and eastern coasts. A new phase of European involvement struck right at the heart of the continent. Until the latter part of the nineteenth century, this territory had been out of bounds for Europeans. The rapids downstream on such strategic rivers as the Congo and the Zambezi made it difficult to move inland, and tropical diseases were lethal to most European explorers. But during the 1870s, a new drive into central Africa produced results. The target was the fertile valleys around the river Congo, and the European colonizers were a privately financed group of Belgians paid by their king, Leopold II (1865–1909). They followed in the footsteps of Henry Morton Stanley, an American newspaperman and explorer who later became a British subject and a knight of the realm. Stanley hacked his way through thick canopy jungle into territory where no European had previously set foot. His "scientific" journeys inspired the creation of a society of researchers and students of African culture in Brussels, in reality a front organization for the commercial company set up by Leopold. The ambitiously named International Association for the Exploration and Civilization of the Congo was set up in 1876 and soon set about signing treaties with local elites, which opened the whole Congo River basin to commercial exploitation. The vast resources of palm oil and natural rubber and the promise of minerals (including diamonds) were now within Europeans' reach.

The strongest resistance that Leopold's company faced came from other colonial powers, particularly Portugal, which objected to this new drive for occupation. In 1884, a conference was called in Berlin to settle the matter of control over the Congo River basin. It was chaired by the master of European power politics, Otto von Bismarck, and attended by all the leading colonial nations as well as by the United States. The conference established ground rules for a new phase of European economic and political expansion. Europe's two great overseas empires, Britain and France, and the strongest emerging power inside Europe, Germany, joined forces in a settlement that seemed to be perfectly in line with nineteenth-century liberalism. The Congo valleys would be open to free trade and commerce; a slave trade still run by some of the Islamic kingdoms in the region would be suppressed in favor of free labor; and a Congo Free State would be set up, denying the region to the formal control of any single European country.

In reality, the Congo Free State was run by Leopold's private company, and the region was opened up to unrestricted exploitation by a series of large European corporations. The older slave trade was suppressed, but the European companies took the "free" African labor guaranteed in Berlin and placed workers in equally bad conditions. Huge tracts of land, larger than whole European countries, became diamond mines or plantations for the extraction of palm oil, rubber, or cocoa. African workers labored in appalling conditions, with no real medicine or sanitation, too little food, and according to production schedules that made European factory labor look mild by comparison. Hundreds of thousands of African workers died from disease and overwork. Because European managers did not respect the different cycle of seasons in central Africa, whole crop years were lost, leading to famines. Laborers working in the heat of the dry season often carried individual loads on their backs that would have been handled by heavy machinery in a European factory. Thousands of Africans were pressed into work harvesting goods Europe wanted. They did so for little or no pay, under the threat of beatings and mutilation for dozens of petty offenses against the plantation companies, who made the laws of the Free State. Eventually the scandal of the Congo became too great to go on unquestioned. A whole generation of authors and journalists, most famously Joseph Conrad in his *Heart of Darkness*, publicized the arbitrary brutality and the vast scale of suffering. In 1908, Belgium was forced to take direct control of the Congo, turning it into a Belgian colony. A few restrictions at least were imposed on the activities of the great plantation companies that had brought a vast new store of raw materials to European industry by using slavery in all but name.

The Partition of Africa

The occupation of Congo, and its promise of great material wealth, pressured other colonial powers into expanding their holdings. By the 1880s, the "scramble for Africa" was well under way, hastened by stories of rubber forests or diamond mines in other parts of central and southern Africa. The guarantees made at the 1884 Berlin conference allowed the Europeans to take further steps. The French and Portuguese increased their holdings. Italy moved into territories along the Red Sea, beside British-held land and the independent kingdom of Ethiopia.

Germany came relatively late to empire overseas. Bismarck was reluctant to engage in an enterprise that he believed would yield few economic or political advantages. Yet he did not want either Britain or France to dominate Africa, and Germany seized colonies in strategic locations. The German colonies in Cameroon and most of modern Tanzania separated the territories of older, more established powers. Though the Germans were not the most enthusiastic colonialists, they were fascinated by the imperial adventure and jealous of their territories. When the Herero people of German Southwest Africa (now Namibia) rebelled in the early 1900s, the Germans responded with a vicious campaign of village burning and ethnic killing that nearly annihilated the Herero.

Great Britain and France had their own ambitions. The French aimed to move west to east across the continent, an important reason for the French expedition to Fashoda (in the Sudan) in 1898 (discussed later). Britain's part in the scramble took place largely in southern and eastern Africa and was encapsulated in the dreams and career of one man: the diamond tycoon, colonial politician, and imperial visionary Cecil Rhodes. Rhodes, who made a fortune from the South African diamond mines in the 1870s and 1880s and founded the diamond-mining company DeBeers, became prime minister of Britain's Cape Colony in 1890. (He left part of this fortune for the creation of the Rhodes scholarships to educate future leaders of the empire at Oxford.) In an uneasy alliance with the Boer settlers in their independent republics and with varying levels of support from London, Rhodes pursued two great personal and imperial goals. The personal goal was to build a southern African empire that was founded on diamonds. "Rhodesia" would fly the Union Jack out of pride but send its profits into Rhodes's own companies. Through bribery, double dealing, careful coalition politics with the British and Boer settlers, warfare, and outright theft, Rhodes helped carve out territories occupying the modern nations of Zambia, Zimbabwe, Malawi, and Botswana—most of the savannah of southern Africa. Rhodes had a broader imperial vision, one that he shared with the new British colonial secretary in the late 1890s, Joseph Chamberlain. The first part of that vision was a British presence along the whole of eastern Africa, symbolized by the goal of a Cape-to-Cairo railway. The second was that the empire should make Britain self-sufficient, with British

"THE RHODES COLOSSUS" (left). This cartoon, which appeared in *Punch* magazine, satirized the ambitions of Cecil Rhodes, the driving force behind British imperialism in South Africa. **"NOW WE SHANT BE LONG TO CAIRO" (right).** So read the banner across Engine No. 1, taking the first train from Umtali to Salisbury, Rhodesia. In Cecil Rhodes's vision, the Capetown-to-Cairo railway symbolized British domination of the African continent.

industry able to run on the goods and raw materials shipped in from its colonies, then exporting many finished products back to those lands. Once the territories of Zambeziland and Rhodesia were taken, Rhodes found himself turning against the European settlers in the region, a conflict that led to the Boer war in 1899 (discussed later in this chapter).

This battle over strategic advantage, diamonds, and European pride was typical of the scramble. As each European power sought its "place in the sun," in the famous phrase of the German kaiser William II, they brought more and more of Africa under direct colonial control. It created a whole new scale of plunder as companies were designed and managed to strip the continent of its resources. African peoples thus faced a combination of direct European control and indirect rule, which allowed local elites friendly to European interests to lord over those who resisted. The partition of Africa was the most striking instance of the new imperialism, with broad consequences for the subject peoples of European colonies and for the international order as a whole.

IMPERIAL CULTURE

Imperialism was thoroughly anchored in the culture of late-nineteenth-century Europe and the United States. Images of empire were everywhere, not just in the propagandist literature of colonialism's supporters but on tins of tea and boxes of cocoa and as background themes in posters advertising everything from dance halls to sewing machines. Museums and world's fairs displayed the products of empire and introduced spectators to "exotic peoples." Music halls rang to the sound of imperialist songs. Empire was present in novels of the period, sometimes appearing as a faraway setting for fantasy, adventure, or stories of self-discovery. Even the tales of Sherlock Holmes, set in London and not overtly imperialist, often used references to empire—tiger carpets, hookahs and opium dens, Malaysian servants—to add mystery and fascination to their plots. The popular literature of empire showed a particular fascination with sexual practices in faraway places—photos and postcards of North African harems and unveiled Arab women were common in European pornography, as were colonial memoirs that chronicled the sexual adventures of their authors.

Empire thus played an important part in establishing European identity during these years. In France, the "civilizing mission" demonstrated to French citizens the grandeur of their nation. Building railroads and "bringing progress to other lands" illustrated the vigor of the French republic. Many British writers spoke in similar tones. One author wrote, "The British race may safely be called a missionary race. The command to go and teach all nations is

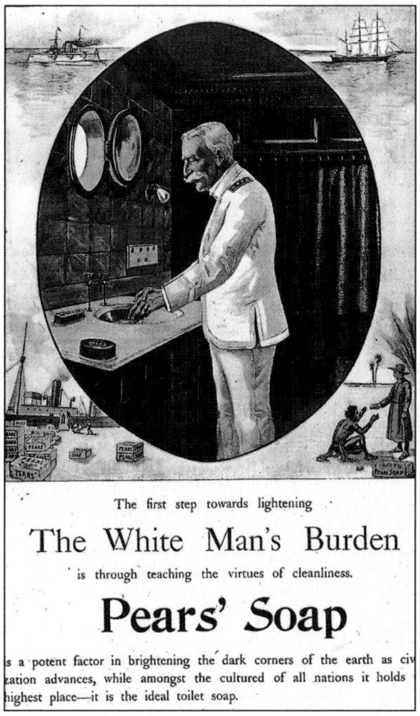

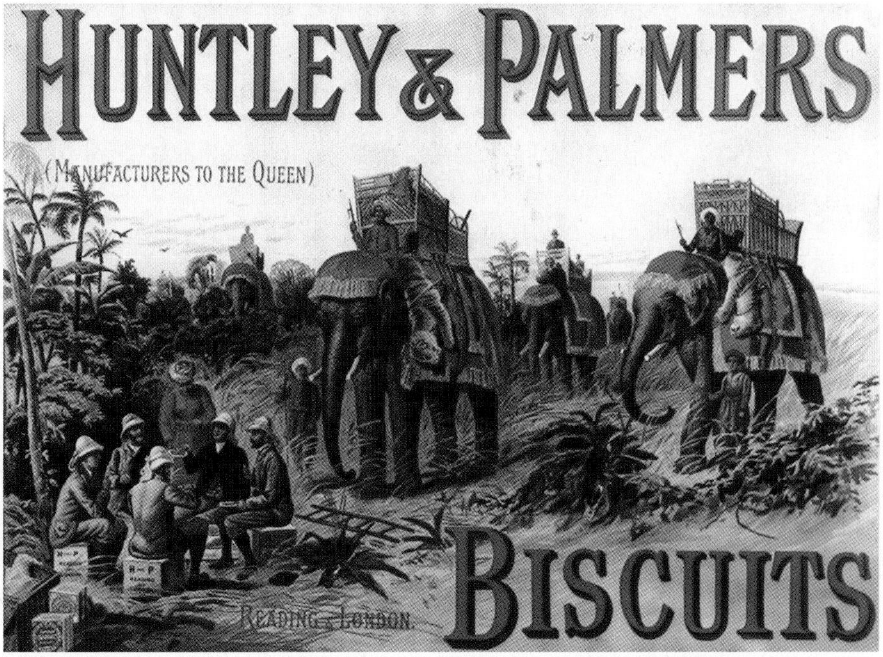

THINKING ABOUT EMPIRE AT HOME. By the end of the nineteenth century, advertisers had begun to use images of empire to sell their products to consumers. The advertisement for Pears' Soap appeared in the American magazine *McClure's* in 1899. The image of the white-uniformed officer washing his hands connects the theme of cleanliness and personal hygiene to notions of racial superiority and the necessity of bringing civilization to "the dark corners of the earth." The packaging of Huntley & Palmers Biscuits, on the other hand, transported the familiar domestic scene of teatime to an exotic imperial location with a supporting cast of elephants. The image, which adorned biscuit boxes in many English parlors during the late Victorian period, seemed to reinforce the idea that essential aspects of British culture could be maintained even as they traveled to distant parts of the globe.

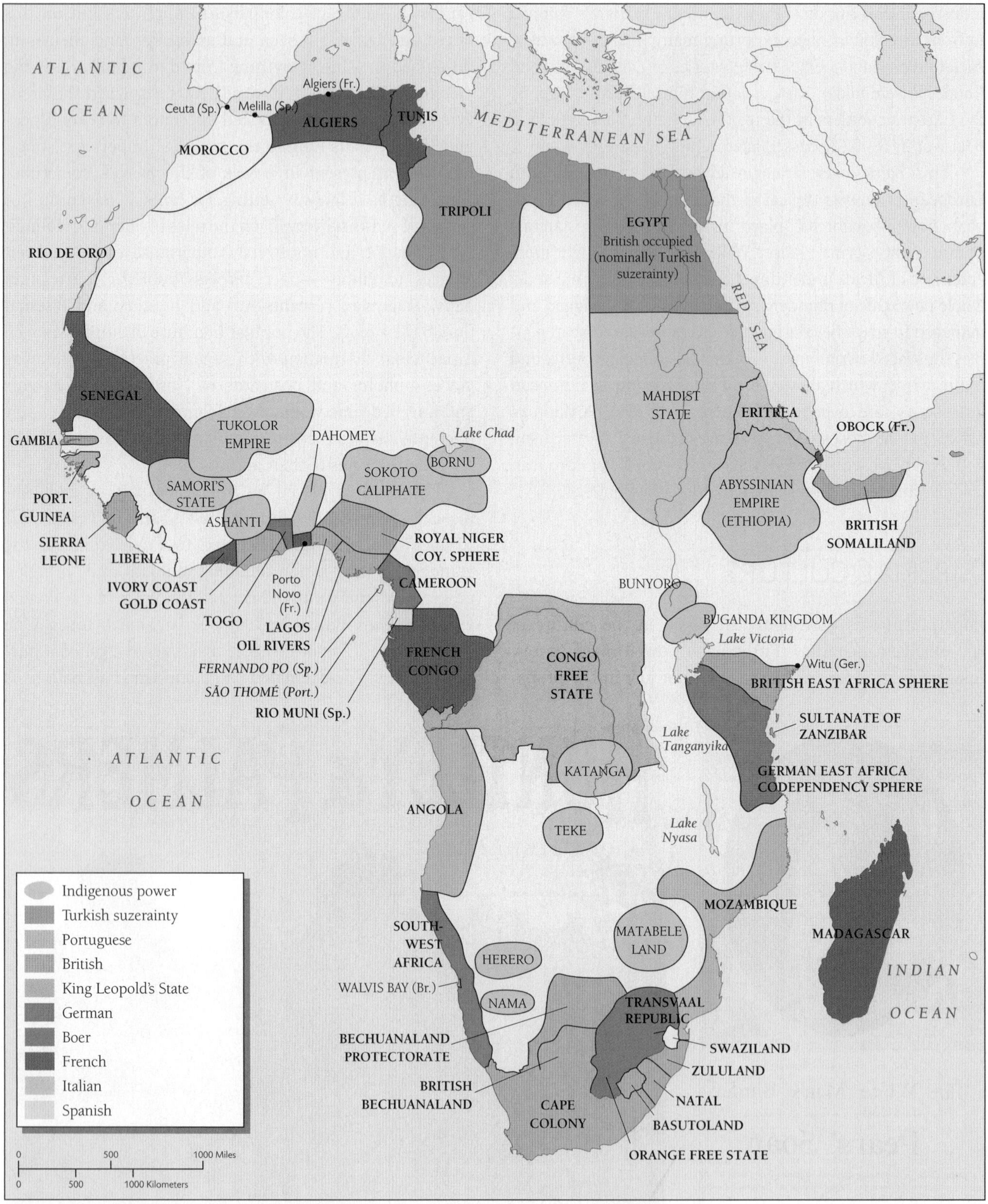

AFRICA, c. 1886. ▪ ***What is the single biggest difference in terms of rulership between the two maps?*** ▪ ***Who were the winners and losers in the scramble for Africa before the First World War?*** ▪ ***What does the result of the scramble for Africa suggest about how European powers regarded each other?***

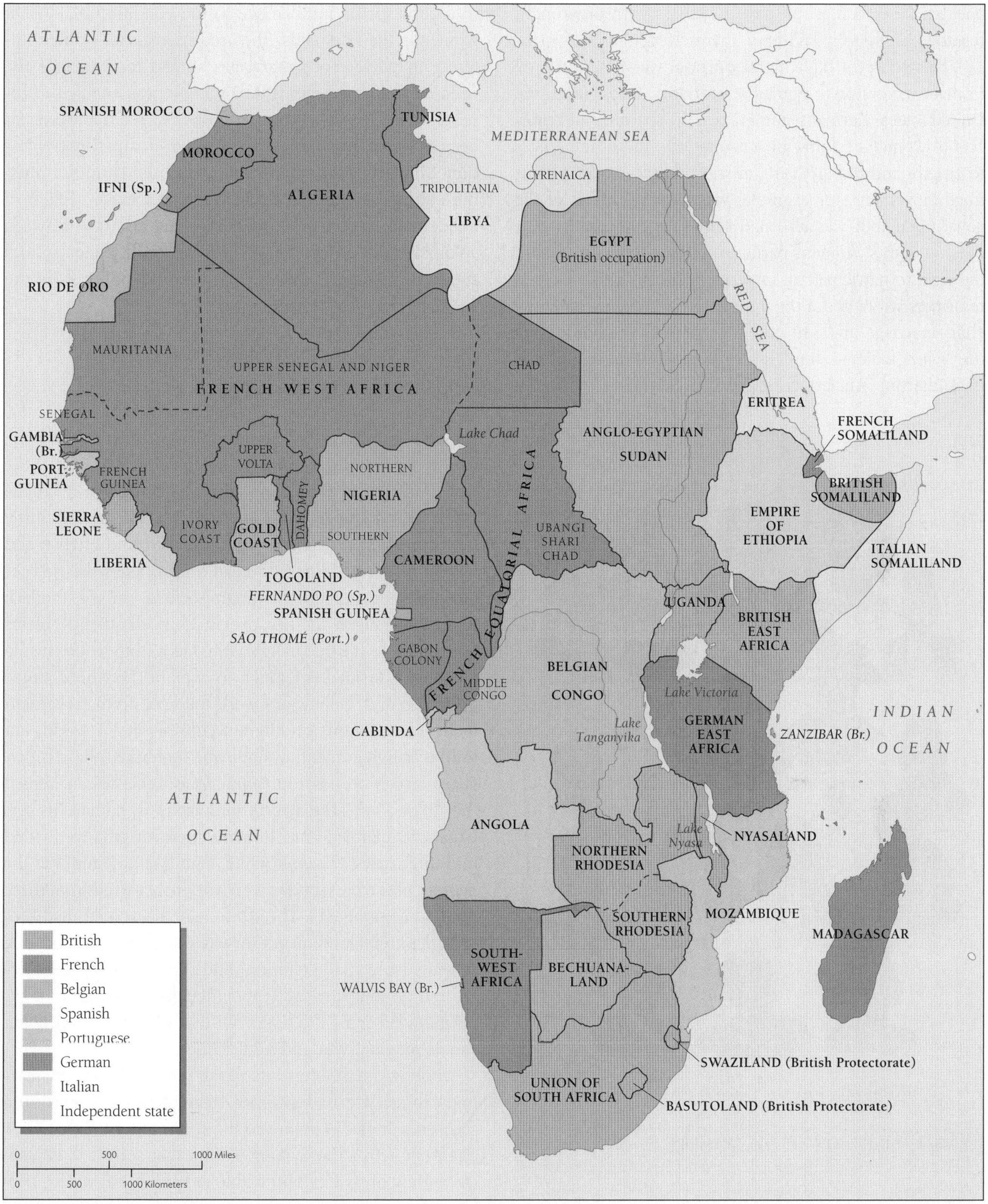

AFRICA, c. 1914.

one that the British people have, whether rightly or wrongly, regarded as specially laid upon themselves."

This sense of high moral purpose was not restricted to male writers or to figures of authority. In England, the United States, Germany, and France, the speeches and projects of women's reform movements were full of references to empire and the civilizing mission. Britain's woman suffrage movement, for example, was fiercely critical of the government but was also nationalist and imperialist. For these militants, women's participation in politics also meant the right to participate in imperial projects. British women reformers wrote about the oppression of Indian women by child marriage and sati and saw themselves shouldering the "white women's burden" of reform. In France, suffragist Hubertine Auclert criticized the colonial government in Algeria for its indifference to the condition of Muslim women in their domains. She used an image of women suffering in polygamous marriages abroad to dramatize the need for reform. Arguments such as these enabled European women in their home countries to see themselves as bearers of progress, as participants in a superior civilization. Similarly, John Stuart Mill often used Hindu or Muslim culture as a foil when he wanted to make a point of freedom of speech and religion. This contrast between colonial backwardness and European civility and cultural superiority shaped Western culture and political debate about liberal ideas in particular.

RACIAL THINKING IN THE AGE OF EMPIRE. This plate was published in 1906 in England and the United States in a geography book that was aimed at a mass audience. It is a good example of the ways that racial categories were given scientific legitimacy and disseminated in a way that lent them credibility in the popular imagination of the reading public. ▪ ***How does this print convey the notion of racial hierarchy, the idea that some "races" were superior to others? Is the idea of "race" contained in this print purely biological? Does it also contain implications about human history?***

Imperialism and Racial Thought

Imperial culture gave new prominence to racial thinking. Count Arthur de Gobineau (*GOH-bih-noh*, 1816–1882) wrote a massive work, *The Inequality of the Races*, in the 1850s, but it sparked little interest until the period of the new imperialism, when it was translated into English and widely discussed. For Gobineau, race offered the "master key" for understanding human societies in the modern world. "The racial question overshadows all other problems of history . . . the inequality of the races from whose fusion a people is formed is enough to explain the whole course of its destiny." Gobineau's work followed from Enlightenment investigations of different cultures in the world, but unlike Enlightenment authors who attributed these differences largely to environmental factors, Gobineau argued that "blood" was the determining factor in human history. Gobineau claimed that humans were originally divided into three races, "black," "white," and "yellow," and that the peoples of the present day were variously mixed from these original components. The white race, he argued, had preserved purer bloodlines and was therefore superior. The others suffered "adulteration" and were therefore degenerate and no longer capable of civilization. Gobineau's readers included some defenders of the confederacy during the American Civil War and Adolf Hitler.

Followers of Gobineau's racial thinking looked increasingly to science to legitimate their theories. The natural scientist Charles Darwin, no racist himself, attracted wide attention with a theory of evolution that sought to explain the variety of species observable in the natural world. Darwin suggested that only the most "fit" individuals in a species survived to bear viable offspring, and that this process of "natural selection" explained how species diverged from one another: variations that made individuals better able to find food and mates were likely to be passed on to future generations. Social scientists such as Herbert Spencer sought to use a similar logic of competition among individuals for scarce resources to explain the evolution of social groups, suggesting that inequalities of wealth or ability could also be explained as the result of a process of "natural selection." Racial theorists and followers of Gobineau such as Houston Stewart Chamberlain (1855–1927) wasted little time in harnessing such scientific arguments to the claim that human "races" evolved over time. Chamberlain's books sold tens of thousands of copies in England and Germany.

Francis Galton (1822–1911), a half cousin of Charles Darwin and a scientist who studied evolution, went so far as to advocate improving the population's racial characteristics by selective breeding of "superior types." Galton and others feared that improvements in health care and hygiene might allow individuals with inferior traits to survive to reproductive age, and his system of racial management, which he called *eugenics*, would save European populations from a decline in their vitality and biological fitness. Theories such as Galton's or Gobineau's did not cause imperialism, and they were closely linked with other developments in European culture, in particular renewed anxieties about social class and a fresh wave of European anti-Semitism. Yet the increasingly scientific racism of late-nineteenth-century Europe made it easier for many to reconcile the rhetoric of progress, individual freedom, and the civilizing mission with contempt for other peoples.

Opposition to Imperialism

Support for imperialism was not unanimous. Hobson and Lenin condemned the entire enterprise as an act of greed and arrogance. Polish-born Joseph Conrad, a British novelist, shared much of the racism of his contemporaries, but he nevertheless believed that imperialism was an expression of deeply rooted pathologies in European culture. Other anti-imperialists were men and women from the colonies themselves who brought their case to the metropole. The British Committee of the Indian National Congress gathered together many members of London's Indian community to educate British public opinion about the exploitation of Indian peoples and resources.

Perhaps the most defiant anti-imperialist action was the London Pan-African Conference of 1900, staged at the height of the scramble for Africa and during the Boer War (discussed on page 000). The conference grew out of an international tradition of African American, British, and American antislavery movements and brought the rhetoric used earlier to abolish slavery to bear on the tactics of European imperialism. They protested forced labor in the mining compounds of South Africa as akin to slavery and asked in very moderate tones for some autonomy and representation for African peoples. The Pan-African Conference of 1900 was small, but it drew delegates from the Caribbean, West Africa, and North America, including the thirty-two-year-old Harvard Ph.D. and leading African American intellectual, W. E. B. Du Bois (1868–1963). The conference issued a proclamation "To the Nations of the World," with a famous introduction written by Du Bois. "In the metropolis of the modern world, in this closing year of the nineteenth century," the proclamation read, "there has been assembled a congress of men and women of African blood, to deliberate solemnly upon the present situation and outlook of the darker races of mankind. The problem of the twentieth century is the problem of the colour-line." The British government ignored the conference, but pan-Africanism, like Indian nationalism, grew rapidly after the First World War.

Colonial Cultures

Imperialism also created new colonial cultures in other parts of the world. Cities such as Bombay, Calcutta, and Shanghai boomed, more than tripling in size. Treaty ports like Hong Kong were transformed as Europeans built banks, shipping enterprises, schools, and religious missions. As Europeans and indigenous peoples encountered and transformed one another, new hybrid cultures emerged. Elsewhere, new social instabilities were produced as European demands for labor brought men out of their villages, away from their families, and crowded them into shantytowns bordering sprawling new cities. Hopes that European rule would create a well-disciplined labor force were quickly dashed.

People on both sides of the colonial divide worried about preserving national traditions and identity in the face of these hybrid and changing colonial cultures. In Africa and the Middle East, Islamic scholars debated the proper response to European control. In China and India, suggestions that local populations adopt European models of education set off fierce controversies. Chinese elites, already divided over such customs as foot-binding and concubinage (the legal practice of maintaining formal sexual partners for men outside their marriage), found their dilemmas heightened as imperialism became a more powerful force. Should they defend such practices as integral to their culture? Should they argue for a Chinese path to reform? Proponents of change in China or India thus had to sort through their stance toward Western culture and traditional popular culture.

For their part, British, French, and Dutch authorities fretted that too much familiarity between colonized and colonizer would weaken European prestige and authority. In Phnom Penh, Cambodia (part of French Indochina),

Analyzing Primary Sources

Address to the Nations of the World by the Pan-African Conference in London, 1900

The Pan-African Conference that met in 1900 in London brought together a group of people of African heritage from many parts of the world who were determined to add their voices to those who were discussing and debating the consequences of European imperialism in the last decades of the nineteenth century. The declaration that they produced gives a clear picture of their vision of history, their sense of the injustices associated with colonial conquest, and their hopes for the future. The chair of the committee who wrote the address was W. E. B. Du Bois (1868–1963), an African American professor of history, sociology, and economics who had studied at Harvard and the University of Berlin and who in 1909 became a founding member of the National Association for the Advancement of Colored People.

In the metropolis of the modern world, in this the closing year of the nineteenth century, there has been assembled a congress of men and women of African blood, to deliberate solemnly upon the present situation and outlook of the darker races of mankind. The problem of the twentieth century is the problem of the colour-line, the question as to how far differences of race—which show themselves chiefly in the colour of the skin and the texture of the hair—will hereafter be made the basis of denying to over half the world the right of sharing to their utmost ability the opportunities and privileges of modern civilization.

To be sure, the darker races are today the least advanced in culture according to European standards. This has not, however, always been the case in the past, and certainly the world's history, both ancient and modern, has given many instances of no despicable ability and capacity among the blackest races of men.

In any case, the modern world must remember that in this age when the ends of the world are being brought so near together the millions of black men in Africa, America, and the Islands of the Sea, not to speak of the brown and yellow myriads elsewhere, are bound to have a great influence upon the world in the future, by reason of sheer numbers and physical contact. If now the world of culture bends itself towards giving Negroes and other dark men the largest and broadest opportunity for education and self-development, then this contact and influence is bound to have a beneficial effect upon the world and hasten human progress. But if, by reason of carelessness, prejudice, greed and injustice, the black world is to be exploited and ravished and degraded, the results must be deplorable, if not fatal—not simply to them, but to the high ideals of justice, freedom and culture which a thousand years of Christian civilization have held before Europe.

And now, therefore, to these ideals of civilization, to the broader humanity of the followers of the Prince of Peace, we, the men and women of Africa in world congress assembled, do now solemnly appeal:

Let the world take no backward step in that slow but sure progress which has successively refused to let the spirit of class, of caste, of privilege, or of birth, debar from life, liberty and the pursuit of happiness a striving human soul.

Let not color or race be a feature of distinction between white and black men, regardless of worth or ability.

Let not the natives of Africa be sacrificed to the greed of gold, their liberties

French citizens lived separated from the rest of the city by a moat, and authorities required "dressing appropriately and keeping a distance from the natives." Sexual relations provoked the most anxiety and the most contradictory responses. "In this hot climate, passions run higher," wrote a French administrator in Algeria. "French soldiers seek out Arab women due to their strangeness and newness." "It was common practice for unmarried Englishmen resident in China to keep a Chinese girl, and I did as the others did," reported a British man stationed in Shanghai. He married an Englishwoman, however, and sent his Chinese mistress and their three children to England to avoid awkwardness. European administrators fitfully tried to prohibit liaisons between European men and local women, labeling such affairs as "corrupting." Such prohibitions only drove these relations underground, increasing the gap between the public facade of colonial rule and the private reality of colonial lives.

taken away, their family life debauched, their just aspirations repressed, and avenues of advancement and culture taken from them.

Let not the cloak of Christian missionary enterprise be allowed in the future, as so often in the past, to hide the ruthless economic exploitation and political downfall of less developed nations, whose chief fault has been reliance on the plighted faith of the Christian Church.

Let the British nation, the first modern champion of Negro Freedom, hasten to crown the work of Wilberforce, and Clarkson, and Buxton, and Sharpe, Bishop Colenso, and Livingstone, and give, as soon as practicable, the rights of responsible government to the black colonies of Africa and the West Indies.

Let not the spirit of Garrison, Phillips, and Douglass wholly die out in America; may the conscience of a great nation rise and rebuke all dishonesty and unrighteous oppression toward the American Negro, and grant to him the right of franchise, security of person and property, and generous recognition of the great work he has accomplished in a generation toward raising nine millions of human beings from slavery to manhood.

Let the German Empire, and the French Republic, true to their great past, remember that the true worth of colonies lies in their prosperity and progress, and that justice, impartial alike to black and white, is the first element of prosperity.

Let the Congo Free State become a great central Negro State of the world, and let its prosperity be counted not simply in cash and commerce, but in the happiness and true advancement of its black people.

Let the nations of the World respect the integrity and independence of the first Negro States of Abyssinia, Liberia, Haiti, and the rest, and let the inhabitants of these States, the independent tribes of Africa, the Negroes of the West Indies and America, and the black subjects of all nations take courage, strive ceaselessly, and fight bravely, that they may prove to the world their incontestible right to be counted among the great brotherhood of mankind.

Thus we appeal with boldness and confidence to the Great Powers of the civilized world, trusting in the wide spirit of humanity, and the deep sense of justice of our age, for a generous recognition of the righteousness of our cause.

ALEXANDER WALTERS (Bishop)
President Pan-African Association
HENRY B. BROWN
Vice-President
H. SYLVESTER-WILLIAMS
General Secretary
W. E. BURGHARDT DU BOIS
Chairman Committee on Address

Source: Ayodele Langley, *Ideologies of Liberation in Black Africa* (London: 1979), pp. 738–39.

Questions for Analysis

1. What value do the authors ascribe to "race" as a description of human difference?
2. According to the authors, what choices do European powers have to make as they exercise their power in Africa? What are their hopes for Africans in a world shaped by European expansion?
3. What are the specific "ideals of civilization" that the authors of this declaration invoke? Do they share these ideals with people from elsewhere?
4. Are there echoes of European liberalism or nationalism in the address's pan-Africanism?

CRISES OF EMPIRE AT THE TURN OF THE TWENTIETH CENTURY

The turn of the twentieth century brought a series of crises to the Western empires. Those crises did not end European rule. They did, however, create sharp tensions among Western nations. The crises also drove imperial nations to expand their economic and military commitments in territories overseas. They shook Western confidence. In all of these ways, they became central to Western culture in the years before the First World War.

Fashoda

In the fall of 1898, British and French armies nearly went to war at Fashoda, in the Egyptian Sudan. The crisis had

Interpreting Visual Evidence

Displays of Imperial Culture: The Paris Exposition of 1889

The French colonies were very visible during the celebration of the centenary of the French Revolution in 1889. In that year, the French government organized a "Universal Exposition" in the capital that attracted over 6 million visitors to a broad esplanade covered with exhibitions of French industry and culture, including the newly constructed Eiffel Tower, a symbol of modern French engineering.

At the base of the Eiffel Tower (image A), a colonial pavilion placed objects from France's overseas empire on display, and a collection of temporary architectural exhibits placed reproductions of buildings from French colonies in Asia and Africa as well as samples of architecture from other parts of the world. The photographs here show a reproduction of a Cairo Street (image B); the Pagoda of Angkor, modeled after

A. The Eiffel Tower in 1889.

the Khmer temples of Angkor Wat in Cambodia, a French protectorate (image C); and examples of West African dwellings (image D). The Cairo Street was the second most popular tourist destination at the fair, after the Eiffel Tower. It contained twenty-five shops and restaurants, and employed dozens of Egyptian servers, shopkeepers, and artisans who had been brought to Paris to add authenticity to the exhibit. Other people on display in the colonial pavilion included Senegalese villagers and a Vietnamese theater troupe.

Questions for Analysis

1. What vision of history and social progress is celebrated in this linkage between France's colonial holdings and the industrial power on display in the Eiffel Tower?
2. What might account for the popularity of the Cairo Street exhibit among the public?
3. Why was it so important for the exposition to place people from European colonies on display for a French audience?

B. Reproduction of a Cairo Street at the Paris World's Fair, 1889.

C. Pagoda of Angkor at the Paris World's Fair, 1889.

D. West African houses at the Paris World's Fair, 1889.

complex causes: in the early 1880s, the British had used a local uprising in the Sudan as an excuse to move southward from Egypt in an attempt to control the headwaters of the Nile River. This project began with grandiose dreams of connecting Cairo to the Cape of Good Hope, but it ran into catastrophe when an army led by Britain's most flamboyant general, Charles Gordon, was massacred in Khartoum in 1885 by the forces of the Mahdi, a Sufi religious leader who claimed to be the successor to the prophet Muhammad. Avenging Gordon's death preoccupied the British for more than a decade, and in 1898 a second large-scale rebellion gave them the opportunity. An Anglo-Egyptian army commanded by General Horatio Kitchener attacked Khartoum and defeated the Mahdi's army using modern machine guns and artillery.

The victory brought complications, however. France, which held territories in central Africa adjacent to the Sudan, saw the British victory as a threat. A French expedition was sent to the Sudanese town of Fashoda (now Kodok) to challenge British claims in the area. The French faced off with troops from Kitchener's army, and for a few weeks in September 1898 the situation teetered on the brink of war. The matter was resolved diplomatically, however, and France ceded the southern Sudan to Britain in exchange for a stop to further expansion. The incident was a sobering reminder of the extent to which imperial competition could lead to international tensions between European powers.

EMPEROR MENELIK II. Ethiopia was the last major independent African kingdom, its prosperity a counter to the European opinion of African cultures. Menelik soundly defeated the Italian attempt to conquer his kingdom in 1896.

Ethiopia

During the 1880s and 1890s, Italy had been developing a small empire on the shores of the Red Sea. Italy annexed Eritrea and parts of Somalia, and shortly after the death of Gordon at Khartoum, the Italians defeated an invasion of their territories by the Mahdi's forces. Bolstered by this success, the Italians set out to conquer Ethiopia in 1896. Ethiopia was the last major independent African kingdom, ruled by a shrewd and capable emperor, Menelik II. His largely Christian subjects engaged in profitable trade on the East African coast, and revenues from this trade allowed Menelik to invest in the latest European artillery. When the Italian army—mostly Somali conscripts and a few thousand Italian troops—arrived, Menelik allowed them to penetrate into the mountain passes of Ethiopia. To keep to the roads, the Italians were forced to divide their forces into separate columns. Meanwhile, the Ethiopians moved over the mountains themselves, and at Adowa in March 1896 Menelik's army attacked, destroyed the Italian armies completely, and killed 6,000. Adowa was a national humiliation for Italy and an important symbol for African political radicals during the early twentieth century.

South Africa: The Boer War

In the late 1800s, competition between Dutch settlers in South Africa—known as Afrikaners or Boers—and the British led to a shooting war between Europeans. The Boers (an appropriation of the Dutch word for farmer) arrived in South Africa in the early nineteenth century and had long had a troubled relationship with their British neighbors in the colony. In the 1830s, the Boers trekked inland from the cape, setting up two republics away from British influence: the Transvaal and the Orange Free State. Gold reserves were found in the Transvaal in the 1880s, and Cecil Rhodes, the diamond magnate, tried to provoke war between Britain and the Boers to gain control of the Afrikaners' diamond mines. The war finally

Competing Viewpoints

Rudyard Kipling and His Critics

Rudyard Kipling (1865–1936) remains one of the most famous propagandists of empire. His novels, short stories, and poetry about the British imperial experience in India were defining texts for the cause in which he believed. Kipling's poem was—and continues to be—widely read, analyzed, attacked, and praised. His immediate goal was to influence American public opinion during the Spanish-American War, but he also wanted to celebrate the moral and religious values of European imperialism in general.

The White Man's Burden

Take up the White Man's burden—
Send forth the best ye breed—
Go, bind your sons to exile
To serve your captives' need;
To wait, in heavy harness,
On fluttered folk and wild—
Your new-caught sullen peoples,
Half devil and half child.

Take up the White Man's burden—
In patience to abide,
To veil the threat of terror
And check the show of pride;
By open speech and simple,
An hundred times made plain,
To seek another's profit
And work another's gain.

Take up the White Man's burden—
The savage wars of peace—
Fill full the mouth of Famine,
And bid the sickness cease;
And when your goal is nearest
(The end for others sought)
Watch sloth and heathen folly
Bring all your hope to nought.

Take up the White Man's burden—
No iron rule of kings,
But toil of serf and sweeper—
The tale of common things.
The ports ye shall not enter,
The roads ye shall not tread,
Go, make them with your living
And mark them with your dead.

Take up the White Man's burden,
And reap his old reward—
The blame of those ye better
The hate of those ye guard—
The cry of hosts ye humour
(Ah, slowly!) toward the light:—
"Why brought ye us from bondage,
Our loved Egyptian night?"

Take up the White Man's burden—
Ye dare not stoop to less—
Nor call too loud on Freedom
To cloak your weariness.
By all ye will or whisper,
By all ye leave or do,
The silent sullen peoples
Shall weigh your God and you.

Take up the White Man's burden!
Have done with childish days—
The lightly-proffered laurel,
The easy ungrudged praise:
Comes now, to search your manhood
Through all the thankless years,
Cold, edged with dear-bought wisdom,
The judgment of your peers.

Source: Rudyard Kipling, "The White Man's Burden," *McClure's Magazine* 12 (Feb. 1899).

To the Editor of *The Nation*

Sir: The cable informs us that "Kipling's stirring verses, the 'Call to America,' have created a . . . profound impression" on your side. What that impression may be, we can only conjecture. There is something almost sickening in this "imperial" talk of assuming and bearing burdens for the good of others. They are never assumed or held where they are not found to be of material advantage or ministering to honor or glory. Wherever empire (I speak of the United Kingdom) is extended, and the climate suits the white man, the aborigines are, for the benefit of the white man, cleared off or held in degradation for his benefit. . . .

Taking India as a test, no one moves a foot in her government that is not well paid and pensioned at her cost. No appointments are more eagerly

contended for than those in the Indian service. A young man is made for life when he secures one. The tone of that service is by no means one "bound to exile," "to serve . . . captives' need," "to wait in heavy harness," or in any degree as expressed in Mr. Kipling's highfalutin lines. It is entirely the contrary: "You are requested not to beat the servants" is a not uncommon notice in Indian hotels. . . . So anxious are we, where good pay is concerned, to save Indians the heavy burden of enjoying them, that, while our sons can study and pass at home for Indian appointments, her sons must study and pass in England; and even in India itself whites are afforded chances closed to natives. . . .

There never was a fostered trade and revenue in more disastrous consequences to humanity than the opium trade and revenue. There never was a more grinding and debilitating tax than that on salt. . . .

Source: Alfred Webb, "Mr. Kipling's Call to America," *The Nation* 68 (Feb. 23, 1899).

Questions for Analysis

1. What benefits did Kipling think imperialism brought, and to whom?
2. What, exactly, was the "burden"?
3. What were Webb's arguments against Kipling? Why did he think that imperial talk was "almost sickening"? Did Europeans really suffer in their colonial outposts? In British India, with its well-established civil service, Webb thought not. Why did he mention the opium trade and the salt tax?

broke out in 1899, but the British were unprepared for the ferocity of Boer resistance. British columns were shot to pieces by Afrikaner forces who knew the territory, and the British towns of Ladysmith and Mafeking were besieged. Angered by these early failures, the British replaced their commanders and began to fight in earnest, using the railroads built to service the diamond mines to bring in modern military hardware.

The Afrikaners responded by taking to the hills, fighting a costly guerilla war that lasted another three years. The British tactics became more brutal as the campaign went on, setting up concentration camps—the first use of the term—where Afrikaner civilians were rounded up and forced to live in appalling conditions so that they would not be able to help the guerillas. Nearly 20,000 civilians died in the camps owing to disease and poor sanitation over the course of two years. Black Africans, despised by both sides, also suffered the effects of famine and disease as the war destroyed valuable farmland.

Meanwhile, the concentration camps aroused opposition in Britain and internationally, and protesters campaigned against these violations of "European" rights, without saying anything about the fate of Africans in the conflict. In the end, the Afrikaners ceded control of their republics to a new British Union of South Africa that gave them a share of political power. In the aftermath of the

AN ENGLISH CONCENTRATION CAMP DURING THE BOER WAR. In an attempt to block support to guerilla fighters, the English restricted Afrikaner civilians to camps where appalling conditions led to the death of nearly 20,000 people over two years. This illustration appeared in a French newspaper, *Le Petit Journal*, in 1901.

war, both British and Afrikaners preserved their high standards of living by relying on cheap African labor and, eventually, a system of racial segregation known as apartheid.

U.S. Imperialism: The Spanish-American War of 1898

Imperialism also brought Spain and the United States to war in 1898. American imperialism in the nineteenth century was closely bound up with nation building, the conquest of new territories, and the defeat of the North American Indians (see Chapter 21). In the 1840s, the United States provoked Mexico into war over Texas and California after unsuccessfully trying to purchase the territories. Mexico's defeat, and the treaty of Guadalupe Hidalgo that followed in 1848, gave the American Southwest to the United States, an enormous territorial gain that made the question of slavery more acute in the years before the American Civil War.

The conflict with Spain followed a similar pattern. In the 1880s and 1890s, Spain's imperial powers were considerably weakened, and they faced rebellion in their colonies in the Caribbean and the Pacific. American economic interests had considerable investments in Cuba, and when an American battleship accidentally exploded at port in Havana, advocates of empire and the press in general

IMPERIALISM IN THE BALANCE. This cartoon, titled "A Study—Imperialism" appeared in the United States in 1899 during the beginning of the Philippine-American War. The image shows the scales of justice weighing imperialism against the many victims of U.S. military action, and demonstrates that the populations of colonial powers were far from unanimous about the virtues of imperial expansion and the "civilizing mission."

After You Read This Chapter

Visit StudySpace for quizzes, additional review materials, and multimedia documents. **wwnorton.com/web/westernciv18**

REVIEWING THE OBJECTIVES

- European imperialism in the nineteenth century differed from earlier phases of colonial expansion. How was it different, and which parts of the globe were singled out for special attention by European imperial powers?
- European nations justified the cost and effort of their colonial policies in many ways. What were the major reasons for colonial expansion in the nineteenth century?
- The subjugated peoples of European colonies faced a choice between resistance and accommodation, though these choices were rarely exclusive of one another. What examples of resistance to colonialism can you identify? Of accommodation?
- Imperialism also shaped cultural developments within Europe in the nineteenth century. How did imperialism change the lives of Europeans and their sense of their place in the world?
- Imperialism unleashed destabilizing competitive forces that drove European colonial powers into conflict with one another by the end of the nineteenth century. Where were the flashpoints of these conflicts?

clamored for revenge. President William McKinley gave in to political necessity, in spite of his misgivings, and the United States declared war on Spain in 1898, determined to protect its economic interests in the Americas and the Pacific. The United States swiftly won.

In Spain, the Spanish-American War provoked an entire generation of writers, politicians, and intellectuals to national soul searching. The defeat undermined the Spanish monarchy, which fell in 1912. The ensuing political tensions resurfaced in the Spanish Civil War of the 1930s, an important episode in the origins of the Second World War.

In the United States, this "splendid little war" was followed by the annexation of Puerto Rico, the establishment of a protectorate over Cuba, and a short but brutal war against Philippine rebels who liked American colonialism no better than the Spanish variety. In the Americas, the United States intervened in a rebellion in Panama in 1903, quickly backing the rebels and helping establish a republic while building the Panama Canal on land leased from the new government. The Panama Canal opened in 1914, and like Britain's canal at Suez, it cemented U.S. dominance of the seas in the Western Hemisphere and the eastern Pacific. Later interventions in Hawaii and Santo Domingo gave further evidence of U.S. imperial power and committed the former colony to a broad role in its new and greater sphere of influence.

CONCLUSION

In the last quarter of the nineteenth century, the long-standing relationship between Western nations and the rest of the world entered a new stage. That stage was distinguished by the stunningly rapid extension of formal Western control, by new forms of economic exploitation, and by new patterns of social discipline and settlement. It was driven by the rising economic needs of the industrial West; by territorial conflict; and by nationalism, which by the late nineteenth century linked nationhood to empire. Among its immediate results was the creation of a self-consciously imperial culture in the West. At the same time, however, it plainly created unease and contributed powerfully to the sense of crisis that swept through the late-nineteenth-century West.

For all its force, this Western expansion was never unchallenged. Imperialism provoked resistance and required constantly changing strategies of rule. During the First World War, mobilizing the resources of empire would become crucial to victory. In the aftermath, reimposing the conditions of the late nineteenth century would become nearly impossible. And over the longer term, the political structures, economic developments, and racial ideologies established in this period would be contested throughout the twentieth century.

PEOPLE, IDEAS, AND EVENTS IN CONTEXT

- What was the **EAST INDIA COMPANY**? How did the British reorganize their rule in India after the **SEPOY MUTINY**?
- What did the French mean when they justified colonial expansion in the name of the **CIVILIZING MISSION**?
- How did the **OPIUM WARS** change the economic and political relationships between Europe and China?
- How did the **BERLIN CONFERENCE** of 1884 shape the subsequent colonization of Africa?
- What limits to the exercise of colonial power were revealed by the **BOXER REBELLION**, the failed **ITALIAN INVASION OF ETHIOPIA**, or the **RUSSO-JAPANESE WAR**?
- What expressions of anti-imperialism emerged from the London **PAN-AFRICAN CONFERENCE**?
- How did the **BOER WAR** and the **FASHODA INCIDENT** contribute to a sense of crisis among European colonial powers?
- What effects did the **SPANISH-AMERICAN WAR** have on attitudes toward imperialism in the United States, itself a former European colony?

THINKING ABOUT CONNECTIONS

- Compare the consequences of late-nineteenth-century European colonial conquest with earlier episodes of imperial expansion such as the Roman Empire or early modern colonization in the Atlantic world. What was similar? What was different?
- What challenges were faced by colonial regimes such as France and Britain, which expanded their institutions of representative and elected government at home even as they subjugated the conquered peoples in their new colonies during the nineteenth century?
- The histories of colonial conquest in the nineteenth century helped to establish a network of political and cultural connections that shaped the history of the world in the twentieth century. What was the legacy of these connections during the period of decolonization?
- How was the history of industrialization connected to the history of colonialism?

Before You Read This Chapter

STORY LINES

- The second industrial revolution intensified the scope and effects of technological innovations, as new techniques for producing steel and chemicals became widespread and new sources of power—electricity and oil—provided alternatives to coal-burning machinery.
- The expansion of the electorate in many European nation-states created a different kind of politics, as workers and peasants were given voting rights for the first time while women continued to be excluded from voting. New political parties on the right and the left engaged in partisan struggles to win the support of new voters.
- Although the advances in technology and industry encouraged a sense of self-confidence about European society and progress, other scientific and cultural movements expressed doubt or anxiety about the effects of rapid modernization on European culture.

CHRONOLOGY

1850s–1870s	Production of steel alloys revolutionized
1859	Publication of Charles Darwin's *On the Origin of Species*
1861	Emancipation of the serfs in Russia
1871	Paris Commune
1871–1878	Bismarck's *Kulturkampf*
1880–1890s	Russia launches industrialization program
1890s	Electricity becomes available in many European cities
1894–1906	Dreyfus Affair
1899	Publication of Sigmund Freud's *The Interpretation of Dreams*
1901	Labour party founded in Britain
1903	Russian Marxists split into Bolsheviks and Mensheviks
1905	The First Russian Revolution

23

Modern Industry and Mass Politics, 1870–1914

CORE OBJECTIVES

- **UNDERSTAND** the origins and consequences of the second industrial revolution.
- **DEFINE** *mass politics* and explain how the expansion of voting rights in European nations led to the development of organized political parties that sought the support of the working classes.
- **UNDERSTAND** the arguments both for and against woman suffrage during this period.
- **IDENTIFY** the ways that European liberalism and conservatism evolved as new social and political tensions emerged with the advent of mass politics and intensified industrial development.
- **EXPLAIN** the contributions of scientists and other cultural figures who came to prominence in the final decades of the nineteenth century and their contributions to debates about human nature, modern society, and the natural world.

"We are on the extreme promontory of ages!" decreed the Italian poet and literary editor F. T. Marinetti in 1909. In a bombastic manifesto—a self-described "inflammatory declaration" printed on the front page of a Paris newspaper—Marinetti introduced Europe to an aggressive art movement called futurism. Revolting against what he considered the tired and impotent conservatism of Italian culture, Marinetti called for a radical renewal of civilization through "courage, audacity, and revolt." Enamored with the raw power of modern machinery, with the dynamic bustle of urban life, he trumpeted "a new form of beauty, the beauty of speed." Most notable, Marinetti celebrated the heroic violence of warfare and disparaged the moral and cultural traditions that formed the bedrock of nineteenth-century liberalism.

Few Europeans embraced the modern era with the unflinching abandon of the futurists, but many would have agreed with Marinetti in his claim that modern life was above all characterized by flux, movement, and an accelerating rate of change. In the last decades of the nineteenth century, a second industrial revolution produced new techniques for manufacturing and new sources of power, including electricity and petroleum-based fuels. These developments transformed the infrastructure of European towns and cities, and people felt the immediate effects of these changes in their daily lives.

At the same time, European nation-states faced new political realities as their electorates expanded and new blocs of voters began participating directly in shaping parliamentary bodies and their legislative agendas. New mass-based political parties brought new demands to the political arena, and national governments struggled to maintain order and legitimacy in the face of these challenges. Socialists mobilized growing numbers of industrial workers, while suffragists demanded the franchise for women. The ability of traditional elites to control the political life of nations was sorely tested, even in nations that continued to be governed by hereditary monarchs.

In the arts and sciences new theories challenged older notions of nature, society, truth, and beauty. Since the eighteenth century at least, science had been a frequent ally of political liberalism, as both liberals and scientists shared a common faith in human reason and an openness to rational inquiry into the laws of society and nature. In the late nineteenth century, however, this common agenda was strained by scientific investigations in new fields such as biology and psychology that challenged liberal assumptions about human nature. Meanwhile, in the arts, a new generation of artists and writers embraced innovation and rejected the established conventions in painting, sculpture, poetry, and literature. A period of intense experimentation in the arts followed, leading artists and writers to develop radically new forms of expression.

The nineteenth century, then, ended in a burst of energy as many Europeans embraced a vision of their society racing headlong into what they hoped was a more promising and better future. Behind this self-confidence, however, lay significant uncertainty about the eventual destination. What aspects of the European past would continue to be relevant in the modern age? In politics and social life and in the culture as a whole, such questions produced more conflict than consensus.

NEW TECHNOLOGIES AND GLOBAL TRANSFORMATIONS

In the last third of the nineteenth century, new technologies transformed the face of manufacturing in Europe, leading to new levels of economic growth and complex realignments among industry, labor, and national governments. Like Europe's first industrial revolution, which began in the late eighteenth century and centered on coal, steam, and iron, this second industrial revolution relied on innovation in three key areas: steel, electricity, and chemicals.

Harder, stronger, and more malleable than iron, steel had long been prized as a construction material. But until the mid-nineteenth century, producing steel cheaply and in large quantities was impossible. That changed between the 1850s and 1870s, as different processes for refining and mass-producing alloy steel revolutionized the metallurgical industry. Britain's shipbuilders made a quick and profitable switch to steel construction and thus kept their lead in the industry. Germany and America dominated the

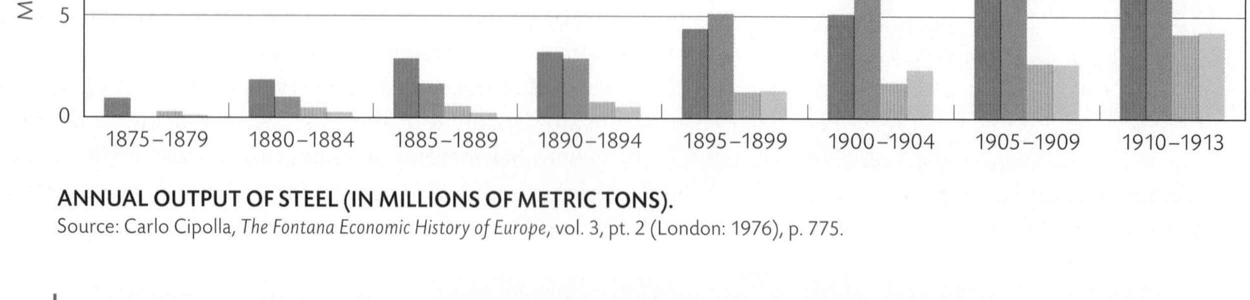

ANNUAL OUTPUT OF STEEL (IN MILLIONS OF METRIC TONS).
Source: Carlo Cipolla, *The Fontana Economic History of Europe*, vol. 3, pt. 2 (London: 1976), p. 775.

rest of the steel industry. By 1901, Germany was producing almost half again as much steel as Britain, allowing Germany to build a massive national and industrial infrastructure.

Like steel, electricity had been discovered earlier, and its advantages were similarly well known. Easily transmitted over long distances to be converted into heat, light, and other types of energy, electricity was made available for commercial and domestic use in the 1880s, after the development of alternators and transformers capable of producing high-voltage alternating current. By century's end, large power stations, which often used cheap water power, could send electric current over vast distances. In 1879, Thomas Edison and his associates invented the incandescent-filament lamp and changed electricity into light. The demand for electricity skyrocketed, and soon entire metropolitan areas were electrified. As a leading sector in the new economy, electrification powered subways, tramways, and, eventually, long-distance railroads; it made possible new techniques in the chemical and metallurgical industries, and gradually, it dramatically altered living habits in ordinary households.

THE SECOND INDUSTRIAL REVOLUTION. A German electrical engineering factory illustrates the scale of production during the second industrial revolution. ▪ ***What changes in business practices and labor management made factories of this size possible?***

The chemical industry was a third sector of important new technologies. The efficient production of alkali and sulfuric acid transformed the manufacture of such consumer goods as paper, soaps, textiles, and fertilizer. Britain and particularly Germany became leaders in the field. Heightened concerns for household hygiene and new techniques in mass marketing enabled the British entrepreneur Harold Lever to market his soaps and cleansers around the world. German production, on the other hand, focused on industrial use, such as developing synthetic dyes and methods for refining petroleum, and came to control roughly 90 percent of the world's chemical market.

Other innovations contributed to the second industrial revolution. The growing demand for efficient power spurred the invention of the liquid-fuel internal combustion engine. By 1914, most navies had converted from coal to oil, as had domestic steamship companies. The new engines' dependence on crude petroleum and distilled gasoline at first threatened their general application, but the discovery of oil fields in Russia, Borneo, Persia, and Texas around 1900 allayed fears. Protecting these oil reserves thus became a vital state prerogative. The adoption of oil-powered machinery had another important consequence: industrialists who had previously depended on nearby rivers or coal mines for power were free to take their enterprises to regions bereft of natural resources. The potential for worldwide industrialization was in place. Of course, the internal combustible engine would bring even more radical changes to twentieth-century transportation in the future, but the automobile and the airplane were both still in their infancies before 1914.

Changes in Scope and Scale

These technological changes were part of a much larger process—impressive increases in the scope and scale of industry. Technologies were both causes and consequences of the race toward a bigger, faster, cheaper, and more efficient world. At the end of the nineteenth century, size mattered. The rise of heavy industry and mass marketing had factories and cities growing hand in hand, while advances in media and mobility spurred the creation of national mass cultures. For the first time, ordinary people followed the news on national and global levels. They watched as European powers divided the globe, enlarging their empires with prodigious feats of engineering mastery; railroads, dams, canals, and harbors grew to monumental proportions. Such projects embodied the ideals of modern European industry. They also generated enormous income for builders, investors, bankers, entrepreneurs, and,

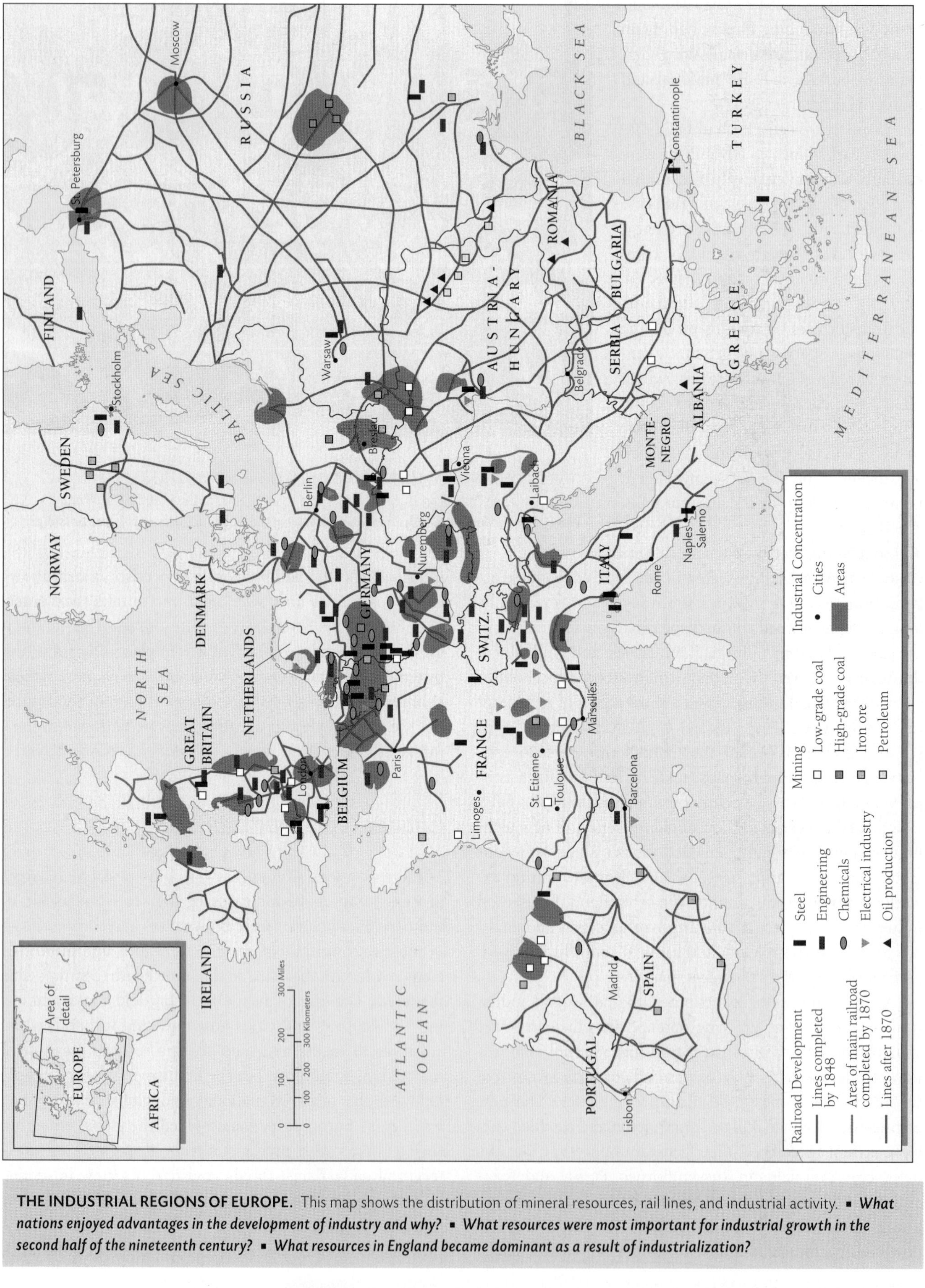

THE INDUSTRIAL REGIONS OF EUROPE. This map shows the distribution of mineral resources, rail lines, and industrial activity. ▪ ***What nations enjoyed advantages in the development of industry and why?*** ▪ ***What resources were most important for industrial growth in the second half of the nineteenth century?*** ▪ ***What resources in England became dominant as a result of industrialization?***

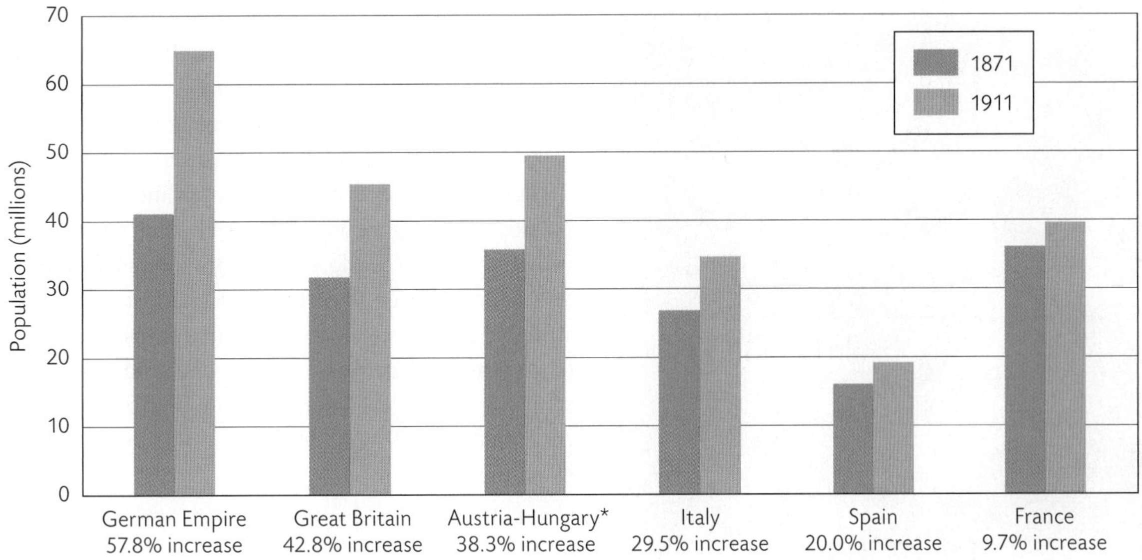

POPULATION GROWTH IN MAJOR STATES BETWEEN 1871 AND 1911 (POPULATION IN MILLIONS).
*Not including Bosnia-Herzegovina.
Source: Colin Dyer, *Population and Society in Twentieth-Century France* (New York: 1978), p. 5.

of course, makers of steel and concrete. Canals in central Europe, railroads in the Andes, and telegraph cables spanning the ocean floors: these "tentacles of empire," as one historian dubs them, stretched across the globe.

Yet industrialization also brought profound, if less spectacular, changes in Europe. The population grew constantly, particularly in central and eastern Europe. Russia's population increased by nearly a quarter and Germany's by half in the space of a generation. Britain's population, too, grew by nearly one-third between 1881 and 1911. Thanks to improvements in both crop yields and shipping, food shortages declined, which rendered entire populations less susceptible to illness and high infant mortality. Advances in medicine, nutrition, and personal hygiene diminished the prevalence of dangerous diseases such as cholera and typhus, and improved conditions in housing and public sanitation transformed the urban environment.

Credit and Consumerism

Changes in scope and scale not only transformed production but also altered consumption. Indeed it was during this period that consumption began to shift, slowly, to the center of economic activity and theory. The era in which economists would worry about consumer confidence and experts could systematically track the public's buying habits did not begin until the middle of the twentieth century, but developments pointed toward that horizon. Department stores offering both practical and luxury goods to the middle class were one mark of the times—of urbanization, economic expansion, and the new importance attached to merchandising. Advertising took off as well. The lavishly illustrated posters of the late nineteenth century that advertised concert halls, soaps, bicycles, and sewing machines were only one sign of underlying economic changes. Even more significant, by the 1880s new stores sought to attract working-class people by introducing the all-important innovation of credit payment. In earlier times, working-class families pawned watches, mattresses, or furniture to borrow money; now they began to buy on credit, a change that would eventually have seismic effects on both households and national economies.

These new late-nineteenth-century patterns of consumption, however, were largely urban. In the countryside, peasants continued to save money under mattresses; pass down a few pieces of furniture for generations; make, launder, and mend their own clothes and linens; and offer a kilo of sugar as a generous household gift. Only slowly did retailers whittle away at these traditional habits. Mass consumption remained difficult to imagine in what was still a deeply stratified society.

The Rise of the Corporation

Economic growth and the demands of mass consumption spurred reorganization, consolidation, and regulation of capitalist institutions. Although capitalist enterprises had been financed by individual investors through the joint-stock

POSTER FOR *MOTOCYCLES COMIOT*, 1899. The rise of consumer spending in the middle class created a new industry and a new art: advertising. This advertisement, like many from the period, contrasted new with old, leisure with toil, and speed, or freedom, with inertia.

principle at least since the sixteenth century, it was during the late nineteenth century that the modern corporation came into its own. To mobilize the enormous funds needed for large-scale enterprises, entrepreneurs needed to offer better guarantees on investors' money. To provide such protection, most European countries enacted or improved their limited-liability laws, which ensured that stockholders could lose only the value of their shares in the event of bankruptcy. Insured in this way, many thousands of middle-class men and women now considered corporate investment a promising venture. After 1870, stock markets ceased to be primarily a clearinghouse for state paper and railroad bonds and instead attracted new commercial and industrial ventures.

Limited liability was one part of a larger trend of incorporation. Whereas most firms had been small or middle size, companies now incorporated to attain the necessary size for survival. In doing so, they tended to shift control from company founders and local directors to distant bankers and financiers. Because financial institutions represented the interests of investors whose primary concern was the bottom line, bankers' control over industrial growth encouraged an ethos of impersonal finance capital.

Equally important, the second industrial revolution created a strong demand for technical expertise, which undercut traditional forms of family management. University degrees in engineering and chemistry became more valuable than on-the-job apprenticeships. The emergence of a white-collar class (middle-level salaried managers who were neither owners nor laborers) marked a significant change in work life and for society's evolving class structure.

The drive toward larger business enterprises was spurred by a desire for increased profits. It was also encouraged by a belief that consolidation protected society against the hazards of boom-and-bust economic fluctuations and against the wasteful inefficiencies of unbridled, "ruinous" competition. Some industries combined vertically, attempting to control every step of production from the acquisition of raw materials to the distribution of finished products. Andrew Carnegie's steel company in Pittsburgh controlled costs by owning the iron and coal mines necessary for steel production as well as by acquiring its own fleet of steamships and railways to transport ore to the mills. A second form of corporate self-protection was horizontal alignment. Organizing into cartels, companies in the same industry would band together to fix prices and control competition, if not eliminate it outright. Coal, oil, and steel companies were especially suited to the organization of cartels, since only a few major players could afford the huge expense of building, equipping, and running mines, refineries, and foundries. In 1894, for example, the Rhenish-Westphalian Coal Syndicate captured 98 percent of Germany's coal market by using ruthless tactics against small competitors, who could join the syndicate or face ruin. Through similar tactics, both legal and illegal, John D. Rockefeller's Standard Oil Company came to control the refined petroleum market in the United States, producing over 90 percent of the country's oil by the 1880s. The monopoly was sustained through the Standard Oil Trust, a legal innovation that enabled Rockefeller to control and manage assets of allied companies through the government. Cartels were particularly strong in Germany and America but less so in Britain, where dedication to free-trade policies made price fixing difficult, and in France, where family firms and laborers both opposed cartels and where there was also less heavy industry.

Though governments sometimes tried to stem the burgeoning power of cartels, the dominant trend of this period was increased cooperation between governments

Analyzing Primary Sources

The Dangers of Consumer Culture

By 1880 the Bon Marché in Paris, the world's first department store, was turning over the astronomical sum of 80 million francs annually and came to embody the new rhythm and tempo of mass consumer culture. The vast scale of selling sparked debate about the decline of the family store, the recreation of browsing and window shopping, and, above all, the "moral disaster" of women's limitless desire for goods. In writing the novel The Ladies' Paradise *(1883), Émile Zola noted he wanted to "write the poem of modern activity." The passage here captures the fascination for Denise, a clerk in her uncle's fabric shop, of the fictitious department store the Ladies' Paradise.*

But what fascinated Denise was the Ladies' Paradise on the other side of the street, for she could see the shop-windows through the open door. The sky was still overcast, but the mildness brought by rain was warming the air in spite of the season; and in the clear light, dusted with sunshine, the great shop was coming to life, and business was in full swing.

Denise felt that she was watching a machine working at high pressure; its dynamism seemed to reach to the display windows themselves. They were no longer the cold windows she had seen in the morning; now they seemed to be warm and vibrating with the activity within. A crowd was looking at them, groups of women were crushing each other in front of them, a real mob, made brutal by covetousness. And these passions in the street were giving life to the materials: the laces shivered, then drooped again, concealing the depths of the shop with an exciting air of mystery; even the lengths of cloth, thick and square, were breathing, exuding a tempting odour, while the overcoats were throwing back their shoulders still more on the dummies, which were acquiring souls, and the huge velvet coat was billowing out, supple and warm, as if on shoulders of flesh and blood, with heaving breast and quivering hips. But the furnace-like heat with which the shop was ablaze came above all from the selling, from the bustle at the counters, which could be felt behind the walls. There was the continuous roar of the machine at work, of customers crowding into the departments, dazzled by the merchandise, then propelled towards the cash-desk. And it was all regulated and organized with the remorselessness of a machine: the vast horde of women were as if caught in the wheels of an inevitable force. . . .

Source: Émile Zola, *The Ladies' Paradise,* trans. Brian Nelson (New York: 1995), pp. 15–16.

Questions for Analysis

1. Why did Zola choose to represent the new department store as a giant machine?
2. The first industrial revolution faced the challenge of production. In what ways was consumption the challenge of the late nineteenth century? What obstacles did merchants confront when encouraging people to consume?

and industry. Contrary to the laissez-faire mentality of early capitalism, corporations developed close relationships with the states in the West—most noticeably in colonial industrial projects, such as the construction of railroads, harbors, and seafaring steamships. These efforts were so costly, or so unprofitable, that private enterprise would not have undertaken them alone. But because they served larger political and strategic interests, governments funded them willingly. Such interdependence was underscored by the appearance of businessmen and financiers as officers of state. The German banker Bernhard Dernburg was the German secretary of state for colonies. Joseph Chamberlain, the British manufacturer and mayoral boss of industrial Birmingham, also served as the colonial secretary. And in France, Charles Jonnart, president of the Suez Canal Company and the Saint-Étienne steelwork, was later governor general of Algeria. Tied to imperial interests, the rise of modern corporations had an impact around the globe.

Global Economics

From the 1870s on, the rapid spread of industrialization heightened competition among nations. The search for markets, goods, and influence fueled much of the imperial expansion and, consequently, often put countries at odds with each other. Trade barriers arose again to protect home markets. All nations except Britain raised tariffs, arguing that the needs of the nation-state trumped laissez-faire doctrine. Yet changes in international economics fueled the continuing growth of an interlocking, worldwide system of manufacturing, trade, and finance. For example, the near universal adoption of the gold standard in currency exchange greatly facilitated world trade. Pegging the value of currencies, particularly Britain's powerful pound sterling, against the value of gold meant that currencies could be readily exchanged. The common standard also allowed nations to use a third country to mediate trade and exchange to mitigate trade imbalances—a common problem for the industrializing West. Almost all European countries, dependent on vast supplies of raw materials to sustain their rate of industrial production, imported more than they exported. To avoid the mounting deficits that this practice would otherwise incur, European economies relied on "invisible" exports: shipping, insurance, and banking services. The extent of Britain's exports in these areas was far greater than that of any other country. London was the money market of the world, to which would-be borrowers looked for assistance before turning elsewhere. By 1914, Britain had $20 billion invested overseas, compared with $8.7 billion for France and $6 billion for Germany. Britain also used its invisible trade to secure relationships with food-producing nations, becoming the major overseas buyer for the wheat of the United States and Canada, the beef of Argentina, and the mutton (lamb) of Australia. These goods, shipped cheaply aboard refrigerated vessels, kept down food prices for working-class families and eased the demand for increased wages.

During this period, the relationship between European manufacturing nations and the overseas sources of their materials—whether colonies or not—was transformed, as detailed in the last chapter. Those changes, in turn, reshaped economies and cultures on both sides of the imperial divide. Europeans came to expect certain foods on their tables; whole regions of Africa, Latin America, and Asia geared toward producing for the European market. This international push toward mass manufacturing and commodity production necessarily involved changes in deep-seated patterns in consumption and in production. It altered the landscape and habits of India as well as those of Britain. It brought new rhythms of life to women working in clothing factories in Germany, to porters carrying supplies to build railways in Senegal, to workers dredging the harbor of Dakar.

LABOR POLITICS, MASS MOVEMENTS

The rapid expansion of late-nineteenth-century industry brought a parallel growth in the size, cohesion, and activism of Europe's working classes. The men and women who worked as wage laborers resented corporate power—resentment fostered not only by the exploitation and inequalities they experienced on the job but also by living "a life apart" in Europe's expanding cities (see Chapter 19). Corporations had devised new methods of protecting and promoting their interests, and workers did the same. Labor unions, which were traditionally limited to skilled male workers in small-scale enterprises, grew during the late nineteenth century into mass, centralized, nationwide organizations. This "new unionism" emphasized organization across entire industries and, for the first time, brought unskilled workers into the ranks, increasing power to negotiate wages and job conditions. More important, though, the creation of national unions provided a framework for a new type of political movement: the socialist mass party.

Why did socialism develop in Europe after 1870? Changing national political structures provide part of the answer. Parliamentary constitutional governments opened the political process to new participants, including socialists. Now part of the legislative process, socialists in Parliament led efforts to expand voting rights in the 1860s and 1870s. Their success created new constituencies of working-class men. At the same time, traditional struggles between labor and management moved up to the national level; governments aligned with business interests, and legislators countered working-class agitation with antilabor and antisocialist laws. To radical leaders, the organization of national mass political movements seemed the only effective way to counter industrialists' political strength. Thus, during this period, socialist movements abandoned their earlier revolutionary traditions (exemplified by the romantic image of barricaded streets) in favor of legal, public competition within Europe's parliamentary systems.

The Spread of Socialist Parties—and Alternatives

The emergence of labor movements in Europe owed as much to ideas as to social changes. The most influential radical thinker was Karl Marx, whose early career was discussed

INDEPENDENT LABOR PARTY DEMONSTRATION IN ENGLAND, c. 1893. Activism among workers swelled in the late nineteenth century. Increasingly powerful labor unions had a profound impact on politics because male workers without property could now vote in local and national elections.

in Chapter 20. Since the 1840s, Marx and his collaborator Friedrich Engels had been intellectuals and activists, participating in the organization of fledgling socialist movements. In 1867, Marx published the first of three volumes of *Capital*, a work he believed was his greatest contribution to human emancipation. *Capital* attacked capitalism using the tools of economic analysis, allowing Marx to claim a scientific validity for his work, and he was contemptuous of other socialists whose opposition to industrial economies were couched only in moral terms. Marx's work claimed to offer a systematic analysis of how capitalism forced workers to exchange their labor for subsistence wages while enabling their employers to amass both wealth and power. Followers of Marx called for workers everywhere to ally with one another to create an independent political force, and few other groups pushed so strongly to secure civil liberties, expand conceptions of citizenship, or build a welfare state. Marxists also made powerful claims for gender equality, though in practice woman suffrage took a backseat to class politics.

Not all working-class movements were Marxist, however. Differences among various left-wing groups remained strong, and the most divisive issues were the role of violence and whether socialists should cooperate with liberal governments—and if so, to what end. Some "gradualists" were willing to work with liberals for piecemeal reform, while anarchists and syndicalists rejected parliamentary politics altogether. When European labor leaders met in 1864 at the first meeting of the International Working Men's Association, Marx argued strongly in favor of political mass movements, which would prepare the working classes for revolution. He was strongly opposed by the anarchist Mikhail Bakunin, who rejected any form of state or party organization and called instead for terror and violence to destabilize society.

Between 1875 and 1905, Marxist socialists founded political parties in Germany, Belgium, France, Austria, and Russia. These parties were disciplined workers' organizations that aimed to seize control of the state to make revolutionary changes in the social order. The most successful was the German Social Democratic party (SPD). Initially intending to work for political change within the parliamentary political system, the SPD became more radical in the face of Bismarck's oppressive antisocialist laws. By the outbreak of the First World War, the German Social Democrats were the largest, best-organized workers' party in the world. Rapid and extensive industrialization, a large urban working class, and a national government hostile to organized labor, made German workers particularly receptive to the goals and ideals of social democracy.

In Britain—the world's first and most industrialized economy—the socialist presence was much smaller and more moderate. Why? The answer lies in the fact that much of the socialist agenda was advanced by radical Liberals in Britain, which forestalled the growth of an independent socialist party. Even when a separate Labour party was formed in 1901, it remained moderate, committed to reforming capitalism with measures such as support for public housing or welfare benefits, rather than a complete overhaul of the economy. For the Labour party, and for Britain's many trade unions, Parliament remained a legitimate vehicle for achieving social change, limiting the appeal of revolutionary Marxism.

Militant workers seeking to organize themselves for political action found alternatives to Marxism in the ideas of anarchists and syndicalists. Anarchists shared many values with Marxist socialists, but they were opposed to centrally organized economies and to the very existence of the state. Rather than participating in parliamentary politics, therefore, the anarchists aimed to establish small-scale, localized, and self-sufficient democratic communities that could guarantee a maximum of individual sovereignty. Renouncing parties, unions, and any form of modern mass organization, the anarchists fell back on the tradition of conspiratorial violence, which Marx had denounced. Anarchists assassinated Tsar Alexander II in 1881 and five other heads of state in the following years, believing that such "exemplary terror" would spark a popular revolt. Syndicalists, on the other hand, did not call for terror but embraced a strategy of strikes and sabotage by workers. Their hope was that a general strike of all workers would bring down the capitalist state and replace it with workers' syndicates or trade associations. Anarchism's opposition to any form of organization kept it from making substantial gains as a movement. Likewise, the syndicalists' refusal to participate in politics limited their ability to command wide influence, but the tradition was kept alive, especially in France, through participation in trade unions.

SOCIALIST PARTY PAMPHLET, c. 1895. Socialism emerged as a powerful political force throughout Europe in the late nineteenth century, although appearing in different forms depending on the region. This German pamphlet quotes from Marx's *Communist Manifesto* of 1848, calling for workers of Asia, Africa, America, and Australia to unite under the banners of equality and brotherhood. ▪ ***What was the significance of this claim for equality, given the image's apparent references to racial difference?***

By 1895, popular socialist movements had made impressive gains in Europe: seven socialist parties had captured between a quarter and third of the votes in their countries. But just as socialists gained a permanent foothold in national politics, they were also straining under limitations and internal conflicts. Working-class movements, in fact, had never gained full worker support. Some workers remained loyal to older liberal traditions or to religious parties, and many others were excluded from socialist politics by its narrow definition of who constituted the working class—male industrial workers.

Furthermore, some committed socialists began to question Marx's core assumptions about the inevitability of workers' impoverishment and the collapse of the capitalist order. A German group of so-called revisionists, led by Eduard Bernstein, challenged Marxist doctrine and called for a shift to moderate and gradual reform, accomplished through electoral politics. Radical supporters of direct action were incensed at Bernstein's betrayal of Marxist theory of revolution, because they feared that the official reforms that favored workers might make the working class more accepting of the status quo. The radicals within the labor movement were inspired by the unexpected (and unsuccessful) revolution in Russia in 1905. German Marxists such as Rosa Luxembourg called for mass strikes, hoping to ignite a widespread proletarian revolution.

Conflicts over strategy peaked just before the First World War, but these divisions did not diminish the strength and appeal of socialism among workers. On the eve of the

"BLOODY RIOTS IN LIMOGES." Labor unions used strikes to draw attention to low wages and dangerous working conditions and to extract concessions from their employers. Some militant groups, known as syndicalists, hoped that a general strike of all workers would lead to a revolutionary change. Fear of labor militancy was a common theme in the popular press, as in this newspaper illustration from Limoges in France, where soldiers are depicted defending the gates of a prison from laborers brandishing the revolutionary red flag of socialism. ▪ ***What connection might this newspaper's readers have made with earlier revolutionary movements in Europe?***

war, governments discreetly consulted with labor leaders about workers' willingness to enlist and fight. Having built impressive organizational and political strength since the 1870s, working-class parties now affected the ability of nation-states to wage war. In short, they had come of age. Much to the disappointment of socialist leaders, however, European laborers—many of whom had voted for socialist candidates in previous elections—nevertheless donned the uniforms of their respective nations and marched off to war in 1914, proving that national identities and class identities were not necessarily incompatible with one another.

DEMANDING EQUALITY: SUFFRAGE AND THE WOMEN'S MOVEMENT

Since the 1860s, the combination of working-class activism and liberal constitutionalism had expanded male suffrage rights across Europe: by 1884, Germany, France, and Britain had enfranchised most men. But nowhere did women have the right to vote. Nineteenth-century political ideology relegated women to the status of second-class citizens, and even egalitarian-minded socialists seldom challenged this entrenched hierarchy. Excluded from the workings of parliamentary and mass party politics, women pressed their interests through independent organizations and through forms of direct action. The new women's movement won some crucial legal reforms during this period; and after the turn of the century, its militant campaign for suffrage fed the growing sense of political crisis, most notably in Britain.

Women's organizations, such as the General German Women's Association, pressed first for educational and legal reforms. In Britain, women's colleges were established at the same time that women won the right to control their own property. (Previously, women surrendered their property, including wages, to their husbands.) Laws in 1884 and 1910 gave Frenchwomen the same right and the ability to divorce their husbands. German women, too, won more favorable divorce laws by 1870, and in 1900 they were granted full legal rights.

After these important changes in women's status, suffrage crystallized as the next logical goal. Indeed, votes became *the* symbol for women's ability to attain full personhood. As the suffragists saw it, enfranchisement meant not merely political progress but economic, spiritual, and moral advancement as well. By the last third of the century, middle-class women throughout western Europe had founded clubs, published journals, organized petitions, sponsored assemblies, and initiated other public activities to press for the vote. The number of middle-class women's societies rapidly multiplied; some, such as the German League of Women's Voting Rights, established in 1902, were founded solely to advocate votes. To the left of middle-class movements were organizations of feminist socialists, women such as Clara Zetkin and Lily Braun who believed that only a socialist revolution would free women from economic as well as political exploitation. Meanwhile, the French celebrity journalist and novelist Gyp (the pseudonym of Sibylle de Riguetti de Mirabeau) carved out a name for herself on the nationalist and anti-Semitic right, with her acerbic commentary on current events.

In Britain, woman suffrage campaigns exploded in violence. Millicent Fawcett, a distinguished middle-class woman with connections to the political establishment, brought together sixteen different organizations into the National Union of Women's Suffrage Societies (1897), committed to peaceful, constitutional reform. But the movement lacked the political or economic clout to sway a male legislature. They became increasingly exasperated by their inability to win over either the Liberal or Conservative party, each of which feared that female suffrage would benefit the other. For this reason Emmeline Pankhurst founded the Women's Social and Political Union (WSPU) in 1903, which adopted tactics of militancy and civil disobedience. WSPU women chained themselves to the visitors' gallery in the House of Commons, slashed paintings in museums, inscribed "Votes for Women" in acid on the greens of golf courses, disrupted political meetings, burned politicians' houses, and smashed department-store windows. The government countered violence with repression. When arrested women went on hunger strikes in prisons, wardens fed them by force—tying them down, holding their mouths open with wooden and metal clamps, and running tubes down their throats. In 1910, the suffragists' attempt to enter the House of Commons set off a six-hour riot with policemen and bystanders, shocking and outraging a nation unaccustomed to such kinds of violence from women. The intensity of suffragists' moral claims was dramatically embodied by the 1913 martyrdom of Emily Wilding Davison who, wearing a "Votes for Women" sash, threw herself in front of the king's horse on Derby Day and was trampled to death.

FEMINIST PROTEST IN THE AGE OF MASS POLITICS. These two images demonstrate the variety of ways that supporters of the vote for women in Britain sought to use the public realm to their political advantage. Emily Davison, shown in the top image being fatally struck by the king's horse at a racetrack, sought to draw attention to the injustice of women's exclusion from political citizenship by disrupting the Epsom Derby, the richest race in Britain and an annual society event. Her death, widely seen as a martyrdom in the cause of women's rights by her supporters, became the occasion for a public funeral procession through London. The image on the bottom shows a woman reading a feminist paper, *Suffragette*, on a British tram. By the end of the nineteenth century, the penny press and growing literacy rates vastly increased the ability of organized political groups to get their message out.

Redefining Womanhood

The campaign for woman suffrage was perhaps the most visible and inflammatory aspect of a larger cultural shift, in which traditional Victorian gender roles were redefined. In the last third of the nineteenth century, economic, political, and social changes were undermining the view that men and women should occupy distinctly different spheres. Women became increasingly visible in the workforce as growing numbers of them took up a greater variety of jobs. Some working-class women joined the new factories and workshops in an effort to stave off their families' poverty, in spite of some working-class men's insistence that stable families required women at home. In addition, the expansion of government and corporate bureaucracies, coupled with a scarcity of male labor owing to industrial growth, brought middle-class women to the workforce as social workers and clerks. The increase in hospital services and the advent of national compulsory education required more nurses and teachers. Again, a shortage of male workers and a need to fill so many new jobs as cheaply as possible made women a logical choice. Thus women, who had campaigned vigorously for access to education, began to see doors opening to them. Swiss universities and medical schools began to admit women in the 1860s. In the 1870s and 1880s, British women established their own colleges at Cambridge and Oxford. Parts of the professional world began to look dramatically different: in Prussia, for instance, 14,600 full-time women teachers were staffing schools by 1896. These changes in women's employment began to deflate the myth of female domesticity.

Women became more active in politics—an area previously termed off limits. This is not to say that female political activity was unprecedented; in important ways, the groundwork for women's new political participation had been laid earlier in the century. Reform movements of the early nineteenth century depended on women and raised women's standing in public. First with charity work in religious associations and later with hundreds of secular associations, women throughout Europe directed their energies toward poor relief, prison reform, Sunday school, temperance, ending slavery and prostitution, and expanding educational opportunities for women. Reform groups brought women together outside the home, encouraging them to speak their minds as freethinking equals and to pursue political goals—a right denied them as individual females. And while some women in reform groups supported political emancipation, many others were drawn into reform politics by appeals to the belief that they had a special moral mission: they saw their public activities as merely an extension of feminine domestic duties. Nonetheless, nineteenth-century reform movements had opened up the world beyond the home, particularly for the middle classes, and widened the scope of possibilities for later generations.

CHANGES IN WHITE-COLLAR WORK. Clerical work was primarily male until the end of the nineteenth century, when cadres of women workers and the emergence of new industries and bureaucracies transformed employment. ▪ ***How might these changing patterns of employment have affected family life or attitudes toward marriage and child-rearing?***

These changes in women's roles were paralleled by the emergence of a new social type, dubbed the "new woman." A new woman demanded education and a job; she refused to be escorted by chaperones when she went out; she rejected the restrictive corsets of mid-century fashion. In other words, she claimed the right to a physically and intellectually active life and refused to conform to the norms that defined nineteenth-century womanhood. The new woman was an image—in part the creation of artists and journalists, who filled newspapers, magazines, and advertising billboards with pictures of women riding bicycles in bloomers (voluminous trousers with a short skirt); smoking cigarettes; and enjoying the cafés, dance halls, tonic waters, soaps, and other emblems of consumption. Very few women actually fit this image: among other things, most were too poor. Still, middle- and working-class women demanded more social freedom and redefined gender norms in the process. For some onlookers, women's newfound independence amounted to shirking domestic responsibilities, and they attacked women who defied convention as ugly "half-men," unfit and unable to marry. For supporters, though, these new women symbolized a welcome era of social emancipation.

Opposition to these changes was intense, sometimes violent, and not exclusively male. Men scorned the women who threatened their elite preserves in universities, clubs, and public offices; but a wide array of female antisuffragists also denounced the movement. Conservatives such as Mrs. Humphrey Ward maintained that bringing women into the political arena would sap the virility of the British Empire. Octavia Hill, a noted social worker, stated that women should refrain from politics and, in so doing, "temper this wild struggle for place and power." Christian commentators criticized suffragists for bringing moral decay through selfish individualism. Still others believed feminism would dissolve the family, a theme that fed into a larger discussion on the decline of the West amid a growing sense of cultural crisis. Indeed, the struggle for women's rights provided a flashpoint for an array of European anxieties over labor, politics, gender, and biology—all of which suggested that an orderly political consensus, so ardently desired by middle-class society, was slipping from reach.

ORGANIZED ANTIFEMINISM. Male students demonstrate against admitting women to Cambridge University in England, 1881. A female figure is hung in effigy to the right of center, and the suspended banner reads (in part): "There's No Place for You Maids."

LIBERALISM AND ITS DISCONTENTS: NATIONAL POLITICS AT THE TURN OF THE CENTURY

Having championed doctrines of individual rights throughout the nineteenth century, middle-class liberals found themselves on the defensive after 1870. Previously, political power had rested on a balance between middle-class interests and traditional elites. The landed aristocracy shared power with industrial magnates; monarchical rule coexisted with constitutional freedoms. During the late nineteenth century, the rise of mass politics upset this balance. An expanding franchise and rising expectations brought newcomers to the political stage. As we have seen, trade unions, socialists, and feminists all challenged Europe's governing classes by demanding that political participation be open to all. Governments responded in turn, with a mix of conciliatory and repressive measures. As the twentieth century approached, political struggles became increasingly fierce, and by the First World War the foundation of traditional parliamentary politics was crumbling. For both the left and the right, for both insiders and outsiders, negotiating this unfamiliar terrain required the creation of new and distinctly modern forms of mass politics.

France: The Third Republic and the Paris Commune

The Franco-Prussian War of 1870, which completed the unification of the victorious Germany, was a bruising defeat for France. The government of the Second Empire folded. In its wake, the French proclaimed a republic whose legitimacy was contested from the start. Crafting a durable republican system proved difficult. The new constitution of the Third Republic, which was finally instituted in 1875, signaled a triumph of democratic and parliamentary principles. Establishing democracy, however, was a volatile process, and the Third Republic faced class conflicts, scandals and the rise of new forms of right-wing politics that would poison politics for decades to come.

No sooner had the government surrendered than it faced a crisis that pitted the nation's representatives against the radical city of Paris. During the war, the city had appointed its own municipal government, the Commune. Paris not only refused to surrender to the Germans but proclaimed itself the true government of France. The city had been besieged by the Germans for four months; most people who could afford to flee had done so; and the rest, hungry and radicalized, defied the French government sitting in Versailles and negotiating the terms of an armistice with the Germans. The armistice signed, the French government turned its attention to the city. After long and fruitless negotiations, in March 1871 the government sent troops to disarm the capital. Since the Commune's strongest support came from the workers of Paris, the conflict became a class war. For a week, the "communards" battled against the government's troops, building barricades to stop the invaders, taking and shooting hostages, and retreating very slowly into the northern working-class neighborhoods of the city. The French government's repression was brutal. At least 25,000 Parisians were executed, killed in fighting, or consumed in the fires that raged through the city; thousands more were deported to the penal colony of New Caledonia in the South Pacific. The Paris Commune was a brief episode, but it cast a long shadow and reopened old political wounds. For Marx, who wrote about the Commune, and for other socialists, it illustrated the futility of an older insurrectionary tradition on the left and the need for more mass-based democratic politics.

The Dreyfus Affair and Anti-Semitism as Politics

On the other side of the French political spectrum, new forms of radical right-wing politics emerged that would foreshadow developments elsewhere. As the age-old foundations of conservative politics, the Catholic Church and the landed nobility, slipped, more radical right-wing politics took shape. Stung by the defeat of 1870 and critical of the republic and its premises, the new right was nationalist, antiparliamentary, and antiliberal (in the sense of commitment to individual liberties). Maurice Barrès, for instance, elected deputy in 1889, declared that parliamentary government had sown "impotence and corruption" and was too weak to defend the nation. During the first half of the nineteenth century, nationalism had been associated with the left (see Chapter 20). Now it was more often invoked by the right and linked to xenophobia (fear of foreigners) in general and anti-Semitism in particular.

The power of popular anti-Semitism in France was made clear by a public controversy that erupted in the 1890s known as the Dreyfus Affair. In 1894, a group of monarchist officers in the army accused Alfred Dreyfus, a Jewish captain on the general staff, of selling military secrets to Germany. Dreyfus was convicted and deported for life to Devil's Island, a ghastly South American prison colony in French Guiana. Two years later, an intelligence officer named Georges Picquart discovered that the documents used to convict Dreyfus were forgeries. The War Department refused to grant Dreyfus a new trial, and the case became an enormous public scandal, fanned on both sides by the involvement of prominent intellectual figures. Republicans, some socialists, liberals, and intellectuals such as the writer Émile Zola backed Dreyfus, claiming that the case was about individual rights and the legitimacy of the republic and its laws. Nationalists, prominent Catholics, and other socialists who believed that the case was a distraction from economic issues, opposed Dreyfus and refused to question the military's judgment. One Catholic newspaper insisted that the question was not whether Dreyfus was guilty or innocent but whether Jews and unbelievers were not the "secret masters of France."

The anti-Semitism of the anti-Dreyfus camp was a combination of three strands of anti-Jewish thinking in Europe: (1) long-standing currents of anti-Semitism within Christianity, which damned the Jewish people as Christ killers; (2) economic anti-Semitism, which insisted that the wealthy banking family of Rothschild was representative of all Jews; and (3) late-nineteenth-century racial thinking, which opposed a so-called Aryan (Indo-European) race to an inferior Semitic race. Anti-Dreyfus propagandists whipped these ideas into a potent form of propaganda in anti-Semitic newspapers such as Edouard Drumont's *La Libre Parole* ("*Free Speech*"), a French daily that claimed a circulation of 200,000 during the height of the Dreyfus Affair.

In 1899, Dreyfus was pardoned and freed by executive order. In 1906, the French Supreme Court declared him free of all guilt, and he was reinstated in the army as a major. A major consequence of the controversy was passage of laws between 1901 and 1905 that separated church and state in France. Convinced that the church and the army were

Competing Viewpoints

Liberalism and the State

In the second half of the nineteenth century, some British liberals responded to calls from an expanding electorate by moving away from a laissez-faire position that called for minimal state interference in society and the economy. This laissez-faire position still had its adherents among liberals, most notably the libertarian social philosopher Herbert Spencer. In the face of a more organized labor movement and what was perceived to be a very real threat of revolution, however, other liberals began to argue that some forms of government action to alleviate social distress were not only compatible with individual liberty in the economic realm but were in fact also necessary to preserve it. Compare Herbert Spencer's arguments against assistance to the poor from 1851 with L. T. Hobhouse's defense of state pension plans in 1911.

Herbert Spencer, *Social Statics* (1851)

In common with its other assumptions of secondary offices, the assumption by a government of the office of Reliever-general to the poor, is necessarily forbidden by the principle that a government cannot rightly do anything more than protect. In demanding from a citizen contributions for the mitigation of distress—contributions not needed for the due administration of men's rights—the state is, as we have seen, reversing its function, and diminishing that liberty to exercise the faculties which it was instituted to maintain. Possibly, unmindful of the explanations already given, some will assert that by satisfying the wants of the pauper, a government is in reality extending *his* liberty to exercise his faculties, inasmuch as it is giving him something without which the exercise of them is impossible; and that hence, though it decreases the rate-payer's sphere of action, it compensates by increasing that of the rate-receiver. But this statement of the case implies a confounding of two widely-different things. To enforce the fundamental law—to take care that every man has freedom to do all that he wills, provided he infringes not the equal freedom of any other man—this is the special purpose for which the civil power exists. Now insuring to each the right to pursue within the specified limits the objects of his desires without let or hindrance, is quite a separate thing from insuring him satisfaction. Of two individuals, one may use his liberty of action successfully—may achieve the gratifications he seeks after, or accumulate what is equivalent to many of them—property; whilst the other, having like privileges, may fail to do so. But with these results the state has no concern. All that lies within its commission is to see that each man is allowed to use such powers and opportunities as he possesses; and if it takes from him who has prospered to give to him who has not, it violates its duty

hostile to the republic, the Republican legislature passed new laws that prohibited any religious orders in France that were not authorized by the state and forbade clerics to teach in public schools.

The French Republic withstood the attacks of radical anti-Semites in the first decade of the twentieth century, but the same right-wing and nationalist forces made their voices known elsewhere in Europe. The mayor of Vienna in 1897 was elected on an anti-Semitic platform. The Russian secret police forged and published a book called *The Protocols of the Learned Elders of Zion* (1903 and 1905), which imagined a Jewish plot to dominate the world and held Jews responsible for the French Revolution and the dislocating effects of industrialization. Political anti-Semitism remained popular among a substantial number of Europeans who accepted its insistence that social and political problems could be understood in racial terms.

Zionism

Among the many people to watch with alarm as the Dreyfus Affair unfolded was Theodor Herzl (1860–1904), a Hungarian-born journalist working in Paris. The rise of

towards the one to do more than its duty towards the other. Or, repeating the idea elsewhere expressed, it breaks down the vital law of society, that it may effect what social vitality does not call for.

Source: Herbert Spencer, *Social Statics: or, The Conditions essential to Happiness specified, and the First of them Developed* (London: John Chapman, 1851), p. 311–12.

L. T. Hobhouse, *Liberalism* (1911)

For the mass of the people, therefore, to be assured of the means of a decent livelihood must mean to be assured of continuous employment at a living wage, or, as an alternative, of public assistance. Now, as has been remarked, experience goes to show that the wage of the average worker, as fixed by competition, is not and is not likely to become sufficient to cover all the fortunes and misfortunes of life, to provide for sickness, accident, unemployment and old age, in addition to the regular needs of an average family. In the case of accident the State has put the burden of making provision on the employer. In the case of old age it has, acting, as I think, upon a sounder principle, taken the burden upon itself. It is very important to realize precisely what the new departure involved in the Old Age Pensions Act amounted to in point of principle. The Poor Law already guaranteed the aged person and the poor in general against actual starvation. But the Poor Law came into operation only at the point of sheer destitution. It failed to help those who had helped themselves. Indeed, to many it held out little inducement to help themselves if they could not hope to lay by so much as would enable them to live more comfortably on their means than they would live in the workhouse. The pension system throws over the test of destitution. It provides a certain minimum, a basis to go upon, a foundation upon which independent thrift may hope to build up a sufficiency. It is not a narcotic but a stimulus to self help and to friendly aid or filial support, and it is, up to a limit, available for all alike. It is precisely one of the conditions of independence of which voluntary effort can make use, but requiring voluntary effort to make it fully available.

Source: L. T. Hobhouse, *Liberalism* (New York: Henry Holt & Co., 1911), pp. 177–78.

Questions for Analysis

1. According to Spencer, what is the primary function of government? Why does he deem assistance to the poor to be a violation of that duty?
2. According to Hobhouse, what circumstances make assistance to the poor, such as of state-sponsored pension plans, necessary?
3. What assumptions lie behind their disagreement about the state's responsibility to remedy social inequalities? What values do they share?

virulent anti-Semitism in the land of the French Revolution troubled Herzl deeply. He considered the Dreyfus Affair "only the dramatic expression of a much more fundamental malaise." Despite Jewish emancipation, or the granting of civil rights, Herzl came to believe Jewish people might never be assimilated into Western culture and that staking the Jewish community's hopes on acceptance and tolerance was dangerous folly. Herzl endorsed the different strategy of Zionism, the building of a separate Jewish homeland outside of Europe (though not necessarily in Palestine). A small movement of Jewish settlers, mainly refugees from Russia, had already begun to establish settlements outside of Europe. Herzl was not the first to voice these goals, but he was the most effective advocate of political Zionism. He argued that Zionism should be recognized as a modern nationalist movement, capable of negotiating with other states. In 1896, Herzl published *The State of the Jews*; a year later he convened the first Zionist Congress in Switzerland. Throughout, he was involved in high politics, meeting with British and Ottoman heads of state. Herzl's vision of a Jewish homeland had strong utopian elements, for he believed that building a new state had to be based on a new and transformed society, eliminating inequality and

JEWISH MIGRATION IN THE LATE NINETEENTH CENTURY. ▪ ***Where did Jews primarily flee from in the late nineteenth century?*** ▪ ***What drove Jewish people to flee from eastern Europe in the late nineteenth century?*** ▪ ***To what areas did Jewish people migrate and why?***

establishing rights. Although Herzl's writings met with much skepticism, they received an enthusiastic reception among Jews who lived in areas of eastern Europe where anti-Semitism was especially violent. During the turmoil of the First World War, specific wartime needs prompted the British to become involved in the issue, embroiling Zionism in international diplomacy (see Chapter 24).

Germany's Search for Imperial Unity

Through deft foreign policy, three short wars, and a groundswell of national sentiment, Otto von Bismarck united Germany under the banner of Prussian conservatism during the years 1864 to 1871. In constructing a federal political system, Bismarck sought to create the centralizing institutions of a modern nation-state while safeguarding

Interpreting Visual Evidence

Anti-Semitism and the Popular Press in France

The Dreyfus Affair lasted twelve years, from 1894, when Captain Alfred Dreyfus was first arrested and convicted of treason by a military court, to 1906, when he was finally absolved of all guilt and reinstated in the army. During the affair, most people in France followed the events of the case through the popular press, which had undergone rapid expansion as public schooling became more general and literacy spread through the population. The newspapers milked every episode of the case for all of its sensational drama, and editors openly took sides in order to increase their circulation and profits. The illustrated press was particularly popular, and the images associated with expressions of anti-Semitism became ubiquitous in both the respectable and the more popular press. Image A shows Jakob Rothschild, a French Jewish banker, stretching his demonic hands around the globe. Edouard Drumont, the anti-Semitic editor of *La Libre Parole* used the scandal to launch his own political career. His celebrity status is evident in a caricature of himself that appeared in a competing paper, *Le Rire* (image B). Even illustrations that did not aim at caricature could carry a powerful message about the intensity of popular anti-Semitism in France during the affair, as in image C, which depicts young people burning Alfred Dreyfus's brother Mathieu in effigy during a demonstration. Mathieu Dreyfus played a key role in the effort to establish his brother's innocence.

Questions for Analysis

1. What fears about the economy are exploited in image A? (Compare this with the image on page 770 of socialists circling the globe, hand in hand.)
2. Is *Le Rire*'s portrait of Edouard Drumont (image B) an anti-Semitic image, or is it critical of Drumont's anti-Semitism?
3. Taken together, what do these images tell us about the connections among anti-Semitism, the popular press, and the definitions of national identity that were current in France during the affair?

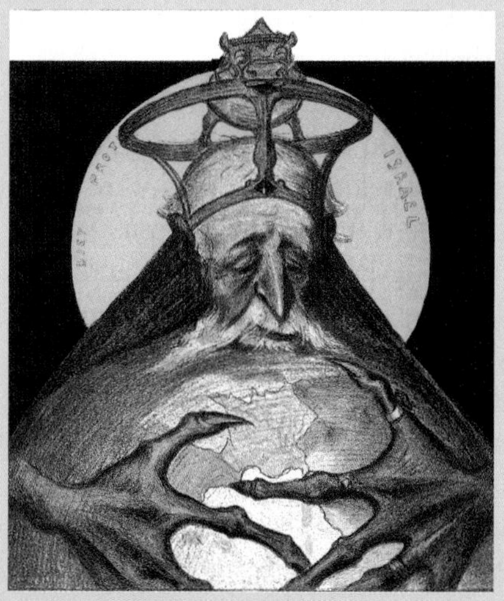

A. Anti-Semitic French cartoon with caricature of Jakob Rothschild, 1898.

B. "The Ogre's Meal," caricature of Edouard Drumont, editor of *La Libre Parole*, from *Le Rire*, 1896.

C. "Anti-Semitic Agitation in Paris: Mathieu Dreyfus burned in effigy in Montmartre (Paris)."

OTTO VON BISMARCK LEAVES OFFICE, 1890. This political cartoon shows Bismarck resigning as Kaiser Wilhelm II childishly plays with "Socialism," a doll made of dynamite. Germany anxiously watches the scene from the background.

the privileges of Germany's traditional elites, including a dominant role for Prussia. Bismarck's constitution assigned administrative, educational, and juridical roles to local state governments and established a bicameral parliament to oversee Germany's national interests. The appointed delegates of the upper house (the Bundesrat) served as a conservative counterbalance to the more democratic lower house (the Reichstag), which was elected through universal male suffrage. In the executive branch, power rested solely with Wilhelm I, the Prussian king and German kaiser (emperor), who wielded full control of foreign and military affairs. Unlike in France or Britain, Germany's cabinet ministers had no responsibility to the Parliament but answered only to the kaiser.

Under a government that was neither genuinely federal nor democratic, building a nation with a sense of common purpose was no easy task. Three fault lines in Germany's political landscape especially threatened to crack the national framework: the divide between Catholics and Protestants; the growing Social Democratic party; and the potentially divisive economic interests of agriculture and industry.

Between 1871 and 1878, Bismarck governed principally with liberal factions interested in promoting free trade and economic growth. To strengthen ties with these liberal coalitions, Bismarck unleashed an anti-Catholic campaign in Prussia. In what is known as the *Kulturkampf*, or "cultural struggle," Bismarck passed laws that imprisoned priests for political sermons, banned Jesuits from Prussia, and curbed the church's control over education and marriage. The campaign backfired, however, and public sympathy for the persecuted clergy helped the Catholic Center party win fully one-quarter of the seats in the Reichstag in 1874.

Bismarck responded by fashioning a new coalition that included agricultural and industrial interests as well as socially conservative Catholics. This new alliance passed protectionist legislation (grain tariffs, duties on iron and steel) that riled both laissez-faire liberals and the German working class, which was represented by the SPD. Just as Bismarck had used anti-Catholic sentiments to solidify his previous alliance, he now turned against a new enemy of the empire—Social Democrats—and couched his protectionist and antisocial legislation in terms of defending a "Christian moral order." In 1878, after two separate attempts on the life of the emperor, Bismarck declared a national crisis to push through a series of antisocialist laws that forbade Social Democrats to assemble or distribute their literature. Additional legislation further expelled socialists from major cities. In effect, these laws obliged the Social Democratic party to become a clandestine organization, fostering a subculture of workers who increasingly viewed socialism as the sole answer to their political needs.

Having made the stick to beat down organized-labor politics, Bismarck now offered a carrot to German workers with an array of social reforms. Workers were guaranteed sickness and accident insurance, rigorous factory inspection, limited working hours for women and children, a maximum workday for men, public employment agencies, and old-age pensions. By 1890, Germany had put together a raft of social legislation, with the exception of unemployment insurance, that became a prototype for the majority of Western nations in the decades to come. The laws nevertheless failed to achieve Bismarck's short-term political goal of winning workers' loyalty: votes for the SPD more than quadrupled between 1881 and 1890, the year that Bismarck resigned.

The embittered atmosphere created by Bismarck's domestic policies prompted the new kaiser, Wilhelm II, to legalize the SPD. By 1912, the Social Democrats were the largest single bloc in the Reichstag, yet the kaiser refused to allow any meaningful political participation beyond a tight-knit circle of elites. Any conclusion to this volatile standoff was preempted by the outbreak of the First World War.

Britain: From Moderation to Militance

During the half century before 1914, the British prided themselves on what they believed to be an orderly and workable system of government. After the passage of the Second Reform Bill in 1867, which extended suffrage to more than a third of the nation's adult males, the two major political parties, Liberal and Conservative, vied with each other to win the support of this growing voting bloc. Parliament responded to new voters' concerns with laws that recognized the legality of trade unions, commissioned the rebuilding of large urban areas, provided elementary education for all children, and permitted male religious dissenters to attend the elite universities of Oxford and Cambridge. In 1884, suffrage expanded to include more than three-fourths of adult males.

Two central figures, the Conservative Benjamin Disraeli and the Liberal William Gladstone, dominated the new parliamentary politics. Disraeli, a converted Jew and bestselling novelist, was eminently pragmatic, whereas Gladstone, a devout Anglican, was committed to political and social reform out of a sense of moral obligation. Despite their opposing sensibilities and bitter parliamentary clashes, the two men led parties that, in retrospect, seem to share largely similar outlooks. Leaders of both parties were drawn from the upper middle class and the landed gentry, and both Liberals and Conservatives offered moderate programs that appealed to the widening electorate. Steered by men whose similar education and outlooks promised middling solutions, the British political system was stable and "reasonable."

Even Britain's working-class movements were notably moderate until the turn of the century, when at last new trade unions and middle-class socialist societies combined to create the independent Labour party in 1901. Pressed from the left, the Liberal ministry that took office in 1906 passed sickness, accident, old-age, and unemployment insurance acts, along with other concessions to trade unions. To pay for the new welfare programs—and for a larger navy to counter the German buildup—the chancellor of the exchequer (finance minister), David Lloyd George, proposed an explosively controversial budget in 1909, which included progressive income and inheritance taxes, designed to make the wealthy pay at higher rates. The bill provoked a rancorous showdown with the House of Lords, which was forced not only to pass the budget but also to surrender permanently its power to veto legislation passed by the Commons. The acrimony of this debate pointed to an increasingly militant tenor in British politics, which to many seemed headed for chaos.

Indeed, after 1900, Britain's liberal parliamentary framework, which had so successfully channeled the rising demands of mass society since the 1860s, began to buckle, as an array of groups rejected legislative activity in favor of radical action. Industrial militants launched enormous labor protests, including nationwide strikes of coal and rail workers and citywide transportation strikes in London and Dublin. Woman suffragists adopted violent forms of direct action (discussed earlier). Meanwhile, in Ireland, disagreements over Irish home rule, or self-government, threatened to produce armed confrontations between increasingly radical Irish nationalists and Protestants opposed to home rule.

Ireland had been put under the direct government of the British Parliament in 1800, and various political and military efforts to regain Irish sovereignty over the course of the nineteenth century had failed. By the 1880s, a modern nationalist party (the Irish Parliamentary party) had begun to make substantial political gains through the legislative process, but as with other reform-minded groups (such as woman suffrage), its agenda was increasingly eclipsed toward the turn of the century by more radical organizers. These proponents of "new nationalism" disdained the party's representatives as ineffectual and out of touch. New groups revived interest in Irish history and culture and provided organizational support to the radical movement, as did such militant political organizations as Sinn Féin and the Irish Republican Brotherhood. Firmly opposed to the nationalists was the Protestant Ulster Volunteer force, led by military officers who were determined to resist the imposition of home rule by force, if necessary. In 1913, as a Liberal plan to grant home rule was once again on the table, Britain now seemed on the verge of a civil war—a prospect delayed only by the outbreak of the First World War in Europe.

Russia: The Road to Revolution

The industrial and social changes that swept Europe proved especially unsettling in Russia. An autocratic political system was ill equipped to handle conflict and the pressures of modern society. Western industrialization challenged Russia's military might. Western political doctrines—liberalism, democracy, socialism—threatened its internal political stability. Like other nations, tsarist Russia negotiated these challenges with a combination of repression and reform.

In the 1880s and 1890s, Russia launched a program of industrialization that made it the world's fifth largest economy by the early twentieth century. The state largely directed this industrial development, for despite the creation of a mobile workforce after the emancipation of the serfs in 1861, no independent middle class capable of raising capital and stewarding industrial enterprises emerged. In fact, the Russian state financed more domestic industrial development than any other major European government during the nineteenth century.

Rapid industrialization heightened social tensions. The transition from country to city life was sudden and harsh. Men and women left agriculture for factory work, straining the fabric of village life and rural culture. In the industrial areas, workers lived in large barracks and were marched, military-style, to and from the factories, where working conditions were among the worst in Europe. They coped by leaving their villages only temporarily and returning to their farms for planting or the harvest. Social change strained Russia's legal system, which did not recognize trade unions or employers' associations. Laws still distinguished among nobles, peasants, clergy, and town dwellers, categories that did not correspond to an industrializing society. Outdated banking and financial laws failed to serve the needs of a modern economy.

Real legal reform, however, would threaten the regime's stability. When Alexander II (r. 1855–81), the liberator of the serfs, was killed by a radical assassin in 1881, his successor, Alexander III (r. 1881–94), steered the country sharply to the right. Russia had nothing in common with western Europe, Alexander III claimed; his people had been nurtured on mystical piety for centuries and would be utterly lost without a strong autocratic system. This principle guided stern repression. The regime curtailed all powers of local assemblies, increased the authority of the secret police, and subjected villages to the governmental authority of nobles appointed by the state. The press and schools remained under strict censorship.

Nicholas II (r. 1894–1917) continued these repressive policies. Like his father, he ardently advocated Russification, or government programs to extend the language, religion, and culture of greater Russia over the empire's non-Russian subjects. Russification amounted to coercion, expropriation, and physical oppression: Finns lost their constitution, Poles studied their own literature in Russian translation, and Jews perished in pogroms. (*Pogrom* is a Russian term for violent attacks on civilians, which in the late nineteenth century were usually aimed at Jewish communities.) The Russian government did not organize pogroms, but it was openly anti-Semitic and made a point of looking the other way when villagers massacred Jews and destroyed their homes, businesses, and synagogues. Other groups whose repression by the state led to long-lasting undercurrents of anti-Russian nationalism included the Georgians, Armenians, and Azerbaijanis of the Caucasus Mountains.

The most important radical political group in late-nineteenth-century Russia was a large, loosely knit group of men and women who called themselves populists. Populists believed that Russia needed to modernize on its own terms, not the West's. They envisioned an egalitarian Russia based on the ancient institution of the village commune (*mir*). Advocates of populism sprang primarily from the middle class; many of its adherents were young students, and women made up about 15 percent—a significantly large proportion for the period. They formed secret bands, plotting the overthrow of tsarism through anarchy and insurrection. They dedicated their lives to "the people," attempting wherever possible to live among common laborers so as to understand and express the popular will. Populism's emphasis on peasant socialism influenced the Social Revolutionary party, formed in 1901, which also concentrated on increasing the political power of the peasant and building a socialist society based on the agrarian communalism of the mir.

The emergence of industrial capitalism and a new, desperately poor working class created Russian Marxism. Organized as the Social Democratic party, Russian Marxists concentrated their efforts on behalf of urban workers and saw themselves as part of the international working-class movement. They made little headway in a peasant-dominated Russia before the First World War, but they provided disaffected urban factory workers and intellectuals alike with a powerful ideology that stressed the necessity of overthrowing the tsarist regime and the inevitability of a better future. Autocracy would give way to capitalism and capitalism to an egalitarian, classless society. Russian Marxism blended radical, activist opposition with a rational, scientific approach to history, furnishing revolutionaries with a set of concepts with which to understand the upheavals of the young twentieth century.

In 1903, the leadership of the Social Democratic party split over an important disagreement on revolutionary strategy. One group, temporarily in the majority and quick

Past and Present

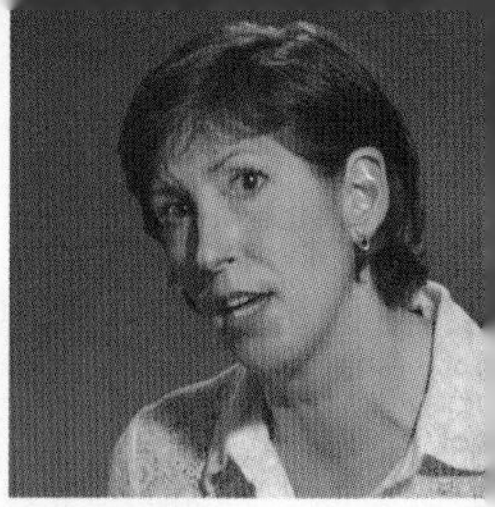

The Age of Mass Politics

Granting the vote to all adult men ushered in an age of mass politics. Political groups competed with one another to gain the support of this new constituency, and to prevent opponents from gaining power (left, in this 1878 cartoon, Otto von Bismarck tries to put socialism back in the box). Then, as now, political groups sought simple messages that would give them an edge, leading to more sharply defined ideological competition, as well as populist demagoguery and scapegoating of minorities (right, Marine Le Pen at rally for the extreme-right party in France, the National Front).

Watch related author interview on StudySpace
wwnorton.com/web/westernciv18

to name itself the Bolsheviks (majority group), believed that the Russian situation called for a strongly centralized party of active revolutionaries. The Bolsheviks also insisted that the rapid industrialization of Russia meant that they did not have to follow Marx's model for the West. Instead of working for liberal capitalist reforms, Russian revolutionaries could skip a stage and immediately begin to build a socialist state. The Mensheviks (which means minority) were more cautious or "gradualist," seeking slow changes and reluctant to depart from Marxist orthodoxy. When the Mensheviks regained control of the Social Democratic party, the Bolsheviks formed a splinter party under the leadership of the young, dedicated revolutionary Vladimir Ilyich Ulyanov, who lived in political exile in western Europe between 1900 and 1917. He wrote under the pseudonym of Lenin, from the Lena River in Siberia, where he had been exiled earlier.

Lenin's theoretical abilities and organizational energy commanded respect, enabling him to remain the leader of the Bolsheviks even while living abroad. From exile, Lenin preached unrelenting class struggle; the need for a coordinated revolutionary socialist movement throughout Europe; and, most important, the belief that Russia was passing into an economic stage that made it ripe for revolution. It was the Bolsheviks' responsibility to organize a revolutionary party on behalf of workers, for without the party's discipline, workers could not effect change. Lenin's treatise *What Is to Be Done?* (1902) set out his vision of Russia's special destiny, and it denounced gradualists who had urged collaboration with moderate parties. Lenin considered revolution the only answer to Russia's problems, and he argued that organizing for revolution needed to be done, soon, by vanguard agents of the party acting in the name of the working class.

AUTOCRACY AND REPRESENTATIVE GOVERNMENT. In response to the revolution of 1905 in Russia, Tsar Nicholas II allowed for the creation of a new legislative body for Russia in 1905, a form of parliament called the Duma. Although he later succeeded in limiting the powers of this body, its very existence indicated that even the autocratic and conservative Russian state was forced to pay lip service to the principle of representative government. In the image above, note the extent to which the opening ceremony evoked the traditional hierarchies of Russian society, exemplified in the presence of the tsar, the military, the aristocracy, and the clergy.

THE FIRST RUSSIAN REVOLUTION

The revolution that came in 1905, however, took all of these radical movements by surprise. Its unexpected occurrence resulted from Russia's resounding defeat in the Russo-Japanese War of 1904–5. But the revolution had deeper roots. Rapid industrialization had transformed Russia unevenly; certain regions were heavily industrial, whereas others were less integrated into the market economy. The economic boom of the 1880s and 1890s turned to bust in the early 1900s, as demand for goods tapered off, prices plummeted, and the nascent working class suffered high levels of unemployment. At the same time, low grain prices resulted in a series of peasant uprisings, which, combined with students' energetic radical organizing, became overtly political.

As dispatches reported the defeats of the tsar's army and navy, the Russian people grasped the full extent of the regime's inefficiency. Hitherto apolitical middle-class subjects clamored for change, and radical workers organized strikes and held demonstrations in every important city. Trust in the benevolence of the tsar was severely shaken on January 22, 1905—"Bloody Sunday"—when a group of 200,000 workers and their families, led by a priest, Father Gapon, went to demonstrate their grievances at the tsar's winter palace in St. Petersburg. When guard troops killed 130 demonstrators and wounded several hundred, the government seemed not only ineffective but arbitrary and brutal.

Over the course of 1905, general protest grew. Merchants closed their stores, factory owners shut down their plants, lawyers refused to plead cases in court. The autocracy lost control of entire rural towns and regions as local authorities were ejected and often killed by enraged peasants. Forced to yield, Tsar Nicholas II issued the October Manifesto, pledging guarantees of individual liberties, a moderately liberal franchise for the election of a Duma, and genuine legislative veto powers for the Duma. Although the 1905 revolution brought the tsarist system perilously close to collapse, it failed to convince the tsar that fundamental political change was necessary. Between 1905 and 1907, Nicholas revoked most of the promises made in the October Manifesto. Above all, he deprived the Duma of its principal powers and decreed that it be elected indirectly on a class basis, which ensured a legislative body of obedient followers.

Nonetheless, the revolt of 1905 persuaded the tsar's more perceptive advisers that reform was urgent. The agrarian programs sponsored by the government's leading minister, Peter Stolypin, were especially significant. Between 1906 and 1911 the Stolypin reforms provided for the sale of 5 million acres of royal land to peasants, granted permission to peasants to withdraw from the mir and form independent farms, and canceled peasant property debts. Further decrees legalized labor unions, reduced the working day (to ten hours in most cases), and established sickness and accident insurance. Liberals could reasonably hope that Russia was on the way to becoming a progressive nation on the Western model, yet the tsar remained stubbornly autocratic. Russian agriculture remained suspended between an emerging capitalist system and the traditional peasant commune; Russian industry, though powerful enough to allow Russia to maintain its status as a world power, had hardly created a modern, industrial society capable of withstanding the enormous strains that Russia would face during the First World War.

Analyzing Primary Sources

Lenin's View of a Revolutionary Party

At the turn of the century, Russian revolutionaries debated political strategy. How could Russian autocracy be defeated? Should revolutionaries follow the programs of their counterparts in the West? Or did the Russian situation require different tactics? In What Is to Be Done? *(1902) Lenin (Vladimir Ilyich Ulyanov, 1870–1924) argued that Russian socialists needed to revise the traditional Marxist view, according to which a large and politically conscious working class would make revolution. In Russia, Lenin argued, revolution required a small but dedicated group of revolutionaries to lead the working class. Lenin's vision was important, for it shaped the tactics and strategies of the Bolsheviks in 1917 and beyond.*

The national tasks of Russian Social-Democracy are such as have never confronted any other socialist party in the world. We shall have occasion further on to deal with the political and organisational duties which the task of emancipating the whole people from the yoke of autocracy imposes upon us. At this point, we wish to state only that the *role of vanguard fighter can be fulfilled only by a party that is guided by the most advanced theory*. . . .

I assert: (1) that no revolutionary movement can endure without a stable organisation of leaders maintaining continuity; (2) that the broader the popular mass drawn spontaneously into the struggle, which forms the basis of the movement and participates in it, the more urgent the need for such an organisation, and the more solid this organisation must be (for it is much easier for all sorts of demagogues to side-track the more backward sections of the masses); (3) that such an organisation must consist chiefly of people professionally engaged in revolutionary activity; (4) that in an autocratic state, the more we *confine* the membership of such an organisation to people who are professionally engaged in revolutionary activity and who have been professionally trained in the art of combating the political police, the more difficult will it be to unearth the organisation; and (5) the *greater* will be the number of people from the working class and from the other social classes who will be able to join the movement and perform active work in it. . . .

Social-Democracy leads the struggle of the working class, not only for better terms for the sale of labour-power, but for the abolition of the social system that compels the propertyless to sell themselves to the rich. Social-Democracy represents the working class, not in its relation to a given group of employers alone, but in its relation to all classes of modern society and to the state as an organised political force. Hence, it follows that not only must Social-Democrats not confine themselves exclusively to the economic struggle. . . . We must take up actively the political education of the working class and the development of its political consciousness.

Source: Vladimir Lenin, *What Is to Be Done?* in *Collected Works of V. I. Lenin*, vol. 5 (Moscow: 1964), pp. 369–70, 373, 375.

Questions for Analysis

1. What were the key features of Lenin's thought?
2. Here Lenin more or less set down the rules for the revolutionary vanguard. What historical experiences and political theories shaped his thinking? In what ways was the Russian experience unique?

Nationalism and Imperial Politics: The Balkans

In southeastern Europe in the last decades of the nineteenth century, nationalism continued to divide the disintegrating Ottoman Empire. When the sultan's government repressed uprisings in Bosnia, Herzegovina, and Bulgaria in 1875–76, the Russians saw an opportunity to intercede following reports of atrocities committed against Christians in the region. In the ensuing Russo-Turkish War (1877–78), the tsar's armies won a smashing victory. The Treaty of San Stefano forced the sultan to surrender nearly all of his European territory, except for a remnant around Constantinople.

BLOODY SUNDAY. Demonstrating workers who sought to bring their grievances to the attention of the tsar were met and gunned down by government troops, January 1905.

Britain and Austria took action to ensure that Russia would not be the only beneficiary of the Ottoman withdrawal, and in 1878 a congress of great powers in Berlin divided the spoils: Bessarabia went to Russia, Thessaly to Greece, and Bosnia and Herzegovina fell under the control of the Austrian Empire. Montenegro, Serbia, and Romania became independent states, launching the modern era of Balkan nationalism. This trend continued in 1908, when the Bulgars succeeded in wresting independence for Bulgaria from the Ottomans—a move that drove the Austrians to annex Bosnia and Herzegovina outright. The power vacuum in the Orient significantly strained Europe's imperial balance of power.

A nationalist movement also emerged in the Ottoman Empire itself. Educated Turks had grown impatient with the sultan's weakness, and some began to call for national rejuvenation through the introduction of Western science and democratic reforms. These reformers called themselves "Young Turks," and in 1908 they successfully forced the sultan to establish a constitutional government. In the following year, they deposed Sultan Abdul Hamid II (1876–1909) and placed his brother, Mohammed V (1909–1918), on the throne. The powers of government were entrusted to a grand vizier and ministers responsible to an elected parliament. Non-Turkish inhabitants of the empire were not given the vote, however; and the Young Turks launched a vigorous effort to "Ottomanize" all their imperial subjects, trying to bring both Christian and Muslim communities under centralized Turkish control. That effort, intended to compensate for the loss of territories in Europe, undercut the popularity of the new reformist regime.

THE SCIENCE AND SOUL OF THE MODERN AGE

Nineteenth-century liberals believed in individualism, progress, and science. Not only did science deliver technological and material rewards but it also confirmed liberals' faith in the power of human reason to uncover and command the laws of nature. Toward the end of the century, however, scientific developments defied these expectations. Darwin's theory of evolution, psychology, and social science all introduced visions of humanity that were sharply at odds with conventional wisdom. At the same time, artists and intellectuals mounted their own revolt against nineteenth-century conventions. Morals, manners, institutions, traditions—all established values and assumptions were under question, as a generation of self-consciously avant-garde artists called for a radical break with the past. These upheavals in the world of ideas unsettled older conceptions of individuality, culture, and consciousness. The modern individual no longer seemed the free and rational agent of Enlightenment thought but rather the product of irrational inner drives and uncontrollable external circumstances. As Georg Simmel, one of the founders of modern sociology, wrote in 1902: "The deepest problems of modern life derive from the claim of the individual to preserve the autonomy and individuality of his existence in the face of overwhelming social forces, of historical heritage, of external culture, and of the technique of life."

Darwin's Revolutionary Theory

If Marx changed conceptions of society, Charles Darwin did him one better, perhaps, for his theory of organic evolution by natural selection transformed conceptions of nature itself. As both a scientific explanation and an imaginative metaphor for political and social change, Darwin's theory of evolution introduced an unsettling new picture of human biology, behavior, and society. As with Marxism, its core concepts were embraced by some and abhorred by others,

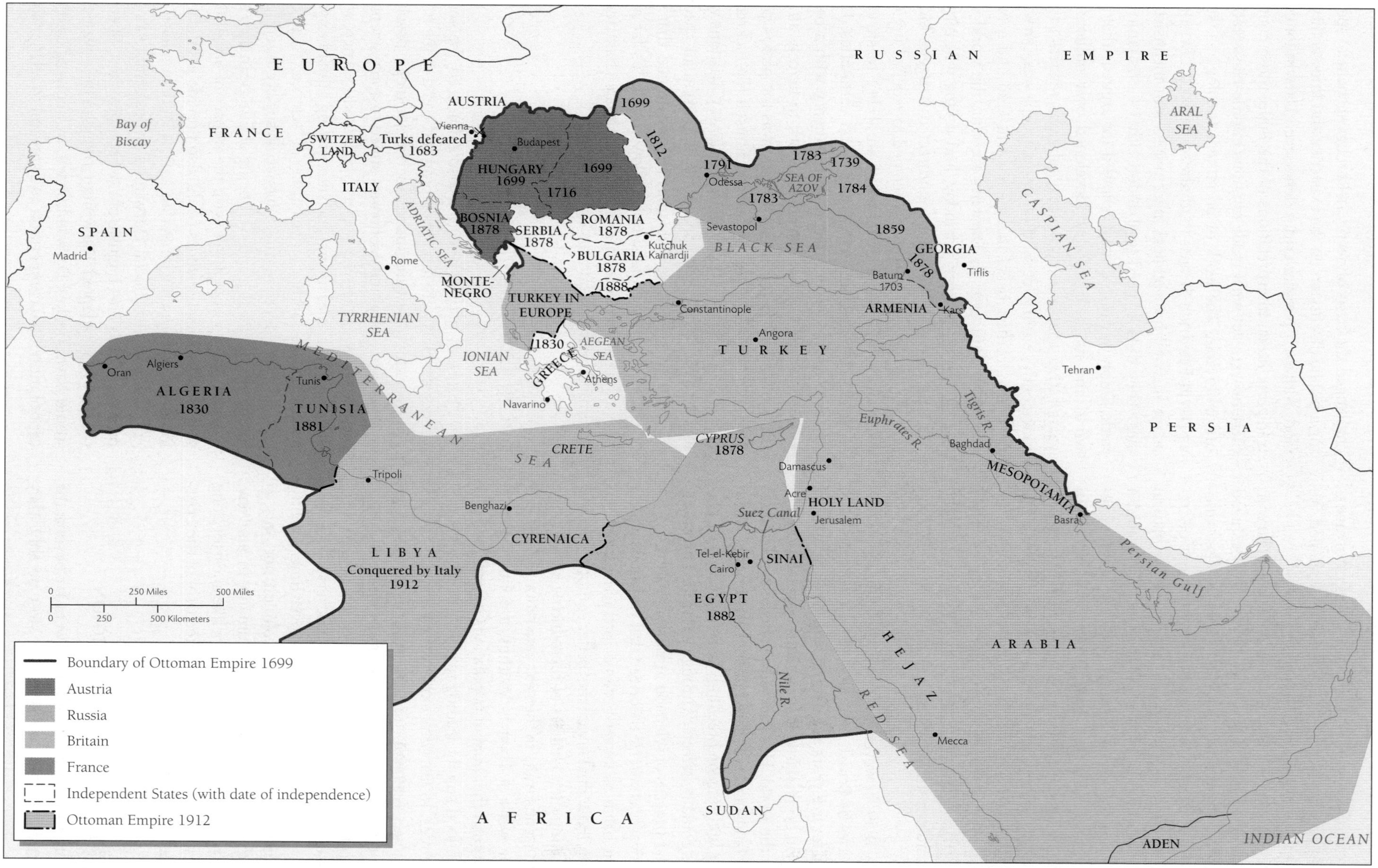

THE DECLINE OF THE OTTOMAN EMPIRE, 1699–1912. ▪ *What were the farthest points that the Ottoman Empire reached into Europe and Africa?* ▪ *How do you explain the slow decline of Ottoman power in relationship to Europe and the emerging global economy?* ▪ *The decline of Ottoman power had enormous significance for relations among European nations themselves. Why?*

and were interpreted and deployed in a variety of unexpected, often conflicting, ways that profoundly shaped the late nineteenth and early twentieth centuries.

Theories of evolution did not originate with Darwin, but none of the earlier theories had gained widespread scientific or popular currency. Geologists in the nineteenth century had challenged the biblical account of creation with evidence that the world was formed by natural processes over millions of years, but no one had found a satisfactory explanation for the existence of different species. One important attempt at an answer was proposed in the early nineteenth century by the French biologist Jean Lamarck, who argued that behavioral changes could alter an animal's physical characteristics within a single generation and that these new traits would be passed on to offspring. Over time, Lamarck suggested, the inheritance of acquired characteristics produced new species of animals.

A more convincing hypothesis of organic evolution appeared in 1859, however, with the publication of *On the Origin of Species* by British naturalist Charles Darwin. Darwin traveled for five years as a naturalist on the HMS *Beagle,* a ship that had been chartered for scientific exploration on a trip around the world. He observed the diversity of species in different lands and wondered about their origins. From a familiarity with pigeon breeding, Darwin knew that particular traits could be selected through controlled breeding. Was a similar process of selection at work in nature?

His answer was yes. He theorized that variations within a population (such as longer beaks or protective coloring) made certain individual organisms better equipped for survival, increasing their chances of reproducing and passing their advantageous traits to the next generation. His theory drew on the work of Thomas Malthus, a political economist who argued that human populations grow faster than the available food supply, leading to a fatal competition for scarce resources. In Darwin's explanation, this Malthusian competition was a general rule of nature, where the strong survived and the weak perished. Competition with other individuals and struggle with the environment produced a "natural selection" of some traits over others, leading to a gradual evolution of different species over time. Eventually, Darwin applied this theory of evolution not only to plant and animal species but also to humans. In his view, the human race had evolved from an apelike ancestor, long since extinct but probably a common precursor of the existing anthropoid apes and humans.

DARWINIAN THEORY AND RELIGION

The implications of Darwin's writings went far beyond the domain of the evolutionary sciences. Most notably, they challenged the basis of deeply held religious beliefs, sparking a public discussion on the existence and knowability of God. Although popular critics denounced Darwin for contradicting literal interpretations of the Bible, those contradictions were not what made religious middle-class readers uncomfortable. The work of prominent theologians, such as David Friedrich Strauss, had already helped Christians adapt their faith to biblical inaccuracies and inconsistencies. They did not need to abandon either Christianity or faith simply because Darwin showed (or argued) that the world and its life forms had developed over millions of years rather than six days. What religious readers in the nineteenth century found difficult to accept was Darwin's challenge to their belief in a benevolent God and a morally guided universe. By Darwin's account, the world was governed not by order, harmony, and divine will but by random chance and constant, undirected struggle. Moreover, the Darwinian worldview seemed to redefine notions of good and bad only in terms of an ability to survive, thus robbing humanity of critical moral certainties. Darwin himself was able to reconcile his theory with a belief in God, but others latched on his work to fiercely attack Christian orthodoxy. One such figure was the philosopher Thomas Henry Huxley, who earned himself the nickname of "Darwin's bulldog" by inveighing against Christians who were appalled by the implications of Darwinian theory. Opposed to all forms of dogma, Huxley argued that the thinking person should simply follow reason "as far as it can take you" and recognize that the ultimate character of the universe lay beyond his or her grasp.

Social Darwinism

The theory of natural selection also influenced the social sciences, which were just developing at the end of the nineteenth century. New disciplines such as sociology, psychology, anthropology, and economics aimed to apply scientific methods to the analysis of society and introduced new ways of quantifying, measuring, and interpreting human experience. Under the authoritative banner of "science," these disciplines exerted a powerful influence on society, oftentimes to improve the health and well-being of European men and women. But, as we will see with the impact of Social Darwinism, the social sciences could also provide justification for forms of economic, imperial, and racial dominance.

The so-called Social Darwinists, whose most famous proponent was the English philosopher Herbert Spencer (1820–1903), adapted Darwinian thought in a way that would have shocked Darwin himself, by applying his concept of individual competition and survival to relationships among classes, races, and nations. Spencer, who coined the phrase *survival of the fittest,* used evolutionary theory to expound the virtues of free competition and attack state welfare programs. As a champion of individualism, Spencer condemned all forms of collectivism as primitive and counterproductive, relics of an earlier stage of social evolution. Government attempts to relieve economic and social hardships—or to place constraints on big business—were, in Spencer's view, hindrances to the vigorous advancement of civilization, which could occur only through individual adaptation and competition. Particularly in America, such claims earned Spencer high praise from some wealthy industrialists, who were no doubt glad to be counted among the fittest.

Unlike the science of biological evolution, a popularized Social Darwinism was easy to comprehend, and its concepts (centering on a struggle for survival) were soon integrated into the political vocabulary of the day. Proponents of laissez-faire capitalism and opponents of socialism used Darwinist rhetoric to justify marketplace competition and the "natural order" of rich and poor. Nationalists embraced Social Darwinism to rationalize imperialist expansion and warfare. Spencer's doctrine also became closely tied to theories of racial hierarchy and white superiority, which claimed that the white race had reached the height of evolutionary development and had thus earned the right to dominate and rule other races (see Chapter 25). Ironically, some progressive middle-class reformers relied on a similar set of racial assumptions: their campaigns to improve the health and welfare of society played to fears that Europe, though dominant, could move down the evolutionary ladder. Despite its unsettling potential, Darwinism was used to advance a range of political objectives and to shore up an array of ingrained prejudices.

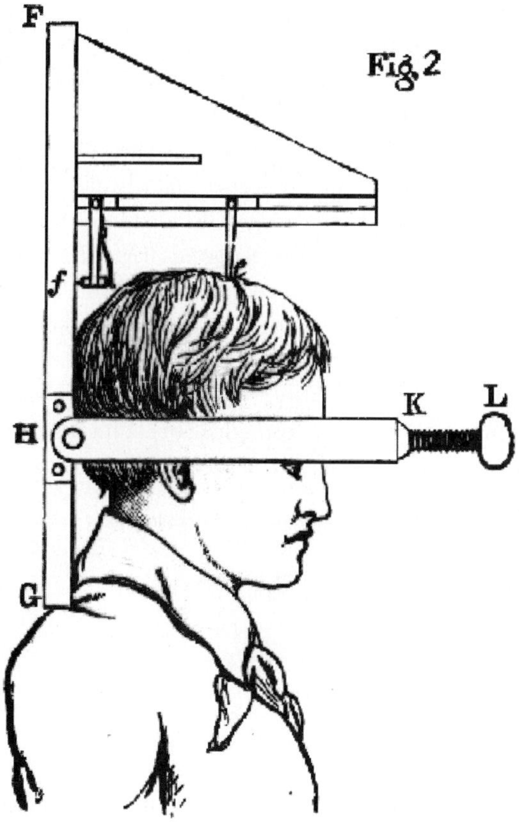

CEPHALOGRAPH. This illustration from Herbert Spencer's autobiography shows a device designed to measure skulls. He believed that the size of one's skull determined brain capacity and applied the idea of "survival of the fittest" to justify theories of white racial superiority.

Challenges to Rationality: Pavlov, Freud, and Nietzsche

Although the new social scientists self-consciously relied on the use of rational, scientific principles, their findings often stressed the opposite: the irrational, even animalistic nature of human experience. Darwin had already called into question the notion that humanity was fundamentally superior to the rest of the animal kingdom, and similarly discomfiting conclusions came from the new field of psychology. The Russian physician Ivan Pavlov (1849–1936) asserted that animal behavior could be understood as a series of trained responses to physical stimuli. Pavlov's famous experiment showed that if dogs were fed after they heard the ringing of a bell, the animals would eventually salivate at the sound of the bell alone, exactly as if they had smelled and saw food. Moreover, Pavlov insisted that such conditioning constituted a significant part of human behavior as well. Known as "behaviorism," this type of physiological psychology avoided vague concepts such as mind and consciousness, concentrating instead on the reaction of muscles, nerves, glands, and visceral organs. Rather than being governed by reason, human activity was recast by behaviorists as a bundle of physiological responses to stimuli in the environment.

Like behaviorism, a second major school of psychology also suggested that human behavior was largely motivated by unconscious and irrational forces. Founded by the Austrian physician Sigmund Freud (1856–1939), the discipline of psychoanalysis posited a new, dynamic, and unsettling theory of the mind, in which a variety of unconscious drives and desires conflict with a rational and moral conscience.

Competing Viewpoints

Darwin and His Readers

Charles Darwin's On the Origin of Species *(1859) and his theory of natural selection transformed Western knowledge of natural history. The impact of Darwin's work, however, extended well beyond scientific circles. It assumed a cultural importance that exceeded even Darwin's scholarly contribution. How Darwinism was popularized is a complex question, for writers and readers could mold Darwin's ideas to fit a variety of political and cultural purposes. The first excerpt comes from the conclusion to* On the Origin of Species *itself, and it sets out the different laws that Darwin thought governed the natural world. The second excerpt comes from the autobiography of Nicholas Osterroth (1875–1933), a clay miner from western Germany. Osterroth was ambitious and self-educated. The passage recounts his reaction to hearing about Darwin and conveys his enthusiasm for late-nineteenth-century science.*

On the Origin of Species

The natural system is a genealogical arrangement, in which we have to discover the lines of descent by the most permanent characters, however slight their vital importance may be.

The framework of bones being the same in the hand of a man, wing of a bat, fin of the porpoise, and leg of the horse,—the same number of vertebrae forming the neck of the giraffe and of the elephant,—and innumerable other such facts, at once explain themselves on the theory of descent with slow and slight successive modifications. The similarity of pattern in the wing and leg of a bat, though used for such different purposes,—in the jaws and legs of a crab,—in the petals, stamens, and pistils of a flower, is likewise intelligible on the view of the gradual modification of parts or organs, which were alike in the early progenitor of each class. . . .

It is interesting to contemplate an entangled bank, clothed with many plants of many kinds, with birds singing on the bushes, with various insects flitting about, and with worms crawling through the damp earth, and to reflect that these elaborately constructed forms, so different from each other, and dependent on each other in so complex a manner, have all been produced by laws acting around us. These laws, taken in the largest sense, being Growth with Reproduction; Inheritance which is almost implied by reproduction; Variability from the indirect and direct action of the external conditions of life, and from use and disuse; a Ratio of Increase so high as to lead to a Struggle for Life, and as a consequence to Natural Selection, entailing Divergence of Character and the Extinction of less-improved forms. Thus, from the war of nature, from famine and death, the most exalted object which we are capable of conceiving, namely, the production of the higher animals, directly follows. There is grandeur in this view of life, with its several powers, having been originally breathed into a few forms or into one; and that, whilst this planet has gone cycling on according to the fixed law of gravity, from so simple a beginning endless forms most beautiful and most wonderful have been, and are being, evolved.

Source: Charles Darwin, *On the Origin of Species* (Harmondsworth, UK: 1968), pp. 450–51, 458–60.

Developed over many years of treating patients with nervous ailments, Freud's model of the psyche contained three elements: (1) the id, or undisciplined desires for pleasure, sexual gratification, aggression, and so on; (2) the superego, or conscience, which registers the prohibitions of morality and culture; and (3) the ego, the arena in which the conflict between id and superego works itself out. Freud believed that most cases of mental disorder result from an irreconcilable tension between natural drives and the restraints placed on individuals. Freud believed that by studying

Nicholas Osterroth: A Miner's Reaction

The book was called *Moses or Darwin?*. . . Written in a very popular style, it compared the Mosaic story of creation with the natural evolutionary history, illuminated the contradictions of the biblical story, and gave a concise description of the evolution of organic and inorganic nature, interwoven with plenty of striking proofs.

What particularly impressed me was a fact that now became clear to me: that evolutionary natural history was monopolized by the institutions of higher learning; that Newton, Laplace, Kant, Darwin, and Haeckel brought enlightenment only to the students of the upper social classes; and that for the common people in the grammar school the old Moses with his six-day creation of the world still was the authoritative world view. For the upper classes there was evolution, for us creation; for them productive liberating knowledge, for us rigid faith; bread for those favored by fate, stones for those who hungered for truth!

Why do the people need science? Why do they need a so-called Weltanschauung [worldview]? The people must keep Moses, must keep religion; religion is the poor man's philosophy. Where would we end up if every miner and every farmhand had the opportunity to stick his nose into astronomy, geology, biology, and anatomy? Does it serve any purpose for the divine world order of the possessing and privileged classes to tell the worker that the Ptolemaic heavens have long since collapsed; that out there in the universe there is an eternal process of creation and destruction; that in the universe at large, as on our tiny earth, everything is in the grip of eternal evolution; that this evolution takes place according to inalterable natural laws that defy even the omnipotence of the old Mosaic Jehovah. . . . Why tell the dumb people that Copernicus and his followers have overturned the old Mosaic creator, and that Darwin and modern science have dug the very ground out from under his feet of clay?

That would be suicide! Yes, the old religion is so convenient for the divine world order of the ruling class! As long as the worker hopes faithfully for the beyond, he won't think of plucking the blooming roses in this world. . . .

The possessing classes of all civilized nations need servants to make possible their godlike existence. So they cannot allow the servant to eat from the tree of knowledge.

Source: Alfred Kelly, ed., *The German Worker: Working-Class Autobiographies from the Age of Industrialization* (Berkeley, CA: 1987), pp. 185–86.

Questions for Analysis

1. Was the theory of evolution revolutionary? If so, how? Would it be fair to say that Darwin did for the nineteenth century what Newton did for the seventeenth and eighteenth centuries?
2. Why did people think the natural world was governed by laws? Was this a religious belief or a scientific fact?
3. What aspects of Darwin appealed to Osterroth and why?

such disorders, as well as dreams and slips of the tongue, scientists could glimpse the submerged areas of consciousness and thus understand seemingly irrational behavior. Freud's seach for an all-encompassing theory of the mind was deeply grounded in the tenets of nineteenth-century science. By stressing the irrational, however, Freud's theories fed a growing anxiety about the value and limits of human reason. Likewise, they brought to fore a powerful critique of the constraints imposed by the moral and social codes of Western civilization.

SIGMUND FREUD. Freud's theory of the mind and the unconscious broke with many of the basic assumptions about human nature during his time. He remained, however, a committed nineteenth-century scientist and believed he had uncovered new laws that governed culture as well as individuals.

No one provided a more sweeping or more influential assault on Western values of rationality than the German philosopher Friedrich Nietzsche (*NEE-chuh*, 1844–1900). Like Freud, Nietzsche had observed a middle-class culture that he believed to be dominated by illusions and self-deceptions, and he sought to unmask them. In a series of works that rejected rational argumentation in favor of an elliptical, suggestive prose style, Nietzsche argued that bourgeois faith in such concepts as science, progress, democracy, and religion represented a futile, and reprehensible, search for security and truth. Nietzsche categorically denied the possibility of knowing truth or reality, since all knowledge comes filtered through linguistic, scientific, or artistic systems of representation. He famously ridiculed Judeo-Christian morality for instilling a repressive conformity that drained civilization of its vitality. Nietzsche's philosophy resounded with themes of personal liberation, especially freedom from the stranglehold of history and tradition. Indeed, Nietzsche's ideal individual, or "superman," was one who abandoned the burdens of cultural conformity and created an independent set of values based on artistic vision and strength of character. Only through individual struggle against the chaotic universe did Nietzsche forecast salvation for Western civilization.

Religion and Its Critics

Faced with these various scientific and philosophical challenges, the institutions responsible for the maintenance of traditional faith found themselves on the defensive. The Roman Catholic Church responded to the encroachments of secular society by appealing to its dogma and venerated traditions. In 1864, Pope Pius IX issued a Syllabus of Errors, condemning what he regarded as the principal religious and philosophical errors of the time. Among them were materialism, free thought, and indifferentism (the idea that one religion is as good as another). The pope also convoked the first Church council since the Catholic Reformation, which in 1871 pronounced the dogma of papal infallibility. This meant that in his capacity "as pastor and doctor of all Christians," the pope was infallible in regard to all matters of faith and morals. Though generally accepted by pious Catholics, the claim of papal infallibility provoked a storm of protest and was denounced by the governments of several Catholic countries, including France, Spain, and Italy. The death of Pius IX in 1878 and the accession of Pope Leo XIII, however, brought a more accommodating climate to the Church. The new pope acknowledged that there was good as well as evil in modern civilization. He added a scientific staff to the Vatican and opened archives and observatories but made no further concessions to liberalism in the political sphere.

Protestants were also compelled to respond to a modernizing world. Since they were taught to understand God with the aid of little more than the Bible and a willing conscience, Protestants, unlike Catholics, had little in the way of doctrine to help them defend their faith. Some fundamentalists chose to ignore the implications of scientific and philosophical inquiry altogether and continued to believe in the literal truth of the Bible. Others were willing to agree with the school of American philosophers known as pragmatists (principally Charles S. Peirce and William James), who taught that "truth" was whatever produced useful, practical results; by their logic, if belief in God provided mental peace or spiritual satisfaction, then the belief was true. Other Protestants sought solace from religious doubt in founding missions, laboring among the poor,

POPULAR RELIGION IN THE MODERN AGE. The political and social changes that accompanied the second industrial revolution and the advent of mass politics transformed European society in fundamental ways, but this did not lead to a waning of traditional religious faith. Instead, the practices of religious devotion changed with the society as a whole. A good example of this is the emergence of new popular destinations for Catholic pilgrimage, such as the Grotto of Lourdes, where a young girl had a series of visions of the Virgin Mary in 1858. After the vision was verified by a local bishop in 1860, the site became a pilgrimage site for the faithful. In 2012, it was estimated that 200 million people had visited the site since 1860. ▪ ***What developments during the second industrial revolution helped to make this pilgrimage a global phenomenon?***

and other good works. Many adherents to this social gospel were also modernists who accepted the ethical teachings of Christianity but discarded beliefs in miracles and original sin.

New Readers and the Popular Press

The effect of various scientific and philosophical challenges on the men and women who lived at the end of the nineteenth century cannot be measured precisely. Millions undoubtedly went about the business of life untroubled by the implications of evolutionary theory, content to believe as they had believed before. Yet the changes we have been discussing eventually had a profound impact. Darwin's theory was not too complicated to be popularized. If educated men and women had neither the time nor inclination to read *On the Origin of Species*, they read magazines and newspapers that summarized (not always correctly) its implications. They encountered some of its central concepts in other places, from political speeches to novels and crime reports.

The diffusion of these new ideas was facilitated by rising literacy rates and by new forms of printed mass culture. Between 1750 and 1870, readership had expanded from the aristocracy to include middle-class circles and, thereafter, to an increasingly literate general population. In 1850, approximately half the population of Europe was literate. In subsequent decades, country after country introduced state-financed elementary and secondary education to provide opportunities for social advancement, to diffuse technical and scientific knowledge, and to inculcate civic and national pride. By 1900, approximately 85 percent of the population in Britain, France, Belgium, the Netherlands, Scandinavia, and Germany could read.

In those countries where literacy rates were highest, commercial publishers such as Alfred Harmsworth in Britain and William Randolph Hearst in the United States hastened to serve the new reading public. New newspapers appealed to the newly literate by means of sensational journalism and spicy, easy-to-read serials. Advertisements drastically lowered the costs of the mass-market newspapers, enabling even workers to purchase one or two newspapers a day. The yellow journalism of the penny presses merged entertainment and sensationalism with the news, aiming to increase circulation and thus secure more lucrative advertising sales. The era of mass readership had arrived, and artists, activists—and above all—governments would increasingly focus their message on this mass audience.

The First Moderns: Innovations in Art

In the crucible of late-nineteenth-century Europe—bubbling with scientific, technological, and social transformations—artists across the Continent began critically and systematically to question the moral and cultural values of liberal, middle-class society. Some did so with grave hesitation, others with heedless abandon. In a dizzying array of experiments, innovations, ephemeral art movements, and bombastic manifestos, the pioneers of what would later be termed "modernism" developed the artistic forms and aesthetic values that came to dominate much of the twentieth century.

***BLACK LINES* BY WASSILY KANDINSKY, 1913.** Kandinsky broke from the traditional representational approach of nineteenth-century painting with his abstractions and was one of a generation of turn-of-the-century artists who reexamined and experimented with their art forms.

Modernism encompassed a diverse and often contradictory set of theories and practices that spanned the entire range of cultural production—from painting, sculpture, literature, and architecture to theater, dance, and musical composition. Despite such diversity, however, modernist movements did share certain key characteristics: first, a sense that the world had radically changed and that change should be embraced (hence the modernists' interest in science and technology); second, a belief that traditional values and assumptions were outdated; and third, a new conception of what art could do, one that stressed expression over representation and insisted on experiment and freedom.

Early modernism was also distinguished by a new understanding of the relationship between art and society. Some artists remained interested in purely aesthetic questions but many others embraced the notion that art could effect profound social and spiritual change. The abstract painter Wassily Kandinsky (1866–1944) believed that the materialism of the nineteenth century was a source of social and moral corruption, and he looked toward a future in which artists would nourish a human spirit that was threatened by the onset of industrial society. Other artists believed they had a duty to document unflinchingly what they saw as the pathological aspects of life in modern cities or the inward chaos of the human mind. In the political arena, modernist hostility toward conventional values sometimes translated into support for antiliberal or revolutionary movements of the extreme right or left.

THE REVOLT ON CANVAS

Like most artistic movements, modernism defined itself in opposition to a set of earlier principles. For painters in particular, this meant a rejection both of mainstream academic art, which affirmed the chaste and moral outlook of museumgoers, and of the socially conscious realist tradition, which strove for rigorous, even scientific exactitude in representing material reality. The rebellion of modern artists went even further, however, by discarding altogether the centuries-old tradition of realist representation. Since the Renaissance, Western art had sought to accurately depict three-dimensional visual reality; paintings were considered to be mirrors or windows on the world. But during the late nineteenth century, artists turned their backs to the visual world, focusing instead on subjective, psychologically oriented, intensely emotional forms of self-expression. As the Norwegian painter Edvard Munch claimed: "Art is the opposite of nature. A work of art can come only from the interior of man."

The first significant breaks with traditional representational art emerged with the French impressionists, who came to prominence as young artists in the 1870s. Strictly speaking, the impressionists were realists. Steeped in scientific theories about sensory perception, they attempted to record natural phenomena objectively. Instead of painting objects themselves, they captured the transitory play of light on surfaces, giving their works a sketchy, ephemeral quality that differed sharply from realist art. And though subsequent artists revolted against what they deemed the cold objectivity of this scientific approach, the impressionist painters, most famously Claude Monet (*moh-NAY*, 1840–1926) and Pierre-Auguste Renoir (1841–1919), left two important legacies to the European avant-garde. First, by developing new techniques without reference to past styles, the impressionists paved

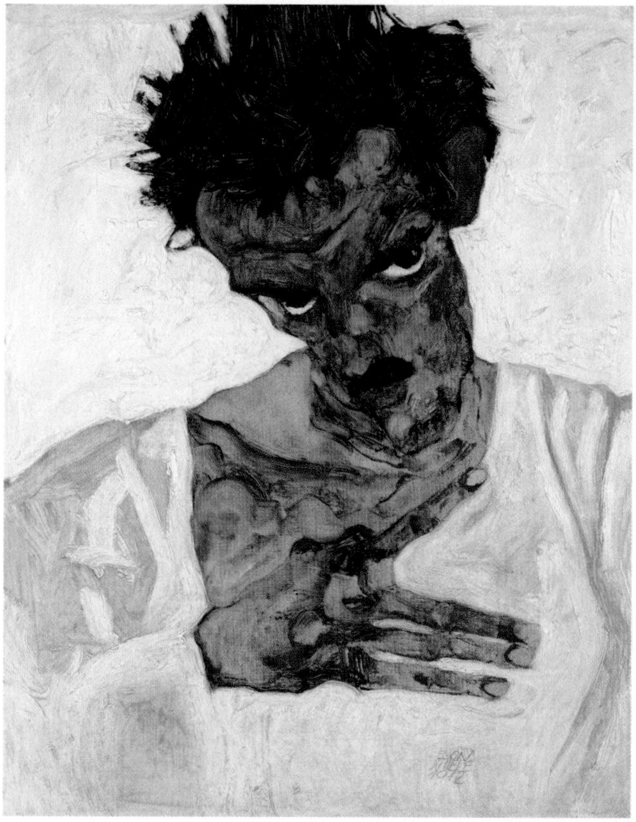

SELF-PORTRAIT, BY EGON SCHIELE, 1912. The Viennese artist Schiele represents another side of early modernism that, instead of moving toward abstraction, sought to portray raw psychological expression.

PORTRAIT OF AMBROISE VOLLARD* BY PABLO PICASSO, 1909.** In the early twentieth century, Picasso and George Braque radically transformed painting with their cubist constructions, breaking the depiction of reality into fragmented planes. Vollard, an important art dealer of the period, loses recognizable form as his figure descends. ▪ ***Compare this portrait with Schiele's self-portrait, at left. What do these paintings say about the task of the artist? ▪ ***What makes them "modern"?***

the way for younger artists to experiment more freely. Second, because the official salons rejected their work, the impressionists organized their own independent exhibitions from 1874 to 1886. These shows effectively undermined the French Academy's centuries-old monopoly on artistic display and aesthetic standards, and they established a tradition of autonomous outsider exhibits, which figures prominently in the history of modernism.

In the wake of impressionism, a handful of innovative artists working at the end of the nineteenth century laid the groundwork for an explosion of creative experimentation after 1900. Chief among them was the Frenchman Paul Cézanne (1839–1906). Perhaps more so than anyone, Cézanne shattered the window of representational art. Instead of a reflection of the world, painting became a vehicle for an artist's self-expression. The Dutchman Vincent van Gogh also explored art's expressive potential, with greater emotion and subjectivity. For Van Gogh, painting was a labor of faith, a way to channel his violent passions. For Paul Gauguin, who fled to the Pacific islands in 1891, art promised a utopian refuge from the corruption of Europe.

After the turn of the century, a diverse crop of avant-garde movements flowered across Europe. In Germany and Scandinavia, expressionists such as Emil Nolde (1867–1956), and Edvard Munch (1863–1944) turned to acid colors and violent figural distortions to express the interior consciousness of the human mind. The Austrian Egon Schiele (1890–1918) explored sexuality and the body with disturbingly raw, graphic imagery. In bohemian Paris, the Frenchman Henri Matisse (1869–1954) and Pablo Picasso (1881–1973), a Catalan Spaniard, pursued their groundbreaking aesthetic experiments in relative quiet. Clamoring for attention, on the other hand, were groups of artists who reveled in the energetic dynamism of modern life.

The cubists in Paris, vorticists in Britain, and futurists in Italy all embraced a hard, angular aesthetic of the machine age. While other modernists sought an antidote to end-of-the-century malaise by looking backward to so-called primitive cultures, these new movements embraced the future in all its uncertainty—often with the kind of aggressive, hypermasculine language that later emerged as a hallmark of fascism. In the futurist *Manifesto,* for instance, F. T. Marinetti proclaimed: "We will glorify war—the only true hygiene of the world—militarism, patriotism, the destructive gesture of anarchist, the beautiful Ideas which kill." In Russia and Holland, meanwhile, a few intensely idealistic painters made perhaps the most revolutionary aesthetic leap of early modernism, into totally abstract, or "object-less" painting.

The breadth and diversity of modern art defy simple categories and explanations. Though they remained the province of a small group of artists and intellectuals before 1914, these radical revisions of artistic values entered the cultural mainstream soon after the First World War (see Chapter 25).

CONCLUSION

Many Europeans who had grown up in the period from 1870 to 1914, but lived through the hardships of the First World War, looked back on the prewar period as a golden age of

After You Read This Chapter

Visit StudySpace for quizzes, additional review materials, and multimedia documents. **wwnorton.com/web/westernciv18**

REVIEWING THE OBJECTIVES

- The second industrial revolution was made possible by technological innovations that stimulated the production of steel and new energy sources. What were the consequences of this era of rapid growth for the economy and for European society?
- Expanded electorates meant that more people were participating in politics, especially among the working classes. What parties and movements emerged to represent European workers, and what were their goals?
- At the end of the nineteenth century, militant agitation in favor of women's suffrage increased. What obstacles faced women who demanded the vote?
- Liberalism and nationalism were changed by the advent of mass politics. How did the expansion of the electorate change political life across Europe?
- Technological innovations and scientific ideas about human nature and modern society changed the way that people thought about their place in the world, stimulating artists and writers to new and revolutionary forms of creative expression. What were these scientific ideas and why were they so controversial at the end of the nineteenth century?

European civilization. In one sense, this retrospective view is apt. After all, the continental powers had successfully avoided major wars, enabling a second phase of industrialization to provide better living standards for the growing populations of mass society. An overall spirit of confidence and purpose fueled Europe's perceived mission to exercise political, economic, and cultural dominion in the far reaches of the world. Yet European politics and culture also registered the presence of powerful—and destabilizing—forces of change. Industrial expansion, relative abundance, and rising literacy produced a political climate of rising expectations. As the age of mass politics arrived, democrats, socialists, and feminists clamored for access to political life, threatening violence, strikes, and revolution. Marxist socialism especially changed radical politics, redefining the terms of debate for the next century. Western science, literature, and the arts explored new perspectives on the individual, undermining some of the cherished beliefs of nineteenth-century liberals. The competition and violence central to Darwin's theory of evolution, the subconscious urges that Freud found in human behavior, and the rebellion against representation in the arts all pointed in new and baffling directions. These experiments, hypotheses, and nagging questions accompanied Europe into the Great War of 1914. They would help shape Europeans' responses to the devastation of that war. After the war, the political changes and cultural unease of the period from 1870 to 1914 would reemerge in the form of mass movements and artistic developments that would define the twentieth century.

PEOPLE, IDEAS, AND EVENTS IN CONTEXT

- Why was the British **LABOUR PARTY** more moderate in its goals than the German **SOCIAL DEMOCRATIC PARTY**?
- What disagreements about political strategy divided **ANARCHISTS** and **SYNDICALISTS** from **MARXISTS** in European labor movements?
- What legal reforms were successfully achieved by **WOMEN'S ASSOCIATIONS** in late-nineteenth-century western European nations?
- What was the **DREYFUS AFFAIR**, and how was it related to the spread of popular **ANTI-SEMITISM** and the emergence of **ZIONISM** in European Jewish communities?
- What were the goals of the **BOLSHEVIKS** and the **MENSHEVIKS** in the **RUSSIAN REVOLUTION OF 1905**?
- Who were the **YOUNG TURKS**?
- What was **CHARLES DARWIN**'s **THEORY OF EVOLUTION**, and why did it stimulate so much debate between religious and secular thinkers?
- Why was the psychology of **SIGMUND FREUD** so troubling for liberals in Europe?
- What common ideas did the artists and writers who came to be known as **MODERNISTS** share?

THINKING ABOUT CONNECTIONS

- How did the expansion of the electorate and the spread of representative political institutions in Europe at the end of the nineteenth century change the nature of debates about the power of public opinion and the responsibility of government for the people?
- Compare the age of mass politics at the end of the nineteenth century in Europe with earlier periods of rapid change, such as the Reformation of the sixteenth century or the period of the French Revolution. What was similar? What was different?
- Compare the age of mass politics in Europe circa 1900 with the political life of Europe or the United States today. What has changed? What remains the same?

Before You Read This Chapter

STORY LINES

- In 1914, the balance of power in Europe collapsed in a total war that mobilized the full resources of modern industrialized nations, their global empires, and their populations.
- The war transformed the relationship between state and society. Governments conscripted an entire generation of young men, encouraged women to work in industry, and took control of the economy to produce goods and material for the military.
- The war provoked the first successful socialist revolution in modern history when the Russian Empire collapsed and the Bolsheviks seized power in October 1917. The Russian Revolution set the stage for the major ideological confrontations of the twentieth century.

CHRONOLOGY

1879	The Dual Alliance (Germany and Austria-Hungary)
1904	The Triple Entente (France, Russia, and Britain)
June 1914	Assassination of Franz Ferdinand in Sarajevo
September 1914	Battle of the Marne
April 1915	Gallipoli campaign begins
May 1915	Italy enters the war against Austria-Hungary
February 1916	Battle of Verdun begins
July 1916	British offensive on the Somme begins
January 1917	Germany begins unrestricted submarine warfare
April 1917	United States enters the war
November 1917	Bolshevik Revolution
March 1918	Treaty of Brest-Litovsk
November 1918	Armistice
June 1919	Treaty of Versailles signed

24

The First World War

CORE OBJECTIVES

- **EXPLAIN** the origins of the First World War.
- **UNDERSTAND** the circumstances that led to trench warfare on the Western Front, and the consequences of the offensive strategy pursued by all sides.
- **IDENTIFY** the major effects of the war on civilian life.
- **EXPLAIN** the war's effects on territories beyond Europe's borders, in the Middle East, in Africa, and in Asia.
- **UNDERSTAND** the origins and goals of the Bolshevik movement in Russia and the circumstances that allowed them to seize power in 1917.
- **IDENTIFY** the people responsible for the final terms of the Versailles Peace Treaty and understand its goals.

The battle of the Somme began on June 24, 1916, with a fearsome British artillery barrage against German trenches along a twenty-five-mile front. Hour after hour, day and night, the British guns swept across the barbed wire and fortifications that faced their own lines, firing 1.5 million rounds over seven days. Mixing gas with explosive rounds, the gunners pulverized the landscape and poisoned the atmosphere. Deep in underground bunkers on the other side, the German defenders huddled in their masks. When the big guns went silent, tens of thousands of British soldiers rose up out of their trenches, each bearing sixty pounds of equipment, and made their way into the cratered No Man's Land that separated the two armies. They had been told that wire-cutting explosives would destroy the labyrinth of barbed wire between the trenches during the barrage, leaving them free to charge across and occupy the front trench before the stunned Germans could recover. To their horror, they found the barbed wire intact. Instead of taking the German trench, they found themselves caught in the open when the German machine-gunners manned the defensive parapets. The result proved all too eloquently the efficiency of the First World

War's mechanized methods of killing. Twenty-one thousand British soldiers were killed on the first day of the battle of the Somme. A further 30,000 were wounded. Because some British units allowed volunteers to serve with their friends—the "Pals Battalions"—there were neighborhoods and villages in Britain in which every married woman became a widow in the space of a few minutes. The British commanders pressed the offensive for nearly five more months, and the combined casualties climbed over a million. The German line never broke.

This contest between artillery and machine gun was a war that was possible only in an industrialized world. Before beginning the assault, the British had stockpiled 2.9 million artillery shells—Napoleon had only 20,000 at Waterloo. Although European armies marched off to war in 1914 with a confidence and ambition bred by their imperial conquests, they soon confronted the ugly face of industrial warfare and the grim capacities of the modern world. In a catastrophic combination of old mentalities and new technologies, the war left 9 million dead soldiers in its wake.

Soldiers were not the only casualties. Four years of fighting destroyed many of the institutions and assumptions of the previous century, from monarchies and empires to European economic dominance. It disillusioned many, even the citizens of the victorious nations. As the British writer Virginia Woolf put it, "It was a shock—to see the faces of our rulers in the light of shell-fire." The war led European states to take over their national economies, as they set quotas for production and consumption and took responsibility for sustaining the civilian population during the crisis. By toppling the Prussian and Austrian monarchies, the war banished older forms of authoritarianism, and by provoking the Russian Revolution of 1917, the war ushered in new ones that bore the distinctive mark of the twentieth century. Finally, the war proved nearly impossible to settle; antagonisms bred in battle only intensified in the war's aftermath and would eventually lead to the Second World War. Postwar Europe faced more problems than peace could manage.

THE JULY CRISIS

In the decades before 1914, Europe had built a seemingly stable peace. Through the complex negotiations of Great Power geopolitics, Europe had settled into two systems of alliance: the Triple Entente (later the Allied Powers) of Britain, France, and Russia rivaled the Triple Alliance (later the Central Powers) of Germany, Austria-Hungary, and Italy. Within this balance of power, the nations of Europe challenged one another for economic, military, and imperial advantage. The scramble for colonies abroad accompanied a fierce arms race at home, where military leaders assumed that superior technology and larger armies would result in a quick victory in a European war. Yet none of the diplomats, spies, military planners, or cabinet ministers of Europe—or any of their critics—predicted the war they eventually got. Nor did many expect that the Balkan crisis of July 1914 would touch off that conflict, engulfing all of Europe in just over a month's time.

The Balkan Peninsula had long been a satellite of the Ottoman Empire. During the nineteenth century, however, Ottoman power became severely weakened, and both the Austro-Hungarian Empire and the Russian monarchy competed with one another to replace the Ottomans as the dominant force in the region. The region was also home to ambitious national movements of Serbs and Bulgarians who took advantage of Ottoman decline to declare their independence in the decades before the First World War. Russia, as the most powerful Slavic monarchy, was the traditional sponsor of these Slavic nationalist movements and had a particularly close relationship with Serbia. Austria-Hungary, on the other hand, sought to minimize the influence of Slavic nationalisms because they constituted a threat to its own multi-ethnic empire. In 1912 and 1913, the region was destabilized by two wars involving the Ottoman Empire and the independent Balkan states of Serbia, Greece, Bulgaria, and Montenegro. The Great Powers steered clear of entanglement and these wars remained localized. The alliance system could only ensure stability, however, if the Great Powers could maintain this posture of nonintervention. Once one of them became embroiled in a local conflict, the system of alliances would lead directly to a wider war.

The spark came from the Balkan province of Bosnia, a multi-ethnic region of Serbs, Croats, and Bosnian Muslims that had been under Austrian rule since 1878. In Bosnia, members of the local Serb population longed to secede from Austrian rule altogether and join the independent state of Serbia. When Bosnian Serbs found their way blocked by the Austrians, some began to conspire with Serbia, and on June 28, 1914, a group of Bosnian Serbs assassinated the heir to the Austro-Hungarian throne, Franz Ferdinand (1889–1914) as he paraded through Sarajevo, the capital of Bosnia.

Shocked by Ferdinand's death, the Austrians treated the assassination as a direct attack by the Serbian government. Three weeks later, the Austrians announced an ultimatum to Serbia, demanding that they denounce the activities of Bosnian Serbs, abstain from propaganda that served their cause, and allow Austro-Hungarian officials to prosecute members of the Serbian government who they believed were involved in the assassination. The demands were deliberately unreasonable—the Austrians wanted war, to crush Serbia and restore order in Bosnia. The Serbs mobilized their army before agreeing to all but the most important demands, and Austria responded with its own mobilization order on July 28, 1914. Shaken from their summer distractions, Europeans began to realize that the treaty system they relied on for stability was actually leading to a much larger confrontation: Austria and its ally Germany were facing a war with Serbia, Serbia's ally Russia, and by extension, Russia's ally France.

Diplomats tried and failed to prevent the outbreak of wider war. When Russia announced a "partial mobilization" to defend Serbia against Austria, the German ministers telegraphed the French to find out if they intended to honor France's defensive treaty with Russia. The French responded that France would "act in accordance with her interests"—meaning that they would immediately mobilize against Germany. Facing the dual threat from both sides that they had long feared, Germany mobilized on August 1 and declared war on Russia—and two days later, on France. The next day, the German army invaded Belgium on its way to take Paris.

EUROPEAN ALLIANCES ON THE EVE OF THE FIRST WORLD WAR. ▪ *What major countries were part of the Triple Alliance?* ▪ *Of the Triple Entente?* ▪ *From the map, why would Germany have declared war on France so quickly once Russia began to mobilize?* ▪ *According to the map, why were the Balkan countries such a volatile region?*

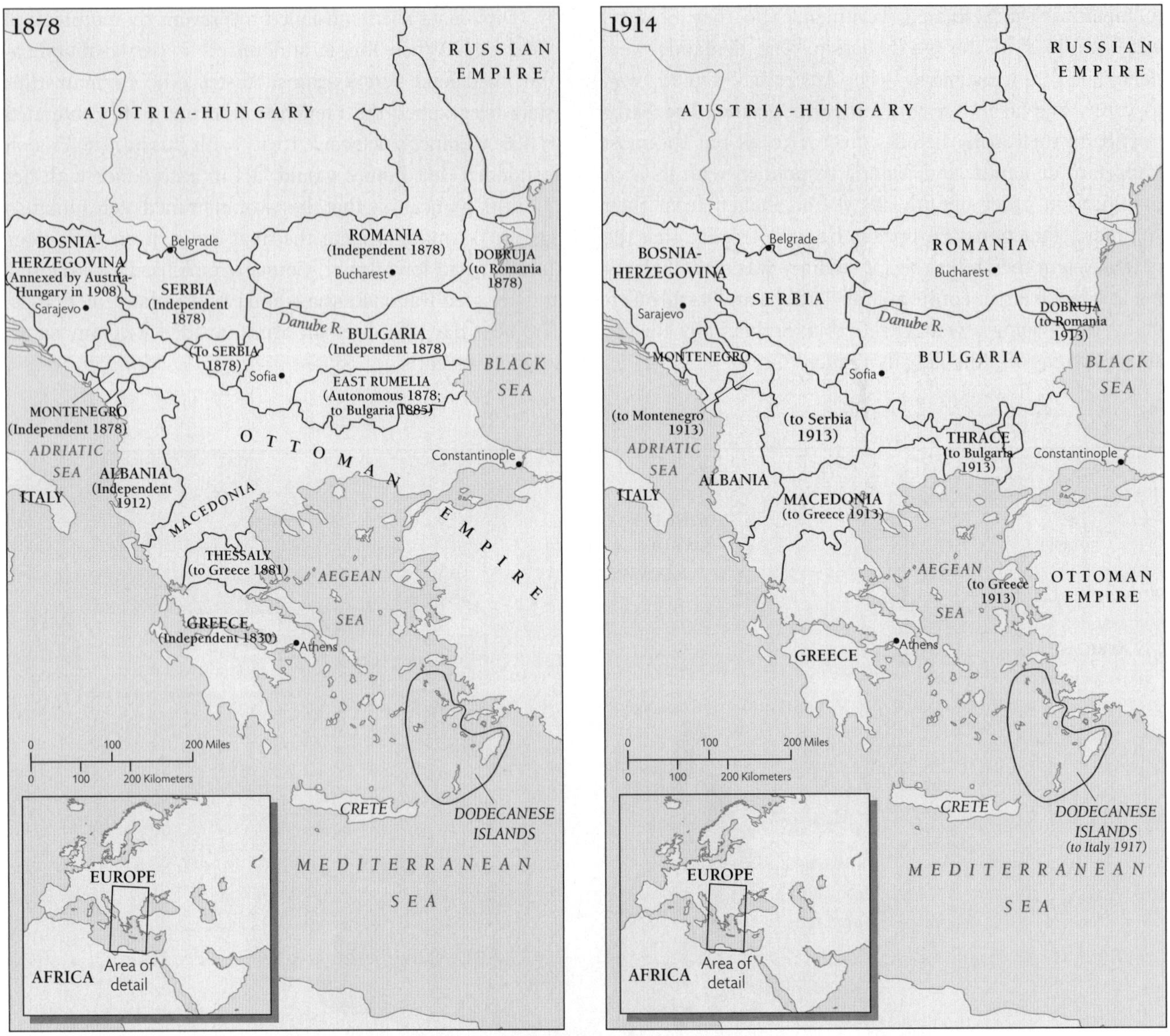

THE BALKAN CRISIS, 1878–1914. ▪ *What major empires were involved in the Balkans during this period?* ▪ *According to the maps, what was the major change in the Balkans between 1878 and 1914?* ▪ *What problems did nationalism, ethnicity, and race create in this region?*

The invasion of neutral Belgium provided a rallying cry for British generals and diplomats who wanted Britain to honor their secret obligations to France and join the war against Germany. This was not a foregone conclusion—the Liberal government was opposed to war and acquiesced partly to avoid being voted out of office. Proponents of war insisted that to maintain the balance of power—a central tenet of British foreign policy—no single nation should be allowed to dominate the continent. On August 4, Britain entered the war against Germany.

Other nations were quickly drawn into the struggle. On August 7, the Montenegrins joined the Serbs against Austria. Two weeks later, the Japanese declared war on Germany, mainly to attack German possessions in the Far East. On August 1, Turkey allied with Germany and in October began the bombardment of Russian ports on the Black Sea. Italy had been allied with Germany and Austria before the war, but at the outbreak of hostilities, the Italians declared neutrality, insisting that since Germany had invaded neutral Belgium, they owed Germany no protection.

The diplomatic maneuvers during the five weeks that followed the assassination at Sarajevo have been called a "tragedy of miscalculation." Austria's determination to punish Serbia, Germany's unwillingness to restrain their

FRANZ FERDINAND AND HIS WIFE, SOPHIE. The Austrian archduke and archduchess, in Sarajevo on June 28, 1914, approaching their car before they were assassinated.
▪ ***What made their deaths the spark that unleashed a general war in Europe?***

Austrian allies, and Russia's desire to use Serbia as an excuse to extend their influence in the Balkans all played a part in making the war more likely. Diplomats were further constrained by the strategic thinking and rigid timetables set by military leaders, and all sides clearly felt that it was important to make a show of force during the period of negotiation that preceded the outbreak of war. It is clear, however, that powerful German officials were arguing that war was inevitable. They insisted that Germany should fight before Russia recovered from their 1905 loss to Japan and before the French army could benefit from its new three-year conscription law, which would put more men in uniform. This sense of urgency characterized the strategies of all combatant countries. The lure of a bold, successful strike against one's enemies, and the fear that too much was at stake to risk losing the advantage created a rolling tide of military mobilization that carried Europe into battle.

THE MARNE AND ITS CONSEQUENCES

Declarations of war were met with a mix of public fanfare and private concern. Though saber-rattling romantics envisioned a war of national glory and spiritual renewal, plenty of Europeans recognized that a continental war put decades of progress and prosperity at risk. Bankers and financiers, who might have hoped to profit from increased wartime production or from captured colonial markets, were among those most opposed to the war. They correctly predicted that a major war would create financial chaos. Many young men, however, enlisted with excitement. On the Continent, volunteer soldiers added to the strength of conscript armies, while in Britain (where conscription wasn't introduced until 1916) over 700,000 men joined the army in the first eight weeks alone. Like many a war enthusiast, these men expected the war to be over by Christmas.

If less idealistic, the expectations of the politicians and generals in charge were also soon to be disproved. Military planners foresaw a short, limited, and decisive war—a tool to be used where diplomacy failed. They thought that a modern economy simply could not function amid a sustained war effort and that modern weaponry made protracted war impossible. They placed their bets on size and speed: bigger armies, more powerful weapons, and faster offensives would win the war. But for all of their planning, they were unable to respond to the uncertainty and confusion of the battlefield.

The Germans based their offensive on what is often called the Schlieffen Plan, named for Count Alfred von Schlieffen (*SHLEE-fen*), chief of the German General Staff from 1890 to 1905. Schlieffen called for attacking France first to secure a quick victory that would neutralize the Western Front and free the German army to fight Russia in the east. With France expecting an attack through Alsace-Lorraine, the Germans would instead invade through Belgium and sweep down through northwestern France to fight a decisive battle near Paris. For over a month, the German army advanced swiftly, but the plan overestimated the army's physical and logistical capabilities. The speed of the operation—advancing twenty to twenty-five miles a day—was simply too much for soldiers and supply lines to keep up with. They were also slowed by the resistance of Belgian forces and by the intervention of Britain's small but highly professional field army. Fearing the Russians would move faster than expected, German commanders altered the offensive plan by dispatching some troops to the east instead of committing them all to the assault on France.

Competing Viewpoints

Toward the First World War: Diplomacy in the Summer of 1914

The assassination of Franz Ferdinand in Sarajevo on June 28, 1914, set off an increasingly desperate round of diplomatic negotiations. As the following exchanges show, diplomats and political leaders on both sides swung from trying to provoke war to attempting to avert or, at least, contain it. A week after his nephew, the heir to the throne, was shot, Franz Joseph set out his interpretation of the long-standing conflict with Serbia and its larger implications—reprinted here.

The second selection comes from an account of a meeting of the Council of Ministers of the Austro-Hungarian Empire on July 7, 1914. The ministers disagreed sharply about diplomatic strategies and about how crucial decisions should be made.

The British foreign secretary Sir Edward Grey, for one, was shocked by Austria's demands, especially its insistence that Austrian officials would participate in Serbian judicial proceedings. The Serbian government's response was more conciliatory than most diplomats expected, but diplomatic efforts to avert war still failed. The Austrians' ultimatum to Serbia included the following demands given in the final extract here.

Emperor Franz Joseph of Austria-Hungary to Kaiser Wilhelm II of Germany, July 5, 1914

The plot against my poor nephew was the direct result of an agitation carried on by the Russian and Serb Pan-Slavs, an agitation whose sole object is the weakening of the Triple Alliance and the destruction of my realm.

So far, all investigations have shown that the Sarajevo murder was not perpetrated by one individual, but grew out of a well-organized conspiracy, the threads of which can be traced to Belgrade. Even though it will probably be impossible to prove the complicity of the Serb government, there can be no doubt that its policy, aiming as it does at the unification of all Southern Slavs under the Serb banner, encourages such crimes, and that the continuation of such conditions constitutes a permanent threat to my dynasty and my lands. . . .

This will only be possible if Serbia, which is at present the pivot of Pan-Slav policies, is put out of action as a factor of political power in the Balkans.

You too are [surely] convinced after the recent frightful occurrence in Bosnia that it is no longer possible to contemplate a reconciliation of the antagonism between us and Serbia and that the [efforts] of all European monarchs to pursue policies that preserve the peace will be threatened if the nest of criminal activity in Belgrade remains unpunished.

Austro-Hungarian Disagreements over Strategy

C [Count Leopold Berchtold, foreign minister of Austria-Hungary] . . . both Emperor Wilhelm and [chancellor] Bethmann Hollweg had assured us emphatically of Germany's unconditional support in the event of military complications with Serbia. . . . It was clear to him that a military conflict with Serbia might bring about war with Russia. . . .

[Count Istvan Tisza, prime minister of Hungary] . . . We should decide what our demands on Serbia will be [but] should only present an ultimatum if Serbia rejected them. These demands must be hard but not so that they cannot be complied with. If Serbia accepted them, we could register a noteworthy diplomatic success and our prestige in the Balkans would be enhanced. If Serbia rejected our demands, then he too would favor military action. But he would already now go on record that we could aim at the down sizing but not the complete annihilation of Serbia because, first, this would provoke Russia to fight to the death and, second, he—as Hungarian premier—could never consent to the monarchy's annexation of a part of Serbia. Whether or not we ought to go to war with Serbia was not a matter for Germany to decide. . . .

[Count Berchtold] remarked that the history of the past years showed that diplomatic successes against Serbia might enhance the prestige of the monarchy temporarily, but that in reality the tension in our relations with Serbia had only increased.

[Count Karl Stürgkh, prime minister of Austria] . . . agreed with the Royal Hungarian Prime Minister that we and not the German government had to determine whether a war was necessary or not . . . [but] Count Tisza should take into account that in pursuing a hesitant and weak policy, we run the risk of not being so sure of Germany's unconditional support. . . .

[Leo von Bilinsky, Austro-Hungarian finance minister] . . . The Serb understands only force, a diplomatic success would make no impression at all in Bosnia and would be harmful rather than beneficial. . . .

Austro-Hungary's Ultimatum to Serbia

The Royal Serb Government will publish the following declaration on the first page of its official *journal* of 26/13 July:

"The Royal Serb Government condemns the propaganda directed against Austria-Hungary, and regrets sincerely the horrible consequences of these criminal ambitions.

"The Royal Serb Government regrets that Serb officers and officials have taken part in the propaganda above-mentioned and thereby imperiled friendly and neighbourly relations.

"The Royal Government . . . considers it a duty to warn officers, officials and indeed all the inhabitants of the kingdom [of Serbia], that it will in future use great severity against such persons who may be guilty of similar doings.

The Royal Serb Government will moreover pledge itself to the following.

1. to suppress every publication likely to inspire hatred and contempt against the Monarchy;

2. to begin immediately dissolving the society called *Narodna Odbrana*,* to seize all its means of propaganda and to act in the same way against all the societies and associations in Serbia, which are busy with the propaganda against Austria-Hungary;

3. to eliminate without delay from public instruction everything that serves or might serve the propaganda against Austria-Hungary, both where teachers or books are concerned;

4. to remove from military service and from the administration all officers and officials who are guilty of having taken part in the propaganda against Austria-Hungary, whose names and proof of whose guilt the I. and R. Government [Imperial and Royal, that is, the Austro-Hungarian empire] will communicate to the Royal Government;

5. to consent to the cooperation of I. and R. officials in Serbia in suppressing the subversive movement directed against the territorial integrity of the Monarchy;

6. to open a judicial inquest [*enquête judiciaire*] against all those who took part in the plot of 28 June, if they are to be found on Serbian territory; the I. and R. Government will delegate officials who will take an active part in these and associated inquiries;

The I. and R. Government expects the answer of the Royal government to reach it not later than Saturday, the 25th, at six in the afternoon. . . .

*Narodna Odbrana, or National Defense, was pro-Serbian and anti-Austrian but nonviolent. The Society of the Black Hand, to which Franz Ferdinand's assassin belonged, considered Narodna Odbrana too moderate.

Source (for all three excerpts): Ralph Menning, *The Art of the Possible: Documents on Great Power Diplomacy, 1814–1914* (New York: 1996), pp. 400, 402–03, and 414–15.

Questions for Analysis

1. Emperor Franz Joseph's letter to Kaiser Wilhelm II tells of the Austrian investigation into the assassination of Archduke Franz Ferdinand. What did Franz seek from his German ally? What did the emperors understand by the phrase "if Serbia . . . is put out of action as a factor of political power in the Balkans"? Why might the Germans support a war against Serb-sponsored terrorism?

2. Could the Serbians have accepted the Austrian ultimatum without total loss of face and sacrifice of their independence? British and Russian foreign ministers were shocked by the demands on Serbia. Others thought the Austrians were justified and that Britain would act similarly if threatened by terrorism. If, as Leo von Bilinsky said, "The Serb understands only force," why didn't Austria declare war without an ultimatum?

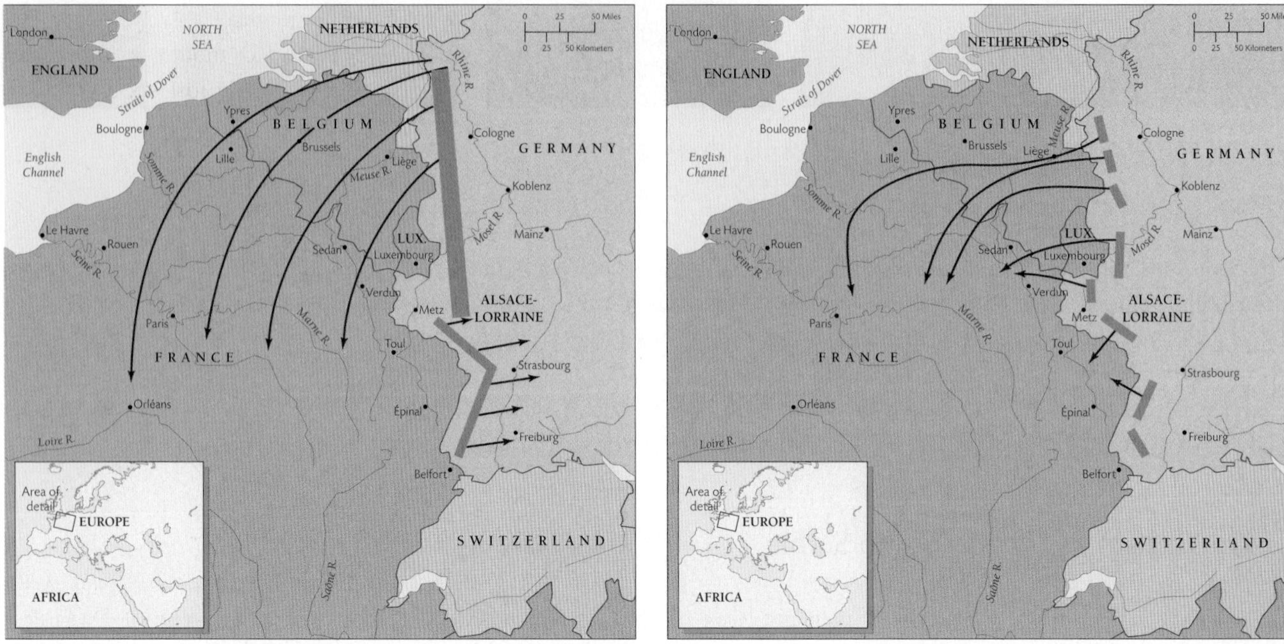

THE SCHLIEFFEN PLAN AND THE GERMAN OFFENSIVE. The map on the left details the offensive strategy developed (and modified several times) by Alfred von Schlieffen, chief of the German General Staff, and Helmuth von Moltke, his successor in the decade after 1890. ▪ ***What strategy did they propose, and why?*** ▪ ***The map on the right shows the German offensive. How was the plan modified, and why?*** ▪ ***With what consequences?*** ▪ ***Why did the German offensive fail to achieve its ultimate goal?***

At first, French counterattacks into Alsace-Lorraine failed, and casualties mounted as the French lines retreated toward Paris. The French commander, Jules Joffre, nevertheless reorganized his armies and slowly drew the Germans into a trap. In September, with the Germans just thirty miles outside of the capital, Britain and France launched a successful counteroffensive at the battle of the Marne. The German line retreated to the Aisne River, and what remained of the Schlieffen Plan was dead.

After the Marne, unable to advance, the armies tried to outflank one another to the north, racing to the sea. After four months of swift charges across open ground, Germany set up a fortified, defensive position that the Allies could not break. Along an immovable front, stretching over 400 miles from the northern border of Switzerland to the English Channel, the Great Powers literally dug in for a protracted battle. By Christmas, trench warfare was born, and the war had just begun.

The Marne proved to be the most strategically important battle of the entire war. This single battle upended Europe's expectations of war and dashed hopes that it would quickly finish. The war of movement had stopped dead in its tracks, where it would remain for four years. Politicians and generals began a continual search for ways to break the stalemate and to bring the war out of trenches, seeking new allies, new theaters, and new weapons. But they also remained committed to offensive tactics on the Western Front. Whether through ignorance, stubbornness, callousness, or desperation, military leaders continued to order their men to go "over the top."

Allied success at the Marne resulted in part from an unexpectedly strong Russian assault in eastern Prussia, which pulled some German units away from the attack on the west. But Russia's initial gains were obliterated at the battle of Tannenberg, August 26–30. Plagued with an array of problems, the Russian army was tired and half-starved; the Germans devastated it, taking 92,000 prisoners and virtually destroying the Russian Second Army. The Russian general killed himself on the battlefield. Two weeks later, the Germans won another decisive victory at the battle of the Masurian Lakes, forcing the Russians to retreat from German territory. Despite this, Russian forces were able to defeat Austrian attacks to their south, inflicting terrible losses and thereby forcing the Germans to commit more troops to Russia. Through 1915 and 1916, the Eastern Front remained bloody and indecisive, with neither side able to capitalize on its gains.

RUSSIAN PRISONERS IN LATE AUGUST 1914, AFTER THE BATTLE OF TANNENBERG. The German army, under Paul von Hindenburg and Erich Ludendorff, crushed the Russians and took 92,000 prisoners. The Russians continued to fight, but the photograph highlights the weakness of even a massive army and the scale of the combat.

STALEMATE, 1915

In the search for new points of attack, both the Allies and the Central Powers added new partners. The Ottoman Empire (Turkey) joined Germany and Austria at the end of 1914. In May 1915, Italy joined the Allies, persuaded by the popular support of its citizens and lured by promises of financial reparations, parts of Austrian territory, and pieces of Germany's African colonies when (and if) the Allies won the war. Bulgaria also hoped to gain territory in the Balkans and joined the war on the side of the Central Powers a few months later. The entry of these new belligerents expanded the geography of the war and introduced the possibility of breaking the stalemate in the west by waging offensives on other fronts.

Gallipoli and Naval Warfare

Turkey's involvement, in particular, altered the dynamics of the war, for it threatened Russia's supply lines and endangered Britain's control of the Suez Canal. To defeat Turkey quickly—and in hopes of bypassing the Western Front—the British first lord of the admiralty, Winston Churchill (1911–15), argued for a naval offensive in the Dardanelles, the narrow strait separating Europe and Asia Minor. Under particularly incompetent leadership, however, the Royal Navy lacked adequate planning, supply lines, and maps to mount a successful campaign, and quickly lost six ships. The Allies then attempted a land invasion of the Gallipoli Peninsula, in April 1915, with a combined force of French, British, Australian, and New Zealand troops. The Turks defended the narrow coast from positions high on fortified cliffs, and the shores were covered with nearly impenetrable barbed wire. During the disastrous landing, a British officer recalled, "the sea behind was absolutely crimson, and you could hear the groans through the rattle of musketry." The battle became entrenched on the beaches at Gallipoli, and the casualties mounted for seven months before the Allied commanders admitted defeat and ordered a withdrawal in December. The Gallipoli campaign—the first large-scale amphibious attack in history—brought death into London's neighborhoods and the cities of Britain's industrial north. Casualties were particularly devastating in the "white dominions"—practically every town and hamlet in Australia, New Zealand, and Canada lost young men, sometimes all the sons of a single family. The defeat cost the Allies 200,000 soldiers and did little to shift the war's focus away from the deadlocked Western Front.

By 1915, both sides realized that fighting this prolonged and costly "modern" war would require countries to mobilize all of their resources. As one captain put it in a letter home, "It is absolutely certainly a war of 'attrition,' as somebody said here the other day, and we have got to stick it out longer than the other side and go on producing men, money, and material until they cry quits, and that's about it, as far as I can see."

The Allies started to wage war on the economic front. Germany was vulnerable, dependent as it was on imports for at least one-third of its food supply. The Allies' naval blockade against all of central Europe aimed to slowly drain their opponents of food and raw materials. Germany responded with a submarine blockade, threatening to attack any vessel in the seas around Great Britain. On May 7, 1915, the German submarine *U-20*, without warning, torpedoed the passenger liner *Lusitania*, which was secretly carrying war supplies. The attack killed 1,198 people, including 128 Americans. The attack provoked the animosity of the United States, and Germany was forced to promise that it would no longer fire without warning. (This promise proved only temporary: in 1917, Germany

Interpreting Visual Evidence

War Propaganda

Poster art was a leading form of propaganda used by all belligerents in the First World War to enlist men, sell war bonds, and sustain morale on the home front. Posters also demonized the enemy and glorified the sacrifices of soldiers to better rationalize the unprecedented loss of life and national wealth. The posters shown here, from a wide range of combatant nations during the war, share a common desire to link the war effort to a set of assumptions about the different roles assigned to men and women in the national struggle.

A. British Poster: "Women of Britain say 'Go!'"

B. Russian Poster: "Women Workers! Take up the Rifle!"

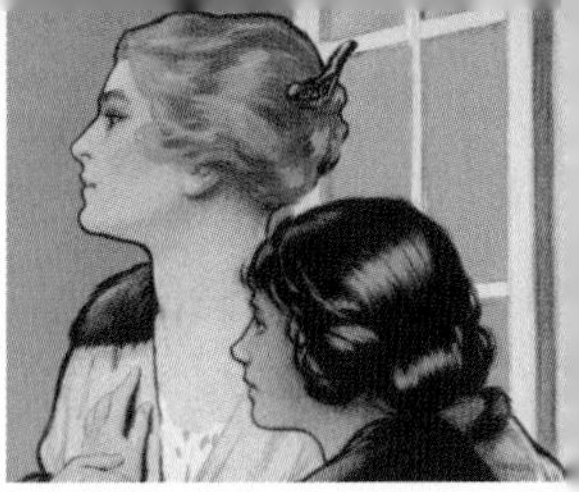

Questions for Analysis

1. Why would nationalists resort to such gendered images in a time of crisis?
2. What do these images tell us about the way that feelings of national belonging are created and sustained in times of urgency?
3. How might the changes that the war brought about—an increase in the number of women working in industry or outside the home, increased autonomy for women in regard to their wages or management of their household affairs—have affected the way that individuals responded to such images?

C. German Poster: "Collect women's hair that has been combed out. Our industry needs it for drive belts."

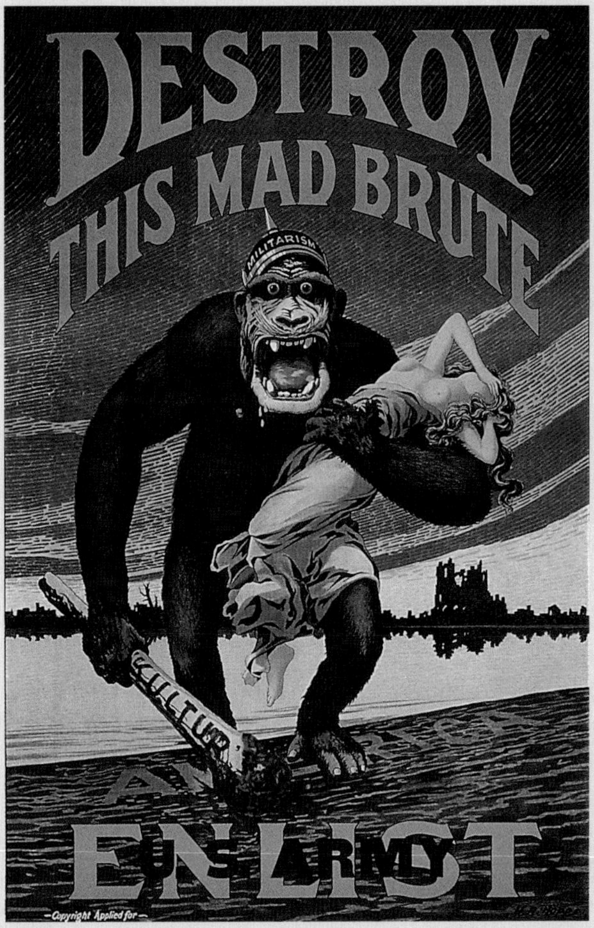

D. American Poster: "Destroy This Mad Brute. Enlist." The mad beast, meant to represent Germany, with *militarism* on his helmet, threatens American civilization with a club of *Kultur* (culture).

THE NEW TECHNOLOGIES OF WAR IN THE AIR AND AT SEA. The use of airplanes and submarines, both produced in large numbers during World War I, changed the nature of warfare. Air war helped dissolve the boundaries between the front line and the home front as civilian populations were brought within range of the enemy's destructive power. Germany's decision to use submarines against merchant ships trading with Britain and France led to the sinking of the *Lusitania* in 1915, which turned public opinion in the United States. The same issue led President Wilson to commit U.S. troops to the Allied side in 1917. The image on the left shows the German submarine base in Kiel, on the Baltic coast. On the right is a German plane attacking an English tank.

would again declare unrestricted submarine warfare, drawing America into the war.) Although the German blockade against Britain destroyed more tonnage, the blockade against Germany was more devastating in the long run, as the continued war effort placed increasing demands on the national economy.

Trench Warfare

While the war escalated economically and politically, life in the trenches—the "lousy scratch holes," as a soldier called them—remained largely the same: a cramped and miserable existence of daily routines and continual killing. Indeed, some 25,000 miles of trenches snaked along the Western Front, normally in three lines on each side of "No Man's Land." The front line was the attack trench, lying anywhere from fifty yards to a mile away from the enemy. Behind the front lay a maze of connecting trenches and lines, leading to a complex of ammunition dumps, telephone exchanges, water points, field hospitals, and command posts. These logistical centers were supposed to allow an army to project its power forward, but just as often, they acted as a tether, making it difficult to advance.

The common assertion that railroads, the central symbol of an industrial age, made war more mobile, is misleading. Trains might take men to the front, but mobility ended there. Machine guns and barbed wire gave well-supplied and entrenched defenders an enormous advantage even against a larger attacking force, but logistics stymied generals' efforts to regain a war of movement.

The British and French trenches were wet, cold, and filthy. Rain turned the dusty corridors into squalid mud pits and flooded the floors up to waist level. "Hell is not fire," was the grim observation of a French soldiers' paper. "The real hell is the mud." Soldiers lived with lice and large black rats, which fed on the dead soldiers and horses that cast their stench over everything. Cadavers could go unburied for months and were often just embedded in the trench walls. It was little wonder that soldiers were rotated out of the front lines frequently—after only three to seven days—to be relieved from what one soldier called "this present, ever-present, eternally present misery, this stinking world of sticky, trickling earth ceilinged by a strip of threatening sky." Indeed, the threat of enemy fire was constant: 7,000 British men were killed or wounded daily. This "wastage," as it was called, was part of the routine, along with the inspections, rotations, and mundane duties of life on the Western Front. Despite this danger, the trenches were a relatively reliable means of protection, especially compared to the casualty rates of going on the offensive.

As the war progressed, new weapons added to the frightening dimensions of daily warfare. Besides artillery, machine guns, and barbed wire, the instruments of war now included exploding bullets, liquid fire, and poison gas. Gas, in particular, brought visible change to the battlefront. First used effectively by the Germans in April 1915 at the second battle of Ypres, poison gas was not only physically devastating—especially in its later forms—but also

POISON GAS. Poison gases (mustard gas, chlorine gas, and phosgene were the most commonly used) caused thousands of casualties in World War I and were greatly feared by the troops. Such weapons led to offensive breakthroughs when first used, but gas was difficult to control and did not change the balance of forces in the war. Both sides developed gas masks to protect their troops. The environmental damage was severe—concentrations of gas residue were intense enough to cause injury to farmers decades after the war ended, and unexploded gas shells are still occasionally found in former battlefields.

psychologically disturbing. The deadly cloud frequently hung over the trenches, although the quick appearance of gas masks limited its effectiveness. Like other new weapons, poison gas solidified the lines and took more lives but could not end the stalemate. The war dragged through its second year, bloody and stagnant. Soldiers grew accustomed to the stalemate, while their leaders plotted ways to end it.

SLAUGHTER IN THE TRENCHES: THE GREAT BATTLES, 1916–17

The bloodiest battles of all—those that epitomize the First World War—occurred in 1916–17, when first the Germans and later the British and French launched major offensives in attempts to end the stalemate. Massive campaigns in the war of attrition, these assaults produced hundreds of thousands of casualties and only minor territorial gains. These battles encapsulated the military tragedy of the war: a strategy of soldiers in cloth uniforms marching against machine guns. The result, of course, was carnage. The common response to these staggering losses was to replace the generals in charge. But though commanders changed, commands did not. Military planners continued to believe that their original strategies were the right ones and that their plans had simply been frustrated by bad luck and German determination. The "cult of the offensive" insisted that a breakthrough was possible with enough troops and enough weapons.

But the manpower needed could not be moved efficiently or protected adequately. Unprotected soldiers armed with rifles, grenades, and bayonets were simply no match for machine guns and deep trenches. Another major problem of military strategy—and another explanation for the continued slaughter—was the lack of effective communication between the front lines and general headquarters. If something went wrong at the front (which happened frequently) it was impossible for the leaders to know in time to make meaningful corrections. As the battles of the Great War illustrate, firepower had outpaced mobility, and the Allied generals simply did not know how to respond.

Verdun

The first of these major battles began with a German attack on the French stronghold of Verdun, near France's eastern border, in February 1916. Verdun had little strategic importance, but it quickly became a symbol of France's strength and was defended at all costs. Germany's goal was not necessarily to take the city but rather to break French morale—France's "remarkable devotion"—at a moment of critical weakness. As the German general Erich von Falkenhayn (1914–16) said, the offensive would "compel the French to throw in every man they have. If they do so the forces of France will bleed to death." One million shells were fired on the first day of battle, inaugurating a ten-month struggle of back-and-forth fighting offensives and counteroffensives of intense ferocity at enormous cost and zero gain. Led by General Henri Pétain (1914–18), the French pounded the Germans with artillery and received heavy bombardment in return. The Germans relied on large teams of horses, 7,000 of which were killed in a single day, to drag their guns through the muddy, cratered terrain. The French moved supplies and troops into Verdun continually. Approximately 12,000 delivery trucks were employed for service. So were 259 out of the 330 regiments of the French army. Neither side could gain a real advantage—one small village on the front changed hands thirteen times in one month alone—but both sides incurred devastating losses of life. By the end of June, over 400,000 French and German soldiers were dead. "Verdun," writes one historian, "had become a place of terror and death that could not yield victory." In the end, the advantage fell to the French, who survived and who bled the Germans as badly as they suffered themselves.

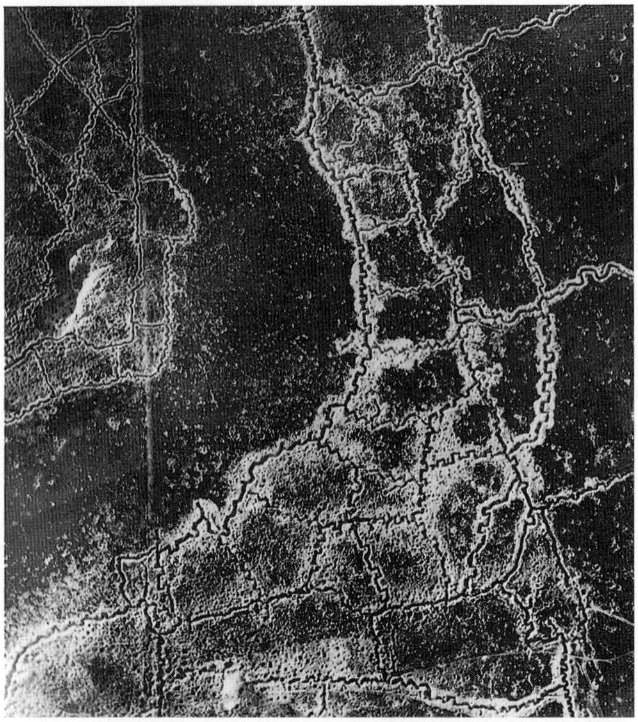

THE LINES OF BATTLE ON THE WESTERN FRONT. A British reconnaissance photo showing three lines of German trenches (right), No Man's Land (the black strip in the center), and the British trenches (partially visible to the left). The upper right-hand quadrant of the photo shows communications trenches linking the front to the safe area. ▪ ***What technologies gave these defenses such decisive advantages?***

The Somme

Meanwhile, the British opened their own offensive against Germany farther west, beginning the battle of the Somme on June 24, 1916. The Allied attack began with a fierce bombardment, blasting the German lines with 1,400 guns. The blasts could be heard all the way across the English Channel. The British assumed that this preliminary attack would break the mesh of German wire, destroy Germany's trenches, and clear the way for Allied troops to advance forward. They were tragically wrong. The shells the British used were designed for surface combat, not to penetrate the deep, reinforced trenches dug by the Germans. The wire and trenches withstood the bombardment. When the British soldiers were ordered over the top toward enemy lines, they found themselves snared in wire and facing fully operational German machine guns. Each man carried sixty pounds of supplies that were to be used during the expected fighting in the German trenches. A few British commanders who had disobeyed orders and brought their men forward before the shelling ended were able to break through German lines. Elsewhere it was hardly a battle; whole British divisions were simply mowed down. Those who made it to the enemy trenches faced bitter hand-to-hand combat with pistols, grenades, knives, bayonets, and bare hands. On the first day of battle alone, a stunning 21,000 British soldiers died, and another 30,000 were wounded. The carnage continued from July until mid-November, resulting in massive casualties on both sides: 500,000 German, 400,000 British, and 200,000 French. The losses were unimaginable, and the outcome was equally hard to fathom: for all their sacrifices, neither side made any real gains. The first lesson of the Somme was offered later, by a war veteran: "Neither side had won, nor could win, the War. The War had won, and would go on winning." The futility of offensive war was not lost on the soldiers, yet morale remained surprisingly strong. Although mutinies and desertions occurred on both sides, they were rare before 1917; and surrenders became an important factor only in the final months of the war.

With willing armies and fresh recruits, military commanders maintained their strategy and pushed for victories on the Western Front again in 1917. The French general Robert Nivelle (1914–17) promised to break through the German lines with overwhelming manpower, but the "Nivelle Offensive" (April–May 1917) failed immediately, with first-day casualties like those at the Somme. The British also reprised the Somme at the third battle of Ypres (July–October 1917), in which a half-million casualties earned Great Britain only insignificant gains—and no breakthrough. The one weapon with the potential to break the stalemate, the tank, was finally introduced into

YPRES. Entrenched in craters, the Sixteenth Canadian Machine Gun Company endures the mud after the third battle of Ypres, usually called the Battle of Passchendaele (July–November 1917). ("Passiondale" in the British pronunciation.) Ypres, along the Yperlee River near the Belgian coast, was the object of three major battles during the war. The third, an Allied offensive, aimed to attack German submarine bases and to strengthen the Allied position if Russia withdrew from the war.

battle in 1916, but with such reluctance by tradition-bound commanders that its halfhearted employment made almost no difference. Other innovations were equally indecisive. Airplanes were used almost exclusively for reconnaissance, though occasional "dogfights" did occur between German and Allied pilots. And though the Germans sent zeppelins to raid London, they did little significant damage.

Off the Western Front, fighting produced further stalemate. The Austrians continued to fend off attacks in Italy and Macedonia, while the Russians mounted a successful offensive against them on the Eastern Front. The initial Russian success brought Romania into the war on Russia's side, but the Central Powers quickly retaliated and knocked the Romanians out of the war within a few months.

The war at sea was equally indecisive, with neither side willing to risk the loss of enormously expensive battleships. The British and German navies fought only one major naval battle early in 1916, which ended in stalemate. Afterward, they used their fleets primarily in the economic war of blockades.

As a year of great bloodshed and growing disillusionment, 1916 showed that not even the superbly organized Germans had the mobility or fast-paced communications to win the western ground war. Increasingly, warfare would be turned against entire nations, including civilian populations on the home front and in the far reaches of the European empires.

WAR OF EMPIRES

Coming as it did at the height of European imperialism, the Great War quickly became a war of empires, with far-reaching repercussions. As the demands of warfare rose, Europe's colonies provided soldiers and material support. Britain, in particular, benefited from its vast network of colonial dominions and dependencies, bringing in soldiers from Canada, Australia, New Zealand, India, and South Africa. Nearly 1.5 million Indian troops served as British forces, some on the Western Front and many more in the Middle East, fighting in Mesopotamia and Persia against the Turks. The French Empire, especially North and West Africa, sent 607,000 soldiers to fight with the Allies; 31,000 of them died in Europe. Colonial recruits were also employed in industry. In France, where even some French conscripts were put to work in factories, the international labor force numbered over 250,000, including workers from China, Vietnam, Egypt, India, the West Indies, and South Africa.

As the war stalled in Europe, colonial areas also became strategically important theaters for armed engagement. Although the campaign against Turkey began poorly for Britain with the debacle at Gallipoli, beginning in 1916 Allied forces won a series of battles, pushing the Turks out of Egypt and eventually capturing Baghdad, Jerusalem, Beirut, and other cities throughout the Middle East. The British commander in Egypt and Palestine was Edmund Allenby (1919–25), who led a multinational army against the Turks. In his campaigns, the support of different Arab peoples seeking independence from the Turks proved crucial. Allenby allied himself to the successful Bedouin (nomadic peoples speaking Arabic) revolts that split the Ottoman Empire; the British officer T. E. Lawrence (1914–18) popularized the Arabs' guerrilla actions. When one of the senior Bedouin aristocrats, the emir Abdullah, captured the strategic port of Aqaba in July 1917, Lawrence took credit and entered popular mythology as "Lawrence of Arabia."

Britain encouraged Arab nationalism for its own strategic purposes, offering a qualified acknowledgment of Arab political aspirations. At the same time, for similar but conflicting strategic reasons, the British declared their support of "the establishment in Palestine of a national home for the Jewish people." Britain's foreign secretary, Arthur Balfour,

A. THE GREAT WAR, 1914–1916. ▪ *What were the farthest points of German expansion on both fronts?* ▪ *Why did the British blockade have a large impact on the war?* ▪ *Why did the war become stalemated?*

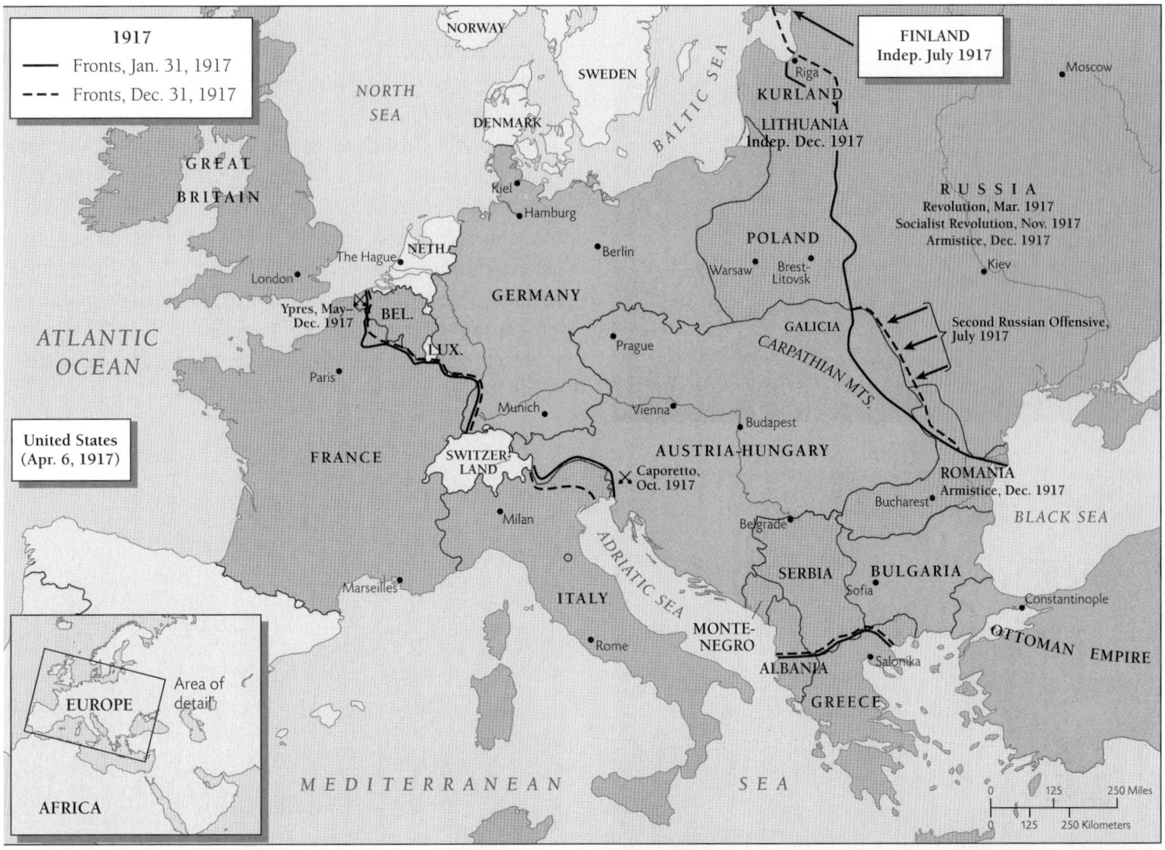

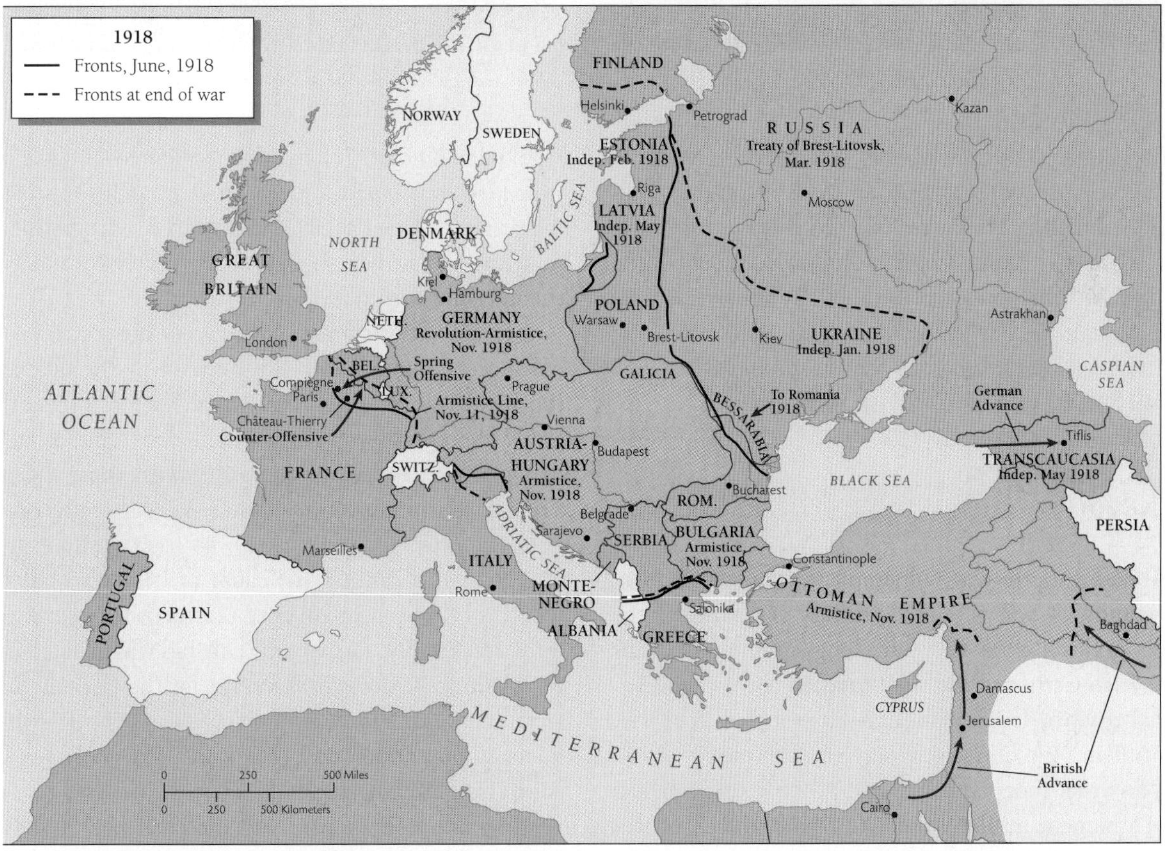

B. THE GREAT WAR, 1917–1918. ▪ *What were the key events of 1917, and how did they change the course of the war?* ▪ *Consider the map of 1918. Why might many German people have believed they nearly won the war?* ▪ *Why were developments in the Middle East significant in the war's aftermath?*

A GLOBAL WAR. The effects of World War 1 were immediately felt in other parts of the world. Japan entered the war in August 1914 on the side of France, Russia, and Britain in order to secure German territory in the Pacific and extend its influence over China. Turkey joined Germany and Austria-Hungary's alliance during the same month. Meanwhile, all the European colonial powers recruited laborers and soldiers from their imperial territories. In the image to the left, Japanese troops land in China at Tsingtao in 1915. In the image at bottom left, an Islamic cleric reads the proclamation of war before a mosque in the Turkish capital of Constantinople in 1914. In the image at bottom right, colonial troops in German East Africa march during World War 1.

made the pledge. European Zionists, who were seeking a Jewish homeland, took the Balfour Declaration very seriously. The conflicting pledges to Bedouin leaders and Zionists sowed the seeds of the future Arab-Israeli conflict. First the war and then the promise of oil drew Europe more deeply into the Middle East, where conflicting dependencies and commitments created numerous postwar problems.

Irish Revolt

The Ottoman Empire was vulnerable; so was the British. The demands of war strained precarious bonds to the breaking point. Before the war, long-standing tensions between Irish Catholics and the Protestant British government had reached fever pitch, and some feared civil war. The Sinn Féin (We Ourselves) party had formed in 1900 to fight for Irish independence, and a home rule bill had passed Parliament in 1912. But with the outbreak of war in 1914, national interests took precedence over domestic politics: the "Irish question" was tabled, and 200,000 Irishmen volunteered for the British army. The problem festered, however, and on Easter Sunday 1916 a group of nationalists revolted in Dublin. The insurgents' plan to smuggle in arms from Germany failed, and they had few delusions of achieving victory. The British army arrived with artillery and machine guns; they shelled parts of Dublin and crushed the uprising within a week.

The revolt was a military disaster but a striking political success. Britain shocked the Irish public by executing the rebel leaders. Even the British prime minister David Lloyd George (1916–22) thought the military governor in Dublin exceeded his authority with these executions. The martyrdom of the "Easter Rebels" seriously damaged Britain's relationship with its Irish Catholic subjects. The deaths galvanized the cause of Irish nationalism and touched off guerrilla violence that kept Ireland in turmoil for years. Finally, a new home rule bill was enacted in 1920, establishing separate parliaments for the Catholic south of Ireland and for Ulster, the northeastern counties where the majority population was Protestant. The leaders of the so-called Dáil Éireann (Irish Assembly), which had proclaimed an Irish Republic in 1918 and therefore been outlawed by Britain, rejected the bill but accepted a treaty that granted dominion status to Catholic Ireland in 1921. Dominion was followed almost immediately by civil war between those who abided by the treaty and those who wanted to

BRITISH REPRESSION OF EASTER REBELLION, DUBLIN, 1916. British troops line up behind a moveable barricade made up of household furniture during their repression of the Irish revolt. The military action did not prevent further conflict.

absorb Ulster, but the conflict ended in an uneasy compromise. The Irish Free State was established, and British sovereignty was partially abolished in 1937. Full status as a republic came, with some American pressure and Britain's exhausted indifference, in 1945.

THE HOME FRONT

When the war of attrition began in 1915, the belligerent governments were unprepared for the strains of sustained warfare. The costs of war—in both money and manpower—were staggering. In 1914, the war cost Germany 36 million marks per day (five times the cost of the war of 1870), and by 1918 the cost had skyrocketed to 146 million marks per day. Great Britain had estimated it would need 100,000 soldiers but ended up mobilizing 3 million. The enormous task of feeding, clothing, and equipping the army became as much of a challenge as breaking through enemy lines; civilian populations were increasingly asked—or forced—to support these efforts. Bureaucrats and industrialists led the effort to mobilize the home front, focusing all parts of society on the single goal of military victory. The term *total war* was introduced to describe this intense mobilization of society. Government propagandists insisted that civilians were as important to the war effort as soldiers, and in many ways they were. As workers, taxpayers, and consumers, civilians were vital parts of the war economy. They produced munitions; purchased war bonds; and shouldered the burden of tax hikes, inflation, and material privations.

The demands of industrial warfare led first to a transition from general industrial manufacturing to munitions production and then to increased state control of all aspects of production and distribution. The governments of Britain and France managed to direct the economy without serious detriment to the standard of living in their countries. Germany, meanwhile, put its economy in the hands of army and industry; under the Hindenburg Plan, named for Paul von Hindenburg (1916–19), the chief of the imperial staff of the German army, pricing and profit margins were set by individual industrialists.

Largely because of the immediate postwar collapse of the German economy, historians have characterized Germany's wartime economy as a chaotic, ultimately disastrous system governed by personal interest. New research, however, suggests that this was not the case: Germany's systems of war finance and commodity distribution, however flawed, were not decisively worse than those of Britain or France.

Women in the War

As Europe's adult men left farms and factories to become soldiers, the composition of the workforce changed: thousands of women were recruited into fields that had previously excluded them. Young people, foreigners, and unskilled workers were also pressed into newly important tasks; in the case of colonial workers, their experiences had equally critical repercussions. But because they were more visible, it was women who became symbolic of many of the changes brought by the Great War. In Germany, one-third of the labor force in heavy industry was female by the end of the war, and in France 684,000 women worked in the munitions industry alone. In England, the "munitionettes," as they were dubbed, numbered nearly 1 million. Women also entered the clerical and service sectors. In the villages of France, England, and Germany, women became mayors, school principals, and mail carriers. Hundreds of thousands of women worked with the army as nurses and ambulance drivers, jobs that brought them very close to the front lines. With minimal supplies and under squalid conditions, they worked to save lives or patch bodies together.

In some cases, war offered new opportunities. Middle-class women often said that the war broke down the restrictions on their lives; those in nursing learned to drive and acquired rudimentary medical knowledge. At home, they could now ride the train, walk the street, or go out to dinner without an older woman present to chaperone them. In terms of gender roles, an enormous gulf sometimes seemed to separate the wartime world from nineteenth-century Victorian society. In one of the most famous autobiographies of the war, *Testament of Youth,* author Vera Brittain (1896–1970) recorded the dramatic new social norms that she and others forged during the rapid changes of wartime. "As a generation of women we were now sophisticated to an extent which was revolutionary when compared with the romantic ignorance of 1914. Where we had once spoken with polite evasion of 'a certain condition,' or 'a certain profession,' we now unblushingly used the words 'pregnancy' and 'prostitution.'" For every Vera Brittain who celebrated the changes, however, journalists, novelists, and other observers grumbled that women were now smoking, refusing to wear the corsets that gave Victorian dresses their hourglass shape, or cutting their hair into the new fashionable bobs. The "new woman" became a symbol of profound and disconcerting cultural transformation.

How long lasting were these changes? In the aftermath of the war, governments and employers scurried to send women workers home, in part to give jobs to veterans, in part to deal with male workers' complaints that women were undercutting their wages. Efforts to demobilize women faced real barriers. Many women wage earners—widowed, charged with caring for relatives, or faced with inflation and soaring costs—needed their earnings more than ever. It was also difficult to persuade women workers who had grown accustomed to the relatively higher wages in heavy industry to return to their poorly paid traditional sectors of employment: the textile and garment industries and domestic service. The demobilization of women after the war, in other words, created as many dilemmas as had their mobilization. Governments passed "natalist" policies to encourage women to go home, marry, and—most important—have children. These policies did make maternity benefits—time off, medical care, and some allowances for the poor—available to women for the first time. Nonetheless, birth rates had been falling across Europe by the early twentieth century, and they continued to do so after the war. One upshot of the war was the increased availability of birth control—Marie Stopes (1880–1958) opened a birth-control clinic in London in 1921—and a combination of economic hardship, increased knowledge, and the demand for freedom made men and women more likely to use it. Universal suffrage, and the vote for all adult men and women, and for women in particular, had been one of the most controversial issues in European politics before the war. At the end of the fighting it came in a legislative rush. Britain was first off the mark, granting the vote to all men and women over thirty with the Representation of the People Act in 1918; the United States gave women the vote with the Nineteenth Amendment the following year. Germany's new republic and the Soviet Union did likewise. France was much slower to offer woman suffrage (1945) but did provide rewards and incentives for the national effort.

Mobilizing Resources

Along with mobilizing the labor front, the wartime governments had to mobilize men and money. All the belligerent countries had conscription laws before the war, except for Great Britain. Military service was seen as a duty,

WOMEN AT WORK. The all-out war effort combined with a manpower shortage at home brought women into factories across Europe in unparalleled numbers. Men and women work side by side in a British shell factory (left); German women assemble military equipment (right). ▪ ***How might the participation of women in the industrial workforce have changed attitudes toward women's labor?*** ▪ ***What tensions might this have created within families or between male and female workers?***

not an option. Bolstered by widespread public support for the war, this belief brought millions of young Europeans into recruitment offices in 1914. The French began the war with about 4.5 million trained soldiers, but by the end of 1914—just four months into the war—300,000 were dead and 600,000 injured. Conscripting citizens and mustering colonial troops became increasingly important. Eventually, France called up 8 million citizens: almost two-thirds of Frenchmen aged eighteen to forty. In 1916, the British finally introduced conscription, dealing a serious blow to civilian morale; by the summer of 1918, half its army was under the age of nineteen.

Government propaganda, while part of a larger effort to sustain both soldier and civilian morale, was also important to the recruitment effort. From the outset, the war had been sold to the people on both sides of the conflict as a moral and righteous crusade. In 1914, the French president Raymond Poincaré (1913–20) assured his fellow citizens that France had no other purpose than to stand "before the universe for Liberty, Justice and Reason." Germans were presented with the task of defending their superior *Kultur* (culture) against the wicked encirclement policy of the Allied nations: "May God punish England!" was practically a greeting in 1914. By the middle of the war, massive propaganda campaigns were under way. Film, posters, postcards, newspapers—all forms of media proclaimed the strength of the cause, the evil of the enemy, and the absolute necessity of total victory. The success of these campaigns is difficult to determine, but it is clear that they had at least one painful effect—they made it more difficult for any country to accept a fair, nonpunitive peace settlement.

Financing the war was another heavy obstacle. Military spending accounted for 3 to 5 percent of government expenditure in the combatant countries before 1914 but soared to perhaps half of each nation's budget during the war. Governments had to borrow money or print more of it. The Allied nations borrowed heavily from the British, who borrowed even more from the United States. American capital flowed across the Atlantic long before the United States entered the war. And though economic aid from the United States was a decisive factor in the Allies' victory, it left Britain with a $4.2 billion debt and hobbled the United Kingdom as a financial power after the war. The situation was far worse for Germany, which faced a total blockade of money and goods. In an effort to get around this predicament, and lacking an outside source of cash, the German government funded its war effort largely by increasing the money supply. The amount of paper money in circulation increased by over 1,000 percent during the war, triggering a dramatic rise in inflation. During the war, prices in Germany rose about

Analyzing Primary Sources

Woman's Work in Wartime

Although women in Europe had worked in some industries—such as textiles—long before World War I, the mobilization of women during the war years brought an unprecedented number of them into the industrial workforce. Inevitably, such profound changes in conceptions of gender and work generated controversy. These two documents provide a window into this debate both from the point of view of the highest government authorities and from women who took advantage of the new opportunities available to them in war work. The first document is a letter from the German chief of the General Staff, General Paul von Hindenburg to Chancellor Bethmann Hollweg, written in October 1916. The second is the testimony taken in 1918 from Helen Ross, an African American woman who had worked in domestic service before taking a wartime job in Topeka, Kansas.

General Paul von Hindenburg to Chancellor Bethmann Hollweg, October 1916

It is also my opinion that women's work should not be overestimated. Almost all intellectual work, heavy physical labour, as well as all real manufacturing work will still fall on men—in addition to the entire waging of the war. It would be good if clear, official expression were given to these facts and if a stop were put to women's agitation for parity in all professions, and thereby, of course, for political emancipation. I completely agree with your Excellency that compulsory labour for women would be an inappropriate measure. After the war, we will need the woman as spouse and mother....

If I *nevertheless* urge that the requirement to work be extended to all women who are either unemployed or working in trivial positions, now and for the duration of the war, I do so because, in my opinion, women can be employed in many areas to a still greater degree than previously and men can thereby be freed for other *work*. But first industry and agriculture must be urged even more to employ women. Further, the choice of occupation must not be left up to the women alone, but rather, it must [be] regulated according to ability, previous experience and social status. In particular, I want to stress again that I consider it especially wrong to keep secondary schools and universities, which have been almost completely emptied of men by conscription, open only for women. It is valueless, because the scholarly gain is minimal; furthermore, because precisely that rivalry with the family that needs to be combated would be promoted; and *finally*, because it would represent the coarsest injustice if the young man, who is giving everything for his Fatherland, is forced behind the woman.

Source: Letter of Chief of the General Staff General Paul von Hindenburg to Chancellor Bethmann Hollweg, October 1916. Quoted in Ute Daniel, *The War from Within: German Working-Class Women in the First World War*, trans. Margaret Ries (Oxford: 1997), pp. 68–69, emphasis in the original.

400 percent, double the inflation in Britain and France. For middle-class people living on pensions or fixed incomes, these price hikes were a push into poverty.

The Strains of War, 1917

The demands of total war worsened as the conflict dragged into 1917. On the front lines, morale fell as war-weary soldiers began to see the futility of their commanders' strategies. After the debacle of the Nivelle Offensive, the French army recorded acts of mutiny in two-thirds of its divisions; similar resistance arose in nearly all major armies in 1917. Military leaders portrayed the mutineers as part of a dangerous pacifist movement, but most were nonpolitical. As one soldier put it: "All we wanted was to call the government's attention to us, make it see that we are men, and not beasts for the slaughterhouse." Resistance within the German army was never organized or widespread but existed in subtler forms. Self-mutilation rescued some soldiers

Helen Ross, Employee of the Santa Fe Railroad, Topeka, Kansas, October 1918

All the colored women like this work and want to keep it. We are making more money at this than any work we can get, and we do not have to work as hard as at housework which requires us to be on duty from six o'clock in the morning until nine or ten at night, with might little time off and at very poor wages. . . . What the colored women need is an opportunity to make money. As it is, they have to take what employment they can get, live in old tumbled down houses or resort to street walking, and I think a woman ought to think more of her blood than to do that. What occupation is open to us where we can make really good wages? We are not employed as clerks, we cannot all be school teachers, and so we cannot see any use in working our parents to death to get educated. Of course we should like easier work than this if it were opened to us. With three dollars a day, we can buy bonds . . . , we can dress decently, and not be tempted to find our living on the streets.

Source: Helen Ross, Freight House, Santa Fe RR, Topeka, Kansas, 28 October 1918, File 55, Women's Service Section, Record Group 14 [Records of the United States Railroad Administration], National Archives, Washington, D.C. Also quoted in M. W. Greenwald, *Women, War and Work: The Impact of World War I on Women Workers in the United States* (Ithaca, NY: 1980, reprinted, 1990), p. 27.

Questions for Analysis

1. What reservations does Hindenburg express about demands made by women for political emancipation, and how does he connect this to the question of women's wartime employment? Why does he nevertheless support women's wartime labor in Germany?
2. How did Helen Ross perceive the opportunity to earn wages in her railroad job compared to her previous work as a domestic servant? How had her life changed?
3. What long-lasting effects might the experience of wartime labor have had for women who worked in such jobs?

from the horror of the trenches; many more were released because of various emotional disorders. Over 6,000 cases of "war neuroses" were reported among German troops—an indication, if not of intentional disobedience, then of the severe physical and psychological trauma that caused the mutinies.

The war's toll also mounted for civilians, who often suffered from the same shortages of basic supplies that afflicted the men at the front. In 1916–17, the lack of clothing, food, and fuel was aggravated in central Europe by abnormally cold, wet weather. These strains provoked rising discontent on the home front. Although governments attempted to solve the problem with tighter controls on the economy, their policies often provoked further hostilities from civilians. "The population has lost all confidence in promises from the authorities," a German official reported in 1917, "particularly in view of earlier experiences with promises made in the administration of food."

In urban areas, where undernourishment was worst, people stood in lines for hours to get food and fuel rations that scarcely met their most basic needs. The price of bread and potatoes—still the central staples of working-class meals—soared. Prices were even higher in the thriving black market that emerged in cities. Consumers worried aloud that speculators were hoarding supplies and creating artificial shortages, selling tainted goods, and profiting from others' miseries. They decried the government's "reckless inattention" to families. Governments, however, were concentrated on the war effort and faced difficult decisions about who needed supplies the most—soldiers at the front, workers in the munitions industry, or hungry and cold families.

Like other nations, Germany moved from encouraging citizens to restrain themselves—"those who stuff themselves full, those who push out their paunches in all directions, are traitors to the Fatherland"—to direct control, issuing ration cards in 1915. Britain was the last to institute control, rationing bread only in 1917 when Germany's submarines sank an average of 630,000 tons per month and brought British food reserves within two

DESPERATION ON THE GERMAN HOME FRONT, 1918. A German photograph of women digging through garbage in search of food. The last year of the war brought starvation to cities in Germany and Austria-Hungary, sending many people into the countryside to forage for provisions. Such foraging was often illegal, a violation of rationing rules. ▪ ***How might the need to break the law in this way have affected support for the war effort and the state?***

weeks of starvation level. But rations indicated only what was allowed, not what was available. Hunger continued despite mass bureaucratic control. Governments regulated not only food but also working hours and wages; and unhappy workers directed their anger at the state, adding a political dimension to labor disputes and household needs. The bread lines, filled mainly by women, were flash points of political dissent, petty violence, even large-scale riots. Likewise, the class conflicts of prewar Europe had been briefly muffled by the outbreak of war and mobilization along patriotic lines, but as the war ground on, political tensions reemerged with new intensity. Thousands of strikes erupted throughout Europe, involving millions of frustrated workers. In April 1917, 300,000 in Berlin went on strike to protest ration cuts. In May, a strike of Parisian seamstresses touched off a massive work stoppage that included even white-collar employees and munitions workers. Shipbuilders and steelworkers in Glasgow went on strike as well, and the British government replied by sending armored cars to "Red Glasgow." Stagnation had given way to crisis on both sides. The strains of total war and the resulting social upheavals threatened political regimes throughout Europe. Governments were pushed to their limits. The Russian Revolution, which resulted in the overthrow of the tsar and the rise of Bolshevism, was only the most dramatic response to widespread social problems.

THE RUSSIAN REVOLUTIONS OF 1917

The first country to break under the strain of total war was tsarist Russia. The outbreak of war temporarily united Russian society against a common enemy, but Russia's military effort quickly turned sour. All levels of Russian society became disillusioned with Tsar Nicholas II who was unable to provide leadership but was nonetheless unwilling to open government to those who could. The political and social strains of war brought two revolutions in 1917. The first, in February, overthrew the tsar and established a transitional government. The second, in October, was a communist revolution that marked the emergence of the Soviet Union.

The First World War and the February Revolution

Like the other participants in the First World War, Russia entered the war with the assumption that it would be over quickly. Autocratic Russia, plagued by internal difficulties before 1914 (see Chapter 23), could not sustain the political strains of extended warfare. In all the warring countries success depended on leaders' ability not only to command but also to maintain social and political cooperation. Tsar Nicholas II's political authority had been shaky for many years, undermined by his unpopular actions following the October Revolution of 1905 and his efforts to erode the minimal political power he had grudgingly granted to the Duma, Russia's parliament. Corruption in the royal court further tarnished the tsar's image. The best Nicholas's supporters could say about him was that he was morally upright and devoted to his family. Once war broke out, the tsar insisted on personally commanding Russian troops, leaving the government in the hands of his court,

GRIGORII RASPUTIN. Rasputin won the trust of the tsar's family by presenting himself as a faith healer and one who could help the tsar's son, Alexei, who suffered from hemophilia. The rising influence of the "holy man" heightened perceptions that the tsar was mired in the past and unable to lead Russia to the future.

especially his wife, Alexandra, and her eccentric spiritual mentor and faith healer, Grigorii Rasputin (1869–1916). Rasputin won the tsarina's sympathy by treating her hemophiliac son, and he used his influence to operate corrupt and self-aggrandizing schemes. His presence only added to the image of a court mired in decadence, incompetent to face the modern world.

In 1914 and 1915, Russia suffered terrible defeats. All of Poland and substantial territory in the Baltics fell to the Germans at the cost of a million Russian casualties. Although the Russian army was the largest in Europe, it was poorly trained and, at the beginning of the war, undersupplied and inadequately equipped. In the first battles of 1914, generals sent soldiers to the front without rifles or shoes, instructing them to scavenge supplies from fallen comrades. By 1915, to the surprise of many, Russia was producing enough food, clothing, and ammunition, but political problems blocked the supply effort. The tsarist government distrusted public initiatives and tried to direct all provisioning itself. Tsarist officials insisted on making crucial decisions about the allocation of supplies without any consultation. Another major offensive in the summer of 1916 brought hope for success but turned into a humiliating retreat. When word came that the government was requisitioning grain from the countryside to feed the cities, peasants began to desert en masse, returning to their farms to guard their families' holdings. By the end of 1916, a combination of political ineptitude and military defeat brought the Russian state to the verge of collapse.

The same problems that hampered the Russian war effort also crippled the tsar's ability to override domestic discontent and resistance. As the war dragged on, the government faced not only liberal opposition in the Duma, soldiers unwilling to fight, and an increasingly militant labor movement but also a rebellious urban population. City dwellers were impatient with inflation and shortages of food and fuel. In February 1917, these forces came together in Petrograd (now St. Petersburg). The revolt began on International Women's Day, February 23, an occasion for a loosely organized march of women—workers, mothers, wives, and consumers—demanding food, fuel, and political reform. The march was the latest in a wave of demonstrations and strikes that had swept through the country during the winter months. This time, within a few days the unrest spiraled into a mass strike of 300,000 people. Nicholas II sent in police and military forces to quell the disorder. When nearly 60,000 troops in Petrograd mutinied and joined the revolt, what was left of the tsar's power evaporated. Nicholas II abdicated the throne on March 2. This abrupt decision brought a century-long struggle over Russian autocracy to a sudden end.

After the collapse of the monarchy, two parallel centers of power emerged. Each had its own objectives and policies. The first was the provisional government, organized by leaders in the Duma and composed mainly of middle-class liberals. The new government hoped to establish a democratic system under constitutional rule. Its main task was to set up a national election for a constituent assembly, and it also acted to grant and secure civil liberties, release political prisoners, and redirect power into the hands of local officials. The other center of power lay with the *soviets,* a Russian term for local councils elected by workers and soldiers. Since 1905, socialists had been active in organizing these councils, which claimed to be the true democratic representatives of the people. A soviet, organized during the 1905 revolution and led by the well-known socialist Leon Trotsky, reemerged after February 1917 and asserted claim to be the legitimate political power in Russia. The increasingly powerful soviets pressed for social reform, the redistribution of land, and a negotiated settlement with Germany and Austria. Yet the provisional government refused to concede military defeat. Continuing the war effort made domestic reform impossible and cost valuable popular support. More fighting during 1917 was just as disastrous as before, and this time the provisional government paid the price. By autumn, desertion in the army was rampant, administering the country was nearly impossible, and Russian politics teetered on the edge of chaos.

The Bolsheviks and the October Revolution

The Bolsheviks, a branch of the Russian socialist movement, had little to do with the events of February 1917. Over the course of the next seven months, however, they became enough of a force to overthrow the provisional government. The chain of events leading to the October revolution surprised most contemporary observers, including the Bolsheviks themselves. Marxism had been quite weak in late-nineteenth-century Russia, although it made small but rapid inroads during the 1880s and 1890s. In 1903, the leadership of the Russian Social Democrats split over revolutionary strategy and the steps to socialism. One group, which won a temporary majority (and chose to call itself the Bolsheviks, or "members of the majority"), favored a centralized party of active revolutionaries. They believed that revolution alone would lead directly to a socialist regime. The Mensheviks (members of the minority), like most European socialists, wanted to move toward socialism gradually, supporting bourgeois or liberal revolution in the short term. Because peasants constituted 80 to 85 percent of the population, the Mensheviks also reasoned that a proletarian revolution was premature and that Russia needed to complete its capitalist development first. The Mensheviks regained control of the party, but the Bolshevik splinter party survived under the leadership of the young, dedicated revolutionary Vladimir Ilyich Ulyanov, who adopted the pseudonym Lenin.

Lenin was a member of the middle class; his father had been an inspector of schools and a minor political functionary. Lenin himself had been expelled from university for engaging in radical activity after his elder brother was executed for involvement in a plot to assassinate Tsar Alexander III. Lenin spent three years as a political prisoner in Siberia. After that, from 1900 until 1917, he lived and wrote as an exile in western Europe.

Lenin believed that the development of Russian capitalism made socialist revolution possible. To bring revolution, he argued, the Bolsheviks needed to organize on behalf of the new class of industrial workers. Without the party's disciplined leadership, Russia's factory workers could not accomplish change on the necessary scale. Lenin's Bolsheviks remained a minority among Social Democrats well into 1917 and industrial workers, a small part of the population. But the Bolsheviks' dedication to the singular goal of revolution and their tight, almost conspiratorial organization gave them tactical advantages over larger and more loosely organized opposition parties. The Bolsheviks merged a peculiarly Russian tradition of revolutionary zeal with Western Marxism, creating a party capable of seizing the moment when the tsar left the scene.

Throughout 1917, the Bolsheviks consistently demanded an end to the war, improvement in working and living conditions for workers, and redistribution of aristocratic land to the peasantry. While the provisional government struggled to hold together the Russian war effort, Lenin led the Bolsheviks on a bolder course, shunning any collaboration with the "bourgeois" government and condemning its imperialist war policies. Even most Bolsheviks considered Lenin's approach too radical. Yet as conditions in Russia deteriorated, his uncompromising calls for "Peace, Land, and Bread, Now" and "All Power to the Soviets" won the Bolsheviks support from workers, soldiers, and peasants. As many ordinary people saw it, the other parties could not govern, win the war, or achieve an honorable peace. While unemployment continued to climb and starvation and chaos reigned in the cities, the Bolsheviks' power and credibility were rising fast.

RUSSIAN REVOLUTION. Russian demonstrators scatter as tsarist troops shoot into the crowd during the February revolution, 1917.

Analyzing Primary Sources

Toward the October Revolution: Lenin to the Bolsheviks

In the fall of 1917, Lenin was virtually the only Bolshevik leader who believed that an insurrection should be launched immediately. As the provisional government faltered, he attempted to convince his fellow Bolsheviks that the time for revolution had arrived.

Having obtained a majority in the Soviets of Workers' and Soldiers' Deputies of both capitals, the Bolsheviks can and *must* take power into their hands.

They can do so because the active majority of the revolutionary elements of the people of both capitals is sufficient to attract the masses, to overcome the resistance of the adversary, to vanquish him, to conquer power and to retain it. For, in offering immediately a democratic peace, in giving the land immediately to the peasants, in re-establishing the democratic institutions and liberties which have been mangled and crushed by Kerensky [leader of the provisional government], the Bolsheviks will form a government which *nobody* will overthrow. . . .

The majority of the people is *with* us. . . . [T]he majority in the Soviets of the capitals is the *result* of the people's progress *to our side*. The vacillation of the Socialist-Revolutionaries and Mensheviks . . . is proof of the same thing . . .

To "wait" for the Constituent Assembly would be wrong. . . . Only our party, having assumed power, can secure the convocation of the Constituent Assembly, and, after assuming power, it could blame the other parties for delaying it and could substantiate its accusations. . . .

It would be naive to wait for a "formal" majority on the side of the Bolsheviks, no revolution ever waits for *this*. . . . History will not forgive us if we do not assume power now.

No apparatus? There is an apparatus: the Soviets and democratic organisations. The international situation *just now*, on the *eve* of a separate peace between the English and the Germans, is *in our favour*. It is precisely now that to offer peace to the peoples means to *win*.

Assume power *at once* in Moscow and in Petrograd . . . ; we will win *absolutely and unquestionably*.

Source: Vladimir Ilyich Lenin, *Bol'sheviki dolzhny vzyat'vlast'* (*The Bolsheviks Must Seize Power*), cited in Richard Sakwa, *The Rise and Fall of the Soviet Union, 1917–1991* (New York and London: 1999), p. 45.

Questions for Analysis

1. Lenin was surprised by the sudden collapse of the tsarist regime in the February revolution of 1917. Why did he think the Bolsheviks could seize power? What were the key elements of his strategy for winning the necessary popular support?
2. Convinced he was right, Lenin returned to Petrograd in disguise and personally presented his arguments for an armed takeover to the Bolshevik Central Committee. What did he mean by saying that "it would be naive to wait for a 'formal' majority on the side of the Bolsheviks, no revolution ever waits for *this*"?

In October 1917, Lenin convinced his party to act. He goaded Leon Trotsky, who was better known among workers, into organizing a Bolshevik attack on the provisional government on October 24–25, 1917. On October 25, Lenin appeared from hiding to announce to a stunned meeting of soviet representatives that "all power had passed to the Soviets." The head of the provisional government fled to rally support at the front lines, and the Bolsheviks took over the Winter Palace, the seat of the provisional government. The initial stage of the revolution was quick and relatively bloodless. In fact, many observers believed they had seen nothing more than a coup d'état, one that might quickly be reversed. Life in Petrograd went on as normal.

The Bolsheviks took the opportunity to rapidly consolidate their position. First, they moved against all political competition, beginning with the soviets. They immediately expelled parties that disagreed with their actions, creating a new government in the soviets composed entirely of Bolsheviks. Trotsky, sneering at moderate socialists who walked out to protest what they saw as an illegal seizure

VLADIMIR ILYICH LENIN. Lenin speaking in Moscow in 1918, at the first anniversary of the October revolution. A forceful speaker and personality, Lenin was the single most powerful politician in Russia between October 1917 and his death in 1924.

of power, scoffed: "You are a mere handful, miserable, bankrupt; your role is finished, and you may go where you belong—to the garbage heap of history." The Bolsheviks did follow through on the provisional government's promise to elect a Constituent Assembly. But when they did not win a majority in the elections, they refused to let the assembly reconvene. From that point on, Lenin's Bolsheviks ruled socialist Russia, and later the Soviet Union, as a one-party dictatorship.

In the countryside, the new Bolshevik regime did little more than ratify a revolution that had been going on since the summer of 1917. When peasant soldiers at the front heard that a revolution had occurred, they streamed home to take land they had worked for generations and believed was rightfully theirs. The provisional government had set up commissions to deal methodically with the legal issues surrounding the redistribution of land, a process that threatened to become as complex as the emancipation of the serfs in 1861. The Bolsheviks simply approved the spontaneous redistribution of the nobles' land to peasants without compensation to former owners. They nationalized banks and gave workers control of factories.

Most important, the new government sought to take Russia out of the war. It eventually negotiated a separate treaty with Germany, signed at Brest-Litovsk in March 1918. The Bolsheviks surrendered vast Russian territories: the rich agricultural region of Ukraine, Georgia, Finland, Russia's Polish territories, the Baltic states, and more. However humiliating, the treaty ended Russia's role in the fighting and saved the fledgling communist regime from almost certain military defeat at the hands of the Germans. The treaty enraged Lenin's political enemies, both moderates and reactionaries, who were still a force to be reckoned with—and who were prepared to wage a civil war rather than accept the revolution. Withdrawing from Europe's war only plunged the country into a vicious civil conflict (see Chapter 25).

Russian autocracy had fended off opposition for the better part of a century. After a long struggle, the regime, weakened by the war, had collapsed with little resistance. By the middle of 1917, Russia was not suffering a crisis of government but rather an absence of government. In June, at the First All-Russian Congress of Soviets, a prominent Menshevik declared, "At the present moment, there is not a political party in Russia that would say: Hand the power over to us, resign, and we will take your place. Such a party does not exist in Russia." Lenin shouted back from the audience, "It does exist!" Indeed, seizing power had been easy for the Bolsheviks, but building the new state proved vastly more difficult.

John Reed, an American journalist covering the Russian Revolution, called the events of October "ten days that shook the world." What had been shaken? First, the Allies, for the revolution allowed the Germans to win the war on the Eastern Front. Second, conservative governments, which in the aftermath of the war worried about a wave of revolution sweeping away other regimes. Third, the expectations of many socialists, startled to see a socialist regime gain and hold power in what many considered a backward country. Over the long run, 1917 was to the twentieth century what the French Revolution had been to the nineteenth century. It was a political transformation, it set the agenda for future revolutionary struggles, and it created the frames of mind on the right and the left for the century that followed.

THE ROAD TO GERMAN DEFEAT, 1918

Russia's withdrawal dealt an immediate strategic and psychological blow to the Allies. Germany could soothe domestic discontent by claiming victory on the Eastern Front, and it could now concentrate its entire army in the west. The Allies feared that Germany would win the war before the United States, which entered the conflict in April 1917, could make a difference. It almost happened. With striking results, Germany shifted its offensive strategy to infiltration by small groups under flexible command. On March 21, Germany initiated a major assault on the west and quickly broke through the Allied lines. The British were hit hardest. Some units, surrounded, fought to the death with bayonets and grenades, but most recognized their plight and surrendered, putting tens of thousands of prisoners in German hands. The British were in retreat everywhere and their commander, Sir Douglas Haig, issued a famous order warning that British troops "now fight with our backs to the wall." The Germans advanced to within fifty miles of Paris by early April. Yet the British—and especially troops from the overseas empire—did just as they were asked and stemmed the tide. As German forces turned southeast instead, the French, who had refused to participate in the foolish attacks over the top, showed stubborn courage on the defensive, where they bogged down in heat, mud, and casualties. It had been a last great try by the well-organized German army; exhausted, it now waited for the Allies to mount their own attack.

When it came in July and August, the Allied counterattack was devastating and quickly gathered steam. New offensive techniques had finally materialized. The Allies improved their use of tanks and the "creeping barrage," in which infantry marched close behind a rolling wall of shells to overwhelm their targets. In another of the war's ironies these new tactics were pioneered by the conservative British, who launched a crushing counterattack in July, relying on the survivors of the armies of the Somme reinforced by troops from Australia, Canada, and India. The French made use of American troops, whose generals attacked the Germans with the same harrowing indifference to casualties shown in 1914. Despite their lack of experience, the American troops were tough and resilient. When combined with more experienced French and Australian forces, they punched several large holes through German lines, crossing into the "lost provinces" of Alsace and Lorraine by October. At the beginning of November, the sweeping British offensive had joined up with the small Belgian army and was pressing toward Brussels.

The Allies finally brought their material advantage to bear on the Germans, who were suffering acutely by the spring of 1918. This was not only because of the continued effectiveness of the Allied blockade but also because of growing domestic conflict over war aims. On the front lines, German soldiers were exhausted. Following the lead of their distraught generals, the troops let morale sink, and many surrendered. Facing one shattering blow after another, the German army was pushed deep into Belgium. Popular discontent mounted, and the government, which was now largely in the hands of the military, seemed unable either to win the war or to meet basic household needs.

Germany's network of allies was also coming undone. By the end of September, the Central Powers were headed for defeat. In the Middle East, Allenby's army, which combined Bedouin guerrillas, Indian sepoys, Scottish highlanders, and Australian light cavalry, decisively defeated Ottoman forces in Syria and Iraq. In the Balkans, France's capable battlefield commander, Louis Franchet d'Espèrey (1914–21), transformed the Allied expedition in Greece and drew that country into the war. The results were remarkable. In September, a three-week offensive by the Greek and Allied forces knocked Bulgaria out of the war. Meanwhile Austria-Hungary faced disaster on all sides, collapsing in Italy as well as the Balkans. Czech and Polish representatives in the Austrian government began pressing for self-government. Croat and Serb politicians proposed a "kingdom of Southern Slavs" (soon known as Yugoslavia). When Hungary joined the chorus for independence the emperor, Karl I, accepted reality and sued for peace. The empire that had started the conflict surrendered on November 3, 1918, and disintegrated soon after.

Germany was now left with the impossible task of carrying on the struggle alone. By the fall of 1918, the country was starving and on the verge of civil war. A plan to use the German surface fleet to attack the combined British and American navies only produced a mutiny among German sailors at the start of November. Revolutionary tremors swelled into an earthquake. On November 8, a republic was proclaimed in Bavaria, and the next day nearly all of Germany was in the throes of revolution. The kaiser's abdication was announced in Berlin on November 9; he fled to

CASUALTY OF WAR. A German soldier killed during the Allies' October 1917 offensive.

Holland early the next morning. Control of the German government fell to a provisional council headed by Friedrich Ebert (1912–23), the socialist leader in the Reichstag. Ebert and his colleagues immediately took steps to negotiate an armistice. The Germans could do nothing but accept the Allies' terms, so at five o'clock in the morning of November 11, 1918, two German delegates met with the Allied army commander in the Compiègne Forest and signed papers officially ending the war. Six hours later the order for cease fire was given across the Western Front. That night, thousands of people danced through the streets of London, Paris, and Rome, engulfed in a different delirium from that four years before, a joyous burst of exhausted relief.

The United States as a World Power

The final turning point of the war had been the entry of the United States in April 1917. Although America had supported the Allies financially throughout the war, its official intervention undeniably tipped the scales. The United States created a fast and efficient wartime bureaucracy, instituting conscription in May 1917. About 10 million men were registered, and by the next year, 300,000 soldiers a month were being shipped "over there." Large amounts of food and supplies also crossed the Atlantic, under the armed protection of the U.S. Navy. This system of convoys effectively neutralized the threat of German submarines to Allied merchant ships: the number of ships sunk fell from 25 to 4 percent. America's entry—though not immediately decisive—gave a quick, colossal boost to British and French morale, while severely undermining Germany's.

The direct cause of America's entry into the war was the German U-boat. Germany had gambled that unrestricted submarine warfare would cripple Britain's supply lines and win the war. But by attacking neutral and unarmed American ships, Germany only provoked an opponent it could not afford to fight. Germany correctly suspected that the British were clandestinely receiving war supplies from U.S. passenger ships; and on February 1, 1917, the kaiser's ministers announced that they would sink all ships on sight, without warning. The American public was further outraged by an intercepted telegram from Germany's foreign minister, Arthur Zimmerman (1916–17), stating that Germany would support a Mexican attempt to capture American territory if the United States entered the war. The United States cut off diplomatic relations with Berlin, and on April 6, President Woodrow Wilson (1913–21) requested and received a declaration of war by Congress.

Wilson vowed that America would fight to "make the world safe for democracy," to banish autocracy and militarism, and to establish a league or society of nations in place of the old diplomatic maneuvering. The Americans' primary interest was maintaining the international balance of power. For years, U.S. diplomats and military leaders believed that American security depended on the equilibrium of strength in Europe. As long as Britain could prevent any one nation from achieving supremacy on the Continent, the United States was safe. But now Germany threatened not only the British navy—which had come to be seen as the shield of American security—but also the international balance of power. American involvement stemmed those threats in 1918, but the monumental task of establishing peace still lay ahead.

Total War

The search for peace was spurred by shock at the murderousness of the war. As early as 1915, contemporaries were speaking of "the Great War"; the transformations were there for all to see. The changing technologies of warfare altered strategic calculations. New artillery was heavier, with a longer range and more deadly results: German mobile

U.S. TROOPS AT THE FRONT. Soldiers in the American Expedition Forces wearing gas masks.

howitzers, such as "Big Bertha," could fire shells of over a thousand pounds at targets nine miles and even farther away. (One shelled Paris from seventy-five miles out.) This was modern, industrialized warfare, first glimpsed in the American Civil War but now more advanced and on a much larger scale. It still deployed cloth-uniformed men, heartbreakingly unprotected against the newly destructive weapons. And it still required human intelligence, speed, brute force—or courage—on a massive scale. The statistics and what they imply still strain the imagination: 74 million soldiers were mobilized on both sides; 6,000 people were killed each day for more than 1,500 days.

The warring nations, Europe's new industrial powerhouses, were also empires, and this "world" war consumed resources and soldiers from all over the globe. Mobilization also reached more deeply into civilian society. Economies bent to military priorities. Propaganda escalated to sustain the effort, fanning old hatreds and creating new ones. Atrocities against civilians came in its wake. Europe had known brutal wars against civilians before, and guerilla war during the time of Napoleon, but the First World War vastly magnified the violence and multiplied the streams of refugees. Minorities who lived in the crumbling Russian, Austro-Hungarian, or Ottoman Empires were especially vulnerable. Jewish populations in Russia had lived in fear of pogroms before 1914; now they were attacked by Russian soldiers who accused them of encouraging the enemy. Austria-Hungary, likewise, summarily executed minorities suspected of Russian sympathies. The worst atrocities came against the Armenian community in Turkey. Attacked by the Allies at Gallipoli and at war with the Russians to the north, the Turkish government turned on its Armenian subjects, labeling them a security risk. Orders came down for "relocation," and relocation became genocide. Armenian leaders were arrested; Armenian men were shot; and entire Armenian villages were force marched to the south, robbed and beaten to death along the way. Over the course of the war, a million Armenians died.

All of these developments—military, economic, and psychological mobilization; a war that tested the powers of a state and its economy; violence against civilians—were the component parts of total war and foreshadowed the conflict to be unleashed in 1939.

The Peace Settlement

The Paris Peace Conference, which opened in January 1919, was an extraordinary moment, one that dramatized just how much the world had been transformed by the war and the decades that preceded it. Gone were the Russian, Austro-Hungarian, and German Empires. That the American president Woodrow Wilson played such a prominent role marked the rise of the United States as a world power. The United States' new status was rooted in the economic development of the second industrial revolution during the nineteenth century. In mass production and technological innovation, it had rivaled the largest European powers (England and Germany) before the war. During the war, American intervention (although it came late) had decisively broken the military-economic deadlock. And in the war's aftermath, American industrial culture, engineering, and financial networks loomed very large on the European continent. Wilson and his entourage spent several months in Paris at the conference—a first for an American president while in office and European leaders' first extended encounter with an American head of state.

American prominence was far from the only sign of global change. Some thirty nations sent delegates to the peace conference, a reflection of three factors: the scope of the war, heightened national sentiment and aspiration, and the tightening of international communication and economic ties in the latter part of the nineteenth century. The world in 1900 was vastly more globalized than it had been fifty years earlier. Many more countries had political, economic, and human investments in the war and its settlement. A belief that peace would secure and be secured by free peoples in sovereign nations represented the full flowering of nineteenth-century liberal nationalism. Delegates came to work for Irish home rule, for a Jewish state in Palestine and for nations in Poland, Ukraine, and Yugoslavia. Europe's colonies, which had been key to the war effort and were increasingly impatient with their status, sent delegates to negotiate for self-determination. They discovered, however, that the western European leaders' commitment to the principle of national self-determination was hedged by their imperial assumptions. Non-state actors—in other words international groups asking for woman suffrage, civil rights, minimum wages, or maximum hours—came to the Paris Peace Conference as well, for these were now seen as international issues. Last, reporters from all over the world wired news home from Paris, a sign of vastly improved communications, transatlantic cables, and the mushrooming of the mass press.

Although many attended, the conference was largely controlled by the so-called Big Four: the U.S. president Woodrow Wilson, the British prime minister David Lloyd George (1916–22), the French premier Georges Clemenceau (1917–20), and the Italian premier Vittorio Orlando (1917–19). The debates among these four personalities were fierce, as they all had conflicting ambitions and interests. In total, five separate treaties were signed, one with each of the

Past and Present

The Legacy of World War I

World War I had severe consequences for civilian populations, resulting not only from military conflict but also from economic dislocation, food shortages, and disease (see photo of a feeding station in Vienna for hungry families in 1918, on left). Recognizing the contribution of civilians to the war effort, states involved in World War I intervened massively in the economy, paying separation allowances to the families of soldiers, unemployment benefits to those thrown out of work, and regulating the sale and production of consumer goods. This example of the ways a government could play a role in the economy set a precedent for later in the twentieth century, and is part of the history of current debates about the role the state can play in remedying inequality (see photo of protesters demonstrating against cuts in social security, on right).

Watch related author interview on StudySpace
wwnorton.com/web/westernciv18

defeated nations: Germany, Austria, Hungary, Turkey, and Bulgaria. The settlement with Germany was called the Treaty of Versailles, after the town in which it was signed.

Wilson's widely publicized Fourteen Points represented the spirit of idealism. Wilson had proposed the Fourteen Points before the war ended, as the foundation of a permanent peace. Based on the principle of "open covenants of peace, openly arrived at," they called for an end to secret diplomacy, freedom of the seas, removal of international tariffs, and reduction of national armaments "to the lowest point consistent with safety." They also called for the "self-determination of peoples" and for the establishment of a League of Nations to settle international conflicts. Thousands of copies of the Fourteen Points had been scattered by Allied planes over the German trenches and behind the lines in an attempt to convince both soldiers and civilians that the Allied nations were striving for a just and durable peace. They shaped the expectations that Germans brought to the peace talks. "The day of conquest and aggrandizement is gone by; so is also the day of secret covenants entered into in the interest of particular governments," Wilson had said. "It is this happy fact . . . which makes it possible for every nation whose purposes are consistent with justice and the peace of the world to avow now or at any other time the objects it has in view."

Idealism, however, was undermined by other imperatives. Throughout the war, Allied propaganda led soldiers and civilians to believe that their sacrifices to the war effort would be compensated by payments extracted from the enemy. Total war demanded total victory. Lloyd George had campaigned during the British election of 1918 on the slogan "Hang the Kaiser!" Clemenceau had twice in his long lifetime seen France invaded and its existence imperiled. With the tables turned, he believed that the French should take full advantage of their opportunity to place Germany under strict control. The devastation of the war and the

"LONG LIVE WILSON!" Paris crowds greet President Wilson after the war. Despite public demonstrations of this sort, Wilson's attempt to shape the peace was a failure.

fiction that Germany could be made to pay for it made compromise impossible. The settlement with Germany was shaped more by this desire for punishment than by Wilson's idealism.

The Versailles treaty required Germany to surrender the "lost provinces" of Alsace and Lorraine to France and to give up other territories to Denmark and the new state of Poland. The treaty gave Germany's coal mines in the Saar basin to France for fifteen years, at which point the German government could buy them back. Germany's province of East Prussia was cut off from the rest of its territory. The port of Danzig, where the majority of the population was German, was put under the administrative control of the League of Nations and the economic domination of Poland. The treaty disarmed Germany, forbid a German air force, and reduced its navy to a token force to match an army capped at 100,000 volunteers. To protect France and Belgium, all German soldiers and fortifications were to be removed from the Rhine Valley.

The most important part of the Versailles treaty, and one of the parts at odds with Wilson's original plan, was the "war-guilt" provision in Article 231. Versailles held Germany and its allies responsible for the loss and damage suffered by the Allied governments and their citizens "as a consequence of the war imposed upon them by the aggression of Germany and her allies." Germany would be forced to pay massive reparations. The exact amount was left to a Reparations Commission, which set the total at $33 billion in 1921. The Germans deeply resented these harsh demands, but others outside of Germany also warned of the dangers of punitive reparations. In *The Economic Consequences of the Peace,* the noted British economist John Maynard Keynes (1883–1946) argued that reparations would undermine Europe's most important task: repairing the world economy.

The other treaties at the Paris Peace Conference were based partly on the Allies' strategic interests, and partly on the principle of national self-determination. The experience of the prewar years convinced leaders that they should draw nations' boundaries to conform to the ethnic, linguistic, and historical traditions of the people they were to contain. Wilson's idealism about freedom and equal representation confirmed these aims. Thus, representatives of Yugoslavia were granted a state. Czechoslovakia was created, Poland reestablished, Hungary separated from Austria, and the Baltic states made independent (see the map on page 000). These national boundaries did not, indeed in most cases could not, follow ethnic divisions; they were created according to facts on the ground, hasty compromises, and political dictates—such as insulating western Europe from the communist threat of the Soviet Union. The peacemakers carved new nations from older, multiethnic empires, especially the Austro-Hungarian Empire, whose fragility had helped spark the war and whose structure had collapsed with the conflict. Creating nations, however, almost invariably created new minorities within those nations. The architects of the new Europe wrestled, briefly, with the problem of minorities, but did not resolve it. The issue would return and undermine European stability in the 1930s.

The Ottoman Empire ended as well, with two results: the creation of the modern Turkish state and a new structure for British and French colonial rule. As territories were taken from the Ottomans, Greece chose to seize some by force. The effort was successful at first, but the Turks counterattacked, driving out Greek forces by 1923 and creating the modern state of Turkey under the charismatic leadership of General Mustafa Kemal Attaturk (1923–38). Ottoman territories placed under French and British control became part of the colonial "mandate system," which legitimized Europe's dominance over territories in the Middle East, Africa, and the Pacific. Territories were divided into groups on the basis of their location and their "level of development," or how far, in European eyes, they would have to travel to earn self-government. Choice pieces of land became mandates held, in principle, by the League of Nations but administered by Britain (Transjordan, Iraq, and Palestine) and France (Lebanon and Syria). The British and French Empires, then, expanded after the war, although those territories held trouble ahead—the British faced revolt in Iraq and escalating tensions in Palestine, where they tried to juggle promises made to Zionist settlers and claims of indigenous Arab communities. Arab leaders, accompanied by their advocate T. E. Lawrence, attended the Versailles conference and listened as their hopes for independence were strictly circumscribed.

The peoples of the Allies' existing colonies were also disappointed. Ho Chi Minh, a young student from Indochina attending a Parisian university, was one of many colonial activists who attended the conference to protest conditions in the colonies and to ask that the rights of nations be extended to their homelands. Well-organized delegations from French West Africa and from the Congress Party of India, which favored dominion status in return for the wartime efforts of millions of Indian soldiers who had fought for the British Empire, were also snubbed. The peacemakers' belief in democracy and self-determination collided with their baseline assumptions—inherited from the nineteenth century—about Western superiority; those assumptions justified imperial rule. Although the European powers spoke about reforming colonialism, little was done. Many nationalists in the colonies who had favored moderate legislative change decided that active struggle might be the only answer to the injustices of colonialism.

Each of the five peace treaties incorporated the Covenant of the League of Nations, an organization envisioned as the arbiter of world peace, but it never achieved the idealistic aims of its founders. The League was handicapped from the start by a number of changes to its original design. The arms-reduction requirement was watered down, and the League's power to enforce it was rendered almost nonexistent. Japan would not join unless it was allowed to keep former German concessions in China. France demanded that both Germany and Russia be excluded from the League. This contradicted Wilson's goals but had already been legitimized in Paris, where neither Soviet Russia nor the defeated Central Powers were allowed at the talks. The League received an even more debilitating blow when the U.S. Congress, citing the long-standing national preference for isolation, refused to approve U.S. membership in the League. Hobbled from the start, the international organization had little potential to avert conflicts.

The League began as a utopian response to global conflict and registered the urgency of reorganizing world governance. Its history, however, reflected the larger problems of power politics that emerged after the war.

CONCLUSION

Europe fought the First World War on every front possible—military, political, social, and economic. Consequently, the war's effects extended far beyond the devastated landscapes of the Western Front. Statistics can only hint at the enormous loss of human life: of the 70 million men who were mobilized, nearly 9 million were killed. Russia, Germany, France, and Hungary recorded the highest number of deaths, but the smaller countries of southeast Europe had the highest percentages of soldiers killed. Almost 40 percent of Serbia's soldiers died in battle. With the addition of war-related deaths caused by privation and disease, Serbia lost 15 percent of its population. In comparison, Britain, France, and Germany lost only 2 to 3 percent of their populations. But the percentages are much more telling if we focus on the young men of the war generation. Germany lost one-third of men aged nineteen to twenty-two in 1914. France and Britain sustained similar losses, with mortality among young men reaching eight to ten times the normal rate. This was the "lost generation."

The breakdown of the prewar treaty system and the scale of the diplomatic failure that produced the war discredited the political classes in many countries. Meanwhile, the war itself planted seeds of political and social discontent around the globe. Relations between Russia and western Europe grew sour and suspicious. The Allies had attempted to overthrow the Bolsheviks during the war and had excluded them from the negotiations afterward; these actions instilled in the Soviets a mistrust of the West that lasted for generations. The Allied nations feared that Russia would dominate the new states of eastern Europe, building a "Red Bridge" across the continent. Elsewhere, the conflicting demands of colonialism and nationalism struck only a temporary balance, while the redrawn maps left ethnic and linguistic minorities in every country. The fires of discontent raged most fiercely in Germany, where the Treaty of Versailles was decried as outrageously unjust. Nearly all national governments agreed that it

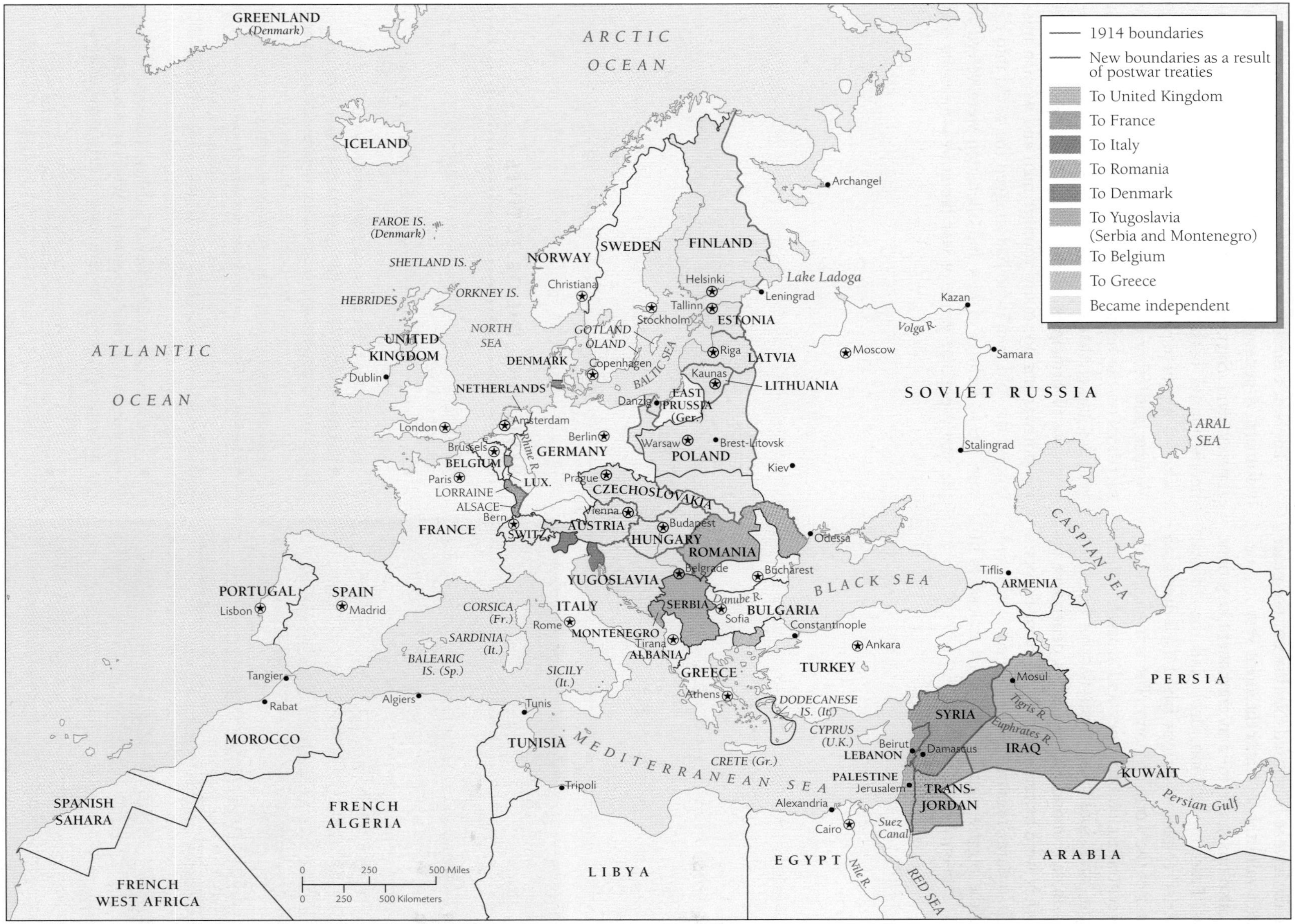

TERRITORIAL CHANGES IN EUROPE AND THE NEAR EAST AFTER THE FIRST WORLD WAR. Note the changes in geography as a result of the First World War. ▪ ***What areas were most affected by the changes within Europe, and why?*** ▪ ***Can you see any obvious difficulties created by the redrawing of the map of Europe?*** ▪ ***What historical circumstances and/or new threats guided the victors to create such geopolitical anomalies?***

would eventually have to be revised. Neither war nor peace had ended the rivalries that caused the Great War.

The war also had powerful and permanent economic consequences. Beset by inflation, debt, and the difficult task of industrial rebuilding, Europe found itself displaced from the center of the world economy. The war had accelerated the decentralization of money and markets. Many Asian, African, and South American nations benefited financially as their economies became less dependent on Europe, and they were better able to profit from Europe's need for their natural resources. The United States and Japan reaped the biggest gains and emerged as leaders in the new world economy.

The war's most powerful cultural legacy was disillusionment. A generation of men had been sacrificed to no apparent end. Surviving soldiers—many of them permanently injured, both physically and psychologically—were sickened by their participation in such useless slaughter. Women and other civilians had also made extraordinary sacrifices on the home front, for little apparent gain. Both veterans and civilians were disgusted by the greedy abandonment of principles by the politicians at Versailles. In the postwar period, many younger men and women mistrusted the "old men" who had dragged the world into the war. These feelings of loss and alienation were voiced in the vastly popular genre of war literature—memoirs and

After You Read This Chapter

Visit StudySpace for quizzes, additional review materials, and multimedia documents. **wwnorton.com/web/westernciv18**

REVIEWING THE OBJECTIVES

- The First World War broke out as a result of conflicts in the Balkans. Why?
- The Western Front was seen by all sides as a crucial theater of the conflict. What measures did the French, British, and Germans take to break the stalemate, and why did they fail?
- European governments intervened in extraordinary ways in the economy to ensure the production of material for the war effort and to remedy the social crisis caused by mobilization. How did governments intervene in the economy?
- The war led European nations to mobilize people and resources from their colonies. How did colonial subjects participate in the war effort, and what did many of them expect in return?
- Russia was devastated by the war, and the population lost confidence in the tsar's government. What circumstances allowed the Bolsheviks to seize power in 1917, and what were their goals?
- The Versailles Peace Treaty blamed the Germans for the war. Who were the most important participants in the peace conference, and who shaped the terms of the treaty the most?

fiction that commemorated the experience of soldiers on the front lines. The German writer and ex-soldier Erich Maria Remarque captured the disillusion of a generation in his novel *All Quiet on the Western Front:* "Through the years our business has been killing;—it was our first calling in life. Our knowledge of life is limited to death. What will happen afterwards? And what shall come out of us?"

That was the main question facing postwar Europe. The German novelist Thomas Mann recognized that 1918 had brought "an end of an epoch, revolution and the dawn of a new age" and that he and his fellow Germans were "living in a new and unfamiliar world." The struggle to define this new world would increasingly be conceived in terms of rival ideologies—democracy, communism, and fascism—competing for the future of Europe. The eastern autocracies had fallen with the war, but liberal democracy was soon on the decline as well. While militarism and nationalism remained strong, calls for major social reforms gained force during worldwide depression. Entire populations had been mobilized during the war, and they would remain so afterward—active participants in the age of mass politics. Europe was about to embark on two turbulent decades of rejecting and reinventing its social and political institutions. As Tomáš Masaryk, the first president of newly formed Czechoslovakia, described it, postwar Europe was "a laboratory atop a graveyard."

PEOPLE, IDEAS, AND EVENTS IN CONTEXT

- Why was **FRANZ FERDINAND** assassinated, and how did his death contribute to the outbreak of the war?
- What was the **SCHLIEFFEN PLAN**, and how was it related to the outbreak of the war?
- What was the significance of the first **BATTLE OF THE MARNE** in 1914?
- Why did the British attempt to attack the Ottoman Empire at **GALLIPOLI**?
- What was the goal of the attacking forces at **VERDUN** and the **SOMME** in 1916? What was accomplished?
- Why did many people in Russia, and especially soldiers in the Russian army, lose faith in **TSAR NICHOLAS II** of Russia?
- Who were the **BOLSHEVIKS** and the **MENSHEVIKS**, and what were their disagreements?
- How did **LENIN** make use of the **SOVIETS** in challenging the **PROVISIONAL GOVERNMENT** in Russia after the fall of the tsar?
- What policies did the **BOLSHEVIKS** follow after seizing power in Russia?
- What were **WOODROW WILSON**'s **FOURTEEN POINTS**?
- What treatment did Germany receive under the terms of the **TREATY OF VERSAILLES**?

THINKING ABOUT CONNECTIONS

- What made World War I different from previous military conflicts in Europe that had involved large numbers of states, such as the Napoleonic Wars of the early nineteenth century (see Chapter 18), or the Thirty Years' War of the seventeenth century (see Chapter 15)?
- In what way might the effects and consequences of World War I have shaped the lives of Europeans in the decades to come? How did it change the lives of various peoples from other parts of the world who were drawn into the conflict?

Before You Read This Chapter

STORY LINES

- With the exception of Bolshevik Russia, European states attempted to find stability in the traumatic aftermath of the First World War by reinforcing democratic institutions and focusing on an orderly transition from wartime production to a peacetime economy.
- The Bolsheviks won the civil war that followed the Russian Revolution in 1917, and by the late 1920s Joseph Stalin embarked on an unprecedented revolution from above, industrializing the nation and transforming rural life through the collectivization of agriculture. The human costs were enormous, as millions died of hunger and millions more were arrested and deported to labor camps in the east.
- The Great Depression undermined political support for Europe's democracies in the 1930s, and the decade saw the consolidation of fascist regimes in Italy and Germany and an anti-capitalist communist regime in the Soviet Union.

CHRONOLOGY

1918	The November Revolution establishes the Weimar Republic
1918–1920	Russian Civil War
1920	National Socialist Worker's party founded in Germany
1922	Mussolini comes to power in Italy
1923	Hitler's Beer Hall Putsch in Munich
1928	First Soviet Five-Year Plan
1928–1929	Stalin gains power in Russia
1929–1933	Collectivization and famine in Soviet Union
1933	Hitler becomes Chancellor of Germany
1937–1938	The Great Terror in Soviet Union

25

Turmoil between the Wars

CORE OBJECTIVES

- **UNDERSTAND** the direction taken by the Russian Revolution after 1917 and the consequences of Stalin's revolution from above in the 1930s.
- **DEFINE** fascism and explain Mussolini's rise to power in Italy in the 1920s.
- **DESCRIBE** the challenges faced by the Weimar Republic and other democracies in Britain, France, and the United States after the First World War.
- **EXPLAIN** Hitler's rise to power in Germany in 1933 and the reasons for the broad support the Nazis enjoyed among many Germans.
- **UNDERSTAND** the ways that the interwar atmosphere of social and political crisis was reflected in the world of the arts, literature, and popular culture.

Käthe Kollwitz, a Berlin painter and sculptor, understood as well as anybody in Europe the terrible costs and futility of the First World War. Her youngest son, Peter, was killed on October 22, 1914, in Germany's failed attack on France. Her diary recorded the last moments she spent with him, an evening walk from the barracks on October 12, the day before his departure for the front: "It was dark, and we went arm in arm through the wood. He pointed out constellations to me, as he had done so often before." Her entry for October 30 was more succinct, a quotation from the postcard she had received from his commanding officer: "Your son has fallen." Kollwitz's pain at this loss found expression in her later work, which explored in naked terms the grief and powerlessness that she and her family had felt during the war years. Her suffering found expression, too, in a commitment to socialism, a political ideology that provided her with an antidote to the nationalism that pervaded German society during the war years and after. Kollwitz's socialism drew her to the attention of the Gestapo after the Nazis came to power in 1933, and she was fired from her position at the Academy of Art. She put up with house searches and harassment but refused invitations from friends abroad to go into exile. She died in Germany in 1945, having survived long enough to see her cherished grandson, also named Peter, killed in a second war while fighting as a German soldier on the Eastern Front in Russia in 1942.

The story of Käthe Kollwitz and her family between 1914 and 1945 is only unusual for the fact that she was a well-known artist. The suffering was all too familiar to others, as was the search for new political ideologies that might save Europeans from their past. The Great War left 9 million dead in its wake and shattered the confidence that had been such a characteristic of nineteenth-century European culture. It led tragically to another world war, even more horrific than the first. Many in the interwar years shared Kollwitz's hope for a socialist or communist future, and many others turned to extremisms of the right. The result in the 1920s was a near collapse of democracy. By the late 1930s, few Western democracies remained. Even in those that did, most notably Britain, France, and the United States, regimes were frayed by the same pressures and strains that wrecked democratic governments elsewhere.

***WIDOWS AND ORPHANS* BY KÄTHE KOLLWITZ, 1919.** Kollwitz (1867–1945), a German artist and socialist activist in Berlin, lost a son in the First World War and a grandson in the Second World War. Her work poignantly displayed the effects of poverty and war on the lives of ordinary people.

The foremost cause of democracy's decline in this period was a series of continuing disruptions in the world economy, caused first by the First World War and later, by the Great Depression of 1929–33. A second source of crisis lay in increased social conflict, exacerbated by the war. Although many hoped that these conflicts would be resolved by the peace and a renewed commitment to democratic institutions, the opposite occurred. Broad swathes of the electorate rallied to extremist political parties that promised radical transformations of nations and their cultures. Nationalism, sharpened by the war, proved a key source of discontent in its aftermath, and in Italy and Germany frustrated nationalist sentiment turned against their governments.

The most dramatic instance of democracy's decline came with the rise of new authoritarian dictatorships, especially in the Soviet Union, Italy, and Germany. The experiences of these three nations differed significantly as a result of varying historical circumstances and personalities. In each case, however, many citizens allowed themselves to be persuaded that only drastic measures could bring order from chaos. Those measures, including the elimination of parliamentary government, strict restrictions on political freedom, and increasingly virulent repression of "enemies" of the state were implemented with a combination of violence, intimidation, and propaganda. That so many citizens seemed willing to sacrifice their freedoms—or those of others—was a measure of their alienation, impatience, or desperation.

THE SOVIET UNION UNDER LENIN AND STALIN

The Russian Civil War

The Bolsheviks seized power in October 1917. They signed a separate peace with Germany in March 1918 (the Treaty of Brest-Litovsk) and then turned to consolidating their own position. The October Revolution and withdrawing from the war, however, had divided Russian society, igniting a war that turned out to be far more costly than conflict with Germany. Fury at the terms of Brest-Litovsk mobilized the Bolsheviks' enemies. Known collectively as "Whites," the Bolsheviks' opponents were only loosely bound by their common goal of removing the "Reds" from power. Their military force came mainly from supporters of the old regime, including tsarist military officers, reactionary monarchists, the former nobility, and disaffected liberal supporters of the monarchy. The Whites were joined by groups as diverse as liberal supporters of the provisional government, Mensheviks, Social Revolutionaries, and anarchist peasant bands known as "Greens" who opposed all central state power. The Bolsheviks also faced insurrections from strong nationalist movements in some parts of the former Russian Empire: Ukraine, Georgia, and the north Caucasus regions. Finally, several foreign powers, including the United States, Great Britain, and Japan, launched small but threatening interventions on the periphery of the old empire. Outside support for the Whites proved to be an insignificant threat to the Bolsheviks, but it heightened Bolshevik mistrust of the capitalist world which, in the Marxists' view, would naturally oppose the existence of the world's first "socialist" state.

The Bolsheviks eventually won the civil war because they gained greater support—or at least tacit acceptance—from the majority of the population and because they were better organized for the war effort itself. Leon Trotsky, the revolutionary hero of 1905 and 1917, became the new commissar of war and created a hierarchical, disciplined military machine that grew to some 5 million men by 1920. Trotsky's Red Army triumphed over the White armies by the end of 1920, although fighting continued into 1922. The Bolsheviks also invaded Poland and nearly reached Warsaw before being thrown back.

When the civil war was over, the country had suffered some 1 million combat casualties, several million deaths from hunger and disease caused by the war, and 100,000–300,000 executions of noncombatants as part of Red and White terror. The barbarism of the war engendered lasting hatreds within the emerging Soviet nation, especially among ethnic minorities, and it brutalized the fledgling society that came into existence under the new Bolshevik regime.

The civil war also shaped the Bolsheviks' approach to the economy. On taking power in 1917, Lenin expected to create, for the short term at least, a state-capitalist system that resembled the successful European wartime economies. The new government took control of large-scale industry, banking, and all other major capitalist concerns while allowing small-scale private economic activity, including agriculture, to continue. The civil war pushed the new government toward a more radical economic stance known as "war communism." The Bolsheviks began to requisition grain from the peasantry, and they outlawed private trade in consumer goods as "speculation," militarized production facilities, and abolished money. Many believed that war communism would replace the capitalist system that had collapsed in 1917.

Such hopes were largely unfounded. War communism sustained the Bolshevik military effort but further disrupted the already war-ravaged economy. The civil war devastated Russian industry and emptied major cities. The population of Moscow fell by 50 percent between 1917 and 1920. The masses of urban workers, who had strongly supported the Bolshevik revolution, melted back into the countryside; and industrial output in 1920–21 fell to only 20 percent of prewar levels. Most devastating were the effects of war communism on agriculture. The peasants had initially benefited from the revolution when they spontaneously seized and redistributed noble lands. Nonetheless, the agricultural system was severely disrupted by the civil war, by the grain requisitioning of war communism, and by the outlawing of all private trade in grain. Large-scale famine resulted in 1921 and claimed some 5 million lives.

LENIN AND STALIN. Under Stalin, this picture was used to show his close relationship with Lenin. In fact, the photograph has been doctored. ▪ ***What opportunities for propaganda and manipulation were offered by new technologies of photography and film?***

Analyzing Primary Sources

Lenin's Theses on the National and Colonial Question, 1920

The success of the Russian Revolution forced the new Soviet leadership to declare what its relationship would be with other movements for revolutionary change, including the movements for national independence that were developing in European colonies in Africa and Asia. These nationalist movements posed a dilemma, however, because many of them were led by middle-class activists, that is, by representatives of the "bourgeois" order that socialists hoped to overthrow. Lenin's Theses on the National and Colonial Question *was the outcome of a debate he had with a young Indian communist, Manabendra Nath Roy (1887–1954), and he argues here that communists might consider temporary alliances with these nationalist movements but that they should never allow them to merge with or subsume the communist movement.*

1. An abstract or formal conception of the question of equality in general and of national equality in particular is in the very nature of bourgeois democracy. Under the guise of the equality of individuals in general, bourgeois democracy proclaims the formal, legal equality of the property owner and the proletarian, the exploiter and the exploited, thereby grossly deceiving the oppressed classes. . . . The real meaning of the demand for equality consists in its being a demand for the abolition of classes.

2. As the conscious expression of the proletarian class struggle to shake off the yoke of the bourgeoisie, the Communist Party, in line with its basic task of struggling against bourgeois democracy and exposing its lies and duplicity, should not base its policy on the national question on abstract and formal principles. Instead, it should first be based on an exact appraisal of specific historical and above all economic conditions. Second, it should clearly differentiate between the interests of the oppressed classes, the toilers, the exploited, and the general concept of the so-called interests of the people, which means the interests of the ruling class. Third, it should with equal precision distinguish between the oppressed, dependent nations that do not have equal rights and the oppressor, exploiting nations that do. . . .

3. The imperialist war of 1914 . . . was justified by both sides with platitudes about national liberation and self-determination. Nonetheless, both the treaties of Brest-Litovsk and Bucharest and those of Versailles and St. Germain showed that the victorious bourgeoisie ruthlessly sets even "national" borders according to its economic interests. For the bourgeoisie even "national" borders are objects of trade . . . [T]he proletariat can achieve genuine national liberation and unity only through revolutionary struggle and by overpowering the bourgeoisie. . . .

4. It follows from these principles that the entire policy of the Communist International on the national and colonial questions must be based primarily upon uniting the proletarians and toiling masses of all nations and countries in common revolutionary struggle to overthrow the landowners and the bourgeoisie. . . .

5. The international political situation has now put the dictatorship of the proletariat on the order of the day. All events in world politics necessarily focus on one single central issue: the struggle of the world bourgeoisie against the Russian Soviet Republic, which rallies around itself both the soviet movement of the advanced workers of all countries and all national liberation movements of the colonies and oppressed peoples. . . .

6. Consequently, we cannot limit ourselves at this time merely to recognizing or proclaiming the friendship of the toilers of various nations. Rather we must pursue a policy of implementing the closest possible alliance of all national and colonial liberation movements with Soviet Russia. The forms of this alliance will be determined by the level of development of the Communist movement within the proletariat of each country or of the revolutionary liberation movement in the backward countries and among the backward nationalities.

7. Federation is a transitional form toward full unity of the toilers of all nations. Federation has already shown its usefulness in practice—in the Russian Soviet Federated Socialist Republic's relations to the other soviet republics . . . and also within the Russian Soviet Federated Socialist Republic itself toward the nationalities that formerly had neither a state nor self-government. . . .

8. . . . [W]e must strive for an ever closer federal association. We must take into consideration first, that the soviet republics, surrounded by imperialist states of the whole world that are considerably stronger militarily, cannot

possibly exist without close association with each other. Second, a close economic alliance of the soviet republics is necessary, without which it is impossible to restore the productive forces destroyed by imperialism and ensure the well-being of the toilers. Third, that there is a tendency to create a world economy unified according to a common plan, controlled by proletarians of all countries. . . .

9. . . . Communist parties must incessantly expose in their entire propaganda and agitation the continually repeated violations of the equality of nations and guaranteed rights of national minorities in all capitalist countries despite their "democratic" constitutions. In addition, it must be explained persistently that only the soviet order can ensure true national equality by uniting first the proletariat and then the whole mass of the toilers in struggle against the bourgeoisie. Moreover, all Communist parties must directly support the revolutionary movement among the nations that are dependent and do not have equal rights (for example Ireland, the Negroes in America, and so forth), and in the colonies. . . .

10. . . . The fight against . . . the most deeply rooted petty-bourgeois, nationalist prejudices (which are expressed in all possible forms, such as racism, national chauvinism, and anti-Semitism) must be given all the more priority as the question becomes more pressing of transforming the dictatorship of the proletariat from a national framework (that is, a dictatorship that exists only in one country and is incapable of carrying out an independent international policy) into an international one (that is, a dictatorship of the proletariat in at least several advanced countries, capable of exercising a decisive influence on all of world politics).

Petty-bourgeois nationalism declares that internationalism consists of the mere recognition of the equality of nations (although this recognition is strictly verbal) and considers national egoism to be sacrosanct. Proletarian internationalism, on the contrary, requires subordinating the interests of the proletarian struggle in one country to the interests of this struggle on a world scale. It also requires that the nation that has overthrown its bourgeoisie has the ability and willingness to make the greatest national sacrifices in order to overthrow international capitalism. . . .

11. With respect to the states and nations that have a more backward, predominantly feudal, patriarchal, or patriarchal-peasant character, the following points in particular must be kept in mind:

a. All Communist parties must support with deeds the revolutionary liberation movement in these countries. . . .

b. A struggle absolutely must be waged against the reactionary and medieval influence of the clergy, the Christian missions, and similar elements.

c. It is necessary to struggle against the Pan-Islamic and Pan-Asian movements and similar currents that try to link the liberation struggle against European and American imperialism with strengthening the power of Turkish and Japanese imperialism and of the nobles, large landowners, clergy, and so forth.

d. It is especially necessary to support the peasant movement in the backward countries against the landowners and all forms and vestiges of feudalism. . . .

Questions for Analysis

1. Why does Lenin begin these theses with a critique of "bourgeois democracy" and "national liberation and self-determination"? What alternative goals does he announce?

2. Why does he say that an alliance between the communist movement and movements for anticolonial liberation is worth pursuing?

3. What possible dangers does he nevertheless identify in some of the anticolonial movements that he mentions?

Source: John Riddell, ed., *Workers of the World and Oppressed Peoples, Unite!: Proceedings and Documents of the Second Congress, 1920,* Vol. 1 (New York: Pathfinder Press, 1991), pp. 283–88.

THE YOUNG GUARD. In the years following 1917, many within the Russian avant-garde wished to aid the revolution with their work. This literary magazine, which here has a constructivist-style cover, promoted Bolshevik values.

As the civil war came to a close, urban workers and soldiers became increasingly impatient with the Bolshevik regime, which had promised socialism and workers' control but had delivered something more akin to a military dictatorship. Large-scale strikes and protests broke out in late 1920, but the Bolsheviks moved swiftly and effectively to subdue the "popular revolts." In crushing dissent, the Bolshevik regime that emerged from the civil war made a clear statement that public opposition would not be tolerated.

The NEP Period

In response to these political and economic difficulties, the Bolsheviks abandoned war communism and in March 1921 embarked on a radically different course known as the New Economic Policy (NEP). The NEP reverted to the state capitalism that had been tried immediately after the revolution. The state continued to own all major industry and financial concerns, while individuals were allowed to own private property, trade freely within limits, and—most important—farm their land for their own benefit. Fixed taxes on the peasantry replaced grain requisitioning; what peasants grew beyond the tax requirements was theirs to do with as they saw fit. The Bolshevik most identified with the NEP was Nikolai Bukharin (1888–1938), a young and brilliant Marxist theoretician who argued that the Bolsheviks could best industrialize the Soviet Union by taxing private peasant economic activity. Lenin himself described the NEP as "one step backward in order to take two steps forward."

The NEP was undeniably successful in allowing Soviet agriculture to recover from the civil war; by 1924, agricultural harvests had returned to prewar levels. Peasants were largely left alone to do as they pleased, and they responded by redividing noble lands among themselves to level wealth discrepancies between rich and poor, by reinforcing traditional social structures in the countryside (especially the peasant commune), and by producing enough grain to feed the country, though they continued to use very primitive farming methods to do so. The NEP was less successful, however, in encouraging peasants to participate in markets to benefit urban areas. The result was a series of shortages in grain deliveries to cities, a situation that prompted many Bolsheviks to call for revival of the radical economic practices of war communism. The fate of these radical proposals, however, was tied to the fate of the man who would, contrary to all expectations, replace Lenin as the leader of the USSR and become one of the most notorious dictators of all time: Joseph Stalin.

Stalin and the "Revolution from Above"

Stalin's rise was swift and unpredicted. His political success was rooted in intraparty conflicts in the 1920s, but it was also closely tied to the abrupt end of the NEP period in the late 1920s and to the beginning of a massive program of social and economic modernization. This "revolution from above," as many call it, was the most rapid social and economic transformation any nation has seen in modern history. It was carried out, however, at unprecedented human cost.

Stalin (1879–1953), the son of a poor shoemaker, was a Bolshevik from the Caucasus nation of Georgia. His real name was Iosep Jughashvili. Receiving his early education in an Orthodox seminary, he participated in revolutionary activity in the Caucasus and spent many years in Siberian exile before the revolution. He was an important member of the Bolshevik party during the Russian Revolution, but

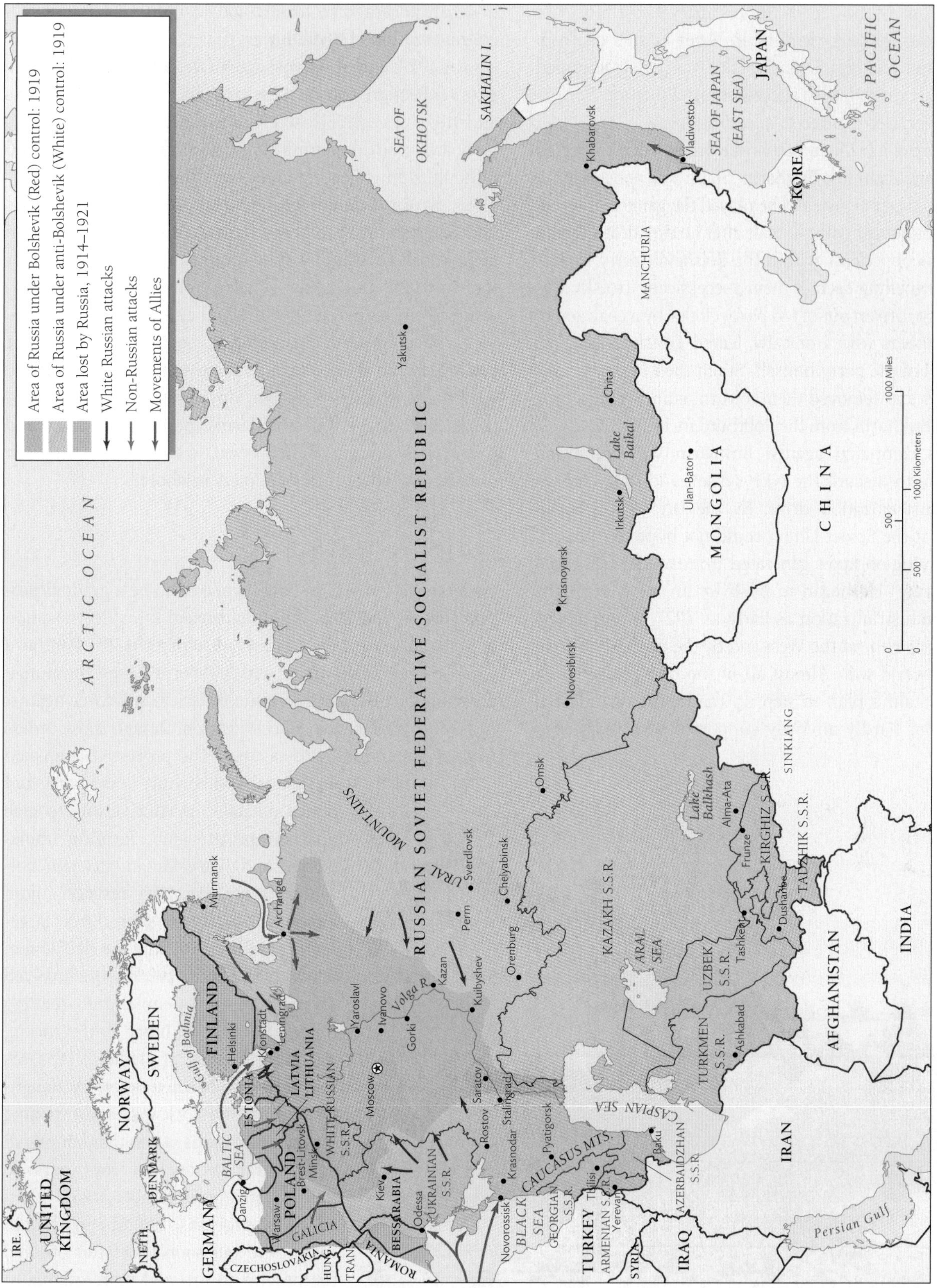

THE SOVIET UNION, 1918–1945. ▪ ***What were the areas lost by Russia in the Treaty of Brest-Litovsk?*** ▪ ***How did the possession of Moscow and Leningrad (St. Petersburg) aid the Bolsheviks in their victory over the Whites?*** ▪ ***How did the civil war of 1917–20 affect the new Soviet state?***

he was not one of the central figures and was certainly not a front runner for party leadership. After Lenin's death in 1924, the civil war hero Leon Trotsky was widely assumed to be the best candidate to succeed him. Other top Bolsheviks, however, also aspired to a leading role.

Though not a brilliant orator like Trotsky or a respected Marxist theoretician like Bukharin, Stalin was nonetheless a master political strategist, and he played the game of internal party politics almost without fault after Lenin's death. Stalin sidelined his opponents within the Bolshevik party by isolating and expelling each of them successively. Trotsky was the first to go, driven out of top party circles by a coalition of Stalin and others who, ironically, feared Trotsky's desire to take control of the party himself. Stalin then turned on his former allies and removed them in turn, culminating in the removal of Bukharin from the Politburo in 1928–29.

Stalin's campaign against Bukharin was connected to his desire to discard the NEP system and to launch an all-out industrialization drive. By the late 1920s, Stalin believed that the Soviet Union could not hope to industrialize by relying on taxes generated from small-scale peasant agriculture. He began to push for an increase in the tempo of industrialization as early as 1927, prompted by fears of falling behind the West and by the perceived threat of another world war. Almost all of the Bolshevik leaders supported Stalin's plan to step up the tempo of industrialization. But hardly anybody supported what happened next: an abrupt turn toward forced industrialization and collectivization of agriculture.

In 1927, a poor harvest caused yet another crisis in the grain-collection system. Low prices for agricultural goods and high prices for scarce industrial goods led peasants to hoard grain, resulting in food shortages in cities and difficulties in collecting taxes from the peasantry. In early 1928, Stalin ordered local officials in the distant Urals and Siberian areas to begin requisitioning grain. He soon applied this revival of war communism to the entire country. In 1929, the upper echelons of the party abruptly reversed the course set by NEP and embarked on the complete collectivization of agriculture, beginning in the major grain-growing areas. Peasants there were to be convinced, by force if necessary, to give up private farmlands. They would either join collective farms, pooling resources and giving a set portion of the harvest to the state, or work on state farms, where they were paid as laborers.

COLLECTIVIZATION

Collectivization was initially expected to be a gradual process, but in late 1929 Stalin embarked on collectivization of agriculture by force. Within a few months, the Politburo (short for political bureau, which governed the Communist party and state) began to issue orders to use force against peasants who resisted collectivization, though those orders were at first shrouded in secrecy. The process that ensued was brutal and chaotic. Local party and police officials forced peasants to give up their private land, farming implements, and livestock and to join collective farms. Peasants resisted, often violently. There were some 1,600 large-scale rebellions in the Soviet Union between 1929 and 1933; some involved several thousand people, and quelling them required military intervention, including the use of artillery. Peasants also resisted collectivization by slaughtering their livestock instead of turning it over to the farms, a loss that hampered agricultural production for years to follow. Sensing a possible crisis, Stalin called the process to a temporary halt in early 1930 but soon thereafter ordered the process to proceed more gradually, and by 1935 collectivization of agriculture was complete in most areas of the Soviet Union.

WINTER DEPORTATIONS, 1929–1930. Ukrainian families charged with being kulaks were deported from their homes because of their refusal to join Stalin's collective farming plan. Many of the evicted families were shipped north by train to the Arctic, where they perished owing to the lack of adequate food and shelter.

To facilitate collectivization, Stalin also launched an all-out attack on peasants designated as *kulaks* (a derogatory term for well-to-do farmers, literally meaning "tight-fisted ones"). Most kulaks, though, were not any better off than their neighbors, and the word became one of many terms for peasants hostile to collectivization. Between 1929 and 1933, some one and a half million peasants were uprooted, dispossessed of their property, and resettled from their farmlands to either inhospitable reaches of the Soviet east and north or to poor farmland closer to their original homes. The land and possessions of these unfortunate peasants were distributed to collective farms or, just as often, to the local officials and peasants participating in the liquidation process. The liquidation of kulaks as a class magnified the disruptive effects of agricultural collectivization, and the two together produced one of the most devastating famines in modern European history. Peasants who were forced into collective farms had little incentive to produce extra food, and exiling many of the most productive peasants not surprisingly weakened the agricultural system. In 1932–33, famine spread across the southern region of the Soviet Union. This was the most productive agricultural area in the country, and the famine that struck there was thus particularly senseless. The 1933 famine cost some 3 million to 5 million lives. During the famine, the Bolsheviks maintained substantial grain reserves in other parts of the country, enough to save many hundreds of thousands of lives at a minimum, but they refused to send this grain to the affected areas, preferring instead to seal off famine-stricken regions and allow people to starve. Grain reserves were instead sold overseas for hard currency and stockpiled in case of war. After 1935, there would never again be any large-scale resistance to Soviet power in the countryside.

"WE SMITE THE LAZY WORKERS!" This Russian propaganda poster was used to mobilize workers to the "Five-Year Plan."

The Five-Year Plans

In Stalin's view, collectivization provided the resources for the other major aspect of his revolution from above: a rapid campaign of forced industrialization. The road map for this industrialization process was the first Five-Year Plan (1928–1932), an ambitious set of goals that Stalin and his cohorts drew up in 1927 and continued to revise upward. The plan called for truly herculean industrialization efforts, and its results rank as one of the most stunning periods of economic growth the modern world has ever seen. Soviet statistics boasted of annual growth rates of 20 percent a year. Even the more cautious Western estimates of 14 percent annual growth were remarkable, given the worldwide depression elsewhere. The Bolsheviks built entirely new industries in entirely new cities. The factory town of Magnitogorsk, for example, emerged from absolutely barren, uninhabited steppes in 1929 to become a steel-producing factory town of some 250,000 residents in 1932; at least in scale, it rivaled anything that the West had built. The industrialization drive transformed the nation's landscape and population as well. Cities such as Moscow and Leningrad doubled in size in the early 1930s, while new cities sprang up across the country. In 1926, only one-fifth of the population lived in towns. Fifteen years later, in 1939, roughly a third did. The urban population had grown from 26 million to 56 million in under fifteen years. The Soviet Union was well on its way to becoming an urban, industrial society.

This rapid industrialization came, however, at enormous human cost. Many large-scale projects were carried out with prison labor, especially in the timber and mining industries. The labor camp system, known as the *gulag*, became a central part of the Stalinist economic system. People were arrested and sent to camps on a bewildering

Competing Viewpoints

Stalin's Industrialization of the Soviet Union

How did the Soviet people experience Stalin's industrialization drive? New archives have helped historians glimpse what the common people lived through and how they responded. The first excerpt is a speech Stalin gave at a Conference of Managers of Socialist Industry in 1931. In his usual style, he invoked fears of Soviet backwardness and Russian nationalism while summoning all to take up the task of industrial production.

The letters in the second selection come from several hundred that workers and peasants sent to Soviet newspapers and authorities recounting their experiences and offering their opinions. Both of the ones printed here were sent to the Soviet paper Pravda.

"The Tasks of Business Executives"

It is sometimes asked whether it is not possible to slow down the tempo somewhat, to put a check on the movement. No, comrades, it is not possible! The tempo must not be reduced! On the contrary, we must increase it as much as is within our powers and possibilities. This is dictated to us by our obligations to the workers and peasants of the USSR. This is dictated to us by our obligations to the working class of the whole world.

To slacken the tempo would mean falling behind. And those who fall behind get beaten. But we do not want to be beaten. No, we refuse to be beaten. One feature of the history of old Russia was the continual beatings she suffered because of her backwardness. She was beaten by the Mongol khans. She was beaten by the Turkish beys. . . . She was beaten by the British and French capitalists. She was beaten by the Japanese barons. All beat her—for her backwardness: for military backwardness, for cultural backwardness, for political backwardness, for industrial backwardness, for agricultural backwardness. . . .

We are fifty or a hundred years behind the advanced countries. We must make good this distance in ten years. Either we do it, or we shall be crushed. . . .

In ten years at most we must make good the distance which separates us from the advanced capitalist countries. We have all the 'objective' possibilities for this. The only thing lacking is the ability to take proper advantage of these possibilities. And that depends on us. *Only* on us! . . . It is time to put an end to the rotten policy of non-interference in production. It is time to adopt a new policy, a policy adapted to the present times—the policy of interfering in everything. If you are a factory manager, then interfere in all the affairs of the factory, look into everything, let nothing escape you, learn and learn again. Bolsheviks must master technique. It is time Bolsheviks themselves became experts. . . .

array of charges, ranging from petty criminal infractions to contact with foreigners to having the ill fortune to be born of bourgeois or kulak parents. The camp system spread throughout the USSR in the 1930s: by the end of the decade, roughly 3.6 million people were incarcerated by the regime. This army of prisoners was used to complete the most arduous and dangerous industrialization tasks, such as the construction of the Moscow–White Sea canal. To save money, the canal connecting Moscow to the seaports of the north was constructed without the use of any machinery. It was literally dug by hand, with human labor used to power everything from conveyor belts to pile drivers. Tens of thousands of individuals lost their lives during construction. One of Stalin's pet projects, it never functioned properly, was too shallow, and froze over in winter. It was bombed early in the Second World War.

The economic system created during this revolution from above was also fraught with structural problems that would plague the Soviet Union for its entire history. The command economy, with each year's production levels entirely planned in advance in Moscow, never functioned in a rational way. Heavy industry was always favored over

There are no fortresses which Bolsheviks cannot capture. We have assumed power. We have built up a huge socialist industry. We have swung the middle peasants to the path of socialism. . . . What remains to be done is not so much: to study technique, to master science. And when we have done that we will develop a tempo of which we dare not even dream at present.

Source: Joseph Stalin, "The Tasks of Business Executives" (speech given at the First All-Union Conference of Managers of Socialist Industry, February 4, 1931), as cited in Richard Sakwa, *The Rise and Fall of the Soviet Union, 1917–1991* (New York: 1999), pp. 187–88.

Stalin's Industrial Development: The View from Below

It should not be forgotten that many millions of workers are participating in the building of socialism. A horse with its own strength can drag seventy-five poods,* but its owner has loaded it with a hundred poods, and in addition he's fed it poorly. No matter how much he uses the whip, it still won't be able to move the cart.

This is also true for the working class. They've loaded it with socialist competition, shock work, over-fulfilling the industrial and financial plan, and so forth. A worker toils seven hours, not ever leaving his post, and this is not all he does. Afterward he sits in meetings or else attends classes for an hour and a half or two in order to increase his skill level, and if he doesn't do these things, then he's doing things at home. And what does he live on? One hundred fifty grams of salted mutton, he will make soup without any of the usual additives, neither carrots, beets, flour, nor salt pork. What kind of soup do you get from this? Mere "dishwater."

—B. N. Kniazev, Tula, Sept. 1930.

Comrade Editor, Please give me an answer. Do the local authorities have the right to forcibly take away the only cow of industrial and office workers? What is more, they demand a receipt showing that the cow was handed over voluntarily and they threaten you by saying if you don't do this, they will put you in prison for failure to fulfill the meat procurement. How can you live when the cooperative distributes only black bread, and at the market goods have the prices of 1919 and 1920? Lice have eaten us to death, and soap is given only to railroad workers. From hunger and filth we have a massive outbreak of spotted fever.

—Anonymous, from Aktybinsk, Kazakhstan

*A pood is a Russian unit of weight, equal to 36.11 pounds.

Source: Lewis Siegelbaum and Andrei Sokolov, *Stalinism as a Way of Life: A Narrative in Documents* (New Haven, CT: 2000), pp. 39–41.

Questions for Analysis

1. What are Stalin's priorities?
2. What images does Stalin use to capture his audience's attention?
3. How did the Soviet people experience Stalin's industrialization drive?

light industry, and the emphasis on quantity made quality practically meaningless. A factory that was charged with producing a certain number of pairs of shoes, for example, could cut costs by producing all one style and size. The consumer would be left with useless goods, but the producer would fulfill the plan. Stalin's industrialization drive did transform the country from an agrarian nation to a world industrial power in the space of a few short years, but in the longer run, the system would become an economic disaster.

The Stalin revolution also produced fundamental cultural and economic changes. The revolution from above altered the face of Soviet cities and the working class populating them. New cities were largely made up of first-generation peasants who brought their rural traditions to the cities with them, changing the fragile urban culture that had existed during the 1920s. Women, too, entered the urban workforce in increasing numbers in the 1930s—women went from 20 percent to almost 40 percent of the workforce in one decade, and in light industry they made up two-thirds of the labor force by 1940.

At the same time, Stalin promoted a sharply conservative shift in all areas of culture and society. In art, the radical

"IMPERIALISTS CANNOT STOP THE SUCCESS OF THE FIVE-YEAR PLAN!" ▪ ***Did propaganda like this also appeal to Russian nationalist pride?***

modernism of the 1920s was crushed by socialist realism, a deadening aesthetic that celebrated the drive toward socialism and left no room for experimentation. Family policy and gender roles underwent a similar reversal. Early Bolshevik activists had promoted a utopian attempt to rebuild one of the basic structures of prerevolutionary society—the family—and to create a genuinely new proletarian social structure. The Bolsheviks in the 1920s legalized divorce, expelled the Orthodox Church from marriage ceremonies, and legalized abortion. Stalin abandoned these ideas of communist familial relations in favor of efforts to strengthen traditional family ties: divorce became more difficult, abortion was outlawed in 1936 except in cases that threatened the life of the mother, and homosexuality was declared a criminal offense. State subsidies and support for mothers, which were progressive for the time, could not change the reality that Soviet women were increasingly forced to carry the double burden of familial and wage labor to support Stalin's version of Soviet society. All areas of Soviet cultural and social policy experienced similar reversals.

The Great Terror

The apogee of Stalinist repression came with the "Great Terror" of 1937–38, which left nearly a million people dead and as many as one and a half million more in labor camps. As Stalin consolidated his personal dictatorship over the country, he eliminated enemies—real and imagined—along with individuals and groups he considered superfluous to the new Soviet society. As we have seen, repression was central to the Stalinist system from the early 1930s, yet the years 1937–38 brought a qualitative and quantitative change—a whirlwind of mass repression unprecedented in scale.

The Terror was aimed at various categories of internal "enemies," from the top to the very bottom of Soviet society. Former and current political elites were perhaps the most visible victims. The top level of the Bolshevik party itself was purged almost completely; some 100,000 party members were removed, most facing prison sentences or execution. Many top party officials, including Bukharin, were condemned at carefully staged show trials and then shot. The purge also struck—with particular ferocity—nonparty elites, industrial managers, and intellectuals. Between 1937 and 1938, Stalin purged the military of people he deemed potential threats, arresting some 40,000 officers and shooting at least 10,000. These purges disrupted the government and the economy but allowed Stalin to promote a new, young cadre of officials who had no experience in the pre-Stalinist era and who owed their careers, if not their lives, to Stalin personally. Whole ethnic groups were viewed with suspicion, including Poles, Ukrainians, Lithuanians, Latvians, Koreans, and others with supposed cross-border ties that, in Stalin's mind, represented a national security threat. From the bottom, some 200,000–300,000 "dekulakized" peasants, petty criminals, and other social misfits were arrested, and many shot.

The Great Terror remains one of the most puzzling aspects of Stalin's path to dictatorial power. The Terror succeeded, with a certain paranoid logic, in solidifying Stalin's personal control over all aspects of social and political life in the Soviet Union, but it did so by destroying the most talented elements in Soviet society.

The results of the Stalin revolution were profound. No other regime in the history of Europe had ever attempted to reorder completely the politics, economy, and society of a major nation. The Soviets had done so in a mere ten years. By 1939, private manufacturing and trade had been almost entirely abolished. Factories, mines, railroads, and public utilities were exclusively owned by the state. Stores were either government enterprises or cooperatives in which consumers owned shares. Agriculture had been almost completely socialized. The decade was not entirely grim, however. There were advances, especially in the area of social reform. Illiteracy was reduced from nearly 50 percent to about 20 percent, and higher education was made available to increasingly large numbers. Government assistance for working mothers and free hospitalization did a great deal to raise the national standard of health. The society that emerged from this terrible decade was industrial, more urban than rural, and more modern than traditional. But it was a society badly brutalized in the process, one in which many of the most productive peasants, gifted intellectuals, and experienced economic and social elites were purged from society in the name of total dictatorial power. The USSR that emerged from this tumultuous period would barely be able to withstand the immense strains placed on it when the Germans struck less than three years after the end of the Terror.

THE EMERGENCE OF FASCISM IN ITALY

Like many European nations, Italy emerged from the First World War as a democracy in distress. Italy was on the winning side, but the war had cost nearly 700,000 Italian lives and over $15 billion. Moreover, Italy had received secret promises of specific territorial gains during the war, only to find those promises withdrawn when they conflicted with principles of self-determination. Italian claims to the west coast of the Adriatic, for instance, were denied by Yugoslavia. Italy received most of the Austrian territories it demanded, but many maintained that these were inadequate rewards for their sacrifices. Groups of militant nationalists seized Fiume, a port city on the Adriatic, and held it for a year before being disbanded by the Italian army. At first, the nationalists blamed the "mutilated victory" on President Wilson, but after a short time they turned on their own rulers and what they considered the weaknesses of parliamentary democracy.

Italy had long-standing problems that were made worse by the war. Since unification, the Italian nation had been rent by an unhealthy economic split—divided into a prosperous industrialized north and a poor agrarian south. Social conflict over land, wages, and local power caused friction in the countryside as well as in urban centers. Governments were often seen as corrupt, indecisive, and defeatist. This was the background for the more immediate problems that Italy faced after the war.

Inflation and unemployment were perhaps the most destructive effects of the war. Inflation produced high prices, speculation, and profiteering. And though normally wages would have risen also, the postwar labor market was glutted by returning soldiers. Furthermore, business elites were shaken by strikes, which became increasingly large and frequent, and by the closing of foreign markets. The parliamentary government that was set up after the war failed to ease these dire conditions, and Italians wanted radical reforms. For the working class, this meant socialism. In 1919, the socialists won about a third of the seats in the Chamber of Deputies. The movement grew increasingly radical: in 1920, the socialist and anarchist workers seized scores of factories, most in the metallurgy sector, and tried to run them for the benefit of the workers themselves. In the countryside, many peasants had no land at all, and worked for wages as rural laborers on large estates. Demands for land reform grew more militant. In some rural areas, so-called Red Leagues tried to break up large estates and force landlords to reduce their rents. In all these actions, the model of the Russian Revolution, although it was only vaguely understood, encouraged the development of local radicalism. In large numbers, voters abandoned the poorly organized parties of the center and the moderate left. They supported two more radical groups: the Socialists and the Catholic People's party (newly formed with the pope's blessing), which appealed to the common people, especially in the countryside. Neither party preached revolution, yet both urged wide-ranging social and economic reforms.

The rising radical tide, especially seen against the backdrop of the Bolshevik revolution, worried other social groups. Industrialists and landowners feared for their property. Small shopkeepers and white-collar workers—social groups that did not think the working-class movement supported their interests—found themselves alienated by business elites on the one hand and by apparently revolutionary radicals on the other. The threat from the left provoked a strong surge to the right. Fascism appeared in the form of vigilante groups breaking up strikes, fighting with workers in the streets, or ousting the Red Leagues from lands occupied in the countryside.

The Rise of Mussolini

"I am fascism," said Benito Mussolini, and indeed, the success of the Italian fascist movement depended heavily on his leadership. Mussolini (1883–1945) was the son of a socialist blacksmith. His mother was a schoolteacher, and he deferentially followed in her footsteps. But he was restless and dissatisfied, soon leaving Italy for further study in Switzerland. There he gave part of his time to his books and the rest to writing articles for socialist newspapers. Expelled from the country for fomenting strikes, he returned to Italy, where he became a journalist and eventually the editor of *Avanti,* the leading socialist daily.

Mussolini did not hold to any particular doctrine, and he reversed himself at several points. When war broke out in August 1914, Mussolini insisted that Italy should remain neutral. He had scarcely adopted this position when he began urging participation on the Allied side. Deprived of his position as the editor of *Avanti,* he founded a new paper, *Il Popolo d'Italia,* and dedicated its columns to arousing enthusiasm for war.

As early as October 1914, Mussolini had organized groups, called fasci, to help drum up support for the war. Members of the fasci were young idealists, fanatical nationalists. After the war, these groups formed the base of Mus-

EUROPE IN 1923. ▪ ***Which countries and empires lost territories after the First World War, and with what consequences?*** ▪ ***How did the Russian Revolution change European politics?*** ▪ ***What problems arose in the central and eastern European nations created after the First World War?***

solini's fascist movement. (The word *fascism* derives from the Latin *fasces:* an ax surrounded by a bundle of sticks that represented the authority of the Roman state. The Italian *fascio* means "group" or "band.") In 1919, Mussolini drafted the original platform of the Fascist party. It had several surprising elements, such as universal suffrage (including woman), an eight-hour workday, and a tax on inheritances. A new platform, adopted in 1920, abandoned all references to economic reforms. Neither platform earned the fascists much political success.

MUSSOLINI REVIEWS A FASCIST YOUTH PARADE. Mobilizing youth was central to fascism and Nazism; it demonstrated the vigor of the movements.

What the fascists lacked in political support, they made up for in aggressive determination. They gained the respect of the middle class and landowners and intimidated many others by forcefully repressing radical movements of industrial workers and peasants. They attacked socialists, often physically, and succeeded in taking over some local governments. As the national regime weakened, Mussolini's coercive politics made him look like a solution to the absence of leadership. In September 1922, he began to negotiate with other parties and the king for fascist participation in government. On October 28, an army of about 50,000 fascist militia, in black-shirted uniforms, marched into Rome and occupied the capital. The premier resigned, and the following day the king, Victor Emmanuel III, reluctantly invited Mussolini to form a cabinet. Without firing a shot the Black Shirts had gained control of the Italian government. The explanation of their success is to be found less in the strength of the fascist movement itself than in the Italian disappointments after the war and the weakness of the older governing classes.

The parliamentary system had folded under pressure. And though Mussolini had "legally" been granted his power, he immediately began to establish a one-party dictatorship. The doctrines of Italian fascism had three components. The first was statism. The state was declared to incorporate every interest and every loyalty of its members. There was to be "nothing above the state, nothing outside the state, nothing against the state." The second was nationalism. Nationhood was the highest form of society, with a life and a soul of its own, transcending the individuals who composed it. The third was militarism. Nations that did not expand would eventually wither and die. Fascists believed that war ennobled man and regenerated sluggish and decadent peoples.

Mussolini began to rebuild Italy in accordance with these principles. The first step was to change electoral laws so they granted his party solid parliamentary majorities and to intimidate the opposition. He then moved to close down parliamentary government and other parties entirely. He abolished the cabinet system and all but extinguished the powers of the Parliament. He made the Fascist party an integral part of the Italian constitution. Mussolini assumed the dual position of prime minister and party leader (*duce*), and he used the party's militia to eliminate his enemies by intimidation and violence. Mussolini's government also controlled the police, muzzled the press, and censored academic activity.

Meanwhile, Mussolini preached the end of class conflict and its replacement by national unity. He began to reorganize the economy and labor, taking away the power of the country's labor movement. The Italian economy was placed under the management of twenty-two corporations, each responsible for a major industrial enterprise. In each corporation were representatives of trade unions, whose members were organized by the Fascist party, the employers, and the government. Together, the members of these corporations were given the task of determining working conditions, wages, and prices. It is not surprising, however, that the decisions of these bodies were closely supervised by the government and favored the position of management. Indeed, the government quickly aligned with big business, creating more of a corrupt bureaucracy than a revolutionary economy.

Mussolini secured some working-class assent with state-sponsored programs, including massive public-works projects, library building, paid vacations for workers, and social security. In 1929, he settled Italy's sixty-year-old conflict with the Roman Catholic Church. He signed a treaty that granted independence to the papal residence in the Vatican City and established Roman Catholicism as the official religion of the state. The treaty also guaranteed religious education in the nation's schools and made religious marriage ceremonies mandatory.

In fact, Mussolini's regime did much to maintain the status quo. Party officers exercised some political supervision over bureaucrats yet did not infiltrate the bureaucracy in significant numbers. Moreover, Mussolini remained on friendly terms with the elites who had assisted his rise to power. Whatever he might proclaim about the distinctions between fascism and capitalism, the economy of Italy remained dependent on private enterprise.

The Italian dictator boasted that fascism had pulled the country back from economic chaos. Like other European economies, the Italian economy did improve in the late 1920s. The regime created the appearance of efficiency, and Mussolini's admirers famously claimed that he had at last "made the trains run on time." Fascism, however, did little to lessen Italy's plight during the worldwide depression of the 1930s.

GERMAN WOMEN SMOKING CIGARS DURING THE WEIMAR REPUBLIC, 1927. The Weimar years were marked by a new atmosphere of cultural experimentation, especially in German cities. The traumatic experience of World War 1, which destroyed so many families and overturned the social and political order, also made prewar social conventions about sex, marriage, and gender seem quaint and outdated. This scene, in which women are smoking and drinking in public, while wearing masculine hairstyles and casually demonstrating their affection for one another was almost unimaginable in 1910. In the 1920s, however, such scenes were common enough to provoke controversy and scandal, becoming fodder for the media, and providing material for best-selling novels. Similar debates over the "New Woman" of the 1920s took place in other European countries, and Hitler and the Nazi party used such images in their campaign to discredit Weimar society as "degenerate."

Like Nazism later, fascism had contradictory elements. It sought to restore traditional authority and, at the same time, mobilize all of Italian society for economic and nationalist purposes—a process that inevitably undercut older authorities. It created new authoritarian organizations and activities that comported with these goals: exercise programs to make the young fit and mobilized, youth camps, awards to mothers of large families, political rallies, and parades in small towns in the countryside. Activities like these offered people a feeling of political involvement though they no longer enjoyed political rights. This mobilized but essentially passive citizenship was a hallmark of fascism.

WEIMAR GERMANY

On November 9, 1918—two days before the armistice ending the First World War—a massive and largely unexpected uprising in Berlin resulted in the kaiser's abdication and the birth of a new German republic. The leader of the new government was Friedrich Ebert, a member of the Social Democratic party (SPD) in the Reichstag. The revolution spread quickly. By the end of the month, councils of workers and soldiers controlled hundreds of German cities. The "November Revolution" was fast and far reaching, though not as revolutionary as many middle- and upper-class conservatives feared. The majority of socialists steered a cautious, democratic course: they wanted reforms but were willing to leave much of the existing imperial bureaucracy intact. Above all, they wanted a popularly elected national assembly to draft a constitution for the new republic.

Two months passed, however, before elections could be held—a period of crisis that verged on civil war. The revolutionary movement that had brought the SPD to power now threatened it. Independent socialists and a nascent Communist party wanted radical reforms, and in December 1918 and January 1919, they staged armed uprisings in the streets of Berlin. Fearful of a Bolshevik-style revolution, the Social Democratic government turned against its former allies and sent militant bands of workers and volunteers to crush the uprisings. During the conflict, the government's fighters murdered Rosa Luxemburg and Karl Liebknecht—two German communist leaders who became instant martyrs. Violence continued into 1920, creating a lasting bitterness among groups on the left.

More important, the revolutionary aftermath of the war gave rise to bands of militant counterrevolutionaries. Veterans and other young nationalists joined so-called *Freikorps* (free corps). Such groups developed throughout the country, drawing as many as several hundred thousand members. Former army officers who led these militias continued their war experience by fighting against Bolsheviks, Poles, and communists. The politics of the Freikorps were fiercely right wing. Anti-Marxist, anti-Semitic, and antiliberal, they openly opposed the new German republic and its parliamentary democracy. Many of the early Nazi leaders had fought in the First World War and participated in Freikorps units.

Germany's new government—known as the Weimar Republic (*VY-mahr*) for the city in which its constitution was drafted—rested on a coalition of socialists, Catholic centrists, and liberal democrats, a necessary compromise since no single party won a majority of the votes in the January 1919 election. The Weimar constitution was based on the values of parliamentary liberalism and set up an open, pluralistic framework for German democracy. Through a series of compromises, the constitution established universal suffrage (for both women and men) and a bill of rights that guaranteed not only civil liberties but also a range of social entitlements. On paper, at least, the revolutionary movement had succeeded.

Yet the Weimar government lasted just over a decade. By 1930, it was in crisis, and in 1933 it collapsed. What happened? Many of Weimar's problems were born from Germany's defeat in the First World War, which was not only devastating but also humiliating. Many Germans soon latched onto rumors that the army hadn't actually been defeated in battle but instead had been stabbed in the back by socialists and Jewish leaders in the German government. Army officers cultivated this story even before the war was over; and though untrue, it helped salve the wounded pride of German patriots. In the next decade, those in search of a scapegoat also blamed the republican regime, which had signed the Versailles treaty. What was needed, many critics argued, was authoritative leadership to guide the nation and regain the world's respect.

The Treaty of Versailles magnified Germany's sense of dishonor. Germany was forced to cede a tenth of its territory, accept responsibility for the war, and slash the size of its army to a mere hundred thousand men—a punishment that riled the politically powerful corps of officers. Most important, the treaty saddled Germany with punitive reparations. Negotiating the $33 billion debt created problems for all the governments involved; it provoked anger from the German public and, in a global economy, had unintended effects on the recipients as well as the debtors. Some opponents of the reparations settlement urged the government not to pay, arguing that the enormous sum would doom Germany's economy. In 1924, Germany accepted a new schedule of reparations designed by an international committee headed by the American financier Charles G. Dawes. At the same time, the German chancellor Gustav Stresemann moved Germany toward a foreign policy of cooperation and rapprochement that lasted throughout the 1920s. Many German people, however, continued to resent reparations, Versailles, and the government that refused to repudiate the treaty.

HYPERINFLATION. German children use stacks of money as toys. In July 1922, the American dollar was worth 670 German marks; in November 1923 it was worth 4,210,500,000,000.
▪ ***How might hyperinflation have affected attitudes in Germany toward the Weimar Republic's government?***

Major economic crises also played a central role in Weimar's collapse. The first period of emergency occurred in the early 1920s. Still reeling from wartime inflation, the government was hard-pressed for revenues. Funding post-war demobilization programs, social welfare, and reparations forced the government to continue to print money. Inflation became nearly unstoppable. By 1923, as one historian writes, the economic situation had "acquired an almost surrealistic quality." A pound of potatoes cost about 9 marks in January, 40 million marks by October. Beef went for almost 2 trillion marks per pound. The government finally took drastic measures to stabilize the currency in 1924, but millions of Germans had already been ruined. For those on fixed incomes, such as pensioners and stockholders, savings and security had vanished. Middle-class employees, farmers, and workers were all hard hit by the economic crisis, and many of them abandoned the traditional political parties in protest. In their eyes, the parties that claimed to represent the middle classes had created the problems and proved incapable of fixing them.

Beginning in 1925, however, Germany's economy and government seemed to be recovering. By borrowing money, the country was able to make its scaled-down reparations payments and to earn money by selling cheap exports. In large cities, socialist municipal governments sponsored building projects that included schools, hospitals, and low-cost worker housing. But such economic and political stability was misleading. The economy remained dependent on large infusions of capital from the United States set up by the Dawes Plan as part of the effort to settle reparations. That dependence made the German economy especially vulnerable to American economic developments. When the U.S. stock market crashed in 1929, beginning the Great Depression (see below), capital flow to Germany virtually stopped.

The Great Depression pushed Weimar's political system to the breaking point. In 1929, there were 2 million unemployed; in 1932, 6 million. In those three years production dropped by 44 percent. Artisans and small shopkeepers lost both status and income. Farmers fared even worse, having never recovered from the crisis of the early 1920s. Peasants staged mass demonstrations against the government's agricultural policies even before the depression hit. For white-collar and civil service employees, the depression meant lower salaries, poor working conditions, and a constant threat of unemployment. Burdened with plummeting tax revenues and spiraling numbers of Germans in need of relief, the government repeatedly cut welfare benefits, which further demoralized the electorate. Finally, the crisis created an opportunity for Weimar's opponents. Many leading industrialists supported a return to authoritarian government, and they were allied with equally conservative landowners, united by a desire for protective economic policies to stimulate the sale of domestic goods and foodstuffs. Those conservative forces wielded considerable power in Germany, beyond the control of the government. So too did the army and the civil service, which were staffed with opponents of the republic—men who rejected the principles of parliamentary democracy and international cooperation that Weimar represented.

HITLER AND THE NATIONAL SOCIALISTS

National Socialism in Germany emerged out of the bitterness of the defeat in the First World War, but Adolf Hitler's political party did not gain mass support until the economic crisis caused by the Depression in 1929 led many Germans to give up on the traditional political parties. At each stage in the movement's development, Hitler found a way to capitalize on the mistakes of his opponents and draw more support to his cause.

Adolf Hitler was born in 1889 in Austria, not Germany. The son of a petty customs official in the Austrian civil service, Hitler dropped out of school and went to Vienna in 1909 to become an artist. That failed. He was rejected by the academy and forced to eke out a dismal existence doing manual labor and painting cheap watercolors in Vienna. Meanwhile, he developed the violent political prejudices that would become the guiding principles of the Nazi regime. He ardently admired the Austrian politicians preaching anti-Semitism, anti-Marxism, and pan-Germanism. When war broke out in 1914, Hitler was among the jubilant crowds in the streets of Munich; and though he was an Austrian citizen, he enlisted in the German army, where he claimed to have finally found meaning in his life. After the war, he joined the newly formed German Workers' party, whose name changed in 1920 to the National Socialist Workers' party (abbreviated in popular usage to Nazi). The Nazis were but one among many small, militant groups of disaffected Germans devoted to racial nationalism and to the overthrow of the Weimar Republic. They grew out of the political milieu that refused to accept the defeat or the November Revolution and that blamed both on socialists and Jews.

Ambitious and outspoken, Hitler quickly moved up the rather short ladder of party leadership as a talented stump orator. By 1921, he was the *Führer*—the leader—to his followers in Bavaria. The wider public saw him as a "vulgar demagogue"—if they noticed him at all. In November 1923, during the worst days of the inflation crisis, the Nazis made a failed attempt (the Beer Hall Putsch in Munich) at overthrowing the state government of Bavaria. Hitler spent the next seven months in prison, where he wrote his autobiography and political manifesto *Mein Kampf* (*myn KAHMPF*;

Past and Present

The Great Depression and Today's Economy

What parallels can one see between the history of the Great Depression in the 1930s and the situation in the world's economy today, after the crisis of 2008? In both cases, the debate has focused on whether or not financial markets can operate without significant government oversight, and what responsibilities the government has to alleviate the pain of those whose jobs or wages are cut as a result of economic collapse. Left, in 1930s France, laborers battle police over wage cuts; right, in 2011, protesters demonstrate in Italy against the government's "austerity" policy, which saw reductions in pension benefits and job cuts.

Watch related author interview on StudySpace
wwnorton.com/web/westernciv18

"*My Struggle*") in 1924. Combining anti-Semitism with anticommunism, the book set out at great length the popular theory that Germany had been betrayed by its enemies and that the country needed strong leadership to regain international prominence. The failed 1923 putsch proved an eye-opening experience for Hitler; he recognized that the Nazis would have to play politics if they wanted to gain power. Released from prison in 1924, Hitler resumed leadership of the party. In the next five years, he consolidated his power over a growing membership of ardent supporters. Actively cultivating the image of the Nazi movement as a crusade against Marxism, capitalism, and Jews, he portrayed himself as the heroic savior of the German people.

An equally important factor in Hitler's rise to power was the Nazis' ambitious and unprecedented campaign program. In the "inflation election" of 1924, the Nazis polled 6.6 percent of the vote as a protest party at the radical fringe. With the economic stabilization of the mid-1920s, their meager share dropped to below 3 percent. But during this time of seeming decline, the Nazis were building an extensive organization of party activists that helped lay the foundation for the party's electoral gains later.

After 1928, political polarization between the right and left worked to Hitler's advantage and made it impossible for the Weimar government to put together a coalition that could support the continuation of democracy in Germany. Alienated voters, especially in rural areas, deserted the traditional political parties. The Nazis quickly learned how to benefit from this splintering of the electorate. Having failed to win over the German working class from the left, the Nazis stepped up their efforts to attract members of the rural and urban middle classes. Guided by their chief propagandist, Joseph Goebbels, the party hammered home its critique of Weimar society: its parliamentary system, the power of the left and the labor movement, liberal moral codes, women wearing "decadent" flapper fashions, and "cosmopolitan" (Jewish or insufficiently nationalist) movies such as *All Quiet on the Western Front*. Presenting itself as young and dynamic, the Nazis built a national profile as an alternative to the parties of middle-class conservatives. By 1930, they were better funded and better organized than ever, winning 18.3 percent of the vote.

Who voted for the Nazis? The Nazis polled highly with small property holders and the rural middle class long before the depression. Other segments of the middle class—notably pensioners, the elderly, and war widows—came to support the Nazis during the economic crisis, when they feared reduction of insurance or pension benefits and when the older conservative parties failed to meet their needs. The Nazis also courted the traditionally elitist civil service. And though they failed to win votes from industrial workers, the Nazis found some of their strongest support among workers in handicrafts and small-scale manufacturing.

In 1930, the Nazi party won 107 of 577 seats in the Reichstag, second only to the Social Democrats, who controlled 143. No party could gain a majority. No governing coalition was possible without Nazi support. And the Nazis refused to join any cabinet that was not headed by Hitler. The chancellor, Heinrich Brüning of the Catholic Center party, continued to govern by emergency decrees, but his deflationary economic policies were disastrous. Industrial production continued to crash and unemployment continued to climb. In 1932, Hitler ran for president and narrowly lost, although he staged an unprecedented campaign by airplane, visiting twenty-one cities in six days. When another parliamentary election was called in July 1932, the Nazis won 37.4 percent of the vote, which, though not a majority, was a significant plurality. The Nazis could claim that they were the party able to draw support across class, geographic, and generational lines. They benefited from their position as outsiders, untainted by involvement in unpopular parliamentary coalitions. Indeed, the failure of the traditional parties was key to the success of the Nazis.

Despite its electoral success in 1932, the Nazi party had not won a majority; Hitler was not in power. Instead, Hitler was appointed chancellor in January 1933 by President Hindenburg, who hoped to create a conservative coalition government by bringing the Nazis into line with the less radical parties. Hindenburg and others in the government had underestimated the Nazis' power and popularity. Legally installed in office, Hitler immediately made the most of it. When a Dutch anarchist with links to the Communist party set fire to the Reichstag on the night of February 27, Hitler seized the opportunity to suspend civil rights "as a defensive measure against communist acts of violence." He convinced Hindenburg to dissolve the Reichstag and to order a new election on March 5, 1933. Under Hitler's sway, the new parliament legally granted him unlimited powers for the next four years. Hitler proclaimed his new government the Third Reich. (The first Reich was the German empire of the Middle Ages; the second was that of the kaisers.)

NAZISM AND THE RURAL MYTH. To stress the rural roots of Aryan Germany, Hitler appeared in lederhosen in the 1920s. ▪ ***Which social groups in Germany were explicitly excluded by this myth?***

Nazi Germany

By the fall of 1933, Germany had become a one-party state. The socialist and communist left was crushed by the new regime. Almost all non-Nazi organizations had been either abolished or forced to become part of the Nazi system. Nazi party leaders took over various government departments; party *Gauleiters,* or regional directors, assumed administrative responsibility throughout the country. Party propaganda sought to impress citizens with the regime's "monolithic efficiency." But in fact, the Nazi government was a tangled bureaucratic maze, with both agencies and individuals vying fiercely for Hitler's favor.

Ironically, at the end of the party's first year in power, the most serious challenges to Hitler came from within the party. Hitler's paramilitary Nazi storm troopers (the SA) had been formed to maintain discipline within the party and impose order in society. SA membership soared after 1933, and many in the SA hailed Hitler's appointment as the beginning of a genuinely Nazi revolution. Such radicalism was alarming to the more traditional conservative groups that had helped make Hitler chancellor. If Hitler was to maintain power, then, he needed to tame the SA. On the night of June 30, 1934, more than a thousand high-ranking SA officials, including several of Hitler's oldest associates, were executed in a bloody purge known as the Night of Long Knives. The purge was accomplished by a second paramilitary organization, the *Schutzstaffel* ("bodyguard"), or SS. Headed by the fanatical Heinrich Himmler, the SS became the most dreaded arm of Nazi terror. As Himmler saw it, the mission of the SS was to fight political and racial enemies of the regime, which included building the system of concentration camps. The first camp, at Dachau, opened in March 1933. The secret state police, known as the Gestapo, were responsible for the arrest, incarceration in camps, and murder of thousands of Germans. But the police force was generally understaffed and deluged with paperwork—as one historian has shown, the Gestapo was not "omniscient, omnipotent, and omnipresent." In fact, the majority of arrests was based on voluntary denunciations made by ordinary citizens against each other, often as petty personal attacks. It was not lost on the Gestapo leadership that these denunciations created a level of control that the Gestapo itself could never achieve.

Hitler and the Nazis enjoyed a sizable amount of popular support. Many Germans approved of Hitler's use of violence against the left. The Nazis could play on deep-seated fears of communism, and they spoke a language of intense national pride and unity that had broad appeal. Many Germans saw Hitler as a symbol of a strong, revitalized Germany. Propagandists fostered a Führer cult, depicting Hitler as a charismatic leader with the magnetic energy to bring people to their knees. Hitler's appeal also rested on his ability to give the German people what they wanted: jobs for workers, a productive economy for industrialists, a bulwark against communism for those who feared the wave of revolution. His appeal lay not so much in the programs he championed, many of which were ill-conceived or contradictory, but in his revolt against politics as they had been practiced in Germany. Finally, he promised to lead Germany back to national greatness and to "overthrow" the Versailles settlement.

Hitler's plans for national recovery called for full-scale rearmament and economic self-sufficiency. With policies similar to those of other Western nations, the Nazis made massive public investments, set strict market controls to stop inflation and stabilize the currency, and sealed Germany off from the world economy. The regime launched state-financed construction projects—highways, public housing, reforestation. Late in the decade, as the Nazis rebuilt the entire German military complex, unemployment dropped from over 6 million to under 200,000. The German economy looked better than any other in Europe. Hitler claimed this as his "economic miracle." Such improvements were significant, especially in the eyes of Germans who had lived through the continual turmoil of war, inflation, political instability, and economic crisis.

Like Mussolini, Hitler moved to abolish class conflict by stripping working-class institutions of their power. He outlawed trade unions and strikes, froze wages, and organized workers and employers into a National Labor Front. At the same time, the Nazis increased workers' welfare benefits, generally in line with the other Western nations. Class distinctions were somewhat blurred by the regime's attempts to infuse a new national "spirit" into the entire society. Popular organizations cut across class lines, especially among the youth. The Hitler Youth, a club modeled on the Boy Scouts, was highly successful at teaching children the values of Hitler's Reich; the National Labor Service drafted students for a term to work on state-sponsored building and reclamation projects. Government policy encouraged women to withdraw from the labor force, both to ease unemployment and to conform to Nazi notions of a woman's proper role. "Can woman," one propagandist asked, "conceive of anything more beautiful than to sit with her husband in her cozy home and listen inwardly to the loom of time weaving the weft and warp of motherhood?"

NAZI RACISM

At the core of Nazi ideology lay a particularly virulent racism. Much of this racism was not new. Hitler and the Nazis drew on a revived and especially violent form of nineteenth-century Social Darwinism, according to which nations and people struggled for survival, with the superior peoples strengthening themselves in the process. By the early twentieth century, the rise of the social sciences had taken nineteenth-century prejudices and racial thinking into new terrain. Just as medical science had cured bodily ills, doctors, criminologists, and social workers sought ways to cure social ills. Across the West, scientists and intellectuals worked to purify the body politic, improve the human race, and eliminate the "unfit." Even progressive-minded individuals sometimes subscribed to eugenics, a program of racial engineering to improve either personal or public fitness. Eugenic policies

Analyzing Primary Sources

Nazi Propaganda

The Nazis promised many things to many people. As the document by Goebbels shows, anti-Semitism allowed them to blend their racial nationalism, vaguely defined (and anti-Marxist) socialism, and disgust with the state of German culture and politics. Joseph Goebbels, one of the early members of the party, became director of propaganda for the party in 1928. Later, Hitler appointed him head of the National Ministry for Public Enlightenment and Propaganda. The Nazis worked hard to win the rural vote, as evidenced by the Nazi campaign pamphlet reprinted in the second excerpt. The Nazis tried to appeal to farmers' economic grievances; their fears of socialism, on the one hand, and big business, on the other; and their more general hostility to urban life and culture.

Joseph Goebbels, "Why Are We Enemies of the Jews?"

We are NATIONALISTS because we see in the NATION the only possibility for the protection and the furtherance of our existence.

The NATION is the organic bond of a people for the protection and defense of their lives. He is nationally minded who understands this IN WORD AND IN DEED. . . .

Young nationalism has its unconditional demands, BELIEF IN THE NATION is a matter of all the people, not for individuals of rank, a class, or an industrial clique. The eternal must be separated from the contemporary. The maintenance of a rotten industrial system has nothing to do with nationalism. I can love Germany and hate capitalism; not only CAN I do it, I also MUST do it. The germ of the rebirth of our people LIES ONLY IN THE DESTRUCTION OF THE SYSTEM OF PLUNDERING THE HEALTHY POWER OF THE PEOPLE.

WE ARE NATIONALISTS BECAUSE WE, AS GERMANS, LOVE GERMANY. And because we love Germany, we demand the protection of its national spirit and we battle against its destroyers.

WHY ARE WE SOCIALISTS?

We are SOCIALISTS because we see in SOCIALISM the only possibility for maintaining our racial existence and through it the reconquest of our political freedom and the rebirth of the German state. SOCIALISM has its peculiar form first of all through its comradeship in arms with the forward-driving energy of a newly awakened nationalism. Without nationalism it is nothing, a phantom, a theory, a vision of air, a book. With it, it is everything, THE FUTURE, FREEDOM, FATHERLAND! . . .

WHY DO WE OPPOSE THE JEWS?

We are ENEMIES OF THE JEWS, because we are fighters for the freedom of the German people. THE JEW IS THE CAUSE AND THE BENEFICIARY OF OUR MISERY. He has used the social difficulties of the broad masses of our people to deepen the unholy split between Right and Left among our people. He has made two halves of Germany. He is the real cause for our loss of the Great War.

The Jew has no interest in the solution of Germany's fateful problems. He CANNOT have any. FOR HE LIVES ON THE FACT THAT THERE HAS BEEN NO SOLUTION. If we would make the German people a unified community and give them freedom before the world, then the Jew can have no place among us. He has the best trumps in his hands when a people lives in inner and outer slavery. THE JEW IS RESPONSIBLE FOR OUR MISERY AND HE LIVES ON IT.

That is the reason why we, AS NATIONALISTS and AS SOCIALISTS, oppose the Jew. HE HAS CORRUPTED OUR RACE, FOULED OUR MORALS, UNDERMINED OUR CUSTOMS, AND BROKEN OUR POWER.

in the Third Reich began with a 1933 law for the compulsory sterilization of "innumerable inferior and hereditarily tainted" people. This "social-hygienic racism" later became the systematic murder of mentally and physically ill patients. Social policy was governed by a basic division between those who possessed "value" and those who did not, with the aim of creating a racial utopia.

The centerpiece of Nazi racism was anti-Semitism. This centuries-old phenomenon was part of Christian society from the Middle Ages on. By the nineteenth century, traditional Christian anti-Semitism was joined by a current of nationalist anti-Jewish theory. A great many of the theorists of European nationalism saw the Jewish people as permanent outsiders who could only be assimilated and

National Socialist Campaign Pamphlet, 1932

GERMAN FARMER YOU BELONG TO HITLER! WHY?

The German farmer stands between two great dangers today:

The one danger is the American economic system—Big capitalism!

it means "world economic crisis"

it means "eternal interest slavery" . . .

it means that the world is nothing more than a bag of booty for Jewish finance in Wall Street, New York, and Paris

it enslaves man under the slogans of progress, technology, rationalization, standardization, etc.

it knows only profit and dividends

it wants to make the world into a giant trust

it puts the machine over man

it annihilates the independent, earth-rooted farmer, and its final aim is the world dictatorship of Jewry [. . .]

it achieves this in the political sphere through parliament and the swindle of democracy. In the economic sphere, through the control of credit, the mortgaging of land, the stock exchange and the market principle [. . .]

The farmer's leagues, the Landvolk and the Bavarian Farmers' League all pay homage to this system.

The other danger is the Marxist economic system of bolshevism:

it knows only the state economy

it knows only one class, the proletariat

it brings in the controlled economy

it doesn't just annihilate the self-sufficient farmer economically—it roots him out [. . .]

it brings the rule of the tractor

it nationalizes the land and creates mammoth factory-farms

it uproots and destroys man's soul, making him the powerless tool of the communist idea—or kills him

it destroys the family, belief, and customs [. . .]

it is anti-Christ, it desecrates the churches [. . .]

its final aim is the world dictatorship of the proletariat, that means ultimately the world dictatorship of Jewry, for the Jew controls this powerless proletariat and uses it for his dark plans

Big capitalism and bolshevism work hand in hand; they are born of Jewish thought and serve the master plan of world Jewry.

Who alone can rescue the farmer from these dangers?

NATIONAL SOCIALISM!

Source (for both documents): Anton Kaes, Matin Jay, and Edward Dimendberg, *The Weimar Republic Sourcebook* (Los Angeles: 1994), pp. 137–38, 142.

Questions for Analysis

1. How did Goebbels use metaphors of illness and health, growth and decay? Do the metaphors suggest what the Nazis would try to do to cure the ills of Germany if they took power?
2. How does Goebbels's anti-Semitism differ from the nineteenth-century French anti-Semitism documented on page 779?
3. The Nazi campaign pamphlet of 1932 targeted German farmers. How did the pamphlet play on their fears of market manipulation by American big business and Bolshevik demands for collectivization and seizure of private land? How did the Nazis identify themselves with Christianity and traditional values, sincerely or not?
4. How, specifically, does the party propose to deal with the "two great dangers of today"?

become citizens if they denied their Jewish identity. At the end of the nineteenth century, during the Dreyfus Affair in France (see Chapter 23), French and European anti-Semites launched a barrage of propaganda against Jews—scores of books, pamphlets, and magazines blamed Jews for all the troubles of modernity, from socialism to international banks and mass culture. The late nineteenth century also brought a wave of pogroms—violent assaults on Jewish communities—especially in Russia. Racial anti-Semitism drew the line between Jews and non-Jews on the basis of erroneous biology. Religious conversion, which traditional Christian anti-Semites encouraged, would not change biology. Nor would assimilation, which was counseled by more secular nationalist thinkers.

NAZI BOYCOTT OF JEWISH SHOPS IN BERLIN, 1933. Nazis stand in front of a Jewish-owned clothing store. "Germans! Buy nothing from the Jews!"

It is important not to generalize, but anti-Semitism in these different forms was a well-established and open political force in most of the West. By attacking Jews, anti-Semites attacked modern institutions—from socialist parties and the mass press to international banking—as part of an "international Jewish conspiracy" to undermine traditional authority and nationality. Conservative party leaders told shopkeepers and workers that "Jewish capitalists" were responsible for the demise of small businesses, for the rise of giant department stores, and for precarious economic swings that threatened their livelihoods. In Vienna, middle-class voters supported the openly anti-Semitic Christian Democrats. In Germany, in 1893, sixteen avowed anti-Semites were elected to the Reichstag, and the Conservative party made anti-Semitism part of its official program. Hitler gave this anti-Semitism an especially murderous twist by tying it to doctrines of war and social-hygienic racism.

To what extent was the Nazis' virulent anti-Semitism shared? Although the "Jewish Question" was clearly Hitler's primary obsession during the early 1920s, he made the theme less central in campaign appearances as the Nazi movement entered mainstream politics, shifting instead to attacks on Marxism and the Weimar democracy. Moreover, anti-Semitic beliefs would not have distinguished the Nazi from any other party on the political right; it was likely of only secondary importance to people's opinions of the Nazis. Soon after Hitler came to power, though, German Jews faced discrimination, exclusion from rights as citizens, and violence. Racial laws excluded Jews from public office as early as April 1933. The Nazis encouraged a boycott of Jewish merchants, while the SA created a constant threat of random violence. In 1935, the Nuremberg Decrees deprived Jews (defined by bloodline) of their German citizenship and prohibited marriage between Jews and other Germans. Violence escalated. In November 1938, the SA attacked some 7,500 Jewish stores, burned nearly 200 synagogues, killed ninety-one Jews, and beat up thousands more in a campaign of terror known as *Kristallnacht,* the Night of Broken Glass. Violence like this did raise some opposition from ordinary Germans. Legal persecution, however, met only silent acquiescence. And from the perspective of Jewish people, *Kristallnacht* made it plain that there was no safe place for them in Germany. Unfortunately, only one year remained before the outbreak of war made it impossible for Jews to escape.

What did national socialism and fascism have in common? Both arose in the interwar period as responses to the First World War and the Russian Revolution. Both were violently antisocialist and anticommunist, determined to "rescue" their nations from the threat of Bolshevism. Both were intensely nationalistic; they believed that national solidarity came before all other allegiances and superseded all other rights. Both opposed parliamentary government and democracy as cumbersome and divisive. Both found their power in mass-based authoritarian politics. Similar movements existed in all the countries of the West, but only in a few cases did they actually form regimes. Nazism, however, distinguished itself by making a racially pure state central to its vision, a vision that would lead to global struggle and mass murder.

THE GREAT DEPRESSION IN THE DEMOCRACIES

The histories of the three major Western democracies—Great Britain, France, and the United States—run roughly parallel during the years after the First World War. In all three countries, governments put their trust in prewar policies and assumptions until the Great Depression forced them to make major social and economic reforms, reforms that would lay the foundations of the modern welfare state. These nations weathered the upheavals of the interwar years, but they did not do so easily.

Both France and Britain sought to keep the price of manufactured goods low in the 1920s, to stimulate demand in the world markets. This policy of deflation kept businessmen happy but placed a great burden on French and British workers, whose wages and living standards remained low. In both countries, class conflict boiled just below the surface, as successive governments refused to raise taxes to pay for social reforms. Workers' resentment in Britain helped elect the first Labour party government in 1924 and again in 1929. A general strike in Britain in 1926 succeeded only in increasing middle-class antipathy toward workers. In France, a period of strikes immediately after the war subsided and was followed by a period in which employers refused to bargain with labor unions. When the French government passed a modified social insurance program in 1930—insuring against sickness, old age, and death—French workers remained unsatisfied.

Among the democracies, the United States was a bastion of conservatism. Presidents Warren G. Harding, Calvin Coolidge, and Herbert Hoover held a social philosophy formulated by the barons of big business in the nineteenth century. The Supreme Court used its power of judicial review to nullify progressive legislation enacted by state governments and occasionally by Congress.

The conservative economic and social policies of the prewar period were dealt their deathblow by the Great Depression of 1929. This worldwide depression peaked during the years 1929–33, but its effects lasted a decade. For those who went through it, the depression was perhaps the formative experience of their lives and the decisive crisis of the interwar period. It was an important factor in the rise of Nazism; but in fact, it forced every country to forge new economic policies and to deal with unprecedented economic turmoil.

The Origins of the Great Depression

What caused the Great Depression? Its deepest roots lay in the instability of national currencies and in the interdependence of national economies. Throughout the 1920s, Europeans had seen a sluggish growth rate. A major drop in world agricultural prices hurt the countries of southern and eastern Europe, where agriculture was small in scale and high in cost. Unable to make a profit on the international market, these agricultural countries bought fewer manufactured goods from the more industrial sectors of northern Europe, causing a widespread drop in industrial productivity. Restrictions on free trade crippled the economy even more. Although debtor nations needed open markets to sell their goods, most nations were raising high trade barriers to protect domestic manufacturers from foreign competition.

Then in October of 1929, prices on the New York Stock Exchange collapsed. On October 24, "Black Thursday," 12 million shares were traded amid unprecedented chaos. Even more surprising, the market kept falling. Black Thursday was followed by Black Monday and then Black Tuesday: falling prices, combined with an enormously high number of trades, made for the worst day in the history of the stock exchange to that point. The rise of the United States as an international creditor during the Great War meant that the crash had immediate, disastrous consequences in Europe. When the value of stocks dropped, banks found themselves short of capital and then, when not rescued by the government, forced to close. International investors called in their debts. A series of banking houses shut their doors, among them Credit Anstalt, the biggest bank in Austria and one with significant interests in two-thirds of Austrian industry. Workers lost their jobs; indeed, manufacturers laid off virtually entire workforces. In 1930, 4 million Americans were unemployed; in 1933, 13 million—nearly a third of the workforce. By then, per capita income in the United States had fallen 48 percent. In Germany, too, the drop was brutal. In 1929, 2 million were unemployed; in 1932, 6 million. Production dropped 44 percent in Germany, 47 percent in the United States. The stock-market collapse led to widespread bank failure and brought the economy virtually to a standstill.

The governments of the West initially responded to the depression with monetary measures. In 1931, Great Britain abandoned the gold standard; the United States followed suit in 1933. By no longer pegging their currencies to the price of gold, these countries hoped to make money cheaper and thus more available for economic recovery programs. This action was the forerunner of a broad program of currency management, which became an important element in a general policy of economic nationalism. In another important move, Great Britain abandoned its time-honored policy of free trade in 1932, raising protective tariffs as high as 100 percent. But monetary policy alone could not end the hardships of ordinary families. Governments were increasingly forced to address their concerns with a wide range of social reforms.

Britain was the most cautious in its relief efforts. A national government composed of Conservative, Liberal, and Labour party members came to power in 1931. To underwrite effective programs of public assistance, however, the government would have to spend beyond its income—something it was reluctant to do. France, on the other hand, adopted the most advanced set of policies to combat the effects of the depression. In 1936, responding to a threat from ultraconservatives to overthrow the republic, a Popular Front government under the leadership of the socialist Léon Blum was formed by the Radical, Radical Socialist, and Communist parties, and lasted for two years. The Popular Front nationalized the munitions industry and reorganized the Bank of France to break the largest stockholders' monopolistic control over credit. The government also decreed a forty-hour week for all urban workers and initiated a program of public works. For the benefit of the farmers, it established a wheat office to fix the price and regulate the distribution of grain. Although the Popular Front temporarily quelled the threat from the political right, conservatives were generally uncooperative and unimpressed by the attempts to aid the French working class. Both a socialist and Jewish, Blum faced fierce anti-Semitism in France. Fearing that Blum was the forerunner of a French Lenin, conservatives declared, "Better Hitler than Blum." They got their wish before the decade was out.

U.S. FARMERS ON THEIR WAY WEST IN THE 1930s. Forced from their land by depression, debts, and drought, thousands of farmers and their families headed to California, Oregon, and Washington in search of employment.

The most dramatic response to the depression came in the United States for two reasons. First, the United States had clung longest to nineteenth-century economic philosophy. Before the depression, the business classes adhered firmly to the creed of freedom of contract. Industrialists insisted on their right to form monopolies, and they used the government as a tool to frustrate the demands of both workers and consumers. Second, the depression was more severe in the United States than in the European democracies. America had survived the First World War unscathed—and, indeed, had benefited enormously—but now its economy was ravaged even more than Europe's. In 1933, Franklin D. Roosevelt succeeded Herbert Hoover as president and announced the New Deal, a program of reform and reconstruction to rescue the country.

The New Deal aimed to get the country back on its feet without destroying the capitalist system. The government would manage the economy, sponsor relief programs, and fund public-works projects to increase mass purchasing power. These policies were shaped by the theories of the British economist John Maynard Keynes, who had already proved influential during the 1919 treaty meetings at Paris. Keynes argued that capitalism could create a just and efficient society if governments played a part in its management. First, Keynes abandoned the sacred cow of balanced budgets. Without advocating continuous deficit financing, he would have the government deliberately operate in the red whenever private investments weren't enough. Keynes also favored the creation of large amounts of venture capital—money for high-risk, high-reward investments—which he saw as the only socially productive form of capital. Finally, he recommended monetary control to promote prosperity and full employment.

Along with Social Security and other programs, the United States adopted a Keynesian program of "currency management," regulating the value of the dollar according to the needs of the economy. The New Deal helped both individuals and the country recover, but it left the crucial problem of unemployment unsolved. In 1939, after six years of the New Deal, the United States still had more than 9 million jobless workers—a figure that exceeded the combined unemployment of the rest of the world. Only with the outbreak of a new world war—which required millions of soldiers and armament workers—did the United States reach the full recovery that the New Deal had failed to deliver.

INTERWAR CULTURE: ARTISTS AND INTELLECTUALS

The interwar period also brought dramatic upheavals in the arts and sciences. Artists, writers, architects, and composers brought the revolutionary artistic forms of the turn of the century into the mainstream as they rejected traditional aesthetic values and experimented with new forms of expression. Scientists and psychologists challenged deeply held beliefs about the universe and human nature. Finally, radio, movies, and advertising created a new kind of mass culture that fed off the atmosphere of crisis in politics and the arts, and contributed to the anxieties of the age.

Interwar Intellectuals

Novelists, poets, and dramatists were disillusioned by the world war. Much literature in the interwar period reflected the themes of frustration, cynicism, and disenchantment that emerged from the failure of victory to fulfill its promises. The mood of the era is captured in the early work of the American Ernest Hemingway, whose novel *The Sun Also Rises* (1926) described a "lost generation." The poetry of the Anglo-American T. S. Eliot explored a peculiarly modern form of despair: life as a living death, to be endured as boredom and frustration. The German author Bertolt Brecht depicted the cynical corruption of elite members of society in plays written for a working-class audience in cabarets.

Other writers focused their attention on consciousness and inner life, often experimenting with new forms of prose. The Irish writer James Joyce perfected a style that became known as "stream of consciousness" in *Ulysses* (1922), a technique also associated with French author Marcel Proust. In the same vein, British author Virginia Woolf offered an eloquent and biting critique of Britain's elite institutions, from the universities that isolated women in separate, underfunded colleges to the suffocating decorum of middle-class families and relationships.

The depression of the 1930s fostered a second wave of more politicized literature, as a new generation felt called on to indict injustice and point the way to a better society. In *The Grapes of Wrath* (1939), the American writer John Steinbeck depicted the plight of impoverished farmers fleeing from the Dust Bowl to California only to find the land monopolized by companies that exploited their workers. Younger British authors such as W. H. Auden, Stephen Spender, and Christopher Isherwood were communist sympathizers who believed that their duty as artists was to support the revolution.

Interwar Artists

The innovations of the prewar avant-garde thrived in the postwar period. Visual art responded to the rapid transformations of twentieth-century society: new technologies, scientific discoveries, the abandonment of traditional beliefs, and the influence of non-Western cultures. Like the writers of the period, visual artists pushed the boundaries,

MARCEL DUCHAMP. In these photos, Duchamp used shaving cream to transform his appearance. Much of Duchamp's artwork showed his questioning of the role of the artist.

ARCHITECTURAL STYLE IN GERMANY BETWEEN THE WARS. The Bauhaus, by Walter Gropius (1883–1969). This school in Dessau, Germany, is a starkly functional prototype of the interwar "international style."

moving far beyond the conventional tastes of average men and women.

Pablo Picasso pursued his experiments in cubist variations and inventions. The "expressionists" argued that color and line expressed inherent psychological qualities by themselves, so paintings did not need a representational subject at all. The Russian Wassily Kandinsky followed this position to its logical conclusion, creating abstract and colorful paintings that he called "improvisations." A second group of expressionists rejected such experiments and claimed that their goal was "objectivity," by which they meant a candid appraisal of the state of humanity. Chief among this group was the German George Grosz (*Grohz*) whose cruel, satiric line has been likened to a "razor lancing a carbuncle." His scathing cartoonlike images became the most popular portraits of the despised Weimar government.

The dadaists went further, rebelling against the very idea of aesthetic principle. Principles were based on reason, and the world had proved that reason did not exist. Pulling their name at random from a dictionary, the dadaists rejected formal artistic conventions, preferring random juxtapositions from cutouts and collage, bizarre assemblages from wood, glass, and metal. The artists—the Frenchman Marcel Duchamp, the German Max Ernst, and the Alsatian Jean (Hans Arp)—claimed their works were meaningless and playful, but critics saw them as expressions of the subconscious. In Germany, dadaism took on political undertones as their anarchistic social critique challenged the very basis of national culture.

Other artists found inspiration for their work in social and political conflict. Mexican muralists Diego Rivera and José Clemente Orozco and the Americans Thomas Hart Benton and Reginald Marsh sought to depict the social conditions of the modern world, presenting in graphic detail the lives of ordinary working people. These artists avoided the experimentalism of the dadaists or the expressionists and aimed instead for an intelligible art, available to all.

Architects, too, rejected tradition, seeking a style that was more in harmony with the needs of modern civilization. Otto Wagner in Austria, Charles Édouard Jeanneret (known as Le Corbusier) in France, and Louis Sullivan and Frank Lloyd Wright in the United States pioneered a style known as "functionalism." Functionalists believed that the appearance of a building should proclaim its use and purpose. Ornament was designed to reflect an age of science and machines. The German functionalist Walter Gropius established a school in 1919—the Bauhaus—to serve as a center for the development of modern architecture. Their style of design, the so-called international style, explored the use of new materials—chromium, glass, steel, and concrete.

Interwar Scientific Developments

One powerful influence on the artists and intellectuals of the day was neither social nor political but scientific. The pioneering work of the German physicist Albert Einstein revolutionized not only the entire structure of physical science but also challenged ordinary people's most basic beliefs about the universe. Quickly recognized as one of the greatest intellects of all time, Einstein began to question the very foundations of traditional physics early in the twentieth century. By 1915, he had proposed entirely new ways of thinking about space, matter, time, and gravity.

Einstein's theories paved the way for another revolutionary development in physics—the splitting of the atom. As early as 1905, Einstein became convinced of the equivalence of mass and energy and worked out a formula for the conversion of one into the other: $E = mc^2$.

The formula had no practical application for years. Then in 1932, when the Englishman Sir James Chadwick discovered the neutron, scientists had an ideal weapon for bombarding the atom—that is, a way to split it. In 1939, two German physicists, Otto Hahn and Fritz Strassman, successfully split atoms of uranium by bombarding them with neutrons. The initial reaction produced a chain of reactions: each atom that was split shot off more neutrons, which split even more atoms. Scientists in Germany, Great Britain, and the United States were spurred on by governments anxious to turn these discoveries into weapons during the Second World War. American scientists soon prepared an atomic bomb, the most destructive weapon ever created. The legacy was ironic for Einstein, a man who devoted much of his life to promoting pacifism, liberalism, and social justice.

Another important contribution to physics that quickly entered popular culture was the "uncertainty principle" posited by the German physicist Werner Heisenberg in 1927. Heisenberg, who was strongly influenced by Einstein, showed that it is impossible—even in theory—to measure both the position and the speed of an object at the same time. The theory was of consequence only when dealing with atoms or subatomic particles. Though the public had little to no understanding of these groundbreaking scientific concepts, metaphorical invocations of relativity and the uncertainty principle fitted the ambiguities of the modern world. For many people, nothing was definite, everything was changing—and science seemed to be proving it.

Mass Culture and Its Possibilities

Cultural change, however, extended far beyond circles of artistic and intellectual elites. The explosive rise of mass media in the interwar years transformed popular culture and the lives of ordinary people. New mass media—especially radio and films—reached audiences of unprecedented size. Political life incorporated many of these new media, setting off worries that the common people, increasingly referred to as the "masses," could be manipulated by demagogues and propaganda. In 1918, mass politics was rapidly becoming a fact of life: that meant nearly universal suffrage (varying by country), well-organized political parties reaching out to voters, and, in general, more participation in political life. Mass politics was accompanied by the rise of mass culture: books, newspapers, films, and fashions were produced in large numbers and standardized formats, which were less expensive and more accessible, appealing not only to more but to more kinds of people. Older forms of popular culture were often local and class specific; mass culture, at least in principle, cut across lines of class and ethnicity, and even nationality. The term, however, can easily become misleading. The world of culture did not suddenly become homogenous. No more than half the population read newspapers regularly. Not everyone listened to the radio, and those who did certainly did not believe everything they heard. The pace of cultural change, however, did quicken perceptibly. And in the interwar years, mass culture showed that it held both democratic and authoritarian potential.

The expansion of mass culture rested on widespread applications of existing technologies. Wireless communication, for instance, was invented before the turn of the twentieth century and saw limited use in the First World War. With major financial investment in the 1920s, though, the radio industry boomed. Three out of four British families had a radio by the end of the 1930s; and in Germany, the ratio was even higher. In every European country, broadcasting rights were controlled by the government; in the United States, radio was managed by corporations. The radio broadcast soon became the national soapbox for politicians, and it played no small role in creating new kinds of political language. President Franklin Roosevelt's reassuring "fireside chats" took advantage of the way that radio bridged the public world of politics with the private world of the home. Hitler cultivated a different kind of radio personality, barking his fierce invectives; he made some fifty addresses in 1933 alone. In Germany, Nazi propagandists beamed their messages into homes or blared them through loudspeakers in town squares, constant and repetitive. Broadcasting created new rituals of political life—and new means of communication and persuasion.

So did advertising. Advertising was not new, but it was newly prominent. Businesses spent vastly more on advertising than they had before. Hard-hitting visual images replaced older ads that simply announced products, prices, and brand names. Many observers considered advertising the most "modern" of art forms. Why? It was efficient communication, streamlined and standardized, producing images that would appeal to all. It was scientific, drawing on modern psychology; advertising agencies claimed to have a science of selling to people. In a world remade by mass politics, and at a moment when the purchasing power of the common people was beginning to rise, however slowly, the high stakes in advertising (as in much of mass culture) were apparent to many.

The most dramatic changes came on movie screens. The technology of moving pictures came earlier; the

Interpreting Visual Evidence

The Fascist Spectacle of Mass Participation

Like other revolutionary movements, fascism in Italy and national socialism in Germany needed to project an image of popular support for their political programs. As far back as the French Revolution of 1789, representations of "the people" as political actors took on special significance in revolutionary propaganda (see ***Interpreting Visual Evidence***, pages 602–03), and both Hitler and Mussolini understood how to use such images to create the impression of an organic and seamless connection between the party's leadership and the rank and file who made up the movement.

A. Benito Mussolini visits a youth camp where recruits to his Black Shirts were in training, 1935.

B. Still image from Leni Riefenstahl, *Triumph of the Will* (1935), a film about a Nazi party rally in Nuremberg, Germany, 1934.

1890s were the era of nickelodeons and short action pictures. And in that period, France and Italy had strong film industries. Further popularized by news shorts during the war, film boomed in the war's aftermath. When sound was added to movies in 1927, costs soared, competition intensified, and audiences grew rapidly. By the 1930s, an estimated 40 percent of British adults went to the movies once a week, a strikingly high figure. Many went more often than that. The U.S. film industry gained a competitive edge in Europe, buoyed by the size of its home market, by huge investments in equipment and distribution, by aggressive marketing, and by Hollywood's star system of long-term contracts with well-known actors who, in a sense, standardized the product and guaranteed a film's success.

Germany, too, was home to a particularly talented group of directors, writers, and actors, and to a major production company, UFA (Universum Film AG), which ran the largest and best-equipped studios in Europe. The UFA's history paralleled the country's: it was run by the government during the First World War, devastated by the economic crisis of the early 1920s, rescued by wealthy German nationalists in the late 1920s, and finally taken over by the Nazis. During the Weimar years, UFA produced some of the most

C. I. M. Swire (right), a leading figure in the women's section of the British Union of Fascists wearing the organization's female black-shirted uniform (1933).

Representations of the people in nineteenth-century liberal revolutionary movements emphasized an activist definition of political participation, as citizens came together to constitute a national body that reflected their will. Both Italian fascism and German national socialism defined themselves in opposition to democratic or parliamentary regimes, and they explicitly rejected the individualism that was the basis for liberal citizenship. In their orchestration of public celebrations for their program, both fascists and national socialists emphasized images of obedience and subordination to the leader (image A), or to the national movement (image B). Though the pageantry of fascism and national socialism typically emphasized an aggressively masculine image of enthusiastic devotion, most fascist movements also organized special female sections within their movements. In these groups, women could clothe themselves in uniforms like their male counterparts and express their own allegiance to the spirit of self-sacrifice that was at the heart of such collective movements (image C).

Questions for Analysis

1. Each of these images was carefully staged and orchestrated to project a specific message. What are the messages contained in each of these images? What details are important?

2. What do these images tell us about the place of the individual in fascist society?

3. What sense of belonging do you think these images are designed to produce? What made such images so attractive to so many people?

remarkable films of the period, including *Der letzte mann* (*"The Last Man"*; released as *"The Last Laugh"* in English), a universally acclaimed film directed by F. W. Murnau, one of the two great masters of German expressionism. Fritz Lang was the other, directing such masterpieces as the science-fiction film *Metropolis* (1926) and his most famous German film, *M* (1931). After Hitler's rise to power, the Nazis took control of UFA, placing it under the control of Joseph Goebbels and the Ministry of Propaganda. Though production continued unabated during the Third Reich, many of the industry's most talented members fled from the oppressive regime, ending the golden age of German cinema.

Many found the new mass culture disturbing. As they perceived it, the threat came straight from the United States, which deluged Europe with cultural exports after the war. Hollywood westerns, cheap dime novels, and jazz music—which became increasingly popular in the 1920s—introduced Europe to new ways of life. Advertising, comedies, and romances disseminated new and often disconcerting images of femininity. With bobbed haircuts and short dresses, "new women" seemed assertive, flirtatious, capricious, and materialistic. The Wild West genre was popular with teenage boys, much to the dismay of their parents and teachers, who saw westerns as an inappropriate,

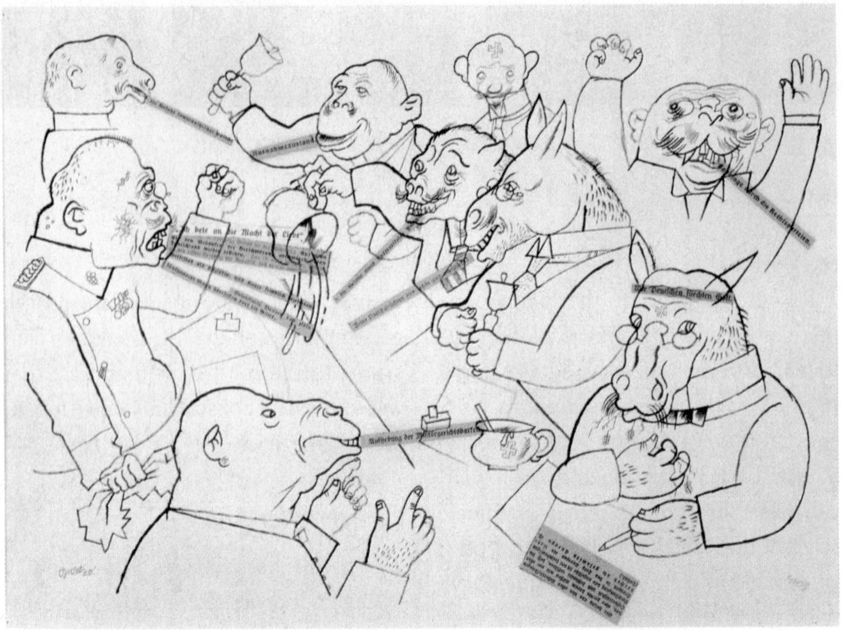

VOICE OF THE PEOPLE, VOICE OF GOD* BY GEORGE GROSZ (1920).** Industrialization, the First World War, and political change combined to make early-twentieth-century Berlin a center of mass culture and communication. In this drawing, the radical artist and social critic George Grosz deplores the newspapers' power over public opinion. That public opinion could be manipulated was a common theme for many who wrote about early-twentieth-century democracy. ▪ ***How does this cynicism about the public sphere compare with earlier defenders of free speech, such as John Stuart Mill?

FRITZ LANG'S *M*. In this film, Peter Lorre, a Jewish actor, played the role of a child murderer, who maintains that he should not be punished for his crimes. Lorre's speech at the end of the film was used in the Nazi propaganda film *The Eternal Jew* as proof that Jews were innate criminals who showed no remorse for their actions.

lower-class form of entertainment. In Europe, the cross-class appeal of American popular culture grated against long-standing social hierarchies. Conservative critics abhorred the fact that "the parson's wife sat nearby his maid at Sunday matinees, equally rapt in the gaze of Hollywood stars." American critics expressed many of the same concerns. Yet the United States enjoyed more social and political stability than Europe. War and revolution had shaken Europe's economies and cultures, and in that context "Americanization" seemed a handy shorthand for economic as well as cultural change. One critic expressed a common concern: "America is the source of that terrible wave of uniformity that gives everyone the same [*sic*]: the same overalls on the skin, the same book in the hand, the same pen between the fingers, the same conversation on the lips, and the same automobile instead of feet."

Authoritarian governments, in particular, decried these developments as decadent threats to national culture. Fascist, communist, and Nazi governments alike tried to control not only popular culture but also high culture and modernism, which were typically out of line with the designs of the dictators. Stalin much preferred socialist realism to the new Soviet avant-garde. Mussolini had a penchant for classical kitsch, though he was far more accepting of modern art than Hitler, who despised its decadence. Nazism had its own cultural aesthetic, promoting "Aryan" art and architecture and rejecting the modern, international style they associated with the "international Jewish conspiracy." Modernism, functionalism, and atonality were banned: the hallmarks of Weimar Germany's cultural preeminence were replaced by a state-sponsored revival of an alleged mystical and heroic past. Walter Gropius's acclaimed experiments in modernist architecture, for example, stood as monuments to everything the Nazis hated. The Bauhaus school was closed in 1933, and Hitler hired Albert Speer as his personal architect, commissioning him to design grandiose neoclassical buildings, including an extravagant plan to rebuild the entire city of Berlin.

The Nazis, like other authoritarian governments, used mass media as efficient means of indoctrination and control. Movies became part of the Nazis' pioneering use of "spectacular politics." Media campaigns, mass rallies, parades

Analyzing Primary Sources

Cinema: Fritz Lang on the Future of the Feature Film in Germany, 1926

Fritz Lang (1890–1976) came from Austria to Berlin after the First World War and became one of the German Weimar Republic's most brilliant movie directors, best known for Metropolis *(1926) and* M *(1931). In this essay, Lang reflects on the technological, artistic, and human potential of film. Like many European filmmakers he was fascinated by American movies. In 1932, Joseph Goebbels, dazzled by Lang's work, asked him to work on movies for the Nazis. Lang immediately left Germany for Paris and, from there, for the United States where he continued to make films in Hollywood.*

There has perhaps never before been a time so determined as ours in its search for new forms of expression. Fundamental revolutions in painting, sculpture, architecture, and music speak eloquently of the fact that people of today are seeking and finding their own means of lending artistic form to their sentiments. . . .

The speed with which film has developed in the last five years makes all predictions about it appear dangerous, for it will probably exceed each one by leaps and bounds. Film knows no rest. What was invented yesterday is already obsolete today. This uninterrupted drive for new modes of expression, this intellectual experimentation, along with the joy Germans characteristically take in overexertion, appear to me to fortify my contention that film as art will first find its form in Germany. . . .

Germany has never had, and never will have, the gigantic human and financial reserves of the American film industry at its disposal. To its good fortune. For that is exactly what forces us to compensate a purely material imbalance through an intellectual superiority. . . .

The first important gift for which we have film to thank was in a certain sense *the rediscovery of the human face*. Film has revealed to us the human face with unexampled clarity in its tragic as well as grotesque, threatening as well as blessed expression.

The second gift is that of visual empathy: in the purest sense the expressionistic representation of thought processes. No longer will we take part purely externally in the workings of the soul of the characters in film. We will no longer limit ourselves to seeing the effects of feelings, but will experience them in our own souls, from the instant of their inception on, from the first flash of a thought through to the logical last conclusion of the idea. . . .

The internationalism of filmic language will become the strongest instrument available for the mutual understanding of peoples, who otherwise have such difficulty understanding each other in all too many languages. To bestow upon film the double gift of ideas and soul is the task that lies before us. . . .

Source: Anton Kaes, Matin Jay, and Edward Dimendberg, *The Weimar Republic Sourcebook* (Los Angeles: 1994), pp. 622–23.

Questions for Analysis

1. Why does Lang suggest that his own time is in search of "new forms of expression"? Do artists always search for new forms, or might this be a specifically twentieth-century phenomenon?
2. What did Lang mean by calling "the rediscovery of the human face" and "visual empathy" gifts of film? Did television, video, and electronic media have comparable effects on how we see the world and other beings in it?
3. How does Lang see the technological, artistic, and human potential of film?

and ceremonies: all were designed to display the strength and glory of the Reich and to impress and intimidate spectators. In 1934, Hitler commissioned the filmmaker Leni Riefenstahl to record a political rally staged by herself and Albert Speer in Nuremberg. The film, titled *Triumph of the Will*, was a visual hymn to the Nordic race and the Nazi regime. Everything in the film was on a huge scale: masses of bodies stood in parade formation, and flags rose and fell in unison; the film invited viewers to surrender to the power of grand ritual and symbolism. The comedian Charlie Chaplin riposted in his celebrated lampoon *The Great Dictator* (1940), an enormously successful parody of Nazi pomposities.

The Nazis also tried to eliminate the influences of American popular culture, which even before 1933 had been decried as an example of biological and cultural degeneracy. For instance, critics associated American dances and jazz (which were increasingly popular in German cities) with what the Nazis deemed "racially inferior" blacks and Jews. With culture, however, the Nazis were forced to strike a balance between party propaganda and popular entertainment. The regime allowed many cultural imports, including Hollywood films, to continue while consciously cultivating German alternatives to American cinema, music, fashions, and even dances. Joseph Goebbels, the minister of propaganda who controlled most film production, placed a high value on economic viability. During the Third Reich, the German film industry turned out comedies, escapist fantasies, and sentimental romances. It developed its own star system and tried to keep audiences happy; meanwhile, it became a major competitor internationally. For domestic consumption, the industry also produced vicious anti-Semitic films, such as *The Eternal Jew* (1940) and *Jew Suss* (1940), a fictional tale of a Jewish moneylender who brings the city of Württemberg to ruin in the eighteenth century. In the final scene of the film, the town expels the entire Jewish community from its midst, asking that "posterity honor this law." Goebbels reported that the entire Reich cabinet had viewed the film and considered it "an incredible success."

After You Read This Chapter

Visit StudySpace for quizzes, additional review materials, and multimedia documents. **wwnorton.com/web/westernciv18**

REVIEWING THE OBJECTIVES

- After 1917, the Bolsheviks in Russia debated how fast they should move to reorganize society along the lines demanded by their revolutionary ideology. What circumstances determined the outcome of this debate and what were the consequences of Stalin's revolution from above in the 1930s?
- Mussolini's Fascist party offered an alternative to Italian voters disappointed with their government in the aftermath of the First World War. What was fascism, and how did Mussolini come to power?
- The Weimar Republic failed in its attempt to establish a stable democracy in Germany while other democracies in France, Britain, and the United States underwent severe strain. What challenges did democratic regimes face during the interwar period?
- Hitler came to power legally in 1933 through the German electoral system. What did he stand for, and why did so many Germans support his cause?
- Artists, writers, and other intellectuals in the interwar period could not help but reflect the atmosphere of social and political crisis in their work. How did artists and writers react to the crisis of the interwar period?

CONCLUSION

The strains of the First World War created a world that few recognized—transformed by revolution, mass mobilization, and loss. In retrospect, it is hard not to see the period that followed as a succession of failures. Capitalism foundered in the Great Depression, democracies collapsed in the face of authoritarianism, and the Treaty of Versailles proved hollow. Stalin's Soviet Union paid a terrible price for the creation of a modern industrial economy in the years of famine, political repression, and state terror. Hitler's Germany and Mussolini's Italy offered a vision of the future that held no comfort for those committed to basic human freedoms and equality under the law. Yet we better understand the experiences and outlooks of ordinary people if we do not treat the failures of the interwar period as inevitable. By the late 1920s, many were cautiously optimistic that the Great War's legacy could be overcome and that problems were being solved. The Great Depression wrecked these hopes, bringing economic chaos and political paralysis. Paralysis and chaos, in turn, created new audiences for political leaders offering authoritarian solutions and brought more voters to their political parties. Finally, economic troubles and political turmoil made contending with rising international tensions, to which we now turn, vastly more difficult. By the 1930s, even cautious optimism about international relations had given way to apprehension and dread.

PEOPLE, IDEAS, AND EVENTS IN CONTEXT

- What is the difference between the Bolshevik policies of **WAR COMMUNISM** and the **NEW ECONOMIC POLICY (NEP)**?
- What were **JOSEPH STALIN**'s goals in implementing his catastrophic plan for **COLLECTIVIZATION** of agriculture, and what did he hope to accomplish with his purging of an entire generation of Bolshevik leaders, along with millions of other Soviet citizens, in the **GREAT TERROR**?
- What was the basis of **BENITO MUSSOLINI**'s rejection of liberal democracy? What kinds of changes in Italian society followed from the adoption of **FASCISM** as the official state ideology?
- How important was **ANTI-SEMITISM** to **ADOLF HITLER**'s political career? What do events like **KRISTALLNACHT** tell us about the depth of German anti-Semitism?
- What effects did the **GREAT DEPRESSION** have on the European economy, and how did this economic crisis affect the political developments of the 1930s?
- How did the **NEW DEAL** attempt to deal with the economic crisis in the United States?

THINKING ABOUT CONNECTIONS

- What did Soviet communism, national socialism in Germany, and Italian fascism have in common during the years 1919–39? What made them different from one another?
- How much of the crisis of the interwar period can be attributed to the effects of World War I? To the economic upheaval of the Great Depression? Is it possible to see the ideological conflicts of these years as the result of a much longer history?

Before You Read This Chapter

STORY LINES

- In the 1930s, Hitler's Germany and Mussolini's Italy allied with imperial Japan to form the Axis. The Axis eventually provoked a Second World War, against a group of Allied powers that included Britain, the United States, Canada, Australia, and the Soviet Union.
- The Nazi regime's military successes in 1939 brought almost all of Europe under German control. The Russian victory at Stalingrad in 1942 proved to be a turning point, and from 1942 to 1945 the Allies progressively rolled back the German and Japanese armies, leading to Allied victory in 1945.
- The Nazi state embarked on a genocidal project of mass murder to exterminate its racial and ideological enemies—Europe's Jews, homosexuals, and the Roma (Gypsies).
- Attacks on civilian populations and the plundering of resources by occupying armies made the Second World War a "total war" in which the distinction between military and home front meant little for many Europeans.

CHRONOLOGY

1931	Japanese invasion of Manchuria
1936–1939	Spanish Civil War
September 1938	Sudeten Crisis and Munich Conference
August 1939	Nazi-Soviet Pact
September 1939	German invasion of Poland
May 1940	German invasion of the Low Countries and France
June 1941	German invasion of the Soviet Union
December 1941	Japanese attack on Pearl Harbor
September 1942–January 1943	Battle of Stalingrad
June 1944	D-Day Invasion
May 1945	German surrender
August 1945	The United States drops atomic bombs on Hiroshima and Nagasaki
August 1945	Japanese surrender

26

The Second World War

CORE OBJECTIVES

- **IDENTIFY** the broader political and economic causes of the Second World War.
- **EXPLAIN** the reasons for the British and French policy of "appeasement," when faced with Hitler's violations of international law.
- **UNDERSTAND** the consequences of German conquest and occupation for European nations and their populations and the challenges facing those who chose to resist.
- **DESCRIBE** how the Holocaust became possible after the conquest of territory in eastern Europe during the invasion of the Soviet Union.
- **UNDERSTAND** the military operations that led to the defeat of the Nazi regime and their allies in Europe.
- **EXPLAIN** the main areas of conflict in Asia and the Pacific and the circumstances that led to Japanese surrender in 1945.

In 1939, Adolf Hitler wanted war. By the spring of that year, he had already revealed to the world the weakness of France and Britain, which had stood by while he dismantled Czechoslovakia, a democratic nation created at the end of World War I. He turned his eyes next to Poland, confident that Britain and France could do little to prevent him from fulfilling his pledge to unleash the full power of a rearmed Germany to conquer *Lebensraum*—"living space"—for the German people in the east. Before he could invade Poland, however, he needed to come to an understanding with another long-standing enemy—the Soviet Union of Josef Stalin. Since 1934, Stalin had participated in a broad-based anti-fascist coalition in Europe, the Popular Front, an alliance that had brought the Soviets to side with the "bourgeois democracies" that were their sworn enemies. The Popular Front had led to Soviet support for the Republican side in the Spanish Civil War, though the Republicans had lost to the Nationalists who were backed by Hitler's Germany and Mussolini's Italian fascists. Hitler's propaganda campaign against the Soviets was relentless. He portrayed the Soviet regime as a cabal run by Jewish communists and referred continuously to Stalin's commissar for foreign affairs, Maxim Litvinov, as "Finkelstein" (his brother was a rabbi). Given this history of conflict, what possible understanding could Hitler hope to achieve with Stalin?

In fact, by 1939, Stalin himself had been forced to recalculate his alliances in Europe. The loss in the Spanish Civil War, and the failure of France and Britain to uphold their obligations to preserve the international order guaranteed by the Versailles peace treaty led the Soviet leader to believe that his regime had no choice but to come to an agreement with Hitler, in an attempt to gain time and preserve the Soviet Union from an immediate war. The hope was that the other European powers—France, Britain, Italy, and Germany—would weaken themselves in a general war, thus benefiting the cause of the Soviet Union. To show his willingness to talk, he fired Litvinov on May 3 and replaced him with his closest adviser, Vyacheslav Molotov (1890–1986), an ethnic Russian. In August, Hitler responded by sending his own foreign minister, Joachim von Ribbentrop (1893–1946), to Moscow to meet with Stalin. When the German envoy arrived, the Moscow airport was decorated with swastikas. The two sides cynically agreed to carve Poland up between them, and when the agreement was announced on August 23, 1939, the world was shocked to discover that these two powers, sworn ideological enemies, had made common cause to destroy Poland. On September 1, 1939, Hitler invaded Poland. Stalin, looking to what was to become a global conflict, had already attacked Japanese forces along the Mongolian border in Central Asia on August 20. The Second World War had begun.

Like the First World War, the Second World War was triggered by threats to the European balance of power. Yet even more than the Great War, the Second World War was a conflict among nations, whole peoples, and fiercely opposing ideals. Adolf Hitler and his supporters in Germany and abroad cast the conflict as a racial war against the twin enemies of national socialism: the democracies in western Europe and the United States, on the one hand, and the communist order of the Soviet Union, on the other. Hitler's opponents in the West and the East believed just as fervently that they were defending a way of life and a vision of justice that was bigger than narrow definitions of national interest.

Belief that the world was now characterized by ideologies and worldviews that were necessarily in mortal combat with one another meant that the scale of the killing overtook even that of the First World War. In 1914, military firepower outmatched mobility, resulting in four years of static, mud-sodden slaughter. In 1939, mobility was joined to firepower on a massive scale, with terrifying results. On the battlefield, the tactics of high-speed armored warfare (*Blitzkrieg*), aircraft carriers sinking ships far below the horizon, and submarines used in vast numbers to dominate shipping lanes changed the scope and the pace of fighting. This was not a war of trenches and barbed wire but a war of motion, dramatic conquests, and terrible destructive power. The devastation of 1914–18 paled in comparison to this new, global conflict.

The other great change involved not tactics but targets. Much of the unprecedented killing power now available was aimed directly at civilians. Cities were laid waste by artillery and aerial bombing. Whole regions were put to the torch, and towns and villages were systematically cordoned off and leveled. Whole populations were targeted as well, in ways that continue to appall. The Nazi regime's systematic murder of gypsies, homosexuals, and other "deviants," along with the effort to exterminate the Jewish people completely, made the Second World War a horrifyingly unique event. So did the United States' use of a weapon whose existence would dominate politics and society for the next fifty years: the atomic bomb. The naive enthusiasm that had marked the outbreak of the Great War was absent from the start. Terrible memories of the first conflict lingered. Yet those who fought against the Axis Powers (and many of those who fought for them) found that their determination to fight and win grew as the war went on. Unlike the seemingly meaningless killing of the Great War, the Second World War was cast as a war of absolutes, of good and evil, of national and global survival. Nevertheless, the scale of destruction brought with it a profound weariness. It also provoked deep-seated questions about the value of Western "civilization" and the terms on which it, and the rest of the world, might live peaceably in the future.

THE CAUSES OF THE WAR: UNSETTLED QUARRELS, ECONOMIC FALLOUT, AND NATIONALISM

Historians have isolated four main causes for the Second World War: the punishing terms of the Versailles peace settlement, the failure to create international guarantees for peace and security after 1918, the successive economic crises of the interwar years, and the violent forms of nationalism that emerged in Europe in the 1930s.

The peace settlement of 1919–20 created as many problems as it solved. The senior Allied heads of state annexed German territory and created satellite states out of the eastern European empires. In doing so, the peacemakers created fresh bitterness and conflict. The Versailles treaty and its champions, such as President Woodrow Wilson, proclaimed the principle of self-determination for the peoples of eastern and southern Europe. Yet the new states created by the treaty crossed ethnic boundaries, created new minorities without protecting them, and frustrated many of the expectations they had raised. The unsteady new boundaries would be redrawn by force in the 1930s. The Allied powers also kept up the naval blockade against Germany after the end of the fighting. This forced the new German government to accept harsh terms that deprived Germany of its political power in Europe and saddled the German economy with the bill for the conflict in a "war guilt" clause. The blockade and its consequences created grievances that many angry, humiliated Germans considered legitimate.

Power politics persisted after the peace conference. Although Woodrow Wilson and other sponsors of the League of Nations acclaimed the League as a means to eliminate power struggles, it did nothing of the sort. The signatures on the peace treaties were hardly dry when the victors began carving out new alliances to maintain their supremacy, interfering in the new central European states and the mandate territories added to the British and French empires in the Middle East. Even the League itself was fundamentally an alliance of the victors against the vanquished. It is not surprising that politicians feared international relations would be undermined by this imbalance of power.

Another cause of the Second World War was the failure to create lasting, binding standards for peace and security. Diplomats spent the ten years after Versailles trying to restore such standards. Some put their faith in the legal and moral authority of the League. Others saw disarmament as the most promising means of guaranteeing peace. In 1925, an effort was made to secure the frontiers on the Rhine established at Versailles in order to reassure the French against any resurgence of German expansionism. In 1928, the Kellogg-Briand Pact attempted to make war an international crime. None of these pacts carried any real weight. Each nation tried to include special provisions and exceptions for "vital interests," and these efforts compromised the treaties from the start. Had the League of Nations been better organized, it might have relieved some of the tensions or at least prevented clashes between nations. But the League was never a league of all nations. Essential members were absent, since Germany and the Soviet Union were excluded for most of the interwar period and the United States never joined.

Economic conditions were a third important cause of renewed conflict. The huge reparations imposed on the Germans and France's occupation of much of Germany's industrial heartland helped slow Germany's recovery. German and French stubbornness about the pace of repayments combined disastrously to bring on the German inflation of the early 1920s. The spiraling inflation made German money nearly worthless, damaging the stability and credibility of Germany's young republic almost beyond repair.

The depression of the 1930s contributed to the coming of the war in several ways. It intensified economic nationalism. Baffled by problems of unemployment and business stagnation, governments imposed high tariffs in an effort to preserve the home market for their own producers. The collapse of investment and terrible domestic unemployment caused the United States to withdraw even further from world affairs. Although France suffered less than some other countries, the depression still inflamed tensions between management and labor. This conflict exacerbated political battles between left and right, making it difficult for either side to govern France. Britain turned to its empire, raising tariffs for the first time and guarding its financial investments jealously.

In Germany, the Great Depression was the last blow to the Weimar Republic. In 1933, power passed to the Nazis, who promised a total program of national renewal. In the fascist states (and, exceptionally, the United States), public works projects of one kind or another were prescribed as an answer to mass unemployment. This produced highways, bridges, and railroads; it also produced a new arms race.

Despite the misgivings of many inside the governments of Britain and France, Germany was allowed to ignore the terms of the peace treaties and rearm. Armaments expansion on a large scale first began in Germany in 1935, with the result that unemployment was reduced and the effects of the depression eased. Other nations followed the German example, not simply as a way to boost their economies but in response to growing Nazi military power. In the Pacific, the decline of Japanese exports meant that the nation did not have enough foreign currency to pay for vital raw materials from overseas. This played into the hands of Japan's military regime. Japanese national ambitions and Japanese leaders' perception of the political and cultural inferiority of the Chinese led Japan to fresh imperial adventures in the name of establishing economic stability in East Asia. They began in 1931 with the invasion of Manchuria and moved from there to create a "Greater Pacific Co-Prosperity Sphere," which involved seizing other territories as Japanese colonies. Raw materials could then be bought with Japanese money and more of Asia would serve the needs of Japan's empire.

Imperial success could serve as consolation when economic methods failed. As the depression dragged on in fascist Italy, Mussolini tried to distract his public with national conquests overseas, culminating in the invasion of Ethiopia in 1935.

In sum, the tremendous economic hardship of the depression, a contested peace treaty, and political weakness undermined international stability. But the decisive factor in the crises of the 1930s and the trigger for another world war lay in a blend of violent nationalism and modern ideologies that glorified the nation and national destiny. This blend, particularly in the forms of fascism and militarism, appeared around the world in many countries. By the middle of the 1930s, recognizing common interests, fascist Italy and Nazi Germany formed an Axis, an alliance binding their goals of national glory and international power. They were later joined by Japan's military regime. In Spain, the ultranationalist forces that tried to overthrow the Spanish Republic, setting off the Spanish Civil War (discussed below), believed they were reviving the stability, authority, and morality of the nation. Fascist, semifascist, or authoritarian regimes spread in eastern Europe, in Yugoslavia, Hungary, and Romania. One exception to this sobering trend toward authoritarianism was Czechoslovakia. Czechoslovakia boasted no ethnic majority. Although the Czechs practiced an enlightened policy of minority self-government, and though their government was remarkably stable, questions of nationality remained a potential source of friction. Those questions became a key factor as international tensions mounted in the late 1930s.

GIANT PORTRAIT OF MUSSOLINI IN ETHIOPIA, 1935. Central to Mussolini's popularity in Italy was his ability to connect a vision of his personal leadership with a militant and expansionist nationalism. This portrait stood over an Italian military camp in Ethiopia in November 1935 during the invasion of this East African nation.

THE 1930s: CHALLENGES TO THE PEACE, APPEASEMENT, AND THE "DISHONEST DECADE"

The 1930s brought the tensions and failures caused by the treaties of 1919–20 to a head, creating a global crisis. Fascist and nationalist governments flouted the League of Nations by launching new conquests and efforts at national expansion. With the memories of 1914–18 still fresh, these new crises created an atmosphere of deepening fear and apprehension. Each new conflict seemed to warn that another, much wider war would follow unless it could somehow be averted. Ordinary people, particularly in Britain, France, and the United States, were divided. Some saw the actions of the aggressors as a direct challenge to civilization, one that had to be met with force if necessary. Others hoped to avoid premature

ANTIFASCIST PROPAGANDA, SPANISH CIVIL WAR. This poster, produced by a left-wing labor organization affiliated with the international anarchist movement, shows a worker delivering a killing blow to a fascist snake.

or unnecessary conflict. Their governments tried instead at several points to negotiate with the fascists and keep a tenuous peace. Writers, intellectuals, and politicians on the left vilified these efforts. Many saw the period as a series of missed opportunities to prevent renewed warfare. In 1939, on the first day of the Second World War, the British poet and leftist W. H. Auden condemned the behavior of Western governments, calling the 1930s "a low, dishonest decade."

The object of Auden's venom was the policy of "appeasement" pursued by Western governments in the face of German, Italian, and Japanese aggression. Appeasement was neither simple power politics nor pure cowardice. It was grounded in three deeply held assumptions. The first assumption was that doing anything to provoke another war was unthinkable. The 1914–18 slaughter and its aftermath left many in the West embracing pacifism and not wanting to deal with the uncompromising aggression of the fascist governments, especially Nazi Germany. Second, many in Britain and the United States argued that Germany had been mistreated by the Versailles treaty and harbored legitimate grievances that should be acknowledged and resolved. Finally, many appeasers were staunch anticommunists. They believed that the fascist states in Germany and Italy were an essential bulwark against the advance of Soviet communism and that division among the major European states only played into the hands of the USSR. One group, however, believed that the Soviets posed the greater threat and that accommodating Hitler might create a common interest against a common enemy. The other faction believed that Nazi Germany presented the true threat to European stability. Nevertheless, they believed, Hitler would have to be placated until Britain and France finished rearming. At that point, they hoped, their greater military power would deter Hitler or Mussolini from risking a general European war. It took most of the 1930s for the debate among appeasers to come to a head. Meanwhile, the League of Nations faced more immediate and pressing challenges.

The 1930s brought three crucial tests for the League: crises in China, Ethiopia, and Spain. In China, the Japanese invasion of Manchuria in 1931 turned into an invasion of the whole country. Chinese forces were driven before the Japanese advance, and the Japanese deliberately targeted civilians to break the Chinese will to fight. In 1937, the Japanese laid siege to the strategic city of Nanjing. Their orders on taking the city were simple: "kill all, burn all, destroy all." More than 200,000 Chinese citizens were slaughtered in what came to be known as the "Rape of Nanjing." The League voiced shock and disapproval but did nothing. In

GUERNICA BY PABLO PICASSO (1937). One of Picasso's most influential paintings, *Guernica* was painted as a mural for the Spanish republican government as it fought for survival in the Spanish Civil War. The Basque town of Guernica had been bombed by German fighters just a few months earlier, in April 1937. Near the center a horse writhes in agony; to the left a distraught woman holds her dead child. Compare Picasso's image to the antifascist propaganda poster on page 876. ▪ ***What is different about the way that the two images deliver their political messages?*** ▪ ***Does Picasso's rejection of realism diminish the power of his political message?*** ▪ ***Does the antifascist poster seek any outcome other than the annihilation of the enemy?***

1935, Mussolini began his efforts to make the Mediterranean an Italian empire by returning to Ethiopia to avenge the defeat of 1896. This time the Italians came with tanks, bombers, and poison gas. The Ethiopians fought bravely but hopelessly, and this imperial massacre aroused world opinion. The League attempted to impose sanctions on Italy and condemned Japan. But for two reasons, no enforcement followed. The first was British and French fear of communism and their hope that Italy and Japan would act as counterweights to the Soviets. The second reason was practical. Enforcing sanctions would involve challenging Japan's powerful fleet or Mussolini's newly built battleships. Britain and France were unwilling, and dangerously close to unable, to use their navies to those ends.

The Spanish Civil War

The third challenge came closer to home. In 1936, civil war broke out in Spain. A series of weak republican governments, committed to large-scale social reforms, could not overcome opposition to those measures and political polarization. War broke out as extreme right-wing military officers rebelled. Although Hitler and Mussolini had signed a pact of nonintervention with the other Western powers, both leaders sent troops and equipment to assist the rebel commander, Francisco Franco (1939–75). The Soviet Union countered with aid to communist troops serving under the banner of the Spanish Republic. Again Britain and France failed to act decisively. Thousands of volunteers from England, France, and the United States—including many working-class socialists and writers, such as George Orwell and Ernest Hemingway—took up arms as private soldiers for the Republican government. They saw the war as a test of the West's determination to resist fascism and military dictatorships. Their governments were much more hesitant. For the British, Franco was anticommunist at least, just like Mussolini and the Japanese. The French prime minister Léon Blum, a committed antifascist, stood at the head of a Popular Front government—an alliance of socialists, communists, and republicans. The Popular Front had been elected on a program of social reform and opposition to Hitler abroad and fascism in France. Yet Blum's margin of support was limited. He feared that intervening in Spain would further polarize his country, bring down his government, and make it impossible to follow through on any commitment to the conflict. In Spain, despite some heroic fighting, the Republican camp degenerated into a hornet's nest of competing factions: republican, socialist, communist, and anarchist.

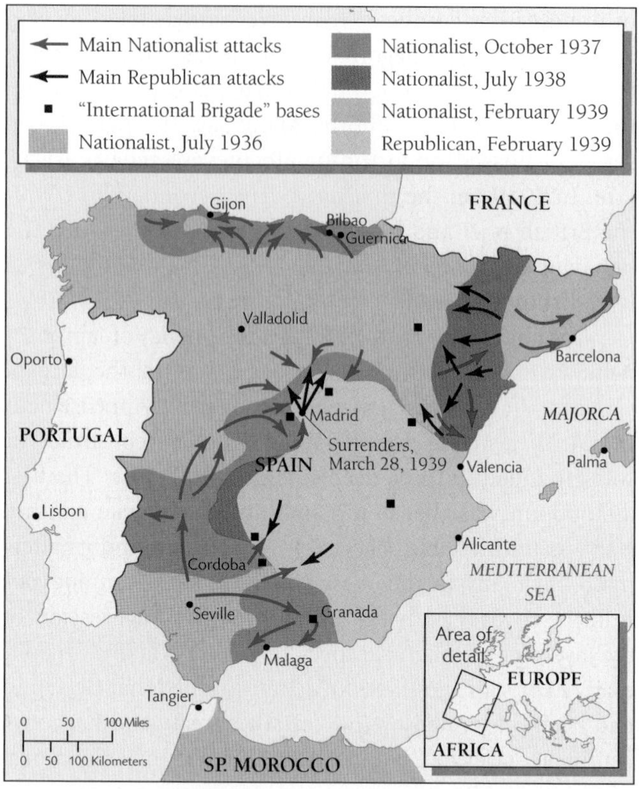

THE SPANISH CIVIL WAR. ▪ ***Why did thousands of foreign fighters join the war?*** ▪ ***How did the strategies and weapons used in the war anticipate those used in the Second World War?*** ▪ ***What were the consequences of Franco's victory?***

The Spanish Civil War was brutal. Both the German and the Soviet "advisers" saw Spain as a "dress rehearsal" for a later war between the two powers. They each brought in their newest weapons and practiced their skills in destroying civilian targets from the air. In April 1937, a raid by German dive bombers utterly destroyed the town of Guernica in northern Spain in an effort to cut off Republican supply lines and terrorize civilians. It shocked public opinion and was commemorated by Pablo Picasso in one of the most famous paintings of the twentieth century. Both sides committed atrocities. The Spanish Civil War lasted three years, ending with a complete victory for Franco in 1939. In the aftermath, Britain and France proved reluctant to admit Spanish Republicans as refugees, even though Republicans faced recriminations from Franco's regime. Franco sent 1 million of his Republican enemies to prison or concentration camps.

Hitler drew two lessons from Spain. The first was that if Britain, France, and the Soviet Union ever tried to contain fascism, they would have a hard time coordinating their efforts. The second was that Britain and France were deeply averse to fighting another European war. This meant that the Nazis could use every means short of war to achieve their goals.

German Rearmament and the Politics of Appeasement

Hitler took advantage of this combination of international tolerance and war weariness to advance his ambitions. As Germany rearmed, Hitler played on Germans' sense of shame and betrayal, proclaiming their right to regain their former power in the world. In 1933, he removed Germany from the League of Nations, to which it had finally been admitted in 1926. In 1935, he defied the disarmament provisions of the Treaty of Versailles and revived conscription and universal military training. Hitler's stated goals were the restoration of Germany's power and dignity inside Europe and the unification of all ethnic Germans inside his Third German Reich. As the first step in this process, Germany reoccupied the Rhineland in 1936. It was a risky move, chancing war with the much more powerful French army. But France and Britain did not mount a military response. In retrospect, this was an important turning point; the balance of power tipped in Germany's favor. While the Rhineland remained demilitarized and German industry in the Ruhr valley was unprotected, France held the upper hand. After 1936, it no longer did so.

In March 1938, Hitler annexed Austria, reaffirming his intention to bring all Germans into his Reich. Once more, no official reaction came from the West. The Nazis' next target was the Sudetenland in Czechoslovakia, a region with a large ethnic German population. With Austria now a part of Germany, Czechoslovakia was almost entirely surrounded by its hostile neighbor. Hitler declared that the Sudetenland was a natural part of the Reich and that he intended to occupy it. The Czechs did not want to give way. Hitler's generals were wary of this gamble. Czechoslovakia had a strong, well-equipped army and a line of fortifications along the border. Many in the French and Polish governments were willing to come to the Czechs' aid. According to plans already being laid for a wider European war, Germany would not be ready for another three to four years. But Hitler gambled, and the British prime minister, Neville Chamberlain, obliged him. Chamberlain decided to take charge of international talks about the Sudetenland and agreed to Hitler's terms. Chamberlain's logic was that this dispute was about the balance of power in Europe. If Hitler were allowed to unify all Germans in one state, he reasoned, then German ambitions would be satisfied. Chamberlain also believed that his country could not commit to a sustained war. Finally, defending eastern European boundaries against Germany ranked low on Great Britain's list of priorities, at least in comparison to ensuring free trade in western Europe and protecting the strategic centers of the British Empire.

On September 29, 1938, Hitler met with Chamberlain, Premier Édouard Daladier (1938–40) of France, and Mussolini in a four-power conference in Munich. The result was another capitulation by France and Britain. The four negotiators bargained away a major slice of Czechoslovakia while Czech representatives were left to await their fate outside the conference room. Chamberlain returned to London proclaiming "peace in our time." Hitler soon proved

GERMAN SOLDIERS ENTER RHINELAND IN COLOGNE, 1936. Hitler's reoccupation of the Rhineland—an area bordering France, Belgium, and the Netherlands—was a direct violation of the Treaty of Versailles, but it was difficult for the French and British governments to respond effectively, because voters in these nations were reluctant to go to war over Hitler's decision to move troops into what was, after all, German territory.

GERMAN AND ITALIAN EXPANSION, 1936–1939. ▪ *What were Hitler's first steps to unify all the ethnic Germans in Europe?* ▪ *How did he use these initial gains to annex territory from the Czechs?* ▪ *After winning Czechoslovakia, why did Hitler choose to invade Poland?*

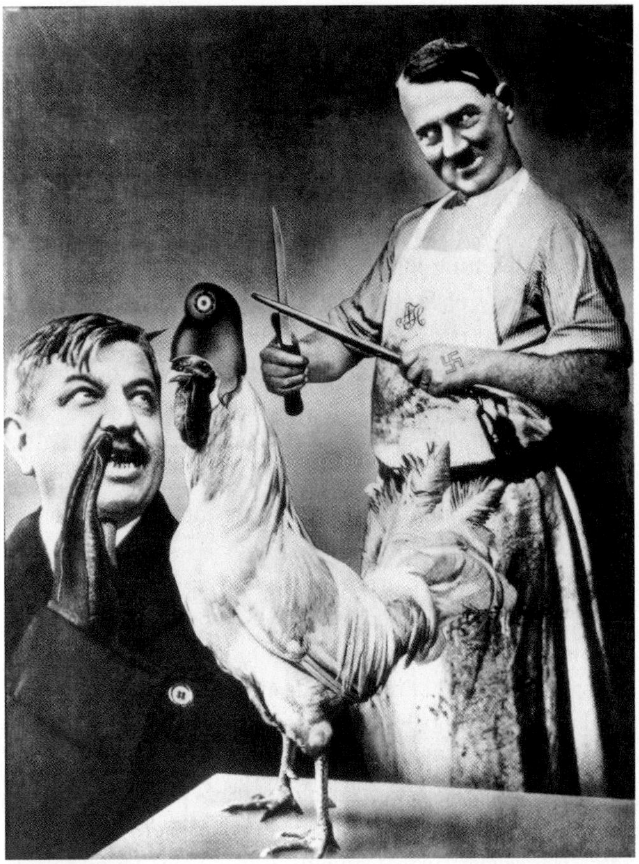

JOHN HEARTFIELD, *HAVE NO FEAR—HE'S A VEGETARIAN.* Heartfield (born Helmut Herzfeld) was a German radical associated with the Dada movement and communism. This photomontage appeared in a French magazine in 1936 as Hitler's warlike intentions became clear. Pierre Laval, then prime minister of France and later architect of French collaboration with the Nazis, whispers reassuringly to a rooster, a symbol for France, as Hitler sharpens his knife.

that boast hollow. In March 1939, Germany invaded what was left of Czechoslovakia, annexed Bohemia and Moravia, and established a puppet regime in Slovakia. This was Germany's first conquest of non-German territory, and it sent shock waves across Europe. It convinced public and political opinion outside Germany of the futility of appeasement. Chamberlain was forced to shift his policies completely. British and French rearmament sped up dramatically. Together with France, Britain guaranteed the sovereignty of the two states now directly in Hitler's path, Poland and Romania.

Meanwhile, the politics of appeasement had fueled Stalin's fears that the Western democracies might strike a deal with Germany at Soviet expense, thus diverting Nazi expansion eastward. The Soviet Union had not been invited to the Munich conference, and suspicious that Britain and France were unreliable allies, Stalin became convinced that he should look elsewhere for security. Tempted by the traditional Soviet desire for territory in Poland, Stalin was promised a share of Poland, Finland, the Baltic states, and Bessarabia by Hitler's representatives. In a cynical reversal of their anti-Nazi proclamations that stunned many, the Soviets signed a nonaggression pact with the Nazis in August 1939. By going to Munich, Britain and France had put their interests first; the Soviet Union would now look after its own.

THE OUTBREAK OF HOSTILITIES AND THE FALL OF FRANCE

After his success in Czechoslovakia, Hitler demanded the abolition of the Polish Corridor. This was a narrow strip of land connecting Poland with the Baltic Sea. The corridor also divided East Prussia from the rest of Germany, separating yet another large German population from union with the Reich. Judging Britain and France by past performance, Hitler believed their pledges to Poland were worthless. With the Soviets now in his camp, he expected that Poland would consent and the Western allies would back down again. When Poland stood firm instead, Hitler attacked. On September 1, 1939, German troops crossed the Polish border. Britain and France sent a joint warning to Germany to withdraw. There was no reply. On September 3, Britain and France declared war.

The conquest of Poland was shockingly quick. It demanded great resources—Germany committed nearly all of its combat troops and planes to the invasion—but the results were remarkable. Well-coordinated attacks by German *panzers* (tanks) and armored vehicles, supported by devastating air power, cut the large but slow-moving Polish army to pieces. German infantry still moved on foot or via horse-drawn transport, but their disciplined advance followed the devastating work of the panzers. The Poles fought doggedly but were so stunned and disorganized that they had little hope of mounting an effective defense. The "lightning war" (*Blitzkrieg, blitz-KREEG*) for which the German officer corps had trained so long was a complete success. Within three weeks German troops were laying siege to Warsaw. German terror bombing, designed to destroy the heart of Warsaw from the air and frighten the population into surrender, was successful. Poland, a large country with a large army, was dismembered in four weeks.

In accordance with its agreement with Nazi Germany, the Soviet Union also invaded Poland from the east, taking its share of Polish territory and using Stalin's signature methods to deal with the enemy: rounding up millions to be deported, imprisoned, or executed. Wary that German aggression would turn on them, the Soviets also hastened to shore up their position to the north, on the Russo-Finnish border. Since at least 1938, the Soviets had demanded from Finland various arrangements to protect Leningrad, from access to strategic locations and permission to build fortifications in Finland to the outright ceding of territory—all of which the Finns had refused. Shortly after the invasion of Poland, then, the Soviets attacked Finland. Despite the Soviets' overwhelming superiority in numbers and material, the Finns fought back tenaciously. The Soviets faced a very difficult campaign—an alarming demonstration of the damaging effects of Stalin's terror on the Soviet military. Although the Soviet Union concluded the undeclared four-month Winter War with a precarious victory in March 1940, Hitler and the rest of the world had made note of Stalin's weaknesses.

After the fall of Poland, the conflict became an ominous "phony war," or *Sitzkrieg*, as it was sometimes called. The fighting in Poland was followed by a winter of anxious nonactivity with occasional headlines about naval skirmishes. In the spring of 1940, that calm was broken by a terrible storm. The Germans struck first in Scandinavia, taking Denmark in a day and invading Norway. Britain and France tried to aid the Norwegian defense and sank a large number of German ships, but the Allied expedition failed. Then the real blow was struck. On May 10, German forces swarmed through Belgium and the Netherlands on their way to France. The two nations were conquered in short order. When the Dutch succeeded in flooding canals that protected their major cities and defended that line with hard-fighting marines, Hitler ordered his air force to bomb the city of Rotterdam. More than 800 Dutch civilians died, and the Netherlands surrendered the next day. The Belgians' stubborn and effective defense of their nation was cut short when King Albert suddenly surrendered after two weeks of fighting, fearing similar destruction. In turn, Albert stayed on as a figurehead for the Nazis, reviled by Belgians who found other ways to carry on the fight against Germany.

JUNE 23, 1940. Hitler and Nazi architect Albert Speer pose across the river from the Eiffel Tower after capturing Paris.

The large French army was carved up by the *Blitzkrieg*. Its divisions were isolated, outflanked, and overwhelmed by German aircraft and armored columns working according to an exacting plan. French units either fought fierce battles until they were hopelessly surrounded or simply collapsed. The French army and French artillery, much of it better built than its German equivalent, were poorly organized and rendered useless in the face of rapid German maneuvers. The defeat turned quickly into a rout. Hundreds of thousands of civilians, each carrying a few precious possessions loaded on carts, fled south. They were joined by thousands of Allied soldiers without weapons, and these columns of refugees were attacked constantly by German dive bombers. The disorganized British made a desperate retreat to the port of Dunkirk on the English Channel, where many of Britain's best troops were sacrificed holding off the panzers. At the beginning of June 1940, despite heavy German air attacks, Britain's Royal Navy evacuated more than 300,000 British and French troops, with the help of commercial and pleasure boats that had been pressed into emergency service.

After Dunkirk, the conflict was bitter but the outcome inevitable. French reservists fought, as their commanders asked, "to the last cartridge," killing thousands of Germans. Without proper organization and more firepower, however, this bravery was useless. The Germans swept through the northwest and the heart of the country, reaching Paris in mid-June 1940. The political will of France's government collapsed along with its armies. Rather than withdrawing to Britain or French colonies in North Africa, the French surrendered on June 22. The armistice cut the country in two. The Germans occupied all of northern France, including Paris and the Channel ports. The south, and French territories in North Africa, lay under the jurisdiction of a deeply conservative government formed at the spa town of Vichy *(VIH-shee)* under the leadership of an elderly First World War hero, Marshal Philippe Pétain. France had fallen. One of Germany's historic enemies, the victor of the previous war, an imperial power and nation of almost 60 million citizens, was reduced to chaos and enemy occupation in forty days.

The penalties exacted on France did not end with defeat. Many liberals within France, and most of the Free French movement quickly established in London, soon felt they had two enemies to fight: Germany and Pétain's regime. The Vichy government proposed to collaborate with the Germans in return for retaining a small measure of sovereignty, or so it believed. The regime also instituted its own National Revolution, which came very close to fascism. Vichy repudiated the republic, accusing it of sapping France's strength. The state proceeded to reorganize French life and political institutions, strengthening the authority of the Catholic Church and the family and helping the Germans crush any resistance. "Work, Family, and Country"—this was Vichy's call to order.

NOT ALONE: THE BATTLE OF BRITAIN AND THE BEGINNINGS OF A GLOBAL WAR

Before launching an invasion across the Channel, the Nazis attempted to establish superiority in the air. From July 1940 to June 1941, in the Battle of Britain, thousands of planes dropped millions of tons of bombs on British targets: first aircraft and airfields and then, as the focus shifted to breaking Britain's will, civilian targets such as London. More than 40,000 British civilians died. Yet the British stood firm. This was possible in part because of a German mistake. After a daring British bombing raid on Berlin, Hitler angrily told his generals to concentrate on civilian targets. This spared the Royal Air Force, whose bases had been steadily devastated up to that point. Given the chance to keep fighting, the R.A.F. forced a costly stalemate in the air. Hitler scrapped the invasion plans, turning his attention east toward Russia.

Another important reason for the determined British resistance was a change of political leadership. In May 1940, Chamberlain's catalog of failures finished his career. He was toppled by a coalition government that brought together Conservative, Liberal, and Labour politicians for the sake of national unity. It was led by the most unlikely of the choices offered to replace him: Winston Churchill (1940–45, 1951–55). Churchill was a political maverick who had changed parties more than once. He was extremely talented but also arrogant. He had a sharp temper and sometimes seemed unstable, and before 1939 his political career was judged to be over. As prime minister, he was not much of an administrator, constantly proposing wild schemes, but he had two genuine gifts. The first was language. Churchill spoke extraordinary words of courage and defiance just when the British public wanted and needed to hear them. He was utterly committed to winning the war.

"You ask what is our policy," Churchill said in his first speech as prime minister in May of 1940, before the Battle of Britain began. "I will say, it is to wage war with all our might, with all the strength that God can give us, to wage war against a monstrous tyranny never surpassed in the dark, lamentable catalogue of human crime."

The second was personal diplomacy. He convinced the American president Franklin Roosevelt (1933–45), who supported the Allies, to break with American neutrality and send massive amounts of aid and weapons to Britain free of charge, under a program called Lend-Lease. Churchill

LONDON DURING THE BATTLE OF BRITAIN. German air raids that lasted from August 1940 to June 1941 wrought destruction but did not achieve Hitler's goal of breaking the British. The Holland House Library in London lost its roof but managed to engage in business as usual.

THE SECOND WORLD WAR IN EUROPE. ▪ ***What parts of the European theater were controlled by the Allies?*** ▪ ***The Axis?*** ▪ ***Which countries were neutral in 1941?*** ▪ ***In what parts of the European theater did the major Axis and Allied campaigns occur?*** ▪ ***What was Germany's greatest geographical challenge during the Second World War?***

also allowed the new government coalition to work to best effect. The ablest Conservative ministers stayed, but Labour politicians were also allowed to take positions of genuine power. Most of the Labour representatives turned out to be excellent administrators and were directly in touch with Britain's huge working class, which now felt fully included in the war effort.

With Britain's survival, the war moved into different theatres: the Atlantic (a battle over sea lanes and supplies), North Africa (strategically important for the Suez Canal and access to oil), the Pacific (the war with Japan), and the Soviet Union (where Hitler's determination to annihilate Stalin merged with his murderous campaign against the Jewish populations of Europe).

The Atlantic and North Africa

The Battle of the Atlantic, launched as a submarine campaign to starve out the British, was a dire threat to the Allies. Learning from the First World War, the Germans sent hundreds of submarines (U-boats) out in "wolf packs" to stalk the major sea lanes to Britain. German submarines sank millions of tons of merchant shipping, as far away as the coasts of Brazil and Florida. Britain's supplies of weapons, raw materials, and food hung in the balance. The British devoted a huge naval effort and great technical resourcefulness to saving their convoys. They developed modern sonar and new systems of aerial reconnaissance and cracked the Germans' codes for communicating with the wolf packs. These efforts kept supplies coming. When the United States entered the war in December 1941 (see below), the British supplied the experience and technology and the Americans the numbers and firepower to sink many more U-boats. By late 1942, the threat receded.

The war in North Africa began because Britain had to protect the Suez Canal, but Britain was soon drawn into a larger conflict. Indian, South African, and West African troops fighting for the British drove the Italians from Ethiopia in May 1941. The Soviets and the British invaded Iran to keep its shah (ruler) from making a deal with Germany over Iranian oil and held the country until 1946. A small, well-led British army in Egypt humiliated a much larger Italian invasion force. The British nearly captured Italy's colony of Libya, and this forced Germany to intervene. An elite armored force called the Afrika Korps, led by Germany's most daring tank commander, Erwin Rommel, drove the British back in the spring of 1941 and started a grudging two-year war in the desert. The British fielded an international army, which included as many Australians, Indians, and New Zealanders as it did Britons, pitted against the Germans and Italians. The fighting swung back and forth for eighteen months, with the British taking the worst of it. Then the momentum shifted. Despite heavy losses from German planes and submarines, the British defeated the Italian navy and took control of the Mediterranean. They also established domination in the air over the desert. When Rommel tried to invade Egypt, his forces were stopped and badly defeated near the town of El Alamein in July, then driven back toward Tunisia later that fall. "This is not the end," said Winston Churchill in his inimitable style, after the British victory at El Alamein. "It is not even the beginning of the end. But it is, perhaps, the end of the beginning."

The United States intervened in November 1942, landing in the French territories of Algeria and Morocco. A conference was held at Casablanca, Morocco, among the Allied powers to discuss the future course of the war and the fate of French territories in North Africa. French administrators in Algeria and Morocco, who had supported Vichy, at least in public, surrendered peacefully or joined the Allied side. Rommel still defended Tunisia against the Allies for four months, but a joint offensive broke the German lines in March 1943, ending the fighting.

The Allies and Japan in the Pacific

The war became truly global when Japan struck the American naval base at Pearl Harbor, Hawaii, on the morning of December 7, 1941. The Japanese had been involved in a costly war in China since the 1930s. To win and to establish a Japanese empire throughout Asia, they would have to destroy America's Pacific fleet and seize the colonies of the British, Dutch, and French Empires. Like Germany, Japan began with lightning blows. The attack on Pearl Harbor

"A DATE WHICH WILL LIVE IN INFAMY," DECEMBER 7, 1941. The U.S.S. *West Virginia* was one of eight battleships sunk during the Japanese surprise attack targeting Battleship Row at the American naval base at Pearl Harbor. More than 2,000 people were killed, but most of the American fleet, en route to or from other locations in the Pacific, was spared.

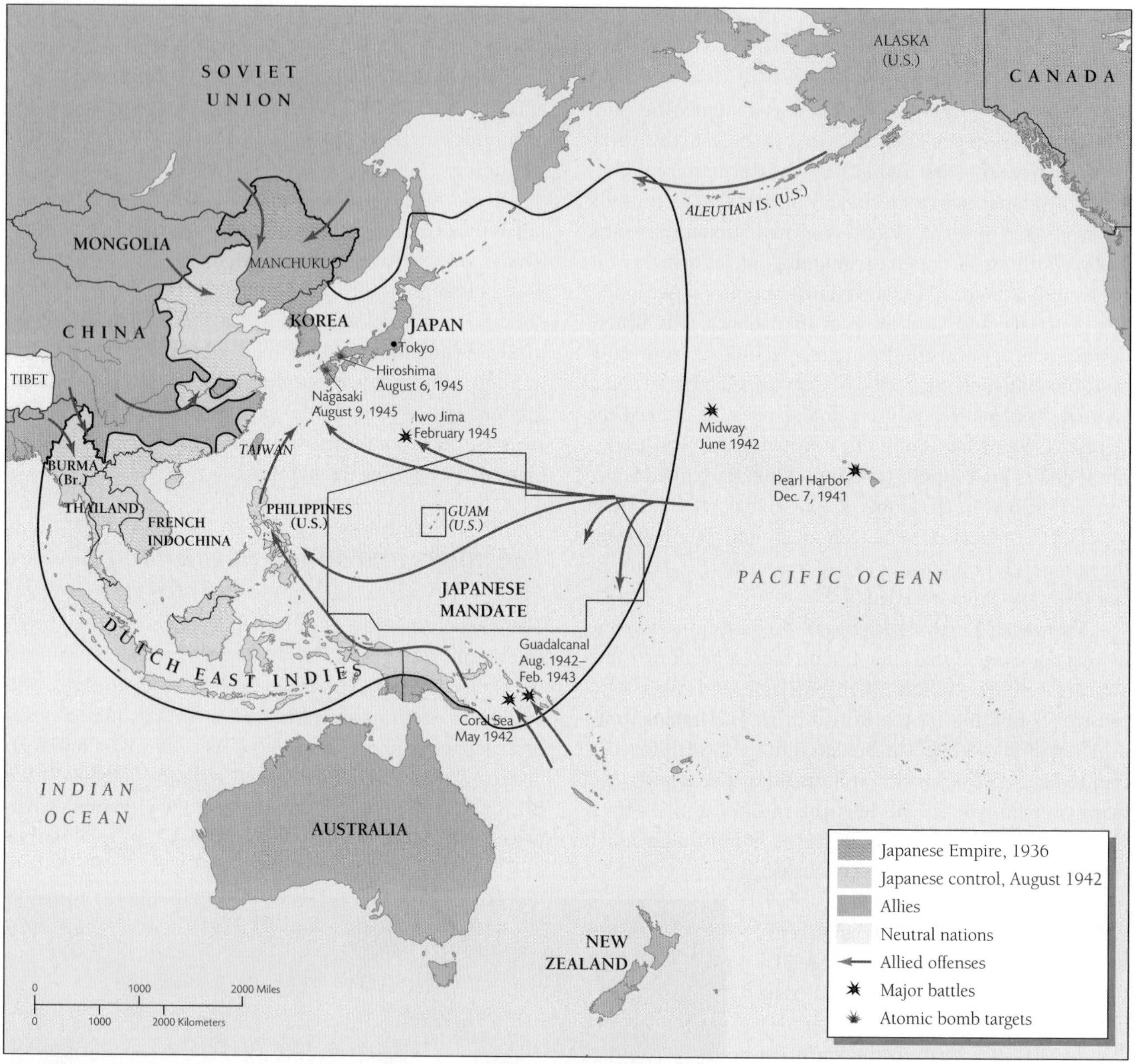

WORLD WAR II IN THE PACIFIC. ▪ *What areas did the Japanese and Allies each control in the Pacific theater during the Second World War?* ▪ *Based on tracing the route of the Allied offense of the map, what did the main Allied strategy appear to be?* ▪ *What factors led the Americans to decide that the dropping of atomic bombs on Hiroshima and Nagasaki was the most expeditious way to end the war rather than invading Japan?*

was a brilliant act of surprise that devastated the American fleet and shocked the American public. It was not, however, the success that the Japanese wanted. Eight U.S. battleships were sunk and more than 2,000 lives lost; but much of the American fleet—including its aircraft carriers, submarines, and many smaller ships—were safely at sea on the day of the strike. The unprovoked attack galvanized American public opinion in a way the war in Europe had not. When Germany rashly declared war on the United States as well, America declared itself ready to take on all comers and joined the Allies.

Despite the mixed results at Pearl Harbor the Japanese enjoyed other, stunning successes. For the European colonial powers, Japan's entry into the war was a catastrophe. Japanese troops swept through the British protectorate of Malaya in weeks, sinking the Pacific squadrons of both the British and Dutch navies in the swift attacks. Britain's fortified island port at Singapore, the keystone of British defenses in the Pacific, fell at the end of December 1941. The shock of the loss nearly took Churchill's government with it. Thousands of British and Australian troops were captured and sent off to four years of torture, forced labor, and starvation in Japanese prison camps. The Japanese also invaded the Philippines in December; and while American soldiers and marines held out on the island of Corregidor for some time, they too were forced to surrender. Some took to the hills to fight as guerrillas; the rest were forced on a death march to Japanese labor camps. The Dutch East Indies fell next, and it seemed there would be no stopping Japanese ships and soldiers before they reached Australia.

Reeling from Japan's blows, the Allies finally reorganized during 1942. After taking Singapore, Japanese troops pressed on into Burma. Several famous British generals tried and failed to defend Burma, with disastrous losses of men and matériel. After these failures, command fell to an obscure Indian army officer, William Slim. For a British officer, Slim had quite humble origins. He was a career soldier, a minor hero in the First World War, and perhaps the best strategist in the British army. Even more important, the millions of nonwhite imperial troops from India and Africa who were under his command liked and respected him as an honest, unprejudiced man. He reorganized imperial defenses, and a joint force of British and Indian troops defeated an attempted Japanese invasion of India at the border near the end of 1942. After that, with an army drawn from around the world, Slim began to push the Japanese back. In New Guinea, Australian troops fresh from North Africa were first to defeat the Japanese on land in bitter hand-to-hand fighting and staged a counterattack through the high mountain jungles. At sea, America's navy benefited from a rapidly increased production schedule that turned out new ships and planes to outnumber the Japanese, and two gifted admirals, Chester Nimitz and William Halsey, who outfought them. In 1942, the United States won crucial victories in the Coral Sea and at Midway, a battle fought at sea and in the air by aircraft flown from each side's carriers. American marines landed on the island of Guadalcanal in early 1942 and captured this strategic Japanese base after months of bitter fighting. Their success began a campaign of island hopping as the marines destroyed Japan's network of island bases throughout the Pacific. This was brutal warfare, often settled with grenades and bayonets. Each side considered the other racially inferior. The Japanese often refused to surrender; the Americans and Australians also took few prisoners. By 1943, the Japanese victories had been halted, the Japanese navy had lost most of its capital ships, and the Allies began a slow march to Singapore and the Philippines.

THE RISE AND RUIN OF NATIONS: GERMANY'S WAR IN THE EAST AND THE OCCUPATION OF EUROPE

While battles ebbed and flowed in the Atlantic and the North African desert, Germany moved southeast into the Balkans. In 1941, Germany took over Yugoslavia almost without a fight. The Germans split Yugoslavia's ethnic patchwork by establishing a Croatian puppet state, pitting Croats against their Serb neighbors who were ruled directly by the Nazis. Romania, Hungary, and Bulgaria joined the Nazis' cause as allies. The Greeks, who had dealt a crushing defeat to an Italian invasion, were suddenly confronted with a massive German force that overran the country. The Greeks stubbornly refused to surrender. An unexpected combination of Greek, British, and New Zealand troops nearly defeated the German paratroopers sent to capture the island of Crete in June of 1941. Many Greeks also took to the mountains as guerrillas, but in the end the country fell. By the summer of 1941, with the exceptions of Spain, Portugal, Sweden, and Switzerland, the whole European continent was either allied with the Nazis or subject to their rule. These victories, and the economy of plunder that enriched Germany with forced labor and other nations' money, won Hitler considerable popularity at home. But these were only the first steps in a larger plan.

Hitler's ultimate goals, and his conception of Germany's national destiny, lay to the east. Hitler had always seen the nonaggression pact with the Soviet Union as an act of convenience, to last only until Germany was ready for this final conflict. By the summer of 1941, it seemed Germany was ready. On June 22, 1941, Hitler began Operation Barbarossa, the invasion of the Soviet Union. The elite of the German army led the way, defeating all the forces the Russians could put in front of them. Stalin's purges of the 1930s had exiled or executed many of his most capable army officers, and the effects showed in Russian disorganization and disaffection in the face of the panzers. Hundreds of thousands of prisoners were taken as German forces pressed deep into Byelorussia (modern Belarus), the Baltic states, and Ukraine. Like Napoleon, the Germans led a multinational army; it included Italians, Hungarians, most of the Romanian army, and freelance soldiers from the Baltics and Ukraine who bore grudges against Stalin's authoritarian regime. During the fall of 1941, the Nazis destroyed much of the Red Army's fighting strength and vigorously pursued their two goals: the destruction of communism and racial purification.

The war against the Soviets was a war of ideologies and of racial hatred. The advancing Nazi forces left burning fields and towns in their wake and methodically wiped the occupied territories clean of "undesirable elements." When Russian guerrillas counterattacked with sniping and sabotage, German forces shot or hanged hundreds of innocent hostages at a time in reprisal, often torturing their victims first. The Russian guerrillas quickly chose to deliver the same punishment to any captured Germans. By the end of 1941, it was clear that the war in the East was a war of destruction and that both sides believed that only one side would be allowed to survive. In 1941, it seemed the victors would be German. Their forces were on the march toward the capital at Moscow. On orders from Berlin, however, some of the German forces pushing toward Moscow were diverted south to attack Russia's industrial heartland in an effort to destroy the Soviets' ability to resist before the Russian winter set in. Moscow was never taken, and the Russian population, its leaders, and its armies began to organize a much more determined resistance.

Hitler nonetheless managed to piece together an empire that stretched across the entire continent of Europe. "We come as the heralds of a New Order and a new justice," his regime announced. Hitler specifically compared his rule to a "new Indian empire," and claimed to have studied British imperial techniques. Much of the New Order was improvised and rested on a patchwork of provisional regimes: military government in Poland and Ukraine, collaborators in France, allied fascists in Hungary, and so on. The clearest principle was German supremacy. "The emphatic German decision to organize Europe hierarchically, like a pyramid with Germany at the top, is known to all," said an Italian diplomat at the time. The empire was meant to feed German citizens and maintain their morale and support for the war, which would prevent the "stab in the back" that Hitler believed had thwarted a German victory in 1914–18. Occupied countries paid inflated "occupation costs" in taxes, food, industrial production, and manpower. More than 2 million foreign workers were brought into Germany in 1942–43 from France, Belgium, Holland, and the Soviet Union. As they conscripted workers, the Nazis spoke of uniting Europe to save it from the "Red Menace" of communism. This propaganda seems to have had little effect. To the contrary, deporting citizens to labor in Germany did more than any other policy to drive individuals into the resistance, especially in France and Greece.

The demands of enemy occupation and the political and moral questions of collaboration and resistance, were issues across occupied Europe. The Nazis set up puppet regimes in a number of occupied territories. Both Norway and the Netherlands were deeply divided by the occupation. In both countries, a relatively small but dedicated party of Nazis governed in the name of the Germans while at the same time well-organized and determined resistance movements gathered information for the Allies and carried out acts of sabotage. In Denmark, the population was much more united against their German occupiers, engaging in regular acts of passive resistance that infuriated German administrators. They also banded together as private citizens to smuggle most of the country's Jewish population out to safety in neutral Sweden.

"CULTURAL TERROR," 1944. Produced in Nazi-occupied Holland, this cultural Frankenstein's monster warns of the looming destruction of European identity with the advance of American troops who will bring American culture with them. The terror of this culture is embodied in a long list of references: aerial bombardment, the violence of lynching and the Ku Klux Klan, African American jazz, Jewish racial threats, sexual license, and common criminality and financial manipulation. ▪ ***What image of European culture was this image designed to defend?***

Elsewhere, the relationship among collaboration, resistance, and self-interested indifference was more complex. In France, collaboration ranged from simple survival tactics under occupation to active support for Nazi ideals and goals. The worst example of this was the Vichy regime's active anti-Semitism and the aid given by French authori-

AXIS EUROPE, 1941. ▪ ***How had Hitler and Mussolini come to dominate the bulk of mainland Europe by the eve of the German invasion of the Soviet Union?*** ▪ ***Why did Hitler choose to annex certain territories to Germany but settle for occupation in others?*** ▪ ***Looking at this map, doesn't a German victory look inevitable? Why or why not?***

ties in isolating, criminalizing, and deporting Jews in France to the concentration camps. Living with the German conquerors forced citizens in France (and elsewhere) to make choices. Many chose to protect their own interests by sacrificing those of others, particularly such "undesirables" as Jews and communists. At the same time, communist activists, some members of the military, and ordinary citizens—such as the people of France's central mountains, who had a long tradition of smuggling and resisting government—became active guerrillas and saboteurs. They established links with the Free French movement in London, led by the charismatic, stiff-necked general Charles de Gaulle, and supplied important intelligence to the Allies. In eastern Europe, resistance movements provoked both open warfare against the fascists and civil war within their own countries. The Germans' system of occupation in Yugoslavia pitted a fascist Croat regime against most Serbs; the Croatian fascist guard, the Ustasha, massacred hundreds of thousands of Orthodox Christian Serbs. Josip Broz (Tito), born in Croatia to a Croatian father and a Slovene mother, emerged as the leader of the most powerful Yugoslavian resistance movement—militarily the most significant resistance in the war. Tito's troops were communists and strong enough to form a guerrilla army. They fought Germans, Italians, and Croat fascists, and they gained support and supplies from the Allies.

Perhaps the most important moral issue facing citizens of occupied Europe was not their national allegiance but rather their personal attitude to the fate of the Nazis' sworn enemies: Jews, communists, gypsies, homosexuals, and political "undesirables." Some French Jews along the Riviera found the Italian Catholic army officers who occupied the area more willing to save them from deportation than their fellow Frenchmen. This deeply personal dilemma—whether to risk family, friends, and careers to aid the deportees or simply to look the other way and allow mass murder—was one of the most powerful of the war.

RACIAL WAR, ETHNIC CLEANSING, AND THE HOLOCAUST

From the beginning, the Nazis had seen the conflict as a racial war. In *Mein Kampf*, Hitler had already outlined his view that war against the *Untermenschen*, or "subhuman" Jews, Gypsies, and Slavs, was natural and necessary. Not only would it purify the German people, but it would also conquer territory for their expansion. Thus, as soon as the war broke out, the Nazis began to implement ambitious plans for redrawing the racial map of the Reich, or what is now called ethnic cleansing. In the fall of 1939, with Poland conquered, Heinrich Himmler directed the SS to begin massive population transfers. Ethnic Germans were moved from elsewhere into the borders of the Reich, while Poles and Jews were deported to specially designated areas in the east. Over 200,000 ethnic Germans from the Baltic states were resettled in western Prussia. Welcoming these ethnic Germans went hand in hand with a brutal campaign of terror against the Poles, especially Polish Jews. The Nazis sought to root out all sources of potential resistance. Professors at the University of Cracow, considered dangerous intellectuals, were deported to concentration camps, where they died. The SS shot "undesirables," such as the inmates of Polish mental asylums, partly to allow SS troops to occupy the asylums' barracks. Poles were deported to forced labor camps. The Nazis began to transport Jews by the thousands to the region of Lublin, south of Warsaw. Special death squads also began to shoot Jews in the streets and in front of synagogues. These Polish campaigns took 100,000 Jewish lives in 1940.

The elimination of European Jewry stood at the center of the Nazis' *Rassenkampf*, or "racial struggle." We have seen the role of anti-Semitism in Hitler's rise to

POLISH JEWS, EVICTED FROM THE WARSAW GHETTO, BEING DEPORTED.
Most of the trains led to death camps.

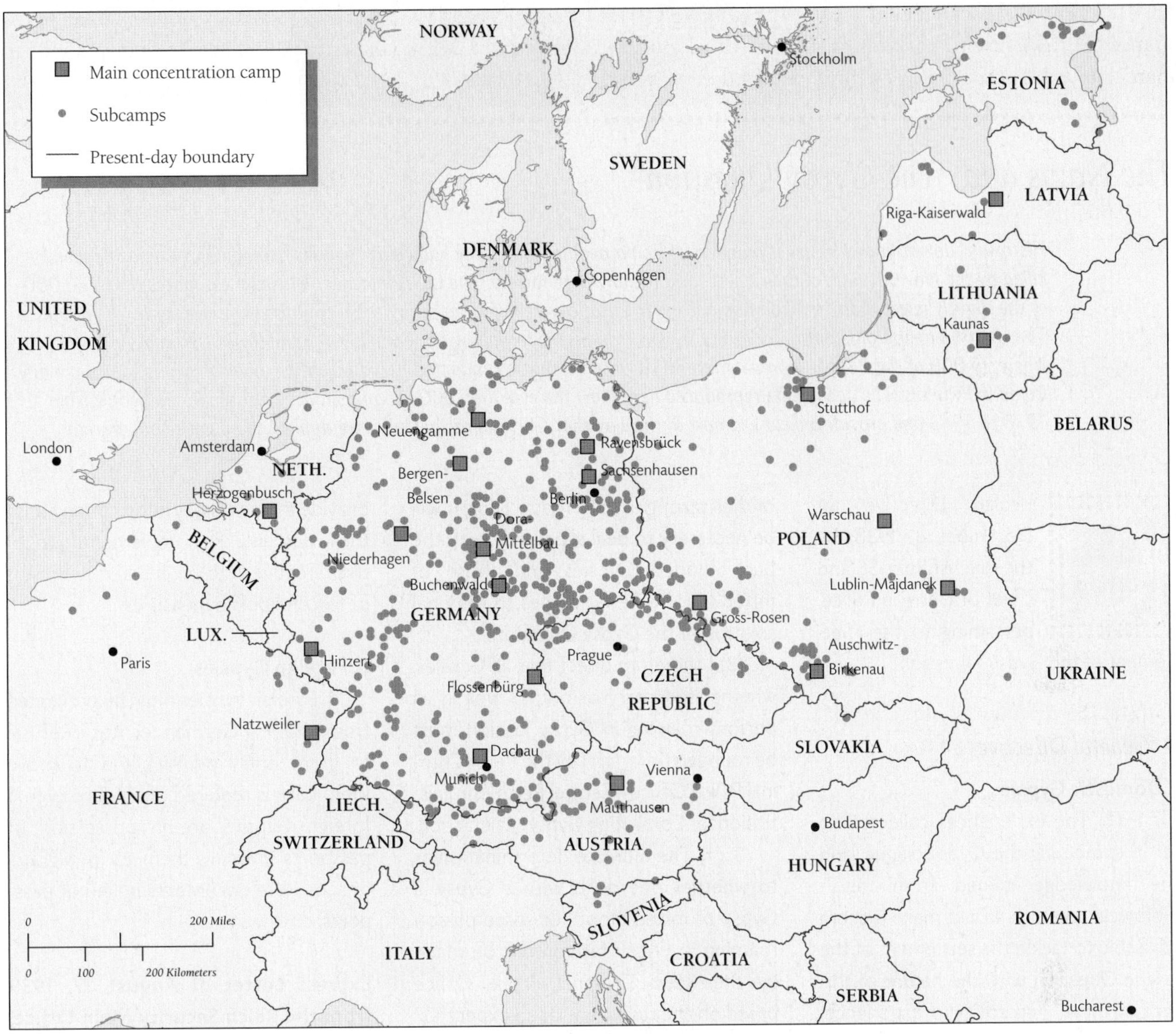

WHERE WERE THE CAMPS? In 2013, historians compiled a list of more than 42,000 separate extermination camps, detention centers, ghettos, and slave labor sites in German-controlled Europe during the war years. Their conclusion, that virtually every population center was close to such a site, has caused historians to revise upward their estimates of who in Europe had knowledge of the extermination policy.

power and the escalating campaign of terror against the Jewish community inside Germany in the 1930s, including the Night of the Broken Glass (see Chapter 25). Most historians now agree that although Hitler and other Nazis verbally announced "war" against the Jews early on, such a policy was not possible until the conquest of territory in the east after 1941 suddenly brought millions of Jews under Nazi control. Until the organized pogroms of 1938, the Nazis' anti-Jewish policy aimed not at extermination but at emigration, and until 1941 the Nazi leadership continued to consider plans to deport Europe's Jews to Madagascar, a French colony off the coast of Africa. These schemes took shape against the background of daily terror and frequent massacres, especially in Poland. The invasion of the Soviet Union turned these atrocities into something much more deadly. Operation Barbarossa was animated by the Nazis' intense ideological and racial hatreds, directed against Slavs, Jews, and Marxists. Goebbels, for example, called the Russians, "not a people but an agglomeration of animals." The invasion of the Soviet Union was thus openly a "war of extermination." The campaign's initial success also created pressing practical problems for the German army in the newly conquered territories, as they debated how to control the millions of people, including military prisoners, eastern

Analyzing Primary Sources

The Nazis and "The Gypsy Question"

Historians do not know the exact numbers of Roma people (commonly known as "gypsies" among non-Roma speakers) killed by the Nazis as part of their quest for a racially pure society. The U.S. Holocaust Museum estimates that 220,000 of the slightly fewer than 1 million Roma living in Europe were killed, either by the Germans themselves or by their allies. The Ustasha militia of Croatia, for example, was responsible for killing between 15,000 and 20,000 Roma. At Auschwitz, where 19,000 of the 23,000 Roma inmates died, Josef Mengele conducted pseudoscientific medical experiments on many Roma individuals. The documents reproduced here show the evolution of German policy toward the Roma people from 1938 to 1943 and provide a clear example of the way that German racial laws were applied to an entire population.

Circular Directive of December 8, 1938, by the Reichsführer-SS and Chief of German Police, pertaining to the "Settlement of the Gypsy Question"

A. General Directives

I. Domestic Gypsies

1. (1) The experiences collected so far in combating the Gypsy plague, and the knowledge gained from racial-biological research would make it seem advisable to tackle the settlement of the Gypsy Question with the nature of this race in mind. According to experience, individuals of mixed race contribute the largest share to Gypsy criminality. Conversely, it has been shown that all attempts to settle Gypsies in a permanent place of residence failed in particular with pure-blooded Gypsies because of their strong urge to roam. Thus, it will be necessary to deal separately with the pure-blooded Gypsies and those of mixed blood when it comes to the final solution of the Gypsy Question.

(3) I therefore direct that all Gypsies, whether sedentary or not, as well as all persons roaming in Gypsy fashion must be rounded up [*erfaßt*] by the Reich Criminal Police Office–Central Reich Administration for Combating Gypsy Malefaction.

3. (1) The ultimate determination as to whether one deals with a Gypsy, a Gypsy of mixed blood, or some person roaming in Gypsy fashion will be made by the Reich Criminal Police Office based on the testimony of an expert.

(2) I therefore direct . . . that all Gypsies, Gypsies of mixed blood, and persons roaming in Gypsy fashion be compelled to submit to a racial-biological examination required for the presentation of a testimony by an expert, and to provide the necessary information about their descent. The implementation of this directive is to be ensured by means of forceful police measures.

. . .

II. Foreign Gypsies

1. Foreign gypsies must be prevented from entering German territory. Refusal to grant entry permits and to move them back is required procedure even if foreign Gypsies are in possession of passports entitling them to immigrate, of substitute documents in lieu of passports, or of visa.

. . .

Express Letter of August 17, 1939 from the Reich Security Main Office, pertaining to the "rounding up" ["Erfassung"] of Gypsies

Berlin, October 10, 1939

Reich Security Main Office
Tgb. No. RKPA. 149/1939-g
Express Letter

European Jews, and other civilians, who had now fallen into Nazi hands. Although Hitler had certainly prepared the way for what followed in his long-nurtured campaigns against Jews, historians now believe that a significant part of the driving force for the Holocaust came from rivalries within the Nazi bureaucracy, which led to a radicalization of persecution and murder on a scale few could have imagined.

As the Nazi army swept into the Soviet Union in 1941, captured communist officials, political agitators, and any hostile civilians were imprisoned, tortured, or shot. About 5.5 million military prisoners were taken and marched to camps. Over half of them died of starvation or were executed. Poles from regions that had been under Soviet rule, Jews, and Russians were deported to Germany to work as slave labor in German factories. On the heels of the army came special battalions of *Einsatzgruppen*, or "death squads." Joined by 11,000 extra SS troops, they stormed through Jewish villages and towns with Russian or Polish populations

To the State Criminal Police—Regional and Local Commands of the Criminal Police . . .

Subject: Rounding Up of Gypsies

By order of the *Reichsführer-SS* and Chief of German Police the Gypsy Question will be fundamentally settled before long within the entire German territory by a uniform standard applied throughout the Reich. I therefore ask you to initiate the following measures at once:

1. The local police stations and the Rural Police must be instructed immediately to notify all Gypsies and Gypsies of mixed blood within their respective districts that effective immediately they may not leave their residence or their present whereabouts until further notice. Anybody in violation of this injunction will be threatened with dispatch to a concentration camp.

. . .

Express letter of January 29, 1943 from the Reich Security Main Office, pertaining to the confinement of "Gypsies of Mixed Blood," "Romany Gypsies" and "Balkan Gypsies" to a concentration camp

Berlin, January 29, 1943

Reich Security Main Office
VA No. 59/43 g
Express Letter

. . .

Subject: Confinement of Gypsies of mixed blood, Romany Gypsies and Balkan Gypsies in a concentration camp

. . .

I. By order of the *Reichsführer-SS* dated December 16, 1942 . . . , Gypsies of mixed blood, Romany Gypsies and members of Gypsy clans of non-German blood and of Balkan origins are to be selected according to fixed guidelines, and in the course of an operation lasting only a few weeks are to be confined in a concentration camp. People affected [*Personenkreis*] will henceforth briefly be referred to as "Persons of Gypsy origin."

Confinement will take place by families, regardless of the degree of mixed blood, in Concentration Camp (Gypsy Camp) Auschwitz.

. . .

(III) 1. Attempts should be made to obtain consent for sterilization from persons of Gypsy origin above 12 years of age and not yet sterilized;

. . .

4. In case of refusal, the Reich Criminal Police Office, after having ascertained the reasons, will decide what steps are to be taken.

Source: Reinhard Rürup, ed., *Topography of Terror: Gestapo, SS, and Reichssicherheitshauptamt on the "Prinz-Albrecht-Terrain"*, translated by Werner T. Augress (Berlin: Arenhövel, 1989).

Questions for Analysis

1. How was the language of racial science used to justify discriminatory practices against the Roma in the 1938 text? Why was it necessary to differentiate among "Gypsies, Gypsies of mixed blood, and persons roaming in Gypsy fashion"?
2. What was the significance of the 1939 document's statement that "the Gypsy Question will be fundamentally settled before long within the entire German territory by a uniform standard applied throughout the Reich"? If the goal was extermination, why use such bureaucratic language? If the goal was other than extermination, why was it necessary to "round up" the Gypsies?
3. By 1943, the extermination policy was already under way—why, then, was it necessary to continue to speak in vague terms of "Gypsies of mixed blood, Romany Gypsies and members of Gypsy clans of non-German blood and of Balkan origins"?

identified as "difficult." The men of the villages were shot; the women and children either deported to labor camps or massacred along with the men. By September 1941, the *Einsatzgruppen* reported that in their efforts at pacification they had killed 85,000 people, most of them Jews. By April 1942, the number was 500,000. This killing began before the gas chambers had gone into operation and continued through the campaigns on the Eastern Front. As of 1943, the death squads had killed roughly 2.2 million Jews.

As Operation Barbarossa progressed, German administrations of occupied areas herded local Jewish populations even more tightly into the ghettos some Jewish communities had occupied for centuries; Warsaw and Lodz in Poland were the largest. There, Nazi administrators, accusing Jewish people in the ghettos of hoarding supplies, refused to allow food to go in. The ghettos became centers of starvation and disease. Those who left the ghetto were shot rather than returned. A German doctor summarized the regime's

THE LIBERATION OF THE CONCENTRATION CAMPS. Many allied soldiers documented the liberation of the concentration camps at the end of the war, taking photographs and films of the appalling scenes they encountered. In many cases, German civilians were brought into the camps and compelled to witness the countless bodies of camp prisoners that remained unburied, before being conscripted to help with the disposal of the corpses to prevent the spread of disease. In this photograph, local residents view the victims of Nazi crimes at the Landesburg camp near Dachau, Germany in 1945. ▪ ***What complications faced the Allies in the task of assigning responsibility for these crimes?***

logic about killing this way: "One must, I can say it quite openly in this circle, be clear about it. There are only two ways. We sentence the Jews in the ghetto to death by hunger or we shoot them. Even if the end result is the same, the latter is more intimidating." In other words, the point was not simply death but terror.

Through the late summer and fall of 1941, Nazi officials discussed and put together plans for mass killings in death camps. The ghettos had already been sealed; now orders came down that no Jews were to leave any occupied areas. That summer, the Nazis had experimented with vans equipped with poison gas, which could kill thirty to fifty people at a time. Those experiments and the gas chambers were designed with the help of scientists from the T-4 euthanasia program, which had already killed 80,000 racially, mentally, or physically "unfit" individuals in Germany. By October 1941, the SS was building camps with gas chambers and deporting people to them. Auschwitz-Birkenau *(OWSH-vihts BIHR-kuh-now),* which had been built to hold Polish prisoners, was built up to be the largest of the camps. Auschwitz eventually held many different types of prisoners—"undesirables" like Jehovah's Witnesses and homosexuals, Poles, Russians, and even some British POWs—but Jews and gypsies were the ones systematically annihilated there. Between the spring of 1942 and the fall of 1944, over 1 million people were killed at Auschwitz-Birkenau alone. The opening of the death camps set off the greatest wave of slaughter from 1942 to 1943. Freight cars hauled Jewish people to the camps, first from the ghettos of Poland, then from France, Holland, Belgium, Austria, the Balkans, and later from Hungary and Greece. Bodies were buried in pits dug by prisoners or burned in crematoria.

The death camps have come to symbolize the horrors of Nazism as a system of modern mass murder. Yet it is worth emphasizing that much of the slaughter was not anonymous, industrialized, or routine and that it took place in

"JEWISH COUPLE IN BUDAPEST," EVGENY KHALDEI (1945). Khaldei, a Soviet photographer and journalist who traveled with the Red Army, left a remarkable and moving account of his encounter with this woman and man. "There was a Jewish couple wearing Stars of David. They were afraid of me. There was still fighting going on in the city, and they thought I might be an SS soldier. So I said *Sholem Aleichem* [hello] to them, and the woman began to cry. After I'd taken the picture, I pulled their stars off and said, 'The fascists are beaten. It's terrible to be marked like that.'"

HITLER'S "FINAL SOLUTION": JEWS MARKED FOR DEATH. On January 20, 1942, German officials met at Wannsee (just outside Berlin) to discuss the "Final Solution" to the "Jewish problem." They also discussed what they believed to be the remaining number of Jewish people in territories they controlled or soon hoped to control. Examine these figures closely. ▪ ***How many millions of innocent people did the Nazis propose to slaughter?*** ▪ ***Based on your reading, what percentage of the Jews did they actually kill?*** ▪ ***What two countries were scheduled for the most executions?***

Competing Viewpoints

The Holocaust: Two Perspectives from the SS

An SS officer charged with inspecting the death camps wrote the first account here of his visit to Belzec, a camp in occupied Poland, near the former Russian border. He opposed the regime. Shortly after leaving this description, in 1945, he committed suicide.

Heinrich Himmler (1900–1945), one of the founding members of the Nazi Party and head of the SS, became one of the most powerful members of the Nazi government. He directed the purge of the rebellious SA in 1934, expanded the SS, supervised the network of death camps, and by 1943—when the speech reprinted here was given—had become minister of the interior for the administration of the Reich. Few represent better the combination of ambition, ideology, and ruthlessness that characterized Nazi leaders. Himmler committed suicide when captured by Allied troops in 1945.

The Death Camps

Next morning, shortly before seven, I was told: 'the first transport will arrive in ten minutes'. And, in fact, after a few minutes, the first train arrived from the direction of Lemberg (Lvov). 45 wagons with 6,700 people, of whom 1,450 were already dead on arrival. Behind the barred hatches stared the horribly pale and frightened faces of children, their eyes full of the fear of death. Men and women were there too. . . .

The chambers fill up. 'Pack them in'—that is what Captain Wirth has ordered. People are treading on each others' toes. 700–800 in an area of twenty-five square metres, in forty-five cubic metres! The SS push them in as far as possible. The doors shut; in the meantime, the others are waiting outside in the open, naked. 'It is the same in winter', I was told. 'But they could catch their death of cold', I say. 'But that's just what they are there for', replied an SS man in dialect. Now at last I understood why the whole apparatus is called the Heckenholt Foundation. Heckenholt is the driver of the diesel engine, a little technician who constructed the installation. The people are going to be killed by the diesel exhaust gases. But the diesel engine won't start! Captain Wirth arrives. He is clearly embarrassed that this should happen just on the day when I am here. Yes indeed, I can see the whole thing. And I wait. My stop watch faithfully records it all. Fifty minutes, 70 seconds [*sic*!]. Still the diesel won't start. The people wait in their gas chambers. In vain. One can hear them crying, sobbing. . . . Captain Wirth hits the Ukrainian who is responsible for helping *Unterscharführer* Heckenholt with the diesel engine twelve or thirteen times in the face with his riding whip. After two hours forty-nine minutes—the stop watch has recorded it all—the engine starts. Up to this moment, the people have been living in these four chambers, four times 750 people in four times forty-five cubic metres. A further twenty-five minutes pass. That's right, many are now dead. One can see through the little peepholes when the electric light illuminates the chambers for a moment. After twenty-eight minutes, only a few are still alive. At last, after thirty-two minutes, they are all dead. . . .

face-to-face encounters outside the camps. Jews and other victims were not simply killed. They were tortured, beaten, and executed publicly while soldiers and other onlookers recorded the executions with cameras—and sent photos home to their families. During the last phases of the war, inmates still in the concentration camps were taken on death marches whose sole purpose was suffering and death. Nor was the killing done by the specially indoctrinated SS and *Einsatzgruppen*. The Nazi regime called up groups of conscripts, such as Reserve Police Battalion 101, from duty in its home city of Hamburg and sent it into occupied territories. Once there, the unit of middle-aged policemen received and obeyed orders to kill, in one day, 1,500 Jewish men, women, and children in one village. The commander offered to excuse men who did not feel they could carry out this assignment; only a few asked for a different task. In one Polish town, occupied first by the Soviets and then retaken by the Nazis, the Polish villagers themselves, with minimal

Himmler's Instructions to the SS

I also want to talk to you quite frankly about a very grave matter. We can talk about it quite frankly among ourselves and yet we will never speak of it publicly. Just as we did not hesitate on 30 June 1934 to do our duty as we were bidden, and to stand comrades who had lapsed up against the wall and shoot them, so we have never spoken about it and will never speak of it. It appalled everyone, and yet everyone was certain that he would do it the next time if such orders should be issued and it should be necessary.

I am referring to the Jewish evacuation programme, the extermination of the Jewish people. It is one of those things which are easy to talk about. "The Jewish people will be exterminated," says every party comrade, "It's clear, it's in our programme. Elimination of the Jews, extermination and we'll do it." And then they come along, the worthy eighty million Germans, and each one of them produces his decent Jew. It's clear the others are swine, but this one is a fine Jew. Not one of those who talk like that has watched it happening, not one of them has been through it. Most of you will know what it means when a hundred corpses are lying side by side, or five hundred or a thousand are lying there. To have stuck it out and—apart from a few exceptions due to human weakness—to have remained decent, that is what has made us tough. This is a glorious page in our history and one that has never been written and can never be written. For we know how difficult we would have made it for ourselves if, on top of the bombing raids, the burdens and the deprivations of war, we still had Jews today in every town as secret saboteurs, agitators and troublemakers. We would now probably have reached the 1916–17 stage when the Jews were still part of the body of the German nation.

We have taken from them what wealth they had. I have issued a strict order, which SS *Obergruppenführer* Pohl has carried out, that this wealth should, as a matter of course, be handed over to the Reich without reserve. We have taken none of it for ourselves. . . . All in all, we can say that we have fulfilled this most difficult duty for the love of our people. And our spirit, our soul, our character has not suffered injury from it. . . .

Source (for both documents): J. Noakes and G. Pridham, *Nazism: A History in Document and Eyewitness Accounts, 1919–1945*, Vol. 2 (New York: 1988), pp. 1151–52, 1199–1200.

Questions for Analysis

1. "This is a glorious page in our history," says Himmler, but one that "can never be written." How does he reconcile that contradiction? What was glorious? To what extent did the Nazis try to conceal what they were doing?
2. What does Himmler's speech suggest about the psychology of Nazism or about the ways in which members of the SS were persuaded to become murderers?

guidance or help from German soldiers, turned on their Jewish neighbors and killed hundreds in a day.

How many people knew of the extent of the Holocaust? No operation of this scale could be carried out without the cooperation or knowledge of many: the Nazi hierarchy; architects who helped build the camps; engineers who designed the gas chambers and crematoria; municipal officials of cities from which people were deported; train drivers; residents of villages near the camps, who reported the smell of bodies burning; and so on. Recent research has shown that the number of extermination camps, ghettos, slave-labor sites, and detention centers in Nazi-controlled Europe was greater than 42,000. Given the difficulty of hiding sites that required guards, logistical support, and access to transportation networks, it is now clear that many more people must have been aware of what was happening. It is not surprising that most who suspected the worst were terrified and powerless. It is also not surprising that

Interpreting Visual Evidence

The Architecture of Mass Murder

The camp at Auschwitz-Birkenau was the largest of the German concentration camps whose central purpose was the murder of Europe's Jews. Almost 1.1 million people, of whom 1 million were Jews, were murdered in Auschwitz.

Auschwitz-Birkenau was in fact a complex of three camps: an extermination center, a prisoner-of-war camp, and a labor camp built with the cooperation of German industrial firms such as IG Farben. Forty other smaller installations and work camps in the surrounding area were also run by the camp's administration. The construction of the Auschwitz-Birkenau complex occupied thousands of workers and continued throughout the war. When the Soviet army arrived in January 1945, they found that the Germans had burned the camp archives before fleeing, but they had not burned the construction archive, which was kept separately. Hundreds of

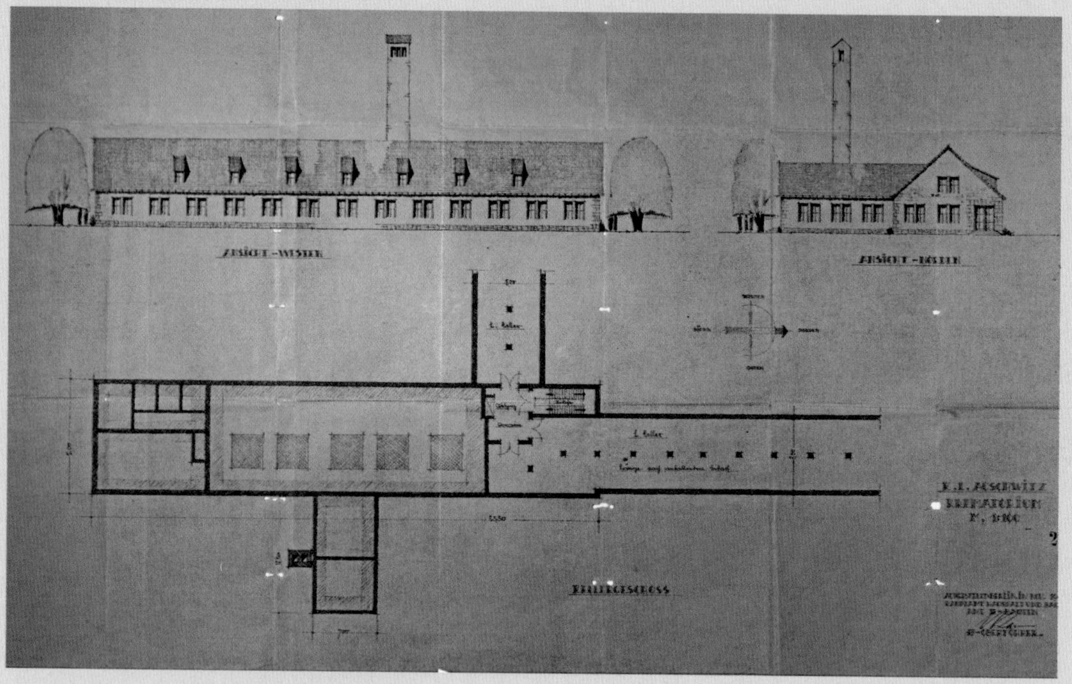

A. Blueprint for Crematorium II, Birkenau, dated November 1941. The five shaded squares in the lower drawing are the gas ovens in the structure's underground level, and the area to the right is labeled "Corpses Room."

many people did not want to know and did their best to ignore evidence and carry on with their lives. Many who continued to support the Nazis did so for other reasons, out of personal opportunism or because they opposed communism and wanted order restored. Yet mere popular indifference does not provide a satisfactory explanation for the Nazis' ability to accomplish the murder of so many people. Many Europeans—German, French, Dutch, Polish, Swiss, and Russian—had come to believe that there was a "Jewish problem" that had to be "solved." The Nazis tried to conceal the death camps. Yet they knew they could count on vocal support for requiring Jews to be specially identified, for restrictions on marriage and property ownership, and for other kinds of discrimination. For reasons that had to do with both traditional Christian anti-Semitism and modern, racialized nationalism, many Europeans had come to see Jewish Europeans as "foreign," no longer members of their national communities.

What of other governments? Their level of cooperation with the Nazis' plans varied. The French Vichy regime, on its

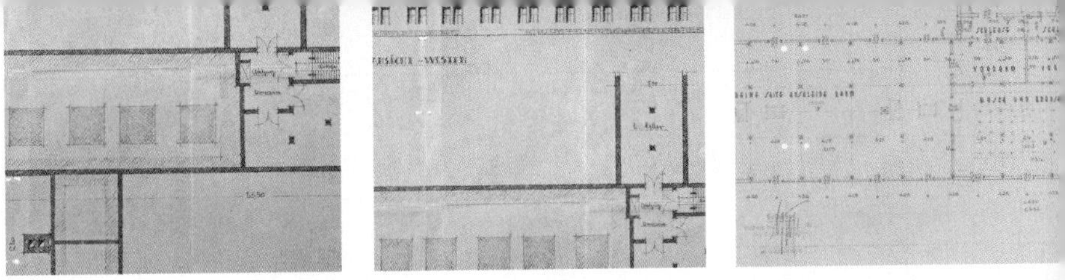

technical drawings were found in this archive, and after the collapse of the Soviet Union in 1991, these drawings became accessible to historians. A further cache of such documents was discovered in an abandoned building in Berlin in 2008. They are now held by Yad Vashem, the Holocaust archive in Jerusalem, Israel.

The discovery of these drawings did not add substantially to what was already known about the murder of Jews and other prisoners at Auschwitz, but they provide an arresting example of the bureaucratic apparatus—and the chilling coldness of the planning—that went into the Nazi extermination policy.

Questions for Analysis

1. Who would have seen these plans and been made aware of their purpose?
2. What do these images tell us about the nature of the effort that went into the Nazi extermination policy?
3. Is there a way to understand the relationship between the careful renderings, the precise measurements, and the rectilinear lines, and the ultimate purpose of the buildings depicted?

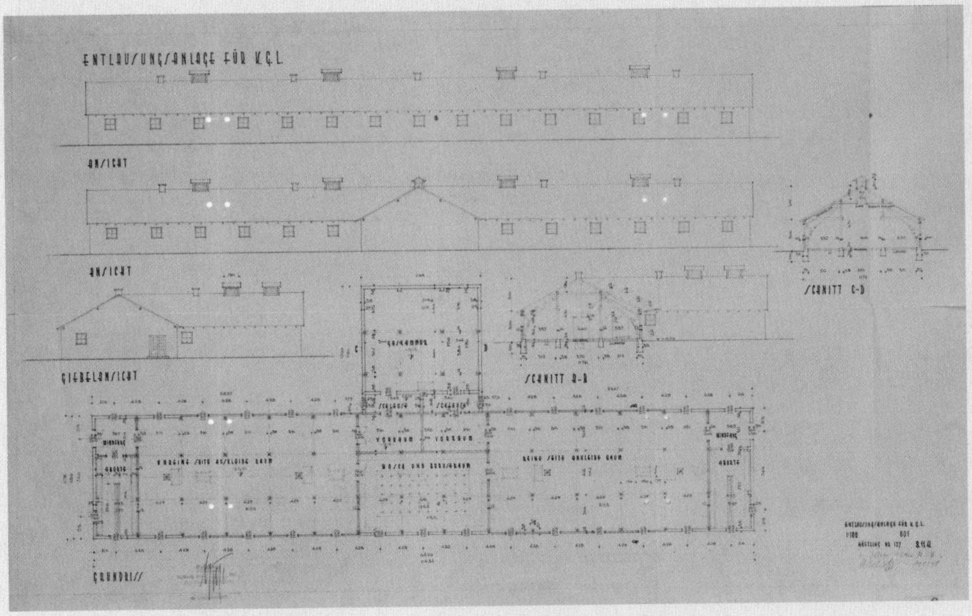

B. Blueprint for the "Delousing Facility" at Auschwitz-Birkenau, showing a room of 11.6 meters by 11.2 meters marked "*Gaskammer*" (gas chamber).

own initiative, passed laws that required Jews to wear identifying stars and strictly limited their movements and activities. When the German government demanded roundups and deportations of Jews, Vichy cooperated. On the other hand, Italy, though a fascist country, participated less actively. Not until the Germans occupied the north of Italy in 1943 were drastic anti-Semitic measures implemented. The Hungarian government, also fascist and allied with the Nazis, persecuted Jews but dragged its heels about deportations. Thus, the Hungarian Jewish community survived—until March 1944, when Germans, disgusted with their Hungarian collaborators, took direct control and immediately began mass deportations. So determined were the Nazis to carry out their "final solution" that they killed up to 12,000 Hungarian Jews a day at Auschwitz in May 1944, contributing to a total death toll of 600,000 Jews from Hungary.

In the face of this Nazi determination, little resistance was possible. The concentration camps were designed to numb and incapacitate their inmates, making them acquiesce in their own slow deaths even if they were not

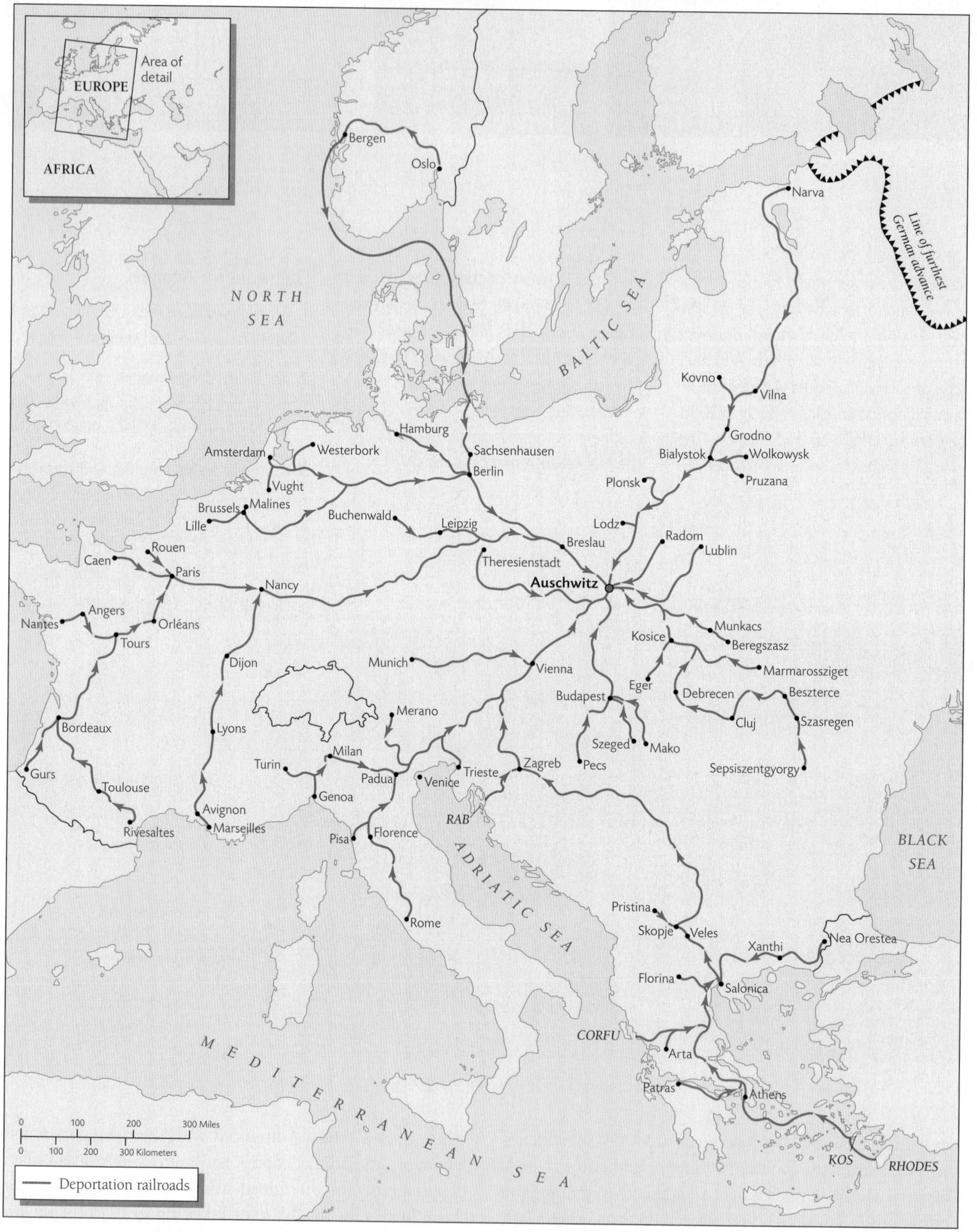

DEPORTATION RAILWAYS. Between March 1942 and November 1944, Jews are known to have been deported from every location on this map—as well as from numerous other locales. Note the effort made by the Nazis to transport Jews from the very frontiers of the empire at the height of a two-front war. ▪ ***According to the map, to which site were most Jews deported?*** ▪ ***Looking back at Hitler's "Final Solution" map on page 895, why was Auschwitz in Poland chosen as the main deportation site?*** ▪ ***What does this say about the Nazi regime in particular and about other states willing to collaborate with the Nazis?***

Past and Present

European Integration Then and Now

Hitler's conquest of Europe was a plan for European integration, based on a theory of racial domination, whereby "pure" Aryan settlements (see photo from "model" Nazi village of Adolf Hitler-Koog) would take over territory from "racially inferior" people who would eventually be eliminated. The great success of European integration after the Second World War (see photo of German Chancellor Konrad Adenauer shaking hands with Jean Monnet, a key figure in European integration) was to create a structure for international cooperation based on democratic institutions and mutual economic interest.

Watch related author interview on StudySpace
wwnorton.com/web/westernciv18

killed right away. In his famous account, the survivor Primo Levi writes: "Our language lacks words to express this offence, the demolition of a man. . . . It is not possible to sink lower than this; no human condition is more miserable than this, nor could it conceivably be so. Nothing belongs to us any more; they have taken away our clothes, our shoes, even our hair; if we speak, they will not listen to us, and if they listen, they will not understand." A few rebellions in Auschwitz and Treblinka were repressed with savage efficiency. In the villages of Poland, Ukraine, and elsewhere, people rounded up to be deported or shot had to make split-second decisions to escape. Saving oneself nearly always meant abandoning one's children or parents, which very few could—or would—do. The countryside offered no shelter; local populations were usually either hostile or too terrified to help. Reprisals horrified all. Families of Jews and gypsies were ordinary people whose lives could not have prepared them for the kind of violence that rolled over them.

The largest Jewish resistance came in the Warsaw ghetto, in the spring of 1943. The previous summer, the Nazis had deported 80 percent of the ghetto's residents to the camps, making it clear that those left behind had little hope of survival. Those in the ghetto had virtually no resources, yet when deportations started again, a small Jewish underground movement—a thousand fighters, perhaps, in a community of 70,000—took on the Nazis with a tiny arsenal of gasoline bombs, pistols, and ten rifles. The Nazis responded by burning the ghetto to the ground and executing and deporting to the camps nearly everyone who was left. Some 56,000 Jews died. "The Warsaw Ghetto is no more," reported the SS commander at the end. Word of the rising did spread, but the repression made it clear that the targets of Nazi extermination could choose only between death in the streets or death in the camps. Sustained resistance, as one person remarked, would have required "the prospect of victory."

The Holocaust claimed between 4.1 and 5.7 million Jewish lives. Even those numbers do not register the nearly total destruction of some cultures. In the Baltic states (Latvia and Lithuania), Germany, Czechoslovakia, Yugoslavia, and Poland, well over 80 percent of the long-established Jewish communities were annihilated. Elsewhere, the figures were closer to 50 percent. The Holocaust was part of a racial war and of an even longer period of ethnically motivated mass murder. Through both world wars and afterward ethnic and religious groups—Jews, Armenians, Poles, Serbian Orthodox, ethnic Germans—were hunted, massacred, and legally deported en masse. Hitler's government had planned to build a "new Europe," safe for ethnic Germans and their allies and secure against communism, on the graveyards of whole cultures.

TOTAL WAR: HOME FRONTS, THE WAR OF PRODUCTION, BOMBING, AND THE BOMB

The Second World War was a "total war." Even more than the First World War, it involved the combined efforts of whole populations, massive resources, and a mobilization of entire economies within combatant nations. Standards of living changed around the world. In the neutral nations of Latin America, which supplied vast amounts of raw materials to the Allies, wartime profits led to a wave of prosperity known as the "dance of the millions." In the lands occupied by Germany or Japan, economies of forced extraction robbed local areas of resources, workers, and even food. In East Asia, deprivations caused rising resentment of the Japanese, who had been seen initially as liberators ending the rule of the old colonial powers. In the United States, Detroit produced no new models of car or truck between 1940 and 1945. Work schedules were grueling. Women and the elderly, pressed back into wage work or working for the first time, put in long shifts (in Britain and Russia, these sometimes ran over twelve hours) before returning home to cook, clean, and care for families and neighbors also affected by enemy bombing and wartime shortages. Diets changed. Though Germany lived comfortably off the farmlands of Europe for several years and the United States could lean on its huge agricultural base, food, gasoline, and basic household goods were still rationed. In occupied Europe and the Soviet Union, rations were just above starvation level and sometimes fell below in areas near the fighting. Britain, dependent on its empire and other overseas sources for food and raw materials, ran a comprehensive rationing system that kept up production and ensured a drab but consistent diet on the table.

Production—the industrial ability to churn out more tanks, tents, planes, bombs, and uniforms than the other side—was essential to winning the war. Britain, the Soviet Union, and America each launched comprehensive, well-designed propaganda campaigns that encouraged the production of war equipment on an unmatched scale. Appeals to patriotism, to communal interests, and to a common stake in winning the war struck a chord. The Allied societies proved willing to regulate themselves and commit to the effort. Despite strikes and disputes with government officials, the Allied powers devoted more of their economies to war production, more efficiently, than any nations in history. They built tanks, ships, and planes capable of competing with advanced German and Japanese designs by the tens of thousands, swamping the enemy with constant reinforcements and superior firepower. Japan nearly reached comparable levels of production but then slowly declined, as Allied advances on land and American subma-

"JUST A GOOD AFTERNOON'S WORK!" A British poster mobilizing women for part-time factory work.

rines cut off overseas sources of vital supplies. Germany, despite its reputation for efficiency and its access to vast supplies of slave labor, was less efficient in its use of workers and materials than the Allied nations. The Germans' ability to produce devastatingly successful weapons led to a damaging side effect—vast amounts of money and time spent developing the pet projects of high-ranking Nazi officials or trying to make unsuccessful designs work. Rather than losing time and resources pursuing perfection, the Allies developed working, standard designs and produced them in overwhelming numbers.

Because industry was essential to winning the war, centers of industry became vital military targets. The Allies began bombing German ports and factories almost as soon as the Germans started their own campaigns. Over time, American and British planners became equally ruthless on an even larger scale. Both of these Allied nations made a major commitment to strategic bombing, developing new planes and technology that allowed them to put thousands of bombers in the air both night and day over occupied Europe. As the war wore on and Germany kept fighting, the Allies expanded their campaign. They moved from pinpoint bombing of the military and industry in Germany to striking such targets across all of occupied Europe and bombing Germany's civilian population in earnest. For the British, despite a public debate about the morality of bombing, it was a war of retribution; for the Americans, it was an effort to grind the Germans down without sacrificing too many Allied lives. The Allies killed tens of thousands of German civilians as they struck Berlin, ports such as Hamburg, and the industrial cities of the Ruhr, but German war production persisted. At the same time, German fighter planes shot down hundreds of Allied bombers, causing heavy losses. After the Allied invasion of Europe, bombing expanded well beyond targets of military value. The German city of Dresden, a center of culture and education that lacked heavy industry, was firebombed with a horrifying death toll. This gave Allied generals and politicians pause, but strategic bombing continued. German industry was slowly degraded, but the German will to keep fighting, like Britain's or the Soviet Union's, remained intact.

The Race to Build the Bomb

Allied scientists in the United States also developed the world's first nuclear weapon during the war years, a bomb that worked by splitting the atom, creating a chain reaction that could release tremendous energy in an explosion. Physicists in Britain and Germany first suggested that such a weapon might be possible, but only the United States had the resources to build such a bomb before the end of the war. A group of physicists at the University of Chicago, under the leadership of Enrico Fermi and including many refugees from fascist regimes in Europe, built the world's first nuclear reactor. In December 1942, Fermi and his group staged the first controlled chain reaction at the site. Fearful that the Germans would develop a bomb of their own, the U.S. government built a laboratory at Los Alamos, New Mexico, and charged the physicists to build an atomic bomb. Physicist J. Robert Oppenheimer directed the top-secret plan, known to the researchers as the Manhattan Project. The idea was to perfect a bomb that could be dropped by plane and detonated above the target. The physicists successfully tested a device on July 16, 1945, in New Mexico, vaporizing the test tower in a wave of heat and fire that rose in a mushroom shape overhead. The United States now possessed the most destructive weapon ever devised.

THE ALLIED COUNTERATTACK AND THE DROPPING OF THE ATOMIC BOMB

Hitler had invaded the Soviet Union in June 1941. Within two years, the war in the East had become his undoing; within four years, it brought about his destruction.

The early successes of the German-led invasion were crippling. Nearly 90 percent of the Soviets' tanks, most of their aircraft, and huge stores of supplies were destroyed or captured. Nazi forces penetrated deep into European Russia. The Soviets fought regardless. By late 1941, German and Finnish forces had cut off and besieged Leningrad (St. Petersburg). Yet the city held out for 844 days—through three winters, massive destruction by artillery and aircraft, and periods of starvation—until a large relief force broke the siege. Russian partisans stepped up their campaigns of ambush and terrorism, and many of the Germans' former allies in Ukraine and elsewhere turned against them in reaction to Nazi pacification efforts.

The Eastern Front

In the East, the character of the war changed as Russians rallied to defend the *rodina*, the Russian motherland. Stalin's efforts were aided by the weather—successive winters took a heavy toll in German lives. At the same time, Soviet industry made an astonishing recovery during the war years. Whole industries were rebuilt behind the safety of the Ural mountains and entire urban populations were sent to work in them, turning out tanks, fighter planes, machine guns, and ammunition. Finally, the Germans were the victims of their own success with their *Blitzkrieg* tactics, as their lines extended deep into Russian territory, spreading their forces more thinly, and opening them up to attack from unexpected angles.

The turning point came in 1942–43, when the Germans attempted to take Stalingrad, in an effort to break the back of Soviet industry. The Russians drew the invading army into the city where they were bogged down in house-to-house fighting that neutralized the German tanks and gave the outnumbered Soviet forces greater chances of success, despite their lack of equipment. The Germans found their supplies running low as winter set in, and in November 1942 large Russian armies encircled the city and besieged the invaders in a battle that continued through a cruel winter. At the end of January 1943, the German commander defied his orders and surrendered. More than a half million German, Italian, and Romanian soldiers had been killed; Russian casualties were over a million, including a hundred thousand civilians.

PRISONERS OF WAR. Over 90,000 captured German troops were forced to march through the streets of Stalingrad after a defeat by the Soviet forces. The combination of the battle and the Russian winter resulted in the German loss of over 300,000 men.

After Stalingrad, a series of Soviet attacks drove the Germans back toward the frontier and beyond. In what may have been the largest battle ever fought, Soviet armies destroyed a German force at Kursk in the summer of 1943—the battle involved over 6,000 tanks and 2 million men. Following this victory, the Russians launched a major offensive into Ukraine, and by the spring of 1944 Ukraine was back in Soviet hands. Meanwhile, Leningrad was liberated and Romania forced to capitulate. Soviet armies entered the Balkans where they met with Tito's partisans in Yugoslavia. In Poland, successive German armies collapsed, and the Soviets, joined by communist partisans from eastern Europe, retook large parts of Czechoslovakia. Hitler's ambitious goal of conquest in the East had brought the downfall of the Nazi regime and death to another generation of German soldiers.

STORMING "FORTRESS EUROPE." American troops landing on Omaha Beach June 6, 1944. In the three months that followed, the Allies poured more than 2 million men, almost a half million vehicles, and 4 million tons of supplies onto the Continent—a measure of how firmly the Germans were established.

The Western Front

When the Nazis invaded Russia, Stalin called on the Allies to open a second front in the West. In response, the Americans led an attack on Italy in 1943, beginning with an invasion of Sicily in July. Italy's government deposed Mussolini and surrendered in the summer of 1943 while the nation collapsed into civil war. Italian partisans, especially the communists, sided with the Americans, while dedicated fascists fought on. The Germans occupied Italy with more than a dozen elite divisions, and the hard-fought and bitter campaign with American and British forces lasted eighteen months.

The most important second front was opened on June 6, 1944, with the massive Allied landings in Normandy. Casualties were high, but careful planning and deception allowed the Allied invasion to gain a foothold in northern Europe, eventually leading to breakthrough of the German lines. A second landing in southern France also succeeded, aided by the resistance. By August, these Allied armies had liberated Paris and pushed into Belgium. In

"RAISING THE RED FLAG OVER THE REICHSTAG," EVGENY KHALDEI (1945). Khaldei was one of several Soviet Jewish photographers to document Nazi atrocities and (in this case) Soviet heroism on the Eastern Front. In this photograph, which became the best-known image of Soviet victory, a Soviet soldier raises a flag over the Reichstag in Berlin. ▪ ***How was the Soviet occupation of the German capital seen from the perspective of the other Allied governments?***

the fall, the Germans managed to defeat a British airborne invasion in the Netherlands and an American thrust into the Rhineland forests before mounting a devastating attack in December 1944, in the Battle of the Bulge. The Allied lines nearly broke, but the American forces held long enough for a crushing counterattack. In April 1945, the Allies crossed the Rhine into Germany, and the last defenders of the German Reich were swiftly overwhelmed. This military success was helped by the fact that most Germans preferred to surrender to Americans or Britons than face the Russians to the east.

Those Soviet troops were approaching fast. The Russian army took Prague and Vienna, and by late April they reached the suburbs of Berlin. In the savage ten-day battle to take the German capital more than 100,000 Russians and Germans died. Adolf Hitler killed himself in a bunker beneath the Chancellery on April 30. On May 2, the heart of the city was captured, and the Soviets' red banner flew from the Brandenburg Gate. On May 7, the German high command signed a document of unconditional surrender. The war in Europe was over.

The War in the Pacific

The war in the Pacific ended four months later. The British pushed the Japanese out of Burma while the Germans were surrendering in the West, and soon after, Australian forces recaptured the Dutch East Indies. In the fall of 1944, the U.S. Navy had destroyed most of Japan's surface ships in the gulfs of the Philippine Islands, and American troops took Manila house by house in bloody fighting. The remaining battles—amphibious assaults on a series of islands running toward the Japanese mainland—were just as brutal. Japanese pilots mounted suicide attacks on American ships while American marines and Japanese soldiers fought over

THE ATOM BOMB. A mushroom cloud hovers over Nagasaki after the city was bombed. Hiroshima was bombed three days earlier.

Competing Viewpoints

The Atomic Bomb and Its Implications

In July 1945, scientists associated with the Manhattan Project became involved in debates about how the atomic bomb could be deployed. Members of the Scientific Panel of the secretary of war's Interim Advisory Committee agreed that a bomb could be used militarily but disagreed about whether it could be used without prior warning and demonstration. Other groups of scientists secretly began to circulate petitions, such as the one reprinted here, in which they set out their views. The petitions never reached the president, but they raised issues that did emerge in the postwar period.

In the section of his memoirs reprinted here, President Harry S Truman sets out the views of other scientists on the secretary of war's advisory committee. He explains the logic of his decision to use the atomic bomb against Hiroshima (August 6, 1945) and Nagasaki (August 9, 1945) and the events as they unfolded.

A Petition to the President of the United States

July 17, 1945

A PETITION TO THE PRESIDENT OF THE UNITED STATES

We, the undersigned scientists, have been working in the field of atomic power. Until recently we have had to fear that the United States might be attacked by atomic bombs during this war and that her only defense might lie in a counterattack by the same means. Today, with the defeat of Germany, this danger is averted and we feel impelled to say what follows:

The war has to be brought speedily to a successful conclusion and attacks by atomic bombs may very well be an effective method of warfare. We feel, however, that such attacks on Japan could not be justified, at least not unless the terms which will be imposed after the war on Japan were made public in detail and Japan were given an opportunity to surrender....

[I]f Japan still refused to surrender our nation might then, in certain circumstances, find itself forced to resort to the use of atomic bombs. Such a step, however, ought not to be made at any time without seriously considering the moral responsibilities which are involved.

The development of atomic power will provide the nations with new means of destruction. The atomic bombs at our disposal represent only the first step in this direction, and there is almost no limit to the destructive power which will become available in the course of their future development. Thus a nation which sets the precedent of using these newly liberated forces of nature for purposes of destruction may have to bear the responsibility of opening the door to an era of devastation on an unimaginable scale.

If after this war a situation is allowed to develop in the world which permits rival powers to be in uncontrolled possession of these new means of destruction, the cities of the United States as well as the cities of other nations will be in continuous danger of sudden annihilation....

The added material strength which this lead [in the field of atomic power] gives to the United States brings with it the obligation of restraint and if we were to violate this obligation our moral position would be weakened in the eyes of the world and in our own eyes. It would then be more difficult for us to live up to our responsibility of bringing the unloosened forces of destruction under control.

In view of the foregoing, we, the undersigned, respectfully petition: first, that you exercise your power as Commander-in-Chief, to rule that the United States shall not resort to the use of atomic bombs in this war unless the terms which will be imposed upon Japan have been made public in detail and Japan knowing these terms has refused to surrender; second, that in such an event the question of whether or not to use atomic bombs be decided by you in the light of the considerations presented in this petition as well as all the other moral responsibilities which are involved.

Source: Michael B. Stoff, Jonathan F. Fanton, and R. Hal Williams, eds., *The Manhattan Project: A Documentary Introduction to the Atomic Age* (New York: 2000), p. 173.

President Truman's Memoirs

I had realized, of course, that an atomic bomb explosion would inflict damage and casualties beyond imagination. On the other hand, the scientific advisers of the committee reported, "We can propose no technical demonstration likely to bring an end to the war; we see no acceptable alternative to direct military use." It was their conclusion that no technical demonstration they might propose, such as over a deserted island, would be likely to bring the war to an end. It had to be used against an enemy target.

The final decision of where and when to use the atomic bomb was up to me. Let there be no mistake about it. I regarded the bomb as a military weapon and never had any doubt that it should be used. The top military advisers to the President recommended its use, and when I talked to Churchill he unhesitatingly told me that he favored the use of the atomic bomb if it might aid to end the war.

In deciding to use this bomb I wanted to make sure that it would be used as a weapon of war in the manner prescribed by the laws of war. That meant that I wanted it dropped on a military target. I had told Stimson that the bomb should be dropped as nearly as possibly upon a war production center of prime military importance.

Stimson's staff had prepared a list of cities in Japan that might serve as targets. Kyoto, though favored by General Arnold as a center of military activity, was eliminated when Secretary Stimson pointed out that it was a cultural and religious shrine of the Japanese.

Four cities were finally recommended as targets: Hiroshima, Kokura, Niigata, and Nagasaki. They were listed in that order as targets for the first attack. The order of selection was in accordance with the military importance of these cities, but allowance would be given for weather conditions at the time of the bombing. Before the selected targets were approved as proper for military purposes, I personally went over them in detail with Stimson, Marshall, and Arnold, and we discussed the matter of timing and the final choice of the first target. . . .

On August 6, the fourth day of the journey home from Potsdam, came the historic news that shook the world. I was eating lunch with members of the *Augusta's* crew when Captain Frank Graham, White House Map Room watch officer, handed me the following message:

> To the President from the Secretary of War
>
> Big bomb dropped on Hiroshima August 5 at 7:15 p.m. Washington time. First reports indicate complete success which was even more conspicuous than earlier test.

I was greatly moved. I telephoned Byrnes aboard ship to give him the news and then said to the group of sailors around me, "This is the greatest thing in history. It's time for us to get home."

Source: Harry S. Truman, *Memoirs*, vol. 1, *Year of Decisions* (Garden City, NY: 1955), pp. 419–21.

Questions for Analysis

1. To express their fears about how the atomic bomb would be used, scientists circulated petitions. Look at the outcomes the scientists proposed. Which came closest to subsequent events? Which was the most prudent? The most honest?

2. Is it appropriate for scientists to propose how new weapons should be used? Are they overreaching in trying to give advice in foreign affairs and military strategy? Or are they obligated to voice moral qualms?

every inch of the shell-blasted rocks in the Pacific. Okinawa fell to the Americans after eighty-two days of desperate fighting, giving the United States a foothold less than 500 miles from the Japanese home islands. The government in Tokyo called on its citizens to defend the nation against an invasion.

On July 26, the U.S., British, and Chinese governments jointly called on Japan to surrender or be destroyed. The United States had already been using long-range B-29 bombers in systematic attacks on Japanese cities, killing hundreds of thousands of Japanese civilians in firestorms produced by incendiary bombs. When the Japanese government refused to surrender, the United States decided to use its atomic bomb.

Many senior military and naval officers argued that the use of the bomb was not necessary, on the assumption that Japan was already beaten. Some of the scientists involved, who had done their part to defeat the Nazis, believed that using the bomb for political ends would set a deadly precedent. Harry Truman, who became president when Roosevelt died in April 1945, decided otherwise. On August 6, a single American plane dropped an atomic bomb on Hiroshima, obliterating 60 percent of the city. Three days later, the United States dropped a second bomb on Nagasaki. On August 14, Japan surrendered unconditionally.

The decision to use the bomb was extraordinary. It did not greatly alter the American plans for the destruction of Japan—in fact many more Japanese died in the earlier fire bombings than in the two atomic blasts. Yet the bomb was an entirely new kind of weapon, revealing a new and terrifying relationship between science and political power. The instant, total devastation of the blasts, and the lingering effects of cancerous radiation that could claim victims decades later was something terribly new. The world now had a weapon that could destroy not just cities and peoples, but humanity itself.

CONCLUSION

After the First World War, many Europeans awoke to find a world they no longer recognized. In 1945, many Europeans came out from shelters or began the long trips back to their homes, faced with a world that hardly existed at all. The products of industry—tanks, submarines, strategic bombing—had destroyed the structures of industrial society—factories, ports, and railroads. The tools of mass culture—fascist and communist appeals, patriotism proclaimed via radios and movie screens, mobilization of mass armies and industry—had been put to full use. In the after-

After You Read This Chapter

Visit StudySpace for quizzes, additional review materials, and multimedia documents. **wwnorton.com/web/westernciv18**

REVIEWING THE OBJECTIVES

- The Second World War stemmed from the political and economic crises of the 1930s. What caused the war?
- British and French leaders in the 1930s hoped to avoid another war in Europe through diplomatic negotiation with Hitler. What were the consequences of these negotiations?
- The populations of nations occupied by the Germans faced a difficult set of choices. What were the consequences of occupation for European nations, and what possibilities existed for resistance?
- The mass murder of European Jews, homosexuals, and Gypsies reached a climax during the invasion of the Soviet Union, though the victims came from every corner of Europe. What efforts did this enormous project entail, and how did it come about?
- The Nazi regime and their allies eventually collapsed after costly defeats in both eastern and western Europe. Where and when did the major defeats take place, and what was their human cost?
- The Japanese government surrendered in August 1945 after the United States dropped two atomic bombs, on Hiroshima and Nagasaki. What events led to the decision to drop these bombs, and what were their consequences?

math, much of Europe lay destroyed and, as we will see, vulnerable to the rivalry of the postwar superpowers: the United States and the Soviet Union.

The two world wars profoundly affected Western empires. Nineteenth-century imperialism had made twentieth-century war a global matter. In both conflicts the warring nations had used the resources of empire to their fullest. Key campaigns, in North Africa, Burma, Ethiopia, and the Pacific, were fought in and over colonial territories. Hundreds of thousands of colonial troops—sepoys and Gurkhas from India and Nepal, Britain's King's African Rifles, French from Algeria and West Africa—served in armies on both sides of the conflict. After two massive mobilizations, many anticolonial leaders found renewed confidence in their own peoples' courage and resourcefulness, and they seized the opportunity of European weakness to press for independence. In many areas that had been under European or Japanese imperial control, from sections of China to Korea, Indochina, Indonesia, and Palestine—the end of the Second World War only paved the way for a new round of conflict. This time, the issue was when imperial control would be ended, and by whom.

The Second World War also carried on the Great War's legacy of massive killing. Historians estimate that nearly 50 million people died. The killing fields of the east took the highest tolls: 25 million Soviet lives. Of those, 8.5 million were in the military, and the rest civilians; 20 percent of the Polish population and nearly 90 percent of the Polish Jewish community; 1 million Yugoslavs, including militias of all sides; 4 million German soldiers and 500,000 German civilians, not including the hundreds of thousands of ethnic Germans who died while being deported west at the end of the war, in one of the many acts of ethnic cleansing that ran through the period. Even the United States, shielded from the full horrors of total war by two vast oceans, lost 292,000 soldiers in battle and more to accidents or disease.

Why was the war so murderous? The advanced technology of modern industrial war and the openly genocidal ambitions of the Nazis offer part of the answer. The global reach of the conflict offers another. Finally, the Second World War overlapped with, and eventually devolved into, a series of smaller, no less bitter conflicts: a civil war in Greece; conflicts among Orthodox, Catholics, and Muslims in Yugoslavia; and political battles for control of the French resistance. Even when those struggles claimed fewer lives, they left deep political scars. So did memories of the war. Hitler's empire could not have lasted as long as it did without active collaboration or passive acquiescence from many, a fact that produced bitterness and recrimination for years.

PEOPLE, IDEAS, AND EVENTS IN CONTEXT

- What was Hitler asking for at the **MUNICH CONFERENCE** of 1938, and what made many people in Europe think that **APPEASEMENT** was their best option?
- What was the **HITLER-STALIN PACT** of 1939?
- What was ***BLITZKRIEG***, and what effect did it have on those who faced Hitler's invasions?
- What were Hitler's goals in **OPERATION BARBAROSSA**, the invasion of the Soviet Union in 1941? What were the consequences of the German defeat at **STALINGRAD**?
- What made the **SECOND WORLD WAR** a global war? Where were the main consequences of the war felt most keenly outside of Europe?
- What was the **MANHATTAN PROJECT**, and how did it affect the outcome of the Second World War?

THINKING ABOUT CONNECTIONS

- What long-term causes going back to the history of Europe in the nineteenth century might one point to in order to understand the outbreak of the Second World War? Can one link the story of this war with the history of European imperialism in the nineteenth century? With the successes and failures of movements for German national unification?
- What circumstances made the Second World War a global conflict?

Before You Read This Chapter

STORY LINES

- Postwar Europeans looked to rebuild their shattered continent in the shadow of a cold war between the United States and the Soviet Union. The new international order sharply curtailed the ability of European nations to act independently.
- After 1945, European imperial powers faced a challenge from movements for national independence in Africa, the Middle East, and Asia. By the early 1960s, almost all of Britain's and France's colonies had gained their independence.
- Western European nations increasingly turned toward political and economic cooperation, leading to unprecedented economic growth in the 1950s and 1960s. In Eastern Europe the socialist regimes of the Eastern bloc sought to chart a different path under Soviet sponsorship, achieving more modest growth in economies that emphasized heavy industries more than the manufacture of consumer goods.

CHRONOLOGY

1946–1964	Twenty French colonies, eleven British colonies, Belgian Congo, and Dutch Indonesia become independent nations
1947	Truman Doctrine
1948	Soviets create the Eastern bloc
1948	Marshall Plan
1949	Chinese Revolution
1949	Formation of NATO
1950–1953	Korean War
1953–1956	Revolts in East Germany, Poland, and Hungary
1955	Formation of Warsaw Pact
1957	Treaty of Rome creates the European Economic Community (EEC, the Common Market)
1961	Building of the Berlin Wall
1964–1975	U.S. Vietnam War

27

The Cold War World: Global Politics, Economic Recovery, and Cultural Change

CORE OBJECTIVES

- **UNDERSTAND** the origins of the Cold War and the ways that the United States and the Soviet Union sought to influence the political and economic restructuring of Europe in the postwar period.
- **IDENTIFY** the policies that led to the economic integration of Western European nations in the postwar decades and the reasons for the rapid economic growth that accompanied this integration.
- **DESCRIBE** the process of decolonization that brought the colonial era in Africa and Asia to an end.
- **EXPLAIN** developments in European postwar culture, as intellectuals, writers, and artists reacted to the loss of European influence in the world and the ideological conflicts of the Cold War.

"The war ended the way a passage through a tunnel ends," wrote Heda Kovály, a Czech woman who survived the concentration camps. "From far away you could see the light ahead, a gleam that kept growing, and its brilliance seemed ever more dazzling to you huddled there in the dark the longer it took to reach it. But when at last the train burst out into the glorious sunshine, all you saw was a wasteland." The war left Europe a land of wreckage and confusion. Millions of refugees trekked hundreds or thousands of miles on foot to return to their homes while others were forcibly displaced from their lands. In some areas, housing was practically nonexistent, with no available means to build anew. Food remained in dangerously short supply; a year after the war, roughly 100 million people in Europe still lived on fewer than 1,500 calories per day. Families scraped vegetables from their gardens or traded smuggled goods on the black market. Governments continued to ration food, and without rationing, a large portion of the Continent's population would have starved. During the winter of 1945–46, many regions had little or no fuel for heat. What coal there was—less than half the prewar supply—could not be transported to the areas that needed it most. The brutality of international war, civil war, and occupation had divided countries against themselves, shredding relations among ethnic groups and fellow citizens. Ordinary people's intense relief at liberation often went hand in hand with recriminations over their neighbors' wartime betrayal, collaboration, or simple opportunism.

How does a nation, a region, or a civilization recover from a catastrophe on the scale of the Second World War? Nations had to do much more than deliver food and rebuild economic infrastructures. They had to restore—or create—government authority, functioning bureaucracies, and legitimate legal systems. They had to rebuild bonds of trust and civility between citizens, steering a course between demands for justice, on the one hand, and the overwhelming desire to bury memories of the past, on the other. On the contrary, rebuilding entailed a commitment to renewing democracy—to creating democratic institutions that could withstand threats such as those the West had experienced in the 1930s. Some aspects of this process were extraordinarily successful, more so than even the most optimistic forecaster might have thought possible in 1945. Others failed or were deferred until later in the century.

The war's devastating effects brought two dramatic changes in the international balance of power. The first change was the emergence of the so-called superpowers, the United States and the Soviet Union, and the swift development of a "cold war" between them. The Cold War divided Europe, with Eastern Europe occupied by Soviet troops, and Western Europe dominated by the military and economic presence of the United States. In both Western and Eastern Europe, the Cold War led to increased political and economic integration, resulting in the emergence of the European Common Market in the West and a socialist bloc dominated by the Soviet Union in the East. The second great change came with the dismantling of the European empires that had once stretched worldwide. The collapse of empires and the creation of newly emancipated nations raised the stakes in the Cold War and brought superpower rivalry to far-flung sections of the globe. Those events, which shaped the postwar recovery and necessarily created a new understanding of what "the West" meant, are the subject of this chapter.

THE REMAINS OF DRESDEN, 1947. Dresden was devastated by a controversial Allied bombing in February 1945. Kurt Vonnegut dramatically portrayed its destruction and the aftermath in his novel *Slaughterhouse-Five.* ▪ ***How did the war's new strategies of aerial bombardment—culminating in the use of atomic weapons—change the customary division between combatants and noncombatant civilians?***

THE COLD WAR AND A DIVIDED CONTINENT

No peace treaty ended the Second World War. Instead, as the war drew to a close, relations between the Allied powers began to fray over issues of power and influence in Central and Eastern Europe. After the war, they descended from mistrust to open conflict. The United States and Soviet Union rapidly formed the centers of two imperial blocs. Their rivalry, which came to be known as the Cold War, pitted against each other two military powers, two sets of state interests, and two ideologies: capitalism and communism. The Cold War's repercussions reached well beyond Europe, for anticolonial movements, sensing the weakness of European colonial powers, turned to the Soviets for help in their struggles for independence. The Cold War thus structured the peace, shaped international relations for four decades, and affected governments and peoples across the globe who depended on either of the superpowers.

The Iron Curtain

The Soviet Union had insisted during the wartime negotiations at Tehran (1943) and Yalta (1945) that it had a legitimate claim to control Eastern Europe, a claim that some Western

TERRITORIAL CHANGES IN EUROPE AFTER THE SECOND WORLD WAR. At the end of the Second World War, the Soviet Union annexed territory in Eastern Europe to create a buffer between it and Western Europe. At the same time, the United States established a series of military alliances in Western Europe to stifle the spread of communism in Europe. ▪ ***What Eastern European countries fell under Russian control?*** ▪ ***Where is Berlin located, and why did its location and control cause so much tension?*** ▪ ***How did these new territorial boundaries aggravate the tensions between the Soviet Union and the United States?***

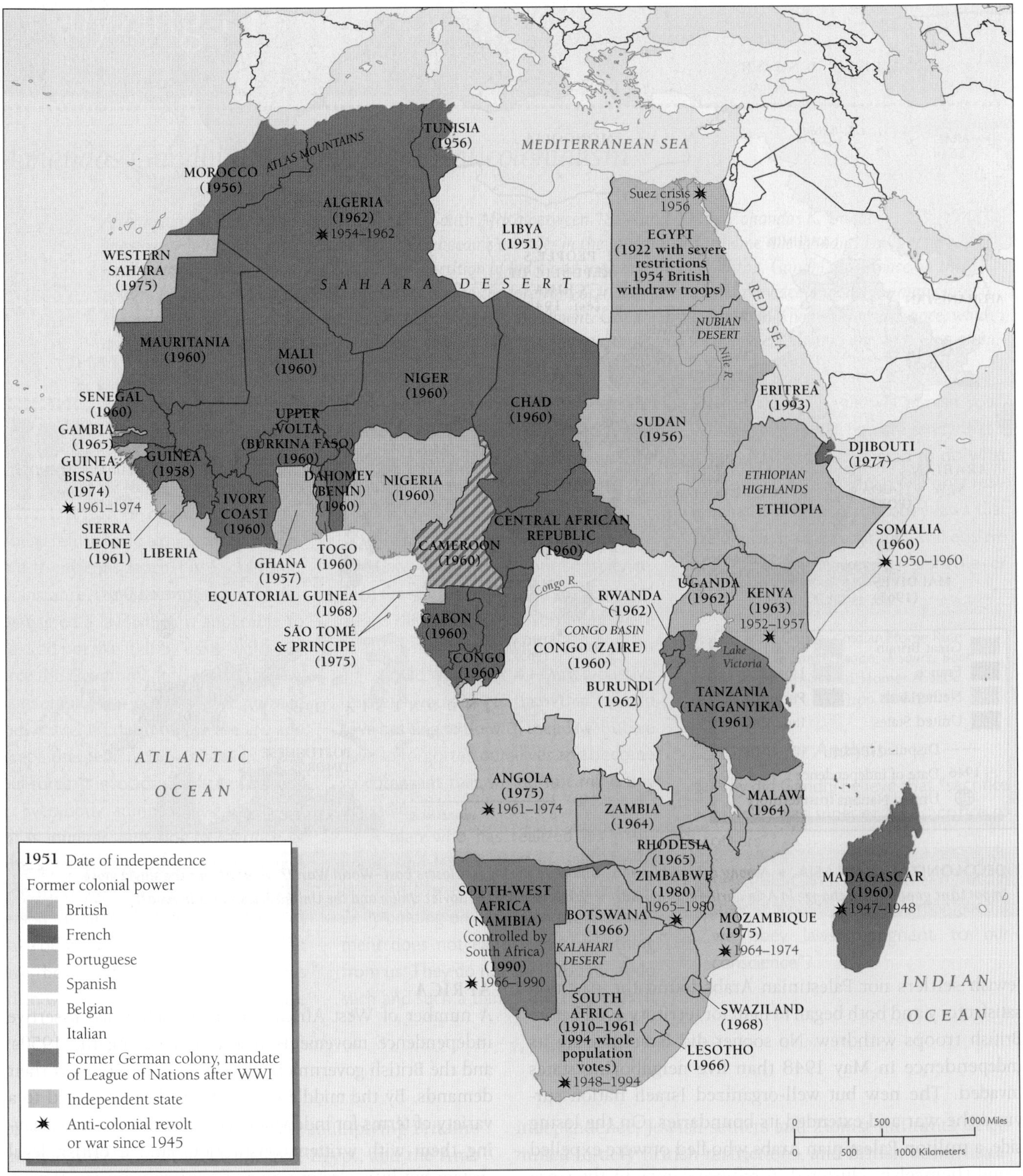

DECOLONIZATION OF AFRICA. ▪ *Who were the biggest imperial losers in the decolonization of Africa?* ▪ *By what decade had most African countries achieved their independence?* ▪ *What were the forces behind decolonization in Africa?*

its president, Kwame Nkrumah, became the first of several African leaders driven from office for corruption and autocratic behavior.

Belgium and France also withdrew from their holdings. By 1965, virtually all of the former African colonies had become independent, and virtually none of them possessed the means to redress losses from colonialism to make that independence work. As Belgian authorities raced out of the Congo in 1960, they left crumbling railways and fewer than two dozen indigenous people with college educations.

The process of decolonization was relatively peaceful—except where large populations of European settlers complicated European withdrawal. In the north, settler resistance made the French exit from Algeria wrenching and complex (discussed below). In the east, in Kenya, the majority Kikuyu population revolted against British rule and against a small group of settlers. The uprising, which came to be known as the Mau Mau rebellion, soon turned bloody. British troops fired freely at targets in rebel-occupied areas, sometimes killing civilians. Internment camps set up by colonial security forces became sites of atrocities that drew public investigations and condemnation by even the most conservative British politicians and army officers. In 1963, a decade after the rebellion began, the British conceded Kenyan independence.

In the late 1950s, the British prime minister Harold Macmillan endorsed independence for a number of Britain's African colonies as a response to powerful winds of change. In southern Africa, the exceptionally large and wealthy population of European settlers set their sails against those winds, a resistance that continued on for decades. These settlers, a mixture of English migrants and the Franco-Dutch Afrikaners who traced their arrival to the eighteenth century, controlled huge tracts of fertile farmland along with some of the most lucrative gold and diamond mines on earth. This was especially true in South Africa. There, during the late 1940s, Britain's Labour government set aside its deep dislike of Afrikaner racism in a fateful political bargain. In return for guarantees that South African gold would be used carefully to support Britain's global financial power, Britain tolerated the introduction of apartheid in South Africa. Even by other standards of segregation, apartheid was especially harsh. Under its terms, Africans, Indians, and colored persons of mixed descent lost all political rights. All the institutions of social life, including marriage and schools, were segregated. What was more, the government tried to block the dramatic social consequences of the expansion of mining and industrialization in general, especially African migration to cities and a new wave of labor militancy in the mines. Apartheid required Africans to live in designated "homelands," forbade them to travel without specific permits, and created elaborate government bureaus to manage the labor essential to the economy. The government also banned any political protest. These measures made Western powers uncomfortable with the segregationist regime, but white South Africans held on to American support by presenting themselves as a bulwark against communism.

To the north, in the territories of Rhodesia, the British government encouraged a large federation, controlled by white settlers but with the opportunity for majority rule in the future. By the early 1960s, however, the federation was on the verge of collapse; the majority-rule state of Malawi was allowed to exit the federation in 1964, and Rhodesia split on northern and southern lines. In the north, the premier relented and accepted majority government under the black populist Kenneth Kaunda. In the south, angry Afrikaners backed by 200,000 right-wing English migrants who had arrived since 1945 refused to accept majority rule. When the British government attempted to force their hand, the settlers unilaterally declared independence in 1965 and began a bloody civil war against southern Rhodesia's black population that lasted a half generation.

CRISIS IN SUEZ AND THE END OF AN ERA

For postwar Britain, empire was not only politically complicated but cost too much. Britain began to withdraw from naval and air bases around the world because they had become too expensive to maintain. The Labour government did try to maintain British power and prestige in the postwar world. In Malaya, British forces repressed a revolt by ethnic Chinese communists and then helped support the independent states of Singapore and Malaysia, maintaining British companies' and banks' ties with Malaysia's lucrative rubber and oil reserves. Labour also launched carefully targeted efforts at "colonial development" to tap local natural resources Britain hoped to sell on world markets. "Development," however, was underfunded and largely disregarded in favor of fulfilling Cold War commitments elsewhere. In the Middle East, the British government protected several oil-rich states with its military and helped overthrow a nationalist government in Iran to ensure that the oil states invested their money in British financial markets.

In Egypt, however, the British refused to yield a traditional point of imperial pride. In 1951, nationalists compelled the British to agree to withdraw their troops from Egyptian territory within three years. In 1952, a group of nationalist army officers deposed Egypt's King Farouk, who had close ties to Britain, and proclaimed a republic. Shortly after the final British withdrawal an Egyptian colonel, Gamal Abdel Nasser (1918–1970), became president of the country (1956–70). His first major public act as president was to nationalize the Suez Canal Company. So doing would help finance the construction of the Aswan Dam on the Nile, and both the dam and nationalizing the canal represented economic independence and Egyptian national pride. Nasser also helped develop the anticolonial ideology of pan-Arabism, proposing that Arab nationalists throughout the Islamic world should create an alliance of modern nations, no longer beholden to the West. Finally, Nasser was also willing to take aid and support from the Soviets to achieve that goal, which made the canal a Cold War issue.

Three nations found Nasser and his pan-Arab ideals threatening. Israel, surrounded on all sides by unfriendly neighbors, was looking for an opportunity to seize the strategic Sinai Peninsula and create a buffer against Egypt. France, already fighting a war against Algerian nationalists, hoped to destroy what it considered the Egyptian source of Arab nationalism. Britain depended on the canal as a route to its strategic bases and was stung by this blow to imperial dignity. Though the British were reluctant to intervene, they were urged on by their prime minister, Sir Anthony Eden; Eden had developed a deep personal hatred of Nasser. In the autumn of 1956, the three nations colluded in an attack on Egypt. Israel occupied the Sinai while British and French jets destroyed Egypt's air force on the ground. The former colonial powers landed troops at the mouth of the canal but lacked the resources to push on in strength toward Cairo. As a result the war left Nasser in power and made him a hero to the Egyptian public for holding the imperialists at bay. The attack was condemned around the world. The United States angrily called its allies' bluff, inflicting severe financial penalties on Britain and France. Both countries were forced to withdraw their expeditions. For policy makers in Great Britain and France, the failure at Suez marked the end of an era.

French Decolonization

In two particular cases, France's experience of decolonization was bloodier, more difficult, and more damaging to French prestige and domestic politics than any in Britain's experience, with the possible exception of Northern Ireland. The first was Indochina, where French efforts to restore imperial authority after losing it in the Second World War only resulted in military defeat and further humiliation. The second case, Algeria, became not only a violent colonial war but also a struggle with serious political ramifications at home.

THE FIRST VIETNAM WAR, 1946–1954

Indochina was one of France's last major imperial acquisitions in the nineteenth century. Here, as elsewhere, the two world wars had helped galvanize first nationalist and then, also, communist independence movements. In Indonesia, nationalist forces rebelled against Dutch efforts to restore colonialism, and the country became independent in 1949. In Indochina, the communist resistance became particularly effective under the leadership of Ho Chi Minh. Ho was French educated and, his expectations raised by the Wilsonian principles of self-determination, had hoped his country might win independence at Versailles in 1919 (see Chapter 24). He read Marx and Lenin and absorbed the Chinese communists' lessons about organizing peasants around social and agrarian as well as national issues. During the Second World War, Ho's movement fought first the Vichy government of the colony and later Japanese occupiers and provided intelligence reports for the Allies. In 1945, however, the United States and Britain repudiated their relationship with Ho's independence movement and allowed the French to reclaim their colonies throughout Southeast Asia. The Vietnamese communists, who were fierce nationalists as well as Marxists, renewed their guerrilla war against the French.

The fighting was protracted and bloody; France saw in it a chance to redeem its national pride. After one of France's most capable generals, Jean de Lattre de Tassigny, finally achieved a military advantage against the rebels in 1951, the French government might have decolonized on favorable terms. Instead, it decided to press on for total victory, sending troops deep into Vietnamese territory to root out the rebels. One major base was established in a valley bordering modern Laos, at a hamlet called Dien Bien Phu. Ringed by high mountains, this vulnerable spot became a base for thousands of elite French paratroopers and colonial soldiers from Algeria and West Africa—the best of France's troops. The rebels besieged the base. Tens of thousands of Vietnamese nationalist fighters hauled heavy artillery by hand up the mountainsides and bombarded the network of forts set up by the French. The siege lasted for months, becoming a protracted national crisis in France.

When Dien Bien Phu fell in May 1954, the French government began peace talks in Geneva. The Geneva Accords, drawn up by the French, Vietnamese politicians including the communists, the British, and the Americans, divided Indochina into three countries: Laos, Cambodia, and Vietnam, which was partitioned into two states. North Vietnam was taken over by Ho Chi Minh's party; South Vietnam by a succession of Western-supported politicians. Corruption, repression, and instability in the south, coupled with Ho

Analyzing Primary Sources

The Vietnam War: American Analysis of the French Situation

At the end of the Second World War, the French government sought to recoup its prestige and empire by reasserting control of the former colony of Indochina. The French faced fierce resistance from nationalist forces under the French-educated leader Ho Chi Minh. Within a few years, American advisers were beginning to shore up the faltering French army. Cold War ideology, anxiety about China and Korea, and a conviction that they could do what the French could not combined to draw the Americans more deeply into the war. In 1950, the Central Intelligence Agency drew up this analysis of the strategic situation.

For more than three years, an intense conflict has been in progress in Indochina in which nationalistic Vietnamese forces under the leadership of the Moscow-trained revolutionist, Ho Chi Minh, have opposed the reimposition of French authority. Within Vietnam . . . a precarious military balance exists between the French and their Vietnamese followers on the one hand and Ho's resistance forces on the other. Thus far, French progress toward both political and military objectives has been substantially less than is necessary to eliminate the threat to French tenure posed by the resistance.

The French position and Bao Dai's [emperor of Vietnam since 1926] prospects have recently been further weakened: politically by Chinese Communist and Soviet recognition of Ho Chi Minh, and militarily by the ability of the Chinese Communist forces to make military supplies available to Ho's forces. Unless the French and Bao Dai receive substantial outside assistance, this combined political and military pressure may accelerate a French withdrawal from all or most of Indochina which, previous to the Chinese Communist and Soviet recognition of Ho, had been estimated as probably occurring within two years. . . .

The fighting in Indochina constitutes a progressive drain on French military resources which is weakening France as a partner in the Western alliance. If France is driven from Indochina, the resulting emergence of an indigenous Communist-oriented regime in Vietnam, in combination with the pressures which will be exerted by the new government of China and the Soviet Union, can be expected to cause adjacent Thailand and Burma to yield to this Communist advance. Under these conditions Malaya and Indonesia would also become highly vulnerable.

The French are trying to halt the present unfavorable trend by according certain aspects of sovereignty to Emperor Bao Dai. . . . The French political aim is to attract non-Communist nationalists from the leadership of Ho Chi Minh to that of Bao Dai.

Meanwhile, Soviet and Chinese Communist recognition of Ho's regime has made it clear that the Kremlin is now prepared to exert greater pressure to achieve its objective of installing a Communist regime in Indochina. France alone is incapable of preventing such a development and can turn only to the US for assistance in thwarting this Communist strategy. Having already publicly proclaimed support of Bao Dai, the US is now faced with the choice of bolstering his weak and vulnerable position or of abandoning him and accepting the far-reaching consequences of Communist control of Indochina.

Source: National Archives, College Park, MD. Record Group 263 (Records of the Central Intelligence Agency), *Estimates of the Office of Research Evaluation, 1946–1950,* box 4.

Questions for Analysis

1. Explain how the author of this CIA report has used George Kennan's policy of containment. What would happen if the French military forces withdrew? Why was Southeast Asia such a hot spot in the decade following the Second World War?

2. Did the French or American military, just coming off a European theater of war, have any idea what it would be like to wage war in a place like Southeast Asia?

"DIEN-BIEN-PHU . . . THEY SACRIFICED THEMSELVES FOR LIBERTY." The sentiments expressed in this poster, which was intended to commemorate the French soldiers who died at Dien Bien Phu in May 1954, helped to deepen French commitments to colonial control in Algeria.

Chi Minh's nationalist desire to unite Vietnam, guaranteed that the war would continue. The U.S. government, which had provided military and financial aid to the French, began to send aid to the South Vietnamese regime. The Americans saw the conflict through the prism of the Cold War: their project was not to restore colonialism but to contain communism and prevent it from spreading through Southeast Asia. The limits of this policy would not become clear until the mid-1960s.

ALGERIA

Still reeling from the humiliation of Dien Bien Phu, France faced a complex colonial problem closer to home, in Algeria. Since the 1830s, the colony had evolved into a settler society of three social groups. First, in addition to a small class of French soldiers and administrators, there were also 1 million European settlers. They typically owned farms and vineyards near the major cities or formed the working-class and merchant communities inside those cities. All of them were citizens of the three administrative districts of Algeria, which were legally part of France. The community produced some of France's best-known writers and intellectuals: Albert Camus, Jacques Derrida, and Pierre Bourdieu, among others. In the small towns and villages of Algeria lived a second group of (largely Muslim) Berbers, whose long history of service in the French army entitled them to certain formal and informal privileges within the colony. Finally, there were millions of Muslim Arabs, some living in the desert south but most crowded into impoverished neighborhoods in the cities. The Arabs were the largest and most deprived group in Algerian society. Between the world wars the French government had offered small reforms to increase their rights and representation, and it had hoped to meld the three groups into a common Algerian society. Reforms came too late and were also undercut by European settlers anxious to maintain their privileges.

At the end of the Second World War, Algerian nationalists called on the Allies to recognize Algeria's independence in return for good service during the war. Public demonstrations became frequent and in several cases turned into attacks on settler-landowners. In one rural town, Setif, celebrations of the defeat of Germany flared into violence against settlers. French repression was harsh and immediate: security forces killed several thousand Arabs. After the war, the French government approved a provincial assembly for all of Algeria, elected by two pools of voters, one made up of settlers and mostly Berber Muslims, the other of Arabs. This very limited enfranchisement gave Arab Algerians no political power. The more important changes were economic. All of Algeria suffered in the difficulties after the war. Many Arab Algerians felt they had to emigrate; several hundred thousand went to work in France. While

COUNTERINSURGENCY IN ALGERIA. An Algerian POW imprisoned by the French in a cellar for animals during the Algerian War of Independence, 1961.

citizens of mainland France read their papers and frowned over the war in Indochina, the situation in Algeria grew more serious. By the middle of the 1950s, a younger generation of Arab activists, unhappy with the leadership of the moderates, had taken charge of a movement dedicated to independence by force. The National Liberation Front (FLN) was organized, which leaned toward socialism and demanded equal citizenship for all.

The war in Algeria became a war on three fronts. The first was a guerrilla war between the regular French Army and the FLN, fought in the mountains and deserts of the country. This war continued for years, a clear military defeat for the FLN but never a clear-cut victory for the French. The second war, fought out in Algeria's cities, began with an FLN campaign of bombing and terrorism. European civilians were killed, and the French administration retaliated with its own campaign. French paratroopers hunted down and destroyed the networks of FLN bombers. The information that allowed the French to break the FLN network was extracted through systematic torture conducted by French security forces. The torture became an international scandal, bringing waves of protest in France. This third front of the Algerian war divided France, brought down the government, and ushered de Gaulle back into power.

De Gaulle visited Algiers to wild cheering from settlers and declared that Algeria would always be French. After another year of violence, he and his advisers had changed their minds. By 1962, talks had produced a formula for independence: a referendum would be held, voted on by the whole population of Algeria. On July 1, 1962, the referendum passed by a landslide vote. Arab political groups and guerrillas from the FLN entered Algiers in triumph. Settlers and Berbers who had fought for the French army fled Algeria for France by the hundreds of thousands. Later, these refugees were joined in France by another influx of Arab economic migrants.

Algeria illustrated the dramatic domestic impact of decolonization. The war cut deep divides through French society, largely because the very identity of France seemed at stake. Withdrawing from Algeria meant reorienting French views of what it meant to be a modern power. De Gaulle summed up the trade-off in his memoirs: to stay in Algeria would "keep France politically, financially, and militarily bogged down in a bottomless quagmire when, in fact, she needed her hands free to bring about the domestic transformation necessitated by the twentieth century and to exercise her influence abroad unencumbered." In France and other imperial powers, the conclusions seemed clear. Traditional forms of colonial rule could not withstand the demands of postwar politics and culture; the leading European nations, once distinguished by their empires, would have to look for new forms of influence. The domestic transformation of which de Gaulle spoke—recovery from the war, economic restructuring, and political renewal—had to take place on a radically changed global stage.

THE STRUGGLE FOR NATIONAL INDEPENDENCE IN ALGERIA. Ben Cherif, a commander in the FLN, handcuffed in 1961. ▪ ***How might this struggle for independence against the French have shaped the generation of political leaders who took power after decolonization?***

POSTWAR CULTURE AND THOUGHT

The postwar period brought a remarkable burst of cultural production. Writers and artists did not hesitate to take up big issues: freedom, civilization, and the human condition itself. The search for democratic renewal gave this literature urgency; the moral dilemmas of war, occupation, and resistance gave it resonance and popular appeal. The process of decolonization, too, forced the issues of race, culture, and colonialism to center stage in Western debates.

The Black Presence

The journal *Présence Africaine* ("*African Presence*"), founded in Paris in 1947, was only one in a chorus of new cultural voices. *Présence Africaine* published such writers as Aimé

Analyzing Primary Sources

Anticolonialism and Violence

Born in the French Caribbean colony of Martinique, Frantz Fanon (1925–1961) studied psychiatry in France before moving on to work in Algeria in the early 1950s. Fanon became a member of the Algerian revolutionary National Liberation Front (FLN) and an ardent advocate of decolonization. Black Skin, White Masks, *published in 1952 with a preface by Jean-Paul Sartre, was a study of the psychological effects of colonialism and racism on black culture and individuals.* The Wretched of the Earth *(1961) was a revolutionary manifesto, one of the most influential of the period. Fanon attacked nationalist leaders for their ambition and corruption. He believed that revolutionary change could come only from poor peasants, those who "have found no bone to gnaw in the colonial system." Diagnosed with leukemia, Fanon sought treatment in the Soviet Union and then in Washington, DC, where he died.*

In decolonization, there is therefore the need of a complete calling in question of the colonial situation. If we wish to describe it precisely, we might find it in the well-known words: "The last shall be first and the first last." Decolonization is the putting into practice of this sentence. . . .

The naked truth of decolonization evokes for us the searing bullets and bloodstained knives which emanate from it. For if the last shall be first, this will only come to pass after a murderous and decisive struggle between the two protagonists. That affirmed intention to place the last at the head of things, and to make them climb at a pace (too quickly, some say) the well-known steps which characterize an organized society, can only triumph if we use all means to turn the scale, including, of course, that of violence.

You do not turn any society, however primitive it may be, upside down with such a program if you have not decided from the very beginning, that is to say from the actual formation of that program, to overcome all the obstacles that you will come across in so doing. The native who decides to put the program into practice, and to become its moving force, is ready for violence at all time. From birth it is clear to him that this narrow world, strewn with prohibitions, can only be called in question by absolute violence.

Source: Frantz Fanon, *The Wretched of the Earth*, trans. Constance Farrington (New York: 1963), pp. 35–37.

Questions for Analysis

1. Why did Fanon believe that violence lay at the heart of both the colonial relationship and anticolonial movements?
2. What arguments would he offer to counter Gandhi?

Césaire (1913–2008), the surrealist poet from Martinique, and Léopold Senghor of Senegal (1906–2001). Césaire and Senghor were brilliant students, educated in the most elite French universities, and elected to the French National Assembly. Césaire became an important political figure in Martinique, a French Caribbean colony that became a department of France in 1946. In 1960, Senghor was elected the first president of Senegal. Both men, in important respects models of Frenchness, became the most influential exponents of *Négritude*, which could be translated as "black consciousness" or "black pride." Senghor wrote:

> Assimilation was a failure. We could assimilate mathematics of the French language, but we could never strip off our black skins or root out black souls. And so we set out on a fervent quest for . . . our collective soul. Negritude is the whole complex of civilized values—cultural, economic, social and political—which characterize the black people.

Césaire's early work took its lead from surrealism and the exploration of consciousness. Later, his work became more political. *Discourse on Colonialism* (1950) was a powerful indictment of the material and spiritual squalor of colonialism, which, he argued, not only dehumanized colonial subjects but degraded the colonizers themselves.

Césaire's student Frantz Fanon (1925–1961), also from Martinique, went further. He argued that withdrawing into an insular black culture (as he interpreted Negritude) was not an effective response to racism. People of color, he believed, needed a theory of radical social change. Fanon trained in psychiatry and worked in Algeria, where he became a member of the National Liberation Front. In *Black Skin, White Masks* (1952), he examined the effects of colonialism and racism from the point of view of a radical psychiatrist. *The Wretched of the Earth* (1961) became one of the most influential revolutionary manifestos of the period. More than Césaire, and bluntly rejecting Gandhi's theories and practice, Fanon argued that violence was rooted in colonialism and, therefore, in anticolonial movements. But he also believed that many anticolonial leaders would be corrupted by their ambition and by collaboration with former colonial powers. Revolutionary change, he believed, could come only from poor peasants, or those who "have found no bone to gnaw in the colonial system."

How did these writers fit into postwar culture? Western intellectuals sought to revive humanism and democratic values after the atrocities of the Second World War. Fanon and others pointed out that the struggles over colonialism made that project more difficult; the violent repression of anticolonial movements in places such as Algeria seemed to be a relapse into brutality. They pointed to the ironies of Europe's "civilizing mission" and demanded a reevaluation of blackness as a central concept in Western culture. The West's postwar recovery would entail eventually facing this challenge to the universal claims of its culture.

SIMONE DE BEAUVOIR (1908–1986). A philosopher, novelist, memoirist, and path-breaking theorist of sex and gender, Beauvoir's work challenged widespread beliefs about femininity and womanhood.

Existentialism

The French existentialist writers, most prominently Jean-Paul Sartre (*SAHR-truh*, 1905–1980) and Albert Camus (*KAM-oo*, 1913–1960), put the themes of individuality, commitment, and choice at center stage. The existentialists took themes from Nietzsche, Heidegger, and Kierkegaard, reworking them in the new context of war-torn Europe. Their starting point was that "existence precedes essence." In other words, meaning in life is not given but created. Thus, individuals were "condemned to be free" and to give their lives meaning by making choices and accepting responsibility. To deny one's freedom or responsibility was to act in "bad faith." War, collaboration and resistance, genocide, and the development of weapons of mass destruction all provided specific points of reference and gave these abstractions new meaning. The existentialists' writing was also clear and accessible, which contributed to their enormous popularity. Although Sartre wrote philosophical treatises, he also published plays and short stories. Camus's own experience in the resistance gave him tremendous moral authority—he became the symbol of a new generation. His novels—including *The Stranger* (1942), *The Plague* (1947), and *The Fall* (1956)—often revolved around metaphors for the war, showing that people were responsible for their own dilemmas and, through a series of antiheroes, exploring the limited ability of men and women to help each other.

Existentialist insights opened other doors. The existentialist approach to race, for instance, emphasized that no meaning inhered in skin color; instead, race derived meaning from a lived experience or situation. As Frantz Fanon wrote, white and black exist "only insofar as they create one another." The same approach could be applied to gender. In her famous introduction to *The Second Sex* (1949), Simone de Beauvoir (*duh bohv-WAHR*, 1908–1986) argued, "One is not born a woman, one becomes one." Women, like men, were condemned to be free. Beauvoir went on to ask why women seemed to accept their secondary status or why, in her words, they "dreamed the dreams of men." The scope and ambition of *The Second Sex* helped make it enormously influential; it was virtually encyclopedic, analyzing history, myth, biology, and psychology, bringing the insights of Marx and Freud to bear on the "woman question." Beauvoir's life also contributed to the book's high profile. A brilliant student from a strict middle-class background, she had a lifelong affair with Sartre but did not marry him, leading many to romanticize her as a liberated and accomplished woman intellectual. She had little to do with feminism, however, until the late 1960s. When *The Second Sex* was published, it was associated with existentialism; only later would it become a key text of the women's movement (see Chapter 28).

Memory and Amnesia: The Aftermath of War

The theme of individual helplessness in the face of state power ran through countless works of the period, beginning, most famously, with George Orwell's *Animal Farm* (1946) and *1984* (1949). The American Joseph Heller's wildly popular *Catch-22* (1961) represented a form of popular existentialism, concerned with the absurdity of war and offering a biting commentary on regimentation and its toll on individual freedom. The Czech author Milan Kundera, who fled the repressive Czech government to live in Paris, eloquently captured the bittersweet efforts to resist senseless bureaucracy. Some writers expressed their despair by escaping into the absurd and fantastic. In Samuel Beckett's deeply pessimistic *Waiting for Godot* (1953, by an Irishman in French) and in the Briton Harold Pinter's *Caretaker* (1960) and *Homecoming* (1965), nothing happens. Characters speak in banalities, paralyzed by the absurdity of modern times.

THE COLD WAR IN EVERYDAY LIFE. A Soviet matchbook label, 1960, depicts a Soviet fist destroying a U.S. plane. Soviet nationalism had been a potent force since the Second World War. ▪ ***Could the Soviet leadership sustain this nationalist sentiment without an external threat?***

Other authors ventured into the realms of hallucination, science fiction, and fantasy. The novels of the Americans William Burroughs and Kurt Vonnegut carry readers from interior fantasies to outer space. One of the most popular books of the period was *The Lord of the Rings* (1954–1955), written before and during the Second World War by the Briton J. R. R. Tolkien. Set in the fantasy world of Middle Earth, Professor Tolkien's tribute to the ancient Celtic and Scandinavian languages he studied and the power of human myths was seized on by a generation of young romantics who rebelled against postwar Western culture for their own reasons.

Questions of terror and dictatorship haunted social and political thought of the postwar era, and especially the work of émigrés from Europe. Representatives of the "Frankfurt school" of German Marxism, by wartime refugees in the United States, sought to understand how fascism and Nazism had taken root in Western culture and politics. Theodor Adorno joined Max Horkheimer in a series of essays, *Dialectic of Enlightenment* (1947), the best known of which indicted the "culture industry" for depoliticizing the masses and crippling democracy. Adorno also coauthored *The Authoritarian Personality* (1950), which used social surveys in an effort to discover how people become receptive to racism, prejudice, and dictatorship. Whatever the specific roots of German Nazism, the Frankfurt school suggested, there were also more general tendencies in modern societies that should give cause for concern.

Hannah Arendt (1906–1975), a Jewish refugee from Germany, was the first to propose that both Nazism and Stalinism should be understood as forms of a novel, twentieth-century form of government: totalitarianism (*The Origins of Totalitarianism,* 1951). Unlike earlier forms of tyranny or despotism, totalitarianism worked by mobilizing mass support. It used terror to crush resistance, break down political and social institutions, and atomize the public. Totalitarianism, Arendt argued, also forged new ideologies. Totalitarian regimes did not concern themselves with whether killing was justified by law; they justified camps and extermination by pointing to the objective laws of history or racial struggle. By unleashing destruction and eliminating entire populations, totalitarian politics made collective resistance virtually impossible. Arendt returned to the same theme in a provocative and disturbing essay on the trial of a Nazi leader, *Eichmann in Jerusalem* (1963). To many readers' distress, she pointedly refused to demonize Nazism. Instead, she explored what she termed "the banality of evil": how the rise of new forms of state power and

Analyzing Primary Sources

The War That Refuses to Be Forgotten

Heda Margolis Kovály was born in Prague and returned to her city after surviving the concentration camps. Like many refugees and survivors, she received an uncertain welcome home. In Czechoslovakia and elsewhere, the Nazi occupation left a legacy of bitterness and division that persisted for decades. Survivors reminded other Europeans of the war and made them defensive. Paradoxically, as Kovály shows, it was common to blame the victims for the war's troubles.

And so ended that horrible long war that refuses to be forgotten. Life went on. It went on despite both the dead and the living, because this was a war that no one had quite survived. Something very important and precious had been killed by it or, perhaps, it had just died of horror, of starvation, or simply of disgust—who knows? We tried to bury it quickly, the earth settled over it, and we turned our backs on it impatiently. After all, our real life was now beginning and what to make of it was up to us.

People came crawling out of their hide-outs. They came back from the forests, from the prisons, and from the concentration camps, and all they could think was, "It's over; it's all over." . . . Some people came back silent, and some talked incessantly as though talking about a thing would make it vanish. . . . While some voices spoke of death and flames, of blood and gallows, in the background, a chorus of thousands repeated tirelessly, "You know, we also suffered. . . . [N]othing but skimmed milk. . . . No butter on our bread. . . ."

Sometimes a bedraggled and barefoot concentration camp survivor plucked up his courage and knocked on the door of prewar friends to ask, "Excuse me, do you by any chance still have some of the stuff we left with you for safekeeping?" And the friends would say, "You must be mistaken, you didn't leave anything with us, but come in anyway!" And they would seat him in their parlor where his carpet lay on the floor and pour herb tea into antique cups that had belonged to his grandmother. . . . He would say to himself, "What does it matter? As long as we're alive? What does it matter?" . . .

It would also happen that a survivor might need a lawyer to retrieve lost documents and he would remember the name of one who had once represented large Jewish companies. He would go to see him and sit in an empire chair in a corner of an elegant waiting room, enjoying all that good taste and luxury, watching pretty secretaries rushing about. Until one of the pretty girls forgot to close a door behind her, and the lawyer's sonorous voice would boom through the crack, "You would have thought we'd be rid of them finally, but no, they're impossible to kill off—not even Hitler could manage it. Every day there're more of them crawling back, like rats. . . ." And the survivor would quietly get up from his chair and slip out of the waiting room, this time not laughing. On his way down the stairs his eyes would mist over as if with the smoke of the furnaces at Auschwitz.

Source: Heda Margolis Kovály, *Under a Cruel Star: A Life in Prague 1941–1968*, trans. Franci Epstein and Helen Epstein with the author (Cambridge, MA: 1986), pp. 45–46.

Questions for Analysis

1. What did Kovály mean when she remarked that the Second World War was "a war that no one had quite survived"? Can such an argument be made about all wars? In what ways was the Second World War distinctive?
2. Kovály describes individual encounters. Do her stories illuminate larger social and cultural developments?

terror had created a world in which Nazis such as Adolf Eichmann could implement genocide as simply one more policy. The crisis of totalitarianism, Arendt argued, was the moral collapse of society, for it destroyed human feeling and the power of resistance in executioners and victims—"tormentors and the tormented"—alike.

Discussions of the war and its legacy, however, were limited. Some memoirs and novels dealing directly with the war and its brutal aftermath did reach a large international public: Jerzy Kosinski's novel about a boy in wartime Poland, *The Painted Bird;* Czesław Miłosz's memoir of intellectual collaboration in Eastern Europe, *The Captive*

Mind (1951); the German Günter Grass's *Tin Drum* (1959), which portrayed the Nazi and war experience in a semi-autobiographical genre and earned Grass recognition as "the conscience of his generation." Of all the memoirs, *The Diary of a Young Girl* by Anne Frank, published in 1947, was undoubtedly the most widely read. Yet the main current in postwar culture ran in a different direction, toward repressing painful issues and bad memories. Postwar governments could not or would not purge all those implicated in war crimes. In France, the courts sentenced 2,640 to death and executed 791; in Austria, 13,000 were convicted of war crimes and 30 executed. Those who called for justice grew demoralized and cynical. Others responded by mythologizing the Resistance and exaggerating participation in it and by avoiding discussion of collaboration. For ten years, French television considered *The Sorrow and the Pity* (1969), Marcel Ophüls's brilliant and unsparing documentary on a French town under Vichy, too controversial for broadcast. Most Jewish survivors, wherever they lived, found that few editors were interested in publishing their stories. In 1947, only a small publishing house would take on the Italian survivor Primo Levi's *Survival in Auschwitz;* the book and Levi's other writings did not find a wide audience until later.

The Cold War was an important factor in burying and distorting memories. West of the Iron Curtain, the eagerness to embrace West Germany as an ally, the single-minded emphasis on economic development, and ardent anticommunism blurred views of the past. One example involved Klaus Barbie, an agent for the Gestapo in occupied France who, among other things, arrested and personally tortured members of the Resistance and deported thousands, including Jewish children, to concentration camps. After the war, American intelligence services recruited Barbie for his anticommunist skills and paid to smuggle him out of Europe, beyond the reach of those who wanted to prosecute him for war crimes. He was finally extradited from Bolivia in 1983, tried in France for crimes against humanity, and convicted. In the Eastern bloc, regimes declared fascism to be a thing of the past and did not scrutinize that past or seek out the many who collaborated with the Nazis. Thus, reckoning with history was postponed until the fall of the Soviet Union. On both sides of the Iron Curtain, the vast majority of people turned inward, cherishing their domestic lives, relieved to have privacy.

THE CUBAN MISSILE CRISIS

One of the last serious and most dramatic confrontations of the Cold War came in 1962, in Cuba. A revolution in 1958 had brought the charismatic communist Fidel Castro to power. Immediately after, the United States began to work with exiled Cubans, supporting, among other ventures, a bungled attempt to invade via the Bay of Pigs in 1961. Castro not only aligned himself with the Soviets but invited them to base nuclear missiles on Cuban soil, only a few minutes' flying time from Florida. When American spy planes identified the missiles and related military equipment in 1962, Kennedy confronted Khrushchev. After deliberating about the repercussions of an air strike, Kennedy ordered a naval blockade of Cuba. On October 22, he appeared on television, visibly tired and without makeup, announced the grave situation to the public, and challenged Khrushchev to withdraw the weapons and "move the world back from the abyss of destruction." Terrified of the looming threat of nuclear war, Americans fled urban areas, prepared for a cramped and uncomfortable existence in fallout shelters, and bought firearms. After three nerve-wracking weeks, the Soviets agreed to withdraw and to remove the bombers and missiles already on Cuban soil. But citizens of both countries spent many anxious hours in their bomb shelters, and onlookers the world over wrestled with their rising fears that a nuclear Armageddon was upon them.

BAY OF PIGS, 1961. American president John F. Kennedy brandishes the combat flag of the Cuban landing brigade.

Past and Present

The Divisions of the Cold War

The Cold War conflict between the United States and the Soviet Union (captured in the image of the Berlin Wall, left) was largely seen as a split between the East and the West, though global competition between the two powers also had profound effects on other regions of the world. The movement of the "Non-Aligned Nations" (represented here by Prime Minister Jawaharlal Nehru of India, President Kwame Nkrumah of Ghana, President Gamal Abdel Nasser of Egypt, President Sukarno of Indonesia, and President Tito of Yugoslavia) was an attempt to provide an alternative to this division.

Watch related author interview on StudySpace
wwnorton.com/web/westernciv18

The Cuban missile crisis provided one inspiration for Stanley Kubrick's classic *Dr. Strangelove* (1964), a devastating and dark comedy with many Cold War themes. The story concerns an "accidental" nuclear attack and the demented characters responsible for it. It also concerns the repression of memory and the sudden reversals of alliances brought about by the Cold War. The wildly eccentric German scientist Dr. Strangelove shuttles between his present life working for the Americans and his barely repressed past as an enthusiastic follower of Hitler. The screenplay was based on the British writer Peter Bryant's *Two Hours to Doom* (1958), one of many 1950s novels with an apocalyptic scenario. The Cuban missile crisis brought the plot so close to home that when the film came out Columbia Pictures felt compelled to issue a disclaimer: "It is the stated position of the United States Air Force that their safeguards would prevent the occurrence of such events as are depicted in this film." Black humor seemed to be a common cultural mechanism for dealing with the terrible possibility of world annihilation. The protagonist of Bob Dylan's 1963 "Talkin' World War III Blues" playfully narrates an apocalyptic dream in which he drives an abandoned Cadillac ("a good car to drive after a war"), approaches the inhabitants of a bunker for a TV dinner, and lights a cigarette on a radioactive parking meter.

CONCLUSION

The Cold War reached deep into postwar culture and it dominated postwar politics. It decisively shaped the development of both the Soviet and American states. Fearful of losing control of territory they had conquered at such cost in the Second World War, the Soviets intervened repeatedly in the politics of their Eastern European allies in the 1940s and 1950s, ensuring the creation of hard-line governments in East Germany, Czechoslovakia, Poland, Hungary, and elsewhere in the Eastern bloc. In the United States, anti-communism became a powerful political force, shaping foreign policy and preparations for military confrontation with the Soviet Union to such an extent that President Eisenhower warned in his farewell address that a "military-industrial complex" had taken shape in the United States and that its "total influence—economic, political, even spiritual—is felt in every city, every statehouse, every office of the federal government."

In Western Europe, rebuilding the economy and creating a new political order in the aftermath of the Second World War meant accepting the new power and influence of the United States, but Europeans also searched for ways to create and express a European identity that would retain some independence and freedom of action. Led by the efforts of France and Germany, Western Europeans eventually found elements of this freedom in increasing integration and economic cooperation. In Eastern Europe, on the other hand, the political leadership found fewer opportunities for independent action and the threat of military intervention by the Soviet

After You Read This Chapter

Visit StudySpace for quizzes, additional review materials, and multimedia documents. **wwnorton.com/web/westernciv18**

REVIEWING THE OBJECTIVES

- The Cold War between the United States and the Soviet Union began as the Second World War ended. How did these two nations seek to influence the postwar political order in Europe?
- Postwar economic growth was accompanied by greater economic integration among Western European nations. What were the goals of those who sought to create the unified European market and which nations played key roles in its development?
- Between the late 1940s and the mid-1960s, almost all the European colonies in Asia and Africa demanded and received their independence, either peacefully or through armed conflict. What combination of events made Europeans less able to defend their colonial empires against the claims of nationalists who sought independence from Europe?
- Decolonization and the Cold War reinforced a sense that Europe's place in the world needed to be rethought. How did intellectuals, writers, and artists react to the loss of European influence in the world?

Union made any innovations or experimentation difficult or impossible.

The sense that Europeans were no longer in a position to act independently or exert their influence in other parts of the world was compounded by the loss of colonies abroad. Former European colonies in Africa and Asia became independent nations, and this loss of influence may have further encouraged the former European imperial powers in their attempts to lay the groundwork for a more integrated Europe. The consensus in the West about the new role that the state should take in economic planning, education, and ensuring social welfare helped lay the groundwork for a Europe that was dedicated to ensuring equal opportunities to its citizens. These commitments were driven by the search for stable forms of democratic government—the memories of the violent ideological conflicts of the 1920s and 1930s were still fresh, and the achievement of an integrated Western Europe (under U.S. sponsorship) on the hinge of Franco-German cooperation must be seen as one of the major victories of the postwar decades. The hard-won stability of this period was to be temporary, however, and beginning in the 1960s a new series of political conflicts and economic crises would test the limits of consensus in Cold War Europe.

PEOPLE, IDEAS, AND EVENTS IN CONTEXT

- When Allied leaders met to discuss the postwar order at **YALTA** and **POTSDAM** in 1945, what were the major issues they discussed?
- What were the goals of the U.S. **MARSHALL PLAN**? How did **JOSEPH STALIN** react to its implementation?
- What was the **TRUMAN DOCTRINE** and how was it related to the creation of **NATO**?
- How did the Soviet Union's successful explosion of an **ATOMIC BOMB** in 1949 change the dynamic of the **COLD WAR**?
- How did the political climate in the Soviet Union and Eastern Europe change under **NIKITA KHRUSHCHEV** during the Thaw that followed Stalin's death?
- What nations were key to the plans for the **EUROPEAN UNION**?
- Why was the decolonization of settler colonies in Africa such as Algeria, Kenya, and Rhodesia more violent than in other colonies on the continent?
- What was apartheid, and why was it adopted by the settler government in South Africa?

THINKING ABOUT CONNECTIONS

- Insofar as one can determine them from today's perspective, what were the long-term consequences of the Cold War for people in both Western and Eastern Europe?
- What challenges did the process of decolonization pose to those who believed that European traditions of democratic rule and individual rights—ideas associated with the Enlightenment and the French Revolution—were universal?

Before You Read This Chapter

STORY LINES

- The postwar economy in Western Europe saw record growth that lasted until the 1970s. Labor shortages led many nations to recruit workers from abroad, causing tensions when unemployment rates went up as the boom came to an end.
- Radio, television, and film combined to create a new kind of global mass culture that contributed to a spirit of novelty and rebellion among young people. More open discussion of sexual matters and an end to restrictions on contraception led some to speak of a "sexual revolution."
- Movements for national independence in the colonial world found an echo in the Civil Rights Movement in the United States and in student protests in Europe and the Americas in the 1960s. These protest movements peaked in 1968, provoking a conservative backlash in the 1970s and 1980s.
- Support for the Soviet Union waned in the 1980s as its economy stagnated and its political system failed to adapt. The Eastern bloc collapsed suddenly in 1989, ending the Cold War.

CHRONOLOGY

1957	Treaty of Rome forms European Common Market
1961	Berlin Wall built
1963	Betty Friedan, *The Feminine Mystique*
1964–1975	Vietnam War
mid-1960s	Birth control pill becomes available
1968	Czech revolt, Prague spring
1968	Student protests in Europe and the Americas
1970s	Détente between Soviet Union and Western powers
1973–1980s	Rising oil prices and worldwide recession
1980	Polish Solidarity workers movement
1989	Berlin Wall falls
1990	Reunification of Germany
1991–1995	Yugoslavian civil wars
1992	Soviet Union dissolved
1993	European Union

28

Red Flags and Velvet Revolutions: The End of the Cold War, 1960–1990

CORE OBJECTIVES

- **DESCRIBE** postwar changes in employment and consumption and their effects on daily life and mass culture in Europe.
- **UNDERSTAND** the shift in attitudes toward sexuality, reproduction, and conceptions of male and female social roles that took place in the postwar decades and the consequences of this shift for women in Europe.
- **IDENTIFY** the motives and goals of the social and political movements that climaxed in 1968 in both Western and Eastern Europe.
- **EXPLAIN** the reasons for the economic downturn that began in the 1970s and its consequences for governments and populations in Europe.
- **UNDERSTAND** the events that led to the collapse of the Soviet bloc in 1989.
- **EXPLAIN** the reasons for the uncertainty and violence that followed the conclusion of the Cold War in Europe in the 1990s.

In 1964, a photograph of a Portuguese laborer named Armando Rodriguez appeared on the cover of the German news magazine *Der Spiegel*. Rodriguez had been met at the border by an official delegation and celebrated as the one millionth "guest worker" to arrive in Germany. As a prize, he received the gift of a motorcycle. The moment reflected the confidence of the West German government that their postwar economic recovery would continue, and that material prosperity would bring a new stability to Europe. In fact, the early 1960s seemed golden and full of promise for many in Western Europe. Despite nearly constant international tension, everyday life seemed to be improving. Full employment drove increases in living standards, the mass availability of consumer items and modern appliances transformed daily life, and a life of relative prosperity and ample leisure now seemed accessible to many. Television, radio, and film promoted images of American middle-class life, and Europeans looked across the Atlantic and saw their own aspirations reflected back at them. Even amid the uncertainties of the Cold War, a new spirit of cooperation animated European governments, party divisions had given way to a broad consensus in favor of an expanded welfare state, and the future looked good.

By the 1990s, however, most of that confidence was gone, and the European landscape had been dramatically transformed. Western Europeans could no longer be so certain of their prosperity or of their leaders' ability to provide the sort of life they took for granted. Already in the late 1960s, the economic boom had come to an end, and movements of social protest, especially among young people, shattered the postwar consensus. The material comforts of a consumer society proved less satisfying than they had once seemed, and environmentalists, feminists, and other cultural critics criticized the assumptions of the older generation. These problems were compounded after 1975 by a continuing economic crisis that threatened the security that the postwar generation had labored so hard to achieve. European societies began to fragment in unexpected ways, well before the epochal transformations that accompanied the end of the Cold War.

The challenges of these decades proved even more fundamental in the Soviet sphere. Economic decay combined with political and social stagnation to produce another wave of revolt. The year 1989 marked the beginning of an extraordinarily rapid and surprising series of events. Communist rule collapsed in Eastern Europe. Hopes for peace were soon replaced by fears of conflict from unexpected quarters. Immigrants were no longer celebrated in Germany and elsewhere—instead they became targets of suspicion or even violence. Shortly after the reunification of Germany in 1991, a wave of attacks against immigrants and refugees in Eastern Germany by right-wing extremists took the lives of seventeen foreigners in Germany, including two Turkish women and a Turkish girl who died in an arson attack by neo-Nazi skinheads in Schleswig-Holstein. Similar attacks took place in France, Britain, Italy, and elsewhere. When postsocialist Yugoslavia collapsed into a brutal civil war in the early 1990s, Europeans faced once again the spectacle of mass political movements motivated by hatred and fear, leading to ethnic violence and mass murder in a European land.

The startlingly sudden dissolution of the Soviet bloc brought an end to the postwar era of superpower confrontation, and observers of European society were forced to confront the uncomfortable fact that the Cold War had provided its own form of stability. Seen from the early 1990s, the future looked much less certain. Could the emerging institutions of an integrated Europe absorb *all* the peoples of the former Soviet sphere? What would such a Europe look like, and who would determine its larger boundaries? What these changes meant for the future of democracy, the stability of the European economy, and definitions of European identity, remained an open question.

SOCIAL CHANGE AND CULTURAL DYNAMISM, 1945–1968

The "boom" of the 1950s, made especially striking by contrast with the bleak years immediately after the Second World War, had profound and far-reaching effects on social life. To begin with, the population expanded, though unevenly. It shifted across the Continent. Both West Germany and France found it necessary to import workers to sustain their production booms. By the mid-1960s, there were 1.3 million foreign workers in West Germany and 1.8 million in France as wages rose and unemployment fell. Most came from the south, particularly from the agrarian areas of southern Italy, where unemployment remained high. Workers from former colonies emigrated to Britain, often to take low-paid, menial jobs and encounter pervasive discrimination at work and in the community. Migrations of this sort, in addition to the vast movement of political and ethnic refugees that occurred during and immediately after the war, contributed to the breakdown of national barriers that was accelerated by the creation of the Common Market.

The most dramatic changes were encapsulated in the transformation of the land and agriculture. Agricultural productivity had barely changed over the first half of the century. After mid-century it soared. To take one example, West German farm land (and labor) sufficient to feed five people in 1900 would feed six in 1950 and thirty-five in 1980. In West Germany and France, Common Market policy; state-sponsored programs of modernization; new agricultural machinery; and new kinds of fertilizer, seed, and animal feed helped produce the transformation. In Poland and the Eastern bloc, socialist regimes replaced small peasant holdings with large-scale agriculture. The effects reached across the economic and social landscape. Abundance meant lower food prices. Families spent a smaller proportion of their budgets on food, freeing up money for other forms of consumption and fueling economic growth. The percentage of the labor force employed in agriculture fell, fueling an expansion in industry and, especially, the service sector. Peasants with large holdings or valuable specialized crops (dairy products or wine), who could withstand debt, adjusted. Others lost ground. The French spoke of an "end of the peasantry"; in the 1960s, a hundred thousand moved from the countryside each year. These changes sparked continuous protest as farmers tried to protect their standard of living. The Common Market agreed to policies of shoring up agricultural prices, but the dynamics remained the same.

Change came in the workplace, eroding traditional social distinctions. Many commentators noted the striking growth in the number of middle-class, white-collar employees—the result, in part, of the dramatic bureaucratic expansion of the state. By 1964, the total number of men and women employed in government service in most European states exceeded 40 percent of the labor force, significantly higher than the number in the 1920s and 1930s. In business and industry, the number of middle-management employees grew as well. In industry, even within the factory workforce, salaried employees—supervisors, inspectors, technicians, and drafters—multiplied. In West Germany, for example, the number of such workers increased by 95 percent between 1950 and 1961. Industrial labor meant something far different from what it had meant in the nineteenth century. Skills were more specialized, based on technological expertise rather than custom and routine. *Skill* meant the ability to monitor automatic controls; to interpret abstract signals; and to make precise, mathematically calculated adjustments. More women entered the workforce, meeting less resistance than they had in the past, and their jobs were less starkly differentiated from men's.

Nineteenth-century society had been marked by clearly defined class cultures. The working class lived "a life apart," with easily identifiable patterns of consumption, dress, leisure, notions of respectability, gender relations, and so on. In 1900, no one would have mistaken a peasant for a worker, and middle-class people had their own schools, recreations, and stores. But economic changes after 1950 chipped away at those distinctive cultures. Trade unions remained powerful institutions: the largest of the French general unions had a membership of 1.5 million; of the Italian, 3.5 million; of the German, 6.5 million. Britain's Trades Union Congress, an affiliation of separate unions, boasted close to 8 million members—including many more women than in the past. Communist parties had powerful electoral clout. But new social movements also grew. Workers still identified themselves as such, but class had a less rigidly defined meaning.

The expansion of education helped shift social hierarchies. All Western nations passed laws providing for the extension of compulsory secondary education—up to the age of sixteen in France, West Germany, and Britain. New legislation combined with rising birthrates to boost school populations dramatically. Between 1950 and 1960, secondary school enrollment in France, Holland, and Belgium doubled. In Britain and West Germany it grew by more than 50 percent. Education did not automatically produce social mobility, but when combined with economic prosperity, new structures of labor, and the consumerist boom, it began to lay the foundation for what would be called "postindustrial" society.

How did patterns differ in the Eastern bloc? Soviet workers were not noted for their specialized skills—in fact, a major factor in the slowdown of the Soviet economy was its failure to innovate. Workers in the "workers' state" commonly enjoyed higher wages than people in middle-class positions (with the exception of managers), but they had far less status. Their relatively high wages owed little to independent trade unions, which had been effectively abolished under Stalin; they were the product of persistent labor shortages and the accompanying fear of labor unrest. As far as the middle classes were concerned, two wars and state socialism devastated traditional, insular bourgeois culture throughout Eastern Europe, though the regimes also created new ways of gaining privilege and status and commentators spoke of a new class of bureaucrats and party members. Educational reforms instituted by Nikita Khrushchev in 1958 encouraged bright children to

MORNING CALISTHENICS AT RUSSIAN FACTORY, 1961. The growing number of industrial workers and women in the workforce in the latter half of the twentieth century was reflected in this Soviet factory. The workers' state still bestowed little status on its workers—a factor that contributed to the weakened Russian economy.

pursue a course of study leading eventually to managerial positions. Soviet education also aimed to unify a nation that remained culturally heterogeneous. Turkish Muslims, for instance, constituted a sizable minority in the Soviet Union. Afraid that the pull of ethnic nationality might tear at the none-too-solid fabric of the Soviet "union" increased the government's desire to impose one unifying culture by means of education, not always with success.

Mass Consumption

Rising employment, higher earnings, and lower agricultural prices combined to give households and individuals more purchasing power. They had more to spend on newspapers, cigarettes, tickets to sporting events, movies, and health and hygiene (which registered the largest increase). Families put money into their homes. Household appliances and cars were the most striking emblems of what was virtually a new world of everyday objects. In 1956, 8 percent of British households had refrigerators. By 1979, that figure had skyrocketed to 69 percent. Vacuum cleaners, washing machines, and telephones all became common features of everyday life. They did not simply save labor or create free time, for household appliances came packaged with more demanding standards of housekeeping and new investments in domesticity—"more work for mother," in the words of one historian. We should not exaggerate the transformation. In 1962, only 40 percent of French households had a refrigerator; in 1975, only 35 percent had a telephone; but even this was still vastly more than the poorer nations of Europe or elsewhere in the world.

In 1948, 5 million Western Europeans had cars; in 1965, 40 million did. In 1950, Italian workers rode bicycles to work; ten years later the factories were building parking lots for their employees' automobiles. Cars captured imaginations throughout the world; in magazines, advertisements, and countless films, the car was central to new images of romance, movement, freedom, and vacation. Of course automobiles alone did not allow workers to take inexpensive holidays; reducing the workweek from forty-eight hours to about forty-two was more important, as was the institution of annual vacations—in most countries workers received over thirty days of paid vacation per year.

These changes marked a new culture of mass consumption. They were boosted by new industries devoted to marketing, advertising, and credit payment. They also entailed shifts in values. In the nineteenth century, a responsible middle-class family did not go into debt; discipline and thrift were hallmarks of respectability. By the second half of the twentieth century, banks and retailers, in the name of mass consumption and economic growth, were persuading middle- and working-class people alike not to be ashamed of debt. Abundance, credit, consumer spending, and standards of living—all these terms became part of the vocabulary of everyday economic life. Most important, the new vocabulary gradually came to reshape how citizens thought about their needs, desires, and entitlements. Standards of living, for instance, created a yardstick for measuring—and protesting—glaring social inequalities. Politicians, economists, and marketing experts paid much closer attention to the spending habits of ordinary people.

In Eastern Europe and the Soviet Union, consumption was organized differently. Governments rather than markets determined how consumer goods would be distributed. Economic policy channeled resources into heavy industry at the expense of consumer durables. This resulted in general scarcity, erratic shortages of even basic necessities, and often poor-quality goods. Women in particular often waited for hours in store lines after finishing a full day of wage work. Though numbers of household appliances

A CAR FOR THE PEOPLE. Originally designed in Hitler's Germany as a car for the people (*das Volk*), the Volkswagen Beetle was produced in large numbers after 1945 and sold in many countries.

PICCADILLY SQUARE, LONDON. In the 1960s and 1970s, a growing consumer culture produced the expansion of the marketing and advertising industries. ▪ ***Why did Europeans associate this kind of commercial culture with the United States?***

increased dramatically in the Soviet Union and in Eastern Europe, the inefficiencies of Soviet consumption made women's double burden of work and housework especially heavy. Citizens' growing unhappiness with scarcities and seemingly irrational policies posed serious problems. As one historian puts it, the failure of policies on consumption was "one of the major dead ends of communism," and it contributed to the downfall of communist regimes.

Mass Culture

New patterns of consumption spurred wide-ranging changes in mass culture. The origins of "mass" culture lay in the 1890s, in the expansion of the popular press, music halls, organized sports, and "Nickelodeons," all of which started the long process of displacing traditional, class-based forms of entertainment: village dances, boulevard theater, middle-class concerts, and so on. Mass culture quickened in the 1920s, its importance heightened by mass politics (see Chapter 25). The social transformations of the 1950s, which we have traced above, meant that families had both more spending money and more leisure time. The combination created a golden opportunity for the growing culture industry. The postwar desire to break with the past created further impetus for change. The result can fairly be called a cultural revolution: a transformation of culture, of its role in the lives of ordinary men and women, and of the power wielded by the media.

MUSIC AND YOUTH CULTURE

Much of the new mass culture of the 1960s depended on the spending habits and desires of the new generation. That new generation stayed in school longer, prolonging the adolescent years. Young people had more distance from their parents and the workforce and more time to be with each other. In the countryside especially, schooling began to break down the barriers that had separated the activities of boys and girls, creating one factor in the "sexual revolution" (discussed later). From the late 1950s on, music became *the* cultural expression of this new generation. The transistor radio came out at the time of the Berlin airlift; by the mid-1950s, these portable radios began to sell in the United States and Europe. Radio sets gave birth to new radio programs and, later, to magazines reporting on popular singers and movie stars. All of these helped create new communities of interest. As one historian puts it, these radio programs were the "capillaries of youth culture." Social changes also affected the content of music: its themes and lyrics aimed to reach the young. Technological changes made records more than twice as long as the old 78s and less expensive. The price of record players fell, multiplying the number of potential buyers. Combined, these developments changed how music was produced, distributed, and consumed. It was no longer confined to the concert hall or cafe but instead reverberated through people's homes or cars and teenagers' rooms—providing a sound track for everyday life.

Postwar youth culture owed much to the hybrid musical style known as rock and roll. During the 1930s and 1940s, the synthesis of music produced by whites and

MUSIC MEETS TELEVISION. Paul McCartney instructs popular variety show host Ed Sullivan on the electric bass, 1964.

MASS CULTURE IN A MEDIA AGE. When John Lennon declared the Beatles were "more popular than Jesus," he raised a storm of protest. Here an American teenager tosses *Meet the Beatles* in a bonfire. ▪ ***What was different about this kind of celebrity when compared with earlier generations of popular entertainers?***

BOB DYLAN POSING FOR THE COVER OF *BLONDE ON BLONDE*, 1966. Dylan's mid-1960s departure from his acoustic folk style into a blues-based rock and roll shocked his original following.

African Americans in the American South found its way into northern cities. After the Second World War, black rhythm and blues musicians and white Southern rockabilly performers found much wider audiences through the use of new technology—electric guitars, better equipment for studio recording, and wide-band radio stations in large cities. The blend of styles and sounds and the cultural daring of white teenagers who listened to what recording studios at the time called "race music" came together to create rock and roll. The music was exciting, sometimes aggressive, and full of energy—all qualities that galvanized young listeners, eager to buy the latest records by their favorite performers.

In Europe, rock and roll found its way into working-class neighborhoods, particularly in Britain and Ireland. There, local youths took American sounds, echoed the inflections of poverty and defiance, and added touches of music-hall showmanship to produce successful artists and bands, collectively referred to as the "British invasion." During the 1960s, British sounds and stars had blended with their American counterparts. As the music's popularity spread, music culture came loose from its national moorings. In France before the 1960s, trendy American songs had been covered by the performer Johnny Hallyday, who sang French popular music as well. The Beatles, though, managed to get their own music on the hit lists in France, Germany, and the United States. By the time of Woodstock (1969), youth music culture was international. Rock became the sound of worldwide youth culture, absorbing Eastern influences such as the Indian sitar and the rebellious energy of a folk-music revival. It provided a bridge across the Cold War divide: despite Eastern bloc limits on importing "capitalist" music, pirated songs circulated—sometimes on X-ray plates salvaged from hospitals. Recording studios latched onto the earning potential of the music and became corporations as powerful as car manufacturers or steel companies.

Art and Painting

The cultural revolution we have been tracing changed high as well as popular art. Record companies' influence reached well beyond rock. New recording techniques made it possible to reissue favorites in classical music, and companies marketed them more aggressively. Record companies buoyed the careers of internationally acclaimed stars, such as the soprano Maria Callas and (much later) the tenor Luciano Pavarotti, staging concerts, using their influence on orchestras, and offering new recordings of their art.

Painting and art, too, were changed by the rise of mass and consumer culture. The art market boomed. The power of the dollar was one factor in the rise of New York as a center of modern art, one of the most striking developments of the period. Immigration was another: a slow stream of immigrants from Europe nourished American art as well as social and political thought (see Chapter 27) and New York proved hospitable to European artists. The creative work of the school of abstract expressionism sealed New York's postwar reputation. The abstract expressionists—William de Kooning (from the Netherlands), Mark Rothko (from Russia), Franz Kline, Jackson Pollock, Helen Frankenthaler, and Robert Motherwell—followed trends established by the cubists and surrealists, experimenting with color, texture, and technique to find new forms of expression. Many of them emphasized the physical aspects of paint and the act of painting. Pollock is a good example. He poured and even threw paint on the canvas, creating powerful images of personal and physical expressiveness. Some dubbed the process "action painting." His huge-scale canvases, which defied conventional artistic structures, gained immediate attention. Critics called the drip paintings "unpredictable, undisciplined, and explosive" and saw in them the youthful exuberance of postwar American culture. Mark Rothko created a series of remote yet extraordinarily compelling abstractions with glowing or somber rectangles of color imposed on other rectangles, saying they represented "no associations, only sensation." The enormous influence of abstract expressionism moved one critic to declare in grandiose fashion that "the main premises of Western art" had moved to the United States, along with "industrial production and political power."

But abstract expressionism also produced its opposite, sometimes called pop art. Pop artists distanced themselves from the moody and elusive meditations of abstract expressionism. They refused to distinguish between avant garde and popular art, or between the artistic and the commercial. They lavished attention on commonplace, instantly recognizable, often commercial images; they borrowed techniques from graphic design; they were interested in the immediacy of everyday art and ordinary people's visual experience. Jasper Johns's paintings of the American flag formed part of this trend. So did the work of Andy Warhol and Roy Lichtenstein, who took objects such as soup cans and images of comic-strip heroes as their subjects. Warhol

ACTION PAINTING. Photographer Martha Holmes reveals the dynamic technique of abstract expressionist Jackson Pollock as he paints, 1950.

did not see his work as a protest against the banality of commercial culture. Instead, he argued that he was continuing to experiment with abstractions. Treating popular culture with this tongue-in-cheek seriousness became one of the central themes of 1960s art.

Film

Mass culture made its most powerful impact in the visual world, especially through film. Film flourished after the Second World War, developing along several different lines. The Italian neorealists of the late 1940s and 1950s, antifascists and socialists, set out to capture authenticity, or "life as it was lived," by which they usually meant working-class existence. They dealt with the same themes that marked the literature of the period: loneliness, war, and corruption. They shot on location, using natural light and little-known actors, deliberately steering away from the artifice and high production values they associated with the tainted cinema of fascist and wartime Europe. Not strictly realists, they played with nonlinear plots, unpredictable characters and motivations. Roberto Rossellini's *Rome: Open City* (1945) was a loving portrait of Rome under Nazi occupation. Vittorio de Sica's *Bicycle Thief* (1948) tells a story of a man struggling against unemployment and poverty, who desperately needs his bicycle to keep his job as a poster hanger.

The film highlighted the contrast between rich and poor—the man's son enviously watches another's family enjoying huge plates of pasta—and between American glamour, represented by movie stars on the posters, and Italy's war-scarred poverty. Federico Fellini came out of the neorealist school and began his career writing for Rossellini. Fellini's break-out film *La Dolce Vita* (1959, starring Marcello Mastroianni) took Italian film to screens throughout Europe and the United States, and it also marked Fellini's transition to his signature surrealist and carnivalesque style, developed in *8½* (1963).

The French directors of the new wave continued to develop this unsentimental, naturalistic, and enigmatic social vision. New wave directors worked closely with each other, casting each other (and their wives and lovers) in their films, encouraged improvisation, and experimented with disjointed narrative. François Truffaut (1932–1984), *400 Blows* (1959) and *The Wild Child* (1969), and Jean-Luc Godard (1930–), *Breathless* (1959) and *Contempt* (1963, with Brigitte Bardot), are leading examples. *Closely Watched Trains* (1966) was the Czech director Jirí Menzel's (1938–) contribution to the new wave. The new wave raised the status of the director, insisting that the film's camera work and vision (rather than the writing) constituted the real art—part, again, of the new value accorded to the visual. France made other contributions to international film by sponsoring the Cannes Film Festival. The first Cannes Festival was held before the Second World War, but the city opened its gates again in 1946 under the banner of artistic internationalism. As one commentator put it, "There are many ways to advance the cause of peace. But the power . . . of cinema is greater than other forms of expression, for it directly and simultaneously touches the masses of the world." Placing itself at the center of an international film industry became part of France's ongoing recovery from the war, and Cannes became one of the world's largest markets for film.

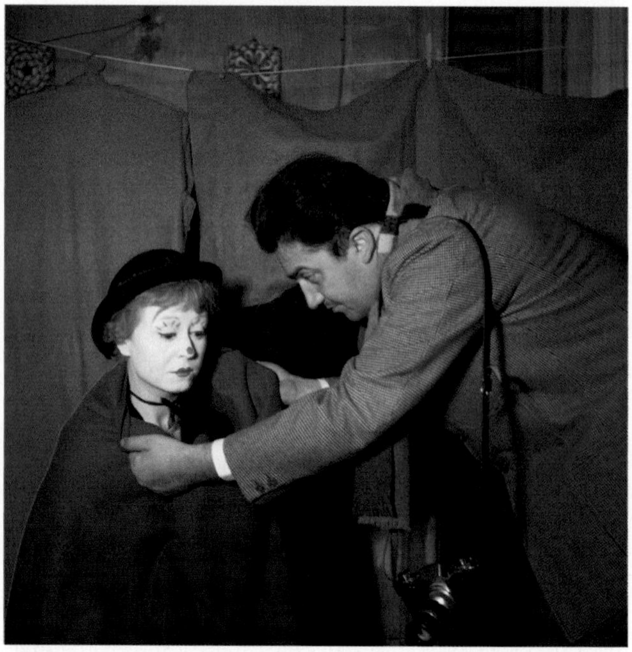

FEDERICO FELLINI ON THE SET OF *LA STRADA*, 1954. Fellini was an Italian neorealist filmmaker who sought to depict life as it was lived.

HOLLYWOOD AND THE AMERICANIZATION OF CULTURE

The American film industry, however, had considerable advantages, and the devastating aftereffects of the Second World War in Europe allowed Hollywood to consolidate its earlier gains (see Chapter 27). The United States' huge domestic market gave Hollywood its biggest advantage. In 1946 an estimated hundred million Americans went to the movies every week. By the 1950s, Hollywood was making 500 films a year and counted for between 40 and 75 percent of films shown in Europe. The same period brought important innovations in filmmaking: the conversion to color and new optical formats, including widescreen. As far as their themes were concerned, some American directors moved in the same direction as the European neorealists. As one critic put it, they tried to "base fictional pictures on fact and, more importantly, to shoot them not in painted studio sets but in actual places."

The domestic politics of the Cold War weighed heavily on filmmaking in the United States. Between 1947 and 1951, the infamous House Un-American Activities Committee called before it hundreds of persons, investigating alleged sympathies with communism or association with any left-wing organization. Hundreds of actors, directors, and writers were blacklisted by the studios. At the same time, paradoxically, American censorship was breaking down, with dramatic consequences on screen. Since the early 1930s, the Motion Picture Production Code had refused to approve "scenes of passion" (including married couples sharing a bed), immorality and profanity (the code banned the words *virgin* and *cripes*), depictions of guns, details of crimes, suicide, or murder. Foreign films, however, came into the United States without the code's seal of approval. The state of New York tried to ban a film (*The Miracle*, directed by Rossellini and written by Fellini) as "sacrilegious," but in 1952 the Supreme Court ruled that film was protected by the First Amendment. A 1955 Otto Preminger movie in which Frank Sinatra played a heroin addict (*The Man with the Golden Arm*) was released despite the disapproval of the Production Code and went on to become a box-office success—a sign of changing mores. *Rebel without a Cause* (1955) made juvenile delinquency a legitimate subject for film. By the 1960s, the Production Code had been scuttled. The extremely graphic violence at the end of Arthur Penn's *Bonnie and Clyde* (1967) marked the scope of the transformation.

Hollywood's expanding influence was but one instance of the "Americanization" of Western culture. Europeans had worried about the United States as a model since at least the 1920s; the United States seemed to be the center for the "production and organization of mass civilization." American films in the 1950s multiplied these worries. So did television, which by 1965 had found its way into 62 million homes in the United States, 13 million in Britain, 10 million in West Germany, and 5 million each in France and Italy and had an even more important impact on everyday life and sociability. The issues were not simply cultural; they included the power of American corporations, American business techniques, aggressive marketing, and American domination of global trade networks. Many concerns were raised, and sometimes they contradicted each other. Some observers believed that the United States and its cultural exports were materialistic, conformist, and complacent. Others considered Americans to be rebellious, lonely, and sexually unhappy. *Rebel without a Cause*, for instance, with James Dean as an alienated teenager in a dysfunctional family and with its scenes of knife fights and car races, provoked cries of outrage from German critics who deplored the permissiveness of American parents and expressed shock that middle-class children behaved like "hoodlums."

Is it helpful, though, to speak of the *Americanization* of culture? First, the term refers to many different processes.

JAMES DEAN IN *REBEL WITHOUT A CAUSE*. Films from the 1950s and 1960s contributed to the romanticization of automobiles, sexuality, and youthful rebellion.

U.S. industrialists openly sought greater economic influence and economic integration: opening markets to American goods, industry to American production techniques, and so on. The U.S. government also aimed to export American political values, above all anticommunism, via organizations such as Radio Free Europe. Yet the farthest-reaching American influences were conveyed, unintentionally, by music and film: images of rebellious teenagers, a society of abundance, cars and the romance of the road, tangled race relations, flirting working girls (who seemed less identifiably working-class than their European counterparts), or bantering couples. These images could not be completely controlled, and they had no single effect. Movies about young Americans might represent the romance of American power, they might represent a rebellion against that power. Second, *American* goods were put to different use in local cultures. Third, journalists, critics, and ordinary men and women tended to use *American* as an all-purpose label for various modern or mass culture developments that were more properly global, such as inexpensive electronics from Asia. As one historian puts it, America was less of a reality than an idea—and a contradictory one at that.

Gender Roles and Sexual Revolution

What some called the sexual revolution of the 1960s had several aspects. The first was less censorship, which we have already seen in film, and fewer taboos regarding discussion of sexuality in public. In the United States, the notorious Kinsey reports on male and female sexuality (in 1948 and 1953, respectively) made morality and sexual behavior front-page news. Alfred Kinsey was a zoologist turned social scientist, and the way in which he applied science and statistics to sex attracted considerable attention. An enthusiastic journalist in Europe reported that the massive numbers Kinsey compiled would, finally, reveal the "truth of sex." The truth, though, was elusive. At the very least Kinsey showed that moral codes and private behaviors did not line up neatly. For instance, 80 to 90 percent of the women he interviewed disapproved of premarital sex, but 50 percent of the women he interviewed had had it. *Time* magazine warned that publicizing disparities between beliefs and behavior might prove subversive—that women and men would decide there was "morality in numbers."

Across Europe and North America, however, young men and women seemed to be reaching rebellious conclusions on their own. As one Italian teenager said, defending her moral codes, "It is our elders who behave scandalously. . . . [W]omen were kept under lock and key, girls married to men who were twice their age. . . . [B]oys, even the very youngest, had total freedom and so queued up at the brothels." Teenage girls in Italy and France told researchers and reporters that taboos were not just old fashioned but damaging, that their mothers had kept them in the dark about matters as rudimentary as menstruation, leaving them unprepared for life.

Was the family crumbling? Transformations in agriculture and life in the countryside did mean that the peasant family was no longer the institution that governed birth, work, courtship, marriage, and death. Yet the family became newly important as the center of consumption, spending, and leisure time, for television took people (usually men) out of bars, cafes, and music halls. It became the focus of government attention in the form of family allowances, health care, and Cold War appeals to family values. People brought higher expectations to marriage, which raised rates of divorce, and they paid more attention to children, which brought smaller families. Despite a postwar spike in the birth rate that produced the "baby boom," over the long term, fertility declined, even in countries that outlawed contraception. The family assumed new meanings as its traditional structures of authority—namely paternal control over wives and children—eroded under the pressure of social change.

A second aspect of the revolution was the centrality of sex and eroticism to mass consumer culture. Magazines, which flourished in this period, offered advice on how to succeed in love and be attractive. Cultivating one's looks, including sexiness, fit with the new accent on consumption; indeed health and personal hygiene was the fastest rising category of family spending. Advertising, advice columns, TV, and film blurred boundaries between buying consumer goods, seeking personal fulfillment, and sexual desire. There was nothing new about appeals to eroticism. But the fact that sexuality was now widely considered a form of self-expression—perhaps even the core of oneself—was new to the twentieth century. These developments helped propel change, and they also made the sexual revolution prominent in the politics of the time.

The third aspect of the revolution came with legal and medical or scientific changes in contraception. Oral contraceptives, first approved for development in 1959, became mainstream in the next decade. The Pill did not have revolutionary effects on the birth rate, which was already falling. It marked dramatic change, however, because it was simple (though expensive) and could be used by women themselves. By 1975, two-thirds of British women between fifteen and forty-four said they were taking the Pill. Numbers like these marked a long, drawn-out end to centuries-old views that to discuss birth control was pornographic, an affront to religion, and an invitation to indulgence and promiscuity. By and large, Western countries legalized contraception in the 1960s and abortion in the 1970s. In 1965, for instance, the U.S. Supreme Court struck down laws banning the use of contraception, though selling contraceptives remained illegal in Massachusetts until 1972. The Soviet Union legalized abortion in 1950, after banning it during most of Stalin's regime. Throughout Eastern Europe, abortion rates were extremely high. Why? Contraceptives proved as difficult to obtain as other consumer goods; men often refused to use them; and women—doubly burdened with long hours of work and housework and facing, in addition, chronic housing shortages—had little choice but to resort to abortion.

SECOND-WAVE FEMINISM. U.S. women celebrating the passage of the Equal Rights Amendment by the House of Representatives in 1970 beneath the Statue of Liberty. The bill did not pass the Senate and never became law. "Second wave" feminists distinguished themselves from the "first wave" of feminism in Europe and the Americas, which had focused on gaining voting rights in the nineteenth and early twentieth centuries. Second-wave feminists argued that votes for women had not ended pervasive gender discrimination. They demanded equal pay for equal work and challenged widespread expectations about the roles that women were expected to play in families and in the workplace.

Legal changes would not have occurred without the women's movements of the time. For nineteenth-century feminists, winning the right to vote was the most difficult practical and symbolic struggle (see Chapter 23). For the revived feminism of the 1960s and 1970s, the family, work, and sexuality—all put on the agenda by the social changes of the period—were central. Since the Second World War, the assumption that middle-class women belonged in the home had been challenged by the steadily rising demand for workers, especially in education and the service sector. Thus, many more married women and many more mothers were part of the labor force. Moreover, across the West young middle-class women, like men, were part of the rising number of university students. But in the United States, to take just one example, only 37 percent of women who enrolled in college in the 1950s finished their degrees, believing they should marry instead. As one of them explained, "We married what we wanted to be": doctor, professor, manager, and so on. Women found it difficult to get nonsecretarial jobs; received less pay for the same work; and, even when employed, had to rely on their husbands to establish credit.

The tension between rising expectations that stemmed from abundance, growth, and the emphasis on self-expression on the one hand and the reality of narrow horizons on the other created quiet waves of discontent. Betty Friedan's *The Feminine Mystique* (1963) brought much of this discontent into the open, contrasting the cultural myths of the fulfilled and happy housewife with the realities of economic inequality, hard work, and narrowed horizons. In 1949, Simone de Beauvoir had asked how Western culture (myth, literature, and psychology) had created an image of woman as the second, and lesser sex; Friedan, using a more journalistic style and writing at a time when social change had made readers more receptive to her ideas, showed how the media, the social sciences, and advertising at once exalted femininity and lowered women's expectations and possibilities. Friedan cofounded NOW (National Organization for Women) in 1966; smaller and often more radical women's movements multiplied across Europe in the following decades. For this generation of feminists, reproductive freedom was both a private matter and a basic right—a key to women's control over their lives. Outlawing contraception and abortion made women alone bear responsibility for the consequences of sweeping changes in Western sexual life. Such measures were ineffective as well as unjust, they argued. French feminists dramatized the point by publishing the names of 343 well-known women, including Beauvoir, who admitted to having had illegal abortions. A similar petition came out in Germany the following year and was followed by petitions from doctors and tens of thousands of supporters. In sum, the legal changes followed from political demands, and those in turn reflected a quiet or subterranean rebellion of many women (and men)—one with longer-term causes. Mass consumption, mass culture, and startlingly rapid transformations in public and private life were all intimately related.

SOCIAL MOVEMENTS DURING THE 1960s

The social unrest of the 1960s was international. Its roots lay in the political struggles and social transformations of the postwar period. Of these, the most important were anticolonial and civil rights movements. The successful anticolonial movements (see Chapter 27) reflected a growing racial consciousness and also helped encourage that consciousness. Newly independent African and Caribbean nations remained wary about revivals of colonialism and the continuing economic hegemony of Western Europe and America. Black and Asian immigration into those nations produced tension and frequent violence. In the West, particularly in the United States, people of color identified with these social and economic grievances.

The Civil Rights Movement

The emergence of new black nations in Africa and the Caribbean was paralleled by growing African American insurgency. The Second World War increased African American migration from the American South to northern cities, intensifying a drive for rights, dignity, and independence that began in the prewar era with organizations such as the National Association for the Advancement of Colored People and the National Urban League. By 1960, various civil rights groups, led by the Congress of Racial Equality (CORE), had started to organize boycotts and demonstrations directed at private businesses and public services that discriminated against blacks in the South. The preeminent figure in the Civil Rights Movement in the United States during the 1960s was Martin Luther King, Jr. (1929–1968). A Baptist minister, King embraced the philosophy of nonviolence promoted by the Indian social and political activist Mohandas K. Gandhi. King's personal participation in countless demonstrations, his willingness to go to jail for a cause that he believed to be just, and his ability as an orator to arouse both blacks and whites with his message led to

Competing Viewpoints

The "Woman Question" on Both Sides of the Atlantic

How did Western culture define femininity, *and did women internalize those definitions? These questions were central to postwar feminist thought, and they were sharply posed in two classic texts: Simone de Beauvoir's* The Second Sex *(1949) and Betty Friedan's* The Feminine Mystique *(1963). Beauvoir (1908–1986) started from the existentialist premise that humans were "condemned to be free" and to give their own lives meaning. Why, then, did women accept the limitations imposed on them and, in Beauvoir's words, "dream the dreams of men"? Although dense and philosophical,* The Second Sex *was read throughout the world. Betty Friedan's equally influential bestseller drew heavily on Beauvoir. Friedan sought the origins of the "feminine mystique," her term for the model of femininity promoted by experts, advertised in women's magazines, and seemingly accepted by middle-class housewives in the postwar United States. As Friedan points out in the excerpt here, the new postwar mystique was in many ways more conservative than prewar ideals had been, despite continuing social change, a greater range of careers opening up to women, the expansion of women's education, and so on. Friedan (1921–2006) cofounded the National Organization for Women in 1966 and served as its president until 1970.*

Simone de Beauvoir, *The Second Sex* (1949)

But first, what is a woman? . . . Everyone agrees there are females in the human species; today, as in the past, they make up about half of humanity; and yet we are told that "femininity is in jeopardy;" we are urged, "Be women, stay women, become women." . . . Although some women zealously strive to embody it, the model has never been patented. It is typically described in vague and shimmering terms borrowed from a clairvoyant's vocabulary. . . .

If the female function is not enough to define woman, and if we also reject the explanation of the "eternal feminine," but if we accept, even temporarily, that there are women on the earth, we then have to ask: what is a woman?

Merely stating the problem suggests an immediate answer to me. It is significant that I pose it. It would never occur to a man to write a book on the singular situation of males in humanity. If I want to define myself, I first have to say, "I am a woman;" all other assertions will arise from this basic truth. A man never begins by positing himself as an individual of a certain sex: that he is a man is obvious. The categories "masculine" and "feminine" appear as symmetrical in a formal way on town hall records or identification papers. The relation of the two sexes is not that of two electrical poles: the man represents both the positive and the neuter. . . . Woman is the negative, to such a point that any determination is imputed to her as a limitation, without reciprocity. . . . [A] man is in his right by virtue of being man; it is the woman who is in the wrong. . . . Woman has ovaries and a uterus; such are the particular conditions that lock her in her subjectivity; some even say she thinks with her hormones. Man vainly forgets that his anatomy also includes hormones and testicles. He grasps his body as a direct and normal link with the world that he believes he apprehends in all objectivity whereas he considers woman's body an obstacle, a prison, burdened by everything that particularises it. "The female is female by virtue of a certain *lack* of qualities," Aristotle said. "We should regard women's nature as suffering from natural defectiveness." And St. Thomas in his turn decreed that woman was an "incomplete man," an "incidental" being. This is what the Genesis story symbolises, where Eve appears as if drawn from Adam's "supernumerary" bone, in Bossuet's words. Humanity is male, and man defines woman, not in herself, but in relation to himself; she is not considered an autonomous being. . . . And she is nothing other than what man decides; she is thus called "the sex," meaning that the male sees her essentially as a sexed being; for him she is sex, so she is it in the absolute. She determines and differentiates herself in relation to man, and he does not in relation to her; she is the inessential in front of the essential. He is the Subject, he is the Absolute. She is the Other.

Source: Simone de Beauvoir, *The Second Sex*, trans. Constance Borde and Sheila Malovany-Chevallier (London: 2009), pp. 3–6.

Betty Friedan, *The Feminine Mystique* (1963)

In 1939, the heroines of women's magazine stories were not always young, but in a certain sense they were younger than their fictional counterparts today. They were young in the same way that the American hero has always been young: they were New Women, creating with a gay determined spirit a new identity for women—a life of their own. There was an aura about them of becoming, of moving into a future that was going to be different from the past. . . .

These stories may not have been great literature. But the identity of their heroines seemed to say something about the housewives who, then as now, read the women's magazines. These magazines were not written for career women. The New Woman heroines were the ideal of yesterday's housewives; they reflected the dreams, mirrored the yearning for identity and the sense of possibility that existed for women then. . . .

In 1949 . . . the feminine mystique began to spread through the land. . . .

The feminine mystique says that the highest value and the only commitment for women is the fulfillment of their own femininity. It says that the great mistake of Western culture, through most of its history, has been the undervaluation of this femininity. . . . The mistake, says the mystique, the root of women's troubles in the past, is that women envied men, women tried to be like men, instead of accepting their own nature, which can find fulfillment only in sexual passivity, male domination, and nurturing maternal love.

But the new image this mystique gives to American women is the old image: "Occupation: housewife." The new mystique makes the housewife-mothers, who never had a chance to be anything else, the model for all women; it presupposes that history has reached a final and glorious end in the here and now, as far as women are concerned. . . .

It is more than a strange paradox that as all professions are finally open to women in America, "career woman" has become a dirty word; that as higher education becomes available to any woman with the capacity for it, education for women has become so suspect that more and more drop out of high school and college to marry and have babies; that as so many roles in modern society become theirs for the taking, women so insistently confine themselves to one role. Why . . . should she accept this new image which insists she is not a person but a "woman," by definition barred from the freedom of human existence and a voice in human destiny?

Source: Betty Friedan, *The Feminine Mystique* (New York: 2001), pp. 38, 40, 42–43, 67–68.

Questions for Analysis

1. Why does Beauvoir ask, "What is a woman?"
2. Why does Friedan think that a "feminine mystique" emerged after the Second World War?

his position as the most highly regarded—and most widely feared—defender of black rights. His inspiring career was tragically ended by assassination in 1968.

King and organizations such as CORE aspired to a fully integrated nation. Other charismatic and important black leaders sought complete independence from white society, fearing that integration would leave African Americans without the spiritual or material resources necessary for a community's pride, dignity, and autonomy. The most influential of the black nationalists was Malcolm X (1925–1965), who assumed the "X" after having discarded his "white" surname (Little). For most of his adult life, Malcolm X, a spokesman for the Black Muslim movement, urged blacks to renew their commitment to their own heritage; to establish black businesses for economic autonomy; and to fortify economic, political, and psychological defenses against white domination. Like King, he was assassinated, in 1965 while addressing a rally in Harlem.

Civil rights laws passed under President Lyndon B. Johnson (1963–1969) in the 1960s did bring African

MARTIN LUTHER KING, JR., 1964. The African American civil rights leader is welcomed in Oslo, Norway, on a trip to accept the Nobel Peace Prize. He would be assassinated four years later. ▪ ***How might Europeans have viewed King's campaign?*** ▪ ***Would it affect their vision of the United States?***

Americans some measure of equality with regard to voting rights—and, to a much lesser degree, school desegregation. In other areas, such as housing and job opportunities, white racism continued. Economic development passed by many African American communities, and subsequent administrations pulled back from the innovative programs of the Johnson era.

These problems were not confined to the United States. West Indian, Indian, and Pakistani immigrants in Britain met with discrimination in jobs, housing, and everyday interaction with the authorities—producing frequent racial disturbances in major British cities. France witnessed hostility toward Algerian immigration, Germany toward the importation of Turkish labor. In Western Europe, as in the United States, struggles for racial and ethnic integration became central to the postcolonial world.

The Civil Rights Movement had enormous significance for the twentieth century, and it galvanized other movements as well. It dramatized as perhaps no other movement could the chasm between the egalitarian promises of American democracy and the real inequalities at the core of the American social and political life—a chasm that could be found in other Western nations as well. African American claims were morally and politically compelling, and the Civil Rights Movement sharpened others' criticisms of what they saw as a complacent, narrowly individualistic, materialist culture.

The Antiwar Movement

The United States' escalating war in Vietnam became a lightning rod for discontent. In 1961, President John F. Kennedy (1917–1963) promised to "bear any burden" necessary to fight communism and to ensure the victory of American models of representative government and free-market economics in the developing nations. Kennedy's plan entailed massive increases in foreign aid, much of it in weapons. It provided the impetus for humanitarian institutions such as the Peace Corps, intended to improve local conditions and show Americans' benevolence and good intentions. Bearing burdens, however, also meant fighting guerrillas who turned to the Soviets for aid. This involved covert interventions in Latin America, the Congo, and, most important, Vietnam.

By the time of Kennedy's death in 1963, nearly 15,000 American "advisers" were on the ground alongside South Vietnamese troops. Kennedy's successor, Lyndon Johnson, began the strategic bombing of North Vietnam and rapidly drew hundreds of thousands of American troops into combat in South Vietnam. The rebels in the south, known as the Viet Cong, were solidly entrenched, highly experienced guerrilla fighters, and were backed by the professional, well-equipped North Vietnamese army under Ho Chi Minh, who also received support from the Soviet Union. The South Vietnamese government resisted efforts at reform, losing popular support. Massive efforts by the United States produced only stalemate, mounting American casualties, and rising discontent.

Vietnam did much to cause the political turmoil of the 1960s in the United States. As Martin Luther King, Jr., pointed out, the war—which relied on a disproportionate number of black soldiers to conduct a war against a small nation of color—echoed and magnified racial inequality at home. Exasperated by troubles in the field, American planners continued to escalate military commitments, with no effect. Peace talks in Paris stalled while the death toll on all sides increased. The involuntary draft of young American men expanded and polarized the public. In 1968, criticism forced President Johnson to abandon his plans to run for a second term. Johnson's successor, Richard M. Nixon, who won a narrow victory on the basis of promises to end the war, expanded it instead. Student protests against the war frequently ended in violence. The government brought criminal conspiracy charges against Benjamin Spock, the nation's leading pediatrician, and William Sloane Coffin, the chaplain of Yale University, for encouraging young people to resist the draft. Avoiding the draft became so widespread that the system was changed in 1970. And from

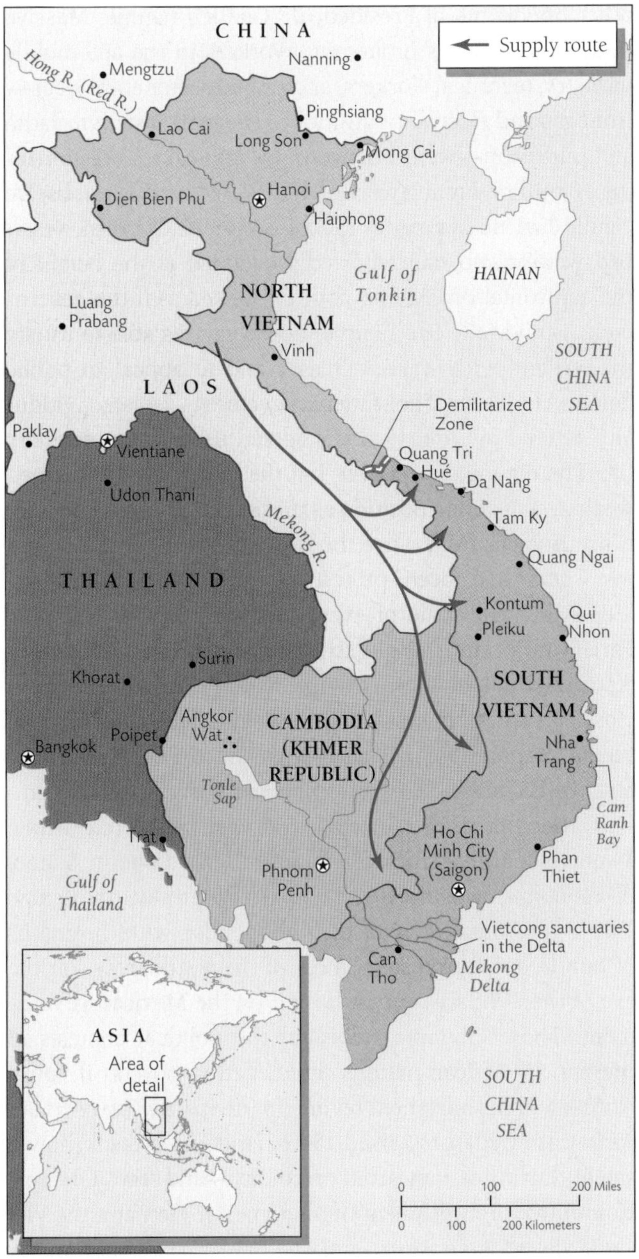

THE WAR IN VIETNAM AND SOUTHEAST ASIA. The 1954 Geneva Accords divided Vietnam at the seventeenth parallel. The north went to Ho Chi Minh, the communist leader, and the south was controlled by Ngo Dinh Diem, an ally of the United States. In 1956, South Vietnam refused to hold the elections mandated in the Geneva Accords. Ho Chi Minh mobilized a guerrilla army, the Viet Cong, and the Vietnam War began. ▪ ***What other countries in this region were drawn into the war?*** ▪ ***How did the Viet Cong use the proximity of Cambodia and Laos to their strategic advantage?*** ▪ ***Why did the United States choose to get involved?***

other countries' points of view, the Vietnam War became a spectacle: one in which the most powerful, wealthiest nation of the world seemed intent on destroying a land of poor peasants in the name of anticommunism, democracy, and freedom. The tarnished image of Western values stood at the center of 1960s protest movements in the United States and Western Europe.

The Student Movement

The student movement itself can be seen as a consequence of postwar developments: a growing cohort of young people with more time and wealth than in the past; generational consciousness heightened, in part, by the marketing of mass youth culture; and educational institutions unable to deal with rising numbers and expectations. In France, the number of students in high school rose from 400,000 in 1949 to 2 million in 1969; in universities, over the same period, enrollments skyrocketed, from 100,000 to 600,000. The same was true in Italy, Britain, and West Germany. Universities, which had been created to educate a small elite, found both their teaching staffs and their facilities overwhelmed. Lecture halls were packed, university bureaucracies did not respond to requests, and thousands of students took exams at the same time. More philosophically, students raised questions about the role and meaning of elite education in a democratic society and about the relationships among the university as a "knowledge factory," consumer culture, and neocolonial ventures such as the Vietnam War and—for the French—the Algerian wars. Conservative traditions made intellectual reform difficult. In addition, student demands for fewer restrictions on personal life—for instance, permission to have a member of the opposite sex in a dormitory room—provoked authoritarian reactions from university representatives. Waves of student protest were not confined to the United States and Western Europe. They swept across Poland and Czechoslovakia where students protested one-party bureaucratic rule, stifling intellectual life, and authoritarianism, and helped sustain networks of dissidents. By the mid-1960s, simmering anger in Eastern Europe had once again reached a dangerous point.

1968

The year 1968 was an extraordinary one, quite similar to 1848 with its wave of revolution (see Chapter 20). It was even more intensely international, a reflection of tightening global ties. International youth culture fostered a sense of collective identity. The new media relayed images of civil rights protests in the United States to Europe, and broadcast news footage of the Vietnam War on television screens from West Virginia to West Germany. The wave of unrest shook both the Eastern and Western blocs. Protest movements assailed bureaucracy and the human costs of the Cold War: on the Soviet side, bureaucracy, authoritarianism, and indifference to civilians; on the Western side, bias and monopolies in the news media, the military-industrial complex, and American imperialism. The Soviet regime, as we have seen, responded with repression. In the United States and Western Europe, traditional political parties had little idea what to make of these new movements and those who participated in them. In both cases, events rapidly overwhelmed political systems.

PARIS

The most serious outbreak of student unrest in Europe came in Paris in the spring of 1968. The French Republic had been shaken by conflicts over the Algerian war in the early 1960s. Even more important, the economic boom had undermined the foundations of the regime and de Gaulle's traditional style of rule. French students at the University of Paris demanded reforms that would modernize their university. Protest first peaked at Nanterre, a new branch of the university built on a former air force depot. Nanterre was in a poor and poorly served neighborhood, starved for funds, and overcrowded with students. Petitions, demonstrations, and confrontations with university authorities traveled quickly from Nanterre to the Sorbonne, in central Paris. In the face of growing disorder, the University of Paris shut down—sending students into the streets and into uglier confrontations with the police. The police reacted with repression and violence, which startled onlookers and television audiences and backfired on the regime. Sympathy with the students' cause expanded rapidly, bringing in other opponents of President de Gaulle's regime. Massive trade-union strikes broke out. Workers in the automobile industry, technical workers, and public-sector employees—from gas and electricity utilities to the mail system to radio and television—went on strike. By mid-May, an astonishing 10 million French workers had walked off their jobs. De Gaulle had no sympathy for the students: "Reform, yes—bed wetting, no," he reportedly declared at the height of the confrontation. At one point, it looked as if the government would fall. The regime, however, was able to satisfy the strikers with wage increases and to appeal to public demand for order. The student movements, isolated, gradually petered out and students agreed to resume university life. The regime did recover, but the events of 1968 helped weaken de Gaulle's position as president and contributed to his retirement from office the following year.

THE PRESS IS POISON. Criticizing the official media was central to the politics of May 1968.

There had been protest and rebelliousness in the 1950s, but the scale of events in 1968 was astonishing. Paris was not the only city to explode in 1968. Student protest broke out in West Berlin, targeting the government's close ties to the autocratic shah of Iran and the power of media corporations. Clashes with the police turned violent. In Italian cities, undergraduates staged several demonstrations to draw attention to university overcrowding. Twenty-six universities were closed. The London School of Economics was nearly shut down by protest. In Mexico City, a confrontation with the police ended with the deaths of hundreds of protesters, most of them students—on the eve of the 1968 Olympics, hosted by the Mexican government. Those Olympics reflected the political contests of the period: African nations threatened to boycott if South Africa, with its apartheid regime, participated. Two African American medalists raised their hands in a black power salute during an awards ceremony—and the Olympic Committee promptly sent them home. In Vietnam, the Viet Cong defied American claims to have turned the tide by launching a new offensive. The Tet offensive, named for the Vietnamese new year, brought the highest casualty rates to date in the Vietnam War and an explosion of protest. Antiwar demonstrations and student rebellions spread across the country. President Johnson, battered by the effects of Tet and already worn down by the war, chose not to run for reelection. The year 1968 also saw damage and trauma for the country's political future, because of the assassinations of Martin Luther King, Jr. (April 4, 1968) and presidential candidate Robert F. Kennedy (June 5, 1968). King's assassination was followed by a wave of rioting in more than fifty cities across the United States, followed in late summer by street battles between police and student protesters at the Democratic National Convention in Chicago. Some saw

Analyzing Primary Sources

1960s Politics: The Situationists

In 1957, a small group of European artists and writers formed a group called the Situationist International. The movement combined the artistic traditions of dada and surrealism with anarchism and Marxism. Unlike traditional Marxists, the situationists did not focus on the workplace. Instead, they developed a broad critique of everyday life, protesting the stifling of art, creativity, and imagination in contemporary society. They denounced the "tyranny" of consumer culture, which constantly invented new needs and desires to fuel consumption. Capitalism, they said, had "colonized" everyday life. The situationists' ideas and especially their unorthodox, surrealist style, became influential during the events of May 1968 in France. All around Paris students painted situationist slogans such as those printed here.

The social movements of 1968 cut across Cold War boundaries, attacking Western consumerism as well as Soviet authoritarianism. A group of students and situationists sent a telegram (second excerpt) to the Politburo of the Communist Party of the Soviet Union in May 1968.

Situationist Anticapitalism, 1968

OCCUPY THE FACTORIES

POWER TO THE WORKERS COUNCILS

ABOLISH CLASS SOCIETY

DOWN WITH THE SPECTACLE-COMMODITY SOCIETY

ABOLISH ALIENATION

ABOLISH THE UNIVERSITY

HUMANITY WON'T BE HAPPY TILL THE LAST BUREAUCRAT IS HUNG WITH THE GUTS OF THE LAST CAPITALIST

DEATH TO THE COPS

FREE ALSO THE 4 GUYS CONVICTED FOR LOOTING DURING THE 6 MAY RIOT

—Occupation committee of the Autonomous and Popular Sorbonne University

Situationist Anticommunist Slogans, 1968

17 MAY 1968 / To the Politburo of the Communist party of the USSR the Kremlin Moscow / Shake in your shoes bureaucrats. The international power of the workers councils will soon wipe you out. Humanity won't be happy till the last bureaucrat is hung with the guts of the last capitalist. Long live the struggle of the Kronstadt sailors and of the Makhnovshchina against Trotsky and Lenin. Long live the 1956 Councilist insurrection of Budapest • Down with the state • Long live revolutionary Marxism. Occupation committee of the Autonomous and Popular Sorbonne

Sources: "Slogans to Be Spread Now by Every Means," in *Situationist International Anthology*, ed. and trans. Ken Knabb (Berkeley, CA: 1981), pp. 334–45.

Questions for Analysis

1. Are there any common themes in these sets of slogans?
2. Why has 1968 often been called "the year of the barricades"?

the flowering of protest as another "springtime of peoples." Others saw it as a long nightmare.

PRAGUE

The student movement in the United States and Western Europe also took inspiration from one of the most significant challenges to Soviet authority since the Hungarian revolt of 1956 (see Chapter 27): the "Prague spring" of 1968. The events began with the emergence of a liberal communist government in Czechoslovakia, led by the Slovak Alexander Dubček (*DOOB-chehk*). Dubček had outmaneuvered the more traditional, authoritarian party leaders. He advocated "socialism with a human face"; he encouraged debate within the party, academic and artistic freedom, and less censorship. As was often the case, party members were

ANTIGOVERNMENT PROTESTS IN MEXICO CITY, 1968. On October 2, 1968, ten days before the opening of the Summer Olympics in Mexico City, police opened fire on student protesters and arrested over one thousand people.

divided between proponents of reform and those fearful that reform would unleash revolution. The reformers, however, also gained support from outside the party, from student organizations, the press, and networks of dissidents. As in Western Europe and the United States, the protest movement overflowed into traditional party politics.

In the Soviet Union, Khrushchev had fallen in 1964, and the reins of Soviet power passed to Leonid Brezhnev as secretary of the Communist party. Brezhnev was more conservative than Khrushchev, less inclined to bargain with the West, and prone to defensive actions to safeguard the Soviet sphere of influence. Initially, the Soviets tolerated Dubček as a political eccentric. The events of 1968 raised their fears. Most Eastern European communist leaders denounced Czech reformism, but student demonstrations of support broke out in Poland and Yugoslavia, calling for an end to one-party rule, less censorship, and reform of the judicial system. In addition, Josip Broz Tito of Yugoslavia and Nicolae Ceaușescu (*chow-SHEHS-koo*) of Romania—two of the more stubbornly independent communists in Eastern Europe—visited Dubček. To Soviet eyes, these activities looked as if they were directed against the Warsaw Pact and Soviet security; they also saw American intervention in Vietnam as evidence of heightened anticommunist activities around the world. When Dubček attempted to democratize the Communist party and did not attend a meeting of members of the Warsaw Pact, the Soviets sent tanks and troops into Prague in August 1968. Again, the world watched as streams of Czech refugees left the country and a repressive government, picked by Soviet security forces, took charge. Dubček and his allies were subjected to imprisonment or "internal exile." Twenty percent of the members of the Czech Communist party were expelled in a series of purges. After the destruction of the Prague spring, Soviet diplomats consolidated their position according to the new Brezhnev Doctrine. The doctrine stated that no socialist state could adopt policies endangering the interests of international socialism and that the Soviet Union could intervene in the domestic affairs of any Soviet bloc nation if communist rule was threatened. In other words, the repressive rules applied to Hungary in 1956 would not change.

What were the effects of 1968? De Gaulle's government recovered. The Republican Richard M. Nixon won the U.S. election of 1968. From 1972 to 1975, the United States withdrew from Vietnam; in the wake of that war came a refugee crisis and a new series of horrific regional conflicts. In Prague, Warsaw Pact tanks put down the uprising, and in the Brezhnev Doctrine the Soviet regime reasserted its right to control its satellites. Serious Cold War confrontations rippled along Czechoslovakia's western border as refugees fled west, and in the Korean peninsula after North Korea's seizure of an eavesdropping ship from the U.S. Navy. Over the long term, however, the protesters' and dissidents' demands proved more difficult to contain. In Eastern Europe and the Soviet Union, dissent was defeated but not eliminated. The crushing of the Czech rebellion proved thoroughly disillusioning, and in important respects the events of 1968 prefigured the collapse of Soviet control in 1989. In Western Europe and the United States, the student movement subsided but its issues and the kinds of politics that it pioneered proved more enduring. Feminism (or, more accurately, "second wave" feminism) really came into its own after 1968, its numbers expanded by women a generation younger than Simone de Beauvoir and Betty Friedan. They had been in student political organizations in the 1960s and their impatience with traditional political parties and, often, their male student allies, sent them into separate groups, where they championed equality in sexual relationships and in the family. In a phrase that captured some of the changes of the 1950s and 1960s, they insisted that "the personal is political." As one English woman said, "We wanted to redefine the meaning of politics to include an analysis of our daily lives," which meant sexuality, health, child care, cultural

A RUSSIAN TANK ATTACKED DURING THE PRAGUE SPRING, 1968. The Soviet-led invasion of Czechoslovakia on August 20–21, 1968 put an end to Alexander Dubčeck's experiment in creating "Socialism with a human face."

images of women, and so on. The antiwar movement took up the issue of nuclear weapons—a particularly volatile issue in Europe. Finally, the environmental movement took hold—concerned not only with pollution and the world's dwindling resources but also with mushrooming urbanization and the kind of unrestrained economic growth that had given rise to the 1960s. Over the long term, in both Europe and the United States, voters' loyalties to traditional political parties became less reliable and smaller parties multiplied; in this way, new social movements eventually became part of a very different political landscape.

ECONOMIC STAGNATION: THE PRICE OF SUCCESS

Economic as well as social problems plagued Europe during the 1970s and 1980s, but these problems had begun earlier. By the middle of the 1960s, for example, the West German growth rate had slowed. Demand for manufactured goods fell, and in 1966 the country suffered its first postwar recession. Volkswagen, the symbol of the German miracle, introduced a shortened workweek; almost 700,000 West Germans were thrown out of work altogether. In France, a persistent housing shortage increased the cost of living. Though new industries continued to prosper, the basic industries—coal, steel, and railways—began to run up deficits. Unemployment was rising in tandem with prices. Prime Minister Harold Wilson's pledge to revive Britain's economy by introducing new technology foundered on crises in the foreign-exchange value of the pound, which were compounded by continued low levels of growth. The Common Market—expanded in 1973 to include Britain, Ireland, and Denmark, and again in the early 1980s to admit Greece, Spain, and Portugal—struggled to overcome problems stemming from the conflict between the domestic economic regulations characteristic of many European states and the free-market policies that prevailed within what would become the European Economic Community (EEC) countries.

Oil prices spiked for the first time in the early 1970s, compounding these difficulties. In 1973, the Arab-dominated

Analyzing Primary Sources

Ludvík Vaculík, "Two Thousand Words" (1968)

During the Prague spring of 1968, a group of Czech intellectuals published a document titled "Two Thousand Words That Belong to Workers, Farmers, Officials, Scientists, Artists, and Everybody" that has become known simply as the "Two Thousand Words." This manifesto called for further reform, including increased freedom of the press. Seen as a direct affront by Moscow, the manifesto heightened Soviet-Czech tensions. In August 1968, Warsaw Pact tanks rolled into Prague, overthrowing the reformist government of Alexander Dubček.

Most of the nation welcomed the socialist program with high hopes. But it fell into the hands of the wrong people. It would not have mattered so much that they lacked adequate experience in affairs of state, factual knowledge, or philosophical education, if only they had enough common prudence and decency to listen to the opinion of others and agree to being gradually replaced by more able people. . . .

The chief sin and deception of these rulers was to have explained their own whims as the "will of the workers." Were we to accept this pretense, we would have to blame the workers today for the decline of our economy, for crimes committed against the innocent, and for the introduction of censorship to prevent anyone writing about these things. The workers would be to blame for misconceived investments, for losses suffered in foreign trade, and for the housing shortage. Obviously no sensible person will hold the working class responsible for such things. We all know, and every worker knows especially, that they had virtually no say in deciding anything. . . .

Since the beginning of this year we have been experiencing a regenerative process of democratization. . . .

Let us demand the departure of people who abused their power, damaged public property, and acted dishonorably or brutally. Ways must be found to compel them to resign. To mention a few: public criticism, resolutions, demonstrations, demonstrative work brigades, collections to buy presents for them on their retirement, strikes, and picketing at their front doors. But we should reject any illegal, indecent, or boorish methods. . . . Let us convert the district and local newspapers, which have mostly degenerated to the level of official mouthpieces, into a platform for all the forward-looking elements in politics; let us demand that editorial boards be formed of National Front representatives, or else let us start new papers. Let us form committees for the defense of free speech. . . .

There has been great alarm recently over the possibility that foreign forces will intervene in our development. Whatever superior forces may face us, all we can do is stick to our own positions, behave decently, and initiate nothing ourselves. We can show our government that we will stand by it, with weapons if need be, if it will do what we give it a mandate to do. . . .

The spring is over and will never return. By winter we will know all.

Source: Jaromir Navratil, *The Prague Spring 1968*, trans. Mark Kramer, Joy Moss, and Ruth Tosek (Budapest: 1998), pp. 177–81.

Questions for Analysis

1. Where, according to the authors of this document, did socialism go wrong?

2. What specific reforms do they demand?

Organization of the Petroleum Exporting Countries (OPEC) instituted an oil embargo against the Western powers. In 1973, a barrel of oil cost \$1.73; in 1975, it cost \$10.46; by the early 1980s, the price had risen to over \$30. This increase produced an inflationary spiral; interest rates rose and with them the price of almost everything else Western consumers were used to buying. Rising costs produced wage demands and strikes. The calm industrial relations of the 1950s and early 1960s were a thing of the past. At the same time, European manufacturers encountered serious competition not only from such highly developed countries as Japan but also from the increasingly active economies of Asia and Africa, in which the West had invested capital eagerly in the previous decades. By 1980, Japan had captured 10 percent of the automobile market in West Germany and 25 percent in Belgium. In 1984, unemployment in Western Europe reached about 19 million. The lean years had arrived.

UNEMPLOYMENT DEMONSTRATION, 1974. A crowd of workers in Rome, Italy, gathered to protest inflation and unemployment, in a strike that lasted twenty-four hours.

Economies in the Soviet bloc also stalled. The expansion of heavy industry had helped recovery in the postwar period, but by the 1970s, those sectors no longer provided growth or innovation. The Soviet Communist party proclaimed in 1961 that by 1970 the USSR would exceed the United States in per capita production. By the end of the 1970s, however, Soviet per capita production was not much higher than in the less industrialized countries of southern Europe. The Soviets were also overcommitted to military defense industries that had become inefficient, though lucrative for the party members who ran them. The Soviet economy did get a boost from the OPEC oil price hikes of 1973 and 1979. (OPEC was founded in 1961; the Soviet Union did not belong, but as the world's largest producer of oil, it benefited from rising prices.) Without this boost, the situation would have been far grimmer.

Following an impressive economic performance during the early 1970s, the Eastern European nations encountered serious financial difficulties. Their success had rested in part on capital borrowed from the West. By 1980, those debts weighed heavily on their national economies. Poland's hard-currency indebtedness to Western countries, for example, was almost four times greater than its annual exports. The solution to this problem, attempted in Poland and elsewhere, was to cut back on production for domestic consumption in order to increase exports. Yet this policy encountered strong popular opposition. Although there was virtually no unemployment in Eastern Europe, men and women were by no means happy with their economic situation. Working hours were longer than in Western Europe, and goods and services, even in prosperous times, were scarce.

Western governments struggled for effective reactions to the abrupt change in their economic circumstances. The new leader of the British Conservative Party, Margaret Thatcher, was elected prime minister in 1979—and reelected in 1983 and 1987—on a program of curbing trade-union power, cutting taxes to stimulate the economy, and privatizing publicly owned enterprises. The economy remained weak, with close to 15 percent of the workforce unemployed by 1986. In West Germany, a series of Social Democratic governments attempted to combat economic recession with job-training programs and tax incentives, both financed by higher taxes. These programs did little to assist economic recovery, and the country shifted to the right.

The fact that governments of right and left were unable to re-create Europe's unprecedented postwar prosperity suggests the degree to which economic forces remain outside the control of individual states. The continuing economic malaise renewed efforts to Europeanize common problems. By the end of the 1980s, the EEC embarked on an ambitious program of integration. Long-term goals, agreed on when the EU (European Union) was formed in 1991, included a monetary union—with a central European bank and a single currency—and unified social policies to reduce poverty and unemployment. As the twenty-first century opened, the European member states had begun to institute several of these steps. It remained unclear whether that new European "federal" state would overcome its members' claims of national sovereignty or whether it would develop the economic and political strength to counter the global domination of the United States.

Solidarity in Poland

In 1980, unrest again peaked in Eastern Europe, this time with the Polish labor movement Solidarity. Polish workers organized strikes that brought the government of the country to a standstill. The workers formulated several key demands. First, they objected to working conditions imposed by the government to combat a severe economic crisis. Second, they protested high prices and especially shortages, both of which had roots in government policy and priorities. Above all, though, the Polish workers in Solidarity demanded truly independent labor unions instead of labor organizations sponsored by the government. Their belief that society had the right to organize itself and, by implication, create its own government, stood at the core of the movement. The strikers were led by an electrician from the Gdansk shipyards, Lech Wałęsa. Wałęsa's charismatic personality appealed not only to the Polish citizenry but to sympathizers in the West. Again, however, the Soviets assisted a military regime in reimposing authoritarian rule. The Polish president, General Wojciech Jaruzelski, had learned from Hungary and Czechoslovakia and played a delicate game of diplomacy to maintain the Polish government's freedom of action while repressing Solidarity itself. But the implied Soviet threat remained.

EUROPE RECAST: THE COLLAPSE OF COMMUNISM AND THE END OF THE SOVIET UNION

One of history's fascinations is its unpredictability. There has been no more telling example of this in recent times than the sudden collapse of the Eastern European communist regimes in 1989, the dramatic end to the Cold War, and the subsequent disintegration of the once-powerful Soviet Union.

Gorbachev and Soviet Reform

This sudden collapse flowed, unintended, from a new wave of reform begun in the mid-1980s. In 1985, a new generation of officials began taking charge of the Soviet Communist party, a change heralded by Mikhail Gorbachev's appointment to the party leadership. In his mid-fifties, Gorbachev was significantly younger than his immediate predecessors and less prey to the habits of mind that had shaped Soviet domestic and foreign affairs. He was frankly critical of the repressive aspects of communist society as well as its sluggish economy, and he did not hesitate to voice those criticisms openly. His twin policies of *glasnost* (intellectual openness) and *perestroika* (economic restructuring) held out hope for a freer, more prosperous Soviet Union. Under Gorbachev, a number of imprisoned dissidents were freed, among them Andrei Sakharov, the scientist known as the "father of the Soviet hydrogen bomb" and later a fierce critic of the Cold War arms race.

The policies of glasnost took aim at the privileges of the political elite and the immobility of the state bureaucracy by allowing greater freedom of speech, instituting competitive elections to official positions, and limiting terms of office. Gorbachev's program of perestroika called for a shift from the centrally planned economy instituted by Stalin to a mixed economy combining planning with the operation of market forces. In agriculture, perestroika accelerated the move away from cooperative production and instituted incentives for the achievement of production targets. Gorbachev planned to integrate the Soviet Union into the international economy by participating in organizations such as the International Monetary Fund.

Even these dramatic reforms, however, were too little too late. Ethnic unrest, a legacy of Russia's nineteenth-century imperialism, threatened to split the Soviet Union apart, while secession movements gathered steam in the Baltic republics and elsewhere. From 1988 onward, fighting between Armenians and Azerbaijanis over an ethnically Azerbaijani region located inside Armenia threatened to escalate into a border dispute with Iran. Only Soviet troops patrolling the border and Gorbachev's willingness to suppress a separatist revolt in Azerbaijan by force temporarily quelled the conflict.

Spurred on by these events in the Soviet Union, the countries of Eastern Europe began to agitate for independence from Moscow. Gorbachev encouraged open discussion—glasnost—not only in his own country but also in the satellite nations. He revoked the Brezhnev Doctrine's insistence on single-party socialist governments and made frequent and inspiring trips to the capitals of neighboring satellites.

Glasnost rekindled the flame of opposition in Poland, where Solidarity had been defeated but not destroyed by the government in 1981. In 1988, the union launched a new series of strikes. These disturbances culminated in an agreement between the government and Solidarity that legalized the union and promised open elections. The results, in June 1989, astonished the world: virtually all of the government's candidates lost; the Citizen's Committee, affiliated with Solidarity, won a sizable majority in the Polish parliament.

In Hungary and Czechoslovakia, events followed a similar course during 1988 and 1989. Janos Kadar, the Hungarian leader since the Soviet crackdown of 1956, resigned in the face of continuing demonstrations in May 1988 and was replaced by the reformist government of the Hungarian Socialist Workers' party. By the spring of 1989, the Hungarian regime had been purged of Communist party supporters. The government also began to dismantle its security fences along the Austrian border. A year later,

GORBACHEV IN POLAND AT THE HEIGHT OF HIS POWER IN 1986. Perestroika aimed at the privileges of the political elite and would eventually lead to his fall from power.

the Hungarian Democratic Forum, pledging it would reinstate full civil rights and restructure the economy, secured a plurality of seats in the National Assembly.

The Czechs, too, staged demonstrations against Soviet domination in late 1988. Brutal beatings of student demonstrators by the police in 1989 radicalized the nations' workers and provoked mass demonstrations. Civic Forum, an opposition coalition, called for the installation of a coalition government to include noncommunists, for free elections, and for the resignation of the country's communist leadership. It reinforced its demands with continuing mass demonstrations and threats of a general strike that resulted in the toppling of the old regime and the election of the playwright and Civic Forum leader Václav Havel as president.

Fall of the Berlin Wall

The most significant political change in Eastern Europe during the late 1980s was the collapse of communism in East Germany and the unification of East and West Germany. Although long considered the most prosperous of the Soviet satellite countries, East Germany suffered from severe economic stagnation and environmental degradation. Waves of East Germans registered their discontent with worsening conditions by massive illegal immigration to the West. This exodus combined with evidence of widespread official corruption to force the resignation of East Germany's longtime, hard-line premier, Erich Honecker. His successor, Egon Krenz, promised reforms, but he was nevertheless faced with continuing protests and continuing mass emigration.

On November 4, 1989, the government, in a move that acknowledged its powerlessness to hold its citizens captive, opened its border with Czechoslovakia. This move effectively freed East Germans to travel to the West. In a matter of days, the Berlin Wall—the embodiment of the Cold War, the Iron Curtain, and the division of East from West—was demolished, first by groups of ordinary citizens and later by the East German government. Jubilant throngs from both sides walked through the gaping holes that now permitted men, women, and children to take the few steps that symbolized the return to freedom and a chance for national unity. Free elections were held throughout Germany in March 1990, resulting in a victory for the Alliance for Germany, a coalition allied with the West German chancellor Helmut Kohl's Christian Democratic Union. With heavy emigration continuing, reunification talks quickly culminated in the formal proclamation of a united Germany on October 3, 1990.

The public mood, in Eastern Europe and perhaps worldwide, was swept up with the jubilation of these peaceful "velvet revolutions" during the autumn of 1989. Yet the end of one-party rule in Eastern Europe was not accomplished without violence. The single most repressive government in the old Eastern bloc, Nicolae Ceaușescu's outright dictatorship in Romania, came apart with much more bloodshed. By December, faced with the wave of popular revolts in surrounding countries and riots by the ethnic Hungarian minority in Transylvania, a number of party officials and army officers in Romania tried to hold

REAGAN AT THE BERLIN WALL. On June 12, 1987, President Reagan challenged Mikhail Gorbachev to tear down the Berlin Wall in a speech given before the Brandenburg Gate in Berlin.

of banditry and separatism against Russian authority that stretched into the nineteenth century. In 1994, the Russian government, weary of this continuing challenge to its authority, launched a concerted effort to quash resistance. As Russian forces moved into the Chechen capital, Grozny, they were ambushed with firepower largely stolen from disused Russian armories. The result was a massacre of the invading Russians, followed by a long and bloody siege to take the city. This in turn fueled a long and particularly bloody guerrilla war between Russian and Chechen forces, marked by repeated atrocities on both sides. After brief pauses in 1995 and 1997, this Chechen war dragged on into the new century, echoing Russia's conflict in Afghanistan on a scale that was both bloodier and closer to home.

The Iron Curtain had established one of the most rigid borders in European history. The collapse of the Soviet Union opened up both Russia and its former imperial dominions. That transformation brought the Cold War to an end. It also created a host of unforeseen problems throughout Eastern Europe and the advanced industrial world: ethnic conflict, diplomatic uncertainty about the new Russian government, and single superpower domination, sometimes called American unilateralism. Within the Russian and several of the former Soviet republics there emerged a new era that some called the Russian "Wild West." Capitalist market relations began to develop without clearly defined property relations or a stable legal framework. Former government officials profited from their positions of power to take over whole sectors of the economy. Corruption ran rampant. Organized crime controlled industries, stock exchanges, a thriving trade in illegal drugs, and even some local governments. Even the most energetic central governments in the large republics such as Russia, Ukraine, and Kazakhstan found themselves faced with enormous problems. Post-Soviet openness could lay the groundwork for a new democratic Russia; it could also set in motion the resurgence of older forms of tyranny.

Postrevolutionary Troubles: Eastern Europe after 1989

The velvet revolutions of Central and Eastern Europe raised high hopes: local hopes that an end to authoritarian government would produce economic prosperity and cultural pluralism and Western hopes that these countries would join them as capitalist partners in an enlarged European Community. The reality was slower and harder than the optimists of 1989 foresaw. The largest struggle, one with continuing implications for the European continent, has been the reunification of Germany. The euphoria of reunification masked uncertainty even among Germans themselves. The foundering East German economy has remained a problem. Piled onto other economic difficulties in the former West Germany during the 1990s, it has produced much resentment of the need to "rescue" the East. What the writer Günter Grass described as the "wall in the mind" still divided the countries. Though there has been great progress in integrating elections and the bureaucracies of the two German states, economic and cultural unity has been much harder to come by.

Adapting to change has been difficult throughout Eastern Europe. Attempts to create free-market economies have brought inflation, unemployment, and—in their wake—anticapitalist demonstrations. Inefficient industries, a workforce resistant to change, energy shortages, lack of venture capital, and a severely polluted environment have combined to hinder progress and dash hopes. Uprisings in Bulgaria and Albania in early 1997 were fueled by the inability of those governments to resolve basic economic and social problems. In addition, racial and ethnic conflicts have continued to divide newly liberated democracies, recalling the divisions that led to the First World War and that have plagued Eastern Europe throughout its history. Minorities waged campaigns for autonomous rights or outright secession that often descended into violence.

Czechoslovakia's velvet revolution collapsed into a "velvet divorce," as Slovakia declared itself independent from the Czechs, forcing Havel's resignation and slowing down the promising cultural and economic reforms begun in 1989. Poland enjoyed an upswing in its economy during the 1990s, after many years of hardship, but most of the rest of Eastern Europe continues to find transformation rough going. These difficulties have been accompanied by revived ethnic tensions formerly suppressed by centralized communist governments. There has been violence against non-European immigrants throughout Eastern Europe, against gypsies (Romani) in the Czech Republic and Hungary, and against ethnic Hungarians in Romania.

The most extreme example of these conflicts came with the implosion of the state of Yugoslavia. After the death of Tito in 1980, the government that had held Yugoslavia's federalist ethnic patchwork together came undone. The 1960s and 1970s brought uneven economic growth, benefiting the capital, Belgrade, and the provinces of Croatia and Slovenia the most; but heavy industrial areas in Serbia, Bosnia-Hercegovina, and the tiny district of Kosovo began to lag far behind. A number of Serb politicians, most notably Slobodan Milosevic, began to redirect Serbs' frustration with economic hardship toward subjects of national pride and sovereignty.

EASTERN EUROPE IN 1989. ▪ ***What political changes in the Soviet Union allowed for the spread of demonstrations throughout Eastern Europe?*** ▪ ***Why did the first political upheavals of 1989 occur in Poland and East Germany?*** ▪ ***In what countries were demonstrations the most widespread and why?***

Nationalism, particularly Serb and Croat nationalism, had long dogged Yugoslavia's firmly federal political system. Feelings ran especially deep among Serbs. Serbian national myths reach back to the Middle Ages, and the country also has more recent traditions of political separatism on ethnic grounds. Milosevic and the Serb nationalists who gathered around him ignited those political flashpoints in ways that caught the fears and frustrations of his times. More important for Milosevic, it catapulted him into crucial positions of authority. In these posts, he alienated representatives from the non-Serb republics. Inspired by the peaceful transformations of 1989, representatives of the small province of Slovenia declared they had been denied adequate representation and economic support inside the republic. In 1991, on a tide of nationalism and reform, the Slovenes seceded from Yugoslavia. After a brief attempt to hold the union together by force, the Yugoslav government relented and let Slovenia claim its independence. Ethnic nationalists in the other republics followed suit. A much deeper, bloodier process of disintegration had begun.

The large republic of Croatia, once part of the Habsburg Empire and briefly an independent state allied with the Nazis during the Second World War, cited injustices by Serb officials in the Yugoslav government and declared independence as a free, capitalist state. War broke out between federal Yugoslav forces and the well-armed militias of independent Croatia, a conflict that ended in arbitration by the United Nations. The religious nature of the conflict—between Catholic Croats and Orthodox Serbs—and the legacies of fighting in the Second World War produced violence on both sides. Towns and villages where Serbs and Croats had lived together since the 1940s were torn apart as each ethnic group rounded up and massacred members of the other.

The next conflict came in the same place that in 1914 had sparked a much larger war: the province of Bosnia-Hercegovina. Bosnia was the most ethnically diverse republic in Yugoslavia. Its capital, Sarajevo, was home to several major ethnic groups and had often been praised as an example of peaceful coexistence. When Bosnia

Interpreting Visual Evidence

Representing the People in Eastern Europe, 1989

The enthusiasm of the mass demonstrations that preceded the revolutionary changes in Eastern Europe in 1989 gave the events a sense of immediate drama, and images of Eastern Europeans massed together in protest, crossing boundaries that had been closed to them, and celebrating the downfall of their repressive governments spread quickly around the world. The symbolism of these images was stark and resonated with a triumphant story about the progress of democratic ideals in an increasingly unified and integrated Europe. In the East, the people's desire to join with the West, long denied, had finally been realized.

The unity of these early days nevertheless obscured a basic uncertainty about the aspirations of the populations of the newly independent nations in Eastern Europe. Many East Germans expressed reservations about the rapid pace of German reunification, and people from the West and the East continued to talk about "the wall in the head" long after the Berlin wall had been torn down. The unity of Czechoslovakia's peaceful velvet revolution in 1989 led quickly to the "velvet divorce" that produced the dissolution of Czechoslovakia into the Czech Republic and Slovakia in 1993. Throughout the region, many commentators continued to speak of a persistent *Ostalgia*—a nostalgia for an alternative Eastern European past that had been lost in the abrupt transition.

We have seen in earlier chapters how representations of the people served to give meaning to moments of rapid social and political change in the French Revolution or in the unification of Germany. The images here, from media coverage of the events of 1989, also serve to frame the interpretations that contemporaries gave to the unfolding events. Image A shows a crowd in Prague waving the Czechoslovakian flag in November 1989. Image B shows a line of East Berliners forming in front of a West Berlin grocery store in the days after the fall of the Berlin Wall. Image C shows the last of the Leipzig Monday demonstrations on March 12, 1990—the caption reads, "Also after the last demonstration: We are the People. We are *one* people."

A. Crowd during Czechoslovakia's Velvet Revolution.

seceded from Yugoslavia in 1992, ethnic coexistence came apart. Bosnia began the war with no formal army: armed bands equipped by the governments of Serbian Yugoslavia, Croatia, and Bosnia battled each other throughout the new country. The Serbs and Croats, both of whom disliked the Muslim Bosnians, were especially well equipped and organized. They rained shells and bullets on towns and villages, burned houses with families inside, imprisoned Muslim men in detention camps and starved them to death, and raped thousands of Bosnian women. All sides committed atrocities. The Serbs, however, orchestrated and carried out the worst crimes. These included what came to

B. East Berliners line up to shop in West Berlin, November 12, 1989.

C. "We Are the People. We Are One People."

"We are the people" was the slogan of the weekly demonstrations in Leipzig in 1989 that did so much to discredit the government in the months before the wall fell. "We are *one* people" became the slogan of Helmut Kohl's government as it pushed for rapid reunification of the two Germanies.

Questions for Analysis

1. In image A, how should one interpret the wave of nationalist enthusiasm that engulfed Czechoslovakia in 1989, in light of what we know of the subsequent failure to keep Czechoslovakia together as a unified nation?
2. Photographs such as image B were extremely common in the media in 1989, showing East Berliners shopping in Western stores. What do such images suggest about how the East's previous isolation was interpreted in the West, and what does it say about how both sides may have viewed the consequences of their newfound freedom?
3. What is the difference between "We are the people" and "We are *one* people" as political slogans?

be called ethnic cleansing. This involved sending irregular troops on campaigns of murder and terror through Muslim and Croat territories to encourage much larger populations to flee the area. During the first eighteen months of the fighting as many as 100,000 people were killed, including 80,000 civilians, mostly Bosnian Muslims. Although the campaigns appalled Western governments, those countries worried that intervention would result only in another Vietnam or Afghanistan with no clear resolution of the horrific ethnic slaughter itself. The outside forces, mostly European troops in United Nations blue helmets, concentrated on humanitarian relief, separating combatants, and creating safe areas for persecuted ethnic populations from all parties.

The crisis came to a head in the autumn of 1995. Sarajevo had been under siege for three years, but a series of mortar attacks on public marketplaces in Sarajevo produced fresh Western outrage and moved the United States to act. Already Croat forces and the Bosnian army had turned the war on the ground against the Serb militias, and now they were supported by a rolling wave of American air strikes. The American bombing, combined with a Croat-Bosnian offensive, forced the Bosnian Serbs to negotiate. Elite French troops supported by British artillery broke the siege of Sarajevo. Peace talks were held at Dayton, Ohio. The agreement divided Bosnia, with the majority of land in the hands of Muslims and Croats and a small, autonomous "Serb Republic" in areas that included land ethnically cleansed in 1992. Stability was restored, but three years of war had killed over 200,000 people.

The legacy of Bosnia flared into conflict again over Kosovo, the medieval homeland of the Orthodox Christian Serbs, now occupied by a largely Albanian, Muslim population. Milosevic accused the Albanians of plotting secession and of challenging the Serb presence in Kosovo. In the name of a "greater Serbia," Serb soldiers fought Albanian separatists rallying under the banner of "greater Albania." Both sides used terrorist tactics. Western nations were anxious lest the conflict might spread to the strategic, ethnically divided country of Macedonia and touch off a general Balkan conflict. Western political opinion was outraged, however, as Serbian forces used many of the same murderous tactics in Kosovo that they had employed earlier in Bosnia. Talks between Milosevic's government and the Albanian rebels were sponsored by the NATO powers but fell apart in early 1999. That failure was followed by a fresh wave of American-led bombing against Serbia itself, as well as against Serbian forces in Kosovo. A new round of ethnic cleansing drove hundreds of thousands of Albanians from their homes. Unwilling to fight a war on the ground in the mountainous, unforgiving terrain of the southern Balkans, the United States and its European allies concentrated on strategic attacks on bridges, power plants, factories, and Serbian military bases. The Russian government, bothered by this unilateral attack on fellow Slavs, nonetheless played an important part in brokering a cease-fire. Milosevic was forced to withdraw from Kosovo, leaving it in the hands of another force of armed NATO peacekeepers.

Finally, Serb-dominated Yugoslavia, worn by ten years of war and economic sanctions, turned against Milosevic's regime. Wars and corruption had destroyed Milosevic's credentials as a nationalist and populist. After he attempted to reject the results of a democratic election in 2000, his government fell to popular protests. He died in 2006, while being tried by a UN tribunal for war crimes.

As we gain perspective on the twentieth century, it is clear that the Yugoslavian wars of the 1990s were not an isolated instance of Balkan violence. The issues are thoroughly Western. The Balkans form one of the West's borderlands, where cultures influenced by Roman Catholicism, Eastern Orthodoxy, and Islam meet, overlap, and contend for political domination and influence. Since the nineteenth century, this region of enormous religious, cultural, and ethnic diversity has struggled with the implications of nationalism. We have seen how conflicts over the creation of new national states drawn

MASS FUNERAL IN KOSOVO, 1999. Ethnic Albanians bury victims of a Serbian massacre toward the end of Yugoslavia's ten years of fighting. ▪ ***Although the nature of war has changed radically in the last hundred years, "ethnic cleansing" has remained remarkably constant and frequent in the modern period. What prevents states from taking effective action to prevent it?***

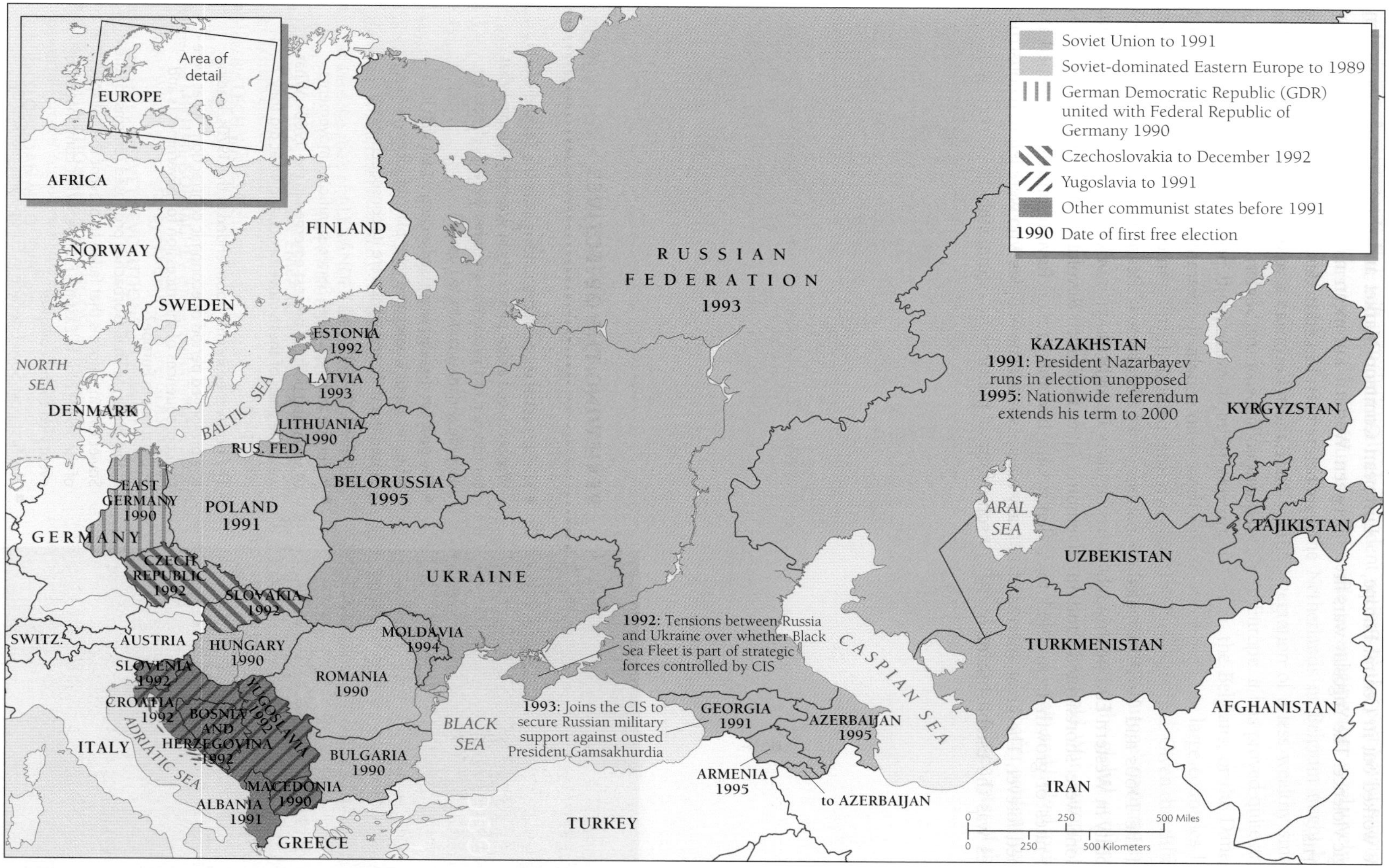

RUSSIAN AND EASTERN EUROPE AFTER THE COLD WAR. Examine closely the geography of southeastern and central Europe. ▪ ***How were political boundaries reorganized?*** ▪ ***How did the collapse of the Soviet Union and the end of the Cold War allow for the reemergence of certain forces in the political landscape of Europe?*** ▪ ***How were the boundaries of the Soviet Union reorganized after 1991?***

Before You Read This Chapter

STORY LINES

- After 1989, the trend toward globalization in the twentieth century became more visible. Improved communications and flows of money and products from one part of the world to another offered many opportunities for economic growth but also reinforced existing inequalities among the world's different regions.
- The legacy of colonialism weighed heavily on former colonies, and some became the arena for conflicts related to the Cold War, such as the end of apartheid in South Africa, civil war and ethnic conflict in Rwanda and Zaire, and postwar economic development in Japan and South Korea.
- In the second half of the twentieth century, events in the Middle East took on global significance. The Arab-Israeli conflict, bitterness against foreign interventions in Muslim countries, and frustration with the first generation of nationalist governments in the region led to the development of modern forms of Islamic radicalism aiming at revolutionary change in the Middle East and confrontation with the West.

CHRONOLOGY

1948	State of Israel formed
1948–1949	First Arab-Israeli War
1960	Formation of OPEC
1967	Israel occupies West Bank
1973	Second Arab-Israeli War
1973	Arab members of OPEC announce oil embargo
1978	Camp David Peace Accords
1979	Soviet invasion of Afghanistan
1979	Islamic revolution in Iran
1980–1988	Iran-Iraq War
1991	Persian Gulf War
1994	Genocide against Tutsis in Rwanda
1997	China reclaims Hong Kong
2001	9/11 terrorist attacks
2003	U.S. invasion of Iraq
2008	Global financial crisis
2011	Arab Spring

29

A World without Walls: Globalization and the West

CORE OBJECTIVES

- **DEFINE** *globalization* and understand what is new about current patterns of interconnection in the world as well as the continuities that can be seen with earlier periods of global connection.
- **EXPLAIN** the continued relevance of the colonial past in shaping the politics, economy, and society of independent states in Asia and Africa and the nature of their ongoing relationships to the societies and states of Europe and North America.
- **UNDERSTAND** the global connections that link societies in other parts of the world to the events and persistent conflicts in the Middle East.

In the twenty-first century, the world has reentered a period in which basic assumptions about the role of nation-states, the roots of prosperity, and the boundaries of cultures are changing fast. We say *reentered* because, as we have seen, a disconcerting sense of seismic and little-understood change has been central to Western culture during several different historical periods. The Industrial Revolution of the nineteenth century is an example, and just as *industrial revolution*, a term coined in the early nineteenth century, seemed to capture contemporaries' perceptions of changes in their own time, so *globalization* seems to capture ours. Globalization is not new, but our acute consciousness of it is.

We know, intuitively, what globalization means: the Internet, protests against the World Trade Organization (WTO), outsourcing of jobs and services, Walmart in Mexico, the dismantling of the Berlin Wall. All of these are powerful images of larger, enormously significant developments. The Internet represents the stunning transformation of global communication, the media, and forms of knowledge. The Berlin Wall once stood for a divided Cold War world; its fall marked a dramatic reconfiguration of international relations, an end to the ideological battle over communism, the creation of new alliances, markets, and communities. The attack on the World Trade Center in 2001 gave the term *globalization* a new and frightening meaning as well. It shattered many Americans' sense of relative isolation and security. Globalization, then, conjures up new possibilities but also new vulnerabilities.

What, precisely, does the term mean? What causes or drives globalization, and what are its effects? To begin simply, globalization means integration. It is the process of creating a rising number of networks—political, social, economic, and cultural—that span larger sections of the globe. New technologies, new economic imperatives, and changing laws have combined to make global exchange faster and, by the same token, to intensify economic, social, and cultural relationships. Information, ideas, goods, and people now move rapidly and easily across national boundaries. Yet *globalization* is not synonymous with *internationalization*, and the distinction is important. International relations are established between nation-states. Global exchange can be quite independent of national control: today trade, politics, and cultural exchange often happen "underneath the radar of the nation-state," in the words of one historian.

Globalization has radically altered the distribution of industry and patterns of trade around the world, as Asian nations in particular emerge as industrial giants and Western powers become increasingly dependent on energy resources drawn from former colonies. Globalization has forced the reorganization of economic enterprises from banking and commerce to manufacturing. Supranational economic institutions such as the International Monetary Fund are examples of globalization and also work to quicken its pace. Likewise, the International Criminal Court represents an important trend in law: the globalization of judicial power. New, rapid, and surprisingly intimate forms of mass communication (blogs, social media sites, Internet-based political campaigns, and so on) have spawned new forms of politics. International human-rights campaigns, for instance, owe an enormous debt to global communications and the communities they create. Perhaps most interesting, the sovereignty of nation-states and the clear boundaries of national communities seem to be eroded by many globalizing trends.

All these developments seem to be characteristic of our time. But are they new? For centuries, religion, empire, commerce, and industry have had globalizing impulses and effects. The East India Companies (Dutch and English), for instance, were to the seventeenth century what Microsoft is to the early twenty-first: the premier global enterprises of the time. Chartered and granted monopolies by the crown, they organized trade, investment of capital, manufacturing enterprises, and commercial agriculture. The Dutch East India Company's networks reached from Amsterdam to South Africa, through to India and Southeast Asia. The economic development of Europe in general was thoroughly enmeshed in global networks that supplied raw materials, markets, and labor. It has always been hard to strip the "West" of its global dimensions. The movement to abolish slavery was certainly transatlantic, if not global.

For another striking example, consider migration and immigration. We think of the contemporary world as fluid, characterized by vast movements of people. Mass, long-distance migration and immigration, however, peaked during the nineteenth century. Between 1846 (when the first reliable statistics were kept) and 1940, 55 million to 58 million people left Europe for the Americas, especially for the United States, Canada, Argentina, and Brazil. During that same period, 48 million to 52 million Indians and southern Chinese migrated to Southeast Asia, the Southern Pacific, and the areas surrounding the Indian Ocean (many of the Indian migrants went to other parts of the British Empire). Roughly another 50 million people left northeastern Asia and Russia for Manchuria, Siberia, central Asia, and Japan. Faster long-distance transportation (railways and steamships) made these long journeys possible; the industrialization of the receiving regions provided the economic dynamics. As the scholar Adam McKeown writes, the nineteenth century was "a world on the move, flowing into factories, construction projects, mines, plantations, agricultural frontiers, and commercial networks across the globe." The demographic, social, economic, and cultural effects of these migrations were transformative. As McKeown also points out, after the First World War, governments set out to close their gates; from the 1920s on, laborers (and refugees) found it much harder to move. If migration is a measure of globalization, our world is less "globalized" than it was a century ago.

What is more, to equate globalization with integration may be misleading. Globalizing trends do not necessarily produce peace, equality, or homogeneity. Their effects are hard to predict. During the early 1900s, many Europeans firmly believed that the world, at least the part of the world dominated by Western empires, would become harmonious, that Western culture would be exported, and that Western standards were universal. History defied those expectations. Some scholars argue that the term *globalization* should be jettisoned because it suggests a uniform, leveling process, one that operates similarly everywhere. Globalization has very different and disparate effects, effects shaped by vast asymmetries of power and wealth among nations or regions. In the last several decades, worldwide inequality has increased. Global processes encounter obstacles and resistance; they sow division as well as unity. At the level of everyday human contact, globalization has hastened new kinds of cultural blending and new forms of sociability, but it has also produced a backlash against that blending. The heady word *global* can distort our analyses or point us in the wrong direction. As one historian argues, although it is crucial to be able to think outside of "national or continental containers," it would be misleading to believe "that there is no container at all, except the planetary one."

In this chapter, we explore three subjects crucial to our early efforts to understand globalization, especially as it relates to the post–Cold War world of the twenty-first century. The first subject is the set of global changes that have accelerated the free flow of money, people, products, and ideas. The second subject is what we have come to call postcolonial politics—the varied trajectories that mark the contemporary experience of former colonies. Finally, we will consider in greater depth the complex and important role of Middle Eastern politics in contemporary global affairs. Throughout, we hope to suggest ways in which recent developments relate to familiar historical issues we have already examined in other contexts.

LIQUID MODERNITY? THE FLOW OF MONEY, IDEAS, AND PEOPLES

A key feature of late-twentieth-century globalization has been the transformation of the world economy, highlighted by the rapid integration of markets since 1970. In a series of historic changes, the international agreements that had regulated the movement of people, goods, and money since the Second World War were overturned. To begin with, the postwar economic arrangements sealed at Bretton Woods (see Chapter 27) steadily eroded in the late 1960s, as Western industrial nations faced a double burden of inflation and economic stagnation. A crucial shift in monetary policy occurred in 1971, when the United States abandoned the postwar gold standard and allowed the dollar—the keystone of the system—to range freely. As a result, formal regulations on currencies, international banking, and lending among states faded away. They were replaced with an informal network of arrangements managed autonomously by large private lenders, their political friends in leading Western states, and independent financial agencies such as the International Monetary Fund and the World Bank. The economists and administrators who dominated these new networks steered away from the interventionist policies that shaped postwar planning and recovery. Instead, they relied on a broad range of market-driven models dubbed "neoliberalism." In a variation on classic liberal economics, neoliberal economists stressed the value of free markets, profit incentives, and sharp restraints on both budget deficits and social welfare programs, whether run by governments or corporations. The new systems of lending they backed had mixed results, funding breakneck growth in some cases and bringing catastrophic debt in others. Industrial development in the globalized economy has created jarring juxtapositions of development and

"CHECKERBOARD OF POVERTY AND AFFLUENCE." Scenes of slums confronting towering skylines, such as this one from Argentina in 2000, are visible around the world as one of the side effects of development and deterioration.

Competing Viewpoints

The Meaning of the "Third World"

Alfred Sauvy, a French demographer, coined the term Third World *in a famous 1952 article about the effects of the Cold War on international relations and economic development. The First World was the West, a world of democratic political institutions and capitalist economies. The Second World, in Sauvy's formulation, was the Soviet sphere, committed to socialist institutions. The Third World was everybody else—the world of European colonies and former colonies, marked by the history of imperialism.*

Though commonly used between the 1950s and 1980s, the term Third World *is less frequently encountered in the present. B. R. Tomlinson, a British economic historian, examines the ways in which the concept was rooted in the ideological world of the Cold War and looks for new vocabulary to tell the history of globalization in the contemporary world.*

Alfred Sauvy, "Three Worlds, One Planet" (1952)

We speak voluntarily about two worlds today, about the possibility of war between them, about their coexistence, etc., forgetting too often that there is a third world [. . .] the collectivity called, in the style of the United Nations, the under-developed countries. . . .

[. . .]

Unfortunately, the struggle for the possession of the third world does not allow the two others to simply pursue their own path, believing it to be obviously the best, the "true" way. The Cold War has curious consequences: over there, a morbid fear of espionage has pushed them to the most ferocious isolation. With us, it has caused a halt in social evolution. What good is it to trouble ourselves or deprive ourselves, at a moment when the fear of communism is holding back those who would like to go further [on the path to equality]? Why should we consider any social reforms at all when the progressive majority is split? [. . .] Why worry about it, since there is no opposition?

In this way, any evolution toward the distant future has been halted in both camps, and this obstacle has one cause: the costs of war.

Meanwhile . . . the under-developed nations, the third world, have entered into a new phase. Certain medical techniques have now been introduced suddenly for a simple reason: they are cheap. [. . .] For a few pennies the life of a man can be prolonged for several years. Because of this, these countries now have the mortality that we had in 1914 and the birthrate that we had in the eighteenth century. Certainly, this has resulted in economic improvement, lower infant mortality, better productivity of adults, etc. Nevertheless, it is easy to see how this demographic increase must be accompanied by important investments in order to adapt the container to what it must contain. Now, these vital investments cost much more than 68 francs per person. They crash right into the financial wall imposed by the cold war. The result is eloquent: the millennial cycle of life and death continues to turn, but it is a cycle of poverty. [. . .]

Since the preparation for war is priority number 1, secondary concerns such as world hunger will only occupy our attention enough to avoid an explosion that might compromise our first priority. But when one remembers the enormous errors that conservatives have committed so many times, we can only have a mediocre confidence in the ability of the Americans to play with the fire of popular anger . . . They have not clearly perceived that under-developed nations of a feudal type might evolve more readily towards a communist regime than toward democratic capitalism. One might console oneself, if one were so inclined, by pointing to the greater advance of capitalism, but the fact remains undeniable. And maybe, in the glare of its own vitality, the first world, even in the absence of any human solidarity, might notice this slow, irresistible, humble and ferocious, push toward life. Because in the end, this ignored, exploited Third World, as despised as the Third Estate [in the French Revolution], wants to be something.

B. R. Tomlinson, "What Was the Third World?" (2003)

The term "Third World" was used frequently in histories of the societies, economies and cultures of many parts of the world in the second half of the twentieth century. [. . .] Like other collective descriptions of Africa, Asia, the Middle East, the Pacific islands and Latin America—such as the "South," the "developing world," or the "less-developed world"—the designation "Third World" was more about what such places were not than what they were. [. . .]

Those who developed a concept of the Third World around a set of measurable criteria usually relied on identifying material circumstances. . . . However, all such attempts to establish a standard measurement of relative poverty that can distinguish various parts of the world from each other run into considerable difficulties. It has often been argued that the various countries of Asia, Africa and Latin America (not to mention the Pacific islands and elsewhere) differ greatly in their size, political ideologies, social structures, economic performance, cultural backgrounds and historical experiences. These differences exist not simply between Third World countries, but within them as well. There are rich and poor people, empowered and disempowered citizens, to be found inside all states and societies in the world.

It was over broad issues of economic development that the fiercest battles for the concept of the Third World were fought. Orthodox development economists in the 1950s and 1960s had suggested that the poverty of non-western economies was the result of low levels of savings and investment, and that these problems could best be resolved by increasing external influence over them to help local élites modernize their societies (in other words, make them more like those of the West) by providing technology and education to increase productivity and output. [. . .]

To many radical critics, these ideas, and the U.S. government's development policies that flowed from them, seemed to mask a narrow political agenda that sought to justify the dominance of free-market capitalism as a model and mechanism for economic, social and cultural development. One powerful reaction to this agenda was to argue that dependence on the West had distorted the economic and social conditions of non-western societies, leading to a common process of historical change in the periphery of the world economy brought about by "a situation in which the economy of certain countries [and hence their social and political structures] is conditioned by the development and expansion of another economy to which the former is subjected." [. . .]

[. . .]

The history of imperialism has been immensely important in shaping our view of the modern world, both from the top down and from the bottom up, but the phenomenon was also historically specific, and represents only one stage in the process of understanding the interaction between the local and the global. To write the history of the "Rest," as well as of the West, we need now to move on, and to construct new narratives of global history that go beyond the models of coherent and distinct communities, nations and states, arranged into hierarchies of material achievement and cultural power, and underpinned by universal institutional ideals of participatory democracy and free markets, that dominated thinking about international and local systems in the world for much of the nineteenth and twentieth centuries. [. . .]

Sources: Alfred Sauvy, "Trois mondes, une planète," first published in *L'Observateur* 14 (August 1952), p. 5. This translation, by Joshua Cole, comes from a French reprint in *Vingtième Siècle*, no. 12 (October–December 1986), pp. 81–83; B. R. Tomlinson, "What Was the Third World?," *Journal of Contemporary History* 38, no. 2 (April 2003), pp. 307–21.

Questions for Analysis

1. In Sauvy's argument, what do the "under-developed nations" have in common? Does Tomlinson agree?
2. Sauvy calls for the First World to invest in the Third World to prevent an explosion of anger. What possible difficulties with this solution did Tomlinson identify?
3. How do Sauvy and Tomlinson see the relationship between the Cold War and the problem of understanding the "Third World?"

deterioration across entire continents and even within single cities—a phenomenon described as a "checkerboard of poverty and affluence."

At the same time, the world's local, national, and regional economies became far more connected and interdependent. Export trade flourished and, with the technological advances of the 1960s and 1980s, came to include an increasing proportion of high-technology goods. The boom in export commerce was tied to important changes in the division of labor worldwide. More industrial jobs emerged in the postcolonial world, not just among the Asian "tigers" but also in India, Latin America, and elsewhere. Although such steady, skilled manual employment started to disappear in Western nations—often replaced by lower-paying menial work—financial and service sector employment leaped ahead. The exchange and use of goods became much more complex. Goods were designed by companies in one country, manufactured in another, and tied into a broader interchange of cultures. Taken together, these global economic changes had deep political effects, forcing painful debates about the nature of citizenship and entitlement inside national borders, about the power and accountability of transnational corporations, and about the human and environmental costs of global capitalism.

Another crucial change involved not only the widespread flow of information but also the new commercial and cultural importance attached to information itself. Electronic systems and devices designed to create, store, and share information multiplied, becoming staggeringly more powerful and accessible—none with so great an impact on the everyday lives of men and women around the world as the personal computer. By the early 1990s, increasingly sophisticated computers brought people into instant communication with each other across continents, not only by new means but also in new cultural and political settings. Electronic communications over the Internet gave a compelling new meaning to the term *global village*. The Internet revolution shared features of earlier print revolutions. It was pioneered by entrepreneurs with utopian ambitions and driven by the new network's ability to deliver personal or commercial messages as well as culturally illicit and politically scandalous material that could be published easily and informally. It offered new possibilities to social and political groups, constituting new "publics." And it attracted large, established corporate interests, eager to cash in on new channels of culture and business.

However common their use seems, the Internet and similar technologies have had wide-ranging effects on political struggles around the globe. Embattled ethnic minorities have found worldwide audiences through online campaign sites. Satellite television arguably sped the sequence of popular revolts in Eastern Europe in 1989. That same year, fax machines brought Chinese demonstrators at Tiananmen Square news of international support for their efforts. Meanwhile, leaps forward in electronic technologies provided new worldwide platforms for commercial interests. Companies such as Sony, RCA, and others produced entertainment content, including music, motion pictures, and television shows as well as the electronic equipment to play that content. Bill Gates's Microsoft emerged as the world's major producer of computer software—with a corporate profit margin that surpassed Spain's gross domestic product. At the level of production, marketing, and management, information industries are global, spread widely across the United States, India, Western Europe, and parts of the developing world. Their corporate headquarters, however, typically remain in the West and support neoliberal politics. The international media, news, and entertainment conglomerates run by the Australian Rupert Murdoch or by Time Warner, for example, are firmly allied to U.S. institutions and worldviews, edging aside state-run companies.

Like the movement of money, goods, and ideas, the flow of labor has become a central aspect of globalization. Since 1945, the widespread migration of peoples, particularly between former colonies and imperial powers, has changed everyday life around the world. Groups of immigrant work-

AN AFGHAN GIRL WEEDS A POPPY FIELD, 2004. Though Afghanistan was historically a center for the silk trade, opium is its most important cash crop today. ▪ ***How is this development related to globalization?***

ers have filled the lower rungs of expanding economies not only in Europe but also in oil-rich Arab states that attracted Asian and Filipino laborers and in the United States, where both permanent and seasonal migrations from Mexico and other Latin American nations have spread across the continent. This fusion of peoples and cultures has produced striking new blends of music, food, language, and other forms of popular culture and sociability. These seem novel until we think of Creole cultures formed in the New World from the sixteenth to the eighteenth centuries. It has also raised tensions over the definition of citizenship and the boundaries of political and cultural communities—familiar themes from modern history. As a result, cycles of violent xenophobic backlash, bigotry, and political extremism have appeared in host countries and regions, but so too have new conceptions of civil rights and cultural belonging.

As suggested earlier, sharp divides exist between the most successful global players and the poorer, disadvantaged, sometimes embattled states and cultures. In one particular area of manufacture, however, poorer postcolonial regions have been able to respond to a steady and immensely profitable market in the West. The production of illegal drugs such as opium, heroin, and cocaine is a thriving industry in countries such as Colombia, Myanmar (formerly Burma), and Malaysia. Though the trade in such substances is banned, the fragile economies of the countries where they are produced have encouraged public and private powers to turn a blind eye to their production—or even to intervene for their own profit. Other, similar forms of illegal commerce have also grown far beyond the old label of "organized crime" in their structure and political importance. Trafficking in illegal immigrants, the management of corrupt financial dealings, trade in illicit animal products, and "conflict" diamonds from several brutal postcolonial civil wars are all indicative of this trend. The organizations behind these criminal trades grew out of the political violence and economic breakdown of failing postcolonial states or from the human and commercial traffic between these parts of the world and leading Western economic powers. They have exploited cracks, loopholes, and unsupervised opportunities in the less regulated system of global trade and carved out centers of power not directly subject to the laws of any single state.

Demographics and Global Health

The developments of globalization are tied in complex ways to the evolving size and health of the world's population. Between 1800 and the middle of the twentieth century, the worldwide population roughly tripled, rising from 1 to 3 billion. Between 1960 and 2012, however, population more than doubled again, to 7 billion. Huge, if uneven, improvements in basic standards of health, particularly for young children and childbearing women, contributed to the increase—as did local efforts to improve the urban-industrial environment. Asia's population as a whole has increased nearly fourfold since 1900, to nearly two-thirds of the world's present population. Such growth has strained underdeveloped social services, public-health facilities, and urban infrastructures, increasing the potential for epidemic disease as well as for cycles of ethnic and ideological violence nursed by poverty and dislocation.

A different type of demographic crisis confronts parts of the West, where steadily shrinking populations erode social welfare systems. Longer life spans, broadened welfare programs, and rising health-care costs have contributed to the challenge. Populations in the United States and Great Britain have been stable or have been slowly expanded by immigration; in Italy, Scandinavia, and, recently, Russia, sharp drops in the birth rate have led to population decline. Declining birth rates have been accompanied by growing populations of older adults, whose health and vitality resulted from decades of improved medical standards and state-run entitlement programs. Maintaining the long-term solvency of such programs poses difficult choices for European countries in particular, as they struggle to balance guarantees of social well-being with fiscal and political realities.

GOVERNMENT EFFORTS TO CURTAIL THE SPREAD OF SEVERE ACUTE RESPIRATORY SYNDROME (SARS). In May 2003, migrant workers at a Beijing railway station line up to have their temperatures checked before boarding the trains.

Analyzing Primary Sources

José Bové, The World Is Not for Sale: Farmers against Junk Food *(2001)*

In 1999, José Bové, a sheep farmer from central France well known for his militancy, helped organize a group of activists from a local agricultural union in a demonstration against a local McDonald's restaurant. Bové claimed that McDonald's was a symbol of "economic imperialism" and his group's protest received much popular support from others in France after its action. Bové himself was imprisoned for three months after the affair and served another ten months in 2003 for destroying transgenic crops.

You've got to link McDonald's to the issue of hormone-treated meat. At our Congress in Vesoul in April 1999, we'd already raised the question of preparing ourselves for American retaliation against Europe's ban on the import of hormone-treated beef. In February 1998, the World Trade Organization had condemned the European Union's ban, and given it fifteen months to get its house back in order—that is to reopen its frontiers. This deadline had expired on 13 May 1999, so the American move came as no surprise. We had already envisaged linking the issue of hormones and McDonald's. What we had not foreseen, however, was that Roquefort, the main produce of the farmers in my area, would be included in the hundred or so products affected by a 100 per cent Customs surcharge on entering the States.

In Washington, the price of Roquefort shot up from $30 a kilo to $60, effectively prohibiting its sale. Around the same time, we found out that a McDonald's was being constructed in Millau. . . .

We sell 440 tonnes of cheese annually to the States, worth 30 million francs. Given that the cost of the milk is half the value of the Roquefort, the producers are losing 15 million francs; this represents 3 million litres of milk out of the 80 million used in the annual production of Roquefort. As a result, the professional association resorted to new measures: 10,000 pamphlets were printed and distributed across the region, including campsites and village fêtes. Posters were put up everywhere, and in Millau itself large banners proclaimed: "No to the US embargo on Roquefort." It was in the spirit of these activities that we decided, at a meeting of the SPLB, to pay a visit to McDonald's. . . .

The objective was to have a non-violent but symbolically forceful action, in broad daylight and with the largest possible participation. We wanted the authorities to be fully aware of what was going to happen, so we explained to the police in advance that the purpose of the rally was to dismantle the McDonald's. The police notified the regional govern-

Globalization has also changed public health and medicine, creating dangerous new threats as well as promising new treatments. Better and more comprehensive health care has generally accompanied other kinds of prosperity and has thus been more accessible in the West. In Africa, Latin America, and elsewhere, political chaos, imbalances of trade, and the practices of some large pharmaceutical companies have often resulted in shortages of medicine and a rickety medical infrastructure, making it difficult to combat deadly new waves of disease. Indeed, the worldwide risk of exposure to epidemic diseases is a new reality of globalization—a product of increased cultural interaction, exposure of new ecosystems to human development, and the speed of intercontinental transportation. By the 1970s, the acceleration of airplane travel led to fears that an epidemic would leapfrog the globe much faster than the pandemics of the Middle Ages. Such fears were confirmed by the worldwide spread of infection by HIV, whose final stage is AIDS, which first appeared at the end of the 1970s. As HIV-AIDS became a global health crisis—particularly in Africa, where the disease spread catastrophically—international organizations recognized the need for an early, swift, and comprehensive response to future outbreaks of disease. In 2003, the successful containment of an outbreak of severe acute respiratory syndrome (SARS) demonstrated the effectiveness of this planning.

Meanwhile, the work of multinational medical research firms continued to extend the ability to prement, and they called back to say they would ask the McDonald's manager to provide a billboard or something similar for us to demolish. This, he said, would allow for a symbolic protest. We replied that this idea was ludicrous, and that it remained our intention to dismantle the doors and windows of the building. The police deemed it unnecessary to mount a large presence. We asked them to make sure that the site would be clear of workers, and that no tools were left lying around.

It all happened as we'd envisaged. The only odd thing was the presence of some ten plainclothes police officers armed with cameras. The demo took place and people, including kids, began to dismantle the inside of the building, taking down partitions, some doors, fuseboxes, and some tiles from the roof—they were just nailed down, and came off very easily; in fact the whole building appeared to have been assembled from a kit. The structure was very flimsy. While some people started to repaint the roof of the restaurant, others began loading bits of the structure on to tractor trailers. One of the trailers was a grain carrier. As soon as the trailers were loaded, everyone left the site. Children clambered on the grain wagon and used wooden sticks to bang on the sides, and the whole lot proceeded in the direction of the prefecture, seat of the regional government.

As the procession wound its way through the town, the festive atmosphere was further heightened by the cheering of local people who had gathered to watch us go by. We unloaded everything in front of the prefecture. It was a beautiful day, everyone was having a good time, and many people ended up on the terraces of Millau's restaurants. . . .

We didn't want McDonald's to be seen as the prime target. It's merely a symbol of economic imperialism. Besides, we never called for a boycott of McDonald's. The journalists grasped that pretty quickly, and most of them latched on to the ideas behind the McDonald's symbol. Our political leaders, however, tried to talk up the anti-American element: some by playing the "typically" Gallic card, others by invoking "sovereignty" in a way that fuelled nationalism. This was the populist side of things: it's easy enough to rubbish America, to discard a problem as not being of direct concern to us, rather than to confront it. From this point of view, it was very easy for our leaders to support our actions.

Source: José Bové and François Dufour, *The World Is Not for Sale: Farmers against Junk Food* (London: 2001), pp. 3–13.

Questions for Analysis

1. Were Bové's motivations strictly economic? Was he simply protesting the surcharge on European goods entering the U.S. market?
2. What made McDonald's a tempting target for the French activists?
3. Is Bové anti-American? What precisely was the target of this protest? What did he think he was defending?

vent and treat disease. One of the most powerful tools in this endeavor was the development of genetic engineering, which stemmed from the monumental discovery of DNA in the 1950s. By the 1990s, several laboratories were engaged in the most ambitious medical research ever attempted: the mapping of the human genome—that is, the entire architecture of chromosomes and genes contained in basic human DNA. Through this process and alongside it, genetic engineers developed methods to alter the biology of living things. Infertile couples, for instance, could now conceive through out-of-body medical procedures. Genetic engineers developed—and patented—strains of mice and other laboratory animals that carried chemical markers, cells, even organs, of other species. By 1997, British researchers succeeded in producing a clone (an exact genetic copy) of a sheep. It is now possible to determine the genetic makeup of any individual human and measure their chances of developing many cancers or other life-threatening diseases and conditions. The rapidly developing field of epigenetics has been able to trace the effects of behaviors such as smoking through more than one generation, demonstrating that the choices made by a grandparent can affect the genes of their grandchildren. These developments raise provocative questions about the relationship between individual responsibility and public health, about how scientists should understand biological "defects" and diversions from genetic norms, and about the privacy of medical information. As a new form of knowledge in an age of global interconnection, genetic engineering leaped across the legal and moral boundaries of human societies. The question of who would govern these advances—nations, international bodies, or local cultural and religious communities—was opened to passionate debate. So were fresh arguments about where to draw lines between lifesaving intervention and cultural preference, between individual agency and biological determinism. Like past scientific investigations directed at humankind, genetics has raised fundamental questions about ethics, citizenship, and the measure of humanity.

Perhaps no issue raises thornier questions about the relationship among population, economic development, and public welfare than the matter of climate change. Climate scientists now largely agree that the average temperature of the planet is rising steadily as a result of increases in carbon dioxide in the atmosphere produced by the burning of fossil fuels. Every year of the twenty-first century has ranked among the fourteen hottest since records were first kept in 1880. Scientists now say that the evidence points to a pattern of global warming produced by human activity. The consequences of this warming are now thought to be substantial: a rise in sea levels as polar ice caps melt; an increase in the frequency of heat waves, droughts, rainfall intensity, coastal flooding; and possibly, increases in the frequency and severity of storms, tornados, and tropical cyclones.

Governments first sounded the alarm about climate change in the early 1990s, but it proved hard to establish a coordinated policy because individual nations worried about compromising their economic competitiveness. Energy producers and economic interests whose profits and growth depended on the burning of fossil fuels were resistant to pollution limits or requirements that they adopt expensive "clean" technologies. Few imagined that it would be easy to change the behavior of consumers in developed countries whose lifestyle depended on easy access to electric power produced by the burning of coal, manufactured goods from distant places, cheap air travel, and the automobile. Changing consumer habits, finding alternative energy sources and developing new technologies to remove carbon from the atmosphere may take years. Finding policy solutions is doubly difficult because those parts of the globe that are most closely associated with pollution caused by the burning of fossil fuels—industrialized societies in Europe and North America—are not necessarily those who will feel its effects the most acutely in the near term. Those impacted will be mainly poorer countries in the global south that have few resources to cope with the effects of climate change on their populations.

Since the 1990s, international efforts to coordinate a response to climate change focused on a UN-sponsored agreement known as the Kyoto Protocol, but the United States never joined the agreement. Current efforts are now focused on allowing market forces to generate incentives for reducing pollution through emissions trading. Under this "cap and trade" system, a central authority would allocate permits to pollute at a certain level (the "cap") and demand that industries hold the necessary permits to maintain their operations. Industries that managed to reduce their emissions could sell the permits that they did not need on the open market to other firms (the "trade"), thus generating incentives to reduce emissions on a global scale while simultaneously allowing for continued economic development. These hotly debated issues about climate change clearly illustrate the necessity of global thinking in the contemporary world.

AFTER EMPIRE: POSTCOLONIAL POLITICS IN THE GLOBAL ERA

Even after the superpower rivalry of the Cold War collapsed, another legacy of the postwar era continued to shape international relations into the twenty-first century. The so-called postcolonial relationships between former colonies and Western powers emerged from the decolonization struggles detailed in Chapter 27. Former colonies, as well as other nations that had fallen under the political and economic sway of imperial powers, gained formal independence at the least, along with new kinds of cultural and political authority. In other respects, however, very little changed for people in the former colonies. The very term *postcolonial* underlines the fact that colonialism's legacies endured even after independence. Within these regions, political communities new and old handled the legacies of empire and the postcolonial future in a variety of ways. In some cases the former colonizers or their local allies retained so much power that formal independence actually meant very little. In others, bloody independence struggles poisoned the political culture. The emergence of new states and new kinds of politics was sometimes propelled by economic goals, sometimes by the revival of cultural identities that preceded colonization, and in other cases by ethnic conflict. The results ranged from breakneck industrial success to ethnic slaughter, from democratization to new local models of absolutism. During the Cold War, these postcolonial regions were often the turf on which the superpower struggle was waged. They benefited from superpower patronage but also became the staging ground for proxy wars funded by the West in the fight against communism. Their various trajectories since 1989 point to the complex legacy of the imperial past in the post–Cold War world of globalization.

Emancipation and Ethnic Conflict in Africa

The legacies of colonialism weighed heavily on sub-Saharan Africa. Most of the continent's former colonies came into their independence after the Second World War with their basic infrastructures deteriorating after decades of imperial negligence. The Cold War decades brought scant improvement, as governments across the continent were plagued by both homegrown and externally imposed corruption, poverty, and civil war. In sub-Saharan Africa, two very different trends began to emerge around 1989, each shaped by a combination of the end of the Cold War and volatile local conditions.

The first trend can be seen in South Africa, where politics had revolved for decades around the brutal racial policies of apartheid, sponsored by the white minority government. The most prominent opponent of apartheid, Nelson Mandela, who led the African National Congress (ANC), had been imprisoned since 1962. Intense repression and violent conflict continued into the 1980s and reached a dangerous impasse by the end of the decade. Then the South African government chose a daring new tack: in early 1990, it released Mandela from prison. He resumed leadership of the ANC and turned the party toward a combination of renewed public demonstrations and plans for negotiation politics changed within the Afrikaner-dominated white regime as well when F. W. de Klerk succeeded P. W. Botha as prime minister. A pragmatist who feared civil war and national collapse over apartheid, de Klerk was well matched to Mandela. In March 1992, the two men began direct talks to establish majority rule. Legal and constitutional reforms followed, and in May 1994, during elections in which all South Africans took part, Nelson Mandela was chosen the country's first black president. Although many of his government's efforts to reform housing, the economy, and public health foundered, Mandela defused the climate of organized racial violence. He also gained and kept tremendous personal popularity among black and white South Africans alike as a living symbol of a new political culture.

NELSON MANDELA VOTES IN SOUTH AFRICA'S FIRST DEMOCRATIC ELECTIONS, 1994. He would be elected the country's president.

Mandela's popularity extended abroad, within sub-Saharan Africa and worldwide. In a number of smaller postcolonial states such as Benin, Malawi, and Mozambique, the early 1990s brought political reforms that ended one-party or one-man rule in favor of parliamentary democracy and economic reform.

The other major trend ran in a different, less encouraging direction. Some former autocracies gave way to calls for pluralism, but other states across the continent collapsed into ruthless ethnic conflict. In Rwanda, a former Belgian colony, conflicts between the Hutu and Tutsi populations erupted into a highly organized campaign of genocide against the Tutsi after the country's president was assassinated. Carried out by ordinary Hutus of all backgrounds, the ethnic slaughter left over 800,000 Tutsi dead in a matter of weeks. International pressure eventually turned local Rwandan politics against the perpetrators. Many of them fled to neighboring Zaire and became hired mercenaries in the many-sided civil war that followed the collapse of

Mobutu Sese Seko, the country's long-time dictator, infamous for diverting billions of dollars in foreign aid into his personal bank accounts. A number of ambitious neighboring countries intervened in Zaire, hoping not only to secure its valuable resources but also to settle conflicts with their own ethnic minorities that spilled over the border. Fighting continued through the late 1990s into the new century, dubbed "Africa's world war" by many observers. Public services, normal trade, even basic health and safety inside Zaire—renamed the Democratic Republic of Congo by an ineffective government in Kinshasa—collapsed. By 2008, 5.4 million people had died in the war and its aftermath, the equivalent of losing the entire population of Denmark in a single decade. As of 2013, the fighting remained unresolved.

Economic Power on the Pacific Rim

By the end of the twentieth century, East Asia had become a center of industrial and manufacturing production. China, whose communist government began to establish commercial ties with the West in the 1970s, was the world's leading heavy industrial producer by the year 2000. Its state-owned companies acquired contracts from Western firms to produce products cheaply and in bulk, for sale back to home markets in the United States and Europe. In a deliberate reversal of Europe's nineteenth-century intrusions on the China trade, Beijing established semicapitalist commercial zones around major port cities like Shanghai, a policy whose centerpiece was the reclamation of Hong Kong from Britain in 1997. The commercial zones were intended to encourage massive foreign investment on terms that left China a favorable balance of trade for its huge volume of cheap exports. In practice, they enjoyed only mixed success. Downturns in farming and a looming energy crisis hampered prosperity and economic growth inland, but Hong Kong worked to maintain its economic and cultural middle ground with the rest of the world as it had since the days of the opium trade (see Chapter 22).

Other Asian nations emerged as global commercial powers as well. Industry flourished in a string of countries, starting with Japan and extending along Asia's Pacific coastline into Southeast Asia and Oceania, during the decades after the Second World War. By the 1980s, their robust industrial expansion and their apparent staying power earned them the collective nickname of "the tigers," taken from the ambitious, forward-looking tiger in Chinese mythology. These Pacific rim states collectively formed the most important industrial region in the world outside the United States and Europe. Among them, Japan not only led the way but also became the most influential model of success, with a postwar revival that eventually surpassed West Germany's economic miracle (see Chapter 28). Japanese firms concentrated on the efficiency and technical reliability of their products: fuel-efficient cars, specialty steel, small electronic goods, and so on. Japanese diplomacy and large state subsidies supported the success of Japanese firms, while a well-funded program of technical education hastened research and development of new goods. Japanese firms also appeared to benefit from collective loyalty among civil servants and corporate managers, attitudes that were encouraged by Japan's long experience of trade guilds and feudal politics. Other East Asian nations, newer or less stable than Japan, tried to mimic its success. Some, such as South Korea and the Chinese Nationalist stronghold of Taiwan, treated the creation of prosperity as a fundamental patriotic duty. In postcolonial nations such as Malaysia and Indonesia, governments parlayed their natural resources and expansive local labor

INDUSTRIALIZATION IN CHINA, 2002. The Three Gorges Dam on the Yan River in Yichang is the largest hydroelectric dam in the world. It has been called the largest construction project in China since the Great Wall.

pools (which had made them attractive to imperial powers in earlier times) into investment for industrialization. As in China, the factories that emerged were either subsidiaries of Western companies or operated on their behalf in new multinational versions of the putting-out system of early industrialization.

The Pacific rim's boom, however, also contained the makings of a first "bust." During the 1990s, a confluence of factors resulted in an enormous slowdown of growth and the near collapse of several currencies. Japan experienced rising production costs, overvalued stocks, and rampant speculation on its high-priced real estate market. When the bubble economy burst in 1991, Japan entered a "lost decade" of economic stagnation that hit bottom in 2003. In Southeast Asia, states such as Indonesia found they had to pay the difference on overvalued industrial capital to Western lenders who set rigid debt repayment schedules. Responses to the economic downturn varied widely. In South Korea, an older generation that remembered economic catastrophe after the Korean War responded to national calls for sacrifice, frequently by investing their own savings to prop up ailing companies. Japan launched programs of monetary austerity to cope with its first serious spike in unemployment in two generations. In Indonesia, inflation and unemployment reignited sharp ethnic conflicts that prosperity and violent state repression had dampened in earlier times. This predominantly Muslim country, with a long tradition of tolerance and pluralism inside the faith, also saw outbursts of violent religious fundamentalism popularly associated with another region—the Middle East.

A NEW CENTER OF GRAVITY: ISRAEL, OIL, AND POLITICAL ISLAM IN THE MIDDLE EAST

Perhaps no other region has drawn more attention from the West in the age of globalization than the Middle East, where a volatile combination of Western military, political, and economic interests converged with deep-seated regional conflicts and transnational Islamic politics. The results of this ongoing confrontation promise to shape the twenty-first century. Here we consider three of the most important aspects of recent history in the region. First is the unfolding of the Arab-Israeli conflict. Second is the region's vital development as the global center of oil production. The third emerges from inside the Arab world, largely as a reaction against the recent relations with the West. This is the development of a specific, modern brand of Islamic radicalism that challenges the legacies of imperialism and promises revolutionary and sometimes apocalyptic change in postcolonial nations and whose most violent elements generate a cycle of fear, anger, and ultimately direct conflict with Western governments.

The Arab-Israeli Conflict

As we saw in Chapter 27, Israel's existence was a battleground from the start. The national aspirations of Jewish immigrants from Europe fleeing the Holocaust and violent postwar anti-Semitism clashed with the motives of pan-Arabists—secular, anticolonial nationalists who urged Arab pride and self-reliance against European domination. By the late 1970s, in the aftermath of two Arab-Israeli wars, it appeared that a generation of fighting might come to an end. American mediators began sponsoring talks to prevent further, sudden outbursts of conflict, while Soviet leaders remained neutral but supportive of peace efforts. Most notably, the Egyptian president Anwar Sadat, who authorized and directed the 1973 war against Israel, decided that coexistence rather than the destruction of Israel was the long-term answer to regional conflict. Aided by the American president Jimmy Carter, Sadat brokered a peace between Egypt and Israel's staunchly conservative leader, Menachem Begin, in 1978. Leaders on both sides of the conflict believed the potential rewards were greater than the obvious risks.

Hopes for a lasting peace were soon dashed. Hostilities escalated between Israel and the Palestinian Arabs displaced by Arab-Israeli warfare, a confrontation that increasingly polarized a much larger group of people. On each side of the Israeli-Palestinian conflict, a potent blend of ethnic and religious nationalism began to control both debate and action. Conservatives in Israel played to a public sentiment that put security ahead of other priorities, particularly among the most recent Jewish immigrants, often from the former Soviet Union. On the other side, younger Palestinians, angered by their elders' failures to provoke revolution, turned against the secular radicalism of the Palestinian Liberation Organization (PLO) and toward radical Islam.

In this combustible political environment, the Palestinians living on the West Bank and in the desperately overcrowded Gaza Strip revolted in an outburst of street rioting in 1987. This rebellion—called the *intifada* (literally, a "throwing off" or uprising)—continued for years in daily battles between stone-throwing Palestinian youths

Interpreting Visual Evidence

Media Representations of Globalization

Because the set of historical developments collectively known as *globalization* are so complex and because the local effects of these developments have often been felt as disruptions of well-entrenched habits or ways of life, debates about globalization are particularly open to manipulation through the presentation of charged imagery. Since the end of the Cold War, provocative images that capture certain aspects of the world's new interconnectedness—and the accompanying need for new kinds of boundaries—have become ubiquitous in the media. The movement of peoples and goods are variously defined as necessary to maintain standards of living or a threat to local jobs and local production. Globalization is defended as good for the economy, good for the consumer, and good for competition, but it is also blamed for hurting workers, destroying local cultures, and eroding long-standing definitions of national identity.

The images here all illustrate essential aspects of globalization. Image A shows ships waiting for loading and unloading at one of the largest container terminals in the world, in Hong Kong. Most of the shipping from China comes through this terminal. Image B shows family members separated by the border fence between the United States and Mexico in Mexicali, Mexico. In the twentieth century, Mexicali grew to be a city of 1.5 million people, in large part on the

A. Cargo ships in Kowloon Bay, 2002.

and armed Israeli security forces. The street fights escalated into cycles of Palestinian terrorism, particularly suicide bombings of civilian targets, and reprisals from the Israeli military. International efforts to broker a peace produced the Oslo Accords of 1993, which established an autonomous Palestinian Authority led by the PLO chief, Yasser Arafat. Yet the peace was always fragile at best—suffering perhaps fatal damage from the assassination of Israel's reformist prime minister Yitzhak Rabin in 1995 by a reactionary Israeli and from continued attacks by Islamist terrorists. By the turn of the twenty-first century the cycle of violence flared again, with a "second intifada" launched by Palestinians in late 2000. In the first decade of the twenty-first century, the Israeli-Palestinian conflict has remained without a solution. The second intifada came to an end after Arafat's death in 2004 and the election of Mahmoud Abbas as the president of the Palestinian Authority in 2005. The electoral victory of a more militant Palestinian organization, Hamas, in the Palestinian parliamentary elections of 2006, however, limited Abbas's power to negotiate with Israel. Meanwhile, continued attacks on Israeli civilians by Hamas—labeled a terrorist organization by the United States and the European Union—led to an Israeli military operation against Palestinians in the Gaza strip that produced at least a three-year suspension of major hostilities along the frontier. In 2013, the UN

B. Mexican family members talk through border fence, 2003.

C. Filipino protester on Labor Day, 2003.

prosperity generated by sending field workers across the border to the United States. Image C shows a Labor Day protester in Manila, Philippines, at a demonstration in which globalization was blamed for amendments to the labor code favorable to employers, a ban on strikes, and antiterrorist measures that were perceived to be an infringement of personal liberties. The medical mask is a reference to the SARS epidemic.

Questions for Analysis

1. Image A is typical of images that emphasize the economic consequences of globalization. Does globalization appear to be a force subject to human control in this image? How do such images shape perceptions of China's place in the global economy?
2. Compare images A and B. Is there a connection between the accelerating flows of money and goods between different parts of the world and restrictions on the movements of people?
3. In image C, the woman's medical mask names globalization as the enemy of Filipino workers. In so doing, who is being targeted? What does this say about the local contest over the conditions of labor in the Philippines?

General Assembly recognized the state of Palestine and granted it nonmember observer status, but a solution to the crisis is still not in sight.

Oil, Power, and Economics

The struggles between the state of Israel and its neighbors have been important in their own right. Yet one of the most compelling reasons that this conflict mattered to outside powers was material: oil. The global demand for oil skyrocketed during the postwar era and has accelerated since. Starting with the consumer boom in the Cold War West, ordinary citizens bought cars and other petroleum-powered consumer durables, while industrial plastics made from petroleum by-products were used to manufacture a wealth of basic household items. Those needs, and the desires for profit and power that went with them, drew Western corporations and governments steadily toward the oil-rich states of the Middle East, whose vast reserves were discovered in the 1930s and 1940s. Large corporations conducted joint diplomacy with Middle Eastern states and their own home governments to design concessions for drilling, refining, and shipping the oil. Pipelines were laid by contractors based around the world, from California to Rome to Russia.

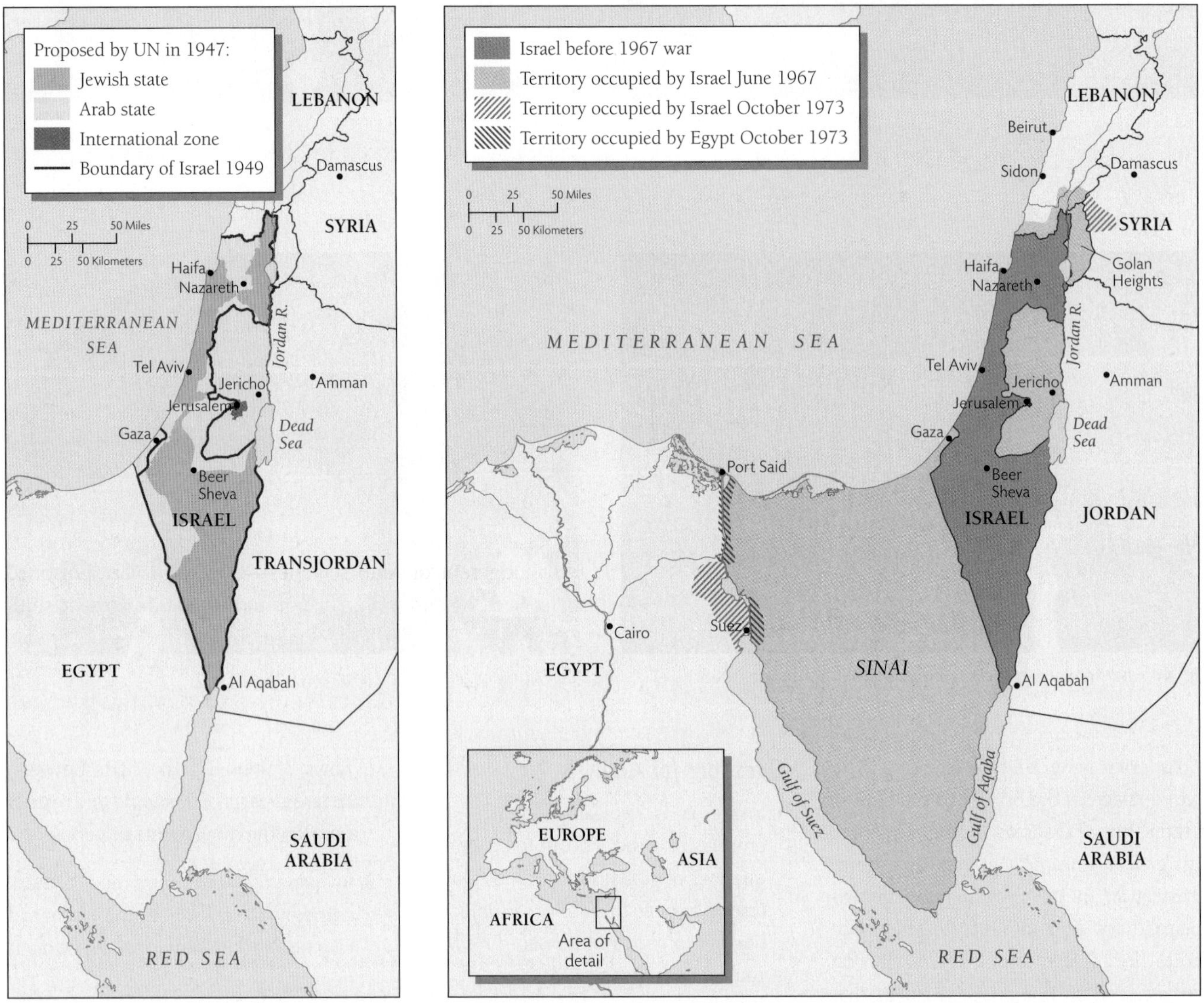

THE ARAB-ISRAELI WARS OF 1967 AND 1973. ▪ ***What were the major changes in the political geography of the Middle East as a result of the Arab-Israeli conflict of 1967?*** ▪ ***Why did the Israelis wish to occupy the Sinai and West Bank regions at the end of the 1967 war?*** ▪ ***What problems did this create, and how might it have led to the conflict in 1973?***

The enormous long-term economic value of the Middle Eastern oil reserves made oil a fundamental tool in new struggles over political power. Many producer states sought to turn their resources into leverage with the West's former imperial powers. In 1960, the leading Middle Eastern, African, and Latin American producers banded together in a cartel to take advantage of this vital resource, forming the Organization of the Petroleum Exporting Countries (OPEC) to regulate the production and pricing of crude oil. During the 1970s, OPEC played a leading role in the global economy. Its policies reflected not only the desire to draw maximum profits out of bottlenecks in oil production but also the militant politics of some OPEC leaders who wanted to use oil as a weapon against the West in the Arab-Israeli conflict. After the 1973 Arab-Israeli war, an embargo inspired by the hard-liners sparked spiraling inflation and economic troubles in Western nations, triggering a cycle of dangerous recession that lasted nearly a decade.

In response, Western governments treated the Middle Eastern oil regions as a vital strategic center of gravity, the subject of constant Great Power diplomacy. If conflict directly threatened the stability of oil production or friendly governments, Western powers were prepared to intervene by force, as the 1991 Gulf War demonstrated. By the 1990s, another new front of competition and potential conflict emerged as the energy demands of other nations also grew. In particular, the new industrial giants China and India eyed the Middle

GAMAL ABDEL NASSER AND SOVIET MINISTER ALEKSEY KOSYGIN, 1966. As the most prominent spokesman for secular pan-Arabism, Nasser became a target for Islamist critics, such as Sayyid Qutb and the Muslim Brotherhood, angered by the Western-influenced policies of his regime.

Eastern oil reserves with the same nervousness as the West. The oil boom also generated violent conflict inside Middle Eastern producer states. Oil revenue produced an uneven form of economic development. The huge gaps between or inside Middle Eastern societies that divided oil's haves and have-nots caused deep resentments, official corruption, and a new wave of radical politics. With the pan-Arab nationalists fading from the scene, the rising revolutionary force gathered instead around modern readings of Islamic fundamentalism, now tied to postcolonial politics.

The Rise of Political Islam

In North Africa and the Middle East, processes of modernization and globalization produced tremendous discontents. The new nations that emerged from decolonization often shared the characteristics of the "kleptocracies" south of the Sahara: corrupt state agencies, cronyism based on ethnic or family kinship, decaying public services, rapid increases in population, and constant state repression of dissent. Disappointment with these conditions ran deep, perhaps nowhere more so than in the seat of pan-Arabism, Nasser's Egypt. During the 1960s, Egyptian academics and cultural critics leveled charges against Nasser's regime that became the core of a powerful new political movement. Their critique offered modern interpretations of certain legal and political currents in Islamic thought, ideas linked loosely across centuries by their association with revolt against foreign interference and official corruption. They denounced Egypt's nationalist government as greedy, brutal, and corrupt.

There was a twist to their claims, however: that the roots of the Arab world's moral failure lay in centuries of colonial contact with the West. The most influential of these Islamist critics, Sayyid Qutb (*Kutb*, 1906–1966), presented these ideas in a series of essays for which he was arrested several times by Egyptian authorities and ultimately executed. His argument ran as follows. As a result of corrupting outside influences, the ruling elites of the new Arab states pursued policies that frayed local and family bonds, deepening economic divides while abandoning the government's responsibility for charity and stability. What was more, the nation's elites were morally bankrupt—their lives defied codes of morality, self-discipline, and communal responsibility rooted in Islamic faith. To maintain power, the elites lived in the pockets of Western imperial and corporate powers. From Qutb's point of view, this collaboration not only caused cultural impurity but also eroded authentic Muslim faith. This dire judgment of Arab societies—that they were poisoned from without and within—required an equally drastic solution. Arab societies should reject not only oppressive postcolonial governments but also all the political and cultural ideas that traveled with them, especially those that could be labeled "Western." After popular revolts, the Arab autocracies would be replaced by an idealized form of conservative Islamic government—a system in which a rigid form of Islam would link law, government, and culture.

In a formula familiar to historians of European politics throughout the nineteenth and twentieth centuries, this particular brand of Islamist politics combined popular anger, intellectual opposition to "foreign" influences, and a highly idealized vision of the past. By the 1970s, it began to express itself openly in regional politics. Qutb's ideas were put into practice by Egypt's Muslim Brotherhood, a secretive but widespread society rooted in anticolonial politics, local charity, and violently fundamentalist Islam. The same ideas spread among similar organizations in other urbanized Arab countries and leading Islamic universities, which were historically centers of debate about political theory and religious law. Radical Islam emerged as a driving force in criticism and defiance of autocratic Arab regimes. Secular critics and more liberal Islamists, who called for open elections and a free press, were more fragmented and thus easier to silence, whereas the new wave of fundamentalists gained concessions that allowed them to preach and publish in public as long as they did not launch actual revolts. Despite the movement's steady rise, the most dramatic turn still managed to surprise observers. Like Protestantism's emergence in the fractious German states, for example, or communism's successful revolution in Russia, radical Islam's defining moment as a political force came in an unexpected place: Iran.

IRAN'S ISLAMIC REVOLUTION

Iran offered one of the most dramatic examples of modernization gone sour in the Middle East. Despite tremendous economic growth in the 1960s and 1970s, Iranians labored with legacies of foreign intervention and corrupt rule at the hands of the shah, Reza Pahlavi, a Western-friendly leader installed during a 1953 military coup supported by Britain and the United States. In exchange for the shah's role as a friend to the West during the Cold War and for providing a steady source of reasonably priced oil, the Iranian government received vast sums in oil contracts, weapons, and development aid. Thousands of Westerners, especially Americans, came to Iran, introducing foreign influences that not only challenged traditional values but also offered economic and political alternatives. The shah, however, kept these alternatives out of reach, consistently denying democratic representation to westernizing middle-class Iranian workers and deeply religious university students alike. He governed through a small aristocracy divided by constant infighting. His army and secret police conducted regular and brutal campaigns of repression. Despite all this, and the public protests it spurred in the West, governments such as the conservative Nixon administration embraced the shah as a strategically vital ally: a key to anti-Soviet alliances and a safe source of oil.

Twenty-five years after the 1953 coup, the shah's autocratic route to an industrial state ended. After a lengthy economic downturn, public unrest, and personal illness, the shah realized he could not continue in power. He retired from public life under popular pressure in February 1979. Eight months of uncertainty followed, most Westerners fled the country, and the provisional government appointed by the shah collapsed. The strongest political coalition among Iran's revolutionaries surged into the vacuum—a broad Islamic movement centered on the ayatollah Ruhollah Khomeini (1902–1989), Iran's senior cleric and theologian, returned from exile in France. Other senior clerics and the country's large population of unemployed, deeply religious university

THE SHAH'S DOWNFALL. Two Iranians symbolically substitute a picture of the shah with one of the ayatollah Khomeini after the Iranian revolution, 1979. ▪ ***What did the Iranian revolutionaries who overthrew the shah have in common with the anti-colonial nationalists in other former European colonies?***

POPULAR SUPPORT FOR IRAN'S ISLAMIC REVOLUTION. A massive crowd awaits the ayatollah Khomeini after the Iranian Revolution, 1979.

students provided the movement's energy. Disenfranchised secular protesters joined the radical Islamists in condemning decades of Western indifference and the shah's oppression. Under the new regime, some limited economic and political populism combined with strict constructions of Islamic law, restrictions on women's public life, and the prohibition of many ideas or activities linked to Western influence.

The new Iranian government also defined itself against its enemies: against the Sunni religious establishment of neighboring states, against "atheistic" Soviet communism, but especially against Israel and the United States. Iranians feared the United States would try to overthrow Khomeini as it had other leaders. Violence in the streets of Tehran reached a peak when militant students stormed the American embassy in November 1979 and seized fifty-two hostages. The act quickly became an international crisis that heralded a new kind of confrontation between Western powers and postcolonial Islamic radicals. Democratic president Jimmy Carter's administration ultimately gained the hostages' release, but not before the catalog of earlier failures led to the election of the Republican Ronald Reagan.

Iran, Iraq, and Unintended Consequences of the Cold War

Iran's victory in the hostage crisis was fleeting. During the later part of 1980, Iran's Arab neighbor and traditional rival Iraq invaded, hoping to seize Iran's southern oil fields during the revolutionary confusion. Iran counterattacked. The result was a murderous eight-year conflict marked by the use of chemical weapons and human waves of young Iranian radicals fighting the Soviet-armed Iraqis. The war ended with Iran's defeat but not with the collapse of its theocratic regime. In the short term, their long defense of Iranian nationalism left the clerics more entrenched at home, while abroad they used oil revenues to back grass-roots radicals in Lebanon and elsewhere who engaged in anti-Western terrorism. The strongest threats to the Iranian regime ultimately came from within, from a new generation of young students and disenfranchised service workers who found their prospects for prosperity and active citizenship had not changed much since the days of the shah.

The Iran-Iraq conflict created another problem for Western interests and the governments of leading OPEC states: Iraq. Various governments—including an unlikely alliance of France, Saudi Arabia, the Soviet Union, and the United States—supported Iraq during the war in an effort to bring down Iran's clerics. Their patronage went to one of the most violent governments in the region, Saddam Hussein's dictatorship. Iraq exhausted itself in the war, politically and economically. To shore up his regime and restore Iraq's influence, Hussein looked elsewhere in the region. In 1990, Iraq invaded its small, oil-rich neighbor Kuwait. With the Cold War on the wane, Iraq's Soviet supporters would not condone Iraqi aggression. A number of Western nations led by the United States reacted forcefully. Within months, Iraq faced the full weight of the United States military—trained intensively since Vietnam to rout much more capable Soviet-armed forces than Iraq's—along with forces from several OPEC states, French troops, and armored divisions from Britain, Egypt, and Syria. This coalition pummeled Iraqi troops from the air for six weeks, then routed them and retook Kuwait in a brief, well-executed ground campaign. This changed the tenor of relations between the United States and Arab oil producers, encouraging not only closeness between governments but also anti-American radicals angry at a new Western presence. It was also the beginning rather than the end of a Western confrontation with Iraq, centered on Hussein's efforts to develop nuclear and biological weapons.

Elsewhere in the region, the proxy conflicts of the Cold War snared both superpowers in the new and growing networks of Islamic radicalism. In 1979, the socialist government of Afghanistan turned against its Soviet patrons. Fearing a result like Iran, with a spread of fundamentalism into the Muslim regions of Soviet Central Asia, Moscow responded by overthrowing the Afghan president and installing a pro-Soviet faction. The new government, backed by more than 100,000 Soviet troops, found itself immediately at war with fighters who combined local

THE IRAN-IRAQ WAR. Iranian guards keep watch over Iraqi prisoners.

Competing Viewpoints

The Place of Islam in Modern Societies

The end of the colonial era and the impact of postcolonial migrations provided the backdrop for a renewed discussion in Europe and the Middle East about the presence of Muslim peoples in European nations and the relationship of religion to politics in traditionally Muslim societies. Among Muslim scholars and clerics, a wide range of opinions have been expressed about the place of Islam in the modern world, and the two figures here represent two distinct voices within this discussion.

Born into a family of Shi'ite Muslim religious leaders, Ruhollah Khomeini (c. 1900–1989) was recognized as the leading Iranian religious authority in the 1950s. He represented a highly conservative Islamic fundamentalism intended to unite Iranian Muslims in violent opposition to the Western-supported government of the shah of Iran and had a powerful influence on Muslims seeking an alternative to Western cultural, political, and economic domination.

Tariq Ramadan (born 1962 in Geneva, Switzerland) is a professor of religion and philosophy and a leading voice speaking for the increasingly large number of Muslims who live in Europe and North America as members of a religious minority in non-Muslim societies. He has taught at the University of Fribourg, the College de Saussure in Geneva, and St. Antony's College, Oxford. In 2004, he was forced to decline an offer to become a professor at the University of Notre Dame in the United States when the State Department denied him a visa. Ramadan argues that Muslims can and should be productive and active citizens in Western societies while remaining true to their religious beliefs.

Ruhollah Khomeini, Islamic Government (1979)

The Islamic government is not similar to the well-known systems of government. It is not a despotic government in which the head of state dictates his opinion and tampers with the lives and property of the people. The prophet, may God's prayers be upon him, and 'Ali, the amir of the faithful, and the other imams had no power to tamper with people's property or with their lives.[1] The Islamic government is not despotic but constitutional. However, it is not constitutional in the well-known sense of the word, which is represented in the parliamentary system or in the people's councils. It is constitutional in the sense that those in charge of affairs observe a number of conditions and rules underlined in the Koran and in the Sunna and represented in the necessity of observing the system and of applying the dictates and laws of Islam.[2] This is why the Islamic government is the government of the divine law. The difference between the Islamic government and the constitutional governments, both monarchic and republican, lies in the fact that the people's representatives or the king's representatives are the ones who codify and legislate, whereas the power of legislation is confined to God, may He be praised, and nobody else has the right to legislate and nobody may rule by that which has not been given power by God. . . .

The government of Islam is not monarchic, . . . and not an empire, because Islam is above squandering and unjustly undermining the lives and property of people. This is why the government of Islam does not have the many big palaces, the servants, the royal courts, the crown prince courts and other trivial requirements that consume half or most of the country's resources and that the sultans and the emperors have. The life of the great prophet was a life of utter simplicity, even though the prophet was the head of the state, who ran and ruled it by himself. . . . Had this course continued until the present, people would have known the taste of happiness and the country's treasury would not have been plundered to be spent on fornication, abomination and the court's costs and expenditures. You know that most of the corrupt aspects of our society are due to the corruption of the ruling dynasty and the royal family. What is the legitimacy of these rulers who build houses of entertainment, corruption, fornication and abomination and who destroy houses which God ordered be raised and in which His name is mentioned? Were it not for what the court wastes and what it embezzles, the country's budget would not experience any deficit that forces the state to borrow from America and England, with all the humiliation and insult that accompany such borrowing. Has our oil decreased or have our minerals that are stored under this good earth run out? We possess everything and we would not need the help of America or of others if it were not for the costs of the court and for its wasteful use of the people's money.

[1] "The prophet" refers to Muhammed; 'Ali was Muhammed's son-in-law and, according to the Shi'ite tradition, his legitimate heir; an amir is a high military official; and an imam, in the Shi'ite tradition, is an important spiritual leader with sole power to make decisions about doctrine.

[2] The Koran is the book of the holy scriptures of Islam; the Sunna is the body of customary Islamic law second only to the Koran in authority.

Source: Ruhollah Khomeini, *Islamic Government*, trans. Joint Publications Research Service (New York: 1979, pp. 17–19.

Tariq Ramadan, Western Muslims and the Future of Islam *(2002)*

. . . [W]ith the emergence of the young Muslim generation . . . it has been deemed necessary to reanalyze the main Islamic sources (Qu'ran and Sunnah) when it comes to interpreting legal issues (*fiqh*) in the European context. Many of these young people intend to stay permanently in a European country, and a large number have already received their citizenship. New forms of interpretation (known as *ijtihad*) have made it possible for the younger generation to practice their faith in a coherent manner in a new context. It is important to note that this has been a very recent phenomenon. Only within the past few years have Muslim scholars and intellectuals felt obliged to take a closer look at the European laws, and at the same time, to think about the changes that have been taking place within the diverse Muslim communities . . . [F]ive main points . . . have been agreed upon by those working on the basis of the Islamic sources and by the great majority of Muslims living in Europe:

1. Muslims who are residents or citizens of a non-Islamic state should understand that they are under a moral and social contract with the country in which they reside. In other words, they should respect the laws of the country.
2. Both the spirit and the letter of the secular model permit Muslims to practice their faith without requiring a complete assimilation into the new culture and, thereby, partial disconnection from their Muslim identity.
3. The ancient division of the world into denominations of *dar al-harb* (abode of war) and *dar al-Islam* (abode of Islam), used by the jurists during a specific geopolitical context, namely the ninth-century Muslim world, is invalid and does not take into account the realities of modern life. Other concepts have been identified as exemplifying more positively the presence of Muslims in Europe.
4. Muslims should consider themselves full citizens of the nations in which they reside and can participate with conscience in the organizational, economic, and political affairs of the country without compromising their own values.
5. With regard to the possibilities offered by European legislation, nothing stops Muslims, like any other citizens, from making choices that respond to the requirements of their own consciences and faith. If any obligations should be in contradiction to the Islamic principles (a situation that is quite rare), the specific case must be studied in order to identify the priorities and the possibility of adaptation (which should be developed at the national level). . . .

For some Muslims, the idea of an "Islamic culture," similar to the concepts of identity and community, connotes the necessity of Muslim isolation from and rejection of European culture. Such an understanding suggests that Muslims are not genuine in their desire to integrate into the society in which they live. They play the citizenship card, while trying to maintain such cultural particularities as dress code, management of space when it comes to men and women, concern about music, and other issues. For them, real integration means becoming European in every aspect of one's character and behavior. This is, in fact, a very narrow vision of integration, almost resembling the notion of assimilation. One admits theoretically that Muslims have the right to practice their religion but revokes these rights when expression of faith becomes too *visible*.

In actuality, the future of Muslim presence in Europe must entail a truly "European Islamic culture" disengaged from the cultures of North Africa, Turkey, and Indo-Pakistan, while naturally referring to them for inspiration. This new culture is just in the process of being born and molded. By giving careful consideration to everything from appropriate dress to the artistic and creative expression of Islam, Muslims are mobilizing a whole new culture. The formation of such a culture is a pioneering endeavor, making use of European energy while taking into account various national customs and simultaneously respecting Islamic values and guidelines.

Source: Tariq Ramadan, "Islam and Muslims in Europe: A Silent Revolution toward Rediscovery," in *Muslims in the West: From Sojourners to Citizens*, ed. Yvonne Yazbeck Haddad (New York: 2002), pp. 160–163.

Questions for Analysis

1. What prevents Islamic government from being despotic, according to Khomeini? Why is there no legislative branch in an Islamic government, in his view?
2. What criticism does Ramadan make of those Muslims who seek to isolate themselves from European culture while living in Europe? What does he mean by "European Islamic culture"?
3. In what ways do these two Muslim thinkers show an engagement with European traditions of political thought?

THE LIBERATION OF KUWAIT. After American forces drove out his Iraqi occupiers, a Kuwaiti celebrates with the victory sign, 1991. Behind him, a defaced poster of Saddam Hussein sits in a garbage heap.

conservatism with militant Islam and who attracted volunteers from radical Islamic movements in Egypt, Lebanon, Saudi Arabia, and elsewhere. These fighters, who called themselves *mujahidin*, viewed the conflict as a holy war. The mujahidin benefited from advanced weapons and training, given by Western powers led by the United States. Those who provided the aid saw the conflict in Cold War terms, as a chance to sap Soviet resources in a fruitless imperial war. On those terms, the aid worked; the war dragged on for nearly ten years, taking thousands of Russian lives and damaging the Soviet government's credibility at home. Soviet troops withdrew in 1989. After five years of clan warfare, hard-line Islamic factions tied to the foreign elements in the mujahidin took over the country. Their experiment in theocracy made Iran's seem mild by comparison.

VIOLENCE BEYOND BOUNDS: WAR AND TERRORISM IN THE TWENTY-FIRST CENTURY

The global networks of communication, finance, and mobility discussed at the beginning of this chapter gave radical political violence a disturbing new character at the end of the twentieth century. In the 1960s, organized sectarian terrorist tactics had become an important part of political conflict in the Middle East, Europe, and Latin America. Most of these early terrorist organizations (including the Irish Republican Army, the Italian Red Brigades, and the different Palestinian revolutionary organizations) had specific goals, such as ethnic separatism or the establishment of revolutionary governments. By the 1980s and increasingly during the 1990s, such groups were complemented and then supplanted by a different brand of terrorist organization, one that ranged freely across territory and local legal systems. These newer, apocalyptic terrorist groups called for decisive conflict to eliminate their enemies and grant themselves martyrdom. Some such groups emerged from the social dislocations of the postwar boom, others were linked directly to brands of radical religion. They often divorced themselves from the local crises that first spurred their anger, roaming widely among countries in search of recruits to their cause.

A leading example of such groups, and soon the most famous, was the radical Islamist umbrella organization al Qaeda. It was created by leaders of the foreign mujahidin who had fought against the Soviet Union in Afghanistan. Its official leader and financial supporter was the Saudi-born multimillionaire Osama bin Laden. Among its operational chiefs was the famous Egyptian radical Ayman al-Zawahiri, whose political career linked him directly to Sayyid Qutb and other founding thinkers in modern revolutionary Islam. These leaders organized broad networks of largely self-contained terrorist cells around the world, from the Islamic regions of Southeast Asia to Europe, East Africa, and the United States, funded by myriad private accounts, front companies, illegal trades, and corporate kickbacks throughout the global economy. Their organization defied borders, and so did their goals. They did not seek to negotiate for territory, or to change the government of a specific state. Instead, they spoke of the destruction of the state of Israel and American, European, and other non-Islamic systems of government worldwide and called for a united, apocalyptic revolt by fundamentalist Muslims to create an Islamic community bounded only by faith. During the 1990s, they involved themselves in a variety of local terrorist campaigns in Islamic countries and organized large-scale suicide attacks against American targets, notably the American embassies in Kenya and Tanzania in 1998.

At the beginning of the twenty-first century, al Qaeda's organizers struck again at their most obvious political enemy, the symbolic seat of globalization: the United States. Small teams of suicidal radicals, aided by al Qaeda's organization, planned to hijack airliners and use them as flying bombs to strike the most strategically important symbols of America's global power. On September 11, 2001, they carried out this mission in the deadliest series of terrorist attacks ever to occur on American soil. In the span of an hour, hijacked planes struck the Pentagon, the headquarters of the U.S. military, and the World Trade Center towers in New York City. A fourth plane, possibly aimed at the U.S. Capitol, crashed in open farmland in Pennsylvania, its attack thwarted when the passengers fought back against their captors. The World Trade Center towers, among the tallest buildings in the world, crumbled into ash and wreckage in front of hundreds of millions of viewers on satellite television and the Internet. In these several simultaneous attacks, roughly 3,000 people died.

The attacks were at once a new brand of terror, deeply indebted to globalization in both its outlook and its method, and something older: the extreme, opportunistic violence of marginal groups against national cultures during a period of general dislocation and uncertainty. The immediate American response was action against al Qaeda's central haven in Afghanistan, a state in total collapse after the warfare of the previous thirty years. The United States' versatile professional soldiers and unmatched equipment, along with armed Afghan militias angry at the country's disarray quickly routed al Qaeda's Taliban sponsors and scattered the terrorists. The search for Osama bin Laden took a decade, during which time the United States and its allies in the war in Afghanistan faced a renewed insurrection by the Taliban beginning in 2003. U.S. forces killed Osama bin Laden at his home in nearby Pakistan in 2011. During the intervening years, the United States succeeded in disrupting, though not completely eliminating, many of the hidden networks of leadership, finance, and information that made Al Qaeda's apocalyptic terrorism possible. Meanwhile, the economic and political rebuilding of Afghanistan, a necessary consequence of American and European military action, began from almost nothing in terms of administration and infrastructure. These efforts were hampered by challenging political circumstances within the country, which made it difficult for the Afghan government to position itself between its U.S. ally and a population with a long tradition of mistrusting foreign powers intervening in their land. U.S. forces are scheduled to leave Afghanistan during 2013, but the stability of the nation after more than three decades of war remains an open question.

TWENTY-FIRST CENTURY TERRORISM. New York City's World Trade Center Towers under attack on September 11, 2001.

One reason for the persistent fears about such groups as al Qaeda has to do with the increasing power and availability of weapons they might use: chemical substances, biological agents that could kill millions, even portable nuclear weapons. With the end of the Cold War, methods and technologies that the superpowers employed to maintain their nuclear balance of power became more available on the margins to displaced groups with the financial or political leverage to seek them out. Other major arms races, centered, for example, around Israel or the conflicts between India and Pakistan, helped spread the availability of production sites and resources for weapons of horrific power, no longer governed absolutely by the legal conventions and deterrent strength of superpowers. Fear that the Iraqi government of Saddam Hussein was reaching for biological and nuclear capabilities helped propel the Gulf War of 1991 and active international efforts to disarm Iraq thereafter. Anxiety that states such as Iraq might transfer such weapons to apocalyptic terrorists, a fear given new life after the attacks on New York and Washington, provided the rationale for an American-led invasion of Iraq in the spring of 2003. The campaign, which used a remarkably small force both on the ground and in the air, quickly took Iraq over and deposed Hussein. No immediate evidence of recent, active weapons development programs was found, however, and in the process the United States inherited the complex reconstruction of a broken state, fractured by guerrilla violence and anti-Western terrorism. After a long struggle against a shifting insurgency that fought the new Iraqi government and the U.S.-led forces that supported it, the last U.S. troops left Iraq in 2011. Since then, continued civil conflict in Iraq has claimed thousands of lives.

A nuclear threat also remained present in North Korea. After the loss of Soviet patronage in 1991, the isolated North Korean state careened from one economic disaster to another, with verified reports of local starvation in some regions of the country and a breakdown of government into military and political fiefdoms. The North Korean government pursued the development of a nuclear arsenal as a bargaining chip against the other major states of northeast Asia and the United States. Those neighbors each understood the grim chance that North Korea might break the last and perhaps most crucial nuclear threshold, providing nuclear

Analyzing Primary Sources

The United Nations, Report of the Fourth World Conference on Women *(1995)*

In September 1995, women representing 185 of the world's nations gathered in Beijing to attend the UN's Fourth World Conference on Women. Delegates to the conference adopted a platform for action that outlined the problems confronting women in the world, including poverty, violence, armed conflict, human rights violations, pollution, and differing access to medical treatment, education, economic advancement, and political power. The passage excerpted here highlights the particular burdens that poverty places on women in many societies throughout the world.

47. More than 1 billion people in the world today, the great majority of whom are women, live in unacceptable conditions of poverty, mostly in the developing countries. . . .

48. In the past decade the number of women living in poverty has increased disproportionately to the number of men, particularly in the developing countries. The feminization of poverty has also recently become a significant problem in the countries with economies in transition as a short-term consequence of the process of political, economic and social transformation. In addition to economic factors, the rigidity of socially ascribed gender roles and women's limited access to power, education, training and productive resources as well as other emerging factors that may lead to insecurity for families are also responsible. The failure to adequately mainstream a gender perspective in all economic analysis and planning and to address the structural causes of poverty is also a contributing factor.

49. Women contribute to the economy and to combating poverty through both remunerated and unremunerated work at home, in the community and in the workplace. The empowerment of women is a critical factor in the eradication of poverty.

50. While poverty affects households as a whole, because of the gender division of labour and responsibilities for household welfare, women bear a disproportionate burden, attempting to manage household consumption and production under conditions of increasing scarcity. Poverty is particularly acute for women living in rural households.

51. Women's poverty is directly related to the absence of economic opportunities and autonomy, lack of access to economic resources, including credit, land ownership and inheritance, lack of access to education and support services and their minimal participation in the decision-making process. Poverty can also force

weapons not to hard-pressed states but instead to stateless organizations. In short, by the early twenty-first century, warfare and the terrifying killing power of modern technology threatened to elude the control of national states and clearly defined political communities.

TRANSFORMATIONS: HUMAN RIGHTS

Some of the same globalizing processes have dramatically expanded our conception of citizenship, rights, and law. High school halls and college walkways are crammed with the tables of international organizations, such as Amnesty International, that promote universal human rights. How has this notion of human rights become so familiar? What older traditions has it built on or replaced?

The contemporary language of human rights is anchored in a tradition of political thought that reaches back to at least the seventeenth century. It took its present form in response to the atrocities of the First World War and, especially, the Second World War. Atrocities and people's shocked responses to them, however, did not create either a new concern with human rights or the institutions dedicated to upholding them. Enforcing *universal* human rights challenges the sovereignty of nation-states and an individual nation-state's power over its citizens. International courts and human rights organizations thus require and hasten what political thinkers call the globalization of judicial power.

women into situations in which they are vulnerable to sexual exploitation.

52. In too many countries, social welfare systems do not take sufficient account of the specific conditions of women living in poverty, and there is a tendency to scale back the services provided by such systems. The risk of falling into poverty is greater for women than for men, particularly in old age, where social security systems are based on the principle of continuous remunerated employment. In some cases, women do not fulfil this requirement because of interruptions in their work, due to the unbalanced distribution of remunerated and unremunerated work. Moreover, older women also face greater obstacles to labour-market re-entry.

53. In many developed countries, where the level of general education and professional training of women and men are similar and where systems of protection against discrimination are available, in some sectors the economic transformations of the past decade have strongly increased either the unemployment of women or the precarious nature of their employment. The proportion of women among the poor has consequently increased. In countries with a high level of school enrolment of girls, those who leave the educational system the earliest, without any qualification, are among the most vulnerable in the labour market. . . .

55. Particularly in developing countries, the productive capacity of women should be increased through access to capital, resources, credit, land, technology, information, technical assistance and training so as to raise their income and improve nutrition, education, health care and status within the household. The release of women's productive potential is pivotal to breaking the cycle of poverty so that women can share fully in the benefits of development and in the products of their own labour.

56. Sustainable development and economic growth that is both sustained and sustainable are possible only through improving the economic, social, political, legal and cultural status of women. Equitable social development that recognizes empowering the poor, particularly women, to utilize environmental resources sustainably is a necessary foundation for sustainable development.

Source: United Nations, *Report of the Fourth World Conference on Women, Beijing*, September 4–15, 1995, accessed June 2010, www.un.org/womenwatch/daw/beijing/platform.

Questions for Analysis

1. According to the UN report, why are women more likely to be poor than men?
2. What are the special challenges faced by women in developing countries?
3. What are the different challenges faced by women residing in more developed nations?

Human rights are part of the Western political tradition. So is opposition to them. The belief that rights were embedded in "nature," "natural order," or "natural law" formed a powerful strain of early modern political thought. John Locke understood natural law as the law of reason (see Chapter 15); others understood it to be the law of God. However conceptualized, it represented a higher authority to which men owed their obedience. Opponents of absolutism in seventeenth- and eighteenth-century Europe were driven by motives that were economic, religious, and social. Natural rights, however, became one of their rallying cries. The English Bill of Rights of 1689, accepted by William and Mary after the Glorious Revolution, insisted on "the true, ancient, and indubitable rights and liberties of the people of this kingdom." A century later, the American Declaration of Independence and the French Declaration of the Rights of Man more broadly proclaimed the "natural, inalienable and sacred rights of man," which in their eyes belonged to all men—not just the colonists of North America or the citizens of France. In point of fact, of course, those bold declarations of rights were not universal: women, slaves, people of color, and people of different religions were excluded, wholly or partially, and many nineteenth-century political theorists and scientists dedicated countless volumes to the proposition that these groups were *not* created equal. Which human beings might receive the "rights of man," then, was bitterly contested for the better part of the nineteenth and twentieth centuries, and only slowly did a more inclusive conception of human rights displace a narrower historical tradition of the rights of man.

As far as the history of human rights is concerned, perhaps the most important development of the nineteenth century was the rise of nationalism and nation-states. Rights, and political movements claiming them, became increasingly inseparable from nationhood. "What is a country . . . but the place in which our demands for individual rights are most secure?" asked the Italian nationalist Giuseppe Mazzini. For nineteenth-century Italians, Germans, Serbs, and Poles and for twentieth-century Indians, Vietnamese, and Algerians—to name just a few—fighting for national independence was the way to secure the rights of citizens. National sovereignty, once achieved, was tightly woven into the fabric of politics and international relations and would not be easily relinquished.

The world wars marked a turning point. The First World War, an unprecedented global conflict, almost inevitably fostered dreams of global peace under the auspices of international organizations. The Peace of Paris aimed for more than a territorial settlement: with the League of Nations it tried, tentatively, to establish an organization that would transcend the power of individual nations and uphold the (ill-defined) principles of "civilization." (Despite this commitment, the League bowed to British and American objections to a statement condemning racial discrimination.) The experiment failed: the fragile League was swept aside by the surge of extreme nationalism and aggression in the 1930s. The shock and revulsion at the atrocities of the war that followed, however, brought forth more decisive efforts. The Second World War's aftermath saw the establishment of the United Nations, an International Court of Justice at the Hague (Netherlands), and the UN's High Commission on Human Rights. Unlike anything attempted after the First World War, the Commission on Human Rights set out to establish the rights of individuals—against the nation-state.

This Universal Declaration of Human Rights, published by the High Commission in 1948, became the touchstone of our modern notion of human rights. It was very much a product of its time. Its authors included Eleanor Roosevelt and the French jurist René Cassin, who had been wounded in the First World War (and held his intestines together during a nearly 400-mile train ride to medical treatment), lost his family in the Holocaust, and had seen his nation collaborate with the Nazis. The High Commission argued that the war and the "barbarous acts which have outraged the conscience of mankind," showed that no state should have absolute power over its citizens. The Universal Declaration prohibited torture, cruel punishment, and slavery. A separate convention, also passed in 1948, dealt with the newly defined crime of genocide. The Universal Declaration of 1948 built on earlier declarations that universalized the rights to legal equality, freedom of religion and speech, and the right to participate in government. Finally, it reflected the postwar period's effort to put democracy on a more solid footing by establishing *social* rights—to education, work, a "just and favorable remuneration," a "standard of living," and social security, among others.

Few nations were willing to ratify the Universal Declaration of Human Rights. For decades after the war, its idealistic principles could not be reconciled with British and French colonialism, American racial segregation, or Soviet dictatorship. For as long as wars to end colonialism continued, declarations of universal principles rang hollow. (Mahatma Gandhi, asked to comment on Western civilization, replied that he thought it was a "good idea.") For as long as the Cold War persisted, human rights seemed only a thinly veiled weapon in the sparring between the superpowers. Thus decolonization and, later, the end of the Cold War began to enhance the legitimacy and luster of human rights. International institutions set up after the Second World War matured, gaining expertise and stature. Global communications and media dramatically expanded the membership and influence of organizations that, like Amnesty International (founded in 1961), operated outside the economic or political boundaries of the nation-state. Memories of the Second World War, distorted or buried by the Cold War, continue to return, and the force of those memories helped drive the creation of International Criminal Tribunals for Yugoslavia and Rwanda in 1993. Finally, as one historian points out, at a time when many feel vulnerable to the forces of globalization, human rights offers a way of talking about rights, goods, and protections (environmental, for example) that the nation-state cannot—or can no longer—provide.

It is nevertheless the case that the troubled era that began with the 9/11 attacks on the United States in 2001 has seen many challenges to the notion of universal human rights. Terrorism, no matter what the ideology of the perpetrator, is a fundamental violation of every human's right to safety and security. In their zeal to punish terrorists, meanwhile, many nations in the world have tacitly turned away from the emerging international legal structures that attempted to defend the rights of all individuals everywhere. The struggle that the United States and its allies waged against al Qaeda and Taliban leadership has raised difficult questions about the tactics used, which included torture, indefinite detention without trial, and the use of pilotless drones to kill suspected militant leaders in distant countries. The use of drone technologies make it easier to avoid U.S. casualties in operations against a dangerous enemy, but many in the United States and abroad have expressed concerns about the government's right to identify, target, and execute individuals, including in some cases U.S. citizens, based on criteria that are never subject to independent legal review. Public opinion in the United States remains strongly in favor of such tactics, but in recent years public anger in Afghanistan and Pakistan has focused on cases of mistaken identity and the deaths of family members and bystanders in drone attacks. Even within the U.S. government and military, some have expressed concern that these methods could be counterproductive.

As the U.S. and European governments pursue their interests abroad, debates about the use of military power in other parts of the world and the form that this power takes have become pressing concerns, and the issues turn on questions that have been a central part of the liberal democratic political tradition since it emerged in opposition to monarchist forms of government in the seventeenth century. How should a nation determine the balance between individual freedoms and national security? What forms of force or violence can the state legitimately use against its enemies at home or abroad? What kinds of information about its citizenry should a government be allowed to keep? Are the terrorist threats that democratic regimes routinely face today so serious that they justify the suspension of internationally recognized human rights? No easy answers to these questions exist—but the answers that governments and societies in Europe and the United States give to them will shape how people everywhere will perceive the legitimacy of the democratic political institutions that they claim to represent.

EUROPE AND THE UNITED STATES IN THE TWENTY-FIRST CENTURY

As the first decade of the twenty-first century drew to a close, the initial confidence that Europeans felt in the aftermath of the revolutions of 1989 seemed badly shaken. The process of European integration, which had contributed so much to the political stability of Europe in the decades after the Second World War, seemed to have reached its limits in the East. Although a few independent nations that were formerly a part of the Soviet Union, such as Ukraine, might be interested in joining the European Union, it is unlikely that Russia would be comfortable with this realignment toward the West. Even the future membership of Turkey, an official candidate for entry into the EU since 1999 and an associate member of the European Union since 1963, remains uncertain because of growing discomfort in many European nations about admitting a historically Muslim nation into Europe. Turkey is a modern industrial nation that has been governed by a secular government since the 1920s, participated in the Marshall Plan after the Second World War, was a member of the Council of Europe in 1949, and became a member of NATO in 1952. A 2010 poll carried out in five European countries nevertheless found that 52 percent of respondents were opposed to Turkish membership in the European Union and only 41 percent in favor.

In the economic realm, the global financial crisis of 2007–2010 caused many in Europe and North America to rethink the central assumptions of late-twentieth-century neoliberalism, especially the belief that markets were by definition self-regulating. The crisis had its origins in a classic bubble in global housing prices, which encouraged banks to make ever-riskier bets in the real estate market while also experimenting with the sale of complicated securities whose risk became difficult to gauge with accuracy. When housing prices fell, many key banks in different parts of the world found themselves unable to state clearly the value of their plummeting investments tied to real estate. Since nobody knew how much money the largest financial institutions had, banks simply stopped lending money to one another, and in the resulting liquidity crisis many businesses failed and trillions of dollars of consumer savings were wiped out. Massive government bailouts of the largest banks with taxpayer money were required to stabilize the global financial system, and popular resentment against the financial industry stimulated many nations to consider widespread reform and government regulation of banks as a result.

Contemporary debates about political integration in Europe or the benefits of free-market capitalism are closely connected with the developments that followed the end of the Cold War in the early 1990s and the period of economic globalization that followed, but they can also be seen as a continuation of debates within the traditions of political and economic liberalism that go back to the eighteenth century. In its classic formulation as put forth by liberal theorists such as Adam Smith, political and economic liberties were best defended in a nation that possessed a small and limited government. The closely related traditions of social democracy that developed in Europe in the nineteenth and twentieth century, on the other hand, arose out of a concern that limited governments in the classic liberal mold could not do enough to remedy the inequalities that emerged from modern industrial societies, and the result was the creation of welfare state institutions that aimed to use the power of the state to maintain a base level of social and economic equality. This tension between the goals of liberty and equality is a constant one within the liberal tradition, and the different trajectories of Europe and the United States in the twentieth century reflect the respective priorities of successive governments in both places.

Many Europeans, therefore, watched the election of Barack Obama in the United States in 2008 with great interest. Since the election of Ronald Reagan in 1980, the divergences between governments in the United States and Europe in their attitudes toward the role that the state might play in remedying social problems had become even more acute. With few exceptions, European governments were much more willing to use the power of the state to assist the unemployed or the aged, to support families, and to provide subsidies for education, public transportation, and national programs for health care. As we have seen, this consensus emerged in part because of a belief that the economic dislocations of the 1920s and 1930s had led directly to the emergence of destabilizing and antidemocratic extremist political movements. In the United States, on the other hand, widespread discontent with attempts by the Johnson administration in the 1960s to use the power of the federal government to end racial segregation and address broad problems such as urban poverty and environmental pollution contributed to a conservative backlash in the 1980s and 1990s. Throughout those years, conservatives in the United States called for an end to welfare programs, repeal of environmental regulations, and less government oversight in the marketplace.

Obama's election in 2008, following on the heels of the financial meltdown earlier the same year, seemed to mark a turning point of sorts in American politics, as his pragmatic campaign was predicated on a claim that government itself was not the problem facing industrial democracies at the outset of the twenty-first century. The Obama administration's ambitious plan to overhaul the health care system faced stiff opposition from many quarters, but a compromise package succeeded in passing the Congress and was signed into law in 2010. Obama's reelection in 2012 has led to the implementation of the law's first measures. The fierceness of the health care debate—which revolved around questions about the power of the state, the responsibilities of elected governments, the nature of the public good, and the balance between liberty and equality—should not obscure the fact that partisans on both sides of these controversies are using a vocabulary and a set of references that are part of the same liberal democratic political traditions that emerged in Europe and North America in the previous two centuries.

If Obama's two-term presidency has given some hope to those who see an important role for the state in solving persistent social and economic problems, the situation in Europe in the aftermath of the 2008 financial crisis has been less comforting. The European welfare state model inherited from the post–Second World War decades was based on a combination of Marshall Plan investment, European economic integration, and cooperation among representatives of labor, employers, and the state. Trade unions agreed to wage moderation in exchange for social protections from the state. Business leaders agreed to higher taxes for social protections in exchange for labor peace. Government officials convinced their electorates to pay higher taxes in exchange for social protections such as universal health care, unemployment, and old age pensions.

This system worked well as long as the economy kept growing. When the economy flattened out beginning in the 1970s, however, businesses reduced their investments, unemployment went up, workers expressed discontent with their former restraint on wages, and European states had less revenue for social protection. In the 1980s and 1990s, European governments resorted to deficit spending to protect their welfare programs, and this system worked well enough as long as the banks that were lending the governments money were confident that they would be repaid. Faith in this system led to the creation of the eurozone as a single currency area in 2002.

After the financial crisis of 2008, however, the delicate balance in Europe between banks and governments in Europe began to crumble. European banks that were already fragile from losses in the real estate bubble demanded extraordinarily high interest rates before they would loan money to governments that were in financial trouble. The crisis was most acute in Greece, Spain, Italy, Ireland, and Portugal, where government debt reached threatening levels. So far, the solution has been for the stronger economies in the eurozone to bail out the weaker economies by providing emergency funds. To receive them, however, the indebted governments are forced to accept steep cuts in state spending, which are deeply unpopular with their populations. The ensuing political crisis has caused some to think that the eurozone might not survive in its present form and that some countries might be forced out or choose to leave of their own will. If that happens, it will mark a significant turning point in the history of European integration, which has provided a template for thinking about the European future since the years after the Second World War.

THE ARAB SPRING OF 2011

The dramatic events that began in Tunisia in December 2010 brought a wave of protest and popular insurrection to much of the Arab Middle East, overthrowing powerful dictators and presidents for life in Tunisia, Egypt, and Libya. The speed of these momentous changes surprised people living in these countries as much as they astonished foreign observers—many had long assumed that political change, when it came to these regimes, would proceed at a glacial pace. Zine al-Abidine Ben Ali of Tunisia, Hosni Mubarak of Egypt, and Muammar Qadhafi of Libya had governed for decades. Ben Ali and Mubarak were establishment figures in the international world, regularly meet-

Past and Present

The Arab Spring in Historical Perspective

With the collapse of the Berlin Wall in 1989 a relatively recent memory, many people in Europe and North America sought to compare the recent protests in the Middle East against authoritarian governments to these European events. Comparisons with 1968 (see left, the Prague Spring), 1989, or 1848 may be instructive, but it is also likely that the forms of democracy that protesters in Tunisia, Egypt (see right, protesters in Tahrir Square, Cairo), and most recently, Turkey, are striving to create will reflect their own values, rather than conform to political models borrowed from elsewhere.

Watch related author interview on StudySpace
wwnorton.com/web/westernciv18

ing with European leaders and U.S. presidents who were among their most loyal supporters. How had this happened so suddenly? Did it mean that a wave of democratic revolution was sweeping through the Middle East?

To explain these events, many observers in Europe and the United States looked for explanations from their own histories. Some people suggested that these revolts were comparable to the movements to overthrow the dictatorial regimes of Eastern Europe that culminated in the fall of the Berlin Wall in 1989 and the collapse of the Soviet Union in 1991. The very name "Arab Spring" recalled the Prague Spring of 1968 when young people in Czechoslovakia attempted, and ultimately failed, to create a different and more democratic form of socialism in that country. Others feared that these revolts might turn out like the Tiananmen Square protests in China of 1989, which ended up in a violent repression of a democratic movement. The continued civil war in Syria is a haunting reminder of the reality of this possibility.

All of these comparisons might be instructive, but they also reveal something significant about the way that many people think about movements for democratic revolutions: there is a tendency to assume that movements for democracy all want the same thing. History shows that it is usually much more complicated than that. Great coalitions can be assembled at a moment of crisis to challenge established regimes, but success brings on new challenges. As the protests in the Middle East and North Africa unfolded in 2011, observers frequently noted how new technologies such as cell phones and new social media such as Facebook and Twitter allowed people to make their voices heard in a new way and to coordinate mass actions almost instantaneously. It remains to be seen, however, what the lasting accomplishments of this movement for change will be. How can this unity be maintained when it comes to building a new political system, a new and different society?

Prior to 2011, many people in the United States, in Europe, and in the Middle East itself had been filled with pessimism about this region of the world. Persistent conflict and the appearance of frightening movements that advocate terrorist violence caused many to give up hope. With the Arab Spring, it became clear, however, that what many people wanted was the right to build a more responsive and accountable form of government that was compatible with their core beliefs and values. Building a consensus around these values is not easy—it is the work of any society that endures. Observers in the United States might pause to remember that it took that country more than 150 years to arrive at a political system in which every adult could vote—a period that witnessed a bloody civil war and persistent violence over questions of race. For Europeans, it took generation after generation of repeated revolutionary and counterrevolutionary violence, not to mention two world wars. The nations of the Arab Middle East have been independent now for less than the lifetime of one person. The form of society that they choose will not be the same as that chosen by the French, the Poles, or the Italians. But in that effort to shape a society that conforms to their beliefs and provides them with security and sustenance, the many people who demonstrated in Tunis or in Tahrir Square in Cairo are no different from anybody else in the world.

CONCLUSION

Globalization—defined loosely as the process by which the economies, societies, and cultures of different parts of the world become increasingly interconnected—has been hailed as a solution to old problems even as it has been criticized as a source of new ones. Although some thought that the end of the Cold War in 1989 meant that economic liberalism—that is, a global free-market capitalist system unfettered by government regulations—had triumphed for good in the world, continued political instability in many parts of the globe and the global economic crisis of 2008 have called into question such optimistic interpretations of world events. In the economic realm, national states have looked for ways to reassert their control over the flow of currencies and goods and protect their populations against decisions made elsewhere by financial speculators and investors. Meanwhile, the danger of radical forms of terrorism, both foreign and domestic, has caused even strongly democratic governments in the West to create new and pervasive surveillance bureaucracies, demonstrating that global threats can have real and seemingly permanent local effects on definitions of

After You Read This Chapter

Visit StudySpace for quizzes, additional review materials, and multimedia documents. **wwnorton.com/web/westernciv18**

REVIEWING THE OBJECTIVES

- Globalization in the second half of the twentieth century was not new. What does globalization mean, and what was similar or different about the most recent phase of globalization in human history?
- The burden of the colonial past continued to weigh heavily on many former colonies after the 1960s. What accounts for the success of some former colonies in the global economy and the continued social and political challenges facing others?
- Since the end of the Second World War, conflicts and events in the Middle East have taken on a global significance far beyond the region's borders. What are the crucial conflicts that occupied the attention of other nations, and what events have proved to be crucial turning points in the emergence of the Middle East as a region that drives developments elsewhere?

citizenship, the permeability of borders, and extensions of state power.

In such uncertain times, it is difficult to remain consistent or to determine national priorities: is the threat of terrorism greater than the threat of a loss of liberty stemming from extensions in government power? Is it fair of the International Monetary Fund to ask developing nations to adhere to austere cuts to their social welfare spending when wealthy private investment banks receive billion-dollar bailouts for making bad bets in the financial markets because they are "too big to fail"? The complexity of the world's interconnections makes it difficult to determine definitive answers to such questions, and even if one could, any ensuing policy decisions would create winners and losers, ensuring that the political struggles implicit in such questions will endure. Globalization, therefore, is not a final destination—it is the new complex reality of human existence, the context for future struggles about the goals of political association, the meanings of liberty or equality, and the possibility of shared values.

The loss of familiar moorings makes fundamental questions about human behavior and political community difficult to answer. History offers no quick solutions. Historians are reluctant to offer what historian Peter Novick calls "pithy lessons that fit on a bumper sticker." As Novick puts it:

> If there is, to use a pretentious word, any wisdom to be acquired from contemplating an historical event, I would think it would derive from confronting it in all its complexity and its contradictions; the ways in which it resembles other events to which it might be compared as well as the way it differs from them. . . . If there are lessons to be extracted from encountering the past, that encounter has to be with the past in all its messiness; they're not likely to come from an encounter with a past that's been shaped so that inspiring lessons will emerge.

The untidy and contradictory evidence that historians discover in the archives rarely yields unblemished heroes or unvarnished villains. Good history reveals the complex processes and dynamics of change over time. It helps us understand the many layers of the past that have formed and constrain us in our present world. At the same time, it shows again and again that these constraints do not preordain what happens next or how we can make the history of the future.

PEOPLE, IDEAS, AND EVENTS IN CONTEXT

- What were the policy goals of **NEOLIBERALISM** after the 1970s, as exemplified by the activities of institutions such as the **INTERNATIONAL MONETARY FUND** and the World Bank?
- How do the **HIV EPIDEMIC** of the 1980s or the **SARS EPIDEMIC** of 2003 illustrate the new realities of public health in a globalized world?
- What was the significance of **NELSON MANDELA**'s election as president of South Africa in 1994?
- How was the **1973 OIL EMBARGO** related to the **ARAB-ISRAELI CONFLICT**, and what were its effects on the global economy?
- What did radical critics dislike about secular forms of **ARAB NATIONALISM** such as that represented by **GAMAL ABDEL NASSER** in Egypt?
- What led the United States and Britain to support the regime of **REZA PAHLAVI** in Iran, and what events brought **RUHOLLAH KHOMEINI** to power in Iran in 1979?
- What circumstances link the Soviet invasion of Afghanistan in 1979 with the origins of **AL QAEDA**?
- What made it difficult for European and North American governments to sign the UN's **UNIVERSAL DECLARATION OF HUMAN RIGHTS** in 1948? What events have occurred since 1948 that indicate that at least some nations might agree to international treaties guaranteeing human rights?

THINKING ABOUT CONNECTIONS

- Many of the global linkages between Europe and the United States, on the one hand, and the independent nations of Asia, Africa, and Latin America, on the other, were first forged during earlier periods of imperial expansion. How does this history continue to be felt in the present?
- Global networks of transport, trade, and communication have long been significant vectors for cultural change, by bringing different peoples into contact and conversation with one another. How have recent developments in technology changed the nature of this global conversation?

Appendix

Rulers of Principal States

THE CAROLINGIAN DYNASTY

Pepin of Heristal, Mayor of the Palace, 687–714
Charles Martel, Mayor of the Palace, 715–741
Pepin III, Mayor of the Palace, 741–751; King, 751–768
Charlemagne, King, 768–814; Emperor, 800–814
Louis the Pious, Emperor, 814–840

West Francia

Charles the Bald, King, 840–877; Emperor, 875–877
Louis II, King, 877–879
Louis III, King, 879–882
Carloman, King, 879–884

Middle Kingdoms

Lothair, Emperor, 840–855
Louis (Italy), Emperor, 855–875
Charles (Provence), King, 855–863
Lothair II (Lorraine), King, 855–869

East Francia

Ludwig, King, 840–876
Carloman, King, 876–880
Ludwig, King, 876–882
Charles the Fat, Emperor, 876–887

HOLY ROMAN EMPERORS

Saxon Dynasty

Otto I, 962–973
Otto II, 973–983
Otto III, 983–1002
Henry II, 1002–1024

Franconian Dynasty

Conrad II, 1024–1039
Henry III, 1039–1056
Henry IV, 1056–1106
Henry V, 1106–1125
Lothair II (Saxony), 1125–1137

Hohenstaufen Dynasty

Conrad III, 1138–1152
Frederick I (Barbarossa), 1152–1190
Henry VI, 1190–1197
Philip of Swabia, 1198–1208 } Rivals
Otto IV (Welf), 1198–1215 } Rivals
Frederick II, 1220–1250
Conrad IV, 1250–1254

Interregnum, 1254–1273

Emperors from Various Dynasties

Rudolf I (Habsburg), 1273–1291
Adolf (Nassau), 1292–1298
Albert I (Habsburg), 1298–1308
Henry VII (Luxemburg), 1308–1313
Ludwig IV (Wittelsbach), 1314–1347
Charles IV (Luxemburg), 1347–1378
Wenceslas (Luxemburg), 1378–1400
Rupert (Wittelsbach), 1400–1410
Sigismund (Luxemburg), 1410–1437

Habsburg Dynasty

Albert II, 1438–1439
Frederick III, 1440–1493

Maximilian I, 1493–1519
Charles V, 1519–1556
Ferdinand I, 1556–1564
Maximilian II, 1564–1576
Rudolf II, 1576–1612
Matthias, 1612–1619
Ferdinand II, 1619–1637
Ferdinand III, 1637–1657
Leopold I, 1658–1705
Joseph I, 1705–1711
Charles VI, 1711–1740
Charles VII (not a Habsburg), 1742–1745
Francis I, 1745–1765
Joseph II, 1765–1790
Leopold II, 1790–1792
Francis II, 1792–1806

RULERS OF FRANCE FROM HUGH CAPET

Capetian Dynasty

Hugh Capet, 987–996
Robert II, 996–1031
Henry I, 1031–1060
Philip I, 1060–1108
Louis VI, 1108–1137
Louis VII, 1137–1180
Philip II (Augustus), 1180–1223
Louis VIII, 1223–1226
Louis IX (St. Louis), 1226–1270
Philip III, 1270–1285
Philip IV, 1285–1314
Louis X, 1314–1316
Philip V, 1316–1322
Charles IV, 1322–1328

Valois Dynasty

Philip VI, 1328–1350
John, 1350–1364
Charles V, 1364–1380
Charles VI, 1380–1422
Charles VII, 1422–1461
Louis XI, 1461–1483
Charles VIII, 1483–1498
Louis XII, 1498–1515
Francis I, 1515–1547
Henry II, 1547–1559
Francis II, 1559–1560
Charles IX, 1560–1574
Henry III, 1574–1589

Bourbon Dynasty

Henry IV, 1589–1610
Louis XIII, 1610–1643
Louis XIV, 1643–1715
Louis XV, 1715–1774
Louis XVI, 1774–1792

After 1792

First Republic, 1792–1799
Napoleon Bonaparte, First Consul, 1799–1804
Napoleon I, Emperor, 1804–1814
Louis XVIII (Bourbon dynasty), 1814–1824
Charles X (Bourbon dynasty), 1824–1830
Louis Philippe, 1830–1848
Second Republic, 1848–1852
Napoleon III, Emperor, 1852–1870
Third Republic, 1870–1940
Pétain regime, 1940–1944
Provisional government, 1944–1946
Fourth Republic, 1946–1958
Fifth Republic, 1958–

RULERS OF ENGLAND

Anglo-Saxon Dynasty

Alfred the Great, 871–899
Edward the Elder, 899–924
Ethelstan, 924–939
Edmund I, 939–946
Edred, 946–955
Edwy, 955–959
Edgar, 959–975
Edward the Martyr, 975–978
Ethelred the Unready, 978–1016
Canute, 1016–1035 (Danish Nationality)
Harold I, 1035–1040
Hardicanute, 1040–1042
Edward the Confessor, 1042–1066
Harold II, 1066

House of Normandy

William I (the Conqueror), 1066–1087
William II, 1087–1100
Henry I, 1100–1135
Stephen, 1135–1154

House of Plantagenet

Henry II, 1154–1189
Richard I, 1189–1199
John, 1199–1216
Henry III, 1216–1272
Edward I, 1272–1307
Edward II, 1307–1327
Edward III, 1327–1377
Richard II, 1377–1399

House of Lancaster

Henry IV, 1399–1413
Henry V, 1413–1422
Henry VI, 1422–1461

House of York

Edward IV, 1461–1483
Edward V, 1483
Richard III, 1483–1485

House of Tudor

Henry VII, 1485–1509
Henry VIII, 1509–1547
Edward VI, 1547–1553
Mary, 1553–1558
Elizabeth I, 1558–1603

House of Stuart

James I, 1603–1625
Charles I, 1625–1649

Commonwealth and Protectorate, 1649–1659

House of Stuart Restored

Charles II, 1660–1685
James II, 1685–1688
William III and Mary II, 1689–1694
William III alone, 1694–1702
Anne, 1702–1714

House of Hanover

George I, 1714–1727
George II, 1727–1760
George III, 1760–1820
George IV, 1820–1830
William IV, 1830–1837
Victoria, 1837–1901

House of Saxe-Coburg-Gotha

Edward VII, 1901–1910
George V, 1910–1917

House of Windsor

George V, 1917–1936
Edward VIII, 1936
George VI, 1936–1952
Elizabeth II, 1952–

RULERS OF AUSTRIA AND AUSTRIA-HUNGARY

*Maximilian I (Archduke), 1493–1519
*Charles V, 1519–1556
*Ferdinand I, 1556–1564
*Maximilian II, 1564–1576
*Rudolf II, 1576–1612
*Matthias, 1612–1619
*Ferdinand II, 1619–1637
*Ferdinand III, 1637–1657
*Leopold I, 1658–1705
*Joseph I, 1705–1711
*Charles VI, 1711–1740
Maria Theresa, 1740–1780
*Joseph II, 1780–1790
*Leopold II, 1790–1792
*Francis II, 1792–1835 (Emperor of Austria as Francis I after 1804)
Ferdinand I, 1835–1848
Francis Joseph, 1848–1916 (after 1867 Emperor of Austria and King of Hungary)
Charles I, 1916–1918 (Emperor of Austria and King of Hungary)
Republic of Austria, 1918–1938 (dictatorship after 1934)
Republic restored, under Allied occupation, 1945–1956
Free Republic, 1956–

*Also bore title of Holy Roman Emperor

RULERS OF PRUSSIA AND GERMANY

*Frederick I, 1701–1713
*Frederick William I, 1713–1740
*Frederick II (the Great), 1740–1786
*Frederick William II, 1786–1797
*Frederick William III,1797–1840
*Frederick William IV, 1840–1861
*William I, 1861–1888 (German Emperor after 1871)
Frederick III, 1888
*William II, 1888–1918
Weimar Republic, 1918–1933
Third Reich (Nazi Dictatorship), 1933–1945
Allied occupation, 1945–1952
Division into Federal Republic of Germany in west and German Democratic Republic in east, 1949–1991
Federal Republic of Germany (united), 1991–

*Kings of Prussia

RULERS OF RUSSIA

Ivan III, 1462–1505
Vasily III, 1505–1533
Ivan IV, 1533–1584
Theodore I, 1534–1598
Boris Godunov, 1598–1605
Theodore II,1605
Vasily IV, 1606–1610
Michael, 1613–1645
Alexius, 1645–1676
Theodore III, 1676–1682
Ivan V and Peter I, 1682–1689
Peter I (the Great), 1689–1725
Catherine I, 1725–1727
Peter II, 1727–1730
Anna, 1730–1740
Ivan VI, 1740–1741
Elizabeth, 1741–1762
Peter III, 1762
Catherine II (the Great), 1762–1796
Paul, 1796–1801
Alexander I,1801–1825
Nicholas I, 1825–1855
Alexander II,1855–1881
Alexander III, 1881–1894
Nicholas II, 1894–1917
Soviet Republic, 1917–1991
Russian Federation, 1991–

RULERS OF UNIFIED SPAIN

Ferdinand { and Isabella, 1479–1504
and Philip I, 1504–1506
and Charles I, 1506–1516 }
Charles I (Holy Roman Emperor Charles V), 1516–1556
Philip II, 1556–1598
Philip III, 1598–1621
Philip IV, 1621–1665
Charles II, 1665–1700
Philip V, 1700–1746
Ferdinand VI, 1746–1759
Charles III, 1759–1788
Charles IV, 1788–1808
Ferdinand VII, 1808
Joseph Bonaparte, 1808–1813
Ferdinand VII (restored), 1814–1833
Isabella II, 1833–1868
Republic, 1868–1870
Amadeo, 1870–1873
Republic, 1873–1874
Alfonso XII, 1874–1885
Alfonso XIII, 1886–1931
Republic, 1931–1939
Fascist Dictatorship, 1939–1975
Juan Carlos I, 1975–

RULERS OF ITALY

Victor Emmanuel II, 1861–1878
Humbert I, 1878–1900
Victor Emmanuel III, 1900–1946
Fascist Dictatorship, 1922-1943 (maintained in northern Italy until 1945)
Humbert II, May 9–June 13, 1946
Republic, 1946–

PROMINENT POPES

Silvester I, 314–335
Leo I, 440–461
Gelasius I, 492–496
Gregory I, 590–604
Nicholas I, 858–867
Silvester II, 999–1003
Leo IX, 1049–1054
Nicholas II, 1058–1061
Gregory VII, 1073–1085
Urban II, 1088–1099
Paschal II, 1099–1118
Alexander III, 1159–1181
Innocent III, 1198–1216
Gregory IX, 1227–1241
Innocent IV, 1243–1254
Boniface VIII, 1294–1303
John XXII, 1316–1334
Nicholas V, 1447–1455
Pius II, 1458–1464
Alexander VI, 1492–1503
Julius II, 1503–1513
Leo X, 1513–1521
Paul III, 1534–1549
Paul IV, 1555–1559
Sixtus V, 1585–1590
Urban VIII, 1623–1644
Gregory XVI, 1831–1846
Pius IX, 1846–1878
Leo XIII, 1878–1903
Pius X, 1903–1914
Benedict XV, 1914–1922
Pius XI, 1922–1939
Pius XII, 1939–1958
John XXIII, 1958–1963
Paul VI, 1963–1978
John Paul I, 1978
John Paul II, 1978–2005
Benedict XVI, 2005–2013
Francis, 2013–

Further Readings

CHAPTER 18

Applewhite, Harriet B., and Darline G. Levy, eds. *Women and Politics in the Age of the Democratic Revolution*. Ann Arbor, MI, 1990. Essays on France, Britain, the Netherlands, and the United States.

Bell, David A. *The First Total War: Napoleon's Europe and the Birth of Warfare as We Know It*. Boston and New York, 2007. Lively and concise study of the "cataclysmic intensification" of warfare.

Blackburn, Robin. *The Overthrow of Colonial Slavery*. London and New York, 1988. A longer view of slavery and its abolition.

Blanning, T. C. W. *The French Revolutionary Wars, 1787–1802*. Oxford, 1996. On the revolution and war.

Blum, Carol. *Rousseau and the Republic of Virtue: The Language of Politics in the French Revolution*. Ithaca, NY, 1986. Excellent on how Rousseau was read by the revolutionaries.

Cobb, Richard. *The People's Armies*. New Haven, CT, 1987. Brilliant and detailed analysis of the popular militias.

Cole, Juan. *Napoleon's Egypt: Invading the Middle East*. New York, 2007. Readable history by a scholar familiar with sources in Arabic as well as European languages.

Connelly, Owen. *The French Revolution and Napoleonic Era*. 3rd ed. New York, 2000. Accessible, lively, one-volume survey.

Darnton, Robert, *The Forbidden Best-Sellers of Pre-Revolutionary France*. New York, 1995. One of Darnton's many imaginative studies of subversive opinion and books on the eve of the revolution.

Desan, Suzanne. *The Family on Trial in Revolutionary France*. Berkeley, CA, 2006. Persuasive study of the ways that women in France were able to take advantage of the revolution and defend their interests in debates about marriage, divorce, parenthood, and the care of children.

Desan, Suzanne, Lynn Hunt, and William Max Nelson, eds. *The French Revolution in Global Perspective*. Ithaca, NY, 2013. Multi-author exploration of the French Revolution's global resonance.

Doyle, William. *Origins of the French Revolution*. New York, 1988. A revisionist historian surveys recent research on the political and social origins of the revolution and identifies a new consensus.

———. *Oxford History of the French Revolution*. New York, 1989.

Dubois, Laurent. *Avengers of the New World. The Story of the Haitian Revolution*. Cambridge, MA, 2004. Now the best and most accessible study.

———, and John D. Garrigus. *Slave Revolution in the Caribbean, 1789–1804: A Brief History with Documents*. New York, 2006. A particularly good collection.

Englund, Steven. *Napoleon, A Political Life*. Cambridge, MA, 2004. Prize-winning biography, both dramatic and insightful.

Forrest, Alan. *The French Revolution and the Poor*. New York, 1981. A moving and detailed social history of the poor, who fared little better under revolutionary governments than under the Old Regime.

Furet, Francois. *Revolutionary France, 1770–1880*. Trans. Antonia Nerill. Cambridge, MA, 1992. Overview by the leading revisionist.

Hunt, Lynn. *The French Revolution and Human Rights*. Boston, 1996. A collection of documents.

———. *Politics, Culture, and Class in the French Revolution*. Berkeley, CA, 1984. An analysis of the new culture of democracy and republicanism.

Hunt, Lynn, and Jack R. Censer. *Liberty, Equality, Fraternity: Exploring the French Revolution*. University Park, PA, 2001. Two leading historians of the revolution have written a lively, accessible study, with excellent documents and visual material.

Landes, Joan B. *Women and the Public Sphere in the Age of the French Revolution*. Ithaca, NY, 1988. On gender and politics.

Lefebvre, Georges. *The Coming of the French Revolution*. Princeton, NJ, 1947. The classic Marxist analysis.

Lewis, G., and C. Lucas. *Beyond the Terror: Essays in French Regional and Social History, 1794–1815*. New York, 1983. Shifts focus to the understudied period after the Terror.

O'Brien, Connor Cruise. *The Great Melody: A Thematic Biography of Edmund Burke*. Chicago, 1992. Passionate, partisan, and brilliant study of Burke's thoughts about Ireland, India, America, and France.

Palmer, R. R. *The Age of the Democratic Revolution: A Political History of Europe and America, 1760–1800*. 2 vols. Princeton, NJ, 1964. Impressive for its scope; places the French Revolution in the larger context of a worldwide revolutionary movement.

———, and Isser Woloch. *Twelve Who Ruled: The Year of the Terror in the French Revolution*. Princeton, NJ, 2005. The terrific collective biography of the Committee of Public Safety, now updated.

Schama, Simon. *Citizens: A Chronicle of the French Revolution*. New York, 1989. Particularly good on art, culture, and politics.

Scott, Joan. *Only Paradoxes to Offer: French Feminists and the Rights of Man*. Cambridge, MA, 1997. A history of feminist engagement with a revolutionary ideology that promised universal liberties while simultaneously excluding women from citizenship.

Soboul, Albert. *The Sans-Culottes: The Popular Movement and Revolutionary Government, 1793–1794*. Garden City, NY, 1972. Dated, but a classic.

Sutherland, D. M. G. *France, 1789–1815: Revolution and Counter-revolution.* Oxford, 1986. An important synthesis of work on the revolution, especially in social history.

Tocqueville, Alexis de. *The Old Regime and the French Revolution.* Garden City, NY, 1955. Originally written in 1856, this remains a provocative analysis of the revolution's legacy.

Trouillot, Michel Rolph. *Silencing the Past.* Boston, 1995. Essays on the Haitian revolution.

Woloch, Isser. *The New Regime: Transformations of the French Civic Order, 1789–1820.* New York, 1994. The fate of revolutionary civic reform.

Woolf, Stuart. *Napoleon's Integration of Europe.* New York, 1991. Technical but very thorough.

CHAPTER 19

Bridenthal, Renate, Claudia Koonz, and Susan Stuard, eds. *Becoming Visible: Women in European History.* 2d ed. Boston, 1987. Excellent, wide-ranging introduction.

Briggs, Asa. *Victorian Cities.* New York, 1963. A survey of British cities, stressing middle-class attitudes toward the new urban environment.

Chevalier, Louis. *Laboring Classes and Dangerous Classes during the First Half of the Nineteenth Century.* New York, 1973. An important, though controversial, account of crime, class, and middle-class perceptions of life in Paris.

Cipolla, Carlo M., ed. *The Industrial Revolution, 1700–1914.* New York, 1976. A collection of essays that emphasizes the wide range of industrializing experiences in Europe.

Clark, Anna. *The Struggle for the Breeches: Gender and the Making of the British Working Class.* Berkeley, CA, 1997. Examines the process of class formation during the industrial revolution in Britain through the lens of gender.

Cott, Nancy. *The Bonds of Womanhood: "Woman's Sphere" in New England, 1780–1935.* New Haven, CT, and London, 1977. One of the most influential studies of the paradoxes of domesticity.

Davidoff, Leonore, and Catherine Hall. *Family Fortunes: Men and Women of the English Middle Class, 1780–1850.* Chicago, 1985. A brilliant and detailed study of the lives and ambitions of several English families.

Ferguson, Niall. "The European Economy, 1815–1914." In *The Nineteenth Century,* ed. T. C. W. Blanning. Oxford and New York, 2000. A very useful short essay.

Gay, Peter. *The Bourgeois Experience: Victoria to Freud.* New York, 1984. A multivolume, path-breaking study of middle-class life in all its dimensions.

———. *Schnitzler's Century: The Making of Middle-Class Culture, 1815–1914.* New York and London, 2002. A synthesis of some of the arguments presented in *The Bourgeois Experience.*

Hellerstein, Erna, Leslie Hume, and Karen Offen, eds. *Victorian Women: A Documentary Account.* Stanford, CA, 1981. Good collection of documents, with excellent introductory essays.

Hobsbawm, Eric J. *The Age of Revolution, 1789–1848.* London, 1962.

———, and George Rudé. *Captain Swing: A Social History of the Great English Agricultural Uprising of 1830.* New York, 1975. Analyzes rural protest and politics.

Horn, Jeff. *The Path Not Taken: French Industrialization in the Age of Revolution, 1750–1830.* Cambridge, 2006. Argues that industrialization in France succeeded in ways that other historians have not appreciated, and was much more than a failed attempt to imitate the British model.

Jones, Eric. *The European Miracle: Environments, Economies and Geopolitics in the History of Europe and Asia.* Cambridge, 2003. Argues that the Industrial Revolution is best understood as a European phenomenon.

Kemp, Tom. *Industrialization in Nineteenth-Century Europe.* London, 1985. Good general study.

Kindelberger, Charles. *A Financial History of Western Europe.* London, 1984. Emphasis on finance.

Landes, David S. *The Unbound Prometheus: Technological Change and Industrial Development in Western Europe from 1750 to the Present.* London, 1969. Excellent and thorough on technological change and its social and economic context.

McNeill, J. R. *Something New under the Sun: An Environmental History of the Twentieth-Century World.* New York and London, 2000. Short section on the nineteenth century.

Mokyr, Joel. *The Lever of Riches: Technological Creativity and Economic Progress.* New York, 1992. A world history, from antiquity through the nineteenth century

O'Gráda, Cormac. *Black '47 and Beyond: The Great Irish Famine.* Princeton, NJ, 1999.

———. *The Great Irish Famine.* Cambridge, 1989. A fascinating and recent assessment of scholarship on the famine.

Kenneth Pomeranz. *The Great Divergence: China, Europe, and the Making of the Modern World Economy.* Princeton, NJ, 2000. Path-breaking global history of the Industrial Revolution that argues that Europe was not as different from other parts of the world as scholars have previously thought.

Rendall, Jane. *The Origins of Modern Feminism: Women in Britain, France and the United States, 1780–1860.* New York, 1984. Helpful overview.

Rose, Sonya O. *Limited Livelihoods: Gender and Class in Nineteenth-Century England.* Berkeley, CA, 1992. On the intersection of culture and economics.

Sabean, David Warren. *Property, Production, and Family Neckarhausen, 1700–1870.* New York, 1990. Brilliant and very detailed study of gender roles and family.

Sabel, Charles, and Jonathan Zeitlin. "Historical Alternatives to Mass Production." *Past and Present* 108 (August 1985): 133–176. On the many forms of modern industry.

Schivelbusch, Wolfgang. *Disenchanted Night: The Instrialization of Light in the Nineteenth Century.* Berkeley, CA, 1988.

———. *The Railway Journey.* Berkeley, 1986. Schivelbusch's imaginative studies are among the best ways to understand how the transformations of the nineteenth century changed daily experiences.

Thompson, E. P. *The Making of the English Working Class.* London, 1963. Shows how the French and Industrial Revolutions fostered the growth of working-class consciousness. A brilliant and important work.

Tilly, Louise, and Joan Scott. *Women, Work and the Family.* New York, 1978. Now the classic study.

Valenze, Deborah. *The First Industrial Woman.* New York, 1995. Excellent and readable on industrialization and economic change in general.

Williams, Raymond. *Keywords: A Vocabulary of Culture and Society.* New York, 1976. Brilliant and indispensable for students of culture, and now updated as *New Keywords: A Revised Vocabulary of Culture and Society* (2005), by Lawrence Grossberg and Meaghan Morris.

Zeldin, Theodore. France, 1848–1945, 2 vols. Oxford, 1973–1977. Eclectic and wide-ranging social history.

CHAPTER 20

Anderson, Benedict. *Imagined Communities: Reflections on the Origin and Spread of Nationalism.* London, 1983. The most influential recent study of the subject, highly recommended for further reading.

Barzun, Jacques. *Classic, Romantic, and Modern.* Chicago, 1943. An enduring and penetrating mid-twentieth-century defense of the Romantic sensibility by a humane and influential cultural historian.

Berlin, Isaiah. *Karl Marx: His Life and Environment.* 4th ed. New York, 1996. An excellent short account.

Briggs, Asa. *The Age of Improvement, 1783–1867.* New York, 1979. A survey of England from 1780 to 1870, particularly strong on Victorian attitudes.

Colley, Linda. *Britons: Forging the Nation, 1707–1837.* New Haven, CT, 1992. An important analysis of Britain's emerging national consciousness in the eighteenth and early nineteenth centuries.

Furet, François. *Revolutionary France, 1770–1880.* New York, 1970. An excellent and fresh overview by one of the preeminent historians of the revolution of 1789.

Gilbert, Sandra M., and Susan Gubar. *The Madwoman in the Attic: The Woman Writer and the Nineteenth-Century Literary Imagination.* New Haven, CT, and London, 1970. A study of the history of women writers and on examination of women writers as historians of their time.

Kramer, Lloyd. *Nationalism: Political Cultures in Europe and America, 1775–1865.* London, 1998. Excellent recent overview.

Langer, William. *Political and Social Upheaval, 1832–1851.* New York, 1969. Long the standard and still the most comprehensive survey.

Laven, David, and Lucy Riall. *Napoleon's Legacy: Problems of Government in Restoration Europe.* London, 2002. A recent collection of essays.

Levinger, Matthew. *Enlightened Nationalism: The Transformation of Prussian Political Culture 1806–1848.* New York, 2000. A nuanced study of Prussian conservatism, with implications for the rest of Europe.

Macfie, A. L. *Orientalism.* London, 2002. Introductory but very clear.

Merriman, John M., ed. *1830 in France.* New York, 1975. Emphasizes the nature of revolution and examines events outside Paris.

Pinkney, David. *The French Revolution of 1830.* Princeton, NJ,1972. A reinterpretation, now the best history of the revolution.

Porter, Roy, and Mikulas Teich, eds. *Romanticism in National Context.* Cambridge, 1988.

Raeff, Marc. *The Decembrist Movement.* New York, 1966. A study of the Russian uprising with documents.

Sahlins, Peter. *Forest Rites: The War of the Demoiselles in Nineteenth-Century France.* Cambridge, MA, 1994. A fascinating study of relations among peasant communities, the forests, and the state.

Said, Edward W. *Orientalism.* New York, 1979. A brilliant and biting study of the imaginative hold of the Orient on European intellectuals.

Saville, John. *1848: The British State and the Chartist Movement.* New York, 1987. A detailed account of the movement's limited successes and ultimate failure.

Schroeder, Paul. *The Transformation of European Politics, 1763–1848.* Oxford and New York, 1994. For those interested in international relations and diplomacy; massively researched and a fresh look at the period. Especially good on the Congress of Vienna.

Sewell, William H. *Work and Revolution in France: The Language of Labor from the Old Regime to 1848.* Cambridge, 1980. A very influential study of French radicalism and its larger implications.

Smith, Bonnie. *The Gender of History: Men, Women, and Historical Practice.* Cambridge, MA, 1998. On Romanticism and the historical imagination.

Sperber, Jonathan. *Karl Marx: A Nineteenth-Century Life.* New York, 2013. A detailed biography examining Marx's public and private engagements, setting him in the context of his time.

Wordsworth, Jonathan, Michael C. Jaye, and Robert Woof. *William Wordsworth and the Age of English Romanticism.* New Brunswick, NJ, 1987. Wide ranging and beautifully illustrated, a good picture of the age.

CHAPTER 21

Agulhon, Maurice. *The Republican Experiment, 1848–1852.* New York, 1983. A full treatment of the revolution in France.

Beales, Derek. *The Risorgimento and the Unification of Italy.* New York, 1971. Objective, concise survey of Italian unification.

Blackbourn, David. *The Long Nineteenth Century: A History of Germany, 1780–1918.* New York, 1998.

Blackbourn, David, and Geoff Eley. *The Peculiarities of German History: Bourgeois Society and Politics in Nineteenth-Century Germany.* Oxford, 1984. Critical essays on the course of German history during the age of national unification and after.

Blackburn, Robin. *The Overthrow of Colonial Slavery.* London, 1988. Brilliant and detailed overview of the social history of slavery and antislavery movements.

Brophy, James M. *Capitalism, Politics, and Railroads in Prussia, 1830–1870.* Columbus, Ohio, 1998. Important, clear, and helpful.

Coppa, Frank. *The Origins of the Italian Wars of Independence.* London, 1992. Lively narrative.

Craig, Gordon. *Germany, 1866–1945.* New York, 1978. An excellent and thorough synthesis.

Davis, David Brian. *Inhuman Bondage: The Rise and Fall of Slavery in the New World.* New York, 2006. As one reviewer aptly puts it, "A gracefully fashioned masterpiece."

Deak, Istvan. *The Lawful Revolution: Louis Kossuth and the Hungarians, 1848–1849.* New York, 1979. The best on the subject.
Eyck, Erich. *Bismarck and the German Empire.* 3d ed. London, 1968. The best one-volume study of Bismarck.
Hamerow, Theodore S. *The Birth of a New Europe: State and Society in the Nineteenth Century.* Chapel Hill, NC, 1983. A discussion of political and social change, and their relationship to industrialization and the increase in state power.
———. *The Social Foundations of German Unification, 1858–1871.* 2 vols. Princeton, NJ, 1969–1972. Concentrates on economic factors that determined the solution to the unification question. An impressive synthesis.
Higonnet, Patrice. *Paris: Capital of the World.* London, 2002. Fascinating and imaginative study of Paris as "capital of the nineteenth century."
Hobsbawm, Eric J. *The Age of Capital, 1848–1875.* London, 1975. Among the best introductions.
———. *Nations and Nationalism since 1870: Programme, Myth, Reality.* 2d ed. Cambridge, 1992. A clear, concise analysis of the historical and cultural manifestations of nationalism.
Howard, Michael. *The Franco-Prussian War.* New York, 1981. The war's effect on society.
Hutchinson, John, and Anthony Smith, eds. *Nationalism.* New York, 1994. A collection of articles, not particularly historical, but with the merit of discussing non-European nationalisms.
Johnson, Susan. *Roaring Camp.* New York, 2000. A history of one mining camp in California and a micro-history of the larger forces changing the West and the world.
Kolchin, Peter. *Unfree Labor: American Slavery and Russian Serfdom.* Cambridge, MA, 1987. Pioneering comparative study.
Mack Smith, Denis. *Cavour and Garibaldi.* New York, 1968.
———. *The Making of Italy, 1796–1870.* New York, 1968. A narrative with documents.
McPherson, James. *Battle Cry of Freedom: The Civil War Era.* New York, 1988. Universally acclaimed and prize-winning book on the politics of slavery and the conflicts entailed in nation building in mid-nineteenth-century United States.
Pflanze, Otto. *Bismarck and the Development of Germany.* 2d ed. 3 vols. Princeton, NJ, 1990. Extremely detailed analysis of Bismarck's aims and policies.
Pinkney, David. *Napoleon III and the Rebuilding of Paris.* Princeton, NJ, 1972. An interesting account of the creation of modern Paris during the Second Empire.
Robertson, Priscilla. *Revolutions of 1848: A Social History.* Princeton, NJ, 1952. Old-fashioned narrative, but very readable.
Sammons, Jeffrey L. *Heinrich Heine: A Modern Biography.* Princeton, NJ, 1979. An excellent historical biography as well as a study of culture and politics.
Scott, Rebecca J. *Degrees of Freedom: Louisiana and Cuba after Slavery.* Cambridge, MA, 2008. Brings the lives of slaves and their owners to life during the era of emancipation in a comparative history that places the southern United States in the context of the Atlantic world.
Sheehan, James J. *German Liberalism in the Nineteenth Century.* Chicago, 1978. Fresh and important synthesis.
Sperber, Jonathan. *The European Revolutions, 1848–1851.* Cambridge, 2005. An excellent synthesis and the best one-volume treatment of the 1848 revolutions, describing the reasons for their failure.
———. *Rhineland Radicals: The Democratic Movement and the Revolution of 1848–1849.* Princeton, NJ, 1993. A detailed study of Germany, by the author of an overview of the revolutions of 1848.
Stearns, Peter N. *1848: The Revolutionary Tide in Europe.* New York, 1974. Stresses the social background of the revolutions.
Zeldin, Theodore. *The Political System of Napoleon III.* New York, 1958. Compact and readable, by one of the major scholars of the period.

CHAPTER 22

Achebe, Chinua. *Things Fall Apart.* Expanded edition with notes. Portsmouth, NH, 1996. An annotated edition of the now classic novel about colonial Africa.
Adas, Michael. *Machines as the Measure of Man: Science, Technology, and Ideologies of Western Dominance.* Ithaca, NY, and London, 1989. An important study of Europeans' changing perceptions of themselves and others during the period of industrialization.
Bayly, C. A. *Indian Society and the Making of the British Empire.* Cambridge, 1988. A good introduction, and one that bridges eighteenth- and nineteenth-century imperialisms.
Burbank, Jane, and Frederick Cooper. *Empires in World History: Power and the Politics of Difference.* Princeton, NJ, 2010. Powerful synthesis that sets European empires in the broader context of world history.
Burton, Antoinette. *Burdens of History: British Feminists, Indian Women, and Imperial Culture, 1865–1915.* Chapel Hill, NC, 1994. On the ways in which women and feminists came to support British imperialism.
Cain, P. J., and A. G. Hopkins. *British Imperialism, 1688–2000.* London, 2002. One of the most influential studies. Excellent overview and exceptionally good on economics.
Chakrabarty, Dipesh. *Provincializing Europe: Postcolonial Thought and Historical Difference.* Princeton, 2000. Sophisticated theoretical challenge to European narratives of social and political progress.
Clancy Smith, Julia, and Frances Gouda. *Domesticating the Empire: Race, Gender, and Family Life in French and Dutch Colonialism.* Charlottesville, VA, and London, 1998. A particularly good collection of essays that both breaks new historical ground and is accessible to nonspecialists. Essays cover daily life and private life in new colonial cultures.
Cohn, Bernard S. *Colonialism and its Forms of Knowledge.* Princeton, 1996. Argues that new forms of cultural knowledge were essential to the project of British imperialism in India.
Conklin, Alice. *A Mission to Civilize: The Republican idea of Empire in France and West Africa, 1895–1930.* Stanford, CA, 1997. One of the best studies of how the French reconciled imperialism with their vision of the Republic.
Cooper, Frederick. *Colonialism in Question: Theory, Knowledge, History.* Berkeley, 2005. Crucial collection of path-breaking essays on the history of colonialism.

Cooper, Frederick, and Ann Laura Stoler. *Tensions of Empire: Colonial Cultures in a Bourgeois World*. Berkeley, CA, 1997. New approaches, combining anthropology and history, with an excellent bibliography.

Darwin, John. *The Empire Project: The Rise and Fall of the British World System*. Cambridge, 2009.

Headrick, Daniel R. *The Tools of Empire: Technology and European Imperialism in the Nineteenth Century*. Oxford, 1981. A study of the relationship between technological innovation and imperialism.

Hobsbawm, Eric. *The Age of Empire, 1875–1914*. New York, 1987. Surveys the European scene at a time of apparent stability and real decline.

Hochschild, Adam. *King Leopold's Ghost: A Story of Greed, Terror, and Heroism in Colonial Africa*. Boston, 1998. Reads like a great novel.

Hull, Isabell. *Absolute Destruction: Military Culture and the Practices of War in Imperial Germany*. Ithaca, 2005. A study of the German military and its role in imperial expansion in Africa, arguing that the experience was crucial in shaping the institution as it entered the twentieth century.

Lorcin, Patricia. *Imperial Identities: Stereotyping, Prejudice and Race in Colonial Algeria*. New York, 1999.

Louis, William Roger. *The Oxford History of the British Empire*. 5 vols. Oxford, 1998. Excellent and wide-ranging collection of the latest research.

Metcalf, Thomas. *Ideologies of the Raj*. Cambridge, 1995.

Pakenham, Thomas. *The Scramble for Africa, 1876–1912*. London, 1991. A well-written narrative of the European scramble for Africa in the late nineteenth century.

Prochaska, David. *Making Algeria French: Colonialism in Bône, 1870–1920*. Cambridge, 1990. One of the few social histories of European settlement in Algeria in English.

Robinson, Ronald, and J. Gallagher. *Africa and the Victorians: The Official Mind of Imperialism*. London, 1961. A classic.

Said, Edward. *Culture and Imperialism*. New York, 1993. A collection of brilliant, sometimes controversial, essays.

Sangari, Kumkum, and Sudesh Vaid. *Recasting Women: Essays in Colonial History*. New Delhi, 1989. A collection of essays on women in India.

Schneer, Jonathan. *London 1900: The Imperial Metropolis*. New Haven, CT, 1999. Excellent study of the empire—and opposition to empire—in the metropole.

Spence, Jonathan. *The Search for Modern China*. New York, 1990. An excellent and readable introduction to modern Chinese history.

CHAPTER 23

Berghahn, Volker. *Imperial Germany, 1871–1914: Economy, Society, Culture, and Politics*. Providence, 1994. Inclusive history that seeks to go beyond standard political accounts.

Berlanstein, Lenard. *The Working People of Paris, 1871–1914*. Baltimore, MD, 1984. A social history of the workplace and its impact on working men and women.

Blackbourn, David. *The Long Nineteenth Century: A History of Germany, 1780–1918*. New York, 1998. Among the best surveys of German society and politics.

Bowler, Peter J. *Evolution: The History of an Idea*. Berkeley, CA, 1984. One of the author's several excellent studies of evolution of Darwinism.

Burns, Michael. *Dreyfus: A Family Affair*. New York, 1992. Follows the story Dreyfus through the next generations.

Clark, T. J. *The Painting of Modern Life: Paris in the Art of Manet and His Followers*. New York, 1985. Argues for seeing impressionism as a critique of French society.

Eley, Geoff. *Forging Democracy*. Oxford, 2002. Wide-ranging and multinational account of European radicalism from 1848 to the present.

Engelstein, Laura. *Slavophile Empire: Imperial Russia's Illiberal Path*. Ithaca, 2009. An examination of Russia's political culture before World War 1, with an eye toward later evolution in the twentieth century.

Frank, Stephen. *Crime, Cultural Conflict, and Justice in Rural Russia, 1856–1914*. Berkeley, CA, 1999. A revealing study of social relations from the ground up.

Gay, Peter. *The Bourgeois Experience: Victoria to Freud*, 5 vols. New York, 1984–2000. Imaginative and brilliant study of private life and middle class culture.

———. *Freud: A Life of Our Time*. New York, 1988. Beautifully written and lucid about difficult concepts; now the best biography.

Harris, Ruth. *Dreyfus: Politics, Emotion, and the Scandal of the Century*. London, 2011. A reassessment of the politics of the Dreyfus affair, with a eye toward its resonance in the culture as a whole.

Herbert, Robert L. *Impressionism: Art, Leisure, and Parisian Society*. New Haven, CT, 1988. An accessible and important study of the impressionists and the world they painted.

Hughes, H. Stuart. *Consciousness and Society*. New York, 1958. A classic study on late-nineteenth-century European thought.

Jelavich, Peter. *Munich and Theatrical Modernism: Politics, Playwriting, and Performance, 1890–1914*. Cambridge, MA, 1985. On modernism as a revolt against nineteenth-century conventions.

Jones, Gareth Stedman. *Outcast London*. Oxford, 1971. Studies the breakdown in class relationships during the second half of the nineteenth century.

Joyce, Patrick. *Visions of the People: Industrial England and the Question of Class, 1848–1914*. New York, 1991. A social history of the workplace.

Kelly, Alfred. *The German Worker: Autobiographies from the Age of Industrialization*. Berkeley, CA, 1987. Excerpts from workers' autobiographies provide fresh perspective on labor history.

Kern, Stephen. *The Culture of Time and Space*. Cambridge, MA, 1983. A cultural history of the late nineteenth century.

Lidtke, Vernon. *The Alternative Culture: Socialist Labor in Imperial Germany*. New York, 1985. A probing study of working-class culture.

Marrus, Michael Robert. *The Politics of Assimilation: A Study of the French Jewish Community at the Time of the Dreyfus Affair*. Oxford, 1971. Excellent social history.

Micale, Mark S. *Approaching Hysteria: Disease and Its Interpretations*. Princeton, NJ, 1995. Important study of the history of psychiatry before Freud.

Rupp, Leila J. *Worlds of Women: The Making of an International Women's Movement*. Princeton, NJ, 1997.

Schivelbusch, Wolfgang. *Disenchanted Night: The Industrialization of Light in the Nineteenth Century.* Berkeley, CA, 1995. Imaginative study of how electricity transformed everyday life.

Schorske, Carl E. *Fin-de-Siècle Vienna: Politics and Culture.* New York, 1980. Classic account of avant-garde art, music, and intellectual culture set against the background of mass politics in the Austrian capital.

Schwartz, Vanessa. *Spectacular Realities: Early Mass Culture in Fin-de-Siècle Paris.* Berkeley, 1998. Innovative approach to the emergence of mass culture in modern France.

Showalter, Elaine. *The Female Malady: Women, Madness, and English Culture, 1890–1980.* New York, 1985. Brilliant and readable on Darwin, Freud, gender, and the First World War.

Silverman, Deborah L. *Art Nouveau in Fin-de-Siècle France: Politics, Psychology, and Style.* Berkeley, CA, 1989. A study of the relationship between psychological and artistic change.

Smith, Bonnie. *Changing Lives: Women in European History since 1700.* New York, 1988. A useful overview of European women's history.

Stern, Fritz. *The Politics of Cultural Despair: A Study of the Rise of the Germanic Ideology.* Berkeley, 1974. Classic account of the rise of nationalist and populist politics in German-speaking lands of central Europe before World War I.

Tickner, Lisa. *The Spectacle of Women: Imagery of the Suffrage Campaign, 1907–14.* Chicago, 1988. A very engaging study of British suffragism.

Verner, Andrew. *The Crisis of Russian Autocracy: Nicholas II and the 1905 Revolution.* Princeton, NJ, 1990. A detailed study of this important event.

Vital, David. *A People Apart: A Political History of the Jews in Europe, 1789-1939.* Oxford and New York, 1999. Comprehensive and extremely helpful.

Walkowitz, Judith. *City of Dreadful Delight: Narratives of Sexual Danger in Late-Victorian London.* Chicago, 1992. Cultural history of the English capital at the end of the nineteenth century.

Weber, Eugen. *Peasants into Frenchmen: The Modernization of Rural France, 1870–1914.* Stanford, CA, 1976. A study of how France's peasantry was assimilated into the Third Republic.

Wehler, Hans-Ulrich. *The German Empire, 1871–1918.* Dover, 1997. Standard account by respected German historian.

CHAPTER 24

Aksakal, Mustapha. *The Ottoman Road to War in 1914: The Ottoman Empire and the First World War.* Cambridge, 2009. A compelling look at Ottoman involvement in the First World War.

Bourke, Joanna. *Dismembering the Male: Men's Bodies, Britain, and the Great War.* Chicago, 1996. A cultural history of the war's effects on male bodies and codes of masculinity.

Chickering, Roger. *Imperial Germany and the Great War, 1914–1918.* New York, 1998. An excellent synthesis.

Clark, Christopher. *The Sleepwalkers: How Europe Went to War in 1914.* New York, 2013. Comprehensive reassessment of the war's origins.

Eksteins, Modris. *Rites of Spring: The Great War and the Birth of the Modern Age.* New York, 1989. Fascinating, though impressionistic, on war, art, and culture.

Ferguson, Niall. *The Pity of War.* London, 1998. A fresh look at the war, including strategic issues, international relations, and economics.

Ferro, Marc. *The Great War, 1914–1918.* London, 1973. Very concise overview.

Figes, Orlando. *A People's Tragedy: A History of the Russian Revolution.* New York, 1997. Excellent, detailed narrative.

Fischer, Fritz. *War of Illusions.* New York, 1975. Deals with Germany within the context of internal social and economic trends.

Fitzpatrick, Sheila. *The Russian Revolution, 1917–1932.* New York and Oxford, 1982. Concise overview.

Fussell, Paul. *The Great War and Modern Memory.* New York, 1975. A brilliant examination of British intellectuals' attitudes toward the war.

Hynes, Samuel. *A War Imagined: The First World War and English Culture.* New York, 1991. The war as perceived on the home front.

Jelavich, Barbara. *History of the Balkans: Twentieth Century.* New York, 1983. Useful for an understanding of the continuing conflict in eastern Europe.

Joll, James. *The Origins of the First World War.* London, 1984. Comprehensive and very useful.

Keegan, John. *The First World War.* London, 1998. The best overall military history.

Macmillan, Margaret, and Richard Holbrooke. *Paris 1919: Six Months That Changed the World.* New York, 2003. Fascinating fresh look at the peace conference.

Mazower, Mark. *Dark Continent: Europe's Twentieth Century.* New York, 1999. An excellent survey, particularly good on nations and minorities in the Balkans and eastern Europe.

Rabinowitch, Alexander. *The Bolsheviks Come to Power.* New York, 1976. A well-researched and carefully documented account.

Roberts, Mary Louise. *Civilization without Sexes: Reconstructing Gender in Postwar France, 1917–1927.* Chicago, 1994. A prize-winning study of the issues raised by the "new woman."

Schivelbusch, Wolfgang. *The Culture of Defeat: On National Trauma, Mourning, and Recovery.* New York, 2001. Fascinating if impressionistic comparative study.

Smith, Leonard. *Between Mutiny and Obedience: The Case of the French Fifth Infantry Division during World War I.* Princeton, NJ, 1994. An account of mutiny and the reasons behind it.

Stevenson, David. *Cataclysm: The First World War as Political Tragedy.* New York, 2003. Detailed and comprehensive, now one of the best single-volume studies.

Stites, Richard. *Revolutionary Dreams: Utopian Visions and Experimental Life in the Russian Revolution.* New York, 1989. The influence of utopian thinking on the revolution.

Suny, Ronald Grigor, Fatma Muge Gocek, and Norman Naimark, eds. *A Question of Genocide: Armenians and Turks at the End of the Ottoman Empire.* Oxford, 2011. Multi-author work offering a comprehensive summary of research on the Armenian genocide.

Williams, John. *The Home Fronts: Britain, France and Germany, 1914–1918.* London, 1972. A survey of life away from the battlefield and the impact of the war on domestic life.

Winter, Jay. *Sites of Memory, Sites of Mourning: The Great War in European Cultural History.* Cambridge, 1998. An essential reference on the legacy of World War I in European cultural history.

Winter, Jay and Jean-Louis Robert. *Capital Cities at War: Paris, London, Berlin, 1914–1919.* Cambridge, 1997 (vol. 1), 2007 (vol. 2). Multi-author work on the demographic, social, and cultural effects of the war on civilian populations of three European capitals.

CHAPTER 25

Bosworth, R. J. B. *Mussolini's Italy: Life under the Fascist Dictatorship, 1915–1945.* New York, 2007. Comprehensive account of "everyday" fascism in Italy.

Conquest, Robert. *The Great Terror: A Reassessment.* New York, 1990. One of the first histories of the Terror, should be read in conjunction with others in this list.

Crew, David F., ed. *Nazism and German Society, 1933–1945.* New York, 1994. An excellent and accessible collection of essays.

de Grazia, Victoria. *How Fascism Ruled Women: Italy, 1922–1945.* Berkeley, 1993. The contradictions between fascism's vision of modernity and its commitment to patriarchal instutions, seen from the point of view of Italian women.

Figes, Orlando. *Peasant Russia Civil War: The Volga Countryside in Revolution, 1917–1921.* Oxford, 1989. Detailed and sophisticated but readable. Study of the region from the eve of the revolution through the civil war.

Fitzpatrick, Shelia. *Everyday Stalinism: Ordinary Life in Extraordinary Times: Soviet Russia in the 1930s.* Oxford and New York, 1999. Gripping on how ordinary people dealt with famine, repression, and chaos.

Friedlander, Saul. *Nazi Germany and the Jews: The Years of Persecution. 1933–1939.* Rev. ed. New York, 2007. Excellent; the first of a two-volume study.

Gay, Peter. *Weimar Culture.* New York, 1968. Concise and elegant overview.

Getty, J. Arch, and Oleg V. Naumov. *The Road to Terror: Stalin and the Self-Destruction of the Bolsheviks, 1932–1939.* New Haven, CT, 1999. Combines analysis with documents made public for the first time.

Goldman, Wendy Z. *Women, the State, and Revolution: Soviet Family Policy and Social Life, 1917–1936.* New York, 1993. On the Bolshevik attempts to transform gender and family.

Kershaw, Ian. *Hitler.* 2 vols: *1889–1936 Hubris,* New York, 1999; *1936–1945: Nemesis,* New York, 2001. The best biography: insightful about politics, culture, and society as well as the man.

———. *The Hitler Myth: Image and Reality in the Third Reich.* New York, 1987. Brilliant study of how Nazi propagandists sold the myth of the Fuhrer and why many Germans bought it.

Klemperer, Victor. *I Will Bear Witness: A Diary of the Nazi Years, 1933–1941.* New York, 1999. *I Will Bear Witness: A Diary of the Nazi Years, 1942–1945.* New York, 2001. Certain to be a classic.

Lewin, Moshe. *The Making of the Soviet System: Essays in the Social History of Interwar Russia.* New York, 1985. One of the best to offer a view from below.

Maier, Charles. *Recasting Bourgeois Europe.* Princeton, 1975. Now classic account of the political and social adjustments made between state and society in the interwar years throughout Europe.

McDermott, Kevin. *Stalin: Revolutionary in an Era of War.* Basingstoke, UK, and New York, 2006. Useful, short, and recent.

Montefior, Simon Sebag. *Stalin: The Court of the Red Tsar.* London, 2004. On the relations among the top Bolsheviks, an interesting personal portrait. Takes you inside the inner circle.

Orwell, George. *The Road to Wigan Pier.* London, 1937. On unemployment and life in the coal mining districts of England, by one of the great British writers of the twentieth century.

———. *Homage to Catalonia.* London, 1938. A firsthand account of the Spanish Civil War.

Payne, Stanley G., *A History of Fascism, 1914–1945.* Madison, WI, 1996. Thorough account of the origins and evolution of fascism in Europe through the end of World War II.

Paxton, Robert O. *The Anatomy of Fascism.* New York, 2004. Excellent introduction to a complex subject by a foremost historian of twentieth century Europe.

Peukert, Detlev. *The Weimar Republic.* New York, 1993. Useful and concise history of Weimar by respected German historian of the period.

Rentschler, Eric. *The Ministry of Illusion: Nazi Cinema and Its Afterlife.* Cambridge, MA, 1996. For the more advanced student.

Service, Robert. *Stalin: A Biography.* London, 2004. Updates Tucker.

Suny, Ronald Grigor. *The Revenge of the Past: Nationalism, Revolution, and the Collapse of the Soviet Union.* Stanford, CA, 1993. Path-breaking study of the issues of nationalism and ethnicity form the revolution to the end of the Soviet Union.

Tucker, Robert C. *Stalin as Revolutionary, 1879–1929.* New York, 1973.

———. *Stalin in Power: The Revolution from Above, 1928–1941.* New York, 1990. With *Stalin as Revolutionary* emphasizes Stalin's purpose and method and sets him in the tradition of Russian dictators.

Weitz, Eric D. *Weimar Germany: Promise and Tragedy.* Princeton, NJ, 2009. A valuable and thorough account that ties together the complex connections between Weimar culture and politics in this transformational period.

CHAPTER 26

The U.S. Holocaust Memorial Museum has an extraordinary collection of articles, photographs, and maps. See www.ushmm.org.

Bartov, Omer. *Hitler's Army: Soldiers, Nazis, and War in the Third Reich.* New York, 1991. A Study of the radicalization of the German army on the Russian front.

Braithwaite, Rodric. *Moscow. 1941: A City and Its People at War.* London, 2006. Readable account of one of the turning points of the war.

Browning, Christopher R. *The Path to Genocide: Essays on Launching the Final Solution.* Cambridge, 1992. Discusses changing interpretations and case studies. See also the author's *Ordinary Men: Reserve Police Battalion 101 and the Final Solution in Poland.*

Burrin, Philippe. *France under the Germans: Collaboration and Compromise.* New York, 1996. Comprehensive on occupation and collaboration.

Carr, Raymond. *The Spanish Tragedy: The Civil War in Perspective.* London, 1977. A thoughtful introduction to the Spanish Civil War and the evolution of Franco's Spain.

Davies, Norman. *Heart of Europe: The Past in Poland's Present.* Oxford, 2001. Revised edition of a classic account of Poland's place in European history, with special attention to the second half of the twentieth century.

Dawidowicz, Lucy S. *The War against the Jews, 1933–1945.* New York, 1975. A full account of the Holocaust.

Divine, Robert A. *Roosevelt and World War II.* Baltimore, MD, 1969. A diplomatic history.

Djilas, Milovan. *Wartime.* New York, 1977. An insider's account of the partisans' fighting in Yugoslavia and a good example of civil war within the war.

Fritzsche, Peter. *Life and Death in the Third Reich.* Cambridge, MA, 2009. A compelling account of the appeal of Nazi ideology and the extent to which it was embraced by ordinary people in Germany.

Gellately, Robert, and Ben Kiernan, eds. *The Specter of Genocide: Mass Murder in Historical Perspective.* New York, 2003. A particularly thoughtful collection of essays.

Graham, Helen. *The Spanish Civil War: A Very Short Introduction.* Oxford and New York, 2005. Excellent and very concise, based on the author's new interpretation in the more detailed *The Spanish Republic at War, 1936–1939.* Cambridge, 2002.

Hilberg, Raul. *The Destruction of the European Jews.* 2nd ed. 3 vols. New York, 1985. An excellent treatment of the Holocaust, its origins, and its consequences.

Hitchcock, William I. *The Bitter Road to Freedom: A New History of the Liberation of Europe.* New York, 2008. The story of Europe's liberation from Hitler's control, seen from the point of view of civilian populations.

Kedward, Roderick. *In Search of the Maquis: Rural Resistance in Southern France, 1942–1944.* Oxford, 1993. An engaging study of French guerilla resistance.

Keegan, John. *The Second World War.* New York, 1990. By one of the great military historians of our time.

Marrus, Michael R. *The Holocaust in History.* Hanover, NH, 1987. Thoughtful analysis of central issues.

Mawdsley, Evan. *Thunder in the East: The Nazi-Soviet War, 1941–1945.* New York, 2005.

Megargee, Geoffrey. *War of Annihilation: Combat and Genocide on the Eastern War, 1941.* Lanham, MD, 2006. Represents some of the new historical work on the eastern front.

Merridale, Catherine. *Ivan's War: Life and Death in the Red Army, 1939–1945.* New York, 2006. Raised many questions and insights.

Michel, Henri. *The Shadow War: The European Resistance, 1939–1945.* New York, 1972. Compelling reading.

Milward, Alan S. *War, Economy, and Society, 1939–1945.* Berkeley, CA, 1977. On the economic impact of the war and the strategic impact of the economy.

Noakes, Jeremy, and Geoffrey Pridham. *Nazism: A History in Documents and Eyewitness Accounts, 1919–1945.* New York, 1975. An excellent combination of analysis and documentation.

Overy, Richard. *Russia's War.* New York, 1998. A very readable account that accompanies the PBS series by the same title.

———. *Why the Allies Won.* New York, 1995. Excellent analysis; succint.

Paxton, Robert O. *Vichy France: Old Guard and New Order, 1940–1944.* New York, 1982. Brilliant on collaboration and Vichy's National Revolution.

Roberts, Mary Louise. *What Soldiers Do: Sex and the American GI in World War II France.* Chicago, 2013. Critical reappraisal of how sex between GIs and civilians became an issue for French and U.S. military personnel after the D-Day invasion.

Snyder, Timothy. *Bloodlands: Europe between Hitler and Stalin.* New York, 2010. Thorough and penetrating account of the methods and motives of Hitler's and Stalin's regimes.

Stoff, Michael B. *The Manhattan Project: A Documentary Introduction to the Atomic Age.* New York, 1991. Political, scientific, and historical; excellent documents and commentary.

Weinberg, Gerhard L. *A World At Arms: A Global History of World War II.* Cambridge, 2005. Second edition of a comprehensive and respected global account of the Second World War.

Wilkinson, James D. *The Intellectual Resistance in Europe.* Cambridge, MA, 1981. A comparative study of the movement throughout Europe.

CHAPTER 27

Aron, Raymond. *The Imperial Republic: The United States and the World, 1945–1973.* Lanham, MD, 1974. An early analysis by a leading French political theorist.

Carter, Erica. *How German Is She? Postwar West German Reconstruction and the Consuming Woman.* Ann Arbor, MI, 1997. A thoughtful examination of gender and the reconstruction of the family in West Germany during the 1950s.

Clayton, Anthony. *The Wars of French Decolonization.* London, 1994. Good survey.

Connelly, Matthew. *A Diplomatic Revolution: Algeria's Fight for Independence and the Origins of the Post–Cold War Era.* New York and Oxford, 2003. An international history.

Cooper, Frederick, and Ann Laura Stoler, eds. *Tensions of Empire: Colonial Cultures in a Bourgeois World.* Berkeley, CA, 1997. Collection of new essays, among the best.

Darwin, John. *Britain and Decolonization: The Retreat from Empire in the Postwar World.* New York, 1988. Best overall survey.

Deák, István, Jan T. Gross, and Tony Judt, eds. *The Politics of Retribution in Europe: World War II and Its Aftermath.* Princeton, NJ, 2000. Collection focusing on the attempt to come to terms with the Second World War in Eastern and Western Europe.

Farmer, Sarah. *Martyred Village: Commemorating the 1944 Massacre at Oradour-sur-Glane.* Berkeley, CA, 1999. Gripping story of French attempts to come to terms with collaboration and complicity in atrocities.

Holland, R. F. *European Decolonization 1918–1981: An Introductory Survey.* New York, 1985. Sprightly narrative and analysis.

Jarausch, Konrad Hugo, ed. *Dictatorship as Experience: Towards a Socio-Cultural History of the GDR.* Trans. Eve Duffy. New York, 1999. Surveys recent research on the former East Germany.

Judt, Tony. *The Burden of Responsibility: Blum, Camus, and the French Twentieth Century.* Chicago and London, 1998. Also on French intellectuals.

———. *A Grand Illusion? An Essay on Europe.* New York, 1996. Short and brilliant.

———. *Past Imperfect: French Intellectuals, 1944–1956.* Berkeley, CA, 1992. Very readable, on French intellectuals, who loomed large during this period.

———. *Postwar. A History of Europe Since 1945.* London, 2005. Detailed, comprehensive, and ground breaking, this single volume surpasses any other account of the entire postwar period.

Koven, Seth, and Sonya Michel. *Mothers of a New World: Maternalist Politics and the Origins of Welfare States.* New York, 1993. Excellent essays on the long history of welfare politics.

LaFeber, Walter. *America, Russia, and the Cold War.* New York, 1967. A classic, now in its ninth edition.

Large, David Clay. *Berlin.* New York, 2000. Accessible and engaging.

Leffler, Melvyn P. *A Preponderance of Power: National Security, the Truman Administration, and the Cold War.* Stanford, CA, 1992. Solid political study.

Louis, William Roger. *The Ends of British Imperialism: The Scramble for Empire, Suez, and Decolonization.* London, 2006. Comprehensive and wide ranging.

Macey, David. *Frantz Fanon.* New York, 2000. Comprehensive recent biography.

Medvedev, Roy. *Khrushchev.* New York, 1983. A perceptive biography of the Soviet leader by a Soviet historian.

Milward, Alan S. *The Reconstruction of Western Europe, 1945–1951.* Berkeley, CA, 1984. A good discussion of the "economic miracle."

Moeller, Robert G. *War Stories: The Search for a Usable Past in the Federal Republic of Germany.* Berkeley, CA, 2001. Revealing analyses of postwar culture and politics.

Reynolds, David. *One World Divisible: A Global History Since 1945.* New York, 2000. Fresh approach, comprehensive, and very readable survey.

Rousso, Henri. *The Vichy Syndrome: History and Memory in France since 1944.* Cambridge, MA, 1991. First in a series of books by one of the preeminent French historians.

Schissler, Hanna, ed. *The Miracle Years: A Cultural History of West Germany, 1949–1968.* Princeton, NJ, 2001. The cultural effects of the economic miracle.

Schneider, Peter. *The Wall Jumper: A Berlin Story.* Chicago, 1998. A fascinating novel about life in divided Berlin.

Shepard, Todd. *The Invention of Decolonization: The Algerian War and the Remaking of France.* Ithaca, NY, 2006. Excellent and original: a study of the deeply wrenching war's many ramifications.

Shipway, Martin. *Decolonization and Its Impact: A Comparative Approach to the End of the Colonial Empires.* Malden, MA, 2008. Accessible account emphasizing the unintended consequences of decolonization.

Trachtenberg, Mark. *A Constructed Peace: The Making of the European Settlement, 1945–1963.* Princeton, NJ, 1999. A detailed study of international relations that moves beyond the Cold War framework.

Tessler, Mark. *A History of the Israeli-Palestinian Conflict.* 2nd ed. Bloomington, IN, 2009. Updated edition of the definitive account from the 1990s.

Westad, Odd Arne. *The Global Cold War.* New York, 2005. An international history that sees the roots of the world's present conflict in the history of the Cold War.

Wilder, Gary. *The French Imperial Nation-State: Negritude and Colonial Humanism between the Two World Wars.* Chicago, 2005. Fascinating new study of the Negritude thinkers in their context.

Yergin, Daniel. *Shattered Peace: The Origins of the Cold War.* New York, 1977. Rev. ed. 1990. Dramatic and readable.

Young, Marilyn B. *The Vietnam Wars, 1945–1990.* New York, 1991. Excellent account of the different stages of the war and its repercussions.

CHAPTER 28

Bailey, Beth. *From Front Porch to Back Seat: Courtship in Twentieth-Century America.* Baltimore, MD, 1988. Good historical perspective on the sexual revolution.

Beschloss, Michael, and Strobe Talbott. *At the Highest Levels: The Inside Story of the End of the Cold War.* Boston, 1993. An analysis of the relationship between presidents Gorbachev and George H. W. Bush and their determination to ignore hard-liners.

Brown, Archie. *The Gorbachev Factor.* Oxford and New York, 1996. One of the first serious studies of Gorbachev, by an Oxford scholar of politics.

Caute, David. *The Year of the Barricades: A Journey through 1968.* New York, 1988. A well-written global history of 1968.

Charney, Leo, and Vanessa R. Schwartz, eds. *Cinema and the Invention of Modern Life.* Berkeley, CA, 1995. Collection of essays.

Dallin, Alexander, and Gail Lapidus. *The Soviet System: From Crisis to Collapse.* Boulder, CO, 1995.

de Grazia, Victoria. *Irresistable Empire: America's Advance through Twentieth-Century Europe.* Cambridge, MA, 2006. Thorough exploration of the history of consumer culture in Europe and its links to relations with the United States.

Echols, Alice. *Daring to Be Bad: Radical Feminism in America, 1967–1975.* Minneapolis, Minn., 1989. Good narrative and analysis.

Eley, Geoff. *Forging Democracy: The History of the Left in Europe, 1850–2000.* Oxford and New York, 2002. Among its other qualities, one of the best historical perspectives on the 1960s.

Fink, Carole, Phillipp Gassert, and Detlef Junker, eds. *1968: The World Transformed.* Cambridge, 1998. A transatlantic history of 1968.

Fulbrook, Mary, ed. *Europe since 1945* (The Short Oxford History of Europe). Oxford, 2001. Particularly good articles on economics and political economy. Structural analysis.

Garton Ash, Timothy. *In Europe's Name: Germany and the Divided Continent.* New York, 1993. An analysis of the effect of German reunification on the future of Europe.

Glenny, Misha. *The Balkans, 1804–1999: Nationalism, War and the Great Powers.* London, 1999. Good account by a journalist who covered the fighting.

Horowitz, Daniel. *Betty Friedan and the Making of the Feminine Mystique: The American Left, the Cold War, and Modern Feminism.* Amherst, MA, 1998. A reconsideration.

Hosking, Geoffrey. *The Awakening of the Soviet Union.* Cambridge, MA, 1990. The factors that led to the end of the Soviet era.

Hughes, H. Stuart. *Sophisticated Rebels: The Political Culture of European Dissent, 1968–1987.* Cambridge, MA, 1990. The nature of dissent on both sides of the disintegrating Iron Curtain in the years 1988–1989.

Hulsberg, Werner. *The German Greens: A Social and Political Profile.* New York, 1988. The origins, politics, and impact of environmental politics.

Jarausch, Konrad. *The Rush to German Unity.* New York, 1994. The problems of reunification analyzed.

Judah, Tim. *The Serbs: History, Myth, and the Destruction of Yugoslavia.* New Haven, CT, 1997. Overview of Serbian history by journalist who covered the war.

Kaplan, Robert D. *Balkan Ghosts: A Journey through History.* New York, 1993. More a political travelogue than a history, but very readable.

Kotkin, Stephen. *Armegeddon Averted: The Soviet Collapse, 1970–2000.* Oxford, 2001. Excellent short account.

Kurlansky, Mark. *1968: The Year that Rocked the World.* New York, 2005. An accessible introduction for nonspecialists.

Lewin, Moshe. *The Gorbachev Phenomenon.* Expanded ed. Berkeley, CA, 1991. Written as a firsthand account, tracing the roots of Gorbachev's successes and failures.

Lieven, Anatol. *Chechnya, Tomb of Russia Power.* New Haven, CT, and London, 1998. Longer view of the region, by a journalist.

Maier, Charles S. *Dissolution: The Crisis of Communism and the End of East Germany.* Princeton, NJ, 1997. Detailed and sophisticated.

Mann, Michael. *The Dark Side of Democracy: Explaining Ethnic Cleansing.* New York, 2005. Brilliant essay on different episodes from Armenia to Rwanda.

Marwick, Arthur. *The Sixties.* Oxford and New York, 1998. An international history.

Pells, Richard. *Not Like Us: How Europeans Have Loved, Hated, and Transformed American Culture since World War II.* New York, 1997. From the point of view of an American historian.

Poiger, Uta G. *Jazz, Rock, and Rebels: Cold War Politics and American Culture in a Divided Germany.* Berkeley, CA, 2000. Pioneering cultural history.

Sheehan, Neil. *A Bright Shining Lie: John Paul Vann and America in Vietnam.* New York, 1988. A study of the war and its escalation through one of the U.S. Army's field advisers.

Strayer, Robert. *Why Did the Soviet Union Collapse? Understanding Historical Change.* Armonk, NY, and London, 1998. A good introduction, with bibliography.

Suri, Jeremi. *Power and Protest.* New ed. Cambridge, MA, 2005. One of the best of the new global histories of the 1960s, looking at relations between social movements and international relations.

Wright, Patrick. *On Living in an Old Country: The National Past in Contemporary Britain.* New York, 1986. The culture of Britain in the 1980s.

CHAPTER 29

Bowen, John R. *Why the French Don't Like Headscarves: Islam, the State, and Public Space.* Princeton, NJ, 2008. An ethnographic account of this volatile debate in France.

Coetzee, J. M. *Waiting for the Barbarians.* London, 1980. A searing critique of apartheid-era South Africa by a leading Afrikaner novelist.

Epstein, Helen. *The Invisible Cure: Africa, the West, and the Fight Against AIDS.* New York, 2007. One of the best recent studies.

Frieden, Jeffrey H. *Global Capitalism: Its Rise and Fall in the Twentieth Century.* New York, 2007. Broad-ranging history for the advanced student.

Geyer, Michael, and Charles Bright. "World History in a Global Age." *American Historical Review* (October 1995). An excellent short discussion.

Glendon, Mary Ann. *A World Made New: Eleanor Roosevelt and the Universal Declaration of Human Rights.* New York, 2001. A fascinating study of the High Commission in its time by a legal scholar.

Harvey, David. *A Brief History of Neoliberalism.* New York, 2007, A critical account of the history of neoliberalism that encompasses the U.S., Europe, and Asia.

Held, David, et al. *Global Transformations: Politics, Economics, and Culture.* Stanford, CA, 1999. Major survey of the globalization of culture, finance, criminality, and politics.

Hopkins, A. G., ed. *Globalization in World History.* New York, 2002. Excellent introduction, written by one of the first historians to engage the issue.

Hunt, Lynn. *Inventing Human Rights: A History.* New York, 2007. A short study of the continuities and paradoxes in the West's human rights tradition, by one of the foremost historians of the French Revolution. On 1776, 1789, and 1948.

Keddie, Nikki. *Modern Iran: Roots and Results of Revolution.* New Haven, CT, 2003. A revised edition of her major study of Iran's 1979 revolution, with added perspective on Iran's Islamic government.

Lacqueur, Walter. *The Age of Terrorism.* Boston, 1987. An important study of the first wave of post-1960s terrorism.

Landes, David. *The Wealth and Poverty of Nations: Why Some Are So Rich and Some So Poor.* New York, 1998. Leading economic historian's account of globalization's effects on the international economy.

Lewis, Bernard. *The Crisis of Islam: Holy War and Unholy Terror.* New York, 2003. Conservative scholar of the Arab world discussing the political crises that fueled terrorism.

Mckeown, Adam. "Global Migration, 1846–1940." *Journal of World History* 15.2 (2004). Includes references to more work on the subject.

McNeill, J. R. *Something New under the Sun: An Environmental History of the Twentieth-Century World.* New York and London, 2000. Fascinating new approach to environmental history.

Merlini, Cesare, and Olivier Roy, eds. *Arab Society in Revolt: The West's Mediterranean Challenge.* Washington DC, 2012. A multi-author attempt to understand the Arab Spring of 2011

Novick, Peter. *The Holocaust in American Life.* Boston, 1999.

Power, Samantha. *The Problem from Hell: America in the Age of Genocide.* A prize-winning survey of the entire twentieth century, its genocides, and the different human rights movements that responded to them.

Reynolds, David. *One World Divisible: A Global History since 1945.* New York and London, 2000. Excellent study of the different dimensions of globalization.

Roy, Olivier. *Globalized Islam: The Search for a New Ummah.* New York, 2006. Examines changes in religious belief and practice as Islam has spread from its historic centers in the Middle East to other areas of the world, including Europe and North America.

Scott, Joan. *The Politics of the Veil.* Princeton, NJ, 2010. A leading feminist scholar analyzes the debate about the veil and the Islamic headscarf in Europe.

Shilts, Randy. *And the Band Played On: Politics, People, and the AIDS Epidemic.* New York, 1987. An impassioned attack on the individuals and governments that failed to come to grips with the early spread of the disease.

Shlaim, Avi. *The Iron Wall: Israel and the Arab World.* New York, 2000. Leading Israeli historian on the evolution of Israel's defensive foreign policy.

Stiglitz, Joseph E. *Globalization and Its Discontents.* New York, 2002. A recent and important consideration of contemporary globalization's character and the conflicts it creates, particularly over commerce and culture.

———. *Freefall: America, Free Markets, and the Sinking of the World Economy.* New York, 2010. Nobel-prize-winning economist gives account of the financial crisis of 2008.

Turkle, Sherry. *Life on the Screen: Identity in the Age of the Internet.* New York, 1995. An important early study of Web culture and the fluid possibilities of electronic communication.

Winter, Jay. *Dreams of Peace and Freedom: Utopian Moments in the Twentieth Century.* New Haven, CT, 2006. One of the leading historians of war and atrocity turns here to twentieth-century hopes for peace and human rights.

Glossary

1973 OPEC oil embargo Some leaders in the Arab-dominated Organization of the Petroleum Exporting Countries (OPEC) wanted to use oil as a weapon against the West in the Arab-Israeli conflict. After the 1972 Arab-Israeli war, OPEC instituted an oil embargo against Western powers. The embargo increased the price of oil and sparked spiraling inflation and economic troubles in Western nations, triggering in turn a cycle of dangerous recession that lasted nearly a decade. In response, Western governments began viewing the Middle Eastern oil regions as areas of strategic importance.

Abbasid Caliphate (750–930) The Abbasid family claimed to be descendants of Muhammad, and in 750 they successfully led a rebellion against the Umayyads, seizing control of Muslim territories in Arabia, Persia, North Africa, and the Near East. The Abbasids modeled their behavior and administration on that of the Persian princes and their rule on that of the Persian Empire, establishing a new capital at Baghdad.

Peter Abelard (1079–1142) Highly influential philosopher, theologian, and teacher, often considered the founder of the University of Paris.

absolutism Form of government in which one body, usually the monarch, controls the right to make war, tax, judge, and coin money. The term was often used to refer to the state monarchies in seventeenth- and eighteenth-century Europe. In other countries the end of feudalism is often associated with the legal abolition of serfdom, as in Russia in 1861.

abstract expressionism The mid-twentieth-century school of art based in New York that included Jackson Pollock, Willem de Kooning, and Franz Kline. It emphasized form, color, gesture, and feeling instead of figurative subjects.

Academy of Sciences This French institute of scientific inquiry was founded in 1666 by Louis XIV. France's statesmen exerted control over the academy and sought to share in the rewards of any discoveries its members made.

Aeneas Mythical founder of Rome, Aeneas was a refugee from the city of Troy whose adventures were described by the poet Virgil in the *Aeneid,* which mimicked the oral epics of Homer.

Aetolian and Achaean Leagues These two alliances among Greek poleis formed during the Hellenistic period in opposition to the Antigonids of Macedonia. Unlike the earlier defensive alliances of the classic period, each league represented a real attempt to form a political federation.

African National Congress (ANC) Multiracial organization founded in 1912 whose goal was to end racial discrimination in South Africa.

Afrikaners Descendants of the original Dutch settlers of South Africa; formerly referred to as Boers.

agricultural revolution Numerous agricultural revolutions have occurred in the history of Western civilizations. One of the most significant began in the tenth century C.E., and increased the amount of land under cultivation as well as the productivity of the land. This revolution was made possible through the use of new technology, an increase in global temperatures, and more efficient methods of cultivation.

AIDS Acquired Immunodeficiency Syndrome. AIDS first appeared in the 1970s and has developed into a global health catastrophe; it is spreading most quickly in developing nations in Africa and Asia.

Akhenaten (r. 1352–1336 B.C.E.) Pharaoh whose attempt to promote the worship of the sun god, Aten, ultimately weakened his dynasty's position in Egypt.

Alexander the Great (356–323 B.C.E.) The Macedonian king whose conquests of the Persian Empire and Egypt created a new Hellenistic world.

Tsar Alexander II (1818–1881) After the Crimean War, Tsar Alexander embarked on a program of reform and modernization, which included the emancipation of the serfs. A radical assassin killed him in 1881.

Alexius Comnenus (1057–1118) This Byzantine emperor requested Pope Urban II's help in raising an army to recapture Anatolia from the Seljuk Turks. Instead, Pope Urban II called for knights to go to the Holy Land and liberate it from its Muslim captors, which launched the First Crusade.

Algerian War (1954–1962) The war between France and Algerians seeking independence. Led by the National Liberation Front (FLN), guerrillas fought the French army in the mountains and desert of Algeria. The FLN also initiated a campaign of bombing and terrorism in Algerian cities that led French soldiers to torture many Algerians, attracting world attention and international scandal.

Dante Alighieri (c. 1265–1321) Florentine poet and intellectual whose *Divine Comedy* was a pioneering work in the Italian vernacular and a vehicle for political and religious critique.

Allied Powers The First World War coalition of Great Britain, Ireland, Belgium, France, Italy, Russia, Portugal, Greece, Serbia, Montenegro, Albania, and Romania.

al Qaeda The radical Islamic organization founded in the late 1980s by former mujahidin who had fought against the Soviet Union in Afghanistan. Al Qaeda carried out the 9/11 terrorist attacks and is responsible as well for attacks in Africa, Southeast Asia, Europe, and the Middle East.

Ambrose (c. 340–397) One of the early "fathers" of the Church, he helped to define the relationship between the sacred authority of bishops and other Church leaders and the secular authority of worldly rulers. He believed that secular rulers were a part of the Church and therefore subject to it.

Americanization The fear of many Europeans, since the 1920s, that U.S. cultural products, such as film, television, and music, exerted too much influence. Many of the criticisms centered on America's emphasis on mass production and organization. The fears about Americanization were not limited to culture. They extended to corporations, business techniques, global trade, and marketing.

Americas The name given to the two great landmasses of the New World, derived from the name of the Italian geographer Amerigo Vespucci. In 1492, Christopher Columbus reached the Bahamas and the island of Hispaniola, which began an era of Spanish conquest in North and South America. Originally, the Spanish sought a route to Asia. Instead they discovered two continents whose wealth they decided to exploit. They were especially interested in gold and silver, which they either stole from indigenous peoples or mined using indigenous peoples as labor. Silver became Spain's most lucrative export from the New World.

Amnesty International Nongovernmental organization formed in 1961 to defend "prisoners of conscience"—those detained for their beliefs, color, sex, ethnic origin, language, or religion.

Anabaptists Protestant movement that emerged in Switzerland in 1521; its adherents insisted that only adults could be baptized Christians.

anarchists In the nineteenth century, they were a political movement with the aim of establishing small-scale, localized, and self-sufficient democratic communities that could guarantee a maximum of individual sovereignty. Renouncing parties, unions and any form of modern mass organization, the anarchists fell back on the tradition of conspiratorial violence.

Anti–Corn Law League This organization successfully lobbied Parliament to repeal Britain's Corn Laws in 1846. The Corn Laws of 1815 had protected British landowners and farmers from foreign competition by establishing high tariffs, which kept bread prices artificially high for British consumers. The league saw these laws as unfair protection of the aristocracy and pushed for their repeal in the name of free trade.

anti-Semitism Anti-Semitism refers to hostility toward Jewish people. Religious forms of anti-Semitism have a long history in Europe, but in the nineteenth century anti-Semitism emerged as a potent ideology for mobilizing new constituencies in the era of mass politics. Playing on popular conspiracy theories about alleged Jewish influence in society, anti-Semites effectively rallied large bodies of supporters in France during the Dreyfus Affair, and then again during the rise of National Socialism in Germany after the First World War. The Holocaust would not have been possible without the acquiescence or cooperation of many thousands of people who shared anti-Semitic views.

apartheid The racial segregation policy of the Afrikaner-dominated South African government. Legislated in 1948 by the Afrikaner National Party, it existed in South Africa for many decades.

appeasement The policy pursued by Western governments in the face of German, Italian, and Japanese aggression leading up to the Second World War. The policy, which attempted to accommodate and negotiate peace with the aggressive nations, was based on the belief that another global war like the First World War was unimaginable, a belief that Germany and its allies had been mistreated by the terms of the Treaty of Versailles, and a fear that fascist Germany and its allies protected the West from the spread of Soviet communism.

Thomas Aquinas (1225–1274) Dominican friar and theologian whose systematic approach to Christian doctrine was influenced by Aristotle.

Arab-Israeli conflict Between the founding of the state of Israel in 1948 and the present, a series of wars has been fought between Israel and neighboring Arab nations: the war of 1948 when Israel defeated attempts by Egypt, Jordon, Iraq, Syria, and Lebanon to prevent the creation of the new state; the 1956 war between Israel and Egypt over the Sinai peninsula; the 1967 war, when Israel gained control of additional land in the Golan Heights, the West Bank, the Gaza strip, and in the Sinai; and the Yom Kippur War of 1973, when Israel once again fought with forces from Egypt and Syria. A particularly difficult issue in all of these conflicts has been the situation of the 950,000 Palestinian refugees made homeless by the first war in 1948 and the movement of Israeli settlers into the occupied territories (outside of Israel's original borders). In the late 1970s, peace talks between Israel and Egypt inspired some hope of peace, but an ongoing cycle of violence between Palestinians and the Israeli military have made a final settlement elusive.

Arab nationalism During the period of decolonization, secular forms of Arab nationalism, or pan-Arabism, found a wide following in many countries of the Middle East, especially in Egypt, Syria, and Iraq.

Arianism A variety of Christianity condemned as a heresy by the Roman Church, it derives from the teaching of a fourth-century priest called Arius, who rejected the idea that Jesus could be the divine equal of God.

aristocracy From the Greek word meaning "rule of the best." By 1000 B.C.E., the accumulated wealth of successful traders in Greece had created a new type of social class, which was based on wealth rather than warfare or birth. These men saw their wealth as a reflection of their superior qualities and aspired to emulate the heroes of old.

Aristotle (384–322 B.C.E.) A student of Plato, his philosophy was based on the rational analysis of the material world. In contrast to his teacher, he stressed the rigorous investigation of real phenomena, rather than the development of universal ethics. He was, in turn, the teacher of Alexander the Great.

Asiatic Society A cultural organization founded in 1784 by British Orientalists who lauded native culture but believed in colonial rule.

Assyrians A Semitic-speaking people that moved into northern Mesopotamia around 2400 B.C.E.

Athens Athens emerged as the Greek polis with the most markedly democratic form of government through a series of political struggles during the sixth century B.C.E. After its key role in the defeat of two invading Persian forces, Athens became the preeminent naval power of ancient Greece and the exemplar of Greek culture. But it antagonized many other poleis, and became embroiled in a war with Sparta and her allies in 431 B.C.E. Called the Peloponnesian War, this bloody conflict lasted until Athens was defeated in 404 B.C.E.

atomic bomb In 1945, the United States dropped atomic bombs on Hiroshima and Nagasaki in Japan, ending the Second World War. In 1949, the Soviet Union tested its first atomic bomb, and in 1953 both superpowers demonstrated their new hydrogen bombs. Strategically, the nuclearization of warfare polarized the world. Countries without nuclear weapons found it difficult to avoid joining either the Soviet or American military pacts. Over time, countries split into two groups: the superpowers with enormous military budgets and those countries that relied on agreements and international law. The nuclearization of warfare also encouraged "proxy wars" between clients of superpowers. Culturally, the hydrogen bomb came to symbolize the age and both humanity's power and vulnerability.

Augustine (c. 354–397) One of the most influential theologians of all time, Augustine described his conversion to Christianity in his autobiographical *Confessions* and articulated a new Christian worldview in *The City of God*, among other works.

Augustus (63 B.C.E.–14 C.E.) Born Gaius Octavius, this grandnephew and adopted son of Julius Caesar came to power in 27 B.C.E. His reign signals the end of the Roman Republic and the beginning of the Principate, the period when Rome was dominated by autocratic emperors.

Auschwitz-Birkenau The Nazi concentration camp in Poland that was designed to systematically murder Jews and Gypsies. Between 1942 and 1944 over 1 million people were killed in Auschwitz-Birkenau.

Austro-Hungarian Empire The dual monarchy established by the Habsburg family in 1867; it collapsed at the end of the First World War.

authoritarianism A centralized and dictatorial form of government, proclaimed by its adherents to be superior to parliamentary democracy. Authoritarian governments claim to be above the law, do not respect individual rights, and do not tolerate political opposition. Authoritarian regimes that have developed a central ideology such as fascism or communism are sometimes termed "totalitarian."

Avignon A city in southeastern France that became the seat of the papacy between 1305 and 1377, a period known as the "Babylonian Captivity" of the Roman Church.

Aztecs An indigenous people of central Mexico; their empire was conquered by Spanish conquistadors in the sixteenth century.

baby boom (1950s) The post–Second World War upswing in U.S. birth rates; it reversed a century of decline.

Babylon An ancient city between the Tigris and Euphrates Rivers, which became the capital of Hammurabi's empire in the eighteenth century B.C.E. and continued to be an important administrative and commercial capital under many subsequent imperial powers, including the Neo-Assyrians, Chaldeans, Persians, and Romans. It was here that Alexander the Great died in 323 B.C.E.

Babylonian captivity Refers both to the Jews' exile in Babylon during the sixth century B.C.E. and the period from 1309 to 1378, when papal authority was subjugated to the French crown and the papal court was moved from Rome to the French city of Avignon.

Francis Bacon (1561–1626) British philosopher and scientist who pioneered the scientific method and inductive reasoning. In other words, he argued that thinkers should amass many observations and then draw general conclusions or propose theories on the basis of these data.

balance of powers The principle that no country should be powerful enough to destabilize international relations. Starting in the seventeenth century, this goal of maintaining balance influenced diplomacy in western and central Europe for two centuries until the system collapsed with the onset of the First World War.

Balfour Declaration A letter dated November 2, 1917, by Lord Arthur J. Balfour, British foreign secretary, that promised a homeland for the Jews in Palestine.

Laura Bassi (1711–1778) She was accepted into the Academy of Science in Bologna for her work in mathematics, which made her one of the few women to be accepted into a scientific academy in the seventeenth century.

Bastille The Bastille was a royal fortress and prison in Paris. In June 1789, a revolutionary crowd attacked the Bastille to show support for the newly created National Assembly. The fall of the Bastille was the first instance of the people's role in revolutionary change in France.

Bay of Pigs (1961) The unsuccessful invasion of Cuba by Cuban exiles, supported by the U.S. government. The rebels intended to incite an insurrection in Cuba and overthrow the communist regime of Fidel Castro.

Cesare Beccaria (1738–1794) An influential writer during the Enlightenment who advocated for legal reforms. He believed that the only legitimate rationale for punishments was to maintain social order and to prevent other crimes. He argued for the greatest possible leniency compatible with deterrence and opposed torture and the death penalty.

Beer Hall Putsch (1923) An early attempt by the Nazi party to seize power in Munich; Adolf Hitler was imprisoned for a year after the incident.

Benedict of Nursia (c. 480–c. 547) Benedict's rule for monks formed the basis of western monasticism and is still observed in monasteries all over the world.

Benedictine Monasticism This form of monasticism was developed by Benedict of Nursia. Its followers adhere to a defined cycle of daily prayers, lessons, communal worship, and manual labor.

Berlin airlift (1948) The transport of vital supplies to West Berlin by air, primarily under U.S. auspices, in response to a blockade of the city that had been instituted by the Soviet Union to force the Allies to abandon West Berlin.

Berlin Conference (1884) At this conference, the leading colonial powers met and established ground rules for the partition of Africa by European nations. By 1914, 90 percent of African territory was under European control. The Berlin Conference ceded control of the Congo region to a private company run by King Leopold II of Belgium. They agreed to make the Congo valleys open to free trade and commerce, to end the slave trade in the region, and to establish a Congo Free State. In reality, King Leopold II's company established a regime that was so brutal in its treatment of local populations that an international scandal forced the Belgian state to take over the colony in 1908.

Berlin Wall The wall built in 1961 by East German Communists to prevent citizens of East Germany from fleeing to West Germany; it was torn down in 1989.

birth control pill This oral contraceptive became widely available in the mid-1960s. For the first time, women had a simple method of birth control that they could take themselves.

Otto von Bismarck (1815–1898) The prime minister of Prussia and later the first chancellor of a unified Germany, Bismarck was the architect of German unification and helped to consolidate the new nation's economic and military power.

Black Death The epidemic of bubonic plague that ravaged Europe, Asia, and North Africa in the fourteenth century, killing one third to one half of the population.

Black Jacobins A nickname for the rebels in Saint-Domingue, including Toussaint L'Ouverture, a former slave who in 1791 led the slaves of this French colony in the largest and most successful slave insurrection.

Blackshirts The troops of Mussolini's fascist regime; the squads received money from Italian landowners to attack socialist leaders.

Black Tuesday (October 29, 1929) The day on which the U.S. stock market crashed, plunging U.S. and international trading systems into crisis and leading the world into the "Great Depression."

William Blake (1757–1827) Romantic writer who criticized industrial society and factories. He championed the imagination and poetic vision, seeing both as transcending the limits of the material world.

Blitzkrieg The German "lightning war" strategy used during the Second World War; the Germans invaded Poland, France, Russia, and other countries with fast-moving and well-coordinated attacks using aircraft, tanks and other armored vehicles, followed by infantry.

Bloody Sunday On January 22, 1905, the Russian tsar's guards killed 130 demonstrators who were protesting the tsar's mistreatment of workers and the middle class.

Giovanni Boccaccio (1313–1375) Florentine author best known for his *Decameron*, a collection of prose tales about sex, adventure, and trickery written in the Italian vernacular after the Black Death.

Jean Bodin (1530–1596) A French political philosopher whose *Six Books of the Commonwealth* advanced a theory of absolute sovereignty, on the grounds that the state's paramount duty is to maintain order and that monarchs should therefore exercise unlimited power.

Boer War (1898–1902) Conflict between British and ethnically European Afrikaners in South Africa, with terrible casualties on both sides.

Boethius (c. 480–524) Member of a prominent Roman family, he sought to preserve aspects of ancient learning by compiling a series of handbooks and anthologies appropriate for Christian readers. His translations of Greek philosophy provided a crucial link between classical Greek thought and the early intellectual culture of Christianity.

Bolsheviks Former members of the Russian Social Democratic Party who advocated the destruction of capitalist political and economic institutions and started the Russian Revolution. In 1918, the Bolsheviks changed their name to the Russian Communist Party. Prominent Bolsheviks included Vladimir Lenin and Josef Stalin. Leon Trotsky joined the Bolsheviks late but became a prominent leader in the early years of the Russian Revolution.

Napoleon Bonaparte (1769–1821) Corsican-born French general who seized power and ruled as dictator from 1799 to 1814. After the successful conquest of much of Europe, he was defeated by Russian and Prussian forces and died in exile.

Boniface VIII During his pontificate (1294–1303), repeated claims to papal authority were challenged by King Philip IV of France. When Boniface died in 1309 (at the hands of Philip's thugs), the French king moved the papal court from Rome to the French city of Avignon, where it remained until 1378.

Sandro Botticelli (1445–1510) An Italian painter devoted to the blending of classical and Christian motifs by using ideas associated with the pagan past to illuminate sacred stories.

bourgeoisie Term for the middle class, derived from the French word for a town-dweller, *bourgeois*.

Boxer Rebellion (1899–1900) Chinese peasant movement that opposed foreign influence, especially that of Christian missionaries; it was finally put down after the Boxers were defeated by a foreign army composed mostly of Japanese, Russian, British, French, and American soldiers.

Tycho Brahe (1546–1601) Danish astronomer who believed that the careful study of the heavens would unlock the secrets of the universe. For over twenty years, he charted the movements of significant objects in the night sky, compiling the finest set of astronomical data in Europe.

British Commonwealth of Nations Formed in 1926, the Commonwealth conferred "dominion status" on Britain's white settler colonies in Canada, Australia, and New Zealand.

Bronze Age (3200–1200 B.C.E.) The name given to the era characterized by the discovery of techniques for smelting bronze (an alloy of copper and tin), which was then the strongest known metal.

Brownshirts Troops of young German men who dedicated themselves to the Nazi cause in the early 1930s by holding street marches, mass rallies, and confrontations. They engaged in beatings of Jews and anyone who opposed the Nazis.

Lord Byron (1788–1824) Writer and poet whose life helped give the Romantics their reputation as rebels against conformity. He was known for his love affairs, his defense of working-class movements, and his passionate engagement in politics, which led to his death in the war for Greek independence.

Byzantium The name of a small settlement located at the mouth of the Black Sea and at the crossroads between Europe and Asia, it was chosen by Constantine as the site for his new imperial capital of Constantinople in 324. Modern historians use this name to refer to the eastern Roman Empire that persisted in this region until 1453, but the inhabitants of that empire referred to themselves as Romans.

Julius Caesar (100–44 B.C.E.) The Roman general who conquered the Gauls, invaded Britain, and expanded Rome's territory in Asia Minor. He became the dictator of Rome in 46 B.C.E. His assassination led to the rise of his grandnephew and adopted son, Gaius Octavius Caesar, who ruled the Roman Empire as Caesar Augustus.

caliphs Islamic rulers who claim descent from the prophet Muhammad.

John Calvin (1509–1564) French-born theologian and reformer whose radical form of Protestantism was adopted in many Swiss cities, notably Geneva.

Canary Islands Islands off the western coast of Africa that were colonized by Portugal and Spain in the mid-fifteenth century, after which they became bases for further expeditions around the African coast and across the Atlantic.

Carbonari An underground organization that opposed the Concert of Europe's restoration of monarchies. They held influence in southern Europe during the 1820s, especially in Italy.

Carolingian Derived from the Latin name Carolus (Charles), this term refers to the Frankish dynasty that began with the rise to power of Charlemagne's grandfather, Charles Martel (688–741). At its height under Charlemagne (Charles the Great), the dynasty controlled what is now France, Germany, northern Italy, Catalonia, and portions of central Europe. The Carolingian Empire collapsed under the combined weight of Viking raids, economic disintegration, and the growing power of local lords.

Carolingian Renaissance A cultural and intellectual flowering that took place around the court of Charlemagne in the late eighth and early ninth centuries.

Carthage The great maritime empire that grew out of Phoenician trading colonies in North Africa and rivaled the power of Rome. Its wars with Rome, collectively known as the Punic Wars, ended in its destruction in 146 B.C.E.

Cassidorus (c. 490–c. 583) Member of an old senatorial family, he was largely responsible for introducing classical learning into the monastic curriculum and for turning monasteries into centers for the collection, preservation, and transmission of knowledge. His *Institutes*, an influential handbook of classical literature for Christian readers, was intended as a preface to more intensive study of theology and the Bible.

Catholic Church The "universal" (catholic) church based in Rome, which was redefined in the sixteenth century, when the Counter-Reformation resulted in the rebirth of the Catholic faith at the Council of Trent.

Margaret Cavendish (1623–1673) English natural philosopher who developed her own speculative natural philosophy. She used this philosophy to critique those who excluded her from scientific debate.

Camillo Benso di Cavour (1810–1861) Prime minister of Piedmont-Sardinia and founder of the Italian Liberal party; he played a key role in the movement for Italian unification under the Piedmontese king, Victor Emmanuel II.

Central Powers The First World War alliance between Germany, Austria-Hungary, Bulgaria, and Turkey.

Charlemagne (742–814) As king of the Franks (767–813), Charles "the Great" consolidated much of western Europe under his rule. In 800, he was crowned emperor by the pope in Rome, establishing a problematic precedent that would have wide-ranging consequences for western Europe's relationship with the eastern Roman Empire in Byzantium and for the relationship between the papacy and secular rulers.

Charles I (1625–1649) The second Stuart king of England, Charles attempted to rule without the support of Parliament, sparking a controversy that erupted into civil war in 1642. The king's forces were ultimately defeated and Charles himself was executed by act of Parliament, the first time in history that a reigning king was legally deposed and executed by his own government.

Charles II of England Nominally King of England, Ireland, and Scotland after his father Charles I's execution in 1649, Charles II lived in exile until he was restored to the throne in 1660. Influenced by his cousin, King Louis XIV of France, he presided over an opulent royal court until his death in 1685.

Chartists A working-class movement in Britain that called for reform of the British political system during the 1840s. They were supporters of the "People's Charter," which had six demands: universal white male suffrage, secret ballots, an end to property qualifications as a condition of public office, annual parliamentary elections, salaries for members of the House of Commons, and equal electoral districts.

Geoffrey Chaucer (1340–1400) English poet whose collection of versified stories, *The Canterbury Tales*, features characters from a variety of different classes.

Christine de Pisan (c. 1364–c. 1431) Born in Italy, Christine spent her adult life attached to the French court and, after her husband's death, became the first laywoman to earn her living by writing. She is the author of treatises in warfare and chivalry as well as of books and pamphlets that challenge long-standing misogynistic claims.

Church of England Founded by Henry VIII in the 1530s, as a consequence of his break with the authority of the Roman pope.

Winston Churchill (1874–1965) British prime minister who led the country during the Second World War. He also coined the phrase "Iron Curtain" in a speech at Westminster College in 1946.

Cicero (106–43 B.C.E.) Influential Roman senator, orator, Stoic philosopher, and prose stylist. His published writings still form the basis of the instruction in classical Latin grammar and usage.

Cincinnatus (519–c. 430 B.C.E.) A legendary citizen-farmer of Rome who reluctantly accepted an appointment as dictator. After defeating Rome's enemies, he allegedly left his political office and returned to his farm.

Civil Constitution of the Clergy Issued by the French National Assembly in 1790, the Civil Constitution of the Clergy decreed that all bishops and priests should be subject to the authority of the state. Their salaries were to be paid out of the public treasury, and they were required to swear allegiance to the new state, making it clear they served France rather than Rome. The Assembly's aim was to make the Catholic Church of France a truly national and civil institution.

civilizing mission An argument made by Europeans to justify colonial expansion in the nineteenth century. Supporters of this idea believed that Europeans had a duty to impose western ideas of economic and political progress on the indigenous peoples they ruled over in their colonies. In practice, the colonial powers often found that ambitious plans to impose European practices on colonial subjects led to unrest that threatened the stability of colonial rule, and by the early twentieth century most colonial powers were more cautious in their plans for political or cultural transformation.

Civil Rights Movement The Second World War increased African American migration from the American South to northern cities, intensifying a drive for rights, dignity, and independence. By 1960, civil rights groups had started organizing boycotts and demonstrations directed at discrimination against blacks in the South. During the 1960s, civil rights laws passed under President Lyndon B. Johnson did bring African Americans some equality with regard to voting rights and, to a much lesser degree, school desegregation. However, racism continued in areas such as housing, job opportunities, and the economic development of African American communities.

Civil War (1861–1865) Conflict between the northern and southern states of America that cost over 600,000 lives; this struggle led to the abolition of slavery in the United States.

classical learning The study of ancient Greek and Latin texts. After Christianity became the only legal religion of the Roman Empire, scholars needed to find a way to make classical learning applicable to a Christian way of life. Christian monks played a significant role in resolving this problem by reinterpreting the classics for a Christian audience.

Cluny A powerful Benedictine monastery founded in 910 whose enormous wealth and prestige would derive from its independence from secular authorities as well as from its wide network of daughter houses (priories).

Cold War (1945–1991) Ideological, political, and economic conflict in which the USSR and Eastern Europe opposed the United States and Western Europe in the decades after the Second World War. The Cold War's origins lay in the breakup of the wartime alliance between the United States and the Soviet Union in 1945 and resulted in a division of Europe into two spheres: the West, commited to market capitalism, and the East, which sought to build Socialist republics in areas under Soviet Control. The Cold War ended with the collapse of the Soviet Union in 1991.

collectivization Stalin's plan for nationalizing agricultural production, begun in 1929. Twenty-five million peasants were forced to give up their land and join 250,000 large collective farms. Many who resisted were deported to labor camps in the Far East, and Stalin's government cut off food rations to those areas most marked by resistance to collectivization. In the ensuing man-made famines, millions of people starved to death.

Columbian Exchange The widespread exchange of peoples, plants, animals, diseases, goods, and culture between the African and Eurasian landmass (on the one hand) and the region that encompasses the Americas, Australia, and the Pacific Islands (on the other); precipitated by voyage of Columbus in 1492.

Christopher Columbus (1451–1506) A Genoese sailor who persuaded King Ferdinand and Queen Isabella of Spain to fund his expedition across the Atlantic, with the purpose of discovering a new trade route to Asia. His miscalculations landed him in the Bahamas and the island of Hispaniola in 1492.

Commercial Revolution A period of economic development in Europe lasting from c. 1500-c.1800. Advances in agriculture and handicraft production, combined with the expansion of trade networks in the Atlantic world, brought new wealth and new kinds of commercial activity to Europe. The commercial revolution prepared the way for the industrial revolution of the 1800s.

Committee of Public Safety Political body during the French Revolution that was controlled by the Jacobins, who defended the revolution by executing thousands during the Reign of Terror (September 1793–July 1794).

commune A community of individuals who have banded together in a sworn association, with the aim of establishing their independence and setting up their own form of representative government. Many medieval towns originally founded by lords or monasteries gained their independence through such methods.

The Communist Manifesto Radical pamphlet by Karl Marx (1818–1883) that predicted the downfall of the capitalist system and its replacement by a classless egalitarian society. Marx believed that this revolution would be accomplished by workers (the proletariat).

Compromise of 1867 Agreement between the Habsburgs and the peoples living in Hungarian parts of the empire that the Habsburg state would be officially known as the Austro-Hungarian Empire.

Concert of Europe (1814–1815) The body of diplomatic agreements designed primarily by Austrian minister Klemens von Metternich between 1814 and 1848 and supported by other European powers until 1914. Its goal was to maintain a balance of power on the Continent and to prevent destabilizing social and political change in Europe.

conciliarism A doctrine developed in the thirteenth and fourteenth centuries to counter the growing power of the papacy, conciliarism holds that papal authority should be subject to a council of the Church at large. Conciliarists emerged as a dominant force after the Council of Constance (1414–1418) but were eventually outmatched by a rejuvenated papacy.

Congress of Vienna (1814–1815) International conference to reorganize Europe after the downfall of Napoleon and the French Revolution. European monarchies restored the Bourbon family to the French throne, agreed to respect each other's borders and to cooperate in guarding against future revolutions and war.

conquistador Spanish term for "conqueror," applied to the mercenaries and adventurers who campaigned against indigenous peoples in central and southern America.

Conservatives In the nineteenth century, conservatives aimed to legitimize and solidify the monarchy's authority and the hierarchical social order. They believed that change had to be slow, incremental, and managed so that the structures of authority were strengthened and not weakened.

Constantine (275–337) The first emperor of Rome to convert to Christianity, Constantine came to power in 312. In 324, he founded a new imperial capital, Constantinople, on the site of a maritime settlement known as Byzantium.

Constantinople Founded by the emperor Constantine on the site of a village called Byzantium, Constantinople became the new capital of the Roman Empire in 324 and continued to be the seat of imperial power after its capture by the Ottoman Turks in 1453. It is now known as Istanbul.

contract theory of government A theory of government written by Englishman John Locke (1632–1704) which posits that government authority was both contractual and conditional; therefore, if a government has abused its given authority, society had the right to dissolve it and create another.

Nicholas Copernicus (1473–1543) Polish astronomer who advanced the idea that the earth moved around the sun.

cosmopolitanism Stemming from the Greek word meaning "universal city," the culture characteristic of the Hellenistic world challenged and transformed the more narrow worldview of the Greek polis.

cotton gin Invented by Eli Whitney in 1793, this device mechanized the process of separating cotton seeds from the cotton fiber, which sped up the production of cotton and reduced its price. This change made slavery profitable in the United States.

Council of Constance (1417–1420) A meeting of clergy and theologians in an effort to resolve the Great Schism within the Roman Church. The council deposed all rival papal candidates and elected a new pope, Martin V, but it also adopted the doctrine of conciliarism, which holds that the supreme authority within the Church rests with a representative general council and not with the pope. However, Martin V himself was an opponent of this doctrine and refused to be bound by it.

Council of Trent The name given to a series of meetings held in the Italian city of Trent (Trento) between 1545 and 1563, when leaders of the Roman Church reaffirmed Catholic doctrine and instituted internal reforms.

Counter-Reformation The movement to counter the Protestant Reformation, initiated by the Catholic Church at the Council of Trent in 1545.

coup d'état French term for the overthrow of an established government by a group of conspirators, usually with military support.

Crimean War (1854–1856) War waged by Russia against Great Britain and France. Spurred by Russia's encroachment on Ottoman territories, the conflict revealed Russia's military weakness when Russian forces fell to British and French troops.

Cuban missile crisis (1962) Diplomatic standoff between the United States and the Soviet Union that was provoked by the Soviet Union's attempt to base nuclear missiles in Cuba; it brought the world closer to nuclear war than ever before or since.

Cuius regio, eius religio A Latin phrase meaning "as the ruler, so the religion." Adopted as a part of the settlement of the Peace of Augsburg in 1555, it meant that those principalities ruled by Lutherans would have Lutheranism as their official religion and those ruled by Catholics must practice Catholicism.

cult of domesticity Concept associated with Victorian England that idealized women as nurturing wives and mothers.

cult of the Virgin The beliefs and practices associated with the veneration of Mary, the mother of Jesus, which became increasingly popular in the twelfth century.

cuneiform An early writing system that began to develop in Mesopotamia in the fourth millennium B.C.E. By 3100 B.C.E., its distinctive markings were impressed on clay tablets using a wedge-shaped stylus.

Cyrus the Great (c. 585–529 B.C.E.) As architect of the Persian Empire, Cyrus extended his dominion over a vast territory stretching from the Persian Gulf to the Mediterranean and incorporating the ancient civilizations of Mesopotamia. His successors ruled this Persian Empire as "Great Kings."

Darius (521–486 B.C.E.) The Persian emperor whose conflict with Aristagoras, the Greek ruler of Miletus, ignited the Persian Wars. In 490 B.C.E., Darius sent a large army to punish the Athenians for their intervention in Persian imperial affairs, but this force was defeated by Athenian hoplites on the plain of Marathon.

Charles Darwin (1809–1882) British naturalist who wrote *On the Origin of Species* and developed the theory of natural selection to explain the evolution of organisms.

D-Day (June 6, 1944) Date of the Allied invasion of Normandy, under General Dwight Eisenhower, to liberate Western Europe from German occupation.

Decembrists Russian army officers who were influenced by events in France and formed secret societies that espoused liberal governance. They were put down by Nicholas I in December 1825.

Declaration of Independence (1776) Historic document stating the principles of government on which the United States was founded.

Declaration of the Rights of Man and of the Citizen (1789) French charter of liberties formulated by the National Assembly during the French Revolution. The seventeen articles later became the preamble to the new constitution, which the assembly finished in 1791.

democracy In ancient Greece, this form of government allowed a class of propertied male citizens to participate in the governance of their polis; but excluded women, slaves, and citizens without property from the political process. As a result, the ruling class amounted to only a small percentage of the entire population.

René Descartes (1596–1650) French philosopher and mathematician who emphasized the use of deductive reasoning.

Denis Diderot (1713–1784) French philosophe and author who was the guiding force behind the publication of the first encyclopedia. His *Encyclopedia* showed how reason could be applied to nearly all realms of thought and aimed to be a compendium of all human knowledge.

Dien Bien Phu (1954) Defining battle in the war between French colonialists and the Viet Minh that secured North Vietnam for Ho Chi Minh and his army and left the south to form its own government, to be supported by France and the United States.

Diet of Worms The select council of the Church that convened in the German city of Worms and condemned Martin Luther on a charge of heresy in 1521.

Diocletian (245–316) As emperor of Rome from 284 to 305, Diocletian recognized that the empire could not be governed by one man in one place. His solution was to divide the empire into four parts, each with its own imperial ruler, but he himself remained the dominant ruler of the resulting tetrarchy (rule of four). He also initiated the Great Persecution, a time when many Christians became martyrs to their faith.

Directory (1795–1799) Executive committee that governed after the fall of Robespierre and held control until the coup of Napoleon Bonaparte.

Discourse on Method Philosophical treatise by René Descartes (1596–1650) proposing that the path to knowledge was through logical deduction, beginning with one's own self: "I think, therefore I am."

Dominican Order Also called the Order of Preachers, it was founded by Dominic of Osma (1170–1221), a Castilian preacher and theologian, and approved by Innocent III in 1216. The order was dedicated to the rooting out of heresy and the conversion of Jews and Muslims. Many of its members held teaching positions in European universities and contributed to the development of medieval philosophy and theology. Others became the leading administrators of the Inquisition.

Dominion in the British Commonwealth Canadian promise to maintain their fealty to the British crown, even after their independence in 1867; later applied to Australia and New Zealand.

Dreyfus Affair The 1894 French scandal surrounding accusations that a Jewish captain, Alfred Dreyfus, sold military secrets to the Germans. Convicted, Dreyfus was sentenced to solitary confinement for life. However, after public outcry, it was revealed that the trial documents were forgeries, and Dreyfus was pardoned after a second trial in 1899. In 1906, he was fully exonerated and reinstated in the army. The affair revealed the depths of popular anti-Semitism in France.

Alexander Dubček (1921–1992) Communist leader of the Czechoslovakian government who advocated for "socialism with a human face." He encouraged debate within the party, academic and artistic freedom, and less censorship, which led to the "Prague spring" of 1968. People in other parts of Eastern Europe began to demonstrate in support of Dubček and demand their own reforms. When Dubček tried to democratize the Communist party and did not attend a meeting of the Warsaw Pact, the Soviets sent tanks and troops into Prague and ousted Dubček and his allies.

Duma The Russian parliament, created in response to the revolution of 1905.

Dunkirk The French port on the English Channel where the British and French forces retreated after sustaining heavy losses against the German military. Between May 27 and June 4, 1940, the Royal Navy evacuated over 300,000 troops using commercial and pleasure boats.

Eastern Front Battlefront between Berlin and Moscow during the First and Second World Wars..

East India Company (1600–1858) British charter company created to outperform Portuguese and Spanish traders in the Far East; in the eighteenth century the company became, in effect, the ruler of a large part of India. There was also a Dutch East India Company.

Edict of Nantes (1598) Issued by Henry IV of France in an effort to end religious violence. The edict declared France to be a Catholic country but tolerated some forms of Protestant worship.

Edward I of England King of England from 1272 to his death in 1307, Edward presided over the creation of new legal and bureaucratic institutions in his realm, violently subjugated the Welsh, and attempted to colonize Scotland. He expelled English Jews from his domain in 1290.

Eleanor of Aquitaine (1122–1204) Ruler of the wealthy province of Aquitaine and wife of Louis VII of France, Eleanor had her marriage annulled in order to marry the young count of Anjou, Henry Plantagenet, who became King Henry of England a year later. Mother of two future kings of England, she was an important patron of the arts.

Elizabeth I (1533–1603) Protestant daughter of Henry VIII and his second wife, Anne Boleyn, Elizabeth succeeded her sister Mary as the second queen regnant of England (1558–1603).

emancipation of the serfs (1861) The abolition of serfdom was central to Tsar Alexander II's program of modernization and reform, but it produced a limited amount of change. Former serfs now had legal rights. However, farm land was granted to the village communes instead of to individuals. The land was of poor quality and the former serfs had to pay for it in installments to the village commune.

emperor Originally the term for any conquering commander of the Roman army whose victories merited celebration in an official triumph. After Augustus seized power in 27 B.C.E., it was the title born by the sole ruler of the Roman Empire.

empire A centralized political entity consolidated through the conquest and colonization of other nations or peoples in order to benefit the ruler and/or his homeland.

Enabling Act (1933) Emergency act passed by the Reichstag (German parliament) that helped transform Hitler from Germany's chancellor, or prime minister, into a dictator, following the suspicious burning of the Reichstag building and a suspension of civil liberties.

enclosure Long process of privatizing what had been public agricultural land in eighteenth-century Britain; it helped to stimulate the development of commercial agriculture and forced many people in rural areas to seek work in cities during the early stages of industrialization.

The Encyclopedia Joint venture of French philosophe writers, led by Denis Diderot (1713–1784), which proposed to summarize all modern knowledge in a multivolume illustrated work with over 70,000 articles.

Friedrich Engels (1820–1895) German social and political philosopher who collaborated with Karl Marx on many publications.

English Civil War (1642–1649) Conflicts between the English Parliament and King Charles I erupted into civil war, which ended in the defeat of the royalists and the execution of Charles on charges of treason against the crown. A short time later, Parliament's hereditary House of Lords was abolished and England was declared a Commonwealth.

English Navigation Act of 1651 Act stipulating that only English ships could carry goods between the mother country and its colonies.

Enlightenment Intellectual movement in eighteenth-century Europe, that believed in human betterment through the application of reason to solve social, economic, and political problems.

Epicureanism A philosophical position articulated by Epicurus of Athens (c. 342–270 B.C.E.), who rejected the idea of an ordered universe governed by divine forces; instead, he emphasized individual agency and proposed that the highest good is the pursuit of pleasure.

Desiderius Erasmus (c. 1469–1536) Dutch-born scholar, social commentator, and Catholic humanist whose new translation of the Bible influenced the theology of Martin Luther.

Estates-General The representative body of the three estates in France. In 1789, King Louis XVI summoned the Estates-General to meet for the first time since 1614 because it seemed to be the only solution to France's worsening economic crisis and financial chaos.

Etruscans Settlers of the Italian peninsula who dominated the region from the late Bronze Age until the rise of the Roman Republic in the sixth century B.C.E.

Euclid Hellenistic mathematician whose *Elements of Geometry* forms the basis of modern geometry.

eugenics A Greek term, meaning "good birth," referring to the project of "breeding" a superior human race. It was popularly championed by scientists, politicians, and social critics in the late nineteenth and early twentieth centuries.

European Common Market (1957) The Treaty of Rome created the European Economic Community (EEC), or Common Market. The original members were France, West Germany, Italy, Belgium, Holland, and Luxembourg. The EEC sought to abolish trade barriers between its members and it pledged itself to common external tariffs, the free movement of labor and capital among the member nations, and uniform wage structures and social security systems to create similar working conditions in all member countries.

European Union (EU) Successor organization to the European Economic Community or European Common Market, formed by the Maastricht Treaty, which took effect in 1993. Currently twenty-eight member states compose the EU, which has a governing council, an international court, and a parliament. Over time, member states of the EU have relinquished some of their sovereignty, and cooperation has evolved into a community with a single currency, the euro.

Exclusion Act of 1882 U.S. congressional act prohibiting nearly all immigration from China to the United States; fueled by animosity toward Chinese workers in the American West.

existentialism Philosophical movement that arose out of the Second World War and emphasized the absurdity of human condition. Led by Jean-Paul Sartre and Albert Camus, existentialists encouraged humans to take responsibility for their own decisions and dilemmas.

expulsion of the Jews European rulers began to expel their Jewish subjects from their kingdoms beginning in the 1280s, mostly due to their inability to repay the money they had extorted from Jewish money-lenders but also as a result of escalating anti-Semitism in the wake of the Crusades, Jews were also expelled from the Rhineland in the fourteenth century and from Spain in 1492.

fascism The doctrine founded by Benito Mussolini, which emphasized three main ideas: statism ("nothing above the state, nothing outside the state, nothing against the state"), nationalism, and militarism. Its name derives from the Latin *fasces*, a symbol of Roman imperial power adopted by Mussolini.

Fashoda Incident (1898) Disagreements between the French and the British over land claims in North Africa led to a standoff between armies of the two nations at the Sudanese town of Fashoda. The crisis was solved diplomatically. France ceded southern Sudan to Britain in exchange for a stop to further expansion by the British.

The Feminine Mystique Groundbreaking book by feminist Betty Friedan (b. 1921), which tried to define *femininity* and explored how women internalized those definitions.

Franz Ferdinand (1863–1914) Archduke of Austria and heir to the Austro-Hungarian Empire; his assassination led to the beginning of the First World War.

Ferdinand (1452–1516) **and Isabella** (1451–1504) In 1469, Ferdinand of Aragon married the heiress to Castile, Isabella. Their union allowed them to pursue several ambitious policies, including the conquest of Granada, the last Muslim principality in Spain, and the expulsion of Spain's large Jewish community. In 1492, Isabella granted three ships to Christopher Columbus of Genoa (Italy), who went on to claim portions of the New World for Spain.

Fertile Crescent An area of fertile land in what is now Syria, Israel, Turkey, eastern Iraq, and western Iran that was able to sustain settlements due to its wetter climate and abundant natural food resources. Some of the earliest known civilizations emerged there between 9000 and 4500 B.C.E.

feudalism A problematic modern term that attempts to explain the diffusion of power in medieval Europe, and the many different kinds of political, social, and economic relationships that were forged through the giving and receiving of fiefs (*feoda*). But because it is anachronistic and inadequate, this term has been rejected by most historians of the medieval period.

First Crusade (1095–1099) Launched by Pope Urban II in response to a request from the Byzantine emperor Alexius Comnenus, who had asked for a small contingent of knights to assist him in fighting Turkish forces in Anatolia; Urban instead directed the crusaders' energies toward the Holy Land and the recapture of Jerusalem, promising those who took the cross (*crux*) that they would merit eternal salvation if they died in the attempt. This crusade prompted attacks against

Jews throughout Europe and resulted in six subsequent—and unsuccessful—military campaigns.

First World War A total war from August 1914 to November 1918, involving the armies of Britain, France, and Russia (the Allies) against Germany, Austria-Hungary, and the Ottoman Empire (the Central Powers). Italy joined the Allies in 1915, and the United States joined them in 1917, helping to tip the balance in favor of the Allies, who also drew upon the populations and raw materials of their colonial possessions. Also known as the Great War.

Five Pillars of Islam The Muslim teaching that salvation is only assured through observance of five basic precepts: submission to God's will as described in the teachings of Muhammad, frequent prayer, ritual fasting, the giving of alms, and an annual pilgrimage to Mecca (the Hajj).

Five-Year Plan Soviet effort launched under Stalin in 1928 to replace the market with a state-owned and state-managed economy in order to promote rapid economic development over a five-year period and thereby "catch and overtake" the leading capitalist countries. The First Five-Year Plan was followed by the Second Five-Year Plan (1933–1937) and so on, until the collapse of the Soviet Union in 1991.

fly shuttle Invented by John Kay in 1733, this device sped up the process of weaving.

Fourteen Points President Woodrow Wilson proposed these points as the foundation on which to build peace in the world after the First World War. They called for an end to secret treaties, "open covenants, openly arrived at," freedom of the seas, the removal of international tariffs, the reduction of arms, the "self-determination of peoples," and the establishment of a League of Nations to settle international conflicts.

Franciscan Order Also known as the Order of the Friars Minor. The earliest Franciscans were followers of Francis of Assisi (1182–1226) and strove, like him, to imitate the life and example of Jesus. The order was formally established by Pope Innocent III in 1209. Its special mission was the care and instruction of the urban poor.

Frankfurt Parliament (1848–1849) Failed attempt to create a unified Germany under constitutional principles. In 1849, the assembly offered the crown of the new German nation to Frederick William IV of Prussia, but he refused the offer and suppressed a brief protest. The delegates went home disillusioned.

Frederick the Great (1712–1786) Prussian ruler (1740–1786) who engaged the nobility in maintaining a strong military and bureaucracy and led Prussian armies to notable military victories. He also encouraged Enlightenment rationalism and artistic endeavors.

French Revolution of 1789 In 1788, a severe financial crisis forced the French monarchy to convene an assembly known as the Estates General, representing the three estates of the realm: the clergy, the nobility, and the commons (known as the Third Estate). When the Estates General met in 1789, representatives of the Third Estate demanded major constitutional changes, and when the king and his government proved uncooperative, the Third Estate broke with the other two estates and renamed themselves the National Assembly, demanding a written constitution. The position of the National Assembly was confirmed by a popular uprising in Paris and the king was forced to accept the transformation of France into a constitutional monarchy. This constitutional phase of the revolution lasted until 1972, when the pressures of foreign invasion and the emergence of a more radical revolutionary movement caused the collapse of the monarchy and the establishment of a Republic in France.

French Revolution of 1830 The French popular revolt against Charles X's July Ordinances of 1830, which dissolved the French Chamber of Deputies and restricted suffrage to exclude almost everyone except the nobility. After several days of violence, Charles abdicated the throne and was replaced by a constitutional monarch, Louis Philippe.

French Revolution of 1848 Revolution overthrowing Louis-Philippe in February, 1848, leading to the formation of the Second Republic (1848–1852). Initially enjoying broad support from both the middle classes and laborers in Paris, the new government became more conservative after elections in which the French peasantry participated for the first time. A workers' revolt was violently repressed in June, 1848, and in December 1848, Napoleon Bonaparte's nephew, Louis-Napoleon Bonaparte, was elected president. In 1852, Louis-Napoleon declared himself emperor and abolished the republic.

Sigmund Freud (1856–1939) The Austrian physician who founded the discipline of psychoanalysis and suggested that human behavior was largely motivated by unconscious and irrational forces.

Galileo Galilei (1564–1642) Italian physicist and inventor; the implications of his ideas raised the ire of the Catholic Church, and he was forced to retract most of his findings.

Gallipoli (1915) In the First World War, a combined force of French, British, Australian and New Zealand troops tried to invade the Gallipoli Peninsula, in the first large-scale amphibious attack in history, and seize it from the Turks. After seven months of fighting, the Allies had lost 200,000 soldiers. Defeated, they withdrew.

Mohandas K. (Mahatma) Gandhi (1869–1948) The Indian leader who advocated nonviolent noncooperation to protest colonial rule and helped win home rule for India in 1947.

Giuseppe Garibaldi (1807–1882) Italian revolutionary leader who led the fight to free Sicily and Naples from the Habsburg Empire; the lands were then peaceably annexed by Sardinia to produce a unified Italy.

Gaul The region of the Roman Empire that was home to the Celtic people of that name, comprising modern France, Belgium, and western Germany.

Geneva Peace Conference (1954) International conference to restore peace in Korea and Indochina. The chief participants were the United States, the Soviet Union, Great Britain, France, the People's Republic of China, North Korea, South Korea, Vietnam, the Viet Minh party, Laos, and Cambodia. The conference resulted in the division of North and South Vietnam.

Genoa Maritime city on Italy's northwestern coast, the Genoese were active in trading ventures along the Silk Road and in the establishment of trading colonies in the Mediterranean. They were also involved in the world of finance and backed the commercial ventures of other powers, especially Spain's.

German Democratic Republic Nation founded from the Soviet zone of occupation of Germany after the Second World War; also known as East Germany.

German Social Democratic party Founded in 1875, it was the most powerful socialist party in Europe before 1917.

Gilgamesh Sumerian ruler of the city of Uruk around 2700 B.C.E., Gilgamesh became the hero of one of the world's oldest epics, which circulated orally for nearly a millennium before being written down.

Giotto (c. 1266–1337) Florentine painter and architect who is often considered a forerunner of the Renaissance.

glasnost Introduced by Soviet leader Mikhail Gorbachev in June 1987, *glasnost* was one of the five major policies that constituted *perestroika*. Often translated into English as "openness," it called for transparency in Soviet government and institutional activities by reducing censorship in mass media and lifting significant bans on the political, intellectual, and cultural lives of Soviet civilians.

globalization The term used to describe political, social, and economic networks that span the globe. These global exchanges are not limited by nation-states and in recent decades are associated with new technologies, such as the Internet. Globalization is not new, however, as human cultures and economies have been in contact with one another for centuries.

Glorious Revolution The overthrow of King James II of England and the installation of his Protestant daughter, Mary Stuart, and her husband, William of Orange, to the throne in 1688 and 1689. It is widely regarded as the founding moment in the development of a constitutional monarchy in Britain, while also establishing a more favorable climate for the economic and political growth of the English commercial classes.

Gold Coast Name that European mariners and merchants gave to that part of West Equatorial Africa from which gold and slaves were exported. Originally controlled by the Portuguese, this area later became the British colony of the Gold Coast.

Mikhail Gorbachev (1931–) Soviet leader who attempted to reform the Soviet Union through his programs of glasnost and perestroika in the late 1980s. He encouraged open discussions in other countries in the Soviet bloc, which helped inspire the velvet revolutions throughout Eastern Europe. Eventually the political, social, and economic upheaval he had unleashed would lead to the breakup of the Soviet Union.

Gothic style A type of graceful architecture emerging in twelfth- and thirteenth-century England and France. The style is characterized by pointed arches, delicate decoration, and large windows.

Olympe de Gouges (1748–1793) French political radical and feminist whose *Declaration of the Rights of Woman* demanded an equal place for women in France.

Great Depression Global economic crisis following the U.S. stock market crash on October 29, 1929, and ending with the onset of the Second World War.

Great Famine A period of terrible hunger and deprivation in Europe that peaked between 1315 and 1317, caused by a cooling of the climate and by the exhaustion of over-farming. It is estimated to have reduced the population of Europe by 10 to 15 percent.

Great Fear (1789) Following the outbreak of revolution in Paris, fear spread throughout the French countryside, as rumors circulated that armies of brigands or royal troops were coming. The peasants and villagers organized into militias, while others attacked and burned the manor houses in order to destroy the records of manorial dues.

Great Schism (1378–1417) Also known as the Great Western Schism, to distinguish it from the longstanding rupture between the Greek East and Latin West. During the schism, the Roman Church was divided between two (and, ultimately, three) competing popes. Each pope claimed to be legitimate and each denounced the heresy of the others.

Great Terror (1936–1938) The systematic murder of nearly a million people and the deportation of another million and a half to labor camps by Stalin's regime in an attempt to consolidate power and remove perceived enemies.

Greek East After the founding of Constantinople, the eastern Greek-speaking half of the Roman Empire grew more populous, prosperous and central to imperial policy. Its inhabitants considered themselves to be the true heirs of Rome, and their own Orthodox Church to be the true manifestation of Jesus's ministry.

Greek independence Nationalists in Greece revolted against the Ottoman Empire and fought a war that ended in Greek independence in 1827. They received crucial help from British, French, and Russian troops as well as widespread sympathy throughout Europe.

Pope Gregory I (r. 590–604) Also known as Gregory the Great, he was the first bishop of Rome to successfully negotiate a more universal role for the papacy. His political and theological agenda widened the rift between the western Latin (Catholic) Church and the eastern Greek (Orthodox) Church in Byzantium. He also articulated the Church's official position on the status of Jews, promoted affective approaches to religious worship, encouraged the Benedictine monastic movement, and sponsored missionary expeditions.

Guernica The Basque town bombed by German planes in April 1937 during the Spanish Civil War. It is also the subject of Pablo Picasso's famous painting from the same year.

guilds Professional organizations in commercial towns that regulated business and safeguarded the privileges of those practicing a particular craft. Often identical to confraternities ("brotherhoods").

Gulag The vast system of forced labor camps under the Soviet regime; it originated in 1919 in a small monastery near the Arctic Circle and spread throughout the Soviet Union. Penal labor was required of both ordinary criminals and those accused of political crimes. Tens of millions of people were sent to the camps between 1928 and 1953; the exact figure is unknown.

Gulf War (1991) Armed conflict between Iraq and a coalition of thirty-two nations, including the United States, Britain, Egypt, France, and Saudi Arabia. The seeds of the war were planted with Iraq's invasion of Kuwait on August 2, 1990.

Johannes Gutenberg European inventor of the printing press, his shop in Mainz produced the first printed book—a Bible—between the years 1453 and 1455.

Habsburg Dynasty A powerful European dynasty which came to power in the eleventh century in a region now part of Switzerland. Early generations of Habsburgs consolidated their control over neighboring German-speaking lands; through strategic marriages with other royal lines, later rulers eventually controlled a substantial part of Europe—including much of central Europe, the Netherlands, and even Spain and all its colonies for a time. In practice, the Holy Roman Emperor chosen from a member of the Habsburg lineage. By the latter half of the seventeenth century, the Austrian Habsburg Empire was made of up nearly 300 nominally autonomous dynastic kingdoms, principalities, duchies, and archbishoprics.

Hagia Sophia The enormous church dedicated to "Holy Wisdom," built in Constantinople at the behest of the emperor Justinian in the sixth century C.E. When Constantinople fell to Ottoman forces in 1453, it became an important mosque.

Haitian Revolution (1802–1804) In 1802, Napoleon sought to reassert French control of Saint-Domingue, but stiff resistance and yellow fever crushed the French army. In 1804, Jean-Jacques Dessalines, a general in the army of former slaves, declared the independent state of Haiti. (See **slave revolt in Saint-Domingue**.)

Hajj The annual pilgrimage to Mecca; an obligation for Muslims.

Hammurabi Ruler of Babylon from 1792 to 1750 B.C.E., Hammurabi issued a collection of laws that were greatly influential in the Near East and which constitute the world's oldest surviving law code.

Harlem Renaissance Cultural movement in the 1920s that was based in Harlem, a part of New York City with a large African American population. The movement gave voice to black novelists, poets, painters, and musicians, many of whom used their art to protest racial subordination.

Hatshepsut (1479–1458 C.E.) As a pharaoh during the New Kingdom, she launched several successful military campaigns and extended trade and diplomacy. She was an ambitious builder who probably constructed the first tomb in the Valley of the Kings. Though she never pretended to be a man, she was routinely portrayed with a masculine figure and a ceremonial beard.

Hebrews Originally a pastoral people divided among several tribes, they were briefly united under the rule of David and his son, Solomon, who promoted the worship of a single god, Yahweh, and constructed the first temple at the new capital city of Jerusalem. After Solomon's death, the Hebrew tribes were divided between the two kingdoms of Israel and Judah, which were eventually conquered by the Neo-Assyrian and Chaldean empires. It was in captivity that the Hebrews came to define themselves through worship of Yahweh and to develop a religion, Judaism, that could exist outside of Judea. They were liberated by the Persian king Cyrus the Great in 539 B.C.E.

Hellenistic art The art of the Hellenistic period bridged the tastes, ideals, and customs of classical Greece and those that would be more characteristic of Rome. The Romans strove to emulate Hellenistic city planning and civic culture and thereby exported Hellenistic culture to their own far-flung colonies in western Europe.

Hellenistic culture The "Greek-like" culture that dominated the ancient world in the wake of Alexander's conquests.

Hellenistic kingdoms Following the death of Alexander the Great, his vast empire was divided into three separate states: Ptolemaic Egypt (under the rule of the general Ptolemy and his successors), Seleucid Asia (ruled by the general Seleucus and his heirs) and Antigonid Greece (governed by Antigonus of Macedonia). Each state maintained its independence, but the shared characteristics of Greco-Macedonian rule and a shared Greek culture and heritage bound them together in a united cosmopolitan world.

Hellenistic world The various Western civilizations of antiquity that were loosely united by shared Greek language and culture, especially around the eastern Mediterranean.

Heloise (c. 1090–1164) One of the foremost scholars of her time, she became the pupil and the wife of the philosopher and teacher Peter Abelard. In later life, she was the founder of a new religious order for women.

Henry IV of Germany King of Germany and Holy Roman Emperor from 1056—when he ascended the throne at the age of six years old—until his death in 1106. Henry'ss reign was first weakened by conflict with the Saxon nobility and later marked by the Investiture Controversy with Pope Gregory VII.

Henry VIII (1491–1547) King of England from 1509 until his death, Henry rejected the authority of the Roman Church in 1534 when the pope refused to annul his marriage to his queen, Catherine of Aragon; he became the founder of the Church of England.

Henry of Navarre (1553–1610) Crowned King Henry IV of France, he renounced his Protestantism but granted limited toleration for Huguenots (French Protestants) by the Edict of Nantes in 1598.

Prince Henry the Navigator (1394–1460) A member of the Portuguese royal family, Henry encouraged the exploration and conquest of western Africa and the trade in gold and slaves.

hieroglyphs The writing system of ancient Egypt, based on a complicated series of pictorial symbols. It fell out of use when Egypt was absorbed into the Roman Empire and was only deciphered after the discovery of the Rosetta Stone in the early nineteenth century.

Hildegard of Bingen (1098–1179) A powerful abbess, theologian, scientist, musician, and visionary who claimed to receive regular revelations from God. Although highly influential in her own day, she was never officially canonized by the Church, in part because her strong personality no longer matched the changing ideal of female piety.

Hiroshima Japanese port devastated by an atomic bomb on August 6, 1945.

Adolf Hitler (1889–1945) The author of *Mein Kampf* and leader of the Nazis who became chancellor of Germany in 1933. Hitler and his Nazi regime started the Second World War and orchestrated the systematic murder of over 5 million Jews.

Hitler-Stalin Pact (1939) Treaty between Stalin and Hitler, which promised Stalin a share of Poland, Finland, the Baltic States, and Bessarabia in the event of a German invasion of Poland, which began shortly thereafter, on September 1, 1939.

HIV epidemic The first cases of HIV-AIDS appeared in the late 1970s. As HIV-AIDS became a global crisis, international organizations recognized the need for an early, swift, and comprehensive response to future outbreaks of disease.

Thomas Hobbes (1588–1679) English political philosopher whose *Leviathan* argued that any form of government capable of protecting its subjects' lives and property might act as an all-powerful sovereign. This government should be allowed to trample over both liberty and property for the sake of its own survival and that of his subjects. For in his natural state, Hobbes argued, man was like "a wolf" toward other men.

Holy Roman Empire The loosely allied collection of lands in central and western Europe ruled by the kings of Germany (and later Austria) from the twelfth century until 1806. Its origins are usually identified with the empire of Charlemagne, the Frankish king who was crowned emperor of Rome by the pope in 800.

homage A ceremony in which an individual becomes the "man" (French: *homme*) of a lord.

Homer (fl. eighth century B.C.E.) A Greek rhapsode ("weaver" of stories) credited with merging centuries of poetic tradition in the epics known as the *Iliad* and the *Odyssey*.

hoplite A Greek foot-soldier armed with a spear or short sword and protected by a large round shield (*hoplon*). In battle, hoplites stood shoulder to shoulder in a close formation called a phalanx.

Huguenots French Protestants who endured severe persecution in the sixteenth and seventeenth centuries.

humanism A program of study associated with the movement known as the Renaissance, humanism aimed to replace the scholastic emphasis on logic and philosophy with the study of ancient languages, literature, history, and ethics.

human rights The belief that all people have the right to legal equality, freedom of religion and speech, and the right to participate in government. Human rights laws prohibit torture, cruel punishment, and slavery.

David Hume (1711–1776) Scottish writer who applied Newton's method of scientific inquiry and skepticism to the study of morality, the mind, and government.

Hundred Years' War (1337–1453) A series of wars between England and France, fought mostly on French soil and prompted by the territorial and political claims of English monarchs.

Jan Hus (c. 1373–1415) A Czech reformer who adopted many of the teachings of the English theologian John Wycliffe, and who also demanded that the laity be allowed to receive both the consecrated bread and wine of the Eucharist. The Council of Constance burned him at the stake for heresy. In response, his supporters, the Hussites, revolted against the Church.

Saddam Hussein (1937–2006) The former dictator of Iraq who invaded Iran in 1980 and started the eight-year-long Iran-Iraq War; invaded Kuwait in 1990, which led to the Gulf War of 1991; and was overthrown when the United States invaded Iraq in 2003. Involved in Iraqi politics since the mid-1960s, Hussein became the official head of state in 1979.

Iconoclast Controversy (717–787) A serious and often violent theological debate that raged in Byzantium after Emperor Leo III ordered the destruction of religious art on the grounds that any image representing a divine or holy personage is prone to promote idol worship and blasphemy. Iconoclast means "breaker of icons." Those who supported the veneration of icons were called iconodules, "adherents of icons."

Il-khanate Mongol-founded dynasty in thirteenth-century Persia.

Indian National Congress Formed in 1885, this Indian political party worked to achieve Indian independence from British colonial control. The Congress was led by Ghandi in the 1920s and 1930s.

Indian Rebellion of 1857 The uprising began near Delhi, when the military disciplined a regiment of Indian soldiers employed by the British for refusing to use rifle cartridges greased with pork fat—unacceptable to either Hindus or Muslims. Rebels attacked law courts and burned tax rolls, protesting debt and corruption. The mutiny spread through large areas of northwest India before being violently suppressed by British troops.

Indo-Europeans A group of people speaking variations of the same language who moved into the Near East and Mediterranean region shortly after 2000 B.C.E.

indulgences Grants exempting Catholic Christians from the performance of penance, either in life or after death. The abusive trade in indulgences was a major catalyst of the Protestant Reformation.

Incas The highly centralized South American empire that was toppled by the Spanish conquistador Francisco Pizarro in 1533.

Innocent III (1160/61–1216) As pope, he wanted to unify all of Christendom under papal hegemony. He furthered this goal at the Fourth Lateran Council of 1215, which defined one of the Church's dogmas as the acknowledgment of papal supremacy. The council also took an unprecedented interest in the religious education and habits of every Christian.

Inquisition Tribunal of the Roman Church that aims to enforce religious orthodoxy and conformity.

International Monetary Fund (IMF) Established in 1945 to ensure international cooperation regarding currency exchange and monetary policy, the IMF is a specialized agency of the United Nations.

Investiture Conflict The name given to a series of debates over the limitations of spiritual and secular power in Europe during the eleventh and early twelfth century, it came to a head when Pope Gregory VII and Emperor Henry IV of Germany both claimed the right to appoint and invest bishops with the regalia of office. After years of diplomatic and military hostility, it was partially settled by the Concordat of Worms in 1122.

Irish potato famine Period of agricultural blight from 1845 to 1849 whose devastating results produced widespread starvation and led to mass immigration to America.

Iron Curtain Term coined by Winston Churchill in 1946 to refer to the borders of Eastern European nations that lay within the zone of Soviet control.

Italian invasion of Ethiopia (1896) Italy invaded Ethiopia, which was the last major independent African kingdom. Menelik II, the Ethiopian emperor, soundly defeated them.

Ivan the Great (1440–1505) Russian ruler who annexed neighboring territories and consolidated his empire's position as a European power.

Jacobins Radical French political group during the French Revolution that took power after 1792, executed the French king, and sought to remake French culture.

Jacquerie Violent 1358 peasant uprising in northern France, incited by disease, war, and taxes.

James I (1566–1625) Monarch who ruled Scotland as James VI, and who succeeded Elizabeth I as king of England in 1603. He oversaw the English vernacular translation of the Bible known by his name.

James II of England King of England, Ireland, and Scotland from 1685–88 whose commitment to absolutism and Catholic zealotry led to his exile to France in the Glorious Revolution of 1688.

Janissaries Corps of enslaved soldiers recruited as children from the Christian provinces of the Ottoman Empire and brought up to display intense personal loyalty to the Ottoman sultan, who used these forces to curb local autonomy and as his personal bodyguards.

Jerome (c. 340–420) One of the early "fathers" of the Church, he translated the Bible from Hebrew and Greek into a popular form of Latin—hence the name by which this translation is known: the Vulgate, or "vulgar" (popular), Bible.

Jesuits The religious order formally known as the Society of Jesus, founded in 1540 by Ignatius Loyola to combat the spread of Protestantism. The Jesuits would become active in politics, education, and missionary work.

Jesus (c. 4 B.C.E.–c. 30 C.E.) A Jewish preacher and teacher in the rural areas of Galilee and Judea who was arrested for seditious political activity, tried, and crucified by the Romans. After his execution, his followers claimed that he had been resurrected from the dead and taken up into heaven. They began to teach that Jesus had been the divine representative of God, the Messiah foretold by ancient Hebrew prophets, and that he had suffered for the sins of humanity and would return to judge all the world's inhabitants at the end of time.

Joan of Arc (c. 1412–1431) A peasant girl from the province of Lorraine who claimed to have been commanded by God to lead French forces against the English occupying army during the Hundred Years' War. Successful in her efforts, she was betrayed by the French king and handed over to the English, who condemned her to death for heresy. Her reputation underwent a process of rehabilitation, but she was not officially canonized as a saint until 1920.

Judaism The religion of the Hebrews as it developed in the centuries after the establishment of the Hebrew kingdoms under David and Solomon, especially during the period of Babylonian Captivity.

Justinian (527–565) Emperor of Rome who unsuccessfully attempted to reunite the eastern and western portions of the empire. Also known for his important codification of Roman law, in the *Corpus Juris Civilis*.

Justinian's Code of Roman Law Formally known as the *Corpus Juris Civilis* or "body of civil law," this compendium consisted of a systematic compilation of imperial statutes, the writings of Rome's great legal authorities, a textbook of legal principles, and the legislation of Justinian and his immediate successors. As the most authoritative collection of Roman law, it formed the basis of canon law (the legal system of the Roman Church) and became essential to the developing legal traditions of every European state as well as of many countries around the world.

Das Kapital (Capital) The 1867 book by Karl Marx that outlined the theory behind historical materialism and attacked the socioeconomic inequities of capitalism.

Johannes Kepler (1571–1630) Mathematician and astronomer who elaborated on and corrected Copernicus's theory and is chiefly remembered for his discovery of the three laws of planetary motion that bear his name.

Keynesian Revolution Postdepression economic ideas developed by the British economist John Maynard Keynes, wherein the state took a greater role in managing the economy, stimulating it by increasing the money supply and creating jobs.

KGB Soviet political police and spy agency, first formed as the Cheka not long after the Bolshevik coup in October 1917. It grew to more than 750,000 operatives with military rank by the 1980s.

Genghis Khan (c. 1167–1227) "Oceanic Ruler," the title adopted by the Mongol chieftain Temujin, founder of a dynasty that conquered much of southern Asia.

Khanate The major political unit of the vast Mongol Empire. There were four Khanates, including the Yuan Empire in China, forged by Chingiz Khan's grandson Kubilai in the thirteenth century.

Ruhollah Khomeini (1902–1989) Iranian Shi'ite religious leader who led the revolution in Iran after the abdication of the shah in 1979. His government allowed some limited economic and political populism combined with strict constructions of Islamic law, restrictions on women's public life, and the prohibition of ideas or activities linked to Western influence.

Nikita Khrushchev (1894–1971) Leader of the Soviet Union during the Cuban missile crisis, Khrushchev came to power after Stalin's death in 1953. His reforms and criticisms of the excesses of the Stalin regime led to his fall from power in 1964.

Kremlin Once synonymous with the Soviet government, it refers to Moscow's walled city center and the palace originally built by Ivan the Great.

Kristallnacht Organized attack by Nazis and their supporters on the Jews of Germany following the assassination of a German embassy official by a Jewish man in Paris. Throughout Germany, thousands of stores, schools, cemeteries and synagogues were attacked on November 9, 1938. Dozens of people were killed, and tens of thousands of Jews were arrested and held in camps, where many were tortured and killed in the ensuing months.

Labour party Founded in Britain in 1900, this party represented workers and was based on socialist principles.

Latin West After the founding of Constantinople, the western Latin-speaking half of the Roman Empire became poorer and more peripheral, but it also fostered the emergence of new barbarian kingdoms. At the same time, the Roman pope claimed to have inherited both the authority of Jesus and the essential elements of Roman imperial authority.

League of Nations International organization founded after the First World War to solve international disputes through arbitration; it was dissolved in 1946 and its assets were transferred to the United Nations.

Leonardo da Vinci (1452–1519) Florentine inventor, sculptor, architect, and painter whose breadth of interests typifies the ideal of "the Renaissance man."

Vladimir Lenin (1870–1924) Leader of the Bolshevik Revolution in Russia (1917) and the first leader of the Soviet Union.

Leviathan A book by Thomas Hobbes (1588–1679) that recommended a ruler have unrestricted power.

liberalism Political and social theory that judges the effectiveness of a government in terms of its ability to protect individual rights. Liberals support representative forms of government, free trade, and freedom of speech and religion. In the economic realm, liberals believe that individuals should be free to engage in commercial or business activities without interference from the state or their community.

lithograph Art form that involves putting writing or design on stone and producing printed impressions.

John Locke (1632–1704) English philosopher and political theorist known for his contributions to liberalism. Locke had great faith in human reason and believed that just societies were those that infringed the least on the natural rights and freedoms of individuals. This led him to assert that a government's legitimacy depended on the consent of the governed, a view that had a profound effect on the authors of the United States' Declaration of Independence.

Louis IX of France King of France from 1226 to his death on Crusade in 1270, Louis was famous for his piety and for his close attention to the administration of law and justice in his realm. He was officially canonized as Saint Louis in 1297.

Louis XIV (1638–1715) Called the "Sun King," he was known for his success at strengthening the institutions of the French absolutist state.

Louis XVI (1754–1793) Well-meaning but ineffectual king of France, finally deposed and executed during the French Revolution.

Ignatius Loyola (1491–1556) Founder of the Society of Jesus (commonly known as the Jesuits), whose members vowed to serve God through poverty, chastity, and missionary work. He abandoned his first career as a mercenary after reading an account of Christ's life written in his native Spanish.

Lucretia According to Roman legend, Lucretia was a virtuous Roman wife who was raped by the son of Rome's last king and who virtuously committed suicide in order to avoid bringing shame on her family.

Luftwaffe Literally "air weapon," this is the name of the German air force, which was founded during the First World War, disbanded in 1945, and reestablished when West Germany joined NATO in 1950.

Lusitania The British passenger liner that was sunk by a German U-boat (submarine) on May 7, 1915. Public outrage over the sinking contibuted to the U.S. decision to enter the First World War.

Martin Luther (1483–1546) A German monk and professor of theology whose critique of the papacy launched the Protestant Reformation.

ma'at The Egyptian term for the serene order of the universe, with which the individual soul (*ka*) must remain in harmony. The power of the pharaoh was linked to *ma'at*, insofar as it ensured the prosperity of the kingdom. After the upheavals of the First Intermediate Period, the perception of the pharaoh's relationship with ma'at was revealed to be conditional, something that had to be earned.

Niccolò Machiavelli (1469–1527) As the author of *The Prince* and the *Discourses on Livy*, he looked to the Roman past for paradigms of greatness while at the same time hoping to win the patronage of contemporary rulers who would restore Italy's political independence.

Magna Carta The "Great Charter" of 1215, enacted during the reign of King John of England and designed to limit his powers. Regarded now as a landmark in the development of constitutional government. In its own time, its purpose was to restore the power of great lords.

Magyar nationalism Lajos Kossuth led this national movement in the Hungarian region of the Habsburg Empire, calling for national independence for Hungary in 1848. With the support of Russia, the Habsburg army crushed the movement and all other revolutionary activities in the empire. Kossuth fled into exile.

Moses Maimonides (c. 1137–1204) Jewish scholar, physician, and scriptural commentator whose *Mishneh Torah* is a fundamental exposition of Jewish law.

Thomas Malthus (1766–1834) British political economist who believed that populations inevitably grew faster than the available food supply. Societies that could not control their population growth would be checked only by famine, disease, poverty, and infant malnutrition. He argued that governments could not alleviate poverty. Instead, the poor had to exercise "moral restraint," postpone marriage, and have fewer children.

Nelson Mandela (b. 1918) The South African opponent of apartheid who led the African National Congress and was imprisoned from 1962 until 1990. After his release from prison, he worked with Prime Minister Frederik Willem De Klerk to establish majority rule. Mandela became the first black president of South Africa in 1994.

Manhattan Project The secret U.S. government research project to develop the first nuclear bomb. The vast project involved dozens of sites across the United States, including New Mexico, Tennessee, Illinois, California, Utah, and Washington. The first test of a nuclear bomb was near Alamogordo, New Mexico on July 16, 1945.

manors Common farmland worked collectively by the inhabitants of entire villages, sometimes on their own initiative, sometimes at the behest of a lord.

Mao Zedong (1893–1976) The leader of the Chinese Revolution who defeated the Nationalists in 1949 and established the Communist regime in China.

Marne A major battle of the First World War in September 1914, which halted the German invasion of France and led to protracted trench warfare on the Western Front.

Marshall Plan Economic aid package given to Europe by the United States after the Second World War to promote reconstruction and economic development and to secure the countries from a feared communist takeover.

Karl Marx (1818–1883) German philosopher and economist who believed that a revolution of the working classes would overthrow the capitalist order and create a classless society. Author of *Das Kapital* and *The Communist Manifesto.*

Marxists Followers of the socialist political economist Karl Marx who called for workers everywhere to unite and create an independent political force. Marxists believed that industrialization produced an inevitable struggle between laborers and the class of capitalist property owners, and that this struggle would culminate in a revolution that would abolish private property and establish a society committed to social equality.

Mary See **cult of the Virgin**.

Mary I (1516–1558) Catholic daughter of Henry VIII and his first wife, Catherine of Aragon, Mary Tudor was the first queen regnant of England. Her attempts to reinstitute Catholicism in England met with limited success, and after her early death she was labeled "Bloody Mary" by the Protestant supporters of her half sister and successor, Elizabeth I.

mass culture The spread of literacy and public education in the nineteenth century created a new audience for print entertainment and a new class of entrepreneurs in the media to cater to this audience. The invention of radio, film, and television in the twentieth century carried this development to another level, as millions of consumers were now accessible to the producers of news, information, and entertainment. The rise of this "mass culture" has been celebrated as an expression of popular tastes but also criticized as a vehicle for the manipulation of populations through clever and seductive propaganda.

Mayans Native American peoples whose culturally and politically sophisticated empire encompassed lands in present-day Mexico and Guatemala.

Giuseppe Mazzini (1805–1872) Founder of Young Italy and an ideological leader of the Italian nationalist movement.

Mecca Center of an important commercial network of the Arabian Peninsula and birthplace of the prophet Muhammad. It is now considered the holiest site in the Islamic world.

Medici A powerful dynasty of Florentine bankers and politicians whose ancestors were originally apothecaries ("medics").

Meiji Empire Empire created under the leadership of Mutsuhito, emperor of Japan from 1868 until 1912. During the Meiji period Japan became a world industrial and naval power.

Mensheviks Within the Russian Social Democratic Party, the Mensheviks advocated slow changes and a gradual move toward socialism, in contrast with the Bolsheviks, who wanted to push for a proletarian revolution. Mensheviks believed that a proletarian revolution in Russia was premature and that the country needed to complete its capitalist development first.

mercantilism A theory and policy for directing the economy of monarchical states between 1600 and 1800 based on the assumption that wealth and power depended on a favorable balance of trade (more exports and fewer imports) and the accumulation of precious metals. Mercantilists advocated forms of economic protectionism to promote domestic production.

Maria Sybilla Merian (1647–1717) A scientific illustrator and an important early entomologist. She conducted research on two continents and published the well-received *Metamorphosis of the Insects of Surinam*.

Merovingian A Frankish dynasty that claimed descent from a legendary ancestor called Merovic, the Merovingians were the only powerful family to establish a lasting kingdom in western Europe during the fifth and sixth centuries.

Mesopotamia The "land between the Tigris and the Euphrates rivers," Tigris and Euphrates where the civilization of Sumer, the first urban society, flourished.

Klemens von Metternich (1773–1859) Austrian foreign minister whose primary goals were to bolster the legitimacy of monarchies and, after the defeat of Napoleon, to prevent another large-scale war in Europe. At the Congress of Vienna, he opposed social and political change and wanted to check Russian and French expansion.

Michelangelo Buonarroti (1475–1564) A virtuoso Florentine sculptor, painter, and poet who spent much of his career in the service of the papacy. He is best known for the decoration of the Sistine Chapel and for his monumental sculptures.

Middle Kingdom of Egypt (2055–1650 B.C.E.) The period following the First Intermediate Period of dynastic warfare, which ended with the reassertion of pharonic rule under Mentuhotep II.

Miletus A Greek polis and Persian colony on the Ionian coast of Asia Minor. Influenced by the cultures of Mesopotamia, Egypt, and Lydia, it produced several of the ancient world's first scientists and sophists. Thereafter, a political conflict between the ruler of Miletus, Aristagoras, and the Persian Emperor, Darius, sparked the Persian Wars with Greece.

John Stuart Mill (1806–1873) English liberal philosopher whose faith in human reason led him to support a broad variety of civic and political freedoms for men and women, including the right to vote and the right to free speech.

Slobodan Milosevic (1941–2006) The Serbian nationalist politician who became president of Serbia and whose policies during the Balkan wars of the early 1990s led to the deaths of thousands of Croatians, Bosnian Muslims, Albanians, and Kosovars. After leaving office in 2000, he was arrested and tried for war crimes at the International Court in The Hague. The trial ended before a verdict with his death in 2006.

Minoan Crete A sea empire based at Knossos on the Greek island of Crete and named for the legendary King Minos. The Minoans dominated the Aegean for much of the second millennium B.C.E.

Modernism There were several different modernist movements in art and literature, but they shared three key characteristics. First, they had a sense that the world had radically changed and that this change should be embraced. Second, they believed that traditional aesthetic values and assumptions about creativity were ill-suited to the present. Third, they developed a new conception of what art could do that emphasized expression over representation and insisted on the value of novelty, experimentation, and creative freedom.

Mongols A nomadic people from the steppes of Central Asia who were united under the ruler Genghis Khan. His conquest of China was continued by his grandson Kubilai and his great-grandson son Ogedei, whose army also seized southern Russia and then moved through Hungary and through Poland toward eastern Germany. The Mongol armies withdrew from eastern Europe after the death of Ogedei, but his descendants continued to rule his vast empire for another half century.

Michel de Montaigne (1533–1592) French philosopher and social commentator, best known for his *Essays*.

Montesquieu (1689–1755) An Enlightenment philosophe whose most influential work was *The Spirit of Laws*. In this work, he analyzed the structures that shaped law and categorized governments into three types: republics, monarchies, and despotisms. His ideas about the separation of powers among the executive, the legislative, and the judicial branches of government influenced the authors of the U.S. Constitution.

Thomas More (1478–1535) Christian humanist, English statesman, and author of *Utopia*. In 1529, he was appointed lord chancellor of England but resigned because he opposed King Henry VIII's plans to establish a national church under royal control. He was eventually executed for refusing to take an oath acknowledging Henry to be the head of the Church of England and has since been canonized by the Catholic Church.

mos maiorum Literally translated as "the code of the elders" or "the custom of ancestors." This unwritten code governed the lives of Romans under the Republic and stressed the importance of showing reverence to ancestral tradition. It was sacrosanct and essential to Roman identity, and an important influence on Roman culture, law, and religion.

Wolfgang Amadeus Mozart (1756–1791) Austrian composer, famous at a young age as a concert musician and later celebrated as a prolific composer of instrumental music and operas that are seen as the apogee of the Classical style in music.

Muhammad (570–632 C.E.) The founder of Islam, regarded as God's last and greatest prophet by his followers.

Munich Conference (1938) Hitler met with the leaders of Britain, France, and Italy and negotiated an agreement that gave Germany a major slice of Czechoslovakia. British prime minister Chamberlain believed that the agreement would bring peace to Europe. Instead, Germany invaded and seized the rest of Czechoslovakia.

Muscovy The duchy centered on Moscow whose dukes saw themselves as heirs to the Roman Empire. In the early fourteenth century, Moscow was under the control of the Mongol Khanate. After the collapse of the Khanate, the Muscovite grand duke, Ivan III, conquered all the Russian principalities between Moscow and the border of Poland-Lithuania, and then Lithuania itself. By the time of his death, Ivan had established Muscovy as a dominant power.

Muslim learning and culture The Crusades brought the Latin West in contact with the Islamic world, which impacted European culture in myriad ways. Europeans adapted Arabic numerals and mathematical concepts as well as Arabic and Persian words. Through Arabic translations, Western scholars gained access to Greek learning, which had a profound influence on Christian theology. European scholars also learned from the Islamic world's accomplishments in medicine and science.

Benito Mussolini (1883–1945) The Italian founder of the Fascist party who came to power in Italy in 1922 and allied himself with Hitler and the Nazis during the Second World War.

Mycenaean Greece (1600–1200 B.C.E.) The term used to describe the civilization of Greece in the late Bronze Age, when territorial kingdoms like Mycenae formed around a king, a warrior caste, and a palace bureaucracy.

Nagasaki Second Japanese city on which the United States dropped an atomic bomb. The attack took place on August 9, 1945; the Japanese surrendered shortly thereafter, ending the Second World War.

Napoleon III (1808–1873) Nephew of Napoleon Bonaparte, Napoleon III was elected president of the French Second Republic in 1848 and made himself emperor of France in 1852. During his reign (1852–70), he rebuilt the French capital of Paris. Defeated in the France-Prussian War of 1870, he went into exile.

Napoleonic Code Legal code drafted by Napoleon in 1804 and based on Justinian's *Corpus Iuris Civilis*. It distilled different legal traditions to create one uniform law. The code confirmed the abolition of feudal privileges of all kinds and set the conditions for exercising property rights.

Napoleon's military campaigns In 1805, the Russians, Prussians, Austrians, Swedes, and British attempted to contain Napoleon, but he defeated them. Out of his victories, Napoleon created a new empire and affiliated states. In 1808, he invaded Spain, but fierce resistance prevented Napoleon from achieving a complete victory. In 1812, Napoleon invaded Russia, and his army was decimated as it retreated from Moscow during the winter. After the Russian campaign, the united European powers defeated Napoleon and forced him into exile. He escaped and reassumed command of his army, but the European powers defeated him for the final time at the Battle of Waterloo.

Gamal Abdel Nasser (1918–1970) Former president of Egypt and the most prominent spokesman for secular pan-Arabism. He became a target for Islamist critics, such as Sayyid Qutb and the Muslim Brotherhood, angered by the Western-influenced policies of his regime.

National Assembly of France Governing body of France that succeeded the Estates General in 1789 during the French Revolution. It was composed of, and defined by, the delegates of the Third Estate.

National Association for the Advancement of Colored People (NAACP) Founded in 1910, this U.S. civil rights organization was dedicated to ending inequality and segregation for black Americans.

National Convention The governing body of France from September 1792 to October 1795. It declared France a republic and then tried and executed the French king. The Convention also confiscated the property of the enemies of the revolution, instituted a policy of de-Christianization, changed marriage and inheritance laws, abolished slavery in its colonies, placed a cap on the price of necessities, and ended the compensation of nobles for their lost privileges.

nationalism Movement to unify a country under one government based on perceptions of the population's common history, customs, and social traditions.

nationalism in Yugoslavia In the 1990s, Slobodan Milosevic and his allies reignited Serbian nationalism in the former Yugoslavia, which led non-Serb republics in Croatia and Slovenia to seek independence. The country erupted into war, with the worst violence taking place in Bosnia, a multi-ethnic region with Serb, Croatian and Bosnian Muslim populations. European diplomats proved powerless to stop attempts by Croatian and Serbian military and paramilitary forces to claim territory through ethnic cleansing and violent intimidation. Atrocities were committed on all sides, but pro-Serb forces were responsible for the most deaths.

NATO The North Atlantic Treaty Organization, a 1949 military agreement among the United States, Canada, Great Britain, and eight Western European nations, which declared that an armed attack against any one of the members would be regarded as an attack against all. Created during the Cold War in the face of the Soviet Union's control of Eastern Europe, NATO continues to exist today and the membership of twenty-eight states includes former members of the Warsaw Pact as well as Albania and Turkey.

Nazi party Founded in the early 1920s, the National Socialist German Workers' Party (NSDAP) gained control over Germany under the leadership of Adolf Hitler in 1933 and continued in power until Germany was defeated in 1945.

Nazism The political movement in Germany led by Adolf Hitler, which advocated a violent anti-Semitic, anti-Marxist, pan-German ideology.

Neo-Assyrian Empire (883–859 B.C.E.–612–605 B.C.E.) Assurnasirpal II laid the foundations of the Neo-Assyrian Empire through military campaigns against neighboring peoples. Eventually, the empire stretched from the Mediterranean Sea to western Iran. A military dictatorship governed the empire through its army, which it used to frighten and oppress both its subjects and its enemies. The empire's ideology was based on waging holy war in the name of its principal god, Assur, and the exaction of tribute through terror.

Neoliberalism Neoliberals believe that free markets, profit incentives, and restraints on both budget deficits and social welfare programs are the best guarantee of individual liberties. Beginning in the 1980s, neoliberal theory was used to structure the policy of financial institutions like the International Monetary Fund and the World Bank, which turned away from interventionist policies in favor of market-driven models of economic development.

Neolithic Revolution The "New" Stone Age, which began around 11,000 B.C.E., saw new technological and social developments, including managed food production, the beginnings of permanent settlements, and the rapid intensification of trade.

Neoplatonism A school of thought based on the teachings of Plato and prevalent in the Roman Empire, which had a profound effect on the formation of Christian theology. Neoplatonists argued that nature is a book written by its creator to reveal the ways of God to humanity. Convinced that God's perfection must be reflected in nature, neoplatonists searched for the ideal and perfect structures that they believed must lie behind the "shadows" of the everyday world.

New Deal President Franklin Delano Roosevelt's package of government reforms that were enacted during the depression of the 1930s to provide jobs for the unemployed, social welfare programs for the poor, and security to the financial markets.

New Economic Policy In 1921, the Bolsheviks abandoned war communism in favor of the New Economic Policy (NEP). Under NEP, the state still controlled all major industry and financial concerns, while individuals could own private property, trade freely within limits, and farm their own land for their own benefit. Fixed taxes replaced grain requisition. The policy successfully helped Soviet agriculture recover from the civil war but was later abandoned in favor of collectivization.

Isaac Newton (1642–1727) One of the foremost scientists of all time, Newton was an English mathematician and physicist; he is noted for his development of calculus, work on the properties of light, and theory of gravitation.

Tsar Nicholas II (1868–1918) The last Russian tsar, who abdicated the throne in 1917. He and his family were executed by the Bolsheviks on July 17, 1918.

Friedrich Nietzsche (1844–1900) The German philosopher who denied the possibility of knowing absolute "truth" or "reality," since all knowledge comes filtered through linguistic, scientific, or artistic systems of representation. He also criticized Judeo-Christian morality for instilling a repressive conformity that drained civilization of its vitality.

nongovernmental organizations (NGOs) Private organizations like the Red Cross that play a large role in international affairs.

Novum Organum Work by English statesman and scientist Francis Bacon (1561–1626) that advanced a philosophy of study through observation.

October Days (1789) The high price of bread and the rumor that the king was unwilling to cooperate with the assembly caused the women who worked in Paris's large central market to march to Versailles along with their supporters to address the king. Not satisfied with their initial reception, they broke through the palace gates and called for the king to return to Paris from Versailles, which he did the following day.

Old Kingdom of Egypt (c. 2686–2160 B.C.E.) During this time, the pharaohs controlled a powerful and centralized bureaucratic state whose vast human and material resources are exemplified by the pyramids of Giza. This period came to an end as the pharaoh's authority collapsed, leading to a period of dynastic warfare and localized rule.

OPEC (Organization of the Petroleum Exporting Countries) Organization created in 1960 by oil-producing countries in the Middle East, South America, and Africa to regulate the production and pricing of crude oil.

Operation Barbarossa The codename for Hitler's invasion of the Soviet Union in 1941.

Opium Wars (1839–1842) War fought between the British and Qing China to protect British trade in opium; resulted in the ceding of Hong Kong to the British.

Oracle at Delphi The most important shrine in ancient Greece. The priestess of Apollo who attended the shrine was believed to have the power to predict the future.

Ottoman Empire (c.1300–1923) During the thirteenth century, the Ottoman dynasty established itself as leader of the Turks. From the fourteenth to sixteenth centuries, they conquered Anatolia, Armenia, Syria, and North Africa as well as parts of southeastern Europe, the Crimea, and areas along the Red Sea. Portions of the Ottoman Empire persisted up to the time of the First World War, but it was dismantled in the years following it.

Reza Pahlavi (1919–1980) The Western-friendly shah of Iran who was installed during a 1953 coup supported by Britain and the United States. After a lengthy economic downturn, public unrest, and personal illness, he retired from public life under popular pressure in 1979.

Pan-African Conference 1900 assembly in London that sought to draw attention to the sovereignty of African people and their mistreatment by colonial powers.

Panhellenism The "all Greek" culture that allowed ancient Greek colonies to maintain a connection to their homeland and to each other through their shared language and heritage. These colonies also exported their culture into new areas and created new Greek-speaking enclaves, which permanently changed the cultural geography of the Mediterranean world.

pan-Slavism Cultural movement that sought to unite native Slavic peoples within the Russian and Habsburg Empires under Russian leadership.

Partition of India (1947) At independence, British India was partitioned into the nations of India and Pakistan. The majority of the population in India was Hindu and the majority of the population in Pakistan was Muslim. The process of partition brought brutal religious and ethnic warfare. More than 1 million Hindus and Muslims died and 12 million became refugees.

Blaise Pascal (1623–1662) A Catholic philosopher who wanted to establish the truth of Christianity by appealing simultaneously to intellect and emotion. In his *Pensées*, he argued that faith alone can resolve the world's contradictions and that his own awe in the face of evil and uncertainty must be evidence of God's existence.

Paul of Tarsus Originally known as Saul, Paul was a Greek-speaking Jew and Roman citizen who underwent a miraculous conversion experience and became the most important proponent of Christianity in the 50s and 60s C.E.

Pax Romana (27 B.C.E.–180 C.E.) Literally translated as "the Roman Peace." During this time, the Roman world enjoyed an unprecedented period of peace and political stability.

Peace of Augsburg A settlement negotiated in 1555 among factions within the Holy Roman Empire, it formulated the principle *cuius regio, eius religio,* "he who rules, his religion": meaning that the inhabitants of any given territory should follow the religion of its ruler, whether Catholic or Protestant.

Peace of Paris The 1919 Paris Peace Conference established the terms to end the First World War. Great Britain, France, Italy, and the United States signed five treaties with each of the defeated nations: Germany, Austria, Hungary, Turkey, and Bulgaria. The settlement is notable for the territory that Germany had to give up, including large parts of Prussia to the new state of Poland, and Alsace and Lorraine to France; the disarming of Germany; and the "war guilt" provision, which required Germany and its allies to pay massive reparations to the victors.

Peace of Westphalia (1648) An agreement reached at the end of the Thirty Years' War that altered the political map of Europe. France emerged as the predominant power on the Continent, while the Austrian Habsburgs had to surrender all the territories they had gained and could no longer use the office of the Holy Roman Emperor to dominate central Europe. Spain was marginalized and Germany became a volatile combination of Protestant and Catholic principalities.

Pearl Harbor The American naval base in Hawaii that was bombed by the Japanese on December 7, 1941, bringing the United States into the Second World War.

peasantry Term used in continental Europe to refer to rural populations that lived from agriculture. Some peasants were free and could own land. Serfs were peasants who were legally bound to the land and subject to the authority of the local lord.

Peloponnesian War The name given to the series of wars fought between Sparta (on the Greek Peloponnesus) and Athens from 431 B.C.E. to 404 B.C.E., and which ended in the defeat of Athens and the loss of her imperial power.

perestroika Introduced by Soviet leader Mikhail Gorbachev in June 1987, *perestroika* was the name given to economic and political reforms begun earlier in his tenure. It restructured the state bureaucracy, reduced the privileges of the political elite, and instituted a shift from the centrally planned economy to a mixed economy, combining planning with the operation of market forces.

Periclean Athens Following his election as *strategos* in 461 B.C.E., Pericles pushed through political reforms in Athens, which gave poorer citizens greater influence in politics. He promoted Athenians' sense of superiority through ambitious public works projects and lavish festivals to honor the gods, thus ensuring his continual reelection. But eventually, Athens' growing arrogance and aggression alienated it from the rest of the Greek world.

Pericles (c. 495–429) Athenian politician who occupied the office of strategos for thirty years and who presided over a series of civic reforms, building campaigns, and imperialist initiatives.

Persian Empire Consolidated by Cyrus the Great in 559, this empire eventually stretched from the Persian Gulf to the Mediterranean and also encompassed Egypt. Persian rulers were able to hold this empire together through a policy of tolerance and a mixture of local and centralized governance. This imperial model of government would be adopted by many future empires.

Persian Wars (490–479 B.C.E.) In 501 B.C.E., a political conflict between the Greek ruler of Miletus, Aristagoras, and the Persian Emperor, Darius, sparked the first of the Persian Wars when Darius sent an army to punish Athens for its intervention on the side of the Greeks. Despite being heavily outnumbered, Athenian hoplites defeated the Persian army at the plain of Marathon. In 480 B.C.E., Darius's son Xerxes invaded Greece but was defeated at sea and on land by combined Greek forces under the leadership of Athens and Sparta.

Peter the Great (1672–1725) Energetic tsar who transformed Russia into a leading European country by centralizing government, modernizing the army, creating a navy, and reforming education and the economy.

Francesco Petrarca (Petrarch) (1304–1374) Italian scholar who revived interest in classical writing styles and was famed for his vernacular love sonnets.

pharaoh A term meaning "household" which became the title borne by the rulers of ancient Egypt. The pharaoh was regarded as the divine representative of the gods and the embodiment of Egypt itself. The powerful and centralized bureaucratic state ruled by the pharaohs was more stable and longlived than any another civilization in world history, lasting (with few interruptions) for approximately 3,000 years.

Pharisees A group of Jewish teachers and preachers who emerged in the third century B.C.E. They insisted that all of Yahweh's (God's) commandments were binding on all Jews.

Philip II (382–336 B.C.E.) King of Macedonia and father of Alexander, he consolidated the southern Balkans and the Greek city-states under Macedonian domination.

Philip II of Spain King of Spain from 1556–98 and briefly King of England and Ireland during his marriage to Queen Mary I of England. As a staunch Catholic, Philip responded with military might to the desecration of Catholic churches in the Spanish Netherlands in the 1560s. When commercial conflict with England escalated, Philip sent the Spanish Armada to conquer England in 1588, but it was largely destroyed by stormy weather.

Philip II Augustus (1165–1223) The first French ruler to use the title "king of France" rather than "king of the French." After he captured Normandy and its adjacent territories from the English, he built an effective system of local administration, which recognized regional diversity while promoting centralized royal control. This administrative pattern would characterize French government until the French Revolution.

Philip IV of France King of France from 1285 until his death, Philip's conflict with Pope Boniface VIII led to the transfer of the papal court to Avignon from 1309 to 1378.

Philistines Descendants of the Sea Peoples who fled to the region that now bears their name, Palestine, after their defeat at the hands of the pharaoh Ramses III. They dominated their neighbors, the Hebrews, who used writing as an effective means of discrediting them (the Philistines themselves did not leave a written record to contest the Hebrews' views).

philosophe During the Enlightenment, this word referred to a person whose reflections were unhampered by the constraints of religion or dogma.

Phoenicians A Semitic people known for their trade in exotic purple dyes and other luxury goods, they originally settled in present-day Lebanon around 1200 B.C.E. and from there established commercial colonies throughout the Mediterranean, notably Carthage.

Plato (429–349 B.C.E.) A student of Socrates, Plato dedicated his life to transmitting his teacher's legacy through the writing of dialogues on philosophical subjects, in which Socrates himself plays the major role. The longest and most famous of these, known as the *Republic*, describes an idealized polis governed by a superior group of individuals chosen for their natural attributes of intelligence and character, who rule as "philosopher-kings."

Plotinus (204–270 C.E.) A Neoplatonist philosopher who taught that everything in existence has its ultimate source in the divine, and that the highest goal of life should be the mystic reunion of the soul with this divine source, something that can be achieved through contemplation and asceticism. This outlook blended with that of early Christianity and was instrumental in the spread of that religion within the Roman Empire.

poleis One of the major political innovations of the ancient Greeks was the *polis*, or city-state (plural *poleis*). These independent social and political entities began to emerge in the ninth century B.C.E., organized around an urban center and fostering markets, meeting places, and religious worship; frequently, poleis also controlled some surrounding territory.

Marco Polo (1254–1324) Venetian merchant who traveled through Asia for twenty years and published his observations in a widely read memoir.

population growth In the nineteenth century, Europe experienced a dramatic population growth. During this period, the spread of rural manufacturing allowed men and women to begin marrying younger and raising families earlier, which increased the size of the average family. As the population grew, the portion of young and fertile people also increased, which reinforced the population growth. By 1900, population growth was strongest in Britain and Germany, and slower in France.

portolan charts Also known as *portolani*, these special charts were invented by medieval mariners during the fourteenth century and were used to map locations of ports and sea routes, while also taking note of prevailing winds and other conditions at sea.

Potsdam (1945) At this conference, Truman, Churchill and Stalin met to discuss their options at the conclusion of the Second World War, including making territorial changes to Germany and its allies and the question of war reparations.

Prague spring A period of political liberalization in Czechoslovakia between January and August 1968 that was initiated by Alexander Dubček, the Czech leader. This period of expanding freedom and openness in this Eastern bloc nation ended on August 20, when the USSR and Warsaw Pact countries invaded with 200,000 troops and 5,000 tanks.

pre-Socratics A group of philosophers in the Greek city of Miletus, who raised questions about humans' relationship with the natural world and the gods and who formulated rational theories to explain the physical universe they observed. Their name reflects the fact that they flourished prior to the lifetime of Socrates.

price revolution An unprecedented inflation in prices in the latter half of the sixteenth century, resulting in part from the enormous influx of silver bullion from Spanish America.

principate Modern term for the centuries of autocratic rule by the successors of Augustus, who seized power in 27 B.C.E. and styled himself *princeps* or Rome's "first man." See **Roman Republic**.

printing press Introduced in Europe by Johannes Gutenberg of Mainz in 1453–55, this new technology quickly revolutionized communication and played a significant role in political, religious, and intellectual revolutions.

Protestantism The name given to the many dissenting varieties of Christianity that emerged during the Reformation in sixteenth-century western Europe. While Protestant beliefs and practices differed widely, all were united in their rejection of papal authority and the dogmas of the Roman Catholic Church.

provisional government After the collapse of the Russian monarchy, leaders in the Duma organized this government and hoped to establish a democratic system under constitutional rule. They also refused to concede military defeat, and it was impossible to institute domestic reforms and fight a war at the same time. As conditions worsened, the Bolsheviks gained support. In October 1917, they attacked the provisional government and seized control.

Claudius Ptolomeus, called Ptolemy (c. 85–165 C.E.) A Greek-speaking geographer and astronomer active in Roman Alexandria, he rejected the findings of previous Hellenistic scientists in favor of the erroneous theories of Aristotle, publishing highly influential treatises that promulgated these errors and suppressed (for example) the accurate findings of Aristarchus (who had discovered the Heliocentric universe) and Erathosthenes (who had calculated the circumference of the earth).

Ptolemaic system Ptolemy of Alexandria promoted Aristotle's understanding of cosmology. In this system, the heavens orbit the earth in an organized hierarchy of spheres, and the earth and the heavens are made of different matter and subject to different laws of motion. A prime mover produces the motion of the celestial bodies.

Ptolemy (c. 367–c. 284 B.C.E.) One of Alexander the Great's trusted generals (and possibly his half brother), he became pharaoh of Egypt and founded a new dynasty that lasted until that kingdom's absorption into the Roman Empire in 30 B.C.E.

public sphere Between the official realm of state activities and the private realm of the household and individual, lies the "public sphere." The public sphere has a political dimension—it is the space of debate, discussion, and expressions of popular opinion. It also has an economic dimension—it is where business is conducted, where commercial transactions take place, where people enter into contracts, search for work, or hire employees.

Punic Wars (264–146 B.C.E.) Three periods of warfare between Rome and Carthage, two maritime empires who struggled for dominance of the Mediterranean. Rome emerged as the victor, destroyed the city of Carthage and took control of Sicily, North Africa and Hispania (Spain).

pyramid Constructed during the third millennium B.C.E., these structures were monuments to the power and divinity of the pharaohs entombed inside them.

Qur'an (often Koran) Islam's holy scriptures, comprised of the prophecies revealed to Muhammad and redacted during and after his death.

Raphael (Raffaelo Sanzio) (1483–1520) Italian painter active in Rome, his works include *The School of Athens*.

realism Artistic and literary style which sought to portray common situations as they would appear in reality.

Realpolitik Political strategy based on advancing power for its own sake.

reason The human capacity to solve problems and discover truth in ways that can be verified intellectually. Philosophers distinguish the knowledge gained from reason from the teachings of instinct, imagination, and faith, which are verified according to different criteria.

Reformation Religious and political movement in sixteenth-century Europe that led to a break between dissenting forms of Christianity and the Roman Catholic Church; notable figures include Martin Luther and John Calvin.

Reich A term for the German state. The First Reich corresponded to the Holy Roman Empire (9th c.–1806), the Second Reich was from 1871 to 1919, and the Third Reich lasted from 1933 through May 1945.

Renaissance From the French word meaning "rebirth," this term came to be used in the nineteenth century to describe the artistic, intellectual, and cultural movement that emerged in Italy after 1300 and that sought to recover and emulate the heritage of the classical past.

Restoration period (1815–1848) European movement after the defeat of Napoleon to restore Europe to its pre–French Revolution status and to prevent the spread of revolutionary or liberal political movements.

Cardinal Richelieu (1585–1642) First minister to King Louis XIII, he is considered by many to have ruled France in all but name, centralizing political power and suppressing dissent.

Roman army Under the Republic, the Roman army was made up of citizen-soldiers who were required to serve in wartime. As Rome's empire grew, the need for more fighting men led to the extension of citizenship rights and, eventually, to the development of a vast, professional, standing army that numbered as many as 300,000 by the middle of the third century B.C.E. By that time, however, citizens were not themselves required to serve, and many legions were made up of paid conscripts and foreign mercenaries.

Roman citizenship The rights and responsibilities of Rome's citizens were gradually extended to the free (male) inhabitants of other Italian provinces and later to most provinces in the Roman world. In contrast to slaves and non-Romans, Romans had the right to be tried in an imperial court and could not be legally subjected to torture.

Roman Republic The Romans traced the founding of their republic to the overthrow of their last king and the establishment of a unique form of constitutional government, in which the power of the aristocracy (embodied by the Senate) was checked by the executive rule of two elected consuls and the collective will of the people. For hundreds of years, this balance of power provided the Republic with a measure of political stability and prevented any single individual or clique from gaining too much power.

Romanticism Beginning in Germany and England in the late eighteenth century and continuing up to the end of the nineteenth century, Romanticism was a movement in art, music, and literature that countered the rationalism of the Enlightenment by placing greater value on human emotions and the power of nature to stimulate creativity.

Jean-Jacques Rousseau (1712–1778) Philosopher and radical political theorist whose *Social Contract* attacked privilege and inequality. One of the primary principles of Rousseau's political philosophy is that politics and morality should not be separated.

Royal Society This British society's goal was to pursue collective research. Members would conduct experiments, record the results, and share them with their peers, who would study the methods, reproduce the experiment, and assess the results. The arrangement gave English scientists a sense of common purpose as well as a system to reach a consensus on facts.

Russian Revolution of 1905 After Russia's defeat in the Russo-Japanese War, Russians began clamoring for political reforms. Protests grew over the course of 1905, and the autocracy lost control of entire towns and regions as workers went on strike, soldiers mutinied, and peasants revolted. Forced to yield, Tsar Nicholas II issued the October Manifesto, which pledged individual liberties and provided for the election of a parliament (called the Duma). The most radical of the revolutionary groups were put down with force, and the pace of political change remained very slow in the aftermath of the revolution.

Russo-Japanese War (1904–1905) Japanese and Russian expansion collided in Mongolia and Manchuria. Russia was humiliated after the Japanese navy sunk its fleet, which helped provoke a revolt in Russia and led to an American-brokered peace treaty.

sacrament A sacred rite. In the Catholic tradition, the administration of the sacraments is considered necessary for salvation.

Saint Bartholomew's Day Massacre The mass murder of French Protestants (Huguenots) instigated by Queen Catherine de' Medici of France and carried out by Catholics. It began in Paris on 24 August 1572 and spread to other parts of France, continuing into October of that year. More than 70,000 people were killed.

salons Informal gatherings of intellectuals and aristocrats that allowed discourse about Enlightenment ideas.

Sappho (c. 620–c. 550 B.C.E.) One of the most celebrated Greek poets, she was revered as "the Tenth Muse" and emulated by many male poets. Ironically, though, only two of her poems survive intact, and the rest must be pieced together from fragments quoted by later poets.

Sargon the Great (r. 2334–2279 B.C.E.) The Akkadian ruler who consolidated power in Mesopotamia.

SARS epidemic (2003) The successful containment of severe acute respiratory syndrome (SARS) is an example of how international health organizations can effectively work together to recognize and respond to a disease outbreak. The disease itself, however, is a reminder of the dangers that exist in a globalized economy with a high degree of mobility in both populations and goods.

Schlieffen Plan Devised by German general Alfred von Schlieffen in 1905 to avoid the dilemma of a two-front war against France and Russia. The Schlieffen Plan required that Germany attack France first through Belgium and secure a quick victory before wheeling to the east to meet the slower armies of the Russians on the Eastern Front. The Schlieffen Plan was put into operation on August 2, 1914, at the outset of the First World War.

scientific revolution of antiquity The Hellenistic period was the most brilliant age in the history of science before the seventeenth century C.E. Aristarchus of Samos posited the existence of a heliocentric universe. Eratosthenes of Alexandria accurately calculated the circumference of the earth. Archimedes turned physics into its own branch of experimental science. Hellenistic anatomists became the first to practice human dissection, which improved their understanding of human physiology. Ironically, most of these discoveries were suppressed by pseudo-scientists who flourished under the Roman Empire during the second century C.E., notably Claudus Ptolomeus Ptolemy) and Aelius Galenus (Galen).

second industrial revolution The technological developments in the last third of the nineteenth century, which included new techniques for refining and producing steel; increased availability of electricity for industrial, commercial, and domestic use; advances in chemical manufacturing; and the creation of the internal combustion engine.

Second World War Worldwide war that began in September 1939 in Europe, and even earlier in Asia (the Japanese invasion of Manchuria began in 1931), pitting Britain, the United States, and the Soviet Union (the Allies) against Nazi Germany, Italy, and Japan (the Axis). The war ended in 1945 with Germany and Japan's defeat.

Seleucus (d. 280 B.C.E.) The Macedonian general who ruled the Persian heartland of Alexander the Great's empire.

Semitic The Semitic language family has the longest recorded history of any linguistic group and is the root for most languages of the Middle and Near East. Ancient Semitic languages include those of the ancient Babylonians and Assyrians, Phoenician, the classical form of Hebrew, early dialects of Aramaic, and the classical Arabic of the Qu'ran.

Sepoy Mutiny of 1857 See **Indian Rebellion of 1857**.

serfdom Peasant labor. Unlike slaves, serfs are "attached" to the land they work, and are not supposed to be sold apart from that land.

William Shakespeare (1564–1616) An English playwright who flourished during the reigns of Elizabeth I and James I, Shakespeare received a basic education in his hometown of Stratford-upon-Avon and worked in London as an actor before achieving success as a dramatist and poet.

Shi'ites An often-persecuted minority within Islam, Shi'ites believe that only descendants of Muhammad's successor Ali and his wife Fatimah (Muhammad's daughter) can have any authority over the Muslim community. Today, Shi'ites constitute the ruling party in Iran and are numerous in Iraq but otherwise comprise only 10 percent of Muslims worldwide.

Abbé Sieyès (1748–1836) In 1789, he wrote the pamphlet "What is the Third Estate?" in which he posed fundamental questions about the rights of the Third Estate and helped provoke its secession from the Estates-General. He was a leader at the Tennis Court Oath, but he later helped Napoleon seize power.

Sinn Féin The Irish revolutionary organization that formed in 1900 to fight for Irish independence.

Sino-Japanese War (1894–1895) Conflict over the control of Korea in which China was forced to cede the province of Taiwan to Japan.

slave revolt in Saint-Domingue (1791–1804) In September of 1791, the largest slave rebellion in history broke out in Saint-Domingue, an important French colony in the Caribbean. In 1794, the revolutionary government in France abolished slavery in the colonies, though this act was essentially only recognizing the liberty that the slaves had seized by their own actions. Napoleon reestablished slavery in the French Caribbean in 1802, but failed in his attempt to reconquer Saint-Domingue. Armies commanded by former slaves succeeded in winning independence for a new nation, Haiti, in 1804, making the revolt in Saint-Domingue the first successful slave revolt in history.

slavery The practice of subjugating people to a life of bondage, and of selling or trading these unfree people. For most of human history, slavery had no racial or ethnic basis, and was widely practiced by all cultures and civilizations. Anyone could become a slave, for example, by being captured in war or by being sold for the payment of a debt. It was only in the fifteenth century, with the growth of the African slave trade, that slavery came to be associated with particular races and peoples.

Adam Smith (1723–1790) Scottish economist and liberal philosopher who proposed that competition between self-interested individuals led naturally to a healthy economy. He became famous for his influential book, *The Wealth of Nations* (1776).

Social Darwinism Belief that Charles Darwin's theory of natural selection (evolution) was applicable to human societies and justified the right of the ruling classes or countries to dominate the weak.

social democracy The belief that democracy and social welfare go hand in hand and that diminishing the sharp inequalities of class society is crucial to fortifying democratic culture.

socialism Political ideology that calls for a classless society with collective ownership of all property.

Society of Jesus See **Jesuits**.

Socrates (469–399 B.C.E.) The Athenian philosopher and teacher who promoted the careful examination of all inherited opinions and assumptions on the grounds that "the unexamined life is not worth living." A veteran of the Peloponnesian War, he was tried and condemned by his fellow citizens for engaging in allegedly seditious activities and was executed in 399 B.C.E. His most influential pupils were the philosopher Plato and the historian and social commentator Xenophon.

Solon (d. 559 B.C.E.) Elected archon in 594 B.C.E., this Athenian aristocrat enacted a series of political and economic reforms that formed the basis of Athenian democracy.

Somme (1916) During this battle of the First World War, Allied forces attempted to take entrenched German positions from July to mid-November of 1916. Neither side was able to make any real gains despite massive casualties: 500,000 Germans, 400,000 British, and 200,000 French.

Soviet bloc International alliance that included the East European countries of the Warsaw Pact as well as the Soviet Union; it also came to include Cuba.

soviets Local councils elected by workers and soldiers in Russia. Socialists started organizing these councils in 1905, and the Petrograd soviet in the capital emerged as one of the centers of power after the Russian monarchy collapsed in 1917 in the midst of World War I. The soviets became increasingly powerful and pressed for social reform, the redistribution of land, and called for Russian withdrawal from the war effort.

Spanish-American War (1898) War between the United States and Spain in Cuba, Puerto Rico, and the Philippines. It ended with a treaty in which the United States took over the Philippines, Guam, and Puerto Rico; Cuba won partial independence.

Spanish Armada Supposedly invincible fleet of warships sent against England by Philip II of Spain in 1588 but vanquished by the English fleet and bad weather in the English Channel.

Sparta Around 650 B.C.E., after the suppression of a slave revolt, Spartan rulers militarized their society in order to prevent future rebellions and to protect Sparta's superior position in Greece, orienting their society toward the maintenance of their army. Sparta briefly joined forces with Athens and other poleis in the second war with Persia in 480–479 B.C.E., but these two rivals ultimately fell out again in 431 B.C.E. when Sparta and her Peloponnesian allies went to war against Athens and her allies. This bloody conflict lasted until Athens was defeated in 404 B.C.E., after Sparta received military aid from the Persians.

Spartiate A full citizen of Sparta, hence a professional soldier of the hoplite phalanx.

spinning jenny Invention of James Hargreaves (c. 1720–1774) that revolutionized the British textile industry by allowing a worker to spin much more thread than was possible on a hand spinner.

SS (Schutzstaffel) Formed in 1925 to serve as Hitler's personal security force and to guard Nazi party (NSDAP) meetings, the SS grew into a large militarized organization that became notorious for their participation in carrying out Nazi policies.

Joseph Stalin (1879–1953) The Bolshevik leader who succeeded Lenin as the leader of the Soviet Union and ruled until his death in 1953.

Stalingrad (1942–1943) The turning point on the Eastern Front during the Second World War came when the German army tried to take the city of Stalingrad in an effort to break the back of Soviet industry. The German and Soviet armies fought a bitter battle, in which more than a half million German, Italian, and Romanian soldiers were killed and the Soviets suffered over a million casualties. The German army surrendered after over five months of fighting. After Stalingrad, the Soviet army launched a series of attacks that pushed the Germans back.

Stoicism An ancient philosophy derived from the teachings of Zeno of Athens (fl. c. 300) and widely influential within the Roman Empire; it also impacted the development of Christianity. Stoics believe in the essential orderliness of the cosmos, and that everything that occurs happens for the best. Since everything is determined in accordance with rational purpose, no individual is master of his or her fate, and the only agency that human beings have consists in their responses to good fortune or adversity.

Sumerians The ancient inhabitants of southern Mesopotamia (modern Iraq and Kuwait) whose sophisticated civilization emerged around 4000 B.C.E.

Sunnis Proponents of Islam's customary religious practices (*sunna*) as they developed under the first two caliphs to succeed Muhammad, his father-in-law Abu-Bakr and his disciple Umar.

Sunni orthodoxy is dominant within Islam but is opposed by the Shi'ites (from the Arabic word *shi'a*, "faction").

syndicalists A nineteenth-century political movement that embraced a strategy of strikes and sabotage by workers. Their hope was that a general strike of all workers would bring down the capitalist state and replace it with workers' syndicates or trade associations. Their refusal to participate in politics limited their ability to command a wide influence.

tabula rasa Term used by John Locke (1632–1704) to describe man's mind before he acquired ideas as a result of experience; Latin for "clean slate."

Tennis Court Oath (1789) Oath taken by representatives of the Third Estate in June 1789, in which they pledged to form a National Assembly and write a constitution limiting the powers of the king.

Reign of Terror (1793–1794) Campaign at the height of the French Revolution in which violence, including systematic executions of opponents of the revolution, was used to purge France of its "enemies" and to extend the revolution beyond its borders; radicals executed as many as 40,000 persons who were judged enemies of the state.

Tetrarchy The result of Diocletian's political reforms of the late third century C.E., which divided the Roman Empire into four quadrants.

Theban Hegemony The term describing the period when the polis of Thebes dominated the Greek mainland, which reached its height after 371 B.C.E., under leadership of the Theban general Epaminondas. It was in Thebes that the future King Philip II of Macedon spent his youth, and it was the defeat of Thebes and Athens at the hands of Philip and Alexander—at the Battle of Chaeronea in 338—that Macedonian hegemony was forcefully asserted.

theory of evolution Darwin's theory that linked biology to history. Darwin believed that competition between different organisms and struggle with the environment were fundamental and unavoidable facts of life. In this struggle, those individuals who were better adapted to their environment survived, whereas the weak perished. This produced a "natural selection," or favoring of certain adaptive traits over time, leading to a gradual evolution of different species.

Third Estate The population of France under the Old Regime was divided into three estates, corporate bodies that determined an individual's rights or obligations under royal law. The nobility constituted the First Estate, the clergy the Second, and the commoners (the vast bulk of the population) made up the Third Estate.

Third Reich The German state from 1933 to 1945 under Adolf Hitler and the Nazi party.

Third World nations—mostly in Asia, Latin America, and Africa—that are not highly industrialized.

Thirty Years' War (1618–1648) Beginning as a conflict between Protestants and Catholics in Germany, this series of skirmishes escalated into a general European war fought on German soil by armies from Sweden, France, and the Holy Roman Empire.

Timur the Lame (1336–1405) Also known as Tamerlane, he was the last ruler of the Mongol Khans' Asian empire.

Marshal Tito (1892–1980) The Yugoslavian communist and resistance leader who became the leader of Yugoslavia and fought to keep his government independent of the Soviet Union. In response, the Soviet Union expelled Yugoslavia from the communist countries' economic and military pacts.

towns Centers for markets and administration. Towns existed in a symbiotic relationship with the countryside. They provided markets for surplus food from outlying farms as well as producing manufactured goods. In the Middle Ages, towns tended to grow up around a castle or monastery which afforded protection.

transatlantic triangle The trading of African slaves by European colonists to address labor shortages in the Americas and the Caribbean. Slaves were treated like cargo, loaded onto ships and sold in exchange for molasses, tobacco, rum, and other precious commodities.

Treaty of Brest-Litovsk (1918) Separate peace between imperial Germany and the new Bolshevik regime in Russia. The treaty acknowledged the German victory on the Eastern Front and withdrew Russia from the war.

Treaty of Utrecht (1713) Resolution to the War of Spanish Succession that reestablished a balance of power in Europe, to the benefit of Britain and in ways that disadvantaged Spain, Holland, and France.

Treaty of Versailles Signed on June 28, 1919, this peace settlement ended the First World War and required Germany to surrender a large part of its most valuable territories and to pay huge reparations to the Allies.

trench warfare Weapons such as barbed wire and the machine gun gave tremendous advantage to defensive positions in World War I, leading to prolonged battles between entrenched armies in fixed positions. The trenches eventually consisted of 25,000 miles of holes and ditches that stretched across the Western Front in northern France, from the Atlantic coast to the Swiss border during the First World War. On the eastern front, the large expanse of territories made trench warfare less significant.

triangular trade The eighteenth-century commercial Atlantic shipping pattern that took rum from New England to Africa, traded it for slaves taken to the West Indies, and brought sugar back to New England to be processed into rum.

Triple Entente Alliance developed before the First World War that eventually included Britain, France, and Russia.

Truman Doctrine (1947) Declaration promising U.S. economic and military intervention to counter any attempt by the Soviet Union to expand its influence. Often cited as a key moment in the origins of the Cold War.

tsar Russian word for "emperor," derived from the Latin *caesar* and similar to the German *kaiser,* it was the title claimed by the rulers of medieval Muscovy and of the later Russian Empire.

Ubaid culture An early civilization that flourished in Mesopotamia between 5500 and 4000 B.C.E., it was characterized by large village settlements and temple complexes: a precursor to the more urban civilization of the Sumerians.

Umayyad Caliphate (661–930) The Umayyad family resisted the authority of the first two caliphs who succeeded Muhammad but eventually placed a member of their own family in that position of power. The Umayyad Caliphate ruled the Islamic world from 661 to 750, modeling their administration on that of the Roman Empire. But after a rebellion led by the rival Abbasid family, the power of the Umayyad Caliphate was confined to their territories in al-Andalus (Spain).

Universal Declaration of Human Rights (1948) United Nations declaration that laid out the rights to which all human beings were entitled.

University of Paris The reputation of Peter Abelard and his students attracted many intellectuals to Paris in the twelfth century, some of whom began offering instruction to aspiring scholars. By 1200, this loose association of teachers had formed themselves into a *universitas,* or corporation. They began collaborating in the higher academic study of the liberal arts with a special emphasis on theology.

Pope Urban II (1042?–1099) Instigator of the First Crusade (1096–1099), who promised that anyone who fought or died in the service of the Church would receive absolution from sin.

urban populations During the nineteenth century, urban populations in Europe increased sixfold. For the most part, urban areas had medieval infrastructures, which new populations and industries overwhelmed. As a result, many European cities became overcrowded and unhealthy.

Utopia Title of a semi-satirical social critique by the English statesman Sir Thomas More (1478–1535); the word derives from the Greek "best place" or "no place."

Lorenzo Valla (1407–1457) One of the first practitioners of scientific philology (the historical study of language), Valla's analysis of the so-called Donation of Constantine showed that the document could not possibly have been written in the fourth century C.E., but must have been forged centuries later.

vassal A person who pledges to be loyal and subservient to a lord in exchange for land, income, or protection.

velvet revolutions The peaceful political revolutions throughout Eastern Europe in 1989.

Verdun (1916) This battle between German and French forces lasted for ten months during the First World War. The Germans saw the battle as a chance to break French morale through a war of attrition, and the French believed the battle to be a symbol of France's strength. In the end, over 400,000 lives were lost and the German offensive failed.

Versailles Conference (1919) Peace conference between the victors of the First World War; resulted in the Treaty of Versailles, which forced Germany to pay reparations and to give up its colonies to the victors.

Queen Victoria (1819–1901) Influential monarch who reigned from 1837 until her death; she presided over the expansion of the British Empire as well as the evolution of English politics and social and economic reforms.

Viet Cong Vietnamese communist group formed in 1954; committed to overthrowing the government of South Vietnam and reunifying North and South Vietnam.

Vikings (800–1000) The collapse of the Abbasid Caliphate disrupted Scandinavian commercial networks and turned traders into raiders (the word *viking* describes the activity of raiding). These raids often escalated into invasions that contributed to the collapse of the Carolingian Empire, resulted in the devastation of settled territories, and ended with the establishment of Viking colonies. By the tenth century, Vikings controlled areas of eastern England, Scotland, the islands of Ireland, Iceland, Greenland, and parts of northern France. They had also established the beginnings of the kingdom that became Russia and made exploratory voyages to North America, founding a settlement at Newfoundland (Canada).

A Vindication of the Rights of Woman Noted work of Mary Wollstonecraft (1759–1797), English republican who applied Enlightenment political ideas to issues of gender.

Virgil (70–19 B.C.E.) An influential Roman poet who wrote under the patronage of the emperor Augustus. His *Aeneid* mimicked the ancient Greek epics of Homer and told the mythical tale of Rome's founding by the Trojan refugee Aeneas.

Visigoths The tribes of "west" Goths who sacked Rome in 410 C.E. and later established a kingdom in the Roman province of Hispania (Spain).

Voltaire Pseudonym of French philosopher and satirist François Marie Arouet (1694–1778), who championed the cause of human dignity against state and Church oppression. Noted deist and author of *Candide*.

Lech Wałęsa (1943–) Leader of the Polish labor movement Solidarity, which organized a series of strikes across Poland in 1980. They protested working conditions, shortages, and high prices. Above all, they demanded an independent labor union. Solidarity's leaders were imprisoned and the union banned, but they launched a new series of strikes in 1988, which led to the legalization of Solidarity and open elections.

war communism The Russian civil war forced the Bolsheviks to take a more radical economic stance. They requisitioned grain from the peasantry and outlawed private trade in consumer goods as "speculation." They also militarized production facilities and abolished money.

Wars of the Roses Fifteenth-century civil conflict between the English dynastic houses of Lancaster and York, each of which was symbolized by the heraldic device of a rose (red and white, respectively). It was ultimately resolved by the accession of the Lancastrian king Henry VII, who married Elizabeth of York.

Warsaw Pact (1955–1991) Military alliance between the USSR and other communist states that was established as a response to the creation of the NATO alliance.

The Wealth of Nations 1776 treatise by Adam Smith, whose laissez-faire ideas predicted the economic boom of the Industrial Revolution.

Weimar Republic The government of Germany between 1919 and the rise of Hitler and the Nazi party.

Western Front Military front that stretched from the English Channel through Belgium and France to the Alps during the First World War.

Whites Refers to the "counterrevolutionaries" of the Bolshevik Revolution (1918–1921) who fought the Bolsheviks (the "Reds"); included former supporters of the tsar, Social Democrats, and large independent peasant armies.

William the Conqueror (1027–1087) Duke of Normandy who laid claim to the throne of England in 1066, defeating the

Anglo-Saxon King Harold at the Battle of Hastings. He and his Norman followers imposed imperial rule in England through a brutal campaign of military conquest, surveillance, and the suppression of the indigenous Anglo-Saxon language.

William of Ockham (d. 1349) An English philosopher and Franciscan friar, he denied that human reason could prove fundamental theological truths, such as the existence of God: he argued that there is no necessary connection between the observable laws of nature and the unknowable essence of divinity. His theories, derived from the work of earlier scholastics, form the basis of the scientific method.

Woodrow Wilson (1856–1924) U.S. president who requested and received a declaration of war from Congress so that America could enter the First World War. After the war, his prominent role in the Paris Peace Conference signaled the rise of the United States as a world power. He also proposed the Fourteen Points, which influenced the peace negotiations.

Maria Winkelmann (1670–1720) German astronomer who worked with her husband in his observatory. Despite discovering a comet and preparing calendars for the Berlin Academy of Sciences, the academy would not let her take her husband's place within the body after he died.

witch craze The rash of persecutions that took place in both Catholic and Protestant countries of early modern Europe and their colonies, facilitated by secular governments and religious authorities.

women's associations Because European women were excluded from the workings of parliamentary and mass politics, some women formed organizations to press for political and civil rights. Some groups focused on establishing educational opportunities for women while others campaigned energetically for the vote.

William Wordsworth (1770–1850) Romantic writer whose central themes were nature, simplicity, and feeling. He considered nature to be man's most trustworthy teacher and source of sublime power that nourished the human soul.

World Bank International agency established in 1944 to provide economic assistance to war-torn nations and countries in need of economic development.

John Wycliffe (c. 1330–1384) A professor of theology at the University of Oxford, Wycliffe urged the English king to confiscate ecclesiastical wealth and to replace corrupt priests and bishops with men who would live according to the apostolic standards of poverty and piety. He advocated direct access to the scriptures and promoted an English translation of the Bible. His teachings played an important role in the Peasants' Revolt of 1381 and inspired the still more radical initiatives of a group known as Lollards.

Xerxes (519?–465 B.C.E.) Xerxes succeeded his father, Darius, as Great King of Persia. Seeking to avenge his father's shame and eradicate any future threats to Persian hegemony, he launched his own invasion of Greece in 480 B.C.E. An allied Greek army defeated his forces in 479 B.C.E.

Yalta Accords Meeting among President Franklin D. Roosevelt, Prime Minister Winston Churchill, and Premier Joseph Stalin that occurred in the Crimea in 1945 shortly before the end of the Second World War to plan for the postwar order.

Young Turks The 1908 Turkish reformist movement that aimed to modernize the Ottoman Empire, restore parliamentary rule, and depose Sultan Abdul Hamid II.

ziggurats Temples constructed under the Dynasty of Ur in what is now Iraq, beginning around 2100 B.C.E.

Zionism A political movement dating to the end of the nineteenth century holding that the Jewish people constitute a nation and are entitled to a national homeland. Zionists rejected a policy of Jewish assimilation and advocated the reestablishment of a Jewish homeland in Palestine.

Zollverein In 1834, Prussia started a customs union, which established free trade among the German states and a uniform tariff against the rest of the world. By the 1840s, the union included almost all of the German states except German Austria. It is considered an important precedent for the political unification of Germany, which was completed in 1870 under Prussian leadership.

Zoroastrianism One of the three major universal faiths of the ancient world, alongside Judaism and Christianity, it was derived from the teachings of the Persian Zoroaster around 600 B.C.E. Zoroaster redefined religion as an ethical practice common to all, rather than as a set of rituals and superstitions that cause divisions among people. Zoroastrianism teaches that there is one supreme god in the universe, Ahura-Mazda (Wise Lord) but that his goodness will be constantly assailed by the forces of evil until the arrival of a final "judgment day." Proponents of this faith should therefore help good to triumph over evil by leading a good life, and by performing acts of compassion and charity. Zoroastrianism exercised a profound influence over many early Christians, including Augustine.

Ulrich Zwingli (1484–1531) A former priest from the Swiss city of Zurich, Zwingli joined Luther and Calvin in attacking the authority of the Roman Catholic Church.

Text Credits

Leon B. Alberti: "On the Family" from *The Family in Renaissance Florence*, trans./ed. by Renée Neu Watkins (University of South Carolina Press, 1969), pp. 208–213. Reprinted by permission of the translator.

Aristophanes: 300 words from *Lysistrata and Other Plays* by Aristophanes, translated with an introduction by Alan H. Sommerstein (Penguin Classics, 1973). Copyright © Alan H. Sommerstein, 1973. Reproduced by permission of Penguin Books Ltd.

Arrian: 300 words from *The Campaigns of Alexander* by Arrian, translated by Aubrey de Sélincourt, revised with an introduction and notes by J.R. Hamilton (Penguin Classics 1958, Revised edition 1971). Copyright © the Estate of Aubrey de Sélincourt, 1958. Introduction and Notes copyright © J.R. Hamilton, 1971. Reproduced by permission of Penguin Books Ltd.

Nels Bailkey (ed.): From Bailkey, *Readings in Ancient History*, 5th Edition. © 1996 Wadsworth, a part of Cengage Learning, Inc. Reproduced by permission. www.cengage.com/permissions.

Armand Bellee (ed.): *Cahiers de plaintes & doleances des paroisses de la province du Maine pour les Etats-generaux de 1789*, 4 vols. (Le Mans: Monnoyer, 1881-92), 2: 578–82. Translated by the American Social History Project, "Liberty, Equality, Fraternity: Exploring the French Revolution" by Jack R. Censer and Lynn Hunt. Reprinted by permission.

Bernard of Angers: "Miracles of Saint Foy" from *Readings in Medieval History, 2nd* Edition, edited by Patrick J. Geary (Toronto, Ont: University of Toronto Press, 2003). Copyright © 2003. Reprinted by permission of the publisher.

Henry Bettenson (ed.): "Obedience as a Jesuit Hallmark" from *Documents of the Christian Church*, 2nd Edition. Copyright © 1967, Oxford University Press. Reprinted by permission of Oxford University Press.

Gabriel Biel: "Execrabilis." Reprinted by permission of the publisher from *Defensorium Obedientiae Apostolicae Et Alia Documenta* by Gabriel Biel, edited and translated by Heiko A. Oberman, Daniel E. Zerfoss and William J. Courtenay, pp. 224–227, Cambridge, Mass.: The Belknap Press of Harvard University Press, Copyright © 1968 by the President and Fellows of Harvard College.

Jose Bove: *The World Is Not for Sale: Farmers Against Junk Food*, pp. 3–13, © Verso, 2001. Reprinted by permission of the publisher.

Walter Bower: "A Declaration of Scottish Independence," from *Scotichronicon*, Volume 7, by Walter Bower. Edited by B. Scott and D. E. R. Watt. Copyright © 1996 Aberdeen University Press. Reprinted with permission.

Boyer, Baker & Kirshner (eds): "Declaration of the Rights of Man and of the Citizen", "Napoleon's Letter to Prince Eugene" and "Circular Letter to Sovereigns" from *University of Chicago Readings in Western Civilization, Vol. 7*, pp. 238–239; 419–420; 426–427, Copyright © 1987 by The University of Chicago. Reprinted by permission of The University of Chicago Press.

Anna Comnena: 340 words from *The Alexiad of Anna Comnena*, translated by E.R.A. Sewter (Penguin Classics, 1969). Copyright © E.R.A. Sewter, 1969. Reproduced by permission of Penguin Books Ltd.

James Cracraft: "Alexander II's Decree Emancipating the Serfs, 1861," *Major Problems in the History of Imperial Russia*. Copyright © 1994 by D.C. Heath and Company.

David Brion Davis: From *Encyclopédie*, Vol. 16, Neuchâtel, 1765, p. 532 as cited in David Brion Davis, *The Problem of Slavery in Western Culture*. (Ithaca, N.Y.: Cornell University Press, 1966), p. 416. Copyright © 1966 by David Brion Davis. Reprinted by permission.

Simone de Beauvoir: From *The Second Sex* by Simone de Beauvoir, translated by Constance Borde & Sheila Malovany-Chevalier, published by Jonathan Cape, translation copyright © 2009 by Constance Borde and Sheila Malovany-Chevalier, Introduction copyright © 2010 by Judith Thurman. Reprinted by permission of Alfred A. Knopf, a division of Random House, Inc. and The Random House Group Ltd.

Geoffrey de Charny: From *The Book of Chivalry of Geoffrey de Charny: Text, Context, and Translation*, translated by Richard W. Kaeuper and Elspeth Kennedy, pp. 99. Copyright © 1996 University of Pennsylvania Press. Reprinted with permission.

Marie de France: "Equitan" in The Lais of Marie de France, translated by Gllyn S. Burgess and Kieth Burgess. Pp. 56–57. Copyright © 1985. Reproduced by permission of Penguin Books Ltd.

Bartolome de las Casas: 500 words from *A Short Account of the Destruction of the Indies* by Bartolome de las Casas, edited and translated by Nigel Griffin, introduction by Anthony Pagden (Penguin Classics, 1992). Translation and Notes copyright © Nigel Griffin, 1992. Introduction copyright © Anthony Pagden 1992. Reproduced by permission of Penguin Books Ltd.

Michel de Montaigne: From *Montaigne: Selections from the Essays*, translated and edited by Donald M. Frame (Harlan Davidson, Inc., 1973), pp. 34–38. Reprinted by permission of Harlan Davidson, Inc.

Alexis de Tocqueville: From *Recollections: The French Revolution of 1848*; trans. George Lawrence, ed. J.P. Mayer, pp. 436–437. Copyright © 1987 by Transaction Publishers. Reprinted by permission of the publisher.

Rene Descartes: From *A Discourse on the Method of Correctly Conducting One's Reason*, trans. Ian Maclean. Copyright © Ian Maclean 2006. Reprinted by permission of Oxford University Press.

Armand J. du Plessis: "Cardinal Richelieu on the Common People of France," pp. 31–32 from Hill, Henry Bertram, *The Political Testament of Cardinal Richelieu*. © 1961 by the Board of Regents of the University of Wisconsin System. Reprinted by permission of The University of Wisconsin Press.

Ecumenical Councils: "Epitome of the Definition of the Iconoclastic Conciliabulum" from *A Select Library of Nicene and Post-Nicene Fathers of the Christian Church, Vol. XIV*, eds. Schaff & Wace (Grand Rapids, MI: Wm. B. Eerdmans Publishing Company, 1955), pp. 543–544.

Frantz Fanon: Excerpt from *The Wretched of the Earth* by Frantz Fanon, copyright © 1963 by *Présence Africaine*. Used by permission of Grove/Atlantic, Inc.

Robert Filmer: "Observations upon Aristotle's Politiques" (1652), in *Divine Right and Democracy: An Anthology of Political Writing in Stuart England*, edited by David Wootton. Pp 110–18. Copyright © 1986. Reproduced by permission of Penguin Books Ltd.

Gregory L. Freeze (ed.): From *From Supplication to Revolution: A Documentary Social History of Imperial Russia*. Copyright © 1988, Oxford University Press, Inc. Reprinted by permission of Oxford University Press.

Betty Friedan: From *The Feminine Mystique* by Betty Friedan. Copyright © 1983, 1974, 1973, 1963 by Betty Friedan. Used by permission of Victor Gollancz, an imprint of The Orion Publishing Group, London and W.W. Norton & Company, Inc.

Galileo Galilei: From *Discoveries and Opinions of Galileo* by Galileo Galilei, translated by Stillman Drake, copyright © 1957 by Stillman Drake. Used by permission of Doubleday, a division of Random House, Inc.

Mohandas K. Gandhi: From *Hind Swaraj* or *Indian Home Rule* by M.K. Gandhi, p. 56, Ahmedabad: Navajivan Trust, 1946. Reprinted by permission of the publisher.

Pierre Gassendi: From *The Selected Works of Pierre Gassendi*, Edited by Craig B. Brush. (New York: Johnson Reprint Corporation, 1972) pp. 334–336. Reprinted with permission.

Joseph Goebbels: "Why are we enemies of the Jews?" from Snyder, Louis, *Documents of German History*. Copyright © 1958 by Rutgers, the State University. Reprinted by permission of Rutgers University Press.

Homer: *Iliad*, translated by Stanley Lombardo, selections from pp. 115–118. Copyright © 1997 by Hackett Publishing Company, Inc. Reprinted by permission of Hackett Publishing Company, Inc. All rights reserved.

Rosemary Horrox (ed.): From *The Black Death*, by Horrox (Trans., Ed.), 1994, Manchester University Press, Manchester, UK. Reprinted with permission.

Juvenal: 224 words from *The Sixteen Satires* by Juvenal, translated by Peter Green (Penguin Classics 1967, Revised edition 1974). Copyright © Peter Green 1967, 1974. Reproduced by permission of Penguin Books Ltd.

Nikita Khrushchev: "Report to the Communist Party Congress (1961)" from *Current Soviet Policies IV*, eds. Charlotte Saikowski and Leo Gruliow, from the translations of the Current Digest of the Soviet Press. Joint Committee on Slavic Studies, 1962, pp. 42–45. Reprinted by permission of the Current Digest of the Soviet Press.

Maureen Gallery Kovacs (trans.): Excerpts from *The Epic of Gilgamesh*, with an Introduction and Notes by Kovacs, Maureen Gallery, translator. Copyright © 1985, 1989 by the Board of Trustees of the Leland Stanford Junior University. All rights reserved. Used with the permission of Stanford University Press, www.sup.org.

Heda Margolius Kovály: *Under a Cruel Star: A Life in Prague 1941–1968*. Translated from the Czech by Franci Epstein and Helen Epstein with the author. (Cambridge, Mass.: Plunkett Lake Press, 1986), pp. 45–46.

Fritz Lang: "The Future of the Feature Film in Germany" from *The Weimar Republic Sourcebook*, edited by Anton Kaes, Martin Jay, and Edward Dimendberg (Berkeley: University of California Press, 1959), pp. 622–623. © 1994 by the Regents of the University of California. Reprinted by permission of the University of California Press.

Carolyne Larrington: "The Condemnation of Joan of Arc by the University of Paris" from *Women and Writing in Medieval Europe*, Carolyne Larrington, Copyright © 1995 Routledge. Reproduced by permission of Taylor & Francis Books UK.

L. R. Loomis (ed. and trans.): "Haec Sancta Synodus" and "Frequens" from *The Council of Constance* (New York: Columbia University Press, 1961), pp. 229, 246–247. Copyright © 1962, Columbia University Press. Reprinted by permission of the publisher. We have made diligent efforts to contact the copyright holder to obtain electronic permission to reprint this selection. If you have information that would help us, please write to Permissions Department, W. W. Norton & Company, Inc., 500 Fifth Avenue, New York, NY 10110.

H. R. Loyn and John Percival: "Capitulary concerning the parts of Saxony" from *The Reign of Charlemagne: Documents on Carolingian Government and Administration* by H.R. Loyn and John Percival, copyright © 1976 by the author and reprinted by permission of St. Martin's Press, LLC.

Niccolo Machiavelli: From *The Prince* by Niccolo Machiavelli, translated and edited by Thomas G. Bergin, pp. 75–76–78. Copyright © 1947 by Harlan Davidson, Inc. Reprinted by permission of Harlan Davidson, Inc.

Mganus Magnusson and Herman Palsson: From *The Vinland Sagas: The Norse Discovery of America*. Pp. 65–67. Copyright © 1965 Penguin Group (USA) Inc. Used by permission of Penguin Group (USA) Inc.

Karl Marx: "Neve Rheinische Zeitung" from *The Class Struggles in France*, pp. 57–58. "Karl Marx and Pierre-Joseph Proudhon, Correspondence" from *Karl Marx, Frederick Engels: Collected Works*, Vol. 38, pp. 38–39. Reprinted by permission of International Publishers, New York.

Jo Ann McNamara and John E. Halborg, E. Gordon Whatley, trans.: "Here Begins the Life of the Blessed Queen Bathild," in *Sainted Women of the Dark Ages*, pp. 268–270. Copyright, 1992, Duke University Press. All rights reserved. Reprinted by permission of the publisher.

Konstantin Mihailovic: *Memoirs of a Janissary*, trans. Benjamin Stolz. Michigan Slavic Translations no. 3 (Ann Arbor: Michigan Slavic Publications, 1975), pp. 157–159. Copyright © 1975, Michigan Slavic Publications. Reprinted by courtesy of Michigan Slavic Publications, Ann Arbor, Mich.

National Council of the Churches of Christ in the USA: 1 Maccabees 1, 2 Maccabees 4, 4 Maccabees 6, 1 Samuel 8:4-22, 10:20-25, 1 Samuel 9:1-10:1, Acts of the Apostles 23:31-24:27, Genesis 6:5-9:1 from the New Revised Standard Version of the Bible, copyright © 1989 the National Council of the Churches of Christ in the USA. Used by permission. All rights reserved.

Nicholas Osterroth: "Clay Miner Autobiography" from *The German Worker: Working-Class Autobiographies from the Age of Industrialization*, translated and edited by Alfred Kelly, pp. 185–186. Copyright © 1987, The Regents of the University of California. Reprinted by permission of the University of California Press.

Denys Page: "The Tawagalawas Letter" from *History and the Homeric Iliad*, by Denys Page (Berkeley: University of California Press, 1959), pp. 11–12. © 1959 by the Regents of the University of California, renewed 1987 by Denys Page. Reprinted by permission of the University of California Press.

Ebenezer Pettigrew: "Notebook containing an account of the death of Ann. B Pettigrew, June 10, 1830," in the Pettigrew Family Papers #592, Southern Historical Collection, Wilson Library, The University of North Carolina at Chapel Hill. Reprinted by permission.

Phintys: From Lefkowitz, Mary R., and Maureen B. Fant, eds. *Women's Life in Greece and Rome*, second edition. pp. 163–164. © 1992 Maureen B. Fant & Mary R. Lefkowitz. Reprinted by permission of Gerald Duckworth & Co. Ltd and The Johns Hopkins University Press.

E.M. Plass: From *What Luther Says, Vol. II*, (pgs. 888-889) © 1959, 1987 Concordia Publishing House. Used with permission of CPH. All rights reserved.

Plato: 365 words from *The Last Days of Socrates* by Plato, translated with an introduction by Hugh Tredennick (Penguin Classics 1954, Third edition 1969). Copyright © Hugh Tredennick, 1954, 1959, 1969. Reproduced by permission of Penguin Books Ltd.

Pliny the Younger, Letters from Book Ten of *Pliny the Younger: Complete Letters*, trans. P.G. Walsh. Copyright © P.G. Walsh 2006. Reprinted by permission of Oxford University Press.

Plutarch: From Lefkowitz, Mary R., and Maureen B. Fant, eds. *Women's Life in Greece and Rome*, second edition. pp. 147–149. © 1992 Maureen B. Fant & Mary R. Lefkowitz. Reprinted by permission of Gerald Duckworth & Co. Ltd and The Johns Hopkins University Press.

Polybius: 350 words from *The Rise of the Roman Empire* by Polybius, translated by Ian Scott-Kilvert, selected with an introduction by F.W. Walbank (Penguin Classics, 1979). Copyright © Ian Scott-Kilvert, 1979. Reproduced by permission of Penguin Books Ltd.

James B. Pritchard (ed.): "Cyrus." From *Ancient Near Eastern Texts Relating to the Old Testament – Third Edition with Supplement*. © 1950, 1955, 1969, renewed 1978 by Princeton University Press. Reprinted by permission of Princeton University Press.

Tariq Ramadan: "Islam and Muslims in Europe: A Silent Revolution toward Rediscovery," *Muslims in the West, From Sojourners to Citizens*, ed. Yvonne Yazbeck Haddad, pp. 160–163. Copyright © 2002 by Oxford University Press. Inc. Reprinted by permission of Oxford University Press, Inc.

Adam Daniel Rotfeld and Walther Stützle (eds.): "A 10-point plan for overcoming the division of Europe and Germany: Speech by the Federal Republic of Germany" from *Germany and Europe in*

Transition, pp. 120–122. Copyright © 1991. Reprinted by permission of Oxford University Press.

Martha T. Roth: Excerpts from "The Code of Hammurabi" from *Law Collections from Mesopotamia and Asia Minor*, edited by Martha T. Roth (Scholars Press, 1997), pp. 76–135. Reprinted by permission of Society of Biblical Literature.

Jean Rousseau: From *Rousseau's Political Writings: A Norton Critical Edition*, edited by Alan Ritter and Julia Conaway Bondanella, translated by Julia Conaway Bondanella. Copyright © 1988 by W.W. Norton & Company, Inc. Used by permission of W.W. Norton & Company, Inc.

Reinhard Rürup (ed.): From *Topography of Terror: Gestapo, SS, and Reichssicherheitshauptamt on the "Prinz-Albrecht-Terrain": A Documentation*, pp. 125–127. (Berlin: Verlag Willmuth Arenhövel, 1991) Reprinted with permission.

Richard Sakwa: "Stalin on Industrialism" and "The Bolsheviks Must Seize Power" from *Rise and Fall of the Soviet Union 1917–1991*, by Richard Sakwa. Copyright © 1999 Routledge. Reproduced by permission of Taylor & Francis Books UK.

Samuel the Nagid: "A Hebrew Poem in Praise of Wine." Reprinted from *Wine, Women, and Death: Medieval Hebrew Poems on the Good Life*, © 1986, by Raymond P. Scheindlin, published by The Jewish Publication Society with the permission of the publisher.

Sappho: "Fragment 16" from *The Poetry of Sappho*, translated and notes by Jim Powell, pp. 6–7. Copyright © 2007 by Jim Powell. Reprinted by permission of Oxford University Press. "Sappho to Her Pupils," translated by Lachlan Mackinnon, *Times Literary Supplement*, July 15, 2005. © Lachlan Mackinnon / The Times Literary Supplement / nisyndication.com. Reprinted with permission.

Second Congress of the Communist International: "Theses on the National and Colonial Questions" from Workers *of the World and Oppressed Peoples, Unite!: Proceedings and Documents of the Second Congress, 1920*, Volume 1, pp. 283–288. Edited by John Riddell. New York: Pathfinder Press, 1991.

Michael Sells (trans.): "81: The Overturning" from *Approaching the Qur'an: The Early Revelations*, translated by Michael Sells, pp. 48, 50. Copyright © 1999 by Michael A. Sells. Reprinted by permission of White Cloud Press.

M. C. Seymour (ed.): "The Legend of Prester John" from *Mandeville's Travels*, pp. 195-199. Copyright © 1967, Clarendon Press. Reprinted by permission of Oxford University Press.

Sidonius: Reprinted by permission of the publishers and the Trustees of the Loeb Classical Library from *Sidonius: Volume II – Letters*, Loeb Classical Library Volume 420, prepared by W.H. Semple and E.H. Warmington from material left by W.B. Anderson, pp. 127–129, 181–183, Cambridge, Mass.: Harvard University Press, Copyright © 1965 by the President and Fellows of Harvard College. Loeb Classical Library ® is a registered trademark of the President and Fellows of Harvard College.

Lewis Siegelbaum and Andrei Sokolov: "Letters from Anonymous Workers to the Newspaper Pravda" from *Stalinism as a Way of Life*, pp. 39–41. Copyright © 2004 by Yale University. Reprinted by permission of Yale University Press.

William Kelly Simpson (ed.): "The Prophecies of Neferty" from *The Literature of Ancient Egypt*, pp. 214–220. Copyright © 2003 by Yale University. All rights reserved. Reprinted by permission of Yale University Press.

Denis Mack Smith: "Building the Italian Nation" from *The Making of Italy, 1796-1870* (New York: Harper & Row, 1968), pp. 47–49, 181–182, 224–225. Reprinted by permission of the author.

St. Ambrose: "The Memorial of Symmachus, Prefect of the City" from *A Select Library of Nicene and Post-Nicene Fathers of the Christian Church, Vol. X*, eds. Schaff & Wace (Grand Rapids, MI: Wm. B. Eerdmans Publishing Company, 1955), pp. 414–415.

St. Francis of Assisi: Excerpts from *St. Francis of Assisi: Omnibus of Sources, Volume One*, edited by Marion A. Habig, © 2008 by St. Anthony Messenger Press, are used by permission. All rights reserved.

Tacitus: 480 words from *The Annals of Imperial Rome* by Tacitus, translated with and introduction by Michael Grant (Penguin Classics 1956, Sixth revised edition 1989). Copyright © Michael Grant Publications Ltd, 1956, 1959, 1971, 1973, 1975, 1977, 1989. Reproduced by permission of Penguin Books Ltd.

Simon Taylor (ed.): "National Socialist Campaign Pamphlet" from *Germany, 1918-1933: Revolution, Counter-Revolution, and the Rise of Hitler* (London: Gerald Duckworth and Co., Ltd), p. 106. We have made diligent efforts to contact the copyright holder to obtain permission to reprint this selection. If you have information that would help us, please write to Permissions Department, W. W. Norton & Company, Inc., 500 Fifth Avenue, New York, NY 10110.

Harry S. Truman: From *Memoirs*, Vol. 1 (Garden City, NY: Doubleday, 1955), pp. 419–421. Reprinted by permission.

Tyrtaeus: "Exhortation to the Young Hoplite" from *University of Chicago Readings in Western Civilization, Vol. 1*, eds. Adkins & White, pp. 23–24. Copyright © 1986 by The University of Chicago. Reprinted by permission of The University of Chicago Press.

United Nations: From *Report of the Fourth World Conference on Women*, United Nations, 4–15 September 1995 and *Global Outlook 2000: An Economic Social & Environmental Perspective*, United Nations, 1993. Reprinted by permission of the United Nations.

Pope Urban II: "Pope Urban II's Call at Clermont, November 1195" from *The Crusades: A Reader*, edited by S.J. Allen and Emilie Amt. © Broadview Press/UTP Higher Education. Reprinted with permission of the publisher.

Paul von Hindenburg: *From The War from Within: German Working-Class Women in the First World War,* translated by Margaret Ries. Pp. 68–69. Copyright © 1997 Bloomsbury Publishing Place. Reprinted with permission.

Peter Waldo: "The Conversion of Peter Waldo" from *The Birth of Popular Heresy*, edited/translated by Robert I. Moore (Edward Arnold, 1975). Copyright © 1975, Edward Arnold Publishers. Reproduced by permission of Edward Arnold (Publishers) Limited.

Sumner Willard and Charity Cannon Willard: From *The Book of the Deeds of Arms and of Chivalry*, pp. 11–13. Copyright © 1999 Pennsylvania State University Press. Reprinted with permission.

Xenophon: "Book I, The Anabasis" from *The Greek Historians* by M.I. Finley, copyright © 1959 by The Viking Press, Inc., renewed © 1987 by Charles Richard Whittaker. Used by permission of Viking Penguin, a division of Penguin Group (USA) Inc.

Emile Zola: "The Dangers of Consumer Culture" from *The Ladies Paradise*, trans. by Brian Nelson. Copyright © 1995, Oxford University Press, Inc. Reprinted by permission of Oxford University Press.

Photo Credits

Chapter 18: p. 580: Erich Lessing / Art Resource, NY; **p. 584 (left):** AKG-Images; **p. 584 (right):** The Art Archive / Musée Carnavalet Paris / Marc Charmet; **p. 585:** Giraudon / The Bridgeman Art Library; **p. 587:** Chateau de Versailles, France / The Bridgeman Art Library; **p. 589:** Musee de la Ville de Paris, Musee Carnavalet, Paris, France / Giraudon / The Bridgeman Art Library; **p. 590:** Musee de la Revolution Francaise, Vizille, France / The Bridgeman Art Library; **p. 596:** Bibliotheque Nationale, Paris, France / The Bridgeman Art Library; **p. 597:** Erich Lessing / Art Resource, NY; **p. 598:** Bettmann/Corbis; **p. 599:** Scala/White Images / Art Resource, NY; **p. 602 (left):** Risma Archivo / Alamy; **p. 602 (right):** The Art Archive; **p. 603 (left):** Musee de la Ville de Paris, Musee Carnavalet, Paris, France/ Lauros / Giraudon/ The Bridgeman Art Library; **p. 603 (right):** Courtesy of the Warden and Scholars of New College, Oxford / The Bridgeman Art Library; **p. 607 (left):** The Gallery Collection/Corbis; **p. 607 (right):** Wikimedia Commons; **p. 608:** Erich Lessing/Art Resource, NY; **p. 609:** © The Trustees of the British Museum / Art Resource, NY; **p. 612 (left):** The Granger Collection, New York; **p. 612 (right):** © Thorsten Strasas/Demotix/Corbis; **p. 613:** © Gianni Dagli Orti/CORBIS.

Chapter 19: p. 616: National Gallery, London / Art Resource, NY; **p. 619:** Peak District National Park; **p. 621:** Stefano Bianchetti/Corbis; **p. 622:** SSPL via Getty Images; **p. 623 (left):** The National Archives of the UK; **p. 623 (right):** The Granger Collection, New York; **p. 624 (top):** Snark / Art Resource, NY; **p. 624 (bottom):** Hulton-Deutsch Collection/Corbis; **p. 625:** Hulton-Deutsch Collection/Corbis; **p. 628:** Wikimedia Commons; **p. 631:** Hulton Deutsch Collection/Corbis; **p. 632:** HIP-Archive / Topham/ The Image Works; **p. 633:** HIP-Archive / Topham/ The Image Works; **p. 634 (left):** © Heritage Images/Corbis; **p. 634 (right):** © ACE STOCK LIMITED / Alamy; **p. 636 (left):** Fotomas / Topham / The Image Works; **p. 363 (right):** Mary Evans / The Image Works; **p. 640:** Geoffrey Clements /Corbis; **p. 641:** Constantin Guys/Wikipedia; **p. 642:** Giraudon / Art Resource, NY; **p. 643:** North Wind / Nancy Carter\North Wind Picture Archives; **p. 647:** The Granger Collection, NY; **p. 649:** The Granger Collection, NY.

Chapter 20: p. 652: Erich Lessing / Art Resource, NY; **p. 657:** Private Collection / Bridgeman Art Library, Archives Charmet; **p. 659:** Photo RMN, Paris; **p. 661:** Erich Lessing / Art Resource, NY; **p. 662:** Reproduced by the Gracious Permission of Her Majesty the Queen; **p. 665:** © The Trustees of the British Museum; **p. 661:** Michael Nicholson/Corbis; **p. 671 (left):** akg-images; **p. 671 (right):** Time & Life Pictures/Getty Images; **p. 672 (top):** The Stapleton Collection / The Bridgeman Art Library; **p. 672 (bottom):** Bettmann/Corbis; **p. 678:** Bettmann/Corbis; **p. 679 (left):** Portrait of Mary Shelley (1797-1851) at the Age of Nineteen, c.1816 (litho) by English School (19th century), Russell-Cotes Art Gallery and Museum, Bournemouth, UK / Bridgeman Art Library; **p. 679 (right):** Illustration from 'Frankenstein' by Mary Shelley (1797-1851) (engraving) (b/w photo) by English School (19th century), Private Collection / Bridgeman Art Library; **p. 681:** Archivo Iconografico S.A./Corbis; **p. 682:** Wikimedia Commons; **p. 683 (top):** Wikimedia Commons; **p. 683 (bottom):** Wikimedia Commons.

Chapter 21: p. 686: Erich Lessing/Art Resource, NY; **p. 692:** Gianni Dagli Orti / The Art Archive at Art Resource, NY; **p. 693 (top):** Erich Lessing / Art Resource, NY; **p. 693 (bottom):** Bildarchiv Preussischer Kulturbesitz / Art Resource, NY; **p. 695 (left):** ullstein bild/ The Granger Collection, New York; **p. 695 (right):** Image Source; **p. 697:** Bildarchiv Preussischer Kulturbesitz / Art Resource, NY; **p. 698 (left);** Bildarchiv Preussischer Kulturbesitz / Art Resource, NY; **p. 698 (right):** Corbis; **p. 700:** Imagno/Getty Images; **p. 704 (top):** Rischgitz/Getty Images; **p. 704 (bottom):** Scala/Art Resource, NY; **p. 706:** Charles E. Rotkin / Corbis; **p. 707:** Hulton-Deutsch Collection / Corbis; **p. 708:** Scala/Art Resource, NY; **p. 710:** Ann Ronan Picture Library / HIP / The Image Works; **p. 712:** Deutsches Historisches Museum; **p. 713 (left):** Bildarchiv Preussischer Kulturbesitz / Art Resource, NY; **p. 713 (right):** Bildarchiv Preussischer Kulturbesitz / Art Resource, NY; **p. 716:** Bettmann / Corbis; **p. 721:** Louie Psihoyos/Corbis; **p. 723 (top):** Corbis; **p. 723 (bottom):** Foto Marburg / Art Resource, NY; **p. 724:** Bettmann/Corbis.

Chapter 22: p. 726: The Granger Collection, New York; **p. 728:** Bibliotheque des Arts Decoratifs, Paris, France / Archives Charmet / The Bridgeman Art Library; **p. 732 (left):** Ken and Jenny Jacobson Orientalist Photography Collection/Research Library, The Getty Research Institute, Los Angeles (2008.R.3); **p. 732 (right):** Hulton Archive/Getty Images; **p. 733 (left):** Bettmann/Corbis; **p. 733 (right):** Punchcartoons.com; **p. 737 (left):** The Granger Collection, New York/The Granger Collection; **p. 737 (right):** © Janine Wiedel Photolibrary/Alamy; **p. 738:** AKG-images; **p. 741 (top):** Oriental and India Office Collections, The British Library/Art Resource, NY; **p. 741 (bottom):** Bettmann/Corbis; **p. 743:** Wikimedia Commons; **p. 744:** Hulton-Deutsch/Corbis; **p. 746 (left):** Wikimedia Commons; **p. 746 (right):** Hulton Archive/Getty Images; **p. 747 (left):** North Wind Picture Archives; **p. 747 (right):** Image Courtesy of The Advertising Archives; **p. 750:** Matthew Fontaine Maury, *New Complete Geography* (New York: University Publishing Company, 1906); **p. 754 (top):** 1999 National Gallery of Art, Washington D.C.; **p. 754**

(left): 1999 National Gallery of Art, Washington D.C.; **p. 754 (center):** 1999 National Gallery of Art, Washington D.C.; **p. 754 (right):** 1999 National Gallery of Art, Washington D.C.; **p. 755:** Bettmann/Corbis; **p. 757:** Bridgeman Art Library; **p. 758:** The Ohio State University Billy Ireland Cartoon Library & Museum.

Chapter 23: p. 760: AKG-images; **p. 763:** AKG-images; **p. 766:** Bildarchiv Preussischer Kulturbesitz / Art Resource, NY; **p. 769:** Hulton-Deutsch Collection / Corbis; **p. 770:** Austrian Archives/Corbis; **p. 771:** Leemage/Getty; **p. 772 (top):** The Hulton Deutsch Collection/Corbis; **p. 772 (bottom):** The Hulton Deutsch Collection/Corbis; **p. 773 (top):** Library of Congress; **p. 773 (bottom):** Bettmann/Corbis; **p. 774:** The Hulton Deutsch Collection/Corbis; **p. 779 (left):** The Granger Collection, New York; **p. 779 (center):** Charles Leandre (1862-1930) Private Collection/ The Bridgeman Art Library Nationality; **p. 779 (right):** Rue des Archives / The Granger Collection , New York; **p. 780:** Bettmann/Corbis; **p. 783 (left):** Universal History Archive/UIG; **p. 783 (right):** © Charles Platiau/Reuters/Corbis; **p. 784:** Hulton-Deutsch Collection/CORBIS; **p. 786:** Staatliche Museen zu Berlin-Preußisher Kulturbesitz; **p. 789:** From *An Autobiography: Herbert Spencer, 1904*; **p. 792:** Bettmann/Corbis; **p. 793:** © Bettmann/Corbis; **p. 794:** *Black Lines,* December 1913. Oil on canvas, 51 x 51 5/8 inches. Solomon R. Guggenheim Museum, Solomon R. Guggenheim Founding Collection, Gift, Solomon R. Guggenheim. 37.241. Vasily Kandinsky © 2007 Artists Rights Society (ARS), New York/ADAGP, Paris; **p. 795 (left):** Erich Lessing / Art Resource, NY; **p. 795 (right):** Scala / Art Resource, NY.

Chapter 24: p. 798: The Art Archive / Imperial War Museum; **p. 803:** Staatliche Museen zu Berlin-Preußisher Kulturbesitz; **p. 807:** Bettmann/Corbis; **p. 808 (left):** Swim Ink 2, LLC/Corbis; **p. 808 (right):** Swim Ink 2, LLC/Corbis; **p. 809 (left):** Hoover Institution, Stanford University; **p. 809 (right):** Wikimedia Commons; **p. 810 (left):** Bundesarchiv; **p. 810 (right):** Bundesarchiv; **p. 811 (left):** Hulton-Deutsch Collection/Corbis; **p. 811 (right):** © Bettmann/CORBIS; **p. 812:** Trustees of the Imperial War Museum, London; **p. 813:** Hulton-Deutsch Collection / Corbis; **p. 814 (top):** Wikimedia Commons; **p. 814 (left):** Bundesarchiv; **p. 814 (right):** Bundesarchiv; **p. 817:** Bettmann/Corbis; **p. 819 (left):** Corbis; **p. 819 (right):** Bundesarchiv; **p. 822:** Bildarchiv Preussischer Kulturbesitz; **p. 823:** Private Collection / Ken Walsh / The Bridgeman Art Library; **p. 824:** Bettmann/Corbis; **p. 826:** Hulton-Deutsch Collection/Corbis; **p. 827:** Bettmann/Corbis; **p. 828:** Bettmann/Corbis; **p. 830 (left):** Bettmann/Corbis; **p. 830 (right):** © Wally McNamee/Corbis; **p. 831:** National Archives.

Chapter 25: p. 836: Erich Lessing / Art Resource, NY, © VAGA; **p. 838:** © 2013 Artists Rights Society (ARS), New York/VG Bild-Kunst, Bonn; **p. 839:** Picture History; **p. 842:** (c) 2010 Estate of Gustav Klutsis/Artists Rights Society (ARS), New York; **p. 844:** Courtesy of Schickler-Lafaille Collection; **p. 845:** Hoover Institution, Stanford University; **p. 848:** Hoover Institution, Stanford University; **p. 851:** Brown Brothers; **p. 852:** © Underwood & Underwood/Corbis; **p. 853:** Hulton-Deutsch Collection/Corbis; **p. 855 (left):** © Daily Mail/Rex/Alamy; **p. 855 (right):** Giorgio Cosulich/Getty Images; **p. 856:** AKG Images; **p. 860:** Hulton-Deutsch Collection/Corbis; **p. 862:** Arthur Rothstein/Corbis; **p. 863:** © 2013 Man Ray Trust/Artists Rights Society (ARS), NY/ADAGP, Paris/Succession Marcel Duchamp. CNAC/MNAM/Dist. Réunion des Musées Nationaux/Art Resource, NY; **p. 864:** The Museum of Modern Art, New York. Photograph courtesy the Museum of Modern Art, New York/Art Resource, NY. © 2013 Artists Rights Society (ARS), New York/VG Bild-Kunst, Bonn; **p. 866 (left):** Topham / The Image Works; **p. 866 (right):** The Kobal Collection; **p. 867:** Photo by William Vanderson/Fox Photos/Getty Images; **p. 868 (top):** Musee National d'Art Moderne, Centre Georges Pompidou, Paris, France. Photo CNAC/MNAM/Dist. RMN/Art Resource, NY; **p. 868 (bottom):** Granger Collection.

Chapter 26: p. 872: Giraudon/Art Resource, NY. © 2013 Estate of Pablo Picasso/Artists Rights Society (ARS), New York; **p. 876 (left):** © Bettmann/CORBIS; **p. 876 (right):** The Southworth Collecion, The Mandeville Special Collections Library of UC San Diego; **p. 877:** Giraudon/Art Resource, NY. © 2013 Estate of Pablo Picasso/Artists Rights Society (ARS), New York; **p. 879:** © Hulton-Deutsch Collection/CORBIS; **p. 881:** The Granger Collection, NYC; **p. 882:** Bettmann/Corbis; **p. 883:** Hulton-Deutsch Collection/Corbis; **p. 885:** Bettmann/Corbis; **p. 888:** Hoover Institution, Stanford University; **p. 890:** AP Photo; **p. 894 (top):** akg-images / ullstein bild; **p. 894 (bottom):** Yevgeny Khaldei; **p. 898:** Yad Vashem Archives; **p. 899:** Yad Vashem Archives; **p. 901 (left):** © Photoshot; **p. 901 (right):** © Egon Steiner/dpa/Corbis; **p. 902:** Public Record Office Image Library, National Archives, UK; **p. 904 (top):** Corbis; **p. 904 (bottom):** National Archives; **p. 905 (top):** Library of Congress; **p. 905 (bottom):** Library of Congress.

Chapter 27: p. 910: Bettmann/Corbis; **p. 912:** Bettmann/Corbis; **p. 914 (left):** Michael Nicholson/Corbis; **p. 914 (right):** Michael Nicholson/Corbis; **p. 915:** Michael Nicholson/Corbis; **p. 916:** Corbis; **p. 918 (left):** The Granger Collection; **p. 918 (right):** © David Pollack/Corbis; **p. 919:** AP Photo; **p. 922 (left):** © Giehr/dpa/Corbis; **p. 922 (right):** © STR/epa/Corbis; **p. 927:** Bettmann/Corbis; **p. 928:** Sovfoto/Eastfoto; **p. 936 (top):** © ADAGP, Paris Corbis; **p.** Marc Garanger/Corbis; **p. 937:** Marc Garanger/Corbis; **p. 939:** Hulton Deutsch Collection/Corbis; **p. 940:** Corbis; **p. 942:** Corbis; **p. 943 (left):** U. Baumgarten via Getty Images; **p. 943 (right):** © Bettman/Corbis.

Chapter 28: p. 946: Peter Turnley/CORBIS; **p. 949:** Bettmann/Corbis; **p. 950:** © Keystone/Corbis; **p. 951 (top):** Paul Almasy/Corbis; **p. 951 (bottom):** Corbis; **p. 952 (left):** Corbis; **p. 952 (right):** Corbis; **p. 953:** Martha Holmes/Time & Life Pictures, Getty Images; **p. 954:** Studio Patellani/Corbis; **p. 955:** Bettmann/Corbis; **p. 956:** © Bettmann/CORBIS; **p. 960:** AP Photo; **p. 962:** Patrick Chauvel/Corbis Sygma; **p. 964:** Abbas/Magnum Photos; **p. 965:** Corbis; **p. 967:** Bettmann/Corbis; **p. 969 (top):** © Peter Turnley/CORBIS; **p. 969 (bottom):** Wally McNamee/Corbis; **p. 972:** © Peter Turnley/CORBIS; **p. 970 (left):** © Boris Yurchenko/AP/AP/Corbis; **p. 970 (right):** © Sysoyev Grigory/ITAR-TASS/Corbis; **p. 976:** Peter Turnley/Corbis; **p. 977 (top):** dpa//Landov; **p. 977 (bottom):** dpa//Landov; **p. 978:** Patrick Robert/Corbis Sygma.

Chapter 29: p. 982: Reuters/Corbis; **p. 985:** Michale Brennan/Corbis; **p. 988:** Shaul Schwaz/Corbis; **p. 989:** Reuters/Corbis; **p. 993:** Reuters/Corbis; **p. 944:** Reuters/Corbis; **p. 996:** Justin Guariglia/Corbis; **p. 996 (left):** Gerd Ludwig/Corbis; **p. 997 (right):** Reuters/Corbis; **p. 999:** Bettmann/Corbis; **p. 1000:** Alain DeJean/Sygma/Corbis; **p. 1001 (top):** Alain DeJean/Sygma/Corbis; **p. 1001 (bottom):** Jean Guichard/Sygma/Corbis; **p. 1004:** Peter Turnley/Corbis; **p. 1005;** Reuters/Corbis; **p. 1011 (left):** © Libor Hajsky/epa/Corbis; **p. 1011 (right):** Associated Press.

Index

Page numbers in *italics* refer to illustrations, maps, and tables.